BOLLINGEN SERIES XLIII

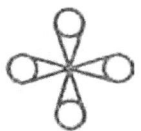

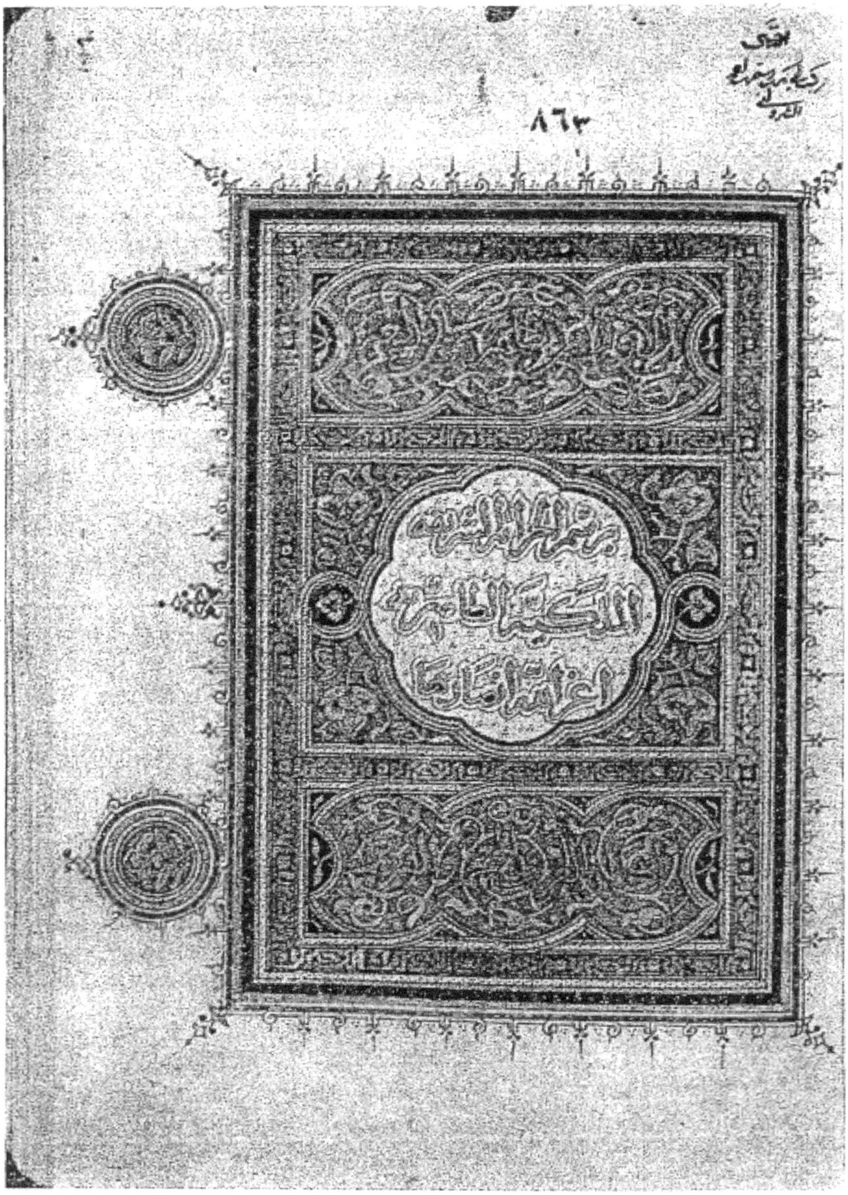

Title Page

From MS. A (Damad Ibrahim 863). Cf. 1:xc, above

IBN KHALDÛN

THE MUQADDIMAH

An Introduction to History

TRANSLATED FROM THE ARABIC BY

FRANZ ROSENTHAL

IN THREE VOLUMES

3

CONTENTS

VOLUME THREE

LIST OF ILLUSTRATIONS *ix*

ABBREVIATIONS AND SYMBOLS *x*

Chapter VI: The various kinds of sciences. The methods of instruction. The conditions that obtain in these connections. The chapter includes a prefatory discussion and appendices [*concluded*]

[12] *Jurisprudence and its subdivision, inheritance laws* 3
The science of inheritance laws, 20

[13] *The science of the principles of jurisprudence and its subdivisions, dialectics and controversial questions* 23
The controversial questions, 30. – *Dialectics,* 32

[14] *The science of speculative theology* 34

[15] *An exposition of ambiguity in the Qur'ân and the Sunnah and of the resulting dogmatic schools among both the orthodox and the innovators* 55

[16] *The science of Sufism* 76

[17] *The science of dream interpretation* 103

[18] *The various kinds of intellectual sciences* 111

[19] *The sciences concerned with numbers* 118
The craft of calculation, 121. – *Algebra,* 124. – *Business arithmetic,* 126. – *Inheritance laws,* 127
[20] *The geometrical sciences* 129
Spherical figures, conic sections, and mechanics, 131. – *Surveying,* 132. – *Optics,* 132
[21] *Astronomy* 133
Astronomical tables, 135
[22] *The science of logic* 137
[23] *Physics* 147
[24] *The science of medicine* 148
[25] *The science of agriculture* 151
[26] *The science of metaphysics* 152
[27] *The sciences of sorcery and talismans* 156
The evil eye, 170
[28] *The science of the secrets of letters* 171
The Zâ'irajah, 182. – *On learning hidden secrets from letter connections,* 214
[29] *The science of alchemy* 227
[30] *A refutation of philosophy. The corruption of the students of philosophy* 246
[31] *A refutation of astrology. The weakness of its achievements. The harmfulness of its goal* 258
[32] *A denial of the effectiveness of alchemy. The impossibility of its existence. The harm that arises from practicing it* 267
[33] *The purposes that must be kept in mind in literary composition and that alone are to be considered valid* 281
[34] *The great number of scholarly works available is an obstacle on the path to attaining scholarship* 288
[35] *The great number of brief handbooks available on scholarly subjects is detrimental to the process of instruction* 290
[36] *The right attitude in scientific instruction and toward the method of giving such instruction* 292
[37] *Study of the auxiliary sciences should not be prolonged, and their problems should not be treated in detail* 298
[38] *The instruction of children and the different methods employed in the Muslim cities* 300
[39] *Severity to students does them harm* 305

[40] *A scholar's education is greatly improved by traveling in quest of knowledge and meeting the authoritative teachers of his time* 307

[41] *Scholars are, of all people, those least familiar with the ways of politics* 308

[42] *Most of the scholars in Islam have been non-Arabs (Persians)* 311

[43] *A person whose first language was not Arabic finds it harder than the native speaker of Arabic to acquire the sciences* 315

[44] *The sciences concerned with the Arabic language* 319

Grammar, 320. – *The science of lexicography*, 325. – *The science of syntax and style and literary criticism*, 332. – *The science of literature*, 339

[45] *Language is a technical habit* 342

[46] *Contemporary Arabic is an independent language different from the languages of the Muḍar and the Ḥimyar* 344

[47] *The language of the sedentary and urban population is an independent language different from the language of the Muḍar* 351

[48] *Instruction in the Muḍar language* 353

[49] *The habit of the Muḍar language is different from Arabic philology and can dispense with it in the process of instruction* 354

[50] *The interpretation and real meaning of the word "taste" according to the technical terminology of literary critics. An explanation of why Arabicized non-Arabs as a rule do not have it* 358

[51] *The urban population is in general deficient in obtaining the linguistic habit that results from instruction. The more remote urban people are from the Arabic language, the more difficult it is for them to obtain it* 363

[52] *The division of speech into poetry and prose* 368

[53] *The ability to write both good poetry and good prose is only very rarely found together in one person* 371

[54] *The craft of poetry and the way of learning it* 373

[55] *Poetry and prose work with words, and not with ideas* 391

[56] *The linguistic habit is obtained by much memorizing. The good quality of the linguistic habit is the result of the good quality of the memorized material* 392

[57] *An explanation of the meaning of natural and contrived speech. How contrived speech may be either good or deficient* 398

[58] *People of rank are above cultivating poetry* 410

[59] *Contemporary Arab poetry, Bedouin and urban* 412
The Spanish muwashshaḥahs *and* zajals, 440

Concluding Remark 481

SELECTED BIBLIOGRAPHY, *by Walter J. Fischel* 483

Addenda (1966) *512*

INDEX OF ARABIC TERMS 525

GENERAL INDEX 533

LIST OF ILLUSTRATIONS

PLATES

FRONTISPIECE. Title Page from MS. A (Damad Ibrahim 863).
P: Courtesy of Dr. Paul A. Underwood.

following p. 204

I. The *Zâ'irajah* (obverse), from MS. E (Ahmet III, 3042, Vol. I, pl. following fol. 237).
The translation is to be found in the pocket at the end of the volume.

II. The *Zâ'irajah* (reverse), from MS. E (Ahmet III, 3042, Vol. I, pl. following fol. 237).

following p. 434

III. Poem in the vulgar language with explicatory notes, from MS. B (Yeni Cami 888, fols. 265*b*–266*a*).

FIGURE

Translation of the *Zâ'irajah* (obverse) *pocket, end of volume*

ABBREVIATIONS AND SYMBOLS

(The use of abbreviations has been avoided as much as possible, but most works cited in the footnotes are provided with full bibliographical data only on their first occurrence in each volume. Thereafter, reference is by short title, with volume and page numbers referring to the edition already cited. The first occurrence of each work can be located with the help of the Index, at the end of Vol. 3.)

A, B, etc.	Sigla used to denote Ibn Khaldûn MSS, described in 1: xc ff., above.
Autobiography	MUḤAMMAD TÂWÎT AṬ-ṬANJÎ (ed.). *at-Ta'rîf bi-Ibn Khaldûn wa-riḥlatuhû gharban wa-sharqan.* Cairo, 1370 [1951].
Bombaci	A. BOMBACI. "Postille alla traduzione De Slane della *Muqaddimah* di Ibn Ḫaldûn," *Annali dell' Istituto Universitario Orientale di Napoli,* N.S. III (1949), 439–72.
Bulaq	NAṢR AL-HÛRÎNÎ (ed.). *Ibn Khaldûn: Muqaddimah.* Bulaq, 1274 [1857].
Concordance	A. J. WENSINCK, J. P. MENSING, *et alii. Concordance et Indices de la tradition musulmane.* Leiden, 1936——.
EI	*Encyclopaedia of Islam.* Leiden and London, 1913–34. (A new edition began to appear in 1954.)
EI Supplement	*Supplement.* Leiden and London, 1938.
GAL	C. BROCKELMANN. *Geschichte der arabischen Litteratur.* Weimar, 1898; Berlin, 1902.
GAL, Suppl.	———. *Supplementbände.* Leiden, 1937–42.
GAL (2nd ed.)	———. Leiden, 1943–49.

Handbook	A. J. Wensinck. *A Handbook of Early Muhammadan Tradition.* Leiden, 1927.
'Ibar	Ibn Khaldûn. *Kitâb al-'Ibar wa-dîwân al-mubtada' wa-l-khabar.* Bulaq, 1284 [1867/68].
de Slane (tr.)	W. M. de Slane (tr.). *Ibn Khaldoun: Histoire des Berbères et des dynasties musulmanes de l'Afrique septentrionale.* Algiers, 1852–56.
Issawi	C. Issawi (tr.). *An Arab Philosophy of History: Selections from the Prolegomena of Ibn Khaldun of Tunis* (1332–1406). London, 1950.
Paris edition	E. Quatremère (ed.). *Prolégomènes d'Ebn-Khaldoun.* Vols. xvi–xviii of the *Notices et Extraits des manuscrits de la Bibliothèque Impériale* (Académie des Inscriptions et Belles-Lettres). Paris, 1858.
( )	Contextual sense supplied. Cf. 1:cxii, above.
[ ]	Translator's interpolations.
< >	MS supplied.
* *	Asterisks enclose passages for which variant (usually, earlier) texts are translated at the foot of the page, in italic.

Chapter VI

(CONCLUDED)

[12] *Jurisprudence and its subdivision, inheritance laws.* III, 1

Jurisprudence is the knowledge of the classification of the laws of God, which concern the actions of all responsible Muslims, as obligatory, forbidden, recommendable, disliked, or permissible. These (laws) are derived from the Qur'ân and the Sunnah (traditions), and from the evidence the Lawgiver (Muḥammad) has established for knowledge of (the laws). The laws evolved from the (whole) of this evidence are called "jurisprudence" (*fiqh*).

The early Muslims evolved the laws from that evidence, though, unavoidably, they differed in (the interpretation of) it. The evidence is mainly derived from texts. The texts are in Arabic. In many instances, and especially with regard to legal concepts,[167] there are celebrated differences among them as to the meaning implicit in the words. Furthermore, the III, 2
traditions (Sunnah) differ widely in respect of the reliability of the recensions. Their legal contents, as a rule, are contradictory. Therefore, a decision is needed. This makes for differences of opinion. Furthermore, evidence not derived from texts causes (still other) differences of opinion. Then, there are new cases which arise and are not covered by the texts. They are referred by analogy to things that are covered by the texts. All of this serves to stir up unavoidable differences of opinion, and this is why differences of opinion occurred among the early Muslims and the religious leaders after them.

Moreover, not all of the men around Muḥammad were qualified to give legal decisions. Not all of them could serve as sources for religious (practice). That was restricted to men who knew the Qur'ân and were acquainted with the abrogating and abrogated, the ambiguous and unambiguous verses,[168] and with all the rest of the evidence that can be

---

167 "And especially . . . concepts" added in D, while the whole sentence is a marginal addition in C.

168 Cf. as-Suyûṭî, *Itqân* (Cairo, 1317/1899), II, 2 ff. (Ch. XLIII), and below, pp. 55 ff.

derived from the Qur'ân, since they had learned (these matters) from the Prophet directly or from their higher ranking colleagues who had learned it from him. These men, therefore, were called "readers," that is, men who (were able to) read the Qur'ân. Because the Arabs were an illiterate nation, those who were able to read the Qur'ân were distinguished by the name of "readers." Their ability to read was a remarkable thing in those days.

It continued to be that way at the beginning of Islam. Then, the cities of Islam grew, and illiteracy disappeared from among the Arabs because of their constant occupation with the Qur'ân. Now the development (of jurisprudence from its sources) took place. Jurisprudence was perfected and came to be a craft and science. The Qur'ân readers were no longer called Qur'ân readers but jurists and religious scholars.

The jurists developed two different approaches to jurisprudence. One was the use of opinion (reasoning) and analogy. It was represented by the 'Irâqîs. The other was the use of traditions. It was represented by the Ḥijâzîs.

As we have stated before,[169] few traditions circulated
III, 3 among the 'Irâqîs. Therefore, they made much use of analogy and became skilled in it. That gave them the name of the representatives of opinion (reasoning). Their chief, around whom and whose followers their school centered, was the imam Abû Ḥanîfah. The leader of the Ḥijâzîs was Mâlik b. Anas and, after him, ash-Shâfi'î.

Later on, a group of religious scholars disapproved of analogy and rejected its use. They were the Ẓâhirites. They restricted the sources of the law to the texts and the general consensus. They considered obvious analogy and causality suggested by the texts as resting in the texts themselves, because a text that indicates a *ratio legis* [170] permits legal decision for all the cases covered by (such a kind of reason-

[169] Cf. 2:461, above.

[170] *An-naṣṣ 'alâ l-'illah* occurs again below, p. 27.

ing).[171] The leaders of this school were Dâwûd b. 'Alî [172] and his son and their followers.

These were the three schools famous among the great mass of Muslims. The 'Alids invented their own school and had their own jurisprudence. They based it upon their dogma requiring abuse of some of the men around Muḥammad, and upon their stated opinion concerning the infallibility of the imams and the inadmissibility of differences in their statements. All these are futile principles. The Khârijites similarly had their own school. The great mass did not care for these (unorthodox) schools, but greatly disapproved of them and abused them. Nothing is known of the opinions of these schools. Their books are not being transmitted. No trace of them can be found except in regions inhabited (by these sectarians). The (legal text) books of the Shî'ah are thus found in Shî'ah countries and wherever Shî'ah dynasties exist, in the West, the East, and in the Yemen. The same applies to the Khârijites. All of them have (legal) writings and books and hold strange opinions on jurisprudence.

The Ẓâhirite school has become extinct today as the result of the extinction of their religious leaders and disapproval of their adherents by the great mass of Muslims. It

---

[171] As de Slane suspected in his note to this passage, the purpose of the sentence is to show that the Ẓâhirites used analogy in a certain sense, but only in cases where the texts of the Qur'ân and the Sunnah seem to imply its use.

A translation of the sentence is given by I. Goldziher, *Die Ẓâhiriten* (Leipzig, 1884), p. 30. If I understand his translation correctly, the main difference between it and the translation above is at the end, where Goldziher says, ". . . because causality [*Gesetzesursache*] mentioned in the text, *wherever it occurs*, is but the determination of a concrete law (not the determination of a legal principle)."

Bombaci, p. 454, translates, "They considered 'evident' analogy and the *ratio legis* resulting from a text in the same way as the (explicit) norms of the texts, in that a text indicating the determining motive is *in each case* equivalent to a text establishing a norm." (Thus, they completely excluded analogy from the sources.)

My italics indicate where I believe Goldziher and Bombaci to have gone wrong, by misunderstanding *maḥâllihâ*.

[172] For Dâwûd b. 'Alî, 202–270 [817/18–884], and his son Muḥammad, 255–297 [869–910], cf. *GAL*, I, 183 f.; *Suppl.*, I, 312 and 249 f.

III, 4 has survived only in books, which have eternal life.[173] Worthless persons occasionally feel obliged to follow this school and study these books in the desire to learn the (Ẓâhirite) system of jurisprudence from them, but they get nowhere and encounter the opposition and disapproval of the great mass of Muslims. In doing so, they often are considered innovators, as they accept knowledge from books for which no key is provided by teachers.[174] That was done by Ibn Ḥazm al-Andalusî,[175] although he occupies a high rank in the expert knowledge of traditions. He turned to the Ẓâhirite school and became skilled in it. He gave his own independent interpretation of their stated opinions. He opposed their leader Dâwûd and attacked most of the Muslim religious leaders. For that, the scholars took their revenge on him. They greatly vilified his school and completely disregarded his books. It went so far that sale of his books on the market was prohibited. At certain times, they were (even) torn up.

Nothing has remained except the schools of the representatives of opinion (reasoning) in the 'Irâq and of the representatives of traditions in the Ḥijâz.

The leading authority of the 'Irâqîs, around whom their school centered, was Abû Ḥanîfah an-Nu'mân b. Thâbit. His place in jurisprudence is unrivaled. This has been attested by persons of his own caliber, in particular, Mâlik and ash-Shâfi'î.

The leading authority of the Ḥijâzîs was Mâlik b. Anas al-Aṣbaḥî, who held the leading position in Medina. He is distinguished by the fact that he added another source of law to those known to other scholars, namely, the practice of the
III, 5 Medinese. He was of the opinion that by virtue of their religion and traditionalism, the Medinese always neces-

[173] Cf. p. 115, below, where the MSS clearly favor *mukhalladah,* and not *mujalladah* "bound." *Mukhalladah* "eternal" is a common epithet of books.

[174] I. Goldziher, *Die Ẓâhiriten*, pp. 193 f., suggests that Ibn Khaldûn was thinking of a contemporary revival of Ẓâhirism in Syria and Egypt. This seems rather improbable.

[175] Cf. 1:414, above.

sarily followed each immediately preceding generation of Medinese, in respect of what they cared [176] to do or not to do. The (process would have gone back) to the generation that was in contact with the actions of the Prophet, and they would have learned from him (what to do and not to do). In (Mâlik's) opinion, the practice of the Medinese, thus, is basic legal evidence.

Many scholars have thought that the (practice of the Medinese) is (rather) one of the problems of the general consensus. Therefore, they have disapproved of (Mâlik's use of) it, because use of the general consensus as a source of law is not restricted to the inhabitants of Medina to the exclusion of other (Muslims), but extends to all Muslims. However, it should be known that general consensus means agreement concerning a religious matter on the strength of independent judgment. Mâlik did not consider the practice of the Medinese in this light. He considered it in the light of the continuity of personal observation over successive generations, (going) back to the time of the Lawgiver (Muḥammad). The necessity of the traditionalism of the Medinese (caused by the fact that they have such excellent models to follow), supports that (attitude). It is true that the problem (of the practice of the Medinese) has been mentioned in the chapter (of legal works) dealing with the general consensus. This is the most appropriate place for it, because both the (practice of the Medinese) and the general consensus are concerned with agreement. However, the agreement of general consensus is the result of independent judgment and opinion (reasoning), in view of the (available) evidence. The agreement of the Medinese, on the other hand, affects their practice in as much as it involves reliance upon personal observation of (the practice of) their predecessors. It would, indeed, have been more appropriate if the problem (of the practice of the

[176] *Yataqayyadûna:* B. The reading *yattafiqûna* "they agreed upon," in A, C, and D, seems to be a simplification. In C it appears to be a correction, though the photostat is not clear enough to say so definitely.

Medinese) were mentioned in the chapter on the actions[177] of the Prophet, or in connection with (the topic of) evidence concerning which there are differences of opinion—as, for example, (the use as legal evidence) of the law of the religions preceding us (Islam), the (legal) opinions of men around Muḥammad, and (the problems of) *praesumptio legis* (*istiṣḥâb*).[178]

God gives success.

Mâlik b. Anas was followed by Muḥammad b. Idrîs al-Muṭṭalibî ash-Shâfi'î. He traveled to the 'Irâq after
III, 6 Mâlik's time. He met the followers of the imam Abû Ḥanîfah and learned from them. He combined the approach of the Ḥijâzîs with those of the 'Irâqîs. He founded his own school and opposed Mâlik on many points.

Mâlik and ash-Shâfi'î were followed by Aḥmad b. Ḥanbal. He was one of the highest-ranking *ḥadîth* scholars.[179] His followers studied with those of Abû Ḥanîfah, notwithstanding the abundant knowledge of traditions they themselves possessed. They founded another school.

These four authorities are the ones recognized by tradition in the (Muslim) cities. Tradition-bound people obliterated all other (authorities), and scholars no longer admit any differences of opinion. The technical terminology of the sciences has become very diversified, and there are obstacles preventing people from attaining the level of independent judgment. It is also feared that (the existence of differences of opinion) might affect unqualified people whose

[177] Bulaq adds: "and assent by silence . . ." The passage appears in the margin of C, and it seems that *wa-taqrîrihî* appears there but has been deleted. Cf. D. Santillana, *Istituzioni di diritto musulmano malichita* (Rome, [1926]-38), I, 36 f.

[178] For *istiṣḥâb*, cf. I. Goldziher in *Wiener Zeitschrift für die Kunde des Morgenlandes*, I (1887), 228–36; D. Santillana, *op. cit.*, II, 621–23.

The Muslim definition of this legal concept runs as follows: "It is the attempt to associate the present (legal situation) with the past by judging the present in the same way as the past is judged, with the result that (the legal situation) is left as it had been, for the reason that no evidence to change it has been found." Cf. at-Tahânawî, *Kashshâf iṣṭilâḥât al-funûn* (Bibliotheca Indica) (Calcutta, 1862), I, 809 f.

[179] Instead of *ḥadîth* scholars, D has "independent scholars."

opinion (reasoning) and religion could not be trusted. Thus, (scholars) came to profess their inability (to apply independent judgment), and had the people adopt the tradition of the (authorities) mentioned and of the respective group of adherents of each. They forbade one to modify his traditional (allegiance), because that would imply frivolity. All that remained after basic textbooks had been produced in the correct manner, and the continuity of their transmission had been established, was to hand down the respective school traditions and, for each individual adherent, to act in accordance with the traditions of his school. Today, jurisprudence means this, and nothing else.[180] The person who would claim independent judgment nowadays would be frustrated and have no adherents.

The Muslims today follow the tradition of one of the four (authorities). The adherents of Ibn Ḥanbal are few in number.[181] Most of them are in Syria and in the 'Irâq, that is,[182] in Baghdad and environs. They are the people who have the best knowledge of the Sunnah and of the transmission of traditions and [183] prefer them to analogical reasoning as a source of law, as far as possible. They [184] were strong and III, 7
numerous in Baghdad, until they clashed with the Shî'ah in the territory of (Baghdad). That caused much unrest in Baghdad. It stopped when the Tatars took possession of Baghdad, and was never resumed later on. The majority of Ḥanbalites are now to be found in Syria.

Abû Ḥanîfah's adherents today are the 'Irâqîs and the Muslims of India, China, Transoxania, and all the non-Arab (Persian-Turkish) countries. His school had formerly been restricted rather to Baghdad and the 'Irâq. There had been

180 Cf. Bombaci, p. 454.

181 Bulaq adds: "because his school makes little use of independent judgment and is so greatly predicated upon the support of transmission and traditions."

182 C and D: "and."

183 The rest of the paragraph is not found in A and Bulaq.

184 The rest of the paragraph is not found in B. It appears in the margin of C, and in the text of D.

pupils of his at the court of the 'Abbâsid caliphs. Their writings were numerous and their disputations with the Shâfi'ites were frequent. Their ways of dealing with controversial questions [185] were excellent. They made a nice discipline out of (the subject of controversial questions) and developed remarkable ideas in this connection. All that is in the hands of scholars. The Maghrib has some knowledge of it. It was brought there by Judge Ibn al-'Arabî [186] and Abû l-Walîd al-Bâjî [187] from their travels.

Ash-Shâfi'î has more adherents in Egypt than anywhere else. His school had formerly spread through the 'Irâq, Khurâsân, and Transoxania. The Shâfi'ites had shared with the Ḥanafites the task of giving legal decisions and teaching in all (Muslim) cities. They had many discussion meetings, and the books on controversial questions are full of the various kinds of (Shâfi'ite) argumentation. Later on, all this stopped when the eastern countries were wiped out.

When the imam Muḥammad b. Idrîs ash-Shâfi'î took up his residence with the 'Abd-al-Ḥakam family [188] in Egypt, a number of them [189] studied with him. His pupils in Egypt included al-Buwayṭî,[190] al-Muzanî,[191] and others. Mâlikites [192]

[185] Cf. pp. 23 ff., below.

[186] Muḥammad b. 'Abdallâh al-Ishbîlî, d. 543 [1148]. Cf. *GAL, Suppl.*, I, 732 f., where his work on controversial questions, and his *Travels*, are mentioned.

[187] Sulaymân b. Khalaf, eleventh century. Cf. *GAL*, I, 419; *Suppl.*, I, 743 f. In MS. D, the order of the names Ibn al-'Arabî and al-Bâjî is reversed.

[188] 'Abdallâh b. 'Abd-al-Ḥakam, d. 214 [830], and his sons 'Abd-ar-Raḥmân, d. 257 [871], 'Abd-al-Ḥakam, d. 851/52, and Muḥammad, 182–268 [798–882]. The last named was a student of ash-Shâfi'î who, after ash-Shâfi'î's death, switched to Mâlikism. Cf. *GAL*, I, 148; *Suppl.*, I, 227 f.; as-Suyûṭî, *Ḥusn al-muḥâḍarah* (Cairo, 1299/1881–82), I, 166 f., 169, 254.

[189] One would expect "a number of Egyptians," but the text hardly permits such an interpretation.

[190] Yûsuf b. Yaḥyâ, d. 231 or 232 [845–47]. Cf. al-Khaṭîb al-Baghdâdî, *Ta'rîkh Baghdâd* (Cairo, 1349/1931), XIV, 299 ff.

[191] Ismâ'îl b. Yaḥyâ, d. 264 [878]. Cf. *GAL*, I, 180; *Suppl.*, I, 305.

[192] The reference to Mâlikites is out of place here, being induced by the preceding reference to the 'Abd-al-Ḥakam family, who wavered between Shâfi'ism and Mâlikism.

in Egypt were certain members of the ʿAbd-al-Ḥakam family,[193] Ashhab,[194] Ibn al-Qâsim,[195] Ibn al-Mawwâz,[196] and, further, al-Ḥârith b. Miskîn [197] and his family; then, Judge III, 8
Abû Isḥâq b. Shaʿbân [198] and his followers. Orthodox jurisprudence was then cut off from Egypt by the appearance of the Shîʿah dynasty. 'Alid jurisprudence came into use there. All the other (schools with their) scholars were on the point of complete disappearance, when [199] Judge ʿAbd-al-Wahhâb [200] came to Egypt from Baghdad at the end of the fourth [tenth] century, because he was in need and had to seek a livelihood. The ʿUbaydid(-Fâṭimid) caliphs proceeded [201] to honor him. They advertised his great qualifications, in order to be able to blame the ʿAbbâsids for driving out such a religious leader, and showed satisfaction with him. As a result, the Mâlikite school saw some flourishing in Egypt, until the extremist [202] Shîʿah ʿUbaydid(-Fâṭimid) dynasty was wiped out by Ṣalâḥ-ad-dîn b. Ayyûb. That meant the end of ʿAlid jurisprudence in Egypt and the return of orthodox jurisprudence among the Egyptians. The jurisprudence of ash-Shâfiʿî and his ʿIrâqî followers now flourished (in Egypt). It turned out to be in a better position than before,

---

193 The beginning of this sentence is not found in Bulaq.

194 Ashab b. ʿAbd-al-ʿAzîz, 140–204 [757/58–820]. Cf. as-Suyûṭî, *Ḥusn al-muḥâḍarah*, I, 166.

195 ʿAbd-ar-Raḥmân b. al-Qâsim, 132–191 [719–806]. Cf. *GAL*, I, 176 f.; *Suppl.*, I, 299.

196 Muḥammad b. Ibrâhîm, d. 281 [894]. Cf. *GAL*, I, 177; *Suppl.*, I, 300.

197 154–250 [771–864]. Cf. as-Suyûṭî, *op. cit.*, I, 168. His son Aḥmad, 239–311 [853/54–923/24], is mentioned by as-Suyûṭi, I, 255.

198 Muḥammad b. al-Qâsim, d. 355 [966]. Cf. Ibn Farḥûn, *Dîbâj* (Fez, 1316/1898–99), pp. 231 f.; as-Suyûṭî, *op. cit.*, I, 172. The reference to Ibn Shaʿbân is not found in Bulaq. "Abû Isḥâq" is omitted in D.

199 The text from here to l. 15 (Egypt) is not found in Bulaq. Cf. pp. 17 f., below.

200 ʿAbd-al-Wahhâb b. ʿAlî, 362–422 [973–1031]. Cf. *GAL*, *Suppl.*, I, 660. Ibn Bassâm mentions ʿAbd-al-Wahhâb's lack of success in Baghdad in the *Dhakhîrah*. Cf. Ibn al-ʿImâd, *Shadharât adh-dhahab* (Cairo, 1350–51/1931–33), III, 223 f.; Ibn Farḥûn, *Dîbâj* (Cairo, 1351/1932), p. 159.

201 *Fa-bâdara*, as in B. The wrong reading *fa-taʾadhdhana* in C and D entered Dozy's *Supplément aux dictionnaires arabes*, I, 15.

202 "Extremist" is not found in D.

and was greatly cultivated.[203] The book of ar-Râfi'î [204] was imported from the 'Irâq into Syria and Egypt. Among famous Shâfi'ites were Muḥyî-ad-dîn an-Nawawî, one of the champions who had grown up in the shadow of the Ayyûbid dynasty in Syria, further, 'Izz-ad-dîn b. 'Abd-as-Salâm,[205] then, Ibn ar-Raf'ah [206] in Egypt, and Taqî-ad-dîn b. Daqîq-al-'îd.[207] After the latter two, there was Taqî-ad-dîn as-Subkî.[208] Finally, (Shâfi'ite leadership) was assumed by the present *Shaykh* of Islam in Egypt, Sirâj-ad-dîn al-Bulqînî.[209] He is the greatest Shâfi'ite in Egypt today and, indeed, the greatest Egyptian religious scholar.

Mâlik's school was restricted to Maghribîs and Spaniards, even though it was also found among other peoples.
III, 9 However, (Maghribîs and Spaniards) very rarely follow other schools. (This situation is explained by the fact that) they mostly traveled to the Ḥijâz. There, their journey ended. Medina, at that time, was the home of religious scholarship, which spread to the 'Irâq from there. The 'Irâq did not lie in the way of (the travels of the Maghribîs and the Spaniards). Thus, they restricted themselves to studying with the scholars of Medina, that is, with Mâlik, the leading Medinese scholar at that time, as with his teachers before him and with his pupils after him. Thus, Maghribîs and Spaniards (always) referred to (Mâlik) and became his adherents and nobody else's, as the methods of other (authorities) did not reach

[203] This sentence follows in B the sentence that is here next.

[204] 'Abd-al-Karîm b. Muḥammad, d. 623 [1226]. Cf. *GAL*, I, 393; *Suppl.*, I, 678. The "book" is the *Kitâb al-Muḥarrar*. The 'Irâq is evidently "the non-Arab 'Irâq."

[205] 'Abd-al-'Azîz b. 'Abd-as-Salâm, 577–660 [1181/82–1262]. Cf. *GAL*, I, 430 f.; *Suppl.*, I, 766 ff.

[206] Aḥmad b. Muḥammad, 645–710 [1247/48–1310]. Cf. *GAL*, II, 133 f.; *Suppl.*, II, 164.

[207] Muḥammad b. 'Alî, 625–702 [1228–1302]. Cf. *GAL*, II, 63; *Suppl.*, II, 66.

[208] 'Alî b. 'Abd-al-Kâfî, 683 [1284] to 755 or 756 [1354/55]. Cf. *GAL*, II, 86 ff.; *Suppl.*, II, 102 ff.

[209] 'Umar b. Raslân, 724–805 [1324–1403]. Cf. *GAL*, II, 93; *Suppl.*, II, 110.

them. Furthermore, the desert attitude was predominant among Maghribîs and Spaniards. They did not care for sedentary culture, such as existed among the 'Irâqîs. Therefore, they were more inclined toward the Ḥijâzîs, because the Ḥijâzîs also had the desert attitude. Thus, the Mâlikite school among them always retained its simplicity and was not affected by the refinement and improvement of sedentary culture that took effect in other schools.

The school doctrine of each authority became, among his adherents, a scholarly discipline in its own right. They were no longer in a position to apply independent judgment and analogy. Therefore, they had to make reference to the established principles from the school doctrine of their authority, in order to be able to analyze problems in their context and disentangle them when they got confused. A firmly rooted habit was required to enable a person to undertake such analysis and disentanglement and to apply the school doctrine of his particular authority to those (processes) according to the best of his ability. This habit is (what is meant) at this time by the science of jurisprudence.

All Maghribîs are adherents of Mâlik. His pupils were formerly spread over Egypt and the 'Irâq. In the 'Irâq, they were represented by Judge Ismâ'îl [210] and his contemporaries, such as Ibn Khuwâzmandâd,[211] Ibn al-Muntâb,[212] Judge Abû III, *10*

[210] Ismâ'îl b. Isḥâq, 199 or 200 [814–16] to 282 [896]. Cf. *GAL, Suppl.*, I, 273, and above, 1:38. The "men of his class" ("his contemporaries"), however, lived a century after him.

[211] Abû 'Abdallâh (Bakr) Muḥammad b. Aḥmad, a pupil of al-Abharî. Cf. I. Goldziher in *Zeitschrift der Deutschen Morgenländischen Gesellschaft*, LVIII (1904), 582–85; Ibn Farḥûn, *Dîbâj* (Cairo ed.), p. 268. According to Goldziher, the correct form of his name would be Ibn Khuwayrmandâd, and that is precisely what we find in Bulaq. The existence of both forms is acknowledged by Ibn Ḥajar, *Lisân al-Mîzân* (Hyderabad, 1329–31/1911–13), V, 291 f. Cf. also aṣ-Ṣafadî, *Wâfî*, ed. S. Dedering (Istanbul, 1949), II, 52.

[212] Ibn al-Muntâb is not identical with either of the two brothers of this name, 'Abdallâh and 'Uthmân b. 'Amr, who lived in the tenth century. He figures as a pupil of Judge Ismâ'îl, teacher of al-Abharî, and contemporary of a man who died in 303 [915/16]. Cf. Ibn Farḥûn, *Dîbâj* (Cairo ed.), pp. 93, 156, 255.

Bakr al-Abharî,[213] Judge Abû l-Ḥasan b. al-Qaṣṣâr,[214] Judge 'Abd-al-Wahhâb,[215] and their successors. In Egypt, there was Ibn al-Qâsim, Ashhab, Ibn 'Abd-al-Ḥakam, al-Ḥârith b. Miskîn, and their contemporaries. Yaḥyâ b. Yaḥyâ al-Laythî[216] traveled from Spain (to the East) and met Mâlik and transmitted the *Muwaṭṭa'* on his authority. He was an important pupil of Mâlik. Also, 'Abd-al-Malik b. Ḥabîb[217] traveled from Spain (to the East) and studied with Ibn al-Qâsim and his contemporaries. He spread the school of Mâlik in Spain. He wrote a systematic work on it, in the *Kitâb al-Wâḍiḥah*. A pupil of his, al-'Utbî,[218] wrote the *'Utbîyah*.

Asad b. al-Furât[219] traveled from Ifrîqiyah (to the East) and studied first with the followers of Abû Ḥanîfah, but then changed over to the school of Mâlik. He studied with Ibn al-Qâsim all the chapters of jurisprudence and wrote down what he learned. He brought his book back to al-Qayrawân. It was called *al-Asadîyah*, after Asad b. al-Furât. Saḥnûn[220] studied it with Asad (himself). He, then, traveled to the East and met Ibn al-Qâsim. He studied with him and confronted him with the problems of the *Asadîyah*. He reconsidered many of them, and Saḥnûn wrote down his own[221] problems in a systematic work, and stated which of the problems of

[213] Muḥammad b. 'Abdallâh, 289–375 [902–986]. Cf. al-Khaṭîb al-Baghdâdî, *Ta'rîkh Baghdâd*, V, 462 f.; Ibn al-Jawzî, *Muntaẓam* (Hyderabad, 1357——/1938——), VII, 131.

[214] 'Alî b. Aḥmad, d. 398 [1007/1008]. Cf. Ibn Farḥûn, *Dîbâj* (Cairo ed.), p. 199; *GAL, Suppl.*, I, 660 (No. 1[5]); II, 963 (No. 49). Cf. also below, p. 32.

[215] Not in D. For 'Abd-al-Wahhâb and the following four men, cf. p. 11, above.

[216] Died 234 or 236 [848–851]. Cf. *GAL, Suppl.*, I, 297; Ibn Ḥajar, *Tahdhîb* (Hyderabad, 1325–27/1907–9), XI, 300 f. The passage concerning Yaḥyâ is found only in C (in the margin) and D.

[217] Died 238 or 239 [853/54]. Cf. *GAL*, I, 149 f.; *Suppl.*, I, 231.

[218] Muḥammad b. Aḥmad, d. 235 [869]. Cf. *GAL*, I, 177; *Suppl.*, I, 300 f. Cf. also below, p. 286.

[219] Born between 142 and 145 [759–63], died in 213 or 214 [828–30]. Cf. Ibn Farḥûn, *Dîbâj* (Cairo ed.), p. 98.

[220] 'Abd-as-Salâm b. Sa'îd, Saḥnûn or Suḥnûn, 160–240 [776/77–854]. Cf. *GAL, Suppl.*, I, 299 f.

[221] Or Ibn al-Qâsim's problems.

the *Asadîyah* he had reconsidered. Ibn al-Qâsim and he together wrote to Asad and asked him to delete from the *Asadîyah* the problems that had been reconsidered (by Ibn al-Qâsim and Saḥnûn) and to accept the book of Saḥnûn. Asad, however, refused to do that. As a result, people disregarded Asad's book and followed the *Mudawwanah* of Saḥnûn, despite the fact that (in the *Mudawwanah*) different problems were (confusingly) lumped together in the various chapters. Therefore, the *Mudawwanah* was called *Mudawwanah*-and-*Mukhtaliṭah* (the "mixed up, confused one"). The inhabitants of al-Qayrawân concentrated upon the *Mudawwanah*, whereas the Spaniards concentrated upon the III, *11*
Wâḍiḥah and the *'Utbîyah*.

Ibn Abî Zayd,[222] then, made a compendium of the *Mudawwanah*-and-*Mukhtaliṭah* in a book entitled *al-Mukhtaṣar*. One of the jurists of al-Qayrawân, Abû Sa'îd al-Barâdhi'î,[223] also made a compendium of it in a book entitled *at-Tahdhîb*. The *shaykh*s of Ifrîqiyah used the *Tahdhîb* as their textbook. They accepted it and disregarded all other works. In the same way, the Spaniards used the *'Utbîyah* as their textbook and kept away from the *Wâḍiḥah* and other works.

Mâlikite scholars have never ceased writing commentaries, explanations, and synopses of these main works. The people of Ifrîqiyah wrote a good deal on the *Mudawwanah*. Scholars such as Ibn Yûnus,[224] al-Lakhmî,[225] Ibn Muḥriz,[226] at-Tûnisî,[227] Ibn Bashîr,[228] and others, wrote on it. The

[222] Cf. 1:223, above.

[223] Khalaf b. Abî l-Qâsim (wrote in 372 [982]). Cf. *GAL*, I, 178; *Suppl.*, I, 302. The reading Barâdhi'î, and not Barâdi'î, is indicated in B and C in this case, though not in the later occurrence of the name, below, p. 286.

[224] Abû 'Abdallâh b. Yûnus, *ca.* 1100. Cf. *GAL*, *Suppl.*, I, 663; II, 963 (No. 53). D. Santillana, *Istituzioni di diritto musulmano malichita*, II, 651, has Abû Bakr Muḥammad b. 'Abdallâh b. Yûnus, d. 451 [1059].

[225] 'Alî b. 'Abdallâh, d. 478 [1085]. Cf. *GAL*, I, 383; *Suppl.*, 300, 661. D. Santillana, *op. cit.*, II, 651, has 'Alî b. Muḥammad.

[226] Abû l-Qâsim, a contemporary of the following Tûnisî. Cf. Ibn Farḥûn, *Dîbâj* (Cairo ed.), pp. 39, 120.

[227] Abû Isḥâq Ibrâhîm b. Ḥasan, died "at the beginning of the disturbances in al-Qayrawân," i.e., during the Arab attacks against the city in the 1050's—possibly in 447 [1055/56] when al-Mu'izz withdrew, or 449

Spaniards wrote a good deal on the *'Utbîyah*. Scholars such as Ibn Rushd[229] and others wrote on it.

Ibn Abî Zayd collected all the problems, contradictions, and statements from the main works in the *Kitâb an-Nawâdir*. He dealt with all the stated opinions of the school and listed in detail in that book the contents of all the main works. Most of it was taken over by Ibn Yûnus into his book on the *Mudawwanah*.

The Mâlikite school was very actively cultivated in the two countries (Spain and northwestern Africa), until the dynasties of Córdoba and al-Qayrawân were destroyed. Later on, the Maghribîs held on to the (Mâlikite tradition of the) two (cities).

III, *12* * There[230] are three different schools within the Mâlikite school:

(1) That of the Qayrawânians. Its founder was Saḥnûn, who studied with Ibn al-Qâsim.

(2) That of the Cordovans. Its founder was Ibn Ḥabîb, who studied with Mâlik, Muṭarrif,[231] Ibn al-Mâjishûn,[232] and Aṣbagh.[233]

Eventually, there appeared the book of Abû 'Amr b. al-Ḥâjib, in which he summarized the various approaches of the Mâlikite (authorities) to every subject and enumerated their

[1057/58] when the Arabs sacked it. Cf. Ibn Farḥûn, *Dîbâj* (Cairo ed.), pp. 88 f.

[228] He apparently is identical with Ibrâhîm b. 'Abd-aṣ-Ṣamad, who lived *ca.* 1100. Cf. Ibn Farḥûn, *op. cit.*, p. 87, who does not, however, mention his work on the *Mudawwanah*. Cf. *GAL*, *Suppl.*, I, 300; II, 960 (No. 22). For this passage, see also below, p. 288.

[229] Muḥammad b. Aḥmad, 450–520 [1058–1126], the philosopher's grandfather. Cf. *GAL*, I, 384; *Suppl.*, I, 300, 662.

[230] The lower text (in italics) is that of Bulaq and A, the upper (between asterisks) that of B, C, and D.

[231] Muṭarrif b. 'Alî, 128 [745/46] to *ca.* 214 [829], son of one of Mâlik's sisters. Cf. Ibn Ḥajar, *Tahdhîb*, X, 175 f.

[232] 'Abd-al-Malik b. 'Abd-al-'Azîz, d. 212 or 214 [827–29]. Cf. Ibn Ḥajar, *Tahdhîb*, VI, 407–409, where 'Abd-al-Malik b. Ḥabîb is mentioned as one of Ibn al-Mâjishûn's students.

[233] Aṣbagh b. al-Faraj, d. 225 [840]. Cf. Ibn Ḥajar, *Tahdhîb*, I, 361 f.

(3) That of the 'Irâqîs. Its founder was Judge Ismâ'îl and his companions.

The Egyptian school followed that of the 'Irâqîs. Judge 'Abd-al-Wahhâb moved from Baghdad to Egypt at the end of the fourth [tenth] century, and the Egyptians studied with him. The Mâlikite school in Egypt had started with al-Ḥârith b. Miskîn, Ibn Muyassar,[234] Ibn al-Lahîb,[235] and Ibn Rashîq.[236] It had remained under cover because of the appearance of the extremist Shî'ah and 'Alid jurisprudence.[237]

The 'Irâqî school was shunned by the inhabitants of al-Qayrawân and Spain, because it was far away, its ways of reaching conclusions were obscure, and they knew little about the sources that (the 'Irâqîs) used. Scholars are (basically) men of independent judgment, even when (their opinion) stands apart (and does not agree with the general opinion), and they do not blindly believe in tradition, nor do they like to use it as (their) method. Therefore, we find that the Maghribîs and Spaniards do not accept the opinion of the 'Irâqîs, whenever they cannot find a tradition of the imam Mâlik or one of his companions to support it.

Later on, the various schools merged with each other. In the sixth [twelfth] century, Abû Bakr aṭ-Ṭurṭûshî [238] traveled from Spain (to the East). He stopped and settled in Jerusalem. The Egyptians and Alexandrians studied with him and took over from him elements of the Spanish school into their own Egyptian school. One of his most important followers was III, *13*

statements on every individual problem. Thus, his work came to be a kind of synopsis of the school.

The Mâlikite school had been in Egypt since the times of al-Ḥârith b. Miskîn, Ibn al-Muyassar, Ibn al-Lahîb, Ibn

---

[234] Aḥmad b. Muḥammad, d. 309 [921/22]. Cf. as-Suyûṭî, *Ḥusn al-muḥâḍarah*, I, 255. C vocalizes Ibn Muyassir.

[235] B has Ibn al-Labîb. No information on him is available to me.

[236] Al-Ḥasan b. 'Atîq, 547–632 [1152/53–1234/35]. Cf. as-Suyûṭî, *op. cit.*, I, 259.

[237] Cf. p. 11, above.

[238] Cf. 1:83, above.

the jurist Sanad, the author of the *Ṭirâz*,[239] and his companions. A number of people studied with them. They included the 'Awf family [240] and their followers. Abû 'Amr b. al-Ḥâjib studied with them. He was followed by Shihâb-ad-dîn al-Qarâfî.[241] In this way, there was a continuity (of Mâlikî teaching) in those times.

The Shâfi'ite school had also been destroyed in Egypt at the time of the 'Alid 'Ubaydid(-Fâṭimid) [242] dynasty. Later on, the work of the Khurâsânian Shâfi'ite ar-Râfi'î [243] made its appearance with the jurists who renewed the Shâfi'ite school. In Syria, one of the Shâfi'ite champions, Muḥyî-ad-dîn an-Nawawî, made his appearance.

Later on, the western school of Mâlikites also took over elements of the 'Irâqî school through ash-Shârimsâḥî.[244] He was outstanding in Alexandria as representative of the Western and Egyptian school. When the 'Abbâsid al-Mustanṣir, the father of al-Musta'ṣim and son of aẓ-Ẓâhir, built his

Rashîq, and Ibn Shâs.[245] *In Alexandria, it was cultivated by the 'Awf and Sanad families, and by Ibn 'Aṭâ'llâh.*[246] *I do not know from whom Abû 'Amr b. al-Ḥâjib* [247] *got his knowledge*

---

[239] Sanad b. 'Inân, d. 541 [1146/47]. Cf. Ibn Farḥûn, *Dîbâj* (Cairo ed.), pp. 126 f.; as-Suyûṭî, *op. cit.*, I, 257. The *Ṭirâz* was a commentary on the *Mudawwanah* in thirty volumes, which he did not live to complete.

[240] Ismâ'îl b. Makkî, 485–581 [1092–1185]. Cf. as-Suyûṭî, *op. cit.*, I, 257 f.; Ibn al-'Imâd, *Shadharât*, IV, 268. This member of the 'Awf family, however, died too early for Ibn al-Ḥâjib to have been his student.

[241] Cf. 2:429 (n. 49), above.

[242] " 'Ubaydid (-Fâṭimid)" added by C (in the margin) and D.

[243] Cf. p. 12, above.

[244] 'Abdallâh b. 'Abd-ar-Raḥmân, 589–669 [1193–1270/71]. Cf. *GAL, Suppl.*, I, 300; as-Suyûṭî, *Ḥusn al-muḥâḍarah*, I, 260. Ibn Khaldûn writes Shârimsâḥî without the long vowel in the first syllable. There existed a place name Shirmasâḥ in Arabia (cf. Yâqût, *Mu'jam al-buldân*, ed. Wüstenfeld [Göttingen, 1866–73], III, 280), but the one to which the *nisbah* here refers is the large village Shârimsâḥ, so vocalized in the Wüstenfeld edition of Yâqût, III, 232. Cf. also Ibn Farḥûn, *Dîbâj* (Cairo ed.), pp. 142 f.

[245] 'Abdallâh b. Najm, d. 616 [1219]. Cf. *GAL, Suppl.*, I, 538; Ibn Kathîr, *Bidâyah* (Cairo, 1351–58/1932–40), XIII, 86; as-Suyûṭî, *op. cit.*, I, 258.

[246] 'Abd-al-Karîm b. 'Aṭâ'llâh, d. 612 [end of 1265 or beginning of 1266]. Cf. as-Suyûṭî, *op. cit.*, I, 260.

[247] 'Uthmân b. 'Umar, d. 646 [1249]. Cf. *GAL*, I, 303 ff.; *Suppl.*, I, 531 ff.

college in Baghdad, he asked the 'Ubaydid(-Fâṭimid) caliphs, who at that time were in Cairo, to send him ash-Shârimsâḥî. They permitted him to go to (al-Mustanṣir). When he arrived in Baghdad, (al-Mustanṣir) appointed him professor in the Mustanṣirîyah College. He remained there until Hûlâgû took possession of Baghdad in 656 [1258]. He escaped the fury of the catastrophe and went free. He remained living there until he died in the days of Hûlâgû's son, Aḥmad Abaghâ.

A compendium of the Egyptian school that had taken over elements of the Western school, was made, as we have mentioned,[248] in the *Mukhtaṣar* of Abû 'Amr b. al-Ḥâjib, which mentions the different problems of every juridical subject and enumerates the various statements on each individual problem. Thus, it came to be a kind of synopsis of the school.*

When his work reached the Maghrib at the end of the III, 14
seventh [thirteenth] century, the majority of Maghribî students, and especially the inhabitants of Bougie, concentrated upon it. The chief teacher of the people of Bougie, Abû 'Alî Nâṣir-ad-dîn az-Zawâwî,[249] had been the one who brought the work of Ibn al-Ḥâjib to the Maghrib. He had studied with (Ibn al-Ḥâjib's) followers in Egypt, had copied his *Mukhtaṣar*, and brought it (to the West). It spread among his pupils in the region of Bougie and was introduced by them into all the other cities of the Maghrib. Contemporary Maghribî students of jurisprudence use and study it, because of the interest the *shaykh* Nâṣir-ad-dîn is said to have aroused in it. A number of Maghribî *shaykhs*, such as Ibn 'Abd-as-

---

of the Mâlikite school, but he lived after the destruction of the 'Ubaydid(-Fâṭimid) dynasty and the disappearance of 'Alid jurisprudence and after the orthodox Shâfi'ite and Mâlikite jurisprudence had reappeared (in Egypt).

[248] Possibly referring back to 2:429? The *Mukhtaṣar* is mentioned in the *Autobiography*, pp. 16 f., 59. Cf. below, pp. 29 f. and 396.

[249] Cf. 2:428 f., above.

Salâm, Ibn Râshid,[250] and Ibn Hârûn,[251] commented on it. All of them are *shaykhs* of Tunis. Their principal champion in this respect is Ibn 'Abd-as-Salâm. In addition, they use the *Kitâb at-Tahdhîb* as textbook in their teaching.

"God guides whomever He wants to guide." [252]

The science of inheritance laws [253]

The science of inheritance laws is the knowledge of estate division and the correct determination of the proper shares in an estate with regard to the relation of the individual shares to the basic divisions. It also includes (the knowledge of) the readjustment of shares (*munâsakhah*). (Such readjustment) is necessary when one of the (original) heirs dies and his portion is to be distributed among his heirs. This requires a calculation to adjust the first division of the estate, so that all the heirs who are entitled to shares in the estate get (to know) their shares without an (actual) distribution (taking
III, *15* place[?]). Such readjustments may have to be undertaken more than once or twice. Thus, there may be a greater number of them. Every time, a (new) calculation is needed.

Also, the division of an estate may have to consider two possibilities, in that, for instance, one heir may acknowledge an(other) heir, while a (third) heir does not acknowledge (that second heir). Then, the division of the estate is adjusted (and figured out) according to the two possibilities, and the amount of the shares is considered. Then, the estate is divided among the heirs in shares proportionate to the basic fractions.[254] All this requires calculation. Therefore,

[250] Muḥammad b. 'Abdallâh al-Qafṣî, d. 736 [1335/36]. Cf. Aḥmad Bâbâ, *Nayl* (Cairo, 1329/1911), pp. 235 f., as quoted by D. Santillana, *Istituzioni di diritto musulmano malichita*, II, 650; *GAL*, *Suppl.*, II, 963 (No. 50); II, 1041 (No. 45).

[251] 'Abdallâh b. Muḥammad, 603–702 [1207–1303]. Cf. *Autobiography*, pp. 19, 306.

[252] Qur'ân 2.142 (136), etc.

[253] Treated again among the intellectual sciences as a part of arithmetic, pp. 127 ff., below.

[254] De Slane explains the situation as follows: A and B are heirs. A acknowledges a third heir, C; B does not. The estate is distributed between

jurists made of it a separate subject, because, in addition to jurisprudence, it requires calculation as the predominant element in it. They considered it a discipline in its own right.

Scholars have written many works on it. The most famous work on the subject among the more recent Spanish Mâlikites is the work of Ibn Thâbit[255] and the *Mukhtaṣar* of Judge Abû l-Qâsim al-Ḥawfî,[256] and then (the one by) al-Ja'dî.[257] Among the more recent Africans who wrote on the subject, there is Ibn al-Munammar aṭ-Ṭarâbulusî,[258] and others.[259]

The Shâfi'ites, Ḥanafites, and Ḥanbalites have (also) written many works on the subject. They have given important and difficult practical instances showing their competence in jurisprudence and calculation. There is, especially, Abû l-Ma'âlî (Imâm al-Ḥaramayn),[260] and similar jurists.

This is a noble discipline. It combines intellectual and traditional knowledge. It figures the claims in inheritance matters in a sound and definite way, whenever those who are charged with the division of an estate do not know the portion (of the estate that should go to each heir) and have difficulties with it.

Religious scholars in the Muslim cities have paid much attention to it. Some authors are inclined to exaggerate the mathematical side of the discipline and to pose problems
requiring for their solution various branches of arithmetic, III, *16*
such as algebra, the use of roots, and similar things. They

A and B, as if they were the only heirs. Then, the individual shares are figured for A, B, and C as heirs, and C receives his share from A's original share.

[255] His identity is not clear to me. Perhaps, he is Aḥmad b. 'Abdallâh, who died in 447 [1055/56]?

[256] Aḥmad b. Muḥammad b. Khalaf, d. 588 [1192]. Cf. *GAL*, I, 384; *Suppl.*, I, 663. Cf. also H. P. J. Renaud in *Hespéris*, XXV (1938), 39.

[257] There is a well-known work that would fit the description, the *Ja'dîyah* by Abû Muḥammad al-Ḥasan b. 'Alî b. Ja'd aṣ-Ṣiqillî, mentioned by Ḥâjjî Khalîfah. However, Ibn Khaldûn would not have quoted an incorrect title, and his al-Ja'dî still remains unidentified. He is mentioned again p. 129, below.

[258] He lived in the first half of the eleventh century. Cf. *'Ibar*, VII, 43; de Slane (tr.), III, 267.

[259] For these men cf. again pp. 128 f., below.

[260] Cf. n. 225 to Ch. III, above.

fill their works with such matters. It is not something that is much used by the people, and it is of no practical use for them in their inheritance matters, because it deals with unusual and rare cases. However, it is useful for practice and offers the best opportunity for acquiring the proper habit, (which can then be) applied to actual cases.

Most of the scholars who are concerned with this discipline refer, in order to prove its excellence, to the following tradition, which is transmitted on the authority of Abû Hurayrah: "The *farâ'iḍ* (inheritance laws) constitute one-third of (religious) scholarship, and they are the first (discipline) to be forgotten." [261] Another recension has: "One-half of (religious) scholarship." The tradition was published by the *ḥadîth* expert Abû Nu'aym.[262] People who are concerned with inheritance laws use it as an argument (in favor of the importance of their science), because they think that *farâ'iḍ* in the tradition quoted refers to estate division (*furûḍ*). However, it is obvious that such an interpretation is farfetched. *Farâ'iḍ* here is intended to mean "obligations" (*furûḍ*) imposed upon Muslims in connection with religious worship, customs, matters of inheritance, and other things. If understood in this sense, it is correct to state that (the *farâ'iḍ*) constitute one-half or one-third of scholarship. The inheritance laws (by themselves) constitute a much lesser portion of religious scholarship as a whole.

This interpretation of the meaning of *farâ'iḍ* in the tradition quoted, is supported by the fact that the application of the word *farâ'iḍ* to a particular discipline, or its restriction to estate division, is part of the technical terminology the jurists created when the various disciplines and terminologies came into existence. At the beginning of Islam, the word (*farâ'iḍ*) was used only in a general way. It was derived from *farḍ*, which means "to determine" or "to cut." [262a] It

[261] Cf. D. Santillana, *op. cit.*, II, 497. Cf. also p. 128, below.

[262] Aḥmad b. 'Abdallâh, 336–430 [948–1038]. Cf. *GAL*, I, 362; *Suppl.*, I, 616 f. His *Musnad* is preserved in MS, but was not available.

[262a] "To determine," rather than "to apportion," is the intended meaning of *taqdîr*, according to Ibn al-Athîr, *Nihâyah* (Cairo, 1322/1904), III, 210;

was intended to be used for all the *furûḍ* "obligations," as we have stated. Such was its actual use in the religious law. (In interpreting the tradition quoted,) the word must not III, 17 be taken to mean anything but what it meant at the time of the (early Muslims). That indicates most correctly what they meant by it.

And God knows better.

[13] *The science of the principles of jurisprudence and its subdivisions, dialectics and controversial questions.*[263]

It should be known that the science of the principles of jurisprudence is one of the greatest, most important, and most useful disciplines of the religious law. It is concerned with the evidence of the religious law from which the laws and legal obligations of the Muslims are derived.

The basic sources of legal evidence are the Book—that is, the Qur'ân—and, then, the Sunnah, which clarifies the Qur'ân. At the time of the Prophet, the laws were received (directly) from him. He possessed the Qur'ânic revelation, and he explained it directly by his words and deeds. No transmission, speculation, or analogical reasoning was needed. After the Prophet's death, direct (explanation of the Qur'ân's legal significance) was no longer possible. The Qur'ân was preserved through a general and continuous transmission. As to the Sunnah, the men around Muḥammad all agreed that it is necessary for us to act in accordance with whatever of it has reached us, as statement or practice, through a sound tradition that can be assumed to be truthful. It is in this sense that legal evidence is determined by Qur'ân and Sunnah.

Then, general consensus (*ijmâ'*) took its place next to

Lisân al-'Arab (Bulaq, 1300–1308/1882–90), IX, 67. *Qaṭ'* is to be understood in its literal meaning, "to cut, to cut off." Cf. the Arabic and general Semitic root *p/f-r-ṣ*.

[263] The section on the principles of jurisprudence has been translated by J.-D. Luciani, "La Théorie du droit musulman (Ouçoul el fiqh) d'après Ibn Khaldûn" in *Revue africaine*, LXIX (1928), 49–64.

(Qur'ân and Sunnah). The men around Muḥammad agreed to disapprove of those who held opinions different from theirs. They would not have done that without some basis for doing so, because people like the men around Muḥammad do not agree upon something without a valid argument. In addition, the evidence attests the infallibility of the whole group. Thus, general consensus became a valid proof in legal matters.

III, *18* Then, we looked into the methods according to which the men around Muḥammad and the early generations made their deductions from Qur'ân and Sunnah. It was found that they compared similar (cases) and drew conclusions from analogy, in that they either all agreed or some of them made concessions in this connection to others. Many of the things that happened after the Prophet are not included in the established texts.[264] Therefore, they compared and combined them with the established indications that are found in the texts, (and drew their conclusions from analogy) according to certain rules that governed their combinations. This assured the soundness of their comparison of two similar (cases), so that it could be assumed that one and the same divine law covered both cases. This became (another kind of) legal evidence, because the (early Muslims) all agreed upon it. This is analogy (*qiyâs*), the fourth kind of evidence.

The great mass of religious scholars is agreed that these are the four basic kinds of evidence. Some scholars differed on the matters of general consensus and analogy. But this is exceptional. Others added further kinds of evidence to the four.[265] We do not have to mention them here, because the basis (upon which they rest) is weak, and they are rarely referred to.

[264] Luciani suggests "les dispositions déjà consacrées" = "precedent cases," but *nuṣûṣ* "texts" evidently refers here to the established texts of the Qur'ân and the Sunnah.

[265] As, for instance, *ʿurf* "common usage," or some subdivisions of the use of opinion, such as *istiṣlâḥ* "considerations of the general welfare." Cf. I. Goldziher, *Die Ẓâhiriten*, pp. 204–6; J. Schacht in *EI*, *s.v.* "Uṣûl."

The first task of this discipline is to study the (right of) existence of the four kinds of evidence.

(1) Proofs for the Qur'ân are the decisively miraculous, (inimitable) character of its text, and the general continuity of its transmission. This leaves no room for any doubt.

(2) The Sunnah, as it has been transmitted to us, is justified[266] by the general consensus (to the effect) that Muslims must act in accordance with traditions that are sound, as we have mentioned before. This is supported by Muḥammad's practice, during his lifetime, of sending letters and messengers to the various regions with legal and religious commands and prohibitions.

(3) The general consensus is justified by the fact that
the men around Muḥammad had agreed to disapprove of III, *19*
those who held opinions different from theirs. In addition, there is the established infallibility of the Muslim nation (as a whole).

(4) Analogy is justified by the general consensus of the men around Muḥammad concerning its (admissibility), as we have mentioned before.

These are the basic kinds of evidence.

The transmitted traditions of the Sunnah need verification through an investigation of the ways of transmission and the probity (*'adâlah*) of transmitters, so that the likelihood of the truthfulness of the transmitted information, which is the basis for the necessity to act in accordance with it, becomes clear. This also is one of the basic subjects of the discipline. Added to this is the knowledge of abrogating and abrogated traditions, when two traditions are mutually contradictory and the earlier one of the two is sought.[267] This, too, is another subject of the discipline.

After that, there comes the study of the meaning of words. This is because one depends upon knowledge of the conventional meanings of single or composite utterances, for

[266] *Leg. fa-li-l-ijmâ'?*
[267] Cf. 2:447 f., above.

deriving ideas in general from word combinations in general. The philological norms needed in this connection are found in the sciences of grammar, inflection, and syntax and style.[268] Now, when speech was a habit of those who used it, these (linguistic matters) were neither sciences nor norms. At that time, jurists did not need them, because linguistic matters were familiar to them by natural habit. But when the habit of the Arabic language was lost,[269] the experts who made it their specialty determined it once and for all with the help of a sound tradition and of sound rules of analogy they evolved. (Linguistic matters,) thus, became sciences the jurists had to know, in order to know the divine laws.

Then, there is certain other, special information to be derived from word combinations. One must derive what constitutes law, among the various ideas, from special indications in word combinations that have a bearing upon law. This is jurisprudence.[270] Knowledge of the conventional
III, 20 meanings in general is not sufficient for that. A knowledge of certain other things on which that special information depends, is needed. The laws can be derived from (those things) in accordance with the principles evolved by expert scholars in the religious disciplines, who established those things as norms for the purpose. Among such norms, for instance, are:

The word meaning is not established by analogy.[271]

A word of two meanings cannot be used to mean both things at the same time.

The use of *wa-* "and" does not imply an order (in time, or classification).[272]

[268] For *bayân*, cf. pp. 332 ff., below.

[269] Cf., for instance, p. 346, below.

[270] Cf. Bombaci, p. 454.

[271] Cf. p. 331, below. The statement means what it says, even though in jurisprudence, analogical reasoning occasionally leads to deducing some particular meaning for a word that it is not otherwise known to have.

[272] Cf. Ibn Ḥazm, *al-Iḥkâm fî uṣûl al-aḥkâm* (Cairo, 1345–48/1926–30), I, 51. "Zayd and 'Amr came" may mean that they came together, or that the one came earlier or later—by some indefinite measure of time—than the other. The *Maḥṣûl* of Fakhr-ad-dîn ar-Râzî, with which Ibn Khaldûn was well acquainted, contains lengthy discussions of this and the other principles mentioned.

If certain special particulars are taken out of some general (term), does it remain proof for the rest?

Does a command imply necessary or voluntary (action),[273] immediate or delayed (action)? Does a prohibition imply corruption or soundness (in an action)?

Is something general applicable to something circumscribed?

Is a text indicating the *ratio legis* [274] sufficient or not for extension (of a rule to other cases)?

There are other such things. All of them are basic in this discipline, but since they are semantic problems, they have to do with philology.

Next, the study of analogy is a very important basis of this discipline. It helps to ascertain the correctness of both principal and special aspects of laws depending on reasoning and analogy; to examine the particular characteristic of a case on which the law is considered probably to depend, as to whether it (exists) in the principle; and to find out whether that characteristic exists in the special case without anything contradicting (it), which would make it impossible to base the law upon it. There are other problems that belong together with this one. All of them are basic in this discipline.

It should be known that this discipline is of recent origin in Islam. The early Muslims could dispense with it. Nothing more than the linguistic habit they possessed was needed for deriving ideas from words. The (early Muslims themselves also) were the source for most of the norms needed in special III, *21*
cases for deriving laws. They had no need to study the chains of transmitters, because they were close to the (transmitters) in time and had personal knowledge and experience of them. Then the early Muslims died, and the first period of Islam was over. All the sciences became technical, as we established earlier.[275] Jurists and religious scholars of independent judg-

[273] Cf., for instance, I. Goldziher, *Die Ẓâhiriten*, pp. 71 ff.

[274] Cf. p. 4, above. Luciani, *op. cit.*, p. 59 (n. 9), translates the Arabic term as "disposition formelle indiquant la raison d'une qualification."

[275] Cf., for instance, 2:444, above.

ment now had to acquire these norms and basic rules, in order to be able to derive the laws from the evidence. They wrote them down as a discipline in its own right and called it "principles of jurisprudence." The first scholar to write on the subject was ash-Shâfi'î. He dictated his famous *Risâlah* on the subject. In it, he discussed commands and prohibitions, syntax and style, traditions, abrogations, and the position of *ratio legis* indicated in a text in relation to analogy.[276]

Later on, Ḥanafite jurists wrote on the subject. They verified the basic rules and discussed them extensively. The speculative theologians also wrote on the subject. However, treatment by jurists is more germane to jurisprudence and more suited for (practical application to) special cases, (than treatment of the subject by speculative theologians), because (juridical works) mention many examples and cases and base their problems on legal points. The theologians, on the other hand, present these problems in their bare outlines, without reference to jurisprudence, and are inclined to use (abstract) logical deduction as much as possible, since that is their scholarly approach and required by their method.

Ḥanafite jurists were especially accomplished in extensive use of legal points and in derivation of the norms from the (actual) problems of jurisprudence, as far as possible. One of their leading scholars, Abû Zayd ad-Dabûsî,[277] wrote more widely on analogical reasoning than any other (Ḥanafite). He completed the research methods and conditions governing this discipline. Thus, the technique of the principles of juris-
III, *22* prudence was perfected. The problems were refined and the basic rules were laid down.

Scholars also occupied themselves with the methods of speculative theologians in connection with this discipline. The best books written by theologians on this subject were the *Kitâb al-Burhân*, by the Imâm al-Ḥaramayn, and the *Mus-*

[276] This refers to the principle mentioned on p. 27.

[277] 'Abdallâh ('Ubaydallâh) b. 'Umar, d. 430 [1038/39]. Cf. *GAL*, I, 175; *Suppl.*, I, 296 f.

taṣfâ, by al-Ghazzâlî. Both authors were Ash'arites. There were two more books, the *Kitâb al-'Umad* by 'Abd-al-Jabbâr,[278] and the commentary on it, entitled *al-Mu'tamad*, by Abû l-Ḥusayn al-Baṣrî.[279] Both authors were Mu'tazilah. These four books were the basic works and pillars of this discipline. They were later on abridged by two excellent recent theologians, the imam Fakhr-ad-dîn Ibn al-Khaṭîb, in the *Kitâb al-Maḥṣûl*,[280] and Sayf-ad-dîn al-Âmidî, in the *Kitâb al-Iḥkâm*.[281] Their approaches to the discipline differed in (the degree of emphasis they placed upon) verification and argumentation. Ibn al-Khaṭîb was more inclined to present many proofs and arguments, while al-Âmidî was eager to verify the views of the schools and to present the problems in detail.

The *Kitâb al-Maḥṣûl* was abridged by such pupils of the imam (Fakhr-ad-dîn) as Sirâj-ad-dîn al-Urmawî,[282] in the *Kitâb at-Taḥṣîl*, and Tâj-ad-dîn al-Urmawî,[283] in the *Kitâb al-Ḥâṣil*. Shihâb-ad-dîn al-Qarâfî [284] selected certain propositions and basic points from these works in a small book which he entitled *at-Tanqîḥât*. The same was done by al-Bayḍâwî in the *Kitâb al-Minhâj*.[285] Beginners occupied themselves with these two books, and many people wrote commentaries on them.

The *Kitâb al-Iḥkâm* by al-Âmidî is more concerned with verifying the problems. It was abridged by Abû 'Amr b. al-Ḥâjib, in the work of his known as the large *Mukhtaṣar*.

[278] 'Abd-al-Jabbâr b. Aḥmad al-Asadâbâdî, d. 415 [1025]. Cf. *GAL*, *Suppl.*, I, 343 f. The title of the work is given as above in A, B, C, and D, with A, C, and D also indicating the vocalization. Bulaq reads *al-'Ahd*.

[279] Muḥammad b. 'Alî, d. 436 [1044]. Cf., for instance, al-Khaṭîb al-Baghdâdî, *Ta'rîkh Baghdâd*, III, 100; Ibn al-Jawzî, *Muntaẓam*, VIII, 126 f.; Ibn Ḥajar, *Lisân al-Mîzân*, V, 298; Ibn al-'Imâd, *Shadharât*, III, 259.

[280] Cf. *GAL*, I, 506 (No. 3), and above, 1:402.

[281] 'Alî b. Abî 'Alî, d. 631 [1233]. Cf. *GAL*, I, 393; *Suppl.*, I, 678. Cf. p. 148, below.

[282] Maḥmûd b. Abî Bakr, 594–682 [1197/98–1283]. Cf. *GAL*, I, 467; *Suppl.*, I, 848 f., 921.

[283] Muḥammad b. al-Ḥasan, d. 656 [1258]. Cf. *GAL*, *Suppl.*, I, 921.

[284] Cf. 2:429 (n. 49), above.

[285] 'Abdallâh b. 'Umar, thirteenth century. Cf. *GAL*, I, 416 ff.; *Suppl.*, I, 738 ff.

Ibn al-Ḥâjib then made another compendium of it, which
III, 23 is used by students.[286] People both in the East and the West studied it and wrote commentaries on it. These compendia represent at its best the approach of the theologians to this discipline.

The Ḥanafites have written a great deal on their approach (to the discipline). The best writings on it by an early scholar are the works of Abû Zayd ad-Dabûsî. The best works on it by a recent scholar are those by Sayf-al-Islâm al-Bazdawî,[287] a leading Ḥanafite. They exhaust the subject. Later on, the Ḥanafite jurist Ibn as-Sâʻâtî [288] combined the approaches of the *Kitâb al-Iḥkâm* and the work of al-Bazdawî in a book entitled *Kitâb al-Badîʻ*. The *Kitâb al-Badîʻ* turned out to be a very well-written and original work. Leading contemporary religious scholars use it for teaching and research. Many non-Arab scholars have been eager to write commentaries on it, and the situation is (still) the same at the present time.

The (foregoing remarks) have explained the real meaning of this discipline, described the subjects with which it deals, and enumerated the works on it known at the present time.

May God let us profit from scholarship and make us scholars through His kindness and generosity.

The controversial questions [289]

It should be known that the jurisprudence described, which is based upon religious evidence, involves many differences of opinion among scholars of independent judgment. Differences of opinion result from the different sources they use and their different outlooks, and are unavoidable, as we have stated before.[290]

[286] Cf. p. 19, above.

[287] ʻAlî b. Muḥammad, d. 482 [1089]. Cf. *GAL*, I, 373; *Suppl.*, I, 637f. He is usually called Fakhr-al-Islâm.

[288] Aḥmad b. ʻAlî, d. after 1291. Cf. *GAL*, I, 382 f.; *Suppl.*, I, 658.

[289] I. Goldziher's suggestion, *Die Ẓâhiriten*, p. 37 (n. 1), that the subject be investigated in its bibliographical aspect, has not yet been followed up.

[290] Cf. p. 3, above.

(These differences) occupied a very large space in Islam. (Originally,) people could adhere to any (juridical authority) they wished. Later on, the matter was in the hands of the four leading authorities in the Muslim cities. They enjoyed a very high prestige. Adherence was restricted to them, and III, 24
people were thus prevented from adhering to anyone else. This situation was the result of the disappearance of independent judgment, because (the exercise of independent judgment) was too difficult a matter and because, in the course of time, the scholarly disciplines constituting material for independent judgment had multiplied. Also, there existed nobody who might have organized a school in addition to the existing four. Thus, they were set up as the basic schools of Islam:

Differences of opinion among their adherents and the followers of their laws received equal status with differences of opinion concerning religious texts and legal principles (in general). The adherents of the four schools held disputations, in order to prove the correctness of their respective founders. These disputations took place according to sound principles and fast rules. Everyone argued in favor of the correctness of the school to which he adhered and which he followed. The disputations concerned all the problems of religious law and every subject of jurisprudence. The difference of opinion was on occasion between ash-Shâfi'î and Mâlik, with Abû Ḥanîfah agreeing with one of them. Or it was between Mâlik and Abû Ḥanîfah, with ash-Shâfi'î agreeing with one of them. Or it was between ash-Shâfi'î and Abû Ḥanîfah, with Mâlik agreeing with one of them. The disputations clarified the sources of the authorities as well as the motives of their differences and the occasions when they exercised independent judgment.

This kind of scholarship was called "controversial questions." The persons who cultivate it must know the basic rules through which laws can be evolved, just as they are known to scholars of independent judgment. However, the latter need those basic rules in order to find the law, while

the former need them in order to guard the legal problems that have been evolved against destruction by the arguments of an opponent. It is, indeed, a very useful discipline. It affords acquaintance with the sources and evidence of the
III, 25 authorities, and gives students practice in arguing whatever they wish to prove. Works by Ḥanafites and Shâfiʻites are more numerous on the subject than those by Mâlikites. As one knows, analogy is for the Ḥanafites a principle on which many details of their school depend. Therefore, they are the people who speculate and investigate. The Mâlikites, on the other hand, mostly rely on tradition. They do not speculate. Furthermore, most of them are Maghribîs who are Bedouins, who care only a little for the crafts.[291]

There are the following works on the subject: the *Kitâb al-Ma'âkhidh*[292] by al-Ghazzâlî, the *Kitâb at-Talkhîṣ* by the Mâlikite Abû Bakr b. al-ʻArabî,[293] who imported (the subject) from the East, the *Kitâb at-Taʻlîqah* by Abû Zayd ad-Dabûsî, and the *ʻUyûn al-adillah* by the Mâlikite *shaykh* Ibn al-Qaṣṣâr.[294] In his *Mukhtaṣar* on the principles of jurisprudence, Ibn as-Sâʻâtî has collected all the controversial law that is based on the principles of jurisprudence.[295] In connection with every problem, he noted the controversial questions that are based on it.

Dialectics

"Dialectics" involves knowledge of the proper behavior in disputations among the adherents of the legal schools and others. The choices of rejection and acceptance in disputations are numerous. In arguing and answering, each disputant lets himself go in his argumentation. Some of it is correct.

[291] Cf., for instance, 2:433, above.

[292] Cf. al-Murtaḍâ, *Itḥâf as-sâdah* (Cairo, 1311/1893–94), I, 43: ". . . *al-Ma'âkhidh* on controversial questions existing between Ḥanafites and Shâfiʻites." C and D seem to suggest the reading *al-Ma'khadh* (?).

[293] Cf. p. 10 (n. 186), above.

[294] Cf. p. 14 (n. 214), above.

[295] Cf. Bombaci, p. 454. It does not seem quite certain whether *Mukhtaṣar* is a title or just refers to a "brief" work on the subject.

Some of it is wrong. Therefore, the authorities had to lay down the proper rules of behavior by which the disputants would have to abide. These concern rejection and acceptance; III, 26
how the person advancing an argument should behave and how the person replying to the argument should behave; when it is permissible for a disputant to advance an argument; how he (should admit) defeat[296] and stop; when he should interrupt or contradict (his opponent); and where he should be silent and permit his opponent to talk and advance his arguments. It has, therefore, been said that this discipline is the knowledge of the basic rules of proper behavior in arguing, which help either to safeguard an opinion or to demolish it, whether that opinion concerns jurisprudence or any other subject.

There are two methods. There is the method of al-Bazdawî, which is limited to the evidence of the religious law from texts, general consensus, and argumentation.[297] And there is the method of al-'Amîdî[298] which applies quite generally to every argument used in argumentation, no matter to which scholarly discipline it belongs.

Most of the (subject) is concerned with argumentation. It is a good procedure, but, by its very nature, it contains much sophistry. If it is considered under the aspect of logic, it is, as a rule, quite similar to sophistical reasoning. However, the (correct) forms of arguments and syllogisms are carefully observed in it, in that the methods of argumentation in this respect are chosen as it is proper.

The 'Amîdî just mentioned was the first to write on his method.[299] Therefore, its (invention) was ascribed to him. He wrote a brief book, entitled *al-Irshâd*. Later on, he was

[296] *Makhṣûman*, as in A, B, and C.

[297] Cf. Bombaci, p. 455.

[298] Muḥammad b. Muḥammad, d. 615 [1218]. Cf. *GAL*, I, 439 f.; *Suppl.*, I, 785 f.

[299] His priority is stated by Ibn Khallikân, *Wafayât* (Cairo, 1299/1882), II, 270 f.; tr. W. M. de Slane (Paris, 1843–71), II, 660; also by 'Abd-al-Qâdir al-Qurashî, *al-Jawâhir al-muḍîyah* (Hyderabad, 1332/1913–14), II, 128.

followed by such recent scholars as an-Nasafî [300] and others who walked in his steps and followed the way he had shown. Many works were written on the method. At this time, no regard is paid to it, because scholarship and scientific instruction have dwindled in the Muslim cities. It is, after all, a luxury, and not a necessity.

"God has the power to execute His commands." [301]

III, 27 [14] *The science of speculative theology.*

This is a science that involves arguing with logical proofs in defense of the articles of faith and refuting innovators who deviate in their dogmas from the early Muslims and Muslim orthodoxy.

The real core of the articles of faith is the oneness of God. Therefore, we shall present here, first, a nice specimen of logical argumentation that will show us the oneness of God in the most direct method and manner. We shall then go back and give a correct description of speculative theology and the (subjects) it studies. We shall also indicate the reason why it developed in Islam and what it was that called for its invention.

We [302] say: It should be known that the things that come into being in the world of existing things, whether they belong to essences or to either human or animal actions, require appropriate causes which are prior to (their coming into being). They introduce the things that come into being into the realm dominated by custom, and effect their coming into being. Each one of these causes, in turn, comes into being and, thus, requires other causes. Causes continue to follow upon causes in an ascending order, until they reach the Causer of causes, Him who brings them into existence and creates them, Praised be He, there is no God but Him.

[300] 'Umar b. Muḥammad, d. 537 [1142]. Cf. *GAL*, I, 427 f.; *Suppl.*, I, 758 ff.

[301] Qur'ân 12.21 (21).

[302] Cf. Issawi, p. 165.

In the process, the causes multiply and widen in extent vertically and horizontally. The intellect becomes confused in the attempt to perceive and enumerate them. Only a comprehensive knowledge can encompass them all, especially (all) human and animal actions. Among the causes of (action), there evidently belong the various kinds of intention and volition, since no action can materialize except through volition and intention. The various kinds of intention and III, 28
volition are matters pertaining to the soul. As a rule, they originate from previous consecutive perceptions (*taṣawwurât*). These perceptions cause the intention to act. The causes of such perceptions are, again, other perceptions. Now, the cause of all the perceptions taking place in the soul is unknown, since no one is able to know the beginnings or order of matters pertaining to the soul. They are consecutive notions that God puts into the mind of man, who is unable to understand their beginnings and ends. As a rule, man is able only to comprehend the causes that are natural and obvious and that present themselves to our perception in an orderly and well-arranged manner, because nature is encompassed by the soul and on a lower level than it. The range of perceptions, however, is too large for the soul, because they belong to the intellect, which is on a higher level than the soul. The soul, therefore, can scarcely perceive very many of them, let alone all of them. This shows the wisdom of the Lawgiver (Muḥammad) when he forbade (us) to speculate about causes and to stop with them. Such speculation is a field in which the mind becomes lost and gets nowhere, nor gains any real insight.[303] "Say: 'God,' and then let them amuse themselves with their idle talk." [304] Man often stops (to speculate about causes) and thereby is prevented from ascending to the next higher stage. His feet slip. He becomes one of those who go astray and perish. We ask God for protection against disappointment and obvious perdition.

[303] C (apparently through later correction) and D add "of it."
[304] Qur'ân 6.91 (91).

One should not think that man has the power, or can choose at will, to stop or to retrace his steps. No! Talking
III, 29 about causes results in giving the soul a fast coloring. We do not know how (this comes about), for if we knew it, we could be on guard against it. Therefore, one must be on guard against it by completely abandoning any speculation about the (causes).

Furthermore, the way in which the causes exercise their influence upon the majority of the things caused is unknown.[305] They are only known through customary (experience) and through conclusions [306] which attest to (the existence of an) apparent (causal) relationship.[307] What that influence really is and how it takes place is not known. "And you were given but little knowledge." [308] Therefore, we have been commanded completely to abandon and suppress any speculation about them and to direct ourselves to the Causer of all causes, who made them and brought them into existence, so that the soul will be firmly colored with the oneness of God. So were we taught by the Lawgiver (Muḥammad) who knows better (than we do) the things that are to the interest of our religion and the ways that lead us to happiness, because he saw that which is beyond sensual perception. He said: "Whoever dies confessing that there is no God but God, enters Paradise." [309]

A man who stops at the causes is frustrated. He is rightly (said to be) an unbeliever. If he ventures to swim in the ocean of speculation and of research into (causes), (seeking) each one of the causes that cause them and the influence they exercise, I can guarantee him that he will return un-

[305] Cf. p. 261, below.

[306] *Qaḍîyat al-iqtirân* is intended by Ibn Khaldûn as a term of logic, probably identical with *qiyâs iqtirânî*, which A.-M. Goichon interprets as categorical syllogism. Cf. her *Lexique de la langue philosophique d'Ibn Sînâ* (Paris, 1938), pp. 363 f.; also her *Vocabulaires comparés d'Aristote et d'Ibn Sînâ* (Paris, 1939), p. 26; and her translation of Ibn Sînâ, *Livre des Directives et Remarques* (Beirut & Paris, 1951), p. 194 (n. 6).

[307] Cf. Bombaci, p. 455.

[308] Qur'ân 17.85 (87).

[309] Cf. also p. 78, below.

successful. Therefore, we were forbidden by the Lawgiver (Muḥammad) to study causes. We were commanded to recognize the absolute oneness of God. "Say: 'God, He is one. God is the *ṣamad*. He did not give birth, and He was not born. He has no one like Him.' "[310]

Man[311] should not trust the suggestion that his mind makes, that it is able to comprehend all existing things and their causes, and to know all the details of existence. Such a suggestion of the mind should be dismissed as stupid. It should be known that every person with perception has the superficial impression that the (whole of) existence is comprised by his perceptions, and that it does not extend beyond (the realm of his perceptions).[312] The matter is different in fact. The truth lies beyond that. One knows that a deaf person
feels that the (whole of) existence is comprised in the per- III, 30
ceptions of his four senses and his intellect. The whole group of audible things constitutes no part of existence for him. The same applies to a blind person. The whole group of visible things constitutes no part of existence for him. If (people with such defects) were not set right by their adherence to information they receive from their fathers and teachers who are their contemporaries, and from the majority of people in general, they would not admit (the existence of audible things, things visible, etc.). They follow the majority in admitting the existence of these groups (of *sensibilia*), but (the admission) is not in their natural disposition nor in the nature of their sense perception. If dumb animals were asked and could speak, we would find that they would ignore the whole group of *intelligibilia*. It would simply not exist for them.

Now, it might be assumed that there exists another kind of perception different from ours, since our sense perceptions are created and brought into existence. God's creation extends beyond the creation of man. Complete knowledge does

[310] Qur'ân, *sûrah* 112. Cf. n. 567 to Ch. III.
[311] Cf. Issawi, pp. 165 f.
[312] Cf. p. 255, below.

not exist (in man). The world of existence is too vast for him. "God has comprehension beyond theirs." [313] Therefore, everyone should be suspicious of the comprehensiveness of his perceptions and the results of his perception, and should follow what the Lawgiver (Muḥammad) commanded him to believe and to do. He is more desirous of his happiness (than man himself) and he knows better what is good for him. His level (of perception) is higher than that of human perception. The territory he covers (in his mind) is wider than that of human intelligence. This does not speak against the intellect and intellectual perceptions. The intellect, indeed, is a correct scale. Its indications are completely certain and in no way wrong. However, the intellect should not be used to weigh such matters as the oneness of God, the other world, the truth of prophecy, the real character of the divine attributes, or anything else that lies beyond the level of the intellect. That would mean to desire the impossible. One might compare it with a man who sees a scale in which gold is being weighed, and wants to weigh mountains in it. The
III, *31* (fact that this is impossible) does not prove that the indications of the scale are not true (when it is used for its proper purpose). However, there is a limit at which the intellect must stop. It cannot go beyond its own level. Thus, it cannot comprehend God and His attributes. It is but one of the atoms of the world of existence which results from (God). This shows that those who give the intellect preference over (traditional) information in such matters are wrong, deficient in understanding, and faulty in reasoning. This, then, explains the true situation in this respect.

If this is clear, it is possible that the ascending sequence of causes reaches the point where it transcends the realm of human perception and existence and thus ceases to be perceivable. The intellect would here become lost, confused, and cut off in the wilderness of conjectures. Thus, (recognition of the) oneness of God is identical with inability to perceive the causes and the ways in which they exercise their

[313] Qur'ân 85.20 (20).

influence, and with reliance in this respect upon the Creator of the causes who comprises them. There is no maker but Him. All (causes) lead up to Him and go back to His power. We know about Him only in as much as we have issued from Him. This is the meaning of the statement transmitted on the authority of a certain truthful (person): "The inability to perceive is perception." [314]

Such (declaration of the) oneness of God does not merely refer to faith, which is affirmation based upon judgment. It belongs to the talk of the soul.[315] Its perfection lies in its acquisition in a form that becomes an attribute of the soul. In the same way, the object of (all human) actions and divine worship is acquisition of the habit of obedience and submissiveness and the freeing of the heart from all preoccupations save the worshiped Master, until the novice on the path to God becomes a holy person.

The difference between "state" [316] and knowledge in questions of dogma is the same as that between talking (about attributes) and having them. This may be explained as follows: Many people know that mercy to the orphans and the poor brings (a human being) close to God and is III, 32
recommendable. They say so and acknowledge the fact.

[314] This statement, which also lends itself to being treated as a verse, appears, for instance, in Hujwîrî, *Kashf al-maḥjûb*, tr. R. A. Nicholson (E. J. W. Gibb Memorial Series, No. 17) (Leiden & London, 1911), p. 18, and in al-Ghazzâlî, *Iḥyâ'* (Cairo, 1352/1934), IV, 262. For Ibn 'Arabî and his school, it became one of the slogans of their mystical philosophy, and as such was constantly quoted. Cf. Ibn 'Arabî, *Futûḥât* (Bulaq, 1293/1876), I, 352; *Dîwân* (Bulaq, 1271/1854–55), p. 10; *Kitâb al-Yâ'*, in *Rasâ'il Ibn 'Arabî* (Hyderabad, 1367/1948), p. 2; *Tarjumân al-ashwâq*, ed. and tr. R. A. Nicholson (London, 1911), pp. 120 f.; H. S. Nyberg, *Kleinere Schriften des Ibn al-'Arabî* (Leiden, 1919), p. 96 (Ar. text). Cf. also Jalâl-ad-dîn Rûmî, *Mathnawî*, ed. and tr. R. A. Nicholson (E. J. W. Gibb Memorial Series, N.S., No. 4) (Cambridge & London, 1925–40), VII, 169, comm. on Bk. 1, vv. 2697 f.

While Ibn Khaldûn ascribes the statement to "a certain truthful person," al-Ghazzâlî mentions as its author "the master of those who are truthful," meaning not 'Alî but Abû Bakr.

[315] On a human level, this seems to be the same as the "essential speech" of the Deity. Cf. 1:199, above, and pp. 49 f., below.

[316] *Ḥâl*, used here in the sense the word originally acquired in mysticism. Cf. p. 78, below.

They quote the sources for it from the religious law. But if they were to see an orphan or a poor person of the destitute classes,[317] they would run away from him and disdain to touch him, let alone show mercy to him or any of the higher "stations" [318] of sympathy, affection, and charity. Their mercy for the orphan was the result of having reached the station of knowledge. It was not the result of the station of "state" nor of an attribute of theirs. Now, there are people who, in addition to the station of knowledge and the realization of the fact that mercy to the poor brings (a human being) close to God, have attained another, higher "station": they have attained the attribute and habit of mercy. When they see an orphan or a poor person, they approach him and show him (mercy). They wish to receive the (heavenly) reward for the compassion they show him. They are hardly able to refrain from (showing compassion), even if they are repulsed. They give as charity whatever they have available from their own property.

The relationship of man's knowledge of the oneness of God to his possession of it as an attribute, is of the same character. Knowledge results by necessity from possession of an attribute. It is a kind of knowledge that exists on a more solid basis than knowledge attained previous to the possession of the attribute. An attribute (on the other hand) is not obtained from knowledge alone. There must be an action, and it must be repeated innumerable times. (Only) this results in a firmly rooted habit, in the acquisition of the attribute and real (knowledge). Another kind of knowledge thus makes its appearance. It is the kind that is useful in the other world. The original knowledge which was devoid of being an attribute is of little advantage or use. It is the (kind of) knowledge that the majority of thinkers (possesses). But the (real) object is knowledge as a "state," and it originates from divine worship.

[317] D: "from among his fellow men."

[318] *Maqâm*, another term borrowed from mysticism. Cf. p. 78, below. Ethical qualities are "stations" during man's ascent to the Divine.

It should be known that, in the opinion of the Lawgiver (Muḥammad), perfection with regard to any of the obligations he has imposed (upon Muslims) requires this (distinction). Perfection in matters of belief depends on the III, *33*
other knowledge, that which results from the possession of (these matters) as an attribute. Perfection in matters of divine worship depends on acquisition of (these matters) as an attribute, on real (knowledge) of them.

Divine worship and its continuous practice leads to this noble result. Muḥammad says concerning the principal act of divine worship: "My consolation lies in prayer." [319] Prayer, for Muḥammad, was an attribute and "state" in which he found his ultimate pleasure and consolation. How different is the prayer of the people! Who could bring them to pray in that way! "Woe unto those who pray, who are careless with regard to their prayer." [320] O God, give us success. "And guide us on the straight path, the path of those to whom you have shown kindness, not of those with whom you are angry, and not of those who go astray." [321] Amen.

It [322] is clear from all the statements we have made that the object of all (religious) obligations is the acquisition of a habit firmly rooted in the soul, from which a necessary knowledge results for the soul. It is the (recognition of the) oneness of God, which is the (principal) article of faith and the thing through which happiness is attained. There is no difference whether the obligations of the heart or those of the body are concerned in this respect.

This shows that faith, which is the basis and source of all the (religious) obligations, is of that type and has several degrees. The first degree is the affirmation by the heart of what the tongue says. The highest degree is the acquisition,

[319] This is the third part of the tradition in which Muḥammad mentions women, perfume, and prayer as the things he likes best. Cf. Ibn Ḥanbal, *Musnad* (Cairo, 1313/1895), III, 128, 199, 285.

[320] Qur'ân 107.4–5 (4–5).

[321] Qur'ân 1.6–8 (6–8).

[322] Cf. Issawi, pp. 174 f.

from the belief of the heart and the resulting actions, of a quality that has complete control over the heart. It commands the actions of the limbs. Every activity takes place in submissiveness to it. Thus, all actions, eventually, become subservient to this affirmation by faith, and this is the highest degree of faith. It is perfect faith. The believer who has it
III, *34* will commit neither a great nor a small sin. The acquisition of the firmly rooted habit (of faith) prevents even the briefest deviation from its ways. Thus, Muḥammad says: "An adulterer does not commit adultery, if he commits adultery while he is a believer." [323]

Then, there is the tradition of Heraclius, who asked Abû Sufyân b. Ḥarb about the Prophet and his position. He asked whether any of the men around Muḥammad would become an apostate, out of displeasure with his religion, after he had become a Muslim.[324] The reply was: "No." (Heraclius) remarked: "The same applies to faith when its cheerfulness has penetrated the hearts." [325] This means that it is as difficult for the soul to oppose the habit of faith, once it has been firmly established, as is the case with all other habits, once they have become firmly established. For they become a kind of natural disposition. This is the highest degree of faith. It comes second after infallibility, because infallibility is a primary necessity of prophets, while this (degree of faith) comes to the believers secondarily, as a result of their actions and of their affirmation.

The (varying) firmness of this habit causes differences in faith, as is known from the statements of the early Muslims. Much of it can be found in the chapter headings of al-Bukhârî's chapter on faith. For instance: "Faith consists of words and actions"; "it may be more or less"; "prayer and fasting are part of faith"; "supererogatory (prayer) in Ramaḍân is part of faith"; and "bashfulness is part of the

[323] According to *Concordance*, II, 343*a*, only the work of Ibn Mâjah (in the Book on *fitan*), among the canonical collections, includes this tradition.

[324] The phrase, "after he had become a Muslim," which appears in al-Bukhârî, is added in C in the margin and is found in the text of D.

[325] Cf. 1:187, above.

faith." [326] All these statements envisage perfect faith. We have referred to it and to how the habit of it can be attained. Perfect faith is something connected with action.

Affirmation, the first degree of perfect faith, admits of no differences (in intensity). Those who consider the first (meanings) of terms and thus think of (faith) as affirmation cannot show any differences (in the intensity of their affirmation), as the leading speculative theologians have stated. But those who consider the final (meanings) of terms and thus think of (faith) as the habit that is perfect faith, do show differences (in the intensity of their faith). This does not speak against the unity of the primary reality of (perfect III, *35*
faith), which is affirmation, since affirmation exists in all degrees of (faith). It is the lowest degree for which the term "faith" may be used. It absolves (the person who has it) from the responsibility of unbelief and is the distinguishing element between unbeliever and believer. Anything less would not be sufficient. Thus, by definition, it is a reality that is uniform and admits of no differences. Differences appear only in the "state" that is the result of action, as we have stated. This should be understood.

It should be known that the Lawgiver (Muḥammad) described to us this first degree of faith which is affirmation. He specified particular matters he charged us to affirm with our hearts and to believe in our souls, while at the same time acknowledging them with our tongues. They are the established articles of the Muslim faith. When Muḥammad was asked about faith, he said: "(Faith is) the belief in God, His angels, His Scriptures, His messengers, the Last Day, and the belief in predestination, be it good or bad." [327]

These are articles of faith as established in the science of speculative theology. Let us describe them in summary

---

[326] Cf. al-Bukhârî, *Ṣaḥîḥ*, ed. Krehl (Leiden, 1862–1908), I, 10 (Ch. i of the Book on *îmân*); I, 10, 19 (Chs. i & xxxiii); I, 18, 17 (Chs. xxx & xxviii); I, 17 (Ch. xxvii); I, 14 (Ch. xvi).

[327] Cf. Muslim, *Ṣaḥîḥ* (Cairo, 1334/1915–16), I, 29 (Book on *îmân*, Ch. i); and, for similar traditions, *Concordance*, I, 29*b*, 260*b*; al-Isfarâyinî, *at-Tabṣîr fî d-dîn* (Cairo, 1359/1940), p. 57.

fashion, so that the real character of speculative theology and the way in which it originated may become clear. We say:

It should be known that the Lawgiver (Muḥammad) commanded us to believe in the Creator whom he considered as the sole source of all actions,[328] as we have mentioned before. He informed us that this belief means our salvation, if we have it when we die. However, he did not inform us about the real being of this worshiped Creator, because it is something too difficult for our perception and above our level. He made it our first obligation to believe that He in His essence cannot be compared with created beings. Otherwise, it would not be correct that He was their creator, since in this way there would be no distinction (between Him and them).

Then, he (made it our obligation to believe that) He cannot be described in any way as deficient. Otherwise, He
III, *36* would be similar to created beings. Then, he (made it our obligation to believe in) His oneness as divine being.[329] Otherwise, the creation (of the world) could not have materialized, on account of mutual antagonism.[330] Then, there are the following articles of faith:

God is knowing and powerful. In this way, (all) actions materialize as witness(es), by syllogism,[331] to the perfection of the act of creation.

He has volition. Otherwise, no created thing would be differentiated from the other.

---

[328] Bulaq: "whom he considered the source of all actions and the sole subject of faith."

[329] *Sic* C and D. Bulaq and B have "as creator."

[330] That is, if there were more than one God, the mutual antagonism of the gods would have prevented the creation of the world, or the world would be destroyed. Cf. 1:394, above; pp. 63 and 144, below.

[331] B vocalizes: *shâhidan qaḍîyatan.* The translation seems not quite certain. De Slane suggested another divine attribute here: "God, having full power to create and produce, is witness (of the execution) of His judgments." Even if one admits the corrections of the text necessary to produce this translation, its meaning is not clear in the context.

He determines the fate of each created thing. Otherwise, volition would be something that comes into being.

He causes our resurrection [332] after death. This constitutes the final touch to His concern with the first [333] creation. If (created things) were destined to disappear completely,[334] their creation would have been frivolous. They are destined for eternal existence after death.[335]

Further articles of faith are: God sent (His) messengers in order to save (us) from trouble on the (Day of) Resurrection, because (that Day) may mean either trouble or happiness (for us), and we would not know about it. He wanted to complete His kindness toward us by informing us about this situation and explaining to us the two possibilities and that Paradise means bliss and Hell punishment.

These main articles of faith are proven by the logical evidence that exists for them. Evidence for them from Qur'ân and Sunnah (also) is ample. The early Muslims derived them from that evidence. The scholars showed the way to them and the religious leaders verified them. However, later on, there occurred differences of opinion concerning details of these articles of faith. Most of the differences concerned ambiguous [336] verses. This led to hostility and disputation. Logical argumentation was used in addition to the traditional (material). In this way, the science of speculative theology originated.

We shall now explain the (preceding) summary statement in detail. In many verses of the Qur'ân, the worshiped Master is described as being absolutely devoid (of human attributes) in obvious terms requiring no interpretation. All those verses are negative (in their statements). They are clear on the sub-

[332] The word translated here and a few lines later as "resurrection" (*ma'âd*) is not only used by Ibn Khaldûn as a mere synonym for *qiyâmah* "resurrection." Cf. below, p. 71. When it occurs together with *qiyâmah,* it has been translated as "revivification."

[333] "First" is added in C and D. Cf. p. 71, below.

[334] *Li-l-fanâ' aṣ-ṣirf,* as in C and D. *Li-amr fânin* "be transitory," in B.

[335] Cf. p. 71, below.

[336] Cf. pp. 55 ff., below.

ject. It is necessary to believe them. Statements of the Lawgiver (Muḥammad) and the men around him and the men of the second generation have explained them in accordance with their plain meaning.

III, 37 Then, there are a few other verses in the Qur'ân suggesting anthropomorphism, with reference to either the essence or the attributes (of God). The early Muslims gave preference to the evidence for God's freedom (from human attributes), because it was ample and clear. They knew that anthropomorphism is absurd. They decided that (those) verses were the word of God, and, therefore, believed in them and did not try to investigate or interpret their meaning. This is what is meant by the statement made by most early Muslims: "Let them pass on as they have come." [337] That is, believe that they are from God, and do not try to interpret or change them; they may be a temptation. It is, thus, necessary to stop [338] and submit to (God).

But there were a few innovators in their time who occupied themselves with the ambiguous verses and [339] delved into anthropomorphism. One group operated with the plain meaning of the relevant verses. They assumed anthropomorphism for God's essence, in that they believed that He has hands, feet, and a face. Thus, they adopted a clear anthropomorphism and were in opposition to the verses stating that God is devoid (of human attributes).

The idea of body entails deficiency and imperfection. It is

[337] Cf. Ibn Fûrak, *Bayân mushkil al-aḥâdîth*, ed. R. Köbert in *Analecta Orientalia* (Rome, 1941), XXII, 7, 12 (Arabic text), where al-Awzâ'î is mentioned among those who made the remark quoted. As-Suyûṭî, *Itqân*, II, 6 (Ch. XLIII), quotes many authorities as saying, with regard to anthropomorphic traditions: "We transmit them as they have come." As a matter of fact, the statement is appropriate in connection with "ambiguous" traditions. In connection with ambiguous verses of the Qur'ân, the wording is improper and disrespectful. There may have been other authors who used the statement in connection with the Qur'ân, but I am inclined to believe that its use here by Ibn Khaldûn is a slight inaccuracy. The editor of Bulaq apparently sensed the difficulty, for the slight correction to "Recite them . . ." appears to be his.

[338] D adds: "with them."

[339] The rest of the sentence is not found in C or D.

more proper to give preference to the negative verses indicating that God is absolutely devoid (of human attributes), which are very numerous and clear, than to cling to the plain meaning of the (anthropomorphic) verses with which we can dispense, and to try to combine the two indications with the help of interpretation of (the anthropomorphic verses). The (people who gave consideration to the anthropomorphic verses) then tried to escape from the anthropomorphic abomination by stating that (God has) "a body unlike (ordinary human) bodies." This is no defense for them, because it is a statement contradictory in itself and a combination of negation and assertion, if both (negation and assertion) are used here for one and the same concept of body. But if the two differ among themselves [340] and (thus) disavow the commonly accepted concept of body, those (people) rather agree with us that God is devoid (of human attributes). They consider the word "bọdy" to be merely one of His names (used in a peculiar sense in connection with Him). Things like that depend on permission.[341]

Another group turned to anthropomorphism with regard to the attributes of God. They assumed direction, sitting,[342] descending, voice, letter (sound), and similar things (for God). Their stated opinions imply anthropomorphism. Like the former group, they took refuge in statements such as: "A voice unlike voices"; "a direction unlike directions"; "descending unlike descending." By that, they meant: "(not as those things are used) in connection with (human) bodies." The refutation here is the same as in the former case. III, *38*

The only thing that remains to be done with the plain (seemingly anthropomorphic) statements is (to follow) the

[340] That is, the negative statement may mean one type of body, and the positive another. The pronoun in *baynahumâ* is reflexive, rather than referring to "two (kinds of body)."

[341] This means that those statements may be authorized.

[342] This refers to the famous statement in the Qur'ân that God "sat upright on the throne," which exercised a great fascination on the imagination of the speculative theologians and, consequently, figures prominently in their discussions of the divine attributes. Qur'ân 7.54 (52), etc. Cf. p. 65, below.

beliefs and theories expressed by the early Muslims. One must believe in the (statements) as they stand, so that it cannot happen that by disavowing their meaning, one disavows them as such, although they are a sound and established part of the Qur'ân.

That is what is behind the statements found in the creed of the *Risâlah* of Ibn Abî Zayd [343] and in his *Mukhtaṣar* and in the books of the *ḥadîth* expert Ibn 'Abd-al-Barr,[344] and others. They try to convey the idea mentioned. One should not close one's eyes to the propositions in their discussion that prove it.

Later on, the sciences and crafts increased. People were eager to write systematic works and to do research in all fields. The speculative theologians wrote on God's freedom (from human attributes). At that juncture, the Mu'tazilah innovation came into being. The Mu'tazilah extended the subject to the negative verses and decided to deny (God's possession of) the ideal attributes [345] of knowledge, power, volition, and life, in addition to (denying) their consequences. Their use (in connection with God) would imply, in (Mu'tazilah) opinion, a manifoldness of things primeval.[346] This (assumption) is refuted by the (assumption) that the attributes are neither identical with the (divine) essence nor different from it.

The [347] Mu'tazilah further decided to deny (God's possession) of the attribute of volition. This forced them to deny predestination, because predestination requires the existence of volition prior to the created things.

They also decided to deny God hearing and vision, because both hearing and vision are corporeal accidents. This
III, 39 (assumption) is refuted by the (assumption) that the meaning of the words (hearing and vision) does not require (the

[343] Cf. L. Bercher's edition of the *Risâlah* (3d ed.; Algiers, 1949), pp. 18–27.

[344] Cf. n. 163 to this chapter, above.

[345] *Ṣifât al-ma'ânî:* "attributes (resulting) from abstract (ideas)."

[346] Whereas the absolute oneness of God requires that only He be primeval.

[347] This paragraph is not found in Bulaq.

existence of) corporeal shape, but merely the perception of audible or visible things.[348]

They further decided to deny God speech for reasons similar to those (they used) in connection with hearing and vision. They did not understand the attribute of speech as an essential function.

Thus, the Mu'tazilah decided that the Qur'ân was created. This was an innovation. The early Muslims had openly expressed the contrary view. The damage done by this innovation was great. Certain leading Mu'tazilah indoctrinated certain caliphs with it, and the people were forced to adopt it. The Muslim religious leaders opposed them. Because of their opposition, it was considered permissible to flog [349] and kill many of them. This caused orthodox people to rise in defense of the articles of faith with logical evidence and to push back the innovations.

The leader of the speculative theologians, Abû l-Ḥasan al-Ash'arî,[350] took care of that. He mediated between the different approaches. He disavowed anthropomorphism and recognized the ideal attributes. He restricted God's freedom (from human attributes) to the extent to which it had been restricted by the early Muslims, and which had been recognized by the proofs stating the general applicability (of the principle) to special cases. He recognized the four ideal attributes, as well as hearing, vision, and speech as an essential function, (and proved his position) with the help of logical and traditional methods. He refuted the innovators in all these respects. He discussed with them (their) stated opinions with regard to (God's concern for human) welfare and with what is best (for man), and their definition of good and evil, which they had invented as the basis for their innovation.[351]

[348] Cf. p. 65, below.

[349] *Abshâr* "bare skins."

[350] 'Alî b. Ismâ'îl, 260 [873/74] to *ca.* 324 [935]. Cf. *GAL*, I, 194 f.; *Suppl.*, I, 345 f. Here, and at its later occurrences, the name is preceded by the title *shaykh*.

[351] This refers to the Mu'tazilah doctrines of *'adl* "divine justice" and *al-wa'd wa-l-wa'îd* "human behavior and its consequences." Cf. p. 61, below.

He perfected the dogmas concerning the rising of the dead, the circumstances of the Resurrection, Paradise, and Hell, and reward and punishment. He added a discussion of the imamate, because the Imâmîyah (Shî'ah) at that time suggested the novel idea that the imamate was one of the articles of faith and that it was the duty of the Prophet as well as the Muslim nation [352] to fix (the succession to) the (imamate) and free the person who would become the imam from any responsibility in this respect. (However, in fact,) the imamate is at best a matter of public interest and social organization.
III, 40 It is not an article of faith. (But, because of the Shî'ah attitude, the question of the imamate) was added to the problems of this discipline.

The whole was called "the science of speculative theology." The reason why this name (which, literally, means "science of speech," or "talk") was chosen, may have been that it included the disputation of innovations. That is merely *talk* and implies no action. Or, the reason may have been that the discipline was invented and cultivated as a consequence of dissension concerning the existence of essential *speech.*[353]

The followers of Abû l-Ḥasan al-Ash'arî became numerous. His approach was later on followed by his pupils, such as Ibn Mujâhid [354] and others. Judge Abû Bakr al-Bâqillânî [355] learned from them. He attacked the problem of the imamate in accordance with the way they had approached it, and improved on it. He laid down the logical premises on which arguments and speculation on the subject depend. He affirmed, for instance, the existence of the atom (*al-jawhar*

[352] But cf. 1:402, above.

[353] Cf. pp. 62 f., below.

[354] Abû 'Abdallâh Muḥammad b. Aḥmad aṭ-Ṭâ'î, d. between 360 and 370 [970–80]. Cf. al-Khaṭîb al-Baghdâdî, *Ta'rîkh Baghdâd*, I, 343. In his biography of al-Bâqillânî, Judge Iyâḍ twice calls him Abû Bakr. The editors of al-Bâqillânî's *Tamhîd* (Cairo, 1366/1947), pp. 242 and 247, recognized this as just a mistake. The date of Ibn Mujâhid's death is indicated in later authors as 370 [980/81]; cf. *Tamhîd*, p. 242 (n. 4); Ibn al-'Imâd, *Shadharât*, III, 74 f. This date, however, is probably deduced merely from the fact that Ibn Mujâhid's biography appears in the *Ta'rîkh Baghdâd* between biographies referring to the years 360 and 370.

[355] Cf. 1:43, above.

al-fard) and of the vacuum. He made statements such as "An accident cannot sustain another accident," and "An accident does not persist two moments." [356] There are similar (premises) on which the arguments of (the Ash'arites) depend. He considered the basic premises as secondary only to the articles of faith, as far as the necessity of believing in them was concerned. The arguments depend on them, and if the arguments are wrong, it is possible to conclude that the thing proven (by them) is also wrong.[357]

Thus, (al-Ash'arî's) approach was perfected and became one of the best speculative disciplines and religious sciences. However, the forms of its arguments are, at times, not technical(ly perfect), because the scholars (of al-Ash'arî's time) were simple and the science of logic which probes arguments and examines syllogisms had not yet made its appearance in Islam. Even if some of it had existed, the theologians would not have used it, because it was so closely related to the philosophical sciences, which are altogether different from the beliefs of the religious law and were, therefore, avoided by them.

The Ash'arite leader, Judge Abû Bakr (al-Bâqillânî), was followed by the Imâm al-Ḥaramayn Abû l-Ma'âlî.[358] He dictated a comprehensive work on the Ash'arite approach. III, *41*
He was very explicit in it. He then abridged the work in the *Kitâb al-Irshâd*. People use the (*Irshâd*) as their guide in matters of (dogmatic) belief.

After that, the science of logic spread in Islam. People studied it. They made a distinction between it and the philosophical sciences, in that (they stated that) logic was merely a norm and yardstick for arguments and served to probe the arguments of the (philosophical sciences) as well as (those of) all other (disciplines).

[356] Cf., for instance, D. B. Macdonald, "Continuous Re-Creation and Atomic Time" in *Isis*, IX (1927), 331. Cf. below, p. 144, or Averroes, *The Incoherence of the Incoherence*, tr. S. van den Bergh (E. J. W. Gibb Memorial Series, N.S. No. 19) (Oxford & London, 1954), I, 82.

[357] Cf. p. 145, below.

[358] Cf. 1:393, above.

(Scholars,) then, studied the basic premises the earlier theologians had established. They refuted most of them with the help of arguments leading them to (a different opinion). Many of these (arguments) were derived from philosophical discussions of physics and metaphysics. When they probed them with the yardstick of logic, it showed that they were applicable (only) to those (other disciplines and not to theology, but) they did not believe that if the arguments were wrong, the thing proven (by the arguments) was also wrong, as had been the opinion of the Judge (al-Bâqillânî). This approach differed in its technical terminology from the older one. It was called "the school of recent scholars." Their approach often included refutation of the philosophers where the (opinions of the) latter differed from the articles of faith. They considered the (philosophers) enemies of the articles of faith, because, in most respects, there is a relationship between the opinions of the innovators and the opinions of the philosophers.

The first (scholar) to write in accordance with the (new) theological approach was al-Ghazzâlî. He was followed by the imam Ibn al-Khaṭîb.[359] A large number of scholars followed in their steps and adhered to their tradition.

The later scholars were very intent upon meddling with philosophical works. The subjects of the two disciplines (theology and philosophy) were thus confused by them. They thought that there was one and the same (subject) in both disciplines, because the problems of each discipline were similar.[360]

It should be known that the theologians most often deduced the existence and attributes of the Creator from the
III, *42* existing things and their conditions. As a rule, this was their line of argument. The physical bodies form part of the existing things, and they are the subject of the philosophical study of physics. However, the philosophical study of them differs from the theological. The philosophers study bodies in so far

[359] Fakhr-ad-dîn ar-Râzî. Cf. 1:402, above.
[360] Cf. p. 153, below.

as they move or are stationary. The theologians, on the other hand, study them in so far as they serve as an argument for the Maker. In the same way, the philosophical study of metaphysics studies existence as such and what it requires for its essence. The theological study (of metaphysics), on the other hand, is concerned with the *existentia*, in so far as they serve as argument for Him who causes existence. In general, to the theologians, the subject of theology is (to find out) how the articles of faith which the religious law has laid down as correct, can be proven with the help of logical arguments, so that innovations may be repulsed and doubts and misgivings concerning the articles of faith be removed.

If one considers how this discipline originated and how scholarly discussion was incorporated within it step by step,[361] and how, during that process, scholars always assumed the correctness of the articles of faith and paraded proofs and arguments (in their defense), one will realize that the character of the subject of this discipline is as we have established it, and one will realize that (the discipline) cannot go beyond it. However, the two approaches have been mixed up by recent scholars. The problems of theology have been confused with those of philosophy. This has gone so far that the one discipline is no longer distinguishable from the other. The student (of theology) cannot learn (theology) from the books of (the recent scholars, and the same situation also confronts the student of philosophy). Such (mixing of theology and philosophy) was done by al-Bayḍâwî, in the *Ṭawâli'*, and by later, non-Arab scholars, in all their works. However, some students have occupied themselves with the (mixed) approach (in spite of its uselessness for the study of theology),
in order to learn the different school opinions and to become III, 43
versed in the knowledge of argumentation, which is amply represented in (the works which follow the mixed approach).

The approach of the early Muslims can be reconciled with the beliefs of the science of speculative theology only if one

361 *Ṣadran ba'da ṣadrin*. For *ṣadr* used by Ibn Khaldûn in the meaning of "some time," cf. also 1:373, above, and p. 171, below.

follows the old approach of the theologians (and not the mixed approach of recent scholars). The basic work here is the *Kitâb al-Irshâd*, as well as works that follow its example. Those who want to inject a refutation of the philosophers into their dogmatic beliefs must use the books of al-Ghazzâlî and the imam [362] Ibn al-Khaṭîb. They do show some divergence from the old technique, but do not make such a confusion of problems and subjects as is found in the approach of the recent scholars who have come after them.

In general, it must be known that this science—the science of speculative theology—is not something that is necessary to the contemporary student. Heretics and innovators have been destroyed. The orthodox religious leaders have given us protection against heretics and innovators in their systematic works and treatments. Logical arguments were needed only when they [363] defended and supported (their own views with them). Now, all that remains of them [364] is a certain amount of discussion, from most of whose ambiguities and inferences the Creator can be considered to be free.[365]

Al-Junayd [366] was once passing a group of theologians discussing the (problem of the freedom of the Creator from human attributes). He asked who they were. He was told that they were people who, by the aid of arguments, were trying to free God from the attributes of createdness and from the qualities that indicate deficiency. Whereupon al-Junayd said: "The denial of a fault where (the existence of) a fault is impossible is (in itself) a fault." [367]

However, the usefulness of (speculative theology) for certain individuals and students is considerable. Orthodox

[362] "The imam" added in C and D.

[363] I.e., the religious leaders, rather than the heretics and innovators. C seems to indicate the reading *li-mâ*, which would make the subordinate clause read: "for the things they refuted and supported"?

[364] I.e., of the logical arguments.

[365] *Sic* B and C (*yunazzahu*). D vocalizes *nunazzihu al-bârî'a* "we consider the Creator to be free."

[366] Cf. 2:187, above.

[367] Cf. 1:51, above.

Muslims should not be ignorant of speculative argumentation in defense of the articles of orthodox faith.

"God is the friend of the believers." [368]

[15] *An exposition of ambiguity in the Qur'ân and the Sunnah and of the resulting dogmatic schools among both the orthodox and the innovators.*[369] III, 44

It should be known that God sent our Prophet Muḥammad to us, in order to call us to salvation and bliss. He revealed to him His noble book in the clear Arabic language. He told us in it about the (religious) obligations that would enable us to attain (salvation and bliss). This process included and necessitated references to God's names and attributes, in order to make us acquainted with His essence. (It also included and necessitated) references to the spirit attaching itself to us, and to the revelation and the angels constituting the connection between God and His messengers who were sent to us. The Day of Resurrection and its warning signs have been mentioned to us (in the Qur'ân), but the exact time when any of these things is to take place is not indicated. Also, at the beginning of certain *sûrahs*, the noble Qur'ân contains, distributed (in various places, combinations of) individual letters of the alphabet the meaning of which we are not able to understand.

All these particulars of the Qur'ân were called "ambiguous" (in the Qur'ân itself). Those who followed them

[368] Qur'ân 3.68 (61).

[369] The section appears first in C and D. Ibn Khaldûn did not add it all at once, for a good deal of the text is still found in the form of marginal additions in C. He may have been asked in his classes to elaborate upon the subject, and hence to have devoted a separate chapter to it supplementing the preceding one. In a sense, it disturbs the arrangement of the discussion.

Cf. D. B. Macdonald in *EI*, *s.v.* "Kalâm": "Ibn Khaldûn evidently added (this section) later from a perception (1) that his view of these passages was essential to his general position and (2) that he had not dealt fully enough with some of the theological matters of controversy. He traced, in fact, the origin, in great part, of the science of Kalâm, viewed as defensive scholasticism, to these ambiguous and obscure passages; it sprang, thus, more from exegetical than from philosophical pressure."

were censured, as indicated in the verse: "It is He who revealed the Book to you. It contains unambiguous verses that are the mother of the Book, and other verses that are ambiguous. Those who are inclined in their hearts toward deviation follow that which is ambiguous in the Qur'ân, because they desire trouble, and they desire to interpret it. But only God knows how to interpret it. Those who are firmly rooted in knowledge say, 'We believe in it. It is all from our Lord.' Only those who have a heart remember." [370]

The early Muslim scholars from among the men around Muḥammad and the men of the second generation understood this verse to mean that the "unambiguous (verses)"
III, *45* are those that are clear and definite. The jurists, therefore, define "unambiguous" in their terminology as "clear in meaning."

Concerning the "ambiguous (verses)," people have different notions. It has been said that they are (verses) requiring study and interpretation in order to establish their correct meaning, because they are in contradiction with other verses or with logic. Therefore, their meaning is obscure and "ambiguous." In this sense, Ibn 'Abbâs said: "One must believe in the 'ambiguous (verses),' but one need not act in accordance with them." [371]

Mujâhid [372] and 'Ikrimah [373] said: "Everything, with the exception of (clearly) unambiguous verses and narrative passages, is ambiguous." This statement was accepted by Judge Abû Bakr (al-Bâqillânî) and by the Imâm al-Ḥaramayn.

Ath-Thawrî,[374] ash-Sha'bî,[375] and a number of early Muslim scholars said: " 'Ambiguous' is what cannot be

[370] Qur'ân 3.6 (5).

[371] Cf. as-Suyûṭî, *Itqân*, II, 2 (Ch. XLIII), whose source is Ibn Abî Ḥâtim,

[372] Cf. 2:179, above. D erroneously adds Ibn 'Abbâs before Mujâhid as another authority for the statement quoted.

[373] Died 104 [722/23] or 107 [725/26]. Cf. al-Bukhârî, *Ta'rîkh* (Hyderabad, 1360——/1941——), IV 1, 49.

[374] Cf. 2:160, above.

[375] 'Âmir b. Sharâḥîl, d. between 103 and 106 [721–25]. Cf. al-Khaṭîb al-Baghdâdî, *Ta'rîkh Baghdâd*, XII, 227 ff.

known, such as the conditions of the Hour, the dates of the warning signs, and the letters at the beginning of certain *sûrahs*."

The phrase "Mother of the Book," in the verse quoted, means "the largest and most prominent part of (the Book)," whereas the "ambiguous (verses)" constitute the smallest part of it, and they have no meaning except with reference to the unambiguous (verses).[376] (The verse,) then, censures those who follow the "ambiguous (verses)" and interpret them or give them a meaning they do not have in the Arabic language which the Qur'ân addresses us in. The verse calls those persons "deviators"—that is, people who turn away from the truth—unbelievers, heretics, stupid innovators. The verse says that they act so in order to cause trouble—that is, polytheism and confusion among the believers—or in order to be able to interpret the (ambiguous verses) to suit their desires and to use (their interpretations) as a model for their innovations.

God then informs (us in the verse quoted) that He has reserved the interpretation of the (ambiguous verses) exclusively to Himself. Nobody knows their interpretation, save only Him. He says: "But only God knows how to interpret them."

The verse then praises scholars for simply believing in the (ambiguous verses). It says: "Those who are firmly rooted in knowledge say, 'We believe in them.' " The early Muslims considered this statement as the beginning of a new sentence. They did not consider it to be coupled (with the preceding statement, in which case it would mean ". . . Only God knows how to interpret them, and so do those who are firmly rooted in knowledge, who say . . .").[377] Belief in
something not known deserves greater praise (than belief in III, 46
something visible). Now, assuming that the two sentences are to be coupled with each other, we would have belief in

[376] Cf. as-Suyûṭî, *Itqân*, II, 5.
[377] Cf. as-Suyûṭî, *Itqân*, II, 3.

something visible, because (this interpretation) implies that (the scholars) know the interpretation, and that it is not something unknown.

This is confirmed by the continuation of the verse, "It is all from our Lord." That shows that human beings do not know the interpretation of the (ambiguous verses). For the words of the language present to the understanding only those meanings given them by the Arabs. Thus, in cases where it is impossible to relate a certain (piece of) information to the (person) who gives it, we do not know what the words mean. When such information comes to us from God, we leave the knowledge of it to Him and do not bother to find out what it might mean. It would not be possible for us anyhow. 'Â'ishah said: "If you see those who dispute about the Qur'ân, they are the ones whom God meant (in the verse quoted)—beware of them!" [378]

This was the opinion of the early Muslims concerning the "ambiguous verses" (of the Qur'ân). The traditions contain similarly (ambiguous) expressions which were considered by them in the same light, because the source is one and the same.

Now that the different kinds of "ambiguous" statements have been established by our remarks, let us return to the differences of opinion regarding them found among people (scholars).

The statements that people consider "ambiguous" and that have reference to the Hour and its conditions, to the dates of the warning signs, to the number of the guardians of Hell,[379] and similar things, hardly are "ambiguous" statements. They contain no equivocal [380] expression or anything else (that may properly be considered ambiguous). They simply (refer to) dates of events, the knowledge of which God has reserved exclusively to Himself, as expressly stated

[378] Cf. al-Bukhârî, *Ṣaḥîḥ*, III, 212 (comm. on Qur'ân 3.7); *Concordance*, III, 62*b*; as-Suyûṭî, *Itqân*, II, 3.

[379] Cf. Qur'ân 96.18 (18).

[380] *Muḥtamil:* C and D.

in His Book and through His Prophet. God says: "The knowledge of them is with God." [381] It is strange that these things could ever have been counted among the "ambiguous" statements.

The (combinations of) individual letters at the beginning of certain *sûrahs* (*al-ḥurûf al-muqaṭṭa'ah*) are, in matter of fact, letters of the alphabet. It is not improbable that they are intended (merely as meaningless letters of the alphabet). Az-Zamakhsharî says: "They indicate the wide sweep of the III, 47
inimitability of the Qur'ân. The revealed Qur'ân is composed of (letters). Anybody could use them, but since their composition (in the Qur'ân), there is a difference in their significance (and they have acquired a superior, divine quality)." [382] Abandonment of the point of view which implies that (these Qur'ânic letters) do in fact indicate (just meaningless letters), would be justified only on the strength of sound tradition. Thus, it is said that *ṭâhâ* is an appellation consisting of *ṭâhir* "pure" and *hâdî* "guide," and so on.[383] But it is difficult to have a sound tradition. In this sense, the letters might be (called) "ambiguous."

The ambiguity in statements concerning the revelation, angels, the spirit, and jinn, results from obscurity in the real meaning of (those terms). They are not commonly accepted (terms). Therefore, they are ambiguous. Some people have

[381] Qur'ân 7.187 (186 f.); 33.63 (63).

[382] As already pointed out by de Slane, az-Zamakhsharî mentions nothing of the sort in his commentary on the beginning of *sûrah* 2, where he discusses the *ḥurûf al-muqaṭṭa'ah* at length. Nor does he say anything in his commentary on *sûrah Ṭâhâ* (20). The interpretation of *ṭâhâ* as *ṭâhir* and *hâdî* does not seem to be generally accepted.

Al-Bâqillânî, *Tamhîd*, pp. 125 f., points out that it is not the letters as such that make the Qur'ân inimitable, but their arrangement.

[383] Similar explanations of the *ḥurûf al-muqaṭṭa'ah*, are found, for instance, in as-Suyûṭî, *Itqân*, II, 9 ff. The unsolved problem of the letters has called forth many ingenious and unproven theories. Cf. T. Nöldeke, F. Schwally, G. Bergsträsser, and O. Pretzl, *Geschichte des Qorâns* (Leipzig, 1909-38), II, 68 ff. For the bitterness with which the supporters of the different theories fight each other to the present day, cf. Ali Nasuh al-Tahir, "Abbreviations in the Holy Qur'ân," *Islamic Review*, Dec. 1950, pp. 8-12. Cf. also 2:192 f. and 205 ff., above.

added (to these things) all related matters, such as the conditions of Resurrection, Paradise, Hell, the Antichrist, the disturbances (preceding the Last Day), the conditions (governing it), and anything that is contrary to familiar custom. They may be right. However, the great mass (of scholars), especially the speculative theologians, do not agree to that. They have determined the significance of those (terms), as we notice, in their works.

Thus, the only ambiguous statements remaining are those concerning the attributes that God has attributed to Himself in His Book and through His Prophet, the plain meaning of which would seem to suggest a deficiency or weakness on the part of God.

After the early Muslims whose opinions (on the subject) we have already clarified, there were differences of opinion among the people concerning these plain statements. There was discussion. Innovations came to affect dogmatic beliefs. Let us explain those opinions and give preference to the sound ones (among them) as against the corrupt ones. I say—and only God can give me success:

It should be known that God described Himself to us in His Book as knowing, powerful, having volition, living, hearing, seeing, speaking, majestic, noble, generous, beneficent,
III, 48 strong, and great. He also established with regard to Himself that He had hands, eyes, a face, a foot, a leg,[384] and other attributes. Some of them imply true divinity, such as knowledge, power, volition, as well as life, which is a condition for all of them. Others are attributes of perfection, such as hearing, vision, and speech. Others, again, seem to suggest deficiency, such as sitting, descending, and coming, as well as face, hands, and eyes, which are attributes of created things. The [385] Lawgiver (Muḥammad) then informed (us) that we shall see our Lord on the Day of Resurrection like the moon on a night when the moon is full, and shall not suffer any

---

[384] *Wa-s-sâq:* C and D, with reference to Qur'ân 68.42 (42).

[385] The rest of the paragraph is found in the margin of C. D inserted it at a wrong place in the text, namely, after the first sentence of the next paragraph.

harm in seeing Him, as is established in sound tradition (the *Ṣaḥîḥ*).[386]

The early Muslims, the men around Muḥammad and the men of the second generation, affirmed God's (possession of) the attributes of divinity and perfection. They left to Him (the question of attributes) that seem to suggest deficiency, and did not say anything as to what they might mean. Later on, people held divergent opinions.

The Mu'tazilah came and affirmed those attributes as abstract data of the mind but did not assume the existence of a (divine) attribute persisting in the (divine) essence. This they called "declaration of the oneness of God" (*tawḥîd*).

Then, they considered man the creator of his own actions, and that the latter have nothing to do with the divine power, especially not man's evil actions and sins, since a wise (Deity) would find it impossible to do them.

They also considered it God's duty to observe what is best for mankind. This they called (divine) justice (*'adl*). Originally, they had denied predestination. They had maintained that everything starts through knowledge which comes into being (in each particular instance), as well as through power and volition which likewise (come into being). This is mentioned in (the sound tradition of) the *Ṣaḥîḥ*,[387] and 'Abdallâh b. 'Umar refused to have anything to do with Ma'bad al-Juhanî [388] and his companions who held those opinions. The denial of predestination was taken up by the Mu'tazilah Wâṣil b. 'Aṭâ al-Ghazzâl,[389] the pupil of al-Ḥasan al-Baṣrî, at the time of 'Abd-al-Malik b. Marwân, and eventually by

[386] Cf. al-Bukhârî, *Ṣaḥîḥ*, I, 148, 153, etc.; and *Concordance*, II, 202. In this often-quoted tradition, the word translated here by "suffer any harm" appears in different forms; the preferred interpretation seems to be: "Everybody will have the privilege of seeing Him." Cf. *Lisân al-'Arab*, VI, 166; XV, 252. Cf. also below, p. 74.

[387] The tradition is found at the beginning of the *Kitâb al-îmân* of Muslim's *Ṣaḥîḥ*.

[388] Died after 80 [699]. Cf. al-Bukhârî, *Ta'rîkh*, IV 1, 399 f.; Ibn Ḥajar, *Tahdhîb*, X, 225 f.

[389] 80–131 [699/700–748/49]. Cf. *GAL*, I, 66; *Suppl.*, I, 103; A. J. Wensinck in *EI*, *s.v.* The correct al-Ghazzâl appears in the MSS.

III, 49 Mu'ammar as-Sullamî.[390] The Mu'tazilah, then, retracted their former opinion in this respect.

One of the Mu'tazilah was Abû l-Hudhayl al-'Allâf.[391] He was the chief of the Mu'tazilah. He had learned the Mu'tazilah approach from 'Uthmân b. Khâlid aṭ-Ṭawîl,[392] who had it from Wâṣil. He was one of those who denied predestination. He followed the opinions of the philosophers in denying the existential attributes, because the philosophical opinions made their appearance at that time.

Then came Ibrâhîm an-Naẓẓâm.[393] He professed (belief in) predestination, and (the Mu'tazilah) followed him. He studied the philosophical works. He strictly denied the (existence of the divine) attributes and firmly established the basic (dogmas) of Mu'tazilism. Then came al-Jâḥiẓ,[394] al-Ka'bî,[395] and the Jubbâ'îyah.[396] Their approach was called "the science of speculative theology." (This name, which,

[390] Mu'ammar b. 'Abbâd, d. 215 [830/31]. Cf. J. Fück, "Neue Materialien zum Fihrist," *Zeitschrift der Deutschen Morgenländischen Gesellschaft*, XC (1936), 318; S. Horovitz, *Über den Einfluss der griechischen Philosophie auf die Entwicklung des Kalams* (Breslau, 1909), pp. 55 ff.

[391] Muḥammad b. al-Hudhayl, d. between 226 and 235 [840–50]. Cf. *GAL, Suppl.*, I, 338.

[392] He is mentioned, for instance, in the biography of al-'Allâf in al-Khaṭîb al-Baghdâdî, *Ta'rîkh Baghdâd*, III, 367. Cf. also ash-Shahrastânî, *Milal*, ed. Cureton (London, 1842–46), p. 34; tr. T. Haarbrücker (Halle, 1850–51), I, 49.

[393] Ibrâhîm b. Sayyâr, d. between 220 and 230 [835–45]. Cf. *GAL, Suppl.*, I, 339; H. S. Nyberg in *EI, Supplement, s.v.* "al-Naẓẓâm." The following statement concerning an-Naẓẓâm's attitude toward predestination is by no means clear. *Qâla bi-l-qadar* literally means "to profess belief in predestination," but in theological usage the phrase had come to mean just the opposite, "to profess belief in free will." Cf., for instance, C. A. Nallino, *Raccolta di scritti* (Rome, 1939–48), II, 176–80. From the preceding remarks by Ibn Khaldûn, if I understand them correctly, it would seem that the above translation expresses what he meant to say, strange as it may seem.

[394] 'Amr b. Baḥr, *ca.* 160 [776] to 255 [869]. Cf. *GAL*, I, 152 f.; *Suppl.*, I, 239 ff.

[395] 'Abdallâh b. Aḥmad al-Balkhî, d. 319 [931]. Cf. *GAL, Suppl.*, I, 343; F. Rosenthal, *A History of Muslim Historiography* (Leiden, 1952), p. 356 (n. 8).

[396] *Sic* C and D. The Jubbâ'îs were Muḥammad b. 'Abd-al-Wahhâb, 235–303 [849/50–916], and his son Abû Hâshim 'Abd-as-Salâm, 275 or 277 [889 or 890/91] to 321 [933]. Cf. *GAL, Suppl.*, I, 342 f. The dates are to be corrected in accordance with al-Khaṭîb al-Baghdâdî, *Ta'rîkh Baghdâd*, XI, 55 f.

literally, means "science of speech," or "talk," was chosen) either because the school implied argumentation and disputation, which is what might be called *talk*, or because it originated from denial of the attribute of *speech*.[397] Therefore, ash-Shâfi'î used to say: "They deserve to be beaten with palm rods and to be led around (in public)."

Those men firmly established the Mu'tazilah school. They confirmed part of it and rejected (other parts). Eventually, Abû l-Ḥasan al-Ash'arî [398] appeared. He disputed (the opinions of) certain Mu'tazilah *shaykhs* concerning the problems of (God's concern for human) welfare and what is best for man. He abolished Mu'tazilism. He followed the opinions of 'Abdallâh b. Sa'îd b. Kullâb,[399] Abû l-'Abbâs al-Qalânisî,[400] and al-Ḥârith b. Asad al-Muḥâsibî,[401] who were followers of the ancient Muslims according [402] to the orthodox approach. He strengthened the statements they had made [403] with speculative theological arguments. He affirmed the existence of knowledge, power, volition, and life, as attributes persisting in the essence of God. (These attributes) are necessary for the argument of mutual antagonism,[404] and they establish the correctness of prophetical miracles.

It also was (Ash'arite) doctrine to affirm the existence of (the divine attributes of) speech, hearing, and vision. On the surface, (these attributes) seem to suggest deficiency, (as they seem to be connected) with corporeal voice and corporeal letter (sound). However, among the Arabs, speech

[397] Cf. p. 50, above.

[398] Cf. p. 49, above.

[399] Second half of the ninth century. Cf. Ibn an-Nadîm, *Fihrist*, ed. Flügel (Leipzig, 1871–72), p. 180; (Cairo, 1348/1929–30), pp. 255 f. The *Fihrist* gives his names as 'Abdallâh b. Muḥammad, instead of 'Abdallâh b. Sa'îd b. Muḥammad.

[400] He is mentioned together with the other two men in ash-Shahrastânî, *Milal*, pp. 20, 65; tr. Haarbrücker, I, 29, 97; W. M. Watt, *Free Will and Predestination in Early Islam* (London, 1948), p. 130.

[401] The famous writer on mysticism, *ca.* 165 [781/82] to 243 [855]. Cf. *GAL*, I, 198; *Suppl.*, I, 351 ff.

[402] C does not have *wa-*, which appears in D.

[403] D and C: *fa-ayyada maqâlâtihim.*

[404] Cf. 1:394, and p. 44, above; p. 144, below.

has another meaning, different from letter (sound) and voice,
III, 50 namely, "that which goes around in the soul" (*khalad*).[405] Speech in it is a reality, in contradistinction to the first (kind of speech). They ascribed such (eternal speech) to God. Thus, the suggestion of deficiency was eliminated. They affirmed the attribute of (speech) as one that is primeval and of general application, as is the case with the other attributes. The Qur'ân, thus, became a term with a double meaning. It is primeval and persisting in the essence of God. This is essential speech. But it is (also) created, in as much as it consists of combinations of letters (sounds) produced in the recital (of the Qur'ân) by (human) voices. When it is called primeval, the first thing is meant. When it is called recitable or audible, this refers to its recitation and written fixation.

His scrupulousness prevented the imam Aḥmad (b. Ḥanbal) from using the word "created" for (the Qur'ân in any way). He had not heard from the ancient Muslims before his time (anything to the effect) that he (was to) say[405a] that written copies of the Qur'ân are primeval, or that the recitation (of the Qur'ân) which is done by (human) tongues was something primeval, as he could observe with his own eyes that it was something created. But only his scrupulousness prevented him from (using the term "created" in those

[405] Cf. ash-Shahrastânî, *Kitâb nihâyat al-iqdâm*, ed. A. Guillaume (Oxford & London, 1934), pp. 320 and 327, where the above explanation of speech is mentioned as Ash'arite doctrine.

[405a] I believe that this renders Ibn Khaldûn's thought accurately. Ibn Ḥanbal was under no obligation to consider the pronunciation of the Qur'ân as uncreated, but he also avoided calling it created, although this would have been the sensible thing to do, because he hesitated to associate the terms "created" and "Qur'ân" in any way whatever. It would not seem correct, for syntactic reasons, to translate: "He had not heard (the word 'created') used by the ancient Muslims before his time. He (also) would not say . . ."

The difficulty we encounter here is caused by the fact that Ibn Ḥanbal's attitude toward this problem was not clearly known to later generations. He is said, on the one hand, to have greatly disapproved of anyone who would say that the pronunciation of the Qur'ân is created, and, on the other hand, he is reported to have vigorously denied a statement attributed to him that it was uncreated. Cf. Ibn al-Jawzî, *Manâqib al-imâm Aḥmad b. Ḥanbal* (Cairo, 1349/1931), pp. 154, 158. Cf. also H. Laoust in the new edition of *EI*, *s.v.* "Aḥmad b. Ḥanbal."

cases). Had he (avoided using it for any other reason), he would have denied something that is necessary. He certainly would not have done that.

Hearing and vision seem to suggest perception by parts of the body. However, linguistically, they also may mean the perception of audible and visible things.[406] This, then, eliminates the suggestion of deficiency, because here we have a real linguistic meaning for the two terms (that may be applicable in connection with the divine attributes).

On the other hand, in the case of the expressions sitting, coming, descending, face, hands, eyes, and the like, the (theologians) abandoned their real linguistic meaning, which would suggest deficiency, anthropomorphically, for metaphoric interpretation. It is the method of the Arabs to resort to metaphoric interpretation whenever the real meanings of words present difficulties. This is done, for instance, in connection with the verse of the Qur'ân: "(A wall) that *wanted* to collapse," [407] and similar cases. It is a well-known method of the Arabs which is not disapproved of and constitutes no innovation. (It is true,) the (metaphoric) interpretation (of the attributes mentioned) is contrary to the opinions of the early Muslims, who left (the matter to God). III, *51*
However, the theologians were led to adopt it by the fact that a number of followers of the early Muslims, namely, the novelty-conscious [408] and more recent Ḥanbalites, erred with regard to the significance of those attributes. They considered them to be definite attributes of God of which it is not known "how" they are. With regard to the statement, "He sat upright upon the throne," [409] they say, "We affirm that He sits, as the word indicates, because we fear to negate Him, but we do not say how, because we fear anthropomorphism,

[406] Cf. p. 49, above.

[407] Qur'ân 18.77 (76).

[408] I believe that the word used here, and again pp. 68 f., below, is to be vocalized *muḥdithûn* and to be understood as a synonym of *mubtadi'ah* "those who create new (opinions)." *Muḥaddithûn* "*ḥadîth* scholars" or *muḥdathûn* "modern" seem less likely interpretations.

[409] Qur'ân 7.54 (52), etc.

which is denied in negative verses such as (these): 'There is nothing like Him';[410] 'Praised be God, beyond the attributes they give (Him)';[411] 'God is above what evildoers say';[412] and 'He did not give birth, and He was not born.' "[413]

These people do not realize that it comes under the subject of anthropomorphism for them to affirm the attribute of sitting, because according to the lexicographers, the word "sitting" implies being firmly settled in a place, which is something corporeal. The negation they hate to bring about would (merely) affect the word, and there is nothing dangerous in that. What is to be avoided is the negation of divinity.[414] They also hate to assume the imposition of an obligation that (human beings) are unable to fulfill.[415] This, however, is a delusion, because ambiguous statements have no bearing upon obligations. Then, they claim that (their opinion) is the opinion of the early Muslims, who, in fact, held no such opinion. Their opinion was the one we established at the beginning,[416] namely, to leave to God (the question of) what is meant by the (attributes), and not to say that one understands them. The (Ḥanbalites) argue in favor of (God's) sitting, using Mâlik's statement, "(The fact of God's) sitting is known, but it is not known how (God sits)." Mâlik did not mean that sitting is known as a definite (attribute) of God. He certainly would not have said such a thing, because he knew the meaning of "sitting." He merely meant that (the meaning of) sitting is known linguistically, and it is something corporeal, but how it takes place—that is, its reality, since
III, *52* the reality of all attributes concerns the how—is not known definitely (in connection) with God.[417]

[410] Qur'ân 42.11 (9).
[411] Qur'ân 23.91 (93); 37.159 (159).
[412] This is not an exact quotation.
[413] Qur'ân 112.3 (3).
[414] C and D: *al-âlihah* "gods"? Text to be corrected?
[415] The impossible obligation, apparently, would be belief in something that is doubtful.
[416] Cf. pp. 58 and 61, above. Cf. also p. 101, below.
[417] Bombaci, p. 455, translates: ". . . since essence and quality (*οὐσία* and *ποιόν*) coincide in the case of the attributes "

These people also argue in favor of a "place" (for God). They do so by using the tradition of the black (slave girl). The Prophet asked her: "Where is God?" She answered: "In heaven." Whereupon (the Prophet) said (to her owner): "Set her free, for she is a believer." [418] Now, the Prophet did not assume that she was a believer because she affirmed the existence of a place for God, but because she believed the plain statements in His Revelation which say that God is in heaven. Thus, she became one of those "firmly rooted (in knowledge)," [419] who believe in ambiguous statements without searching for their meaning. It is definite that one has to disavow the existence of a "place" for God. This follows from the logical argument denying (God's) need (for anything), and from the negative evidence that calls for freeing (God from attributes), as found, for instance, (in the verse), "There is nothing like Him," [420] and similar statements. It also follows from the Qur'ânic statement,[421] "He, God, is in the heavens and upon earth." [422] Nothing that exists can be in two places (at the same time). Thus, the verse is not a definite indication that God is located in a certain place, but must mean something else.

These people then extended the interpretation they had invented to the plain meaning of face, eyes, hands, coming, descending, and speech with letter (sound) and voice. They assumed that these words had meanings that were more general than (mere) references to the body. They declared God free from the corporeal meaning of these attributes. However, this is something that is not recognized in the language.

All of them followed this course. The orthodox Ash'arites and the Ḥanafite theologians shunned them and tried to uproot their dogmatic belief in this respect. An episode that

[418] Cf. Averroes, *Faṣl al-maqâl*, ed. and tr. L. Gauthier (3d ed.; Algiers, 1948), p. 19.

[419] Cf. pp. 56 f., above.

[420] Qur'ân 42.11 (9).

[421] D adds quite pointlessly a reference to Qur'ân 3.109 (105).

[422] Qur'ân 6.3 (3).

happened between Ḥanafite speculative theologians in Bukhara and the imam Muḥammad b. Ismâʻîl al-Bukhârî,[423] is well known.

The anthropomorphists (*mujassimah*) did something similar in affirming that God has a body but not one like (ordinary human) bodies. The word "body" is not [424] used
III, 53 in connection with (God) in the Muslim religio-legal tradition, but they were emboldened in their statement by the fact that they affirmed the (literal) existence of these plain statements. They did not restrict themselves to them,[425] but went deeper into the matter and affirmed the corporeality (of God).[426] They assumed something like (what has just been mentioned) concerning (the meaning of corporeality). They (wanted to) free (God from human attributes) by the contradictory, nonsensical statement, "A body not like (ordinary human) bodies." But in the language of the Arabs, body is something that has depth and is limited. Other interpretations, such as the one that (body) is something persisting in itself, or is something composed of the elements, and other things, reflect the technical terms of speculative theology, through which (the theologians) want to get at another meaning than that indicated by the language. Thus, the anthropomorphists are more involved (than others) in innovation, and, indeed, in unbelief. They assume puzzling attributes for God which suggest deficiency (on His part) and which are not mentioned in either the Word of God or that of His Prophet.

The differences between the dogmatic opinions of the early Muslims, the orthodox theologians, the novelty-conscious (scholars),[427] and the innovators among [428] the Muʻtazilah, has thus become clear through our remarks.

[423] Al-Khaṭîb al-Baghdâdî, *Ta'rîkh Baghdâd*, II, 30–33, mentions discussions concerning the divine attributes that al-Bukhârî had in Nîsâbûr.

[424] C and D: *lam* (for the misprint *lahû* of the Paris ed., which was recognized as such by de Slane and Bombaci).

[425] *Sic:* C and D.

[426] Cf. Bombaci, pp. 455 f.

[427] Cf. p. 65 (n. 408), above.

[428] D adds: "anthropomorphists and

Among the novelty-conscious (scholars), there are extremists who are called *al-mushabbihah*, because they come out openly for anthropomorphism (*tashbîh*).[429] The story goes that one of them even said: "Spare me from speaking about God's beard and genitals. Rather ask me about anything else, whatever you please." [430] Unless one tries to explain such (a remark) in their own interest, by assuming that they want to deal exhaustively with these puzzling plain attributes, and that they consider all of them in the same light as their authorities, it is clear unbelief. God help us!

The books of orthodox scholars are full of argumentations against such innovations and of lengthy refutations of (innovators) with the help of sound evidence. But we have briefly referred to the (subject) in a way that will help to distinguish the details and general outlines of dogmatics. "Praised be God who guided us to this. We would not be persons who are guided aright, had God not guided us." [431] III, *54*

The plain (words) the evidence for and meaning of which are obscure—such as revelation, angels, spirit, jinn, Purgatory (*barzakh*),[432] the conditions of the Resurrection, the Antichrist, the disturbances (preceding the Last Day), the conditions (governing it), and everything else that is difficult to understand or contrary to custom—are considered by us in the same light as the Ash'arites, who are orthodox people, considered such details. There is no ambiguity in it, even though we speak of it as ambiguous. Therefore, we want to elucidate the matter and speak clearly about it. We say:

It should be known that the world of man is the most noble and exalted of the worlds of existent things. Even though human reality is a uniform (element) in (the world),

[429] For the difference between *tashbîh* and *tajsîm*, cf. p. 84, below.

[430] This statement is ascribed to a certain Dâwûd al-Jawâribî. Cf. al-Isfarâyinî, *at-Tabṣîr fî d-dîn*, p. 71; ash-Shahrastânî, *Milal*, ed. Cureton, pp. 77, 143; tr. Haarbrücker, I, 115, 215. In a slightly different form, but still ascribed to Dâwûd al-Jawâribî, it appears in 'Abd-al-Qâhir al-Baghdâdî, *Farq*, tr. A. S. Halkin (Tel Aviv, 1935), pp. 33 f.; as-Sam'ânî, *Ansâb* (E. J. W. Gibb Memorial Series, No. 20)(Leiden & London, 1912), fol. 590*b*.

[431] Qur'ân 7.43 (41).

[432] Cf. 1:199, above; pp. 70 f., below.

it contains different levels which differ from each other through conditions peculiar to them, to such a degree that the realities at each level are different ones.

The [433] first level is constituted by the human world of the body including (man's) external sense perception, his thinking which is directed toward making a living, and all the other activities which are granted to him by his present existence.

The second level is constituted by the world of sleep (dream visions). It involves perception by the imagination. Man lets the perceptions of his imagination rove in his inward (being). With his external senses, he perceives some of them as unencumbered by time, place, or any other condition of the body. He sees them in places where he (himself) is not. If they are good, they present him with the glad tidings of pleasure he may expect in this world and the other world as our truthful (Prophet) promised.

These two levels are shared by all human individuals, but, as one has seen, they differ as to the way perceptions are attained in them.

The third level is that of prophecy. It is restricted to the noblest representatives of humankind by virtue of the fact that God has distinguished them through the knowledge of Himself and (the declaration of) His oneness, through His revelation brought to them by His angels, and through the obligation to achieve the improvement of mankind with
III, *55* respect to conditions altogether different from the outward human conditions.

The fourth level is that of death. Here, human individuals leave their outward life for an(other) existence before the Resurrection. (That existence) is called Purgatory (*barzakh*).[434] In it, they enjoy bliss or receive punishment, depending on their activities (while alive). Then, they come to the Great Resurrection, where they receive the great

[433] For the following discussion, cf. 1:194 ff., above.
[434] Cf. 1:199, above.

reward, that is, either bliss in Paradise or punishment in Hell.

The first two levels are attested by (concrete) intuition.[435] The third level, that of prophecy, is attested to by the prophetic miracle(s) and the conditions peculiar to the prophets. The fourth level is attested to by the divine revelation given to the prophets (and which speaks) of revivification,[436] the conditions of Purgatory (*barzakh*), and the Resurrection. Moreover, logic requires its (existence). God has called our attention to that in many verses concerned with the rising (of the dead). The best argument for the correctness (of these verses) is that if, apart from their visible (existence in this world), human individuals had no existence after death, where they will encounter conditions befitting them, it would have been something frivolous to create them in the first place. If death is non-existence, it would mean the return of the individual to non-existence. In that case, there would have been no sense in creating them in the first place. It is, however, absurd to assume that the wise (Deity) would act frivolously.[437]

Now, after (the existence of) the four levels has been established, we want to explain how human perceptions with regard to those four levels clearly differ. This will reveal the intricacy of (the problem of) ambiguity.

At the first level, human perceptions are clear and obvious. God says: "God brought you forth from the wombs of your mothers. You did not then know anything. And He gave you hearing and vision and hearts." [438] With the help of these perceptions, man is able to master the habits of knowledge, to perfect his human reality, and to satisfy the require- III, *56*
ments of divine worship which brings him to salvation.

At the second level—that of sleep (dream visions)—human perceptions are the same as those of external sense

[435] Cf. 1:198 (n. 277), above.
[436] Cf. p. 45 (n. 332), above.
[437] Cf. p. 45, above.
[438] Qur'ân 16.78 (80).

perception. Although the limbs of the body are not used as they are in the waking state, yet the person who has a (dream) vision ascertains everything perceived by him in his sleep without any doubt or misgiving. The limbs of the body are not employed in their ordinary manner.

Concerning the real character of this state, people are divided into two groups:

The philosophers assume that imaginary pictures are transmitted by the imagination through the motion of thinking to the "common sense" which constitutes the connecting link between external and inner sensual perception. As a result, (these pictures) are represented as something perceived in the external (world) by all the senses. The difficulty here is that true visions from God or the angels are more firmly and definitely perceived than visions of Satanic imaginations, although the imagination active in both is one and the same, as the (philosophers) have established.

The second group is that of the speculative theologians. Their summary statement of the problem is that it is a kind of perception created by God in (the realm of) the senses, and thus takes place in the same way that (perception) takes place in the waking state. This (explanation) is better, even though we are not able to perceive how it takes place.

Perception in sleep is the clearest evidence (we have) for the fact that sensual perception operates at the subsequent levels.

It is not known to us [439] how sensual perception takes place on the third level—that of the prophets—but they themselves have a more than certain (knowledge of) perception through intuition. The Prophet sees God and the angels. He hears God's speech from God Himself or from the angels. He sees Paradise, Hell, and the divine throne and chair. He
III, *57* breaks through the seven heavens in his ascension.[440] He rides al-Burâq [441] and meets the prophets in (the seven

[439] *'Indanâ:* C and D.
[440] Cf. B. Schrieke in *EI*, *s.v.* "Isrâ'."
[441] Cf. B. Carra de Vaux in *EI*, *s.v.*

heavens) and prays with them. He perceives all kinds of sensual perceptions, exactly as he perceives them at the levels of body and sleep, (but) through a kind of necessary knowledge that God creates for him, and not through ordinary human perception by means of the limbs of the body.

In this connection, no attention should be paid to Avicenna's remarks. He brings prophecy down to the level of sleep and says that the imagination transmits a picture to the "common sense." [442] The argument against the (philosophers) in this connection is (even) stronger in the case of sleep (dream visions). As we have established, that process of transmission (by the imagination) is by nature one and the same. In this way, revelation and prophetic dream vision would in reality be identical as to their certainty and reality. However, this is not so, as one knows from the dream vision of the Prophet just six months before the Revelation. The dream was the beginning of the Revelation and the prelude to it, which shows that, in reality, it is inferior to (revelation). The same follows from the process of revelation itself. It was a very difficult matter for the Prophet, as is stated in sound tradition (the *Ṣaḥîḥ*).[443] The Qur'ân was (at the beginning) revealed to him in individual verses. Later on, the (long) ninth *sûrah* (*al-Barâ'ah*) was revealed to him in one piece during the expedition to Tabûk while he was riding on his camel.[444] If the revelation had merely been the result of a process whereby thinking descends to the imagination and from the imagination to the "common sense," there would not have been any difference between those stages (of the revelation).

At the fourth level—that of the dead in Purgatory (*barzakh*), which starts with the grave when they are free
from the body, or during their rising when they reassume a III, *58*

[442] Cf. Ibn Sînâ, *Ishârât*, ed. Forget (Leiden, 1892), pp. 213–15; tr. A.-M. Goichon (Beirut & Paris, 1951), p. 514. Cf. also the references given by the translator.

[443] The reference is to the traditions at the beginning of al-Bukhârî's *Ṣaḥîḥ*. Cf. 1:185 and 201, above.

[444] Cf. 1:202, above.

body—the dead do have sensual perceptions. In his grave, a dead person sees two angels who question him.[445] With the two eyes of his head, he sees the seat he will occupy in either Paradise or Hell. He sees the persons who attend the burial and hears what they say, and he hears the tapping of their shoes when they leave him. He hears the (declaration of the) oneness of God or the affirmation of the two confessions of faith which they suggest to him,[446] and other things. According to sound tradition (the *Ṣaḥîḥ*), the Messenger of God was standing at the well of Badr into which the dead Qurashite polytheists had been thrown.[447] When he called them by their names, 'Umar asked him: "O Messenger of God, are you speaking to those dead bodies?" Muḥammad replied, "By Him in Whose hand my soul rests, you people do not hear what I am saying any better than they." [448]

Furthermore, during the rising of the dead and on the Day of Resurrection, the dead behold the different grades of bliss in Paradise and punishment in Hell with their own eyes and ears, exactly as they used to behold (things) during their life. They see the angels and they see their Lord. Thus, sound tradition (in the *Ṣaḥîḥ*) mentions, "You will see your Lord on the Day of Resurrection like the moon on a night when the moon is full. You will not suffer any harm in seeing Him." [449]

The dead did not have such perceptions while they were alive. (Still,) they are sensual perceptions like those (they had while they were alive). They take place in the limbs of the body by means of (some kind of) necessary knowledge that God creates, as we have stated. The (explanation for the)

[445] Cf. A. J. Wensinck in *EI*, *s.v.* "Munkar wa-Nakîr."

[446] This refers to the *talqîn*, the formulas declaring God's oneness and the prophethood of Muḥammad, which are spoken into the ear of the deceased. References to the *talqîn* in the canonical collections of traditions are found in *Handbook*, p. 52. C correctly vocalizes: *yudhakkirûnahû*.

[447] Ibn Hishâm, *Sîrah*, ed. Wüstenfeld (Göttingen, 1858–60), I, 453.

[448] Cf. al-Bukhârî, *Ṣaḥîḥ*, III, 64. Further references in *Handbook*, p. 28; *Concordance*, II, 541*b*.

[449] Cf. pp. 60 f., above.

secret of it lies in the knowledge that the human soul grows in the body and through the perceptions of the body. When it leaves the body in sleep or in death, or when a prophet, in the state of revelation, changes from human perceptions to angelic ones, the soul takes its means of perceptions along, but free of the limbs of the body. With (these means of perception), the soul perceives, on the (other) level, whatever perceptions it wants to perceive, but these perceptions III, *59*
are on a higher plane than those that the soul had while it was in the body. This was stated by al-Ghazzâlî, who added that the human soul has a form that it retains after its separation (from the body) and that, just like the body's own structure, includes two eyes, two ears, and all the rest of the limbs of the body serving (man) to attain perception.[450] I would say, (however,) that al-Ghazzâlî here refers to the habits obtained through using all those limbs of the body in addition to (mere) perception.[451]

When one understands all this, one will realize that perceptions exist on all four levels. However, they are not everywhere the same as in the life of this world. They differ in intensity according to the conditions affecting them. The theologians have indicated this fact in the summary statement that God creates in (the senses) a necessary knowledge of the thing perceived, whatever it may be. By that, they are referring to the same thing we have been explaining.

This is our brief attempt at classifying the problem of "ambiguity." To attempt to discuss it more widely, would take us beyond comprehension. Let us beseech[452] God that He may guide us and that we may learn through His prophets and His Book how to acknowledge His oneness properly and how to attain salvation.

"God guides whomever He wants to guide."[453]

---

[450] The above statement hardly agrees with what al-Ghazzâlî says about the *rûḥ* ("spirit," for al-Ghazzâlî a synonym of *nafs* "soul") in connection with death. Cf. *Iḥyâ'*, IV, 419.

[451] Al-Ghazzâlî does not refer to the limbs as such.

[452] Both MSS. C and D have *fa-l-naḍra'*.

[453] Qur'ân 2.142 (136), etc.

[16] *The science of Sufism.*[454]

This science belongs to the sciences of the religious law that originated in Islam. Sufism is based on (the assumption) that the method of those people (who later on came to be called Sufis) had always been considered by the important early Muslims, the men around Muḥammad and the men of the second generation, as well as those who came after them, as the path of truth and right guidance. The (Sufi) approach
III, 60 is based upon constant application to divine worship, complete devotion to God, aversion to the false splendor of the world, abstinence from the pleasure, property, and position to which the great mass aspires, and retirement from the world into solitude for divine worship. These things were general among the men around Muḥammad and the early Muslims.

Then, worldly aspirations increased in the second [eighth] century and after. People now inclined toward worldly affairs. At that time, the special name of Sufis (*Ṣûfîyah* and *Mutaṣawwifah*) was given to those who aspired to divine worship. Al-Qushayrî says: "No etymology or analogy can be found for this term in the Arabic language. It is obvious that it is a nickname. Theories deriving the word from *aṣ-ṣafâ'* (purity, sincerity), or from *aṣ-ṣuffah* (bench), or from *aṣ-ṣaff* (row) [455] are improbable from the point of view of linguistic analogy." (Al-Qushayrî) continued: "The same applies to the derivation from *aṣ-ṣûf*

[454] This section was treated in monograph form in a doctoral dissertation by H. Frank, *Beitrag zur Erkenntniss des Sufismus nach Ibn Ḫaldûn* (Leipzig, 1884). However, at the time Frank wrote his dissertation, no beginner could be expected to make any substantial contribution to the subject.

[455] The "bench" refers to "the people of the bench," ascetics of Muḥammad's time whose gathering place was the benches in the Mosque of Medina.

The "row" refers to the rows formed by the Muslims in prayer. The Sufis were supposed to be always in the first row, because of their constant practice of divine worship. But there are also slightly different explanations. Cf., for instance, Hujwîrî, *Kashf al-maḥjûb*, tr. R. A. Nicholson, p. 37: "Sufis are those who have 'cleansed' (*ṣafat*) their spirits and thus entered the first 'row' (*ṣaff*) before the Truth."

(wool), because the Sufis were not the only ones who wore wool." [456]

I say: The most obvious etymology, if one uses one, is that which connects the word with *aṣ-ṣûf*, because Sufis as a rule were characterized by the fact that they wore woolen garments. They were opposed to people wearing gorgeous garments, and, therefore, chose to wear wool.

The Sufis came to represent asceticism, retirement from the world, and devotion to divine worship. Then, they developed a particular kind of perception which comes about through ecstatic experience.[457] This comes about as follows. Man, as man, is distinguished from all the other animals by his ability to perceive. His perception is of two kinds. He can perceive sciences and matters of knowledge, and these may be certain, hypothetical, doubtful, or imaginary. Also, he can

[456] Ibn Khaldûn's rather free quotation is derived from the beginning of the chapter on *taṣawwuf* in ʿAbd-al-Karîm b. Hawâzin al-Qushayrî, *Risâlah* (Cairo, 1367/1948), p. 126. His dates are 376–465 [986–1072]; cf. *GAL*, I, 432 ff.; *Suppl.*, I, 770 ff. For these and other etymologies of *Ṣûfî*, cf. L. Massignon in *EI*, *s.v.* "Taṣawwuf." Modern scholarship is inclined to share Ibn Khaldûn's opinion that Sufi is derived from *ṣûf* "wool."

[457] *Mawâjid* is by no means as common a term in Sufi literature as Ibn Khaldûn's casual use of it suggests. The form *mawâjîd* is occasionally found in the older sources. At least, this is the form used in the printed editions at our disposal. Silvestre de Sacy paid no attention to the difference in form between *mawâjid* and *mawâjîd*, both of which he knew, and considered *mawâjid* a plural of *wajd*. Cf. *Notices et extraits des manuscrits de la Bibliothèque du Roi*, XII (1831), 299 (n. 1), 315 (n. 1). He was followed in this respect by de Slane, in his translation of the *Muqaddimah*, I, 84 (n. 1); III, 86 (n. 4); and by Dozy, in his *Supplément aux dictionnaires arabes*, II, 782. The meaning "ecstatic experience" thus obtained, certainly renders Ibn Khaldûn's understanding of the word accurately. However, Silvestre de Sacy's suggestion oversimplifies matters too much, and it still remains to be seen how, precisely, Ibn Khaldûn derived *mawâjid* from the many-colored root *w-j-d*. Al-Qushayrî's use of *mawâjîd* seems to suggest that *mawâjîd* are the result of *wajd*. Cf. his *Risâlah*, p. 34. As-Suhrawardî, whose *ʿAwârif al-maʿârif* Ibn Khaldûn mentions as another standard work on Sufism, occasionally refers to *mawâjîd*. In one passage, *mawâjîd* is paired with *mawâhib* "(divine) gifts," and both *mawâjîd* and *mawâhib*, as "found" and "given" states of mystical illumination, are contrasted with "acquired" states. Cf. his *ʿAwârif* (Cairo, 1352/1933, in the margin of al-Ghazzâlî, *Iḥyâʾ*), IV, 249 f. This presupposes that *mawâjîd* is considered a plural of *mawjûd*, in the meaning of "things found." The form *mawâjid* may have resulted from association of the term with *mawâhib*.

perceive "states" persisting in himself, such as joy and grief, anxiety and relaxation, satisfaction, anger, patience, gratefulness, and similar things. The reasoning part[458] active in the body originates from perceptions, volitions, and states.
III, *61* It is through them that man is distinguished (from the other animals), as we have stated.[459] They originate from each other. Thus, knowledge originates from evidence, grief and joy from the perception of what is painful or pleasurable, energy from rest, and inertia from being tired. In the same way, the exertion and worship of the Sufi novice must lead to a "state" that is the result of his exertion. That state may be a kind of divine worship. Then, it will be firmly rooted in the Sufi novice and become a "station" for him. Or, it may not be divine worship, but merely an attribute affecting the soul, such as joy or gladness,[460] energy or inertia, or something else.

The "stations" (form an ascending order). The Sufi novice continues to progress from station to station, until he reaches the (recognition of the) oneness of God (*tawḥîd*) and the gnosis (*ma'rifah*) which is the desired goal of happiness. Muḥammad says: "Whoever dies confessing that there is no God but God, enters Paradise."[461]

Thus, the novice must progress by such stages. The basis of all of them is obedience and sincerity. Faith precedes and accompanies all of them. Their result and fruit are states and attributes. They lead to others, and again others, up to the station of the (recognition of the) oneness of God and of gnosis (*'irfân*). If the result[462] shows some shortcoming or defect, one can be sure that it comes from some shortcoming that existed in the previous stage. The same applies to the ideas of the soul and the inspirations of the heart.

The novice, therefore, must scrutinize (*muḥâsabah*) him-

[458] *Sic* B. A, C, and D: "idea." Bulaq: "spirit."
[459] Cf., for instance, 2:411, above.
[460] Bulaq corrects the text to: "grief or joy . . ."
[461] Cf. 2:36, above.
[462] As a technical term in Sufism, *natîjah* "result" is identical with "state" or "station."

self in all his actions and study their concealed import, because the results, of necessity, originate from actions, and shortcomings in the results, thus, originate from defects in the actions. The Sufi novice finds out about that through his III, *62*
mystical experience,[463] and he scrutinizes himself as to its reasons.

Very few people share the (self-scrutiny) of the Sufis, for negligence in this respect is almost universal. Pious people who do not get that far perform, at best, acts of obedience [464] freed from the juridical study of how to be satisfactory [465] and conforming (in the execution of the acts of divine worship). The (Sufis), however, investigate the results of (acts of obedience) with the help of mystical and ecstatic experience, in order to learn whether they are free from deficiency or not. Thus, it is evident that the Sufis' path in its entirety depends upon self-scrutiny with regard to what they do or do not do, and upon discussion of the various kinds of mystical and ecstatic experience that result from their exertions. This, then, crystallizes for the Sufi novice in a "station." From that station, he can progress to another, higher one.

Furthermore, the Sufis have their peculiar form of behavior and a (peculiar) linguistic terminology which they use in instruction.[466] Linguistic data apply only to commonly accepted ideas. When there occur ideas not commonly accepted, technical terms facilitating the understanding of those ideas are coined to express them.

Thus, the Sufis had their special discipline, which is not discussed by other representatives of the religious law. As a consequence, the science of the religious law came to consist of two kinds. One is the special field of jurists and muftis. It is

[463] Lit., "taste," the common mystical term for mystical experience. For "taste" as a term of literary criticism, see pp. 358 ff., below.

[464] The opposite of "acts of disobedience," i.e., sins. Acts of obedience are as positively required as sins are forbidden.

[465] The suggested reading *al-ijrâ'* "to perform" (Bombaci, p. 456) is not supported by MSS. B, C, or D, which clearly indicate the reading *al-ijzâ'*.

[466] "In instruction" is added by C in the margin, and appears in D in the text.

concerned with the general laws governing the acts of divine worship, customary actions, and mutual dealings. The other is the special field of the "people" (Sufis). It is concerned with pious exertion, self-scrutiny with regard to it, discussion of the different kinds of mystical and ecstatic experience occurring in the course of (self-scrutiny), the mode of ascent from one mystical experience to another, and the interpretation of the technical terminology of mysticism in use among them.

When the sciences were written down systematically and when the jurists wrote works on jurisprudence and the
III, 63 principles of jurisprudence, on speculative theology, Qur'ân interpretation, and other subjects, the Sufis, too, wrote on their subject. Some Sufis wrote on the laws governing asceticism and self-scrutiny, how to act and not act in imitation of model (saints). That was done by al-Muḥâsibî, in his *Kitâb ar-Ri'âyah*.[467] Other (Sufi authors) wrote on the behavior of (Sufis) and their different kinds of mystical and ecstatic experience in the "states." Al-Qushayrî in his *Kitâb ar-Risâlah*, and as-Suhrawardî[468] in the *Kitâb 'Awârif al-ma'ârif*, as well as others, did this.

Al-Ghazzâlî combined the two matters in the *Kitâb al-Iḥyâ'*. In it, he dealt systematically with the laws governing asceticism and the imitation of models. Then, he explained the behavior and customs of the people (Sufis) and commented on their technical vocabulary.

Thus, the science of Sufism became a systematically treated discipline in Islam. Before that, mysticism had merely consisted of divine worship, and its laws had existed in the breasts of men. The same had been the case with all other disciplines, such as Qur'ân interpretation, the science of tradition, jurisprudence, the principles of jurisprudence, and

[467] Cf. p. 63, above. The *Ri'âyah* was edited by Margaret Smith in 1940 as No. 15 of the E. J. W. Gibb Memorial Series, N.S. A translation has been prepared by K. Schoonover; cf. *Muslim World*, XXXIX (1949), 26–35.

[468] 'Umar b. Muḥammad, 539–632 [1145–1234/35]. Cf. *GAL*, I, 440 f.; *Suppl.*, I, 788 ff. Cf. also A. J. Arberry in *Bulletin of the School of Oriental Studies*, XIII (1950), 339–56.

other disciplines. (They were only later on) treated systematically.

Mystical [469] exertion, retirement,[470] and *dhikr* exercises [471] are as a rule followed by the removal of the veil (*kashf*) of sensual perception. The Sufi beholds divine worlds which a person subject to the senses cannot perceive at all. The spirit belongs to those worlds. The reason for the removal of (the veil) is the following. When the spirit turns from external sense perception to inner (perception), the senses weaken, and the spirit grows strong. It gains predominance and a new growth. The *dhikr* exercise helps to bring that about. It is like food to make the spirit grow. The spirit continues to grow and to increase. It had been knowledge. Now, it becomes vision. The veil of sensual perception is removed, and the soul realizes its essential existence. This is identical III, 64
with perception. (The spirit) now is ready for the holy gifts, for the sciences of the divine presence, and for the outpourings of the Deity. Its essence realizes its own true character and draws close to the highest sphere, the sphere of the angels. The removal of (the veil) often happens to people who exert themselves (in mystical exercise). They perceive the realities of existence as no one else (does).

They also perceive many (future) happenings in advance. With the help of their minds and psychic powers they are active among the lower *existentia*, which thus become obedient to their will. The great Sufis do not think much of the removal (of the veil) and of activity (among the low *existentia*). They give no information about the reality of anything they have not been ordered to discuss. They consider it a tribulation, when things of that sort happen to them, and try to escape them whenever they afflict them.[472]

The men around Muḥammad practiced that kind of

469 Cf. Issawi, pp. 175 f.
470 Omitted in C and D.
471 The famous Sufi ritual. Cf. D. B. Macdonald in *EI*, *s.v.* "Dhikr."
472 Cf. p. 102, below.

(mystical) exertion. They had a very abundant share in the acts of divine grace, but they did not bother with them. (The description of) the virtues of Abû Bakr, 'Umar,[473] and 'Alî contain much (information) to this effect. They were followed in this respect by the Sufis who are mentioned in the *Risâlah* of al-Qushayrî,[474] and their later successors.

Recent mystics, then, have turned their attention to the removal of the veil and the discussion of perceptions beyond (sensual perception). Their ways of mystical exercise in this respect differ. They have taught different methods of mortifying the powers of sensual perception and nourishing the reasoning spirit with *dhikr* exercises, so that the soul might
III, *65* fully grow and attain its own essential perception. When this happens, they believe that the whole of existence is encompassed by the perceptions of the soul, that the essences of existence are revealed to them, and that they perceive the reality of all the essences from the (divine) throne to light rain.[475] This was said by al-Ghazzâlî in the *Kitâb al-Iḥyâ'*, after he had mentioned the forms of mystical exercise.

The[476] (Sufis) do not consider removal (of the veil) sound, unless it originates in straightforwardness.[477] People who do not eat and who retire (from the world), such as sorcerers, Christians, and other ascetics, may obtain removal (of the veil) without the existence of straightforwardness. However, we mean only that removal (of the veil) which originates in straightforwardness. It may be compared with (the reflections of) a mirror. If it is convex or concave, the object reflected by it appears in a distorted form different

[473] Bulaq adds "'Uthmân"!

[474] Cf. 1:460, above; pp. 85 and 102, below.

[475] *Min al-'arsh ilâ ṭ-ṭashsh.* Bombaci, p. 456, accepts the ingenious emendation found in some Egyptian editions of the *Muqaddimah*, of *ṭashsh* to *farsh* "field, earth." Cf. *ibid.*, (Cairo, 1327/1909), p. 524. However, the MSS do not support this emendation. C even explains *ṭashsh* in the margin as "light rain."

The book on *riyâḍat an-nafs* (mystical exercise) in al-Ghazzâlî's *Iḥyâ'*, III, 42 ff., does not contain the phrase, nor have I succeeded in locating the passage elsewhere in the *Iḥyâ'*.

[476] Cf. Issawi, p. 176.

[477] Used in approximately the sense of "staunch faith."

from the actual form of the object, but if the mirror is flat, the object appears in its correct form. As far as the "states" impressed upon the soul are concerned, straightforwardness means to the soul what flatness means in a mirror.

The recent (Sufis) who have occupied themselves with this kind of removal (of the veil) talk about the real character of the higher and lower *existentia* and about the real character of the (divine) kingdom, the spirit, the (divine) throne, the (divine) seat, and similar things. Those who did not share their approach were not able to understand their mystical and ecstatic experiences in this respect. The muftis partly disapprove of these Sufis and partly accept them. Arguments and proofs are of no use in deciding whether the Sufi approach should be rejected or accepted, since it belongs to intuitive [478] experience.

Some [479] details in explanation:

Ḥadîth scholars and jurists who discuss the articles of faith often mention that God is separate from His creatures. The speculative theologians say that He is neither separate III, *66* nor connected. The philosophers say that He is neither in the world nor outside it. The recent Sufis say that He is one with the creatures, in the sense that He is incarnate in them, or in the sense that He is identical with them and there exists nothing but Himself either (in the) whole or (in) any part (of it).

Let us explain in detail these dogmatic opinions and the real meaning of each of them, so that their significance will be clarified. We say:

Separateness has two meanings. It may mean "separateness in space and direction." [479a] The opposite, then, would be connectedness. In this sense, the statement of (separa-

---

[478] Cf. I:198 (n. 277), above. However, when Ibn Khaldûn uses *wijdânî* in connection with Sufism, he probably associates it in his mind with *mawâjid*, translated here as "ecstatic (experience)." Cf. p. 77, above.

[479] The following discussion, down to p. 87, l. 5, is found on a special inserted slip in C, and appears incorporated in the text of D.

[479a] The second meaning of separateness is discussed on p. 85, ll. 12 ff.

tion)[480] implies (that God is in some) place, either directly—which would be direct anthropomorphism (*tajsîm*)—or indirectly—which would be indirect anthropomorphism (*tashbîh*)[481]—in the way in which one speaks about (God's having) direction. It has been reported that an early Muslim scholar similarly professed the separateness of God, but a different interpretation is possible.

The speculative theologians, therefore, did not acknowledge this (kind of) separateness. They said: It cannot be said that the Creator is separate from His creatures, and it cannot be said that He is connected with them, because such a statement can be made only about things in space. The statement that a particular thing[482] can be described as devoid of one concept and at the same time of the opposite of that concept depends upon whether the description is sound in the first place (or not). If it is impossible, (the statement is) not (correct). It is, in fact, permissible to describe (a certain thing) as devoid of one concept and at the same time of the opposite of that concept. Thus, a solid substance may be described as not wise and not ignorant, not powerful and not weak, not causing harm [?] and not being harmed.[483] Now, the correctness of describing God as separate in the way mentioned is predicated upon the possibility of ascribing direction to Him in the proper meaning of the word, but this cannot be done with the Creator, who is free from (such a description).

This was mentioned by Ibn at-Tilimsânî[484] in his com-

[480] *Hâdhihî l-maqâlah 'alâ hâdhâ t-taqdîr:* C and D.

[481] *Tajsîm:* declaring that God is corporeal. *Tashbîh:* declaring that God is similar (to human beings).

[482] *Maḥall* is especially familiar to Ibn Khaldûn as a legal term. Cf. p. 5 (n. 171), above, and D. Santillana, *Istituzioni di diritto musulmano malichita*, II, 729.

[483] C and D read *wa-lâ mudrik wa-lâ ma'ûf* (D: *mas'ûf* or *ma'sûf?*). Possibly the last word must be corrected to mean "not perceiving and not unperceiving." In the above translation *mudrik* has been corrected to *muḍirr*. The Paris edition has a completely different text: "not able to write and not illiterate."

[484] 'Abdallâh b. Muḥammad, d. 658 [1260]. Cf. *GAL*, I, 389; *Suppl.*, I, 672. His work was not available for checking, so that the exact character and extent of the quotation could not be ascertained. It probably extends to the end of the paragraph.

mentary on the *Luma'* of the Imâm al-Ḥaramayn. He said: The Creator can neither be said to be separate from the world, nor to be connected with it. He is not in it and not outside it. That is what is meant by the philosophers when they say that He is neither in the world nor outside it. They base themselves (on the assumption) that there exist substances (atoms) that exist not in space. The speculative theologians did not acknowledge their (existence), because they would have to be considered equal to the Creator in the most specific qualities. That is fully dealt with in the science of speculative theology. III, 67

The other meaning of separateness is "being distinct and different." The Creator is called separate from His creatures in His essence, identity, existence, and attributes. The opposite is being one, mingled, and merged (with something else).

(God's) separateness in this sense is assumed in the dogmas of all orthodox people, such as the great mass of early Muslims, the religious scholars, the speculative theologians, and the ancient Sufis, such as the men mentioned in (al-Qushayrî's) *Risâlah*, and those who follow them.

A number of recent Sufis who consider intuitive [485] perceptions to be scientific and logical, hold the opinion that the Creator is one with His creatures in His identity, His existence, and His attributes. They often assume that this was the opinion of the philosophers before Aristotle, such as Plato and Socrates.

That is what the speculative theologians mean when they speak about the (oneness of God with His creatures) in theology and try to refute it. They do not [486] mean that there could be a question of two essences, one of which must be negated or comprised (in the other) as a part (in the whole). That would be clear distinctness, and they do not maintain that to be the case.

The oneness (assumed by the Sufis) is identical with the

[485] Cf. 1:198, and p. 83, above.
[486] *Lâ annahû:* C and D.

incarnation the Christians claim for the Messiah. It is even stranger, in that it is the incarnation of something primeval in something created and the oneness of the former with the latter.

(The oneness assumed by the Sufis) is also identical with the stated opinion of the Imâmîyah Shî'ah concerning their imams.[487] In their discussion, the (Shî'ah) [488] consider two ways in which the oneness (of the Deity with the imams) is achieved. (1) The essence of the primeval (Deity) is hidden
III, *68* in all created things, both *sensibilia* and *intelligibilia*, and is one with them in both kinds of perception. All of them are manifestations of it, and it has control over them—that is, it controls their existence in the sense that, without it, they would not exist. Such is the opinion of the people who believe in incarnation.

(2) There is the approach of those who believe in absolute oneness. It seems as if in the exposition of the people who believe in incarnation, they have sensed the existence of a differentness contradicting the concept of oneness. Therefore, they disavowed the (existence of differentness) between the primeval (Deity) and the creatures in essence, existence, and attributes. In (order to explain) the differentness of the manifestations perceived by the senses and the intellect, they used the specious argument that those things were human perceptions that are imaginary. By imaginary, they do not mean imaginary as part of the sequence: known, hypothetical, doubtful, but they mean that all those things do not exist in reality and exist only in human perception. Only the primeval (Deity) has real existence (and nothing else) either outwardly or inwardly. Later on, we shall, as far as possible,[489] establish this.

In order to understand this intellectually, it is useless to rely upon speculation and argumentation, as is done in con-

[487] Only C has "concerning their imams."

[488] The suffix clearly refers to the immediately preceding "Shî'ah." However, Ibn Khaldûn does not speak only of the Shî'ah, but includes the Sufis who hold similar opinions.

[489] Cf. pp. 90 f., below.

nection with human perceptions. This (sort of insight corresponds to) angelic perceptions and is transferred from them (to human beings). Prophets have it through natural disposition. After them, saints have it through divine guidance. But one errs if one wants to obtain it by scientific methods.

Authors have occasionally tried to explain the (Sufi) opinions concerning the revelation (*kashf*) of existence and the order of the realities of existence according to the approach of the people who (have the theory of) "manifestations" (*maẓâhir*).[490] As compared to people who cultivate speculation, technical terminology, and the sciences, (it must be said that) they have always added obscurity to obscurity. An example is al-Farghânî,[491] the commentator on Ibn al- III, 69
Fâriḍ's *Poem*.[492] He wrote a preface at the beginning of his commentary. In connection with the origin of the world of existence from the Maker and its order, he mentions that all existence comes forth from the attribute of uniqueness (*waḥdânîyah*) which is the manifestation of unity (*aḥadîyah*).[493] Both of them together issue from the noble essence that is identical with oneness and nothing else. This process is called "revelation" (*tajallî*). The first degree of revelation (*tajallî*), in (Sufi) opinion, is the revelation, as such,[494] of the essence. This implies perfection, because it emanates creation and appearance, according to (God's) statement in the prophetic tradition transmitted by (the Sufis): "I was a

[490] *Maẓhar* is understood by al-Farghânî as the "place where something manifests itself." Cf. also p. 88 (n. 496), below.

[491] According to the edition of his *Muntahâ al-madârik* ([Istanbul,] 1293/1876), his names were Sa'îd-ad-dîn Muḥammad b. Aḥmad. *GAL*, I, 262; *Suppl.*, I, 463, gives, apparently incorrectly, Sa'îd b. 'Abdallâh. He lived *ca.* 700 [1300]. Ibn Khaldûn bravely tries to compress al-Farghânî's highly involved discussion into a few words. However, he is not quite successful in reproducing the terminology of his source with complete exactness.

[492] The famous *Tâ'îyah* of 'Umar b. al-Fâriḍ, 577–632 [1182–1235]. Cf. *GAL*, I, 262 f.; *Suppl.*, I, 462 ff.

[493] Al-Farghânî, *op. cit.*, I, 9 ff., says that *aḥadîyah* and *wâḥidîyah* result from *waḥdah*.

[494] "As such" refers to revelation. The masculine pronoun of the Arabic text, unless one wants to correct it to the feminine, can hardly be taken to refer to "essence": "revelation of the essence as such."

concealed treasure. I wanted to be known. Therefore, I created the creatures, so that they might know Me." [495] This is perfection in creation descending to the level of existence and particularization of the realities. It is, in (Sufi) opinion, the world of ideas, the nubilous (*'amâ'îyah*) presence,[496] and Muḥammadan reality. It contains the realities of the attributes, the writing tablet and the pen, the realities of all the prophets and messengers, and the whole of the people of the Muḥammadan nation. All this is the particularization of the Muḥammadan reality. From these realities, other realities issue in the atomic (*habâ'îyah*) presence,[497] which is the level of the ideas (*mithâl*). From there, then, issue in succession the (divine) throne, the (divine) seat, the spheres, the world of the elements, and the world of composition. All this is (originally) in the world of mending (*ratq*), but when these

[495] This *ḥadîth qudsî* ("tradition in which God appears as the speaker"; cf. 1:193, above) is quoted by al-Farghânî, *op. cit.*, I, 5. It appears in Ibn 'Arabî's *Futûḥât;* cf. M. Asín Palacios, "Ibn Masarra y su escuela," in *Obras Escogidas* (Madrid, 1946), I, 163 (n. 4). Jalâl-ad-dîn Rûmî quotes it over and over again in his *Mathnawî.* Cf. R. A. Nicholson's edition (E. J. W. Gibb Memorial Series, N.S. No. 4)(London, 1925–40), Bk. I, v. 2862; Bk. II, v. 364; Bk. IV, vv. 2540 ff., 3029. Cf. also H. S. Nyberg, *Kleinere Schriften des Ibn al-'Arabî,* p. 139.

[496] Cf. al-Farghânî, *op. cit.*, I, 23. The expression *'amâ'îyah* "nubilous" is based upon the following tradition. "Muḥammad was asked: 'Where was God before the creation?' He replied: 'He was in a cloud (*'amâ'*) above which there was no air and underneath which there was no air.' " The tradition is also quoted, for instance, in al-Mas'ûdî, *Akhbâr az-zamân* (Cairo, 1357/1938), p. 5; Ibn Kathîr, *Bidâyah,* I, 8. Cf. also A. J. Wensinck, *Bar Hebraeus' Book of the Dove* (Leiden, 1919), pp. CIII–CV.

The terms *'amâ'îyah* and *habâ'îyah* are those of Ibn 'Arabî. Cf. Asín Palacios, *op. cit.*, I, 97 and 146 f., and the references in the index to A. E. Affifi, *The Mystical Philosophy of Muhyid dín-Ibnul 'Arabi* (Cambridge, 1939). Al-Farghânî was a pupil of Ṣadr-ad-dîn al-Qônawî, d. 672 [1273]; cf. *GAL,* I, 449 f.; *Suppl.*, I, 807 f. The latter, in turn, was a pupil of Ibn 'Arabî.

The word "presence" (*ḥaḍrah*) in al-Farghânî is nearly synonymous with *'âlam* "world," *maḥall* "place," and *maẓhar* "manifestation." Cf. Asín Palacios, *op. cit.*, I, 204 ff. ("La teoria de los 'ḥaḍras' de Ibn 'Arabî y las 'dignitates' de Lulio.")

Cf. also p. 177, below.

[497] For *habâ'îyah*, cf. the preceding note and al-Farghânî, *op. cit.*, I, 55 ff. *Habâ'* means "dust particle" and also "atom." Cf. P. Kraus, *Jâbir Ibn Ḥayyân* (Mémoires de l'Institut d'Egypte, Nos. 44–45)(Cairo, 1942–43), II, 154.

things manifest themselves, they are in the world of rending (*fatq*). End of the quotation.

This school is called that of the people of revelation, manifestations, and presences. It is a theory that people cultivating (logical) speculation cannot properly grasp, be- III, 70
cause it is obscure and cryptic. There also is a great gap between the theories of people who have vision and intuitive experience and those of people who cultivate logical reasoning.[498] (Sufi) systems (like the one mentioned) are often disapproved of on the strength of the plain wording of the religious law, for no indication of them can be found in it anywhere.

Other (Sufis) turned to affirming absolute oneness. This is a theory (even) stranger than the first one to understand in its implications and details. They believe the components of everything in existence to possess powers that bring the realities, forms, and matters of the existing things into being. The elements come into being through the powers that are in them. The same is the case with matter, which has in itself a power that has brought about its existence. Composite things contain such powers implicit in the power that brought about (their) composition. For instance, the mineral power contains the powers of the elements of matter and, in addition, the mineral power. The animal power contains the mineral power and, in addition, its own power. The same is the case with the human power as compared to animal power. The firmament contains the human power and something in addition. The same applies to the spiritual essences.

Now, the power combining everything without any particularization is the divine power. It is the power distributed over all existing things, whether they are universals or particulars, combining and comprising them in every aspect, with regard to appearance and hiddenness and with regard to form and matter. Everything is one. (Oneness) is

[498] Cf. p. 155, below.

identical with the divine essence. In reality, (the divine essence) is one and simple. The thing that divides it is the way (we) look at it. For instance, as to the relationship of humanity to animality, it is clear that the former is included under the latter and comes into being when it comes into
III, *71* being. At times, (the Sufis) represent the relationship as that of genus to species, (which exists) in every existing thing, as we have mentioned.[499] Or, they represent it as that of the universal to the particular, according to the theory of ideas (*mithâl*). At any rate, they always try to get away from any thought of composition or manifoldness. They think that (manifoldness) is brought about by fancy and imagination.

It appears from the discussion of Ibn Dihâq,[500] who explains this (Sufi) theory, that what the (Sufis) say about oneness is actually similar to what the philosophers say about colors, namely, that their existence is predicated upon light. When there is no light, no colors whatever exist. Thus, the (Sufis) think that all existing *sensibilia* are predicated upon the existence of some (faculty of) sensual perception [501] and, in fact, that all existing *intelligibilia* and objects of imagination are predicated upon the existence of some (faculty of) intellectual perception. Thus, every particular in existence is predicated upon (the existence of) [502] the human (faculty) that perceives it. If we assumed that no human being with perception exists, there would be no particularization in existence. Existence would be simple and one.

Thus, heat and cold, solidity and softness, and, indeed, earth, water, fire, heaven, and the stars, exist only because the senses perceiving them exist, because particularization that does not exist in existence is made possible for the (person) who perceives. It exists only in perception. If there were no perceptions to create distinctions, there would be no

[499] Cf. 1:9 [?], above, and p. 138, below.

[500] * Or Dahhâq, i.e., Ibrâhîm b. Yûsuf Ibn al-Mar'ah, d. 611 [1214–15].

[501] The vocalization in C, here and in the following lines, is *madrak*, not *mudrik*, as one might expect.

[502] Bulaq actually has the words in brackets.

particularization, but just one single perception, namely, the
"I" and nothing else. They consider this comparable to the
condition of a sleeper. When he sleeps and has no external
sense perception, he loses in that condition all (perception of)
sensibilia, with the exception of the things that the imagination particularizes for him. They continued by saying that a
person who is awake likewise experiences particularized
perceptions only through the type of human perception (that
exists) in him. If he had not that something in him that per- III, 72
ceives, there would be no particularization. This is what the
(Sufis) mean when they say "imaginary." They do not mean
"imaginary" as a part (in the sequence) of human perceptions.[503]

This is a short exposition of (Sufi) opinion, as gathered from the discussion of Ibn Dihâq. It is most erroneous. We know for certain that a country which we have quitted on our travels or to which we are traveling, exists, despite the fact that we do not see it any more. We also have definite knowledge of the existence of heaven that overlooks[504] (everything), and of the stars, and of all the other things that are remote from us. Man knows these things for certain. No one would deny to himself (the existence of) certain knowledge. In addition, competent recent Sufis say that during the removal (of the veil), the Sufi novice often has a feeling of the oneness (of existence). Sufis call that the station of "combination" (*jam'*).[505] But then, he progresses to distinguishing between existent things. That is considered by the Sufis the station of "differentiation" (*farq*). That is the station of the competent gnostic. The (Sufis) believe that the novice cannot avoid the ravine of "combination," and this ravine causes difficulties

[503] Cf. p. 86, above.

[504] *Al-muṭillah,* though A and C read *al-muẓillah* "gives shade to."

[505] The Sufi terms translated here as "combination" and "differentiation" may be understood literally either as "combining" and "differentiating," or, more likely, as "where something (some one) is combined (united) or differentiated (separated)." For some of the many Sufi interpretations of *jam'* and *farq* (*tafriqah*), cf., for instance, Hujwîrî, *Kashf al-maḥjûb,* pp. 252 ff.

for him because there is danger that he might be arrested at it and his enterprise thus come to nought.[506]

The different kinds of mystics have thus been explained.

The recent Sufis who speak of the removal (of the veil) and supersensory perception have delved deeply into these (subjects). Many of them turned to (the theory of) incarnation and oneness, as we have indicated. They have filled many pages with (their exposition of) it. That was done, for instance, by al-Harawî,[507] in the *Kitâb al-Maqâmât*, and by others. They were followed by Ibn al-ʽArabî and Ibn Sabʽîn[508] and their pupils, and then by Ibn al-ʽAfîf (ʽAfîf-ad-dîn),[509] Ibn al-Fâriḍ, and Najm-ad-dîn al-Isrâʼîlî,[510] in the poems they composed.

The early (Sufis) had had contact with the Neo-Ismâʽîlîyah
III, 73 Shîʽah extremists who also believed in incarnation and the divinity of the imams, a theory not known to the early (Ismâʽîlîyah). Each group came to be imbued with the dogmas of the other. Their theories and beliefs merged and were assimilated. In Sufi discussion, there appeared the theory of the "pole" (*quṭb*), meaning the chief gnostic. The Sufis assumed that no one can reach his station in gnosis, until God takes him unto Himself and then gives his station to another gnostic who will be his heir. Avicenna referred to this in the sections on Sufism in the *Kitâb al-Ishârât*. He said: "The majestic Truth is too exalted to be available equally to all

[506] Consequently, even according to Sufi theory itself, particularized existence is not only possible, but the knowledge of it still more desirable than that of the oneness of existence.

For "ravine" as a Sufi term, cf., for instance, al-Qushayrî, *Risâlah*, p. 49, and al-Ghazzâlî, *Iḥyâʼ*, I, 48, 112.

[507] ʽAbdallâh b. Muḥammad, *ca.* 401 [1010/11] to 481 [1089]. Cf. *GAL*, I, 433; *Suppl.*, I, 773 f. The *Maqâmât* are identical with the work entitled *Manâzil as-sâʼirîn*. Cf. p. 95, below.

[508] Cf. 2:187 f., above.

[509] Shams-ad-dîn Muḥammad b. ʽAfîf-ad-dîn Sulaymân b. ʽAlî at-Tilimsânî, *ca.* 658 [1260] to 688 [1289]. Cf. *GAL*, I, 258; *Suppl.*, I, 458. Or, perhaps, rather his father ʽAfîf-ad-dîn himself, 613–690 [1216/17–1291].

[510] Not the famous Ibn Sahl (p. 393, below), but Najm-ad-dîn Ibn Isrâʼîl, 603–677 [1206–1278]. Cf. *GAL*, I, 257; Ibn Kathîr, *Bidâyah*, XIII, 283 ff.

who seek it,[511] or to be seen save by one person at a time." [512]

The theory of (successive "poles") is not confirmed by logical arguments or evidence from the religious law. It is a sort of rhetorical figure of speech. It is identical with the theory of the extremist Shî'ah about the succession [513] of the imams through inheritance. Clearly, mysticism has plagiarized this idea from the extremist Shî'ah and come to believe in it.

The (Sufis), furthermore, speak about the order of existence of the "saints" who come after the "pole," exactly as the Shî'ah speak about their "chiefs." [514] They go so far (in the identification of their own concepts with those of the Shî'ah) that when they construed a chain of transmitters for the wearing of the Sufi cloak (*khirqah*) as a basic requirement of the mystic way and practice, they made it go back to 'Alî.[515] This points in the same direction and can only (be explained as Shî'ah influence). Among the men around Muḥammad, 'Alî was not distinguished by any particular practice or way of dressing or by any special condition. Abû Bakr and 'Umar were the most ascetic and pious people after the Messenger of God. Yet, none of these men was distinguished by the possession of any particular religious practice exclusively peculiar to him. In fact, all the men around Muḥammad were models of religion, austerity, asceticism,[516] and (pious) exertion. This is attested by their way of life III, 74
and history. Indeed, with the help of these stories, the Shî'ah try to suggest that 'Alî is distinguished from the other men around Muḥammad by being in possession of particular virtues, in conformity with well-known Shî'ah beliefs.

---

[511] Lit., "to be a watering place for anybody who comes down to it,

[512] Cf. *Ishârât*, ed. Forget, p. 207; tr. Goichon, p. 501.

[513] The rest of the paragraph is not found in Bulaq.

[514] *Abdâl* "saints," lit., "representatives." *Nuqabâ'*, pl. of *naqîb*, referring to the 'Alid nobility. Cf. 2:165 and 187, above.

[515] Cf. L. Massignon, *Essai sur les origines du lexique technique de la mystique musulmane* (Paris, 1922), pp. 108 f.

[516] "Asceticism" is added in C and D..

It [517] is obvious that the Sufis in the 'Irâq derived their comparison between the manifest and the inner (world) from the Ismâ'îlîyah Shî'ah and their well-known theory concerning the imamate and connected matters, at the time when the Ismâ'îlîyah Shî'ah made its appearance. The (Ismâ'îlîyah Shî'ah) considered the leadership of mankind and its guidance toward the religious law a duty of the imam. Therefore, they assumed that there could be no more than one imam if the possibility of a split were to be avoided, as is established in the religious law. (Correspondingly, the Sufis) then regarded as a duty of the "pole," who is the chief gnostic, the instruction (of mankind) in the gnosis of God. Therefore, they assumed that there could be only one, on analogy from the imam in the manifest (world), and that he was the counterpart of the imam.[518] They called him "pole," because the gnosis revolves around him, and they equated the "saints" with the 'Alid "chiefs," in their exaggerated desire to identify (their concepts with those of the Shî'ah).

An instance of what I have just been saying is the lengthy discussion of the Fâṭimid in Sufi works.[519] The early Sufis made neither negative nor affirmative statements on the Fâṭimid. The lengthy discussion of (recent) Sufis was derived from the discussion (of the subject) and the dogmas (concerning it) expressed by the extremist Shî'ah in their works.

"God guides to the truth." [520]

I [521] consider it appropriate to quote here a remark made by our *shaykh*, the gnostic and chief saint in Spain, Abû Mahdî 'Îsâ b. az-Zayyât.[522] He repeated it very often. It concerns

[517] This paragraph appears first in C and D, in the margin of the former and in the text of the latter.

[518] MSS. C and D do not have the additional "in the inner (world)," which appears in the Paris ed., but is of doubtful correctness.

[519] Cf. 2:186 ff., above.

[520] Qur'ân 10.35 (36); 46.30 (29).

[521] The following quotation extends to p. 98. It is not found in Bulaq. C and D add: "Additional note."

[522] I have no further information on him.

some verses from the *Kitâb al-Maqâmât* of al-Harawî which suggest, and almost profess openly, the theory of absolute oneness. These are the verses:[523]

The oneness of the Unique One has never been declared (properly) by anyone, III, *75*
Since anyone who declares His oneness is one who denies (His true oneness).
Declaration of the divine oneness by a person who speaks about His attributes,
Is dualism,[524] which the Unique One has nullified.
His (Own) declaration of His (Own) oneness is the (true) declaration of His oneness.
And to describe Him with attributes is deviation.[525]

Abû Mahdî says in defense of al-Harawî: People have found it difficult to (explain how one could) use the expression "one who denies" for those who "declare the oneness of the Unique One," and the expression "deviation, heresy," for those who describe Him with attributes. They have disapproved of the verses quoted. They have attacked the author and contemned him. But we say that, according to the view of that group (of Sufis to whom al-Harawî belongs), declaration of the divine oneness means the negation of the very

[523] The verses are from the end of al-Harawî's *Manâzil as-sâ'irîn* (Cairo, 1327/1909), p. 52. Cf. W. Ahlwardt, *Die Handschriften-Verzeichnisse der Königlichen Bibliothek zu Berlin: Verzeichniss der arabischen Handschriften* (Berlin, 1891), III, 12, No. 2826. Cf. also Ibn Qayyim al-Jawzîyah's lengthy commentary on the verses in his *Madârij as-sâlikîn* (Cairo, 1331–33/1913–15), III, 332 f.; the brief commentary by Maḥmûd al-Firkâwî, ed. S. De Laugier de Beaurecueil (Textes et traductions d'auteurs orientaux, No. 17) (Cairo, 1953), pp. 150 f.; E. Berthels in *Islamica*, III (1927), 12 f.

For the biography of 'Abdallâh al-Anṣârî al-Harawî, 396–481 [1006–1089], cf. *GAL*, I, 433; *Suppl.*, I, 773 ff., and S. De Laugier de Beaurecueil in *Mélanges de l'Institut Dominicain d'Etudes Orientales du Caire*, II (1955), 5 f.

[524] The original text of al-Harawî does not have *tathniyah* "dualism" but *'âriyah* "loan." It is a "loan," and not his property but God's property. God's true oneness, not recognized by the person who speaks about God's attributes, nullifies and cancels this loan. This is the explanation of Ibn Qayyim al-Jawzîyah. *Tathniyah*, which was Ibn az-Zayyât's reading, is a simplification.

[525] Cf. Ibn 'Arabî, *Futûḥât*, IV, 473: "Whoever declares the oneness of God is a deviator (heretic), because of the 'whoever' that requires numerical plurality."

essence of createdness through affirmation of the very essence of primevalness. The whole existence is one reality and one being (*annîyah*). The great mystic, Abû Sa'îd al-Kharrâz,[526] thus said, "The Truth is the very essence of that which is manifest, and the very essence of that which is inwardly hidden."

The (Sufis) are of the opinion that the occurrence of any numerical plurality in that (divine) reality and [527] the existence of duality are imaginary and, compared with sensual data, are on the level of shadow pictures, or the pictures [528] in mirrors. Everything, except the very essence of primevalness, if one follows it up, turns out to be non-existent. This, they think, is the meaning (of the statement), "God was, and nothing (was) with Him. He is now in the same state in which He was." [529] This, too, is what is meant by the verse of Labîd, which the Messenger of God considered to be true:

Indeed, everything but God is vanity.[530]

(This is what) the (Sufis) say. Consequently, a person who "declares the divine oneness and describes God with attributes" speaks about: (1) a created being who declares the divine oneness — that is, he himself; (2) a created declaration of the divine oneness — that is, his action (of declaring the divine oneness); and (3) a primeval being who is declared to be one — that is, his worshiped Master. Now, it has been

---

[526] Aḥmad b. 'Îsâ, d. *ca.* 286 [899]. Cf. *GAL, Suppl.*, I, 354. The quotation is not contained in al-Kharrâz' *Kitâb aṣ-ṣidq*, published by A. J. Arberry (Islamic Research Association, No. 6) (Oxford, 1937). As is quite usual in the case of Muslim mystics, their published work would hardly make it seem likely that they made the rather unorthodox statements attributed to them.

A reads: "The Truth is not (*ghayr*) that which is manifest, and not (*ghayr*) that which . . ."

[527] *Sic* MSS.

[528] *Sic* MSS.

[529] Cf. H. S. Nyberg, *Kleinere Schriften des Ibn al-'Arabî*, p. 139 (p. 47 of the Arabic text); H. Ritter, *Das Meer der Seele* (Leiden, 1955), p. 602.

[530] Cf. Labîd, *Dîwân*, ed. A. Hubert and C. Brockelmann (Leiden, 1891), No. 41, v. 9. Muḥammad's approval of the verse is noted by al-Bukhârî, *Ṣaḥîḥ*, IV, 228.

mentioned before that declaration of divine oneness is negation of the very essence of createdness, but now, the very essence of createdness is (here) definitely stated (in connection with the declaration of divine oneness) and, in fact, in more than one (way). Thus, the divine oneness is actually denied, and the claim (to have declared the divine oneness) is false. It is the same as if someone were to say to someone else who is with him in a house, "There is nobody in the III, 76
house except you." Whereupon the other person would reply at once, "This could be correct only if you were non-existent." And a competent (scholar) remarked in connection with the statement, "God created time," that these words contain a basic contradiction, because the creation of time precedes time, yet is an action that must take place in time.

These things are caused by the difficulty of expressing the realities and the inability of language to convey the truth with regard to them and give them their due. If it is certain that he who declares (the divine) oneness is identical with Him whose oneness is declared,[531] and that anything else is altogether non-existent, then the (declaration of) divine oneness is truly a sound one. This is what is meant by the (Sufi) statement, "Only God knows God." [532]

There is no objection to a person's declaring the oneness of the Truth, while retaining the outlines and traces (of worldliness). This belongs to the chapter (dealing with the fact) that the good actions of pious people may be the bad actions of persons who are close to the Divine. It results from the lack of freedom, servitude, and doubleness [533] (of the

[531] *Al-muwaḥḥid huwa al-muwaḥḥad*, as vocalized in C. The last word is vocalized in the same manner in A, too.

[532] Aḥmad al-Ghazzâlî is credited with a very similar statement: "The Truth is known only through the Truth." Cf. L. Massignon, *Recueil de textes inédits concernant l'histoire de la mystique en pays d'Islam* (Collection de textes inédits relatifs à la mystique musulmane, No. 1) (Paris, 1929), p. 98. Cf. also *EI*, *s.v.* "Shaṭḥ."

[533] *Shaf'îyah* goes back to the incomprehensible oath, "by the *even* and the odd," in Qur'ân 89.3 (2); cf. R. Bell's translation (Edinburgh, 1937–39), II, 654. Ibn 'Arabî, *Kitâb al-isrâ'*, in the *Rasâ'il Ibn al-'Arabî*, p. 58, speaks of the "veil of *shaf'*." *Shaf'* is opposed to *fard* (and *wâḥid*) in Ibn Arabî, *Futûḥât*, IV, 110 f., 355 f.

human condition). For those who have ascended to the station of "combination," it constitutes a defect. They are conscious of their rank and know that (their imperfection) is a deception resulting from (human) servitude, that vision can eliminate it, and that the very essence of "combination" can cleanse them from the uncleanliness of their createdness. The type (of persons) most firmly rooted in this assumption is that of those who hold the theory of absolute oneness and who say that gnosis, however interpreted, revolves around reaching the Unique One.

The poet uttered the remark (quoted) as an incitement and exhortation, referring to a higher station in which doubleness is eliminated and absolute oneness in (its) essence, not merely as a figure of speech or (some kind of) expression, is attained. Those who are safe and sound [534] can rest. Those who have trouble with the reality of (oneness [535] ought to become) familiar with (God's) statement, "I am his [536] hearing and vision." [537] If the concepts are known, there can be no quarrels about the words. All this teaches realization of the
III, 77 fact that there is something above this level, something about which one cannot speak and about which there is no information.

This much of a hint is sufficient. Going deeply into matters like this (lowers) the veil. That is the gist of the well-known (Sufi) statements.

Here ends the quotation from *shaykh* Abû Mahdî b. az-Zayyât. I quoted it from the book on love by the wazir Ibn

[534] De Slane reads, with A, *sallama* "accepts (it)."

[535] It might be possible to translate, "Those who have trouble with *their* reality . . ." i.e., those whose real being is not safe and sound and fully prepared for oneness, but who have trouble with it. This, however, seems much less likely than the translation above.

[536] That is, of the human being whom God loves.

[537] Cf. al-Bukhârî, *Ṣaḥîḥ*, IV, 231, quoted by Ibn 'Arabî, for instance; cf. L. Massignon, *Recueil de textes inédits . . .*, p. 118. According to Massignon, *Essai sur les origines du lexique technique de la mystique musulmane* (Paris, 1922), p. 107, this *ḥadîth qudsî* was adopted by Ibrâhîm b. Adham.

al-Khaṭîb,[538] entitled *at-Ta'rîf bi-l-ḥubb ash-sharîf* ("Information on the Noble Love [of God]"). I heard it from our *shaykh* Abû Mahdî himself several times. However, I think that the written form (in Ibn al-Khaṭîb's work) preserves it better (than my memory), because it has been a long time (since I heard Abû Mahdî tell it).

God gives success.

Many jurists and muftis have undertaken to refute these and similar statements by recent Sufis. They summarily disapproved of everything they came across in the (Sufi) path. The truth is that discussion with the (Sufis) requires making a distinction. (The Sufis) discuss four topics. (1) Firstly, they discuss pious exertions, the resulting mystical and ecstatic experiences, and self-scrutiny concerning (one's) actions. (They discuss these things) in order to obtain mystical experiences, which then become a station from which one progresses to the next higher one, as we have stated.[539] (2) Secondly, they discuss the removal (of the veil) and the perceivable supernatural realities, such as the divine attributes, the (divine) throne, the (divine) seat, the angels, revelation, prophecy, the spirit, and the realities of everything in existence, be it supernatural or visible; furthermore, they discuss the order of created things, how they issue from the Creator Who brings them into being, as mentioned before.[540] (3) The third topic is concerned with activities in the various worlds and among the various created things connected with different kinds of acts of divine grace. (4) The

[538] Muḥammad b. 'Abdallâh, 713–776 [1313–1374]. Cf. *GAL*, II, 260 ff.; *Suppl.*, II, 372 f., and above, 1:xliv. The work quoted was not available for checking. Cf. *GAL, Suppl.*, II, 373, No. 24.

In a letter to Ibn Khaldûn, dated January 24, 1368, Ibn al-Khaṭîb speaks about the work he had just written, hoping to surpass the *Dîwân aṣ-ṣabâbah* of Ibn Abî Ḥajalah at-Tilimsânî (cf. *GAL*, II, 13 f.; *Suppl.*, II, 5 f.). Cf. *Autobiography*, pp. 120 f., and also al-Ghuzûlî, *Maṭâli' al-budûr* (Cairo, 1299–1300/1881–82), II, 72 f.

[539] Cf. p. 79, above.

[540] The reference is apparently to pp. 81 f.

fourth topic (finally) is concerned with expressions that are suspect (if understood) in their plain meaning. Such (expressions) have been uttered by most Sufi leaders. In Sufi technical terminology, they are called "ecstatic utterances" (*shaṭaḥât*).[541] Their plain meaning is difficult to understand.
III, 78 They may be something that must be disapproved of, or something that can be approved, or something that requires interpretation.

As for their discussion of pious exertions and stations, of the mystical and ecstatic experiences that result, and of self-scrutiny with regard to (possible) shortcomings in the things that cause these (experiences), this is something that nobody ought to reject. These mystical experiences of (the Sufis) are sound ones. Their realization is the very essence of happiness.[542]

As for their discussion of the acts of divine grace experienced by Sufis, the information they give about supernatural things, and their activity among the created things, these (also) are sound and cannot be disapproved of, even though some religious scholars tend to disapprove. That is not right. Professor Abû Isḥâq al-Isfarâyinî, a leading Ash'arite, argued that these things should be disapproved of, since they might be confused with the (prophetical) miracles. However, competent orthodox scholars have made a distinction between (miracles and acts of divine grace) by referring to "the (advance) challenge" (*taḥaddî*),[543] that is, the claim (made by a prophet in advance) that the miracle would occur in agreement with the prophetic revelation. It is not possible, they said, that a miracle could happen in agreement with the claim of a liar. Logic requires that a miracle indicate truthfulness. By definition, a (miracle is something that) can be verified. If it were performed by a liar, it (could not be verified, and thus) would have changed its character, which is absurd. In addition, the world of existence attests the occurrence of many

---

[541] Cf. L. Massignon in *EI*, *s.v.* "Shaṭḥ."
[542] Apparently there is no separate discussion of point two.
[543] Cf. 1:188 ff. and 223, above; pp. 167 and 170, below.

such acts of divine grace. Disapproval of them would be a kind of negative approach. Many such acts of divine grace were experienced by the men around Muḥammad and the great early Muslims. This is a well-known and famous (fact).

Most of the (Sufi) discussion of the removal (of the veil), of the reception of the realities of the higher things, and of the order in which the created things issue, falls, in a way, under the category of ambiguous statements.[544] It is based upon the intuitive experience of (Sufis), and those who lack such intuitive experience cannot have the mystical experience that the (Sufis receive from) it. No language can express the things that (Sufis) want to say in this connection, because languages have been invented only for (the expression of) III, 79
commonly accepted concepts, most of which apply to the *sensibilia*.[545] Therefore, we must not bother with the (Sufi) discussion of those matters. We ought merely to leave it alone, just as we leave alone the ambiguous statements (of the Qur'ân and the Sunnah).[546] Those to whom God grants some understanding of those (mystical) utterances in a way that agrees with the plain meaning of the religious law do, indeed, enjoy happiness.

(Finally,) there are the suspect expressions which the Sufis call "ecstatic utterances" (*shaṭaḥât*) and which provoke the censure of orthodox Muslims. As to them, it should be known that the attitude that would be fair to the (Sufis) is (to observe) that they are people who are removed from sense perception. Inspiration grips them. Eventually, they say things about their inspiration that they do not intend to say. A person who is removed (from sense perception) cannot be spoken to. He who is forced (to act) is excused (when he acts, no matter what he does). (Sufis) who are known for their excellence and exemplary character are considered to act in good faith in this and similar respects. It is difficult to express ecstatic experiences, because there are no conventional

544 Cf. the preceding section, pp. 55 ff.
545 Cf. p. 79, above.
546 Cf. pp. 58, 61 and 66, above.

ways of expressing them. This was the experience of Abû Yazîd al-Bisṭâmî [547] and others like him. However, (Sufis) whose excellence is not known and famous deserve censure for utterances of this kind, since the (data) that might cause us to interpret their statements (so as to remove any suspicion attached to them) are not clear to us. (Furthermore, any Sufis) who are not removed from sense perception and are not in the grip of a state when they make utterances of this kind, also deserve censure. Therefore, the jurists and the great Sufis decided that al-Ḥallâj [548] was to be killed, because he spoke (ecstatically) while not removed (from sense perception) but in control of his state. And God knows better.

The early Sufis who are mentioned in (al-Qushayrî's) *Risâlah*,[549] those outstanding Muslims to whom we have referred above, had no desire to remove the veil and to have such (supernatural) perception. Their concern was to follow their models and to lead an exemplary life as far as possible. Whenever they had a (supernatural) experience, they turned away from it and paid no attention to it. Indeed, they tried to
III, 80 avoid it.[550] They were of the opinion that it was an obstacle and a tribulation and belonged to the (ordinary) perceptions of the soul, and, as such, was something created. They also thought that human perception could not comprise all the *existentia* and that the knowledge of God was wider, His creation greater, and His religious law more certain for guidance (than any mystical experience).[551] Therefore, they did not speak about any of their (supernatural) perceptions. In fact, they forbade the discussion of those things and pre-

[547] The famous mystic, who died *ca.* 260 [874]. Cf. *GAL*, *Suppl.*, I, 353; R. A. Nicholson in *EI*, *Supplement*, *s.v.* "al-Bisṭâmî." Cf. also pp. 179 f., below. "Al-Bisṭâmî" is found in C and D.

[548] Al-Ḥusayn b. Manṣûr, 244–309 [858/59–922]. Cf. *GAL*, I, 199; *Suppl.*, I, 355. L. Massignon, "Nouvelle bibliographie Hallagienne," in *I. Goldziher Memorial Volume* (Budapest, 1948), I, 252–79.

[549] Cf. p. 82, above.

[550] An illustration is given below, pp. 179 f. Cf. also 1:222, above, and, for instance, A. Mez, *Die Renaissance des Islâms* (Heidelberg, 1922), p. 284.

[551] Cf. Bombaci, p. 456.

vented their companions, for whom the veil (of sense perception) was removed, from discussing the matter or from giving it the slightest consideration. They continued following their models and leading exemplary lives as they had done in the world of sensual perception before the removal (of the veil), and they commanded their companions to do the same.[552] Such ought to be the state of the Sufi novice.

God gives success.

[17] *The science of dream interpretation.*

This science belongs to the sciences of the religious law. It originated in Islam when the sciences became crafts [553] and scholars wrote books on them. Dream visions and dream interpretation existed among the ancients, as among later generations. It existed among former (pre-Islamic) religious groups and nations. However, their dream interpretation did not reach us,[554] because we have been satisfied with the discussions of Muslim dream interpreters. In any case, all human beings can have dream visions, and these visions must be interpreted.

Truthful Joseph already interpreted visions, as is mentioned in the Qur'ân.[555] (Sound tradition in) the *Ṣaḥîḥ*, on the authority of the Prophet and on the authority of Abû Bakr, likewise establishes (the existence of dream visions). Dream vision is a kind of supernatural perception. Muḥammad said: "A good dream vision is the forty-sixth part of prophecy." [556] III, 81
He also said: "The only remaining bearer of glad tidings is a good dream vision, beheld by—or shown to—a good man." [557] The revelation given to the Prophet began with a

[552] Cf. Bombaci, pp. 456 f.

[553] Cf. Bombaci, p. 457.

[554] Of course, Greek works on dream interpretation, such as Artemidorus, were translated into Arabic. A fourteenth-century copy of his work, containing the first three books, is preserved in Istanbul University (Arabca yazma 4726). Artemidorus is also quoted, for instance, by ad-Damîrî, *Ḥayawân*; cf. J. de Somogyi in *Journal asiatique*, CCXIII (1928), 113. Cf. also M. Steinschneider, *Centralblatt für Bibliothekswesen* (Leipzig, 1893), Beiheft XII, 105.

[555] Cf. *sûrah* 12.

[556] Cf. 1:208 f., above, and p. 107, below.

[557] Cf. 1:209, above.

dream vision. Every dream vision he saw appeared to him like the break of dawn. When Muḥammad went away from the morning prayer, he used to ask the men around him, "Did any one of you see a dream vision during the night?" He asked this question in order to derive good news from dream visions, which might refer to the victory of Islam and the growth of its power.[558]

The reason for perception of the supernatural in dream visions is as follows: [559] The spirit of the heart, which is the fine vapor coming from the cavity in the flesh of the heart, spreads into the veins and, through the blood, to all the rest of the body. It serves to perfect the actions and sensations of the animal powers. The (spirit) may be affected by lassitude, because it is very busy with the sensual perception of the five senses and with the employment of the external powers. When the surface of the body, then, is covered by the chill of night, the spirit withdraws from all the other regions of the body to its center, the heart. It rests, in order to be able to resume its activity, and all the external senses are (for the time being) unemployed. This is the meaning of sleep, as was mentioned before at the beginning of the book. Now, the spirit of the heart is the vehicle of man's rational spirit. Through its essence, the rational spirit perceives everything that is in the divine world, since its reality and its essence are identical with perception. It is prevented from
III, 82 assimilating any supernatural perception by the veil of its preoccupation with the body and the corporeal powers and senses. If it were without that veil or stripped of it, it would return to its reality, which is identical with perception. It would thus be able to assimilate any object of perception. If it were stripped of part of it, its preoccupation would be less. It is thus able to catch a glimpse of its own world, since external sense perception, its greatest preoccupation, now

[558] Cf. Abû Dâwûd, *Sunan* (Cairo, 1310/1892–93, in the margin of az-Zurqânî, *Sharḥ al-Muwaṭṭa'*), IV, 236, who reports Muḥammad's question and continues with Muḥammad saying that "the only (kind of) prophecy remaining after my death will be good dream visions."

[559] For the following discussion, cf. 1:209 ff., above.

occupies it less. Its (supernatural perception) corresponds (in intensity) to the degree to which the veil is withdrawn from it. Thus it becomes prepared to receive the available perceptions from its own world that are appropriate for it. When it has perceived these perceptions from its own worlds, it returns with them to its body, since, as long as it remains in its corporeal body, it cannot be active except through corporeal means of perception.

The faculties through which the body perceives knowledge are all connected with the brain. The active part among them is the imagination. It derives imaginary pictures from the pictures perceived by the senses and turns them over to the power of memory, which retains them until they are needed in connection with speculation and deduction. From the (imaginary pictures), the soul also abstracts other spiritual-intellectual pictures. In this way, abstraction ascends from the *sensibilia* to the *intelligibilia*. The imagination is the intermediary between them. Also, when the soul has received a certain number of perceptions from its own world, it passes them on to the imagination, which forms them into appropriate pictures and turns those perceptions over to the common sense. As a result, the sleeper sees them as if they were perceived by the senses. Thus, the perceptions come down from the rational spirit to the level of sensual perception, with the imagination again being the intermediary. This is what dream visions actually are.

The (preceding) exposition shows the difference between true dream visions and false, "confused dreams." All of them are pictures in the imagination while an individual is asleep. III, *83*
However, if these pictures come down from the rational spirit that perceives (them), they are dream visions. But if they are derived from the pictures preserved in the power of memory, where the imagination deposits them when the individual is awake, they are "confused dreams." [560]

[560] Cf. 1:211 f., above. The distinction Artemidorus makes at the beginning of his work, between different kinds of dreams, appears in the Arabic translation under the heading of "Distinction between dream visions and confused dreams."

It[561] should be known that true dream visions have signs indicating their truthfulness and attesting their soundness, so that the person who has the dream vision becomes conscious of the glad tidings from God given him in his sleep.

The first of these signs is that the person who has the dream vision wakes up quickly, as soon as he has perceived it. It seems as if he is in a hurry to get back to being awake and having sensual perception. Were he (to continue) to sleep soundly, the perception given him would weigh heavily on him. Therefore, he tries to escape from the state (in which he has supernatural perception) to the state of sensual perception in which the soul is always fully immersed in the body and the corporeal accidents.

Another sign is that the dream vision stays and remains impressed with all its details in the memory of (the person who perceived it). Neither neglect nor forgetfulness affects it. No thinking or remembering is required, in order to have it present (to one's mind). The (dream vision) remains pictured in the mind of (the dreamer) when he awakes. Nothing of it is lost to him. This is because perception by the soul does not take place in time and requires no consecutive order, but takes place all at once and within a single time element.[562] "Confused dreams," on the other hand, take place in time, because they rest in the powers of the brain and are brought from the power of memory to the common sense by the imagination, as we have stated. (The process is an action of the body,) and all actions of the body take place in time. Thus, they (require) a consecutive order, in order to perceive anything, with something coming first and something else coming later. Forgetfulness, which always affects the powers of the brain, affects (them). That is not the case with the perceptions of the rational soul. They do not take place in time and have no consecutive order. Perceptions that are impressed in
III, 84 (the rational soul) are impressed all at once in the briefest

[561] The following discussion, down to p. 107, l. 21, is not found in Bulaq or A.

[562] *Zaman fard* "time atom" or "atomic time." Cf. p. 144, below.

moment. Thus, after (the sleeper) is awake, (his) dream vision remains present in his memory for quite some time. In no way does it slip his mind as the result of neglect, if it originally made a strong impression. However, if it requires thinking and application to remember a dream vision after a sleeper is awake, and if he has forgotten many of its details before he can remember them again, the dream vision is not a true one but a "confused dream."

These signs belong in particular to (prophetic) revelation. God said to His Prophet: "Do not set your tongue in motion to make haste with (the revelation of the Qur'ân). It is up to us to put it together and to recite it. And when we recite it, follow its recitation. Then, it is up to us to explain it." [563] Dream visions are related to prophecy and revelation, as is stated in (the sound tradition of) the *Ṣaḥîḥ*. Thus, Muḥammad said: "A dream vision is the forty-sixth part of prophecy." [564] In the same way, the characteristics of dream visions are related to the characteristics of prophecy. One should not consider that as unlikely. It appears to be this way.

God creates whatever He wishes to create.

As to the idea of dream interpretation, the following should be known. The rational spirit has its perceptions and passes them on to the imagination. (The imagination) then forms them into pictures but it forms them only into such pictures as are somehow related to the (perceived) idea. For instance, if the idea of a mighty ruler is perceived, the imagination depicts it in the form of an ocean. Or, the idea of hostility is depicted by the imagination in the form of a serpent. A person wakes up and knows only that he saw an ocean or a serpent. Then, the dream interpreter, who is certain that the ocean is the picture conveyed by the senses and that the perceived idea is something beyond that picture, puts the power of comparison to work. He is guided by

[563] Qur'ân 75.16–19 (16–19).

[564] Cf. 1:208 f., and p. 103, above.

III, *85* further data that establish the character of the perceived idea for him. Thus, he will say, for instance, that the ocean means a ruler, because an ocean is something big with which a ruler can appropriately be compared. Likewise, a serpent can appropriately be compared with an enemy, because it does great harm. Also, vessels can be compared with women, because they are receptacles, and so on.[565]

Dream visions may be evident and require no interpretation, because they are clear and distinct, or because (the ideas) perceived in them may be very similar to (the pictures) by which they are represented. Therefore, it has been said in (the sound tradition of) the *Ṣaḥîḥ*, "There are three kinds of dream visions. There are dream visions from God, dream visions from the angels, and dream visions from Satan." [566] Dream visions from God are those that are evident and need no explanation. Dream visions from an angel are true dreams that require interpretation. And dream visions from Satan are "confused dreams."

It should be known that when the spirit passes its perceptions on to the imagination, (the latter) depicts them in the customary molds of sensual perception. Where such molds never existed in sensual perception, (the imagination) [567] cannot form any pictures. A (person who was) born blind could not depict a ruler by an ocean, an enemy by a serpent,

---

565 The interpretation of the ocean as ruler and the serpent as enemy was known to Artemidorus *Oneirocritica* iii. 16. ii. 13. The comparison of women with vessels in this context is of Islamic origin, but does not appear to have been generally accepted in Muslim works on dream interpretation. It is not mentioned by (Pseudo-)Ibn Sîrîn, in *Ta'bîr ar-ru'yâ* (Cairo, 1298/1881), or in his *Muntakhab al-kalâm fî tafsîr al-aḥlâm* (Cairo, 1301/1883–84, in the margin of Vol. I of 'Abd-al-Ghanî an-Nâbulusî, *Ta'ṭîr al-anâm fî ta'bîr al-manâm*). But al-Kirmânî, as quoted by Ibn Shâhîn, *al-Ishârât fî 'ilm al-'ibârât* (Cairo, 1301/1883–84, in the margin of Vol. II of 'Abd-al-Ghanî an-Nâbulusî), II, 383, compares vessels and the like with women and servants. The equation of ocean with ruler and serpent with enemy appears in Ibn Sîrîn, *Ta'bîr,* pp. 12, 43; *Muntakhab,* I, 186 f.; Ibn Shâhîn, *op. cit.*, II, 102, 359; 'Abd-al-Ghanî an-Nâbulusî, *op. cit.*, I, 56 ff., 200 ff.

566 Cf. 1:211 f., above.

567 Cf. Bombaci, p. 457.

or women by vessels, because he had never perceived any such things. For him, the imagination would depict those things through similarly appropriate (pictures) derived from the type of perceptions with which he is familiar—that is, things which can be heard or smelled. The dream interpreter must be on guard against such things. They often cause confusion in dream interpretation and spoil its rules.

The science of dream interpretation implies a knowledge of general norms upon which the dream interpreter bases the interpretation and explanation of what he is told. For instance, they say that an ocean represents a ruler. Elsewhere,
they say that an ocean represents wrath. Again, elsewhere, III, 86
they say that it represents worry and calamity. Or, they say that a serpent represents an enemy, but elsewhere they say that it represents one who conceals a secret. Elsewhere again, they say that it represents life, and so on.[568]

The dream interpreter knows these general norms by heart and interprets the dreams in each case as required by the data establishing which of these norms fits a particular dream vision best. The data may originate in the waking state. They may originate in the sleeping state. Or, they may be created in the soul of the dream interpreter himself by the special quality with which he is endowed.

Everyone is successful at the things for which he was created.[569]

This science never ceased being transmitted in the circles

568 An agitated ocean may indicate worry and fear, and a snake is said to indicate an enemy who conceals his enmity. Cf. Ibn Sîrîn, *Ta'bîr*, pp. 12, 42; and *Muntakhab*, I, 187; 'Abd-al-Ghanî an-Nâbulusî, *op. cit.*, I, 58. The various possibilities of interpreting ocean and snake, quoted by Ibn Shâhîn (II, 203, 360) in the name of Ja'far aṣ-Ṣâdiq, agree with Ibn Khaldûn's statement only in so far as the snake may indicate a livelihood (*'aysh*). However, Ibn Khaldûn may have found his examples in the literature quoted on p. 110, which was not available to me.

In C and D the reference to life precedes that to concealing a secret. It may be noted that the snake, as a symbol of Asclepius, signified length of life. Cf. F. Rosenthal, "An Ancient Commentary on the Hippocratic Oath," *Bulletin of the History of Medicine*, XXX (1956), 70 f.

569 Cf. 2:332, above, and p. 300, below.

of the early Muslims. Muḥammad b. Sîrîn [570] was one of the most famous experts in (dream interpretation) among them. Certain norms of dream interpretation were written down on his authority. People have transmitted them down to this time.

Al-Kirmânî [571] wrote on the subject after Ibn Sîrîn. Recent scholars have written many works on it. The books in use among contemporary Maghribîs are the *Mumti'* and other works by Ibn Abî Ṭâlib al-Qayrawânî,[572] a scholar from al-Qayrawân, and the *Kitâb al-Ishârah* by as-Sâlimî [573] which is one of the most useful and briefest [574] books on the subject. There also is the *Kitâb al-Marqabah al-'ulyâ* by Ibn Râshid,[575] who belonged to (the circle of) our *shaykhs* in Tunis.

Dream interpretation is a science resplendent with the light of prophecy, because prophecy and dreams are related to each other, and (dreams) played a part in the (prophetic) revelation, as has been established in sound tradition.

"God knows the supernatural." [576]

[570] He died in 110 [778/79]. Cf. *GAL*, I, 66; *Suppl.*, I, 102. There can be no doubt that his fame as dream interpreter is unhistorical, and the works ascribed to him pseudepigraphical.

A large list of titles of Muslim works on dream interpretation is found at the end of W. Ahlwardt's description of such works preserved in Berlin: *Die Handschriften-Verzeichnisse . . . Verzeichniss der arabischen Handschriften*, III, 574 ff.

[571] Al-Kirmânî's work is mentioned in the tenth century, in Ibn an-Nadîm, *Fihrist* (ed. Flügel), p. 316; (Cairo, 1348/1929–30), p. 439. As-Sâlimî, who quotes it, gives his names as Abû Isḥâq Ibrâhîm; cf. W. Ahlwardt, *op. cit.*, III, 578, No. 4270. Quotations of his work seem also to be preserved in a MS in Paris, referred to in *GAL*, *Suppl.*, II, 1039 (No. 21). Cf. also *ibid.*, I, 433.

[572] No further information on him is available.

[573] Muḥammad b. Aḥmad b. 'Umar. Cf. *GAL*, *Suppl.*, I, 102 (where Isḥâq al-Qaramânî should read Abû Isḥâq al-Kirmânî), and II, 1040 (No. 32). He was a contemporary of Ibn Khaldûn, as shown by the fact that he quotes Ibn Râshid in his work. Cf. W. Ahlwardt, *loc. cit.*

[574] "And briefest" (*wa-akhṣariha*) in C and D. The reading is not quite certain. The work could hardly be called the "briefest." It may be "most comprehensive" (*aḥṣar*). "Most accessible" (*aḥḍar*) seems unlikely.

[575] Cf. n. 250 to this chapter, above. His *Marqabah al-'ulyâ* is quoted by as-Sâlimî; cf. n. 573 to this chapter, above. Is it identical with the work mentioned in *GAL*, *Suppl.*, II, 1041, under the title *ad-Durr ath-thamîn fî 'ilm at-tafsîr?*

The sentence referring to Ibn Râshid is found in D.

[576] Qur'ân 9.78 (79). Cf. also Qur'ân 5.109 (108), 116 (116); 34.48 (47).

[18] *The various kinds of intellectual sciences.*

The intellectual sciences are natural to man, in as much as he is a thinking being. They are not restricted to any par- III, 87
ticular religious group. They are studied by the people of all religious groups who are all equally qualified to learn them and to do research in them. They have existed (and been known) to the human species since civilization had its beginning in the world. They are called the sciences of philosophy and wisdom. They comprise four different sciences.

(1) The first science is logic. It is a science protecting the mind from error in the process of evolving unknown facts one wants to know from the available, known facts. Its use enables the student to distinguish right from wrong wherever he so desires in his study of the essential and accidental perceptions and apperceptions.[577] Thus, he will be able to ascertain the truth concerning created things, negatively or positively,[578] within the limits of his ability to think.

(2) Then, philosophers may study the elemental substances perceivable by the senses, namely, the minerals, the plants, and the animals which are created from (the elemental substances), the heavenly bodies, natural motions, and the soul from which the motions originate, and other things. This discipline is called "physics." It is the second of the intellectual sciences.

(3) Or they may study metaphysical, spiritual matters. This science is called "metaphysics" (*al-'ilm al-ilâhî*). It is the third of the intellectual sciences.

(4) The fourth science is the study of quantities (measurements). It comprises four different sciences, which are called the "mathematical sciences" (*ta'âlîm*).

The first mathematical science is geometry. It is the study of quantities (measurements) in general.[579] The quantities

[577] *Sic* C and D. The earlier texts read: "the existing things and their accidents."

[578] "Negatively or positively" is added in C and D.

[579] Cf. p. 129, below.

(measurements) may be either discontinuous, in as much as they constitute numbers, or continuous (as geometrical
III, *88* figures). They may be of one dimension—the line; of two dimensions—the plane; or of three dimensions—the mathematical solid. These quantities (measurements) and the qualities they possess, either by themselves or in combination with each other, are (what is) studied (in geometry).

The second mathematical science is arithmetic. It is the knowledge of the essential and accidental properties of the discontinuous quantity, number.

The third mathematical science is music. It is the knowledge of the proportions of sounds and modes and their numerical measurements. Its fruit is the knowledge of musical melodies.[580]

The fourth mathematical science is astronomy. It fixes the (various) shapes of the spheres, determines the position and number of each planet and fixed star, and makes it possible to learn these things from the visible heavenly motions of each (sphere), their motions, both retrograde and direct, their precession and recession.

These are the basic philosophical sciences. They are seven (in number). Logic comes first. Then comes mathematics, beginning with arithmetic, followed in succession by geometry, astronomy, and music. Then comes physics and, finally, metaphysics. Each of these sciences has subdivisions. One subdivision of physics is medicine. Subdivisions of arithmetic are calculation,[581] the inheritance laws, and business (arithmetic). A subdivision of astronomy is the astronomical tables (*zîj*). They are norms for computing the motions of the stars and adjusting (the data) in order to be able to know their positions, whenever desired. Another subdivision of the study of the stars is the science of stellar judgments (astrology).

We shall discuss all these sciences, one after the other.

---

580 Ibn Khaldûn devotes no special section to music, though he seems originally to have intended to do so. Cf. 2:339, above.

581 That is, elementary arithmetic.

It should be known that as far as our historical information goes, these sciences were most extensively cultivated by the two great pre-Islamic nations, the Persians and the Greeks (Rûm). According to the information we have, the sciences were greatly in demand among them, because they possessed an abundant civilization and were the ruling nations immediately before Islam and its time. In their regions and cities, the sciences flourished greatly. III, 89

The Chaldaeans and, before them, the Syrians, as well as their contemporaries, the Copts, were much concerned with sorcery and astrology and the related subjects of powerful (charms) and talismans. The Persian and Greek nations learned these things from them. The Copts especially cultivated those things, which enjoyed great prominence among them. The Qur'ân (*al-matlûw*) mentions this fact in the story of Hârût and Mârût,[582] and the affair of the sorcerers.[583] There also are the reports of informed persons on the temples of Upper Egypt.[584] Later on, these things were declared forbidden and illegal by successive religious groups. As a result, the sciences concerned with them were wiped out and vanished, as if they had never been. Only a small remnant, transmitted by the practitioners of those crafts, has remained. And God knows better whether those crafts are sound. The sword of the religious law hangs over them and prevents choice of them (as a subject of study).[585]

Among the Persians, the intellectual sciences played a large and important role, since the Persian dynasties were powerful and ruled without interruption. The intellectual sciences are said to have come to the Greeks from the Persians, (at the time) when Alexander killed Darius and gained

[582] Cf. Qur'ân 2.102 (96). The passage refers to Babel, but it would be difficult to include the Persians and the Greeks, in addition to the Copts, among the antecedents of "them" in the preceding sentence. Cf. p. 159, below. For *al-matlûw*, cf. 1:192, 260, and 437, above; p. 284, below.

[583] The sorcerers of Pharaoh, as described in the Qur'ân.

[584] Cf. p. 160, below. Instead of "informed persons," A and B simply have "people" (*ahl al-'âlam*).

[585] The translation follows the reading *ikhtiyârihâ* of C and D. *Ikhtibârihâ* "their exploration," as in A and B, also yields a satisfactory meaning.

control of the Achaemenid empire. At that time, he appropriated the books and sciences of the Persians. However,[586] when the Muslims conquered Persia and came upon an indescribably large number of books and scientific papers, Sa'd b. Abî
III, 90 Waqqâṣ wrote to 'Umar b. al-Khaṭṭâb, asking him for permission to take them and distribute them as booty among the Muslims. On that occasion, 'Umar wrote him: "Throw them into the water. If what they contain is right guidance, God has given us better guidance. If it is error, God has protected us against it." [587] Thus, the (Muslims) threw them into the water or into the fire, and the sciences of the Persians were lost and did not reach us.

The dynasty of the Rûm originally belonged to the Greeks, among whom the intellectual sciences occupied a large place. They were cultivated by famous Greek personalities, among them the pillars of philosophy, and others. The Peripatetic philosophers, in particular the Stoics,[588] possessed a good method of instruction in the intellectual sciences. It has been assumed that they used to study in a stoa, which protected them from the sun and the cold. Their school tradition is assumed to have passed from the sage Luqmân [589]

[586] The word "however," which is not found in the slightly different text of Bulaq, seems to express some misgivings as to how the Muslims could have found so many books if Alexander had appropriated (and, after their translation, destroyed) them at a much earlier date.

[587] This is a variant of the famous legend, according to which 'Umar ordered the destruction of the celebrated library in Alexandria. Cf., for instance, M. Meyerhof, "Joannes Grammatikos (Philoponos) von Alexandrien und die arabische Medizin," *Mitteilungen des Deutschen Instituts für Ägyptische Altertumskunde in Kairo*, II (1931), 9 f.

Ibn Khaldûn, *'Ibar*, III, 537, mentions that after the conquest of Baghdad in 1258, the Tatars threw many scientific books into the Tigris, thus imitating what the Muslims had done at the beginning of Islam with the books and sciences of the Persians. Cf. also 2:219, above.

[588] Cf. *'Ibar*, II, 188: Since Plato (*sic*) walked while teaching in a stoa, his pupils were called "Peripatetics." Knowing little about the Stoics, the inability of the Arabs to distinguish clearly between Stoics and Peripatetics is easily explained.

[589] Cf. B. Heller in *EI*, *s.v.* "Luḳmân." The Greek sage considered to have lived at the time of King David and to have studied with Luqmân, is said to have been Empedocles. Cf. M. Asín Palacios, "Ibn Masarra y su escuela," in *Obras Escogidas*, I, 55.

and his pupils to Socrates of the barrel,[590] and then, in succession, to Socrates' pupil, Plato, to Plato's pupil, Aristotle, to Aristotle's pupils, Alexander of Aphrodisias and Themistius, and others.

Aristotle was the teacher of Alexander, the ruler of the (Greeks) who defeated the Persians and deprived them of their realm. He was the greatest Greek scientist and enjoyed the greatest prestige and fame. He has been called "the First Teacher." [591] He became world-famous.

When the Greek dynasty was destroyed and the Roman emperors seized power and adopted Christianity, the intellectual sciences were shunned by them, as religious groups and their laws require. (But) they continued to have a permanent life [592] in scientific writings and treatments which were preserved in their libraries.

The (Roman emperors) [593] later on took possession of Syria. The (ancient) scientific books continued to exist dur- III, *91*
ing their (rule). Then, God brought Islam, and its adherents gained their incomparable victory. They deprived the Byzantines (Rûm), as well as all other nations, of their realms. At the beginning, they were simple (in their ways) and disregarded the crafts. Eventually, however, the Muslim rule and dynasty flourished. The Muslims developed a sedentary culture, such as no other nation had ever possessed. They became versed in many different crafts and sciences. Then, they desired to study the philosophical disciplines. They had heard some mention of them by the bishops and priests among (their) Christian subjects, and man's ability to think has (in any case) aspirations in the direction of the intellectual sciences. Abû Ja'far al-Manṣûr, therefore, sent to the Byzantine Emperor and asked him to send him translations of mathe-

590 For this confusion of Socrates with Diogenes, cf., for instance, al-Mubashshir b. Fâtik, *Mukhtâr al-ḥikam*, on the life of Socrates; al-Qifṭî, *Ta'rîkh al-ḥukamâ'*, ed. Müller-Lippert (Leipzig, 1903), p. 197; F. Rosenthal in *Islamic Culture*, XIV (1940), 388.

591 Cf. also 1:275 (n. 75), above, and pp. 116, 139, 153, and 249, below.

592 Cf. p. 6, above. *Mukhalladah* is clearly indicated in A, B, and C.

593 Cf. Bombaci, p. 457.

matical works. The Emperor sent him Euclid's book and some works on physics. The Muslims read them and studied their contents. Their desire to obtain the rest of them grew. Later on, al-Ma'mûn came. He had some (scientific knowledge). Therefore, he had a desire for science. His desire aroused him to action in behalf of the (intellectual) sciences. He sent ambassadors to the Byzantine emperors. (These ambassadors were) to discover the Greek sciences and to have them copied in Arabic writing. He sent translators for that purpose (into Byzantine territory). As a result, a good deal of the material was preserved and collected.

Muslim scientists assiduously studied the (Greek sciences).[594] They became skilled in the various branches. The (progress they made in the) study of those sciences could not have been better. They contradicted the First Teacher (Aristotle) on many points. They considered him[595] the decisive authority as to whether an opinion should be rejected or accepted, because he possessed the greatest fame. They wrote systematic works on the subject. They surpassed their predecessors in the intellectual sciences.

III, 92 Abû Naṣr al-Fârâbî and Abû 'Alî Ibn Sînâ (Avicenna) in the East, and Judge Abû l-Walîd b. Rushd (Averroes) and the wazir Abû Bakr b. aṣ-Ṣâ'igh (Avempace)[596] in Spain, were among the greatest Muslim (philosophers), and there were others who reached the limit in the intellectual sciences. The men mentioned enjoy especial fame and prestige.

Many (scientists) restricted themselves to cultivating the mathematical disciplines and the related sciences of astrology, sorcery, and talismans. The most famous practitioners of these sciences were Jâbir b. Ḥayyân in the East,[597] and the Spaniard, Maslamah b. Aḥmad al-Majrîṭî, and his pupils.

The intellectual sciences and their representatives suc-

594 For the following remarks, cf. p. 250, below.

595 *Ikhtaṣṣûhu*, as in Bulaq, A, B, and C.

596 Muḥammad b. Yaḥyâ, d. 533 [1138/39]. Cf. *GAL*, I, 460; *Suppl.*, I, 830. Cf. also p. 443, below.

597 The reference to Jâbir was added when Ibn Khaldûn was in the East. It is found in the margin of C and in the text of D.

ceeded to some degree in penetrating Islam. They seduced many people who were eager to study those sciences and accept the opinions expressed in them. In this respect, the sin falls upon the person who commits it. "If God had wanted it, they would not have done it." [598]

Later on, civilizational activity stopped in the Maghrib and in Spain. The sciences decreased with the decrease of civilization. As a consequence, scientific activity disappeared there, save for a few remnants that may be found among scattered individuals and that are controlled by orthodox religious scholars.

We hear that the intellectual sciences are still amply represented among the inhabitants of the East,[599] in particular in the non-Arab 'Irâq and, farther east, in Transoxania. The people there are said to be very successful in the intellectual and traditional sciences, because their civilization is abundant and their sedentary culture firmly established.

In Egypt, I have become acquainted with numerous works by a great scholar of Herât in Khurâsân, by name Sa'd-ad-dîn at-Taftazânî.[600] Some of his works are on speculative theology, the principles of jurisprudence, and syntax and style (*bayân*). They show that he is well grounded in these sciences. They (also) contain things proving that he has studied and knows the philosophical sciences and is well versed in all the intellectual disciplines. "God aids whomever He wishes to aid." [601] III, *93*

We further hear now that the philosophical sciences are greatly cultivated in the land of Rome and along the adjacent

[598] Qur'ân 6.137 (138). Cf. also Qur'ân 6.112 (112).

[599] Cf. Bombaci, p. 457.

[600] Mas'ûd b. 'Umar, 722–792 [1322–1390]. Cf. *GAL*, II, 215; *Suppl.*, II, 301 ff. The date of his birth seems to be correct as indicated (cf. C. A. Storey in *EI*, *s.v.* "al-Taftazânî"), although Ibn Ḥajar, *ad-Durar al-kâminah* (Hyderabad, 1348–50/1929–31), IV, 350, and the other biographers cited in *GAL*, who follow Ibn Ḥajar, have 712 [1312/13]. Cf. also p. 315, below.

Ibn Khaldûn seems to have said, "numerous works *on the intellectual sciences*," but Bulaq is certainly correct in omitting this addition. A correction to "on the traditional sciences," found in a minor MS, has nothing to recommend itself.

[601] Qur'ân 3.13 (11). Bulaq completes the quotation.

northern shore of the country of the European Christians. They are said to be studied there again and to be taught in numerous classes. Existing systematic expositions of them are said to be comprehensive, the people who know them numerous, and the students of them very many. God knows better what exists there. "He creates whatever He wishes, and His is the choice." [602]

[19] *The sciences concerned with numbers.*

The first of them is arithmetic. Arithmetic is the knowledge of the properties of numbers combined in arithmetic or geometric progressions.

For instance, in an arithmetic progression, in which each number is always higher by one than the preceding number, the sum of the first and last numbers of the progression is equal to the sum of any two numbers (in the progression) that are equally far removed from the first and the last number, respectively, of the progression.[603]

Or, (the sum of the first and last numbers of a progression) is twice the middle number of the progression, if the total number of numbers (in the progression) is an odd number. It can be a progression of even and odd numbers, or of even numbers, or of odd numbers.[604]

Or, if the numbers of a (geometrical) progression are such that the first is one-half of the second and the second one-half of the third, and so on, or if the first is one-third of the second and the second one-third of the third, and so on, the result of multiplying the first number by the last number of the progression is equal to the result of multiplying any two

---

[602] Qur'ân 28.68 (68).

[603] In the progression $a\,(a+1)\,(a+2)\,(a+3)\cdots(a+n)$, if x is the distance from the first or last number, we get:

$$a+(a+n)=(a+x)+(a+n-x).$$

[604] In the progression $a(a+1)(a+2)(a+3)\cdots(a+2n)$, then

$$a+(a+2n)=2\,(a+n).$$

In the progression $2a\,(2a+2)(2a+4)(2a+6)\cdots(2a+2n)$, then

$$2a+(2a+2n)=2\,(2a+n).$$

In the progression $(2a+1)(2a+3)(2a+5)(2a+7)\cdots(2a+[2n+1])$, then $(2a+1)+(2a+[2n+1])=2\,(2a+[n+1])$.

numbers of the progression that are equally far removed from the first and the last number, respectively, (of the progression).[605] III, 94

Or, (the result of multiplying the first number by the last number of a geometrical progression,) if the number of numbers (in the progression) is odd, is equal to the square of the middle number of the progression. For instance, the progression may consist of the powers of two: two, four, eight, sixteen.[606]

Or, there are the properties of numbers that originate in the formation of numerical *muthallathah* (triangle), *murabba'ah* (square), *mukhammasah* (pentagon), and *musaddasah* (hexagon) progressions,[607] where the numbers are arranged

605 In the progression $a\ \frac{a}{2}\ \frac{a}{4}\ \frac{a}{8} \cdots \frac{a}{2^{(n-1)}}$, if x is the distance from the first or last number, we get:

$$a \cdot \frac{a}{2^{(n-1)}} = \frac{a}{2^x} \cdot \frac{a \cdot 2^x}{2^{(n-1)}}.$$

In the progression $a\ \frac{a}{3}\ \frac{a}{9}\ \frac{a}{27} \cdots \frac{a}{3^{(n-1)}}$, we get:

$$a \cdot \frac{a}{3^{(n-1)}} = \frac{a}{3^x} \cdot \frac{a \cdot 3^x}{3^{(n-1)}}.$$

606 In the progression $a\ a^2\ a^3\ a^4 \cdots a^n$, then

$$a \cdot a^n = (a^{\frac{n+1}{2}})^2$$

607 Cf. al-Khuwârizmî, *Mafâtîḥ al-'ulûm* (Cairo, 1349/1930), p. 111; al-Bîrûnî, *Kitâb at-tafhîm*, ed. and tr. R. R. Wright (London, 1934), pp. 29 f. As al-Khuwârizmî explains it, a *muthallathah* results from adding the numbers from one on; a *murabba'ah* results from adding every second number (or from adding up the adjacent numbers of a *muthallathah*); a *mukhammasah* results from adding every third number; a *musaddasah* from adding every fourth; and so on.

Thus, the progression 1 2 3 4 5 6 7 8 9 10 11 12 13 . . . yields the *muthallathah* 1 3 6 10 15 21 28 and so on. The progression 1 3 5 7 9 11 13 . . . yields the *murabba'ah* 1 4 9 16 25 36 49 and so on. The progression 1 4 7 10 13 . . . yields the *mukhammasah* 1 5 12 22 35 and so on. The progression 1 5 9 13 . . . yields the *musaddasah* 1 6 15 28 and so on.

Ibn Khaldûn, however, proceeds in a slightly different manner. He always adds a *muthallathah* to a given progression, in order to obtain the next higher one. Thus, he has:

progressively in their rows by [608] adding them up from one to the last number. Thus, a *muthallath(ah)* is formed. (Other) *muthallathahs* (are placed) successively in rows under the "sides." Then, each *muthallathah* is increased by the "side" in front of it. Thus, a *murabba'ah* is formed. Then, each *murabba'(ah)* is increased (by the "side") in front of it. Thus, a *mukhammasah* is formed, and so on. The (various) progressions of "sides" form figures. Thus, a table is formed with vertical and horizontal rows. The horizontal rows are constituted by the progression of the numbers (one, two, etc.), followed by the *muthallathah, murabba'ah, mukhammasah* progressions, and so on. The vertical rows contain all the numbers and certain numerical combinations. The totals and (the results of) dividing some of the numbers by others, both vertically and horizontally, (reveal) remarkable numerical properties. They have been evolved by the inductive method. The problems connected with them have been laid down in the systematic treatments of (arithmeticians).

The same applies to special properties originating in connection with even numbers, odd numbers, the powers of two,

1 2 3 4 5 6 7 8 9 10 11 12 13

Muthallathah		3	6	10	15	21	28
			3	6	10	15	21
Murabba'ah		4	9	16	25	36	49
			3	6	10	15	21
Mukhammasah		5	12	22	35	51	70
			3	6	10	15	21
Musaddasah	1	6	15	28	45	66	91

A perusal of the largely unpublished Arabic literature on arithmetic will certainly provide an exact presentation of the table that Ibn Khaldûn has in mind. The theory of polygonal numbers (as well as all the other theorems mentioned in this section) came to the Arabs through the work of Nicomachus of Gerasa, which was translated into Arabic and is preserved but not yet published in its Arabic form. However, though Ibn Khaldûn seems to refer to the geometrical figures of Nicomachus, which provided the terminology for the subject, his table would appear to be one made up of numerical progressions. Cf. Nicomachus *Introduction to Arithmetic* ii. 8–11. M. L. D'Ooge (tr.), (University of Michigan Studies, Humanistic Series, No. 16) (New York, 1926), pp. 241 ff. [* Ar. translation, ed. W. Kutsch (Beirut, 1959)].

608 Actually, a new sentence should begin here ("By adding them up, a triangle is formed"), but the text does not permit such a construction, and no correction is permissible.

odd numbers multiplied by two,[609] and odd numbers multiplied by multiples of two.[610] They are dealt with in this discipline, and in no other discipline.

This discipline is the first and most evident part of mathematics. It is used in the proofs of the mathematicians.[611] Both early and later philosophers have written works on it. Most III, *95* of them include it under mathematics in general and, therefore, do not write monographs on it. This was done by Avicenna in the *Kitâb ash-Shifâ'* and the *Kitâb an-Najâh*, and by other early scholars. The subject is avoided by later scholars, since it is not commonly used (in practice), being useful in (theoretical mathematical) proofs rather than in (practical) calculation. (They handled the subject the way) it was done, for instance, by Ibn al-Bannâ' [612] in the *Kitâb Raf' al-ḥijâb*. They extracted the essence of the subject (as far as it was useful) for the theory of (practical) calculation and then avoided it. And God knows better.

The craft of calculation [613]

A subdivision of arithmetic is the craft of calculation. It is a scientific craft concerned with the counting operations of "combining," and "separating." The "combining" may take place by (adding the) units. This is addition. Or it may take place by increasing a number as many times as there are units in another number. This is multiplication. The "separating"

---

[609] That is, $2(2n + 1)$.

[610] That is, $2(m + 1)(2n + 1)$.

In literal translation, the Arabic terms, derived from the Greek, read: even, odd, evenly-even, unevenly-even, and evenly-even-odd. Ibn Khaldûn does not mention oddly-odd, i.e., odd numbers multiplied by each other:

$$(2n + 1)(2n + 1).$$

Cf. al-Bîrûnî, *op. cit.*, p. 25.

[611] That is, in theoretical mathematics.

[612] Cf. 1:238, above, and pp. 123 and 137, below.

[613] Ibn Khaldûn is said to have written a work on the subject himself; cf. 1:xliv, above. The first two paragraphs of this section are quoted by J. Ruska, "Zur ältesten arabischen Algebra und Rechenkunst," in *Sitzungsberichte der Heidelberger Akademie der Wissenschaften, Philos.-hist. Kl.* (Heidelberg, 1917), pp. 19 f.

may take place by taking away one number from another and seeing what remains. This is subtraction. Or it may take place by separating a number into equal parts of a given number. This is division.

These operations may concern either whole numbers or fractions. A fraction is the relationship of one number to another number. Such relationship is called fraction. Or they may concern "roots." "Roots" are numbers that, when multiplied by themselves, lead to square numbers.[614] Numbers that are clearly expressed are called "rational," and so are their squares. They do not require (special) operations in
III, 96 calculation. Numbers that are not clearly expressed are called "surds." Their squares may be rational, as, for instance, the root of three whose square is three. Or, they may be surds, such as the root of the root of three, which is a surd. They require (special) operations in calculation. Such roots are also included in the operations of "combining" and "separating."

This craft is something newly created. It is needed for business calculations. Scholars have written many works on it. They are used in the cities for the instruction of children. The best method of instruction is to begin with (calculation), because it is concerned with lucid knowledge and systematic proofs. As a rule, it produces an enlightened intellect that is trained along correct lines. It has been said that whoever applies himself to the study of calculation early in his life will as a rule be truthful, because calculation has a sound basis and requires self-discipline. (Soundness and self-discipline) will, thus, become character qualities of such a person. He will get accustomed to truthfulness and adhere to it methodically.

In the contemporary Maghrib, one of the best simple [615]

[614] A "root" is $\sqrt{n^2}$, not $\sqrt{n}$, which might be irrational. The following discussion of rational numbers and surds appears in the margin of C and the text of D, and is not yet found in the earlier texts.

[615] The word *mabsûṭ* as such can also mean "extensive," but in view of the character of the work, Renaud (see n. 616, below) suggests the above translation.

works on the subject is the small work by al-Ḥaṣṣâr.[616] Ibn al-Bannâ' al-Marrâkushî deals with the (subject) in an accurate and useful brief description (*talkhîṣ*) of the rules of calculation.[617] Ibn al-Bannâ' later wrote a commentary on it in a book which he entitled *Raf' al-ḥijâb*.[618] The (*Raf' al-ḥijâb*)[619] is too difficult for beginners, because it possesses a solid groundwork of (theoretical) proofs. It is an important book. We have heard our teachers praise it. It deserves that. In [620] the (work), the author competed with the *Kitâb Fiqh al-ḥisâb* by Ibn Mun'im,[621] and the *Kâmil* by al-Aḥdab. He gave a résumé of the proofs dealt with in these two works, but he changed them in as much as, instead of ciphers, he used clear III, 97 theoretical reasons in the proofs. They bring out the real meaning and essence of (what in the work itself is expressed by calculations with ciphers).[622] All of them are difficult. The difficulty here lies in the attempt to bring proof. This is usually the case in the mathematical sciences. All the problems and operations are clear, but if one wants to comment on them—that is, if one wants to find the reasons for the operations—it causes greater difficulties to the understanding than

[616] Muḥammad b. 'Abdallâh b. 'Ayyâsh. Cf. *GAL, Suppl.*, II, 363; and esp., H. P. J. Renaud, "Sur un passage d'Ibn Khaldûn relatif à l'histoire des mathématiques," *Hespéris*, XXXI (1944), 35–47, where Renaud corrects statements he had made earlier in *Hespéris*, XXV (1938), 24 (n. 6). Renaud shows that a *large* work by al-Ḥaṣṣâr, whose existence we should expect from Ibn Khaldûn's reference to the "small" work, actually did exist.

[617] The work referred to is Ibn al-Bannâ''s well-known *Talkhîṣ a'mâl al-ḥisâb*.

[618] At the beginning of the *Raf'*, Ibn al-Bannâ' states that the work was intended to "explain the scientific contents and comment on" the apparent difficulties of the *Talkhîṣ*. Cf. MS. or., Princeton, 1032-A (80 B).

[619] The pronoun found in the Arabic text must refer to the *Raf'*, but the statement would seem to apply rather to the *Talkhîṣ*.

[620] The following eight lines are not found in Bulaq, and in A they are still in the form of a marginal note. There is no reference in Ibn al-Bannâ''s works to the effect that he used the sources mentioned. However, it is clear from Ibn Khaldûn's attitude toward Ibn al-Bannâ' that he would not think of accusing him of plagiarism.

[621] Muḥammad b. 'Îsâ b. 'Abd-al-Mun'im, who lived at the court of Roger II of Sicily. Cf. H. P. J. Renaud in *Hespéris*, XXV (1938), 33–35. Nothing is known about al-Aḥdab and his work.

[622] The translation follows that suggested by Renaud in *Hespéris*, XXXI (1944), 42 f.

(does) practical treatment of the problems. This should be taken into consideration.

God guides with His light whomever He wants (to guide).[623]

Algebra

Another subdivision of arithmetic is algebra. This is a craft that makes it possible to discover the unknown from the known data, if there exists a relationship between them requiring it. Special technical terms have been invented in algebra for the various multiples (powers) of the unknown. The first of them is called "number," [624] because by means of it one determines the unknown one is looking for, discovering its value from the relationship of the unknown to it. The second is (called) "thing," [625] because every unknown as such refers to some "thing." It also is called "root," because (the same element) requires multiplication in second degree (equations). The third is (called) "property." [626] It is the square of the unknown. Everything beyond that depends on the exponents of the two (elements) that are multiplied.[627]

Then, there is the operation that is conditioned by the problem. One proceeds to create an equation between two or more different (units) of the (three) elements (mentioned). The various elements are "confronted," and "broken" portions (in the equation) are "set" [628] and thus become

---

[623] Cf. Qur'ân 24.35 (35).

[624] *'Adad:* i.e., n, the part of the equation that is not a multiple (or fraction) of the unknown.

[625] *Shay':* Latin *res*, that is, x (the unknown).

[626] *Mâl:* Latin *substantià, census*, that is, x^2.

[627] That is, the higher powers are expressed by multiplying two or more times the second and third (*ka'b* "cube," not mentioned by Ibn Khaldûn) powers. Thus, x^4 is *mâl mâl*, x^5 is *mâl ka'b*, etc. For *uss*, cf. P. Luckey, *Die Rechenkunst bei Ǧamšîd b. Mas'ûd al-Kâšî* (Abhandlungen für die Kunde des Morgenlandes, No. 31[1]) (Wiesbaden, 1951), pp. 59, 70 f., 104 f. According to Luckey, *uss* has two meanings, that of exponent, and another referring to the position of the numbers (one for the units, two for the tens, three for the hundreds, etc.). Cf. also 1:241, above, and pp. 203 ff., below.

[628] *Jabr*, hence Algebra.

"healthy." The degrees of equations are reduced to the fewest possible basic forms. Thus, they come to be three. Algebra revolves around these three basic forms. They are "number," "thing," and "property." [629] III, 98

When an equation consists of one (element) on each side, the value of the unknown is fixed. The value of "property" or "root" becomes known and fixed, when equated with "number." [630] A "property" equated with "roots" is fixed by the multiples of those "roots." [631]

When an equation consists of one (element) on one side and two on the other,[632] there is a geometrical solution for it by multiplication in part on the unknown side of the equation with the two (elements). Such multiplication in part fixes the (value) of (the equation). Equations with two (elements) on one side and two on the other are not possible.[633]

The largest number of equations recognized by algebraists is six. The simple and composite equations of "numbers," "roots," and "properties" come to six.[634]

The first to write on this discipline was Abû ʻAbdallâh al-Khuwârizmî.[635] After him, there was Abû Kâmil Shujâʻ b. Aslam.[636] People followed in his steps. His book on the six problems of algebra is one of the best books written on the subject. Many Spanish scholars wrote good commentaries

[629] I.e., n, x, x^2, and the three basic equations: $ax = n$, $bx^2 = n$, and $ax^2 = bx$. Cf. L. C. Karpinski, "Robert of Chester's Translation of the Algebra of al-Khowarizmi," in *Contributions to the History of Science* (University of Michigan Studies, Humanistic Series, No. 11) (Ann Arbor, 1930), p. 69.

[630] $ax = n$; $bx^2 = n$.

[631] $x^2 = bx$; $x = b$, b being the multiple of the "root."

[632] $ax^2 + bx = n$, or rather: $x^2 + n = ax$. The geometrical solution for the equation $x^2 + 21 = 10x$ is explained by al-Khuwârizmî; cf. Karpinski, *op. cit.*, pp. 83 ff. The expressions *tafṣîl aḍ-ḍarb* and *aḍ-ḍarb al-mufaṣṣal* are not quite clear to me. They have been rendered tentatively by "multiplication in part," since they seem to refer to the addition of $(\frac{10}{2})^2$ which is necessary for finding the value of x.

[633] Apparently, $ax^3 + bx^2 = cx + n$, or the like.

[634] The simple equations are: $ax = n$; $bx^2 = n$; and $ax^2 = bx$. The composite equations are: $ax^2 + bx = n$; $ax^2 + n = bx$; and $ax^2 = bx + n$. Cf. Karpinski, *op. cit.*, pp. 69 and 71.

[635] Muḥammad b. Mûsâ, who lived in the first half of the ninth century. Cf. *GAL*, I, 215 f.; *Suppl.*, I, 381 f.

[636] *Ca.* 900? Cf. *GAL*, *Suppl.*, I, 390.

on it. One of the best Spanish commentaries is the book of al-Qurashî.[637]

We have heard that great eastern mathematicians have extended the algebraic operations beyond the six types and brought them up to more than twenty. For all of them, they discovered solutions based on solid geometrical proofs.[638]

God "gives in addition to the creatures whatever He wishes to give to them."[639]

III, 99

Business (arithmetic)

Another subdivision of arithmetic is business (arithmetic). This is the application of arithmetic to business dealings in cities. These business dealings may concern the sale (of merchandise), the measuring (of land), the charity taxes, as well as other business dealings that have something to do with numbers. In this connection, one uses both arithmetical techniques,[640] (and one has to deal) with the unknown and the known, and with fractions, whole (numbers), roots, and other things.

In this connection, very many problems have been posed. Their purpose is to give (the student) exercise and experience through repeated practice, until he has the firm habit of the craft of arithmetic.

Spanish mathematicians have written numerous works on the subject. The best known of these works are the business arithmetics of az-Zahrâwî,[641] Ibn as-Samḥ,[642] Abû Muslim b.

[637] He is referred to as Abû l-Qâsim al-Qurashî of Bougie, and was a source of Ibn al-Bannâ'’s *Talkhîṣ*. Cf. H. P. J. Renaud in *Hespéris*, XXV (1938), 35–37.

[638] Cf. 'Umar al-Khayyâm, *Algebra*, ed. F. Woepcke (Paris, 1851).

[639] Qur'ân 35.1 (1).

[640] I.e., calculation (elementary arithmetic) and algebra.

[641] 'Alî b. Sulaymân. Cf. Ṣâ'id al-Andalusî, *Ṭabaqât al-umam*, tr. R. Blachère (Publications de l'Institut des Hautes Etudes Marocaines, No. 28) (Paris, 1935), pp. 131 f.

[642] Aṣbagh b. Muḥammad, d. 426 [979–1035]. Cf. *GAL*, I, 472; *Suppl.*, I, 861; Ṣâ'id al-Andalusî, *Ṭabaqât*, pp. 130 f., where his age is incorrectly given as fifty (instead of fifty-six) solar years.

Khaldûn,[643] who were pupils of Maslamah al-Majrîṭî, and others.

Inheritance laws [644]

Another subdivision of arithmetic is inheritance laws. It is a craft concerned with calculation, that deals with determining the correct shares of an estate for the legal heirs. It may happen that there is a large number of heirs, and one of the heirs dies and his portions have to be (re-)distributed among his heirs. Or, the individual portions, when they are counted together and added up, may exceed the whole estate.[645] Or, there may be a problem when one heir ac-

[643] ʿAmr (ʿUmar?) b. Aḥmad, d. 449 [1057/58], a member of Ibn Khaldûn's family. Cf. Ṣâʿid al-Andalusî, *Ṭabaqât*, p. 133, and above, 1:xxxiv. Ibn Faḍlallâh al-ʿUmarî, d. 749 [1349], states in his *Masâlik al-abṣâr* that he had seen very good astrolabes signed by Ibn Khaldûn, and had personally copied a work of his, which, however, he lost later on. (MS, Topkapusaray, Ahmet III, 2797, Vol. V, p. 417.)

[644] The subject was treated as a part of jurisprudence, pp. 20 ff., above.

[645] In such cases, the process called *ʿawl* "reduction," mentioned below, is applied. The total of the inheritance shares, as stipulated by the Qur'ân, may be greater than the entire estate. Thus, according to the famous example, if a man leaves two daughters, his two parents, and one wife, the daughters would be entitled to two-thirds, the parents to one-third, and the wife to one-eighth of the estate. Qur'ân 4.11 f. (12–14). Therefore, the following procedure is used. The fractions are reduced to their common denominator: $\frac{2}{3} = \frac{16}{24}$; $\frac{1}{3} = \frac{8}{24}$; $\frac{1}{8} = \frac{3}{24}$; the new numerators are added up ($16 + 8 + 3 = 27$); and the total is made the new denominator. Thus, the new shares are $\frac{16}{27}$, $\frac{8}{27}$, and $\frac{3}{27}$. The wife's share, which was one-eighth, is "reduced" (*ʿawl*) to one-ninth, but the proportion of the shares to each other is preserved.

In our symbols, the procedure can be expressed as follows (for the sake of simplicity only two fractions are assumed):

$$(1)\quad \frac{a}{m}, \frac{b}{n} \quad \left(\frac{a}{m} + \frac{b}{n} \lessgtr 1\right)$$

$$\frac{a \cdot m \cdot n}{m} \quad \frac{b \cdot m \cdot n}{n}$$

$$(3)\quad \frac{an}{an+bm}, \frac{bm}{an+bm} \quad \left(\frac{an}{an+bm} + \frac{bm}{an+bm} = \right.$$

The correctness of the procedure can be proven as follows:

$$(1)\quad \frac{a}{m} : \frac{b}{n} :: x : y \qquad x + y = 1$$

$$(2)\quad bmx = any \qquad x = 1 - y$$

$$(3)\quad bm - bmy = any$$

$$(4)\quad y = \frac{bm}{an+bm}, \qquad x = \frac{an}{an+bm}.$$

knowledges, but the others do not acknowledge, (another heir, and vice versa). All this requires solution, in order to determine the correct amount of the shares in an estate and the correct share that goes to each relative, so that the heirs get the amounts of the estate to which they are entitled in view of the total amount of the shares of the estate. A good
III, *100* deal of calculation comes in here. It is concerned with whole (numbers), fractions, roots, knowns and unknowns; it is arranged according to the chapters and problems of inheritance law.

This craft, therefore, has something to do with jurisprudence, namely, with inheritance law, as far as it is concerned with the laws concerning the legal shares of inheritance, the reduction of the individual shares (*'awl*), the acknowledgement or non-acknowledgement (of heirs), wills, manumission by will, and other problems. And it has also a good deal [646] to do with arithmetic, in as much as it is concerned with determining the correct amount of the shares in accordance with the law evolved by the jurists.

It is a very important discipline. The scholars who cultivate it have produced traditions attesting to its excellence, such as, for instance: "The *farâ'iḍ* (inheritance laws) constitute one-third of (religious) scholarship, and they are the first science to be abolished," [647] and other such traditions. However, as was mentioned before, I am of the opinion that according to their plain meaning, all those traditions refer to individual "obligations" (*farâ'iḍ*), and not to the inheritance laws (*farâ'iḍ*). The latter are too few in number to constitute one-third of (religious) scholarship, whereas individual obligations are numerous.

Scholars, in early and late times, have written extensive works on the subject. Among the best works on the subject according to the school of Mâlik are the book of Ibn Thâbit, the *Mukhtaṣar* of Judge Abû l-Qâsim al-Ḥawfî, and the books

[646] *Sic* C and D.

[647] Cf. p. 22, above.

of Ibn al-Munammar, al-Ja'dî,[648] aẓ-Ẓawdî,[649] and others. But al-Ḥawfî is pre-eminent. His book is preferable to all the others. A clear and comprehensive commentary on it was written by one of our teachers, Abû 'Abdallâh Muḥammad b. Sulaymân as-Saṭṭî,[650] the leading *shaykh* of Fez. The Imâm al-Ḥaramayn wrote works on the subject according to the school of ash-Shâfi'î. They attest to his great scholarly capability and his firm grounding in scholarship. The Ḥanafites and the III, *101*
Ḥanbalites also (wrote works on the subject). The positions of scholars in scholarship vary.[651]

"God guides whomever He wants to guide." [652]

[20] *The geometrical sciences.*

This science studies quantities (measurements).[653] Quantities (measurements) may be continuous, like lines, planes, and (geometrical) solids, or discontinuous, like numbers. It also studies the essential properties of the quantities (measurements), as, for instance:

The angles of any triangle are equal to two right angles.

Parallel lines do not intersect anywhere, even when they extend to infinity.

The opposite angles formed when two lines intersect are equal to each other.

The result of multiplying the first and the third of four quantities in a proportion is equal to that of multiplying the second and the fourth.[654] And so on.

[648] All these scholars were mentioned above, p. 21. This passage was used by Ḥâjjî Khalîfah, *Kashf aẓ-ẓunûn*, ed. Flügel (Leipzig & London, 1835–58), III, 64.

[649] This Berber name is spelled with a *ṣ* into which a small *z* is inserted. Cf. 1:67 (n. 183), above. He is 'Abdallâh b. Abî Bakr b. Yaḥyâ, who was born *ca.* 643 [1245/46] and who was still alive in 699 [1299/1300]. Cf. Aḥmad Bâbâ, *Nayl al-ibtihâj* (Cairo, 1351/1932, in the margin of Ibn Farḥûn, *Dîbâj*), pp. 140 f.

[650] Cf. the *Autobiography*, pp. 31 f.

[651] This remark would seem to imply that Ḥanafite and Ḥanbalite works are inferior.

[652] Cf. Qur'ân 2.142 (136), 213 (209), etc.

[653] Cf. p. 311, above.

[654] This is not correct.

The Greek work on this craft which has been translated (into Arabic) is the book of Euclid. It is entitled *Kitâb al-uṣûl wa-l-arkân* ("Book of Basic Principles and Pillars").[655] It is the simplest [656] book on the subject for students. It was the first Greek work to be translated in Islam in the days of Abû Ja'far al-Manṣûr. The existing recensions differ, depending on the respective translators. There are the recensions of Ḥunayn b. Isḥâq,[657] Thâbit b. Qurrah,[658] and Yûsuf b. al-Ḥajjâj.[659]

The work contains fifteen books, four on the planes, one on proportions, another one on the relationship of planes to
III, *102* each other, three on numbers, the tenth on rational and irrational (quantities) [660]—the "roots"—and five on solids.

Many abridgments of Euclid's work have been written. Avicenna, for instance, devoted a special monograph treatment to it in (the section on) the mathematical disciplines in the *Shifâ'*. Ibn aṣ-Ṣalt [661] made another abridgment in the *Kitâb al-Iqtiṣâr*, and the same was done by others. Many scholars have also written commentaries on it. It is the starting point of the geometrical sciences in general.

It should be known that geometry enlightens the intellect and sets one's mind right. All its proofs are very clear and

---

655 This is a translation of *stoicheia, elementa.* In addition to the bibliographical references in *GAL*, there is a recent study by E. B. Plooij, *Euclid's Conception of Ratio and his Definition of Proportional Magnitudes as Criticized by Arabian Commentators*, (Leiden dissertation) (Rotterdam, [1950]). Cf. also, 2:365, above.

656 Or "most extensive." However, since it is considered as an introduction to geometry, the above translation may be preferable.

657 He died *ca.* 260 [873]. Cf. *GAL*, I, 205 f.; *Suppl.*, I, 366 ff.

658 He died in 288 [901]. Cf. *GAL*, I, 217 f.; *Suppl.*, I, 384 ff.

659 That is, al-Ḥajjâj b. Yûsuf b. Maṭar. Cf. *GAL*, I, 203; *Suppl.*, I, 363.

660 As explained in the definitions of the tenth book of Euclid, a square is called *ῥητόν, munṭaq* "rational," whereas its sides belong among the elements that "have power over" (*αἱ δυνάμεναι, al-qawîyah 'alâ*) the production of rational quantities and are called "irrational."

661 This cannot be the early translator Ibrâhim b. aṣ-Ṣalt; cf. *GAL*, *Suppl.*, I, 371. Ibn Khaldûn presumably had in mind Abû ṣ-Ṣalt Umayyah b. 'Abd-al-'Azîz b. Abî ṣ-Ṣalt, who lived *ca.* 460 [1067/68]. Cf. *GAL*, I, 486 f.; *Suppl.*, I, 889. He is credited with a work on geometry by Ibn Abî Uṣaybi'ah, *'Uyûn al-anbâ'*, ed. Müller (Königsberg & Cairo, 1882–84), II, 62, l. 22. Cf. also below, p. 135.

orderly. It is hardly possible for errors to enter into geometrical reasoning, because it is well arranged and orderly. Thus, the mind that constantly applies itself to geometry is not likely to fall into error. In this convenient way, the person who knows geometry acquires intelligence. It has been assumed that the following statement was written upon Plato's door: "No one who is not a geometrician may enter our house." [662]

Our teachers used to say that one's application to geometry does to the mind what soap does to a garment. It washes off stains and cleanses it of grease and dirt. The reason for this is that geometry is well arranged and orderly, as we have mentioned.

Spherical figures, conic sections, (and mechanics)

A subdivision of this discipline is the geometrical study of spherical figures (spherical trigonometry) and conic sections. There are two Greek works on spherical figures, namely, the works of Theodosius and Menelaus on planes and sections of (spherical figures).[663] In (mathematical) instruction, the book by Theodosius is (studied) before the III, *103*
book by Menelaus, since many of the (latter's) proofs depend on the former. Both works are needed by those who want to study astronomy, because the astronomical proofs depend on (the material contained in) them. All astronomical discussion is concerned with the heavenly spheres and the sections and circles found in connection with them as the result of the various motions, as we shall mention. (Astronomy,) therefore, depends on knowledge of the laws governing planes and sections of spherical figures.

[662] The famous ἀγεωμέτρητος μηδεὶς εἰσίτω, which appears in Elias' commentary on the *Categories* and was well known to the Arabs. It entered Arabic literature in connection with the introductions to Aristotelian philosophy. Cf. al-Fârâbî, *Fî-mâ yanbaghî an yuqaddam qabl ʿilm al-falsafah*, ed. and tr. F. Dieterici: *Alfârâbî's Philosophische Abhandlungen* (Leiden, 1890, 1892), pp. 52, 87.

[663] Cf. also 2:365, above.

Conic sections also are a branch of geometry. This discipline is concerned with study of the figures and sections occurring in connection with cones. It proves the properties of cones by means of geometrical proofs based upon elementary geometry. Its usefulness is apparent in practical crafts that have to do with bodies, such as carpentry and architecture. It is also useful for making remarkable statues and rare large objects (effigies, *hayâkil*) [664] and for moving loads and transporting large objects (*hayâkil*) with the help of mechanical contrivances, engineering (techniques), pulleys, and similar things.

There exists a book on mechanics that mentions every astonishing, remarkable technique and nice mechanical contrivance. It is often difficult to understand, because the geometrical proofs occurring in it are difficult. People have copies of it. They ascribe it to the Banû Shâkir.[665]

Surveying

Another subdivision of geometry is surveying. This discipline is needed to survey the land. This means that it
III, 104 serves to find the measurements of a given piece of land in terms of spans, cubits, or other (units), or to establish the relationship of one piece of land to another when they are compared in this way. Such surveying is needed to determine the land tax on (wheat) fields, lands, and orchards. It is also needed for dividing enclosures [666] and lands among partners or heirs, and similar things.

Scholars have written many good works on the subject.

Optics

Another subdivision of geometry is optics. This science explains the reasons for errors in visual perception, on the

664 For *haykal*, pl. *hayâkil*, cf. 1:151 (n. 172), above.

665 They lived in the ninth century. Cf. *GAL*, I, 216 f.; *Suppl.*, I, 382 f.

666 *Ḥawâʾiṭ* "gardens." Or does Ibn Khaldûn mean the fixing of the boundaries of buildings?

basis of knowledge as to how they occur. Visual perception takes place through a cone formed by rays, the top of which is the point of vision and the base of which is the object seen. Now, errors often occur. Nearby things appear large. Things that are far away appear small. Furthermore, small objects appear large under water or behind transparent bodies. Drops of rain as they fall appear to form a straight line, flame a circle, and so on.

This discipline explains with geometrical proofs the reasons for these things and how they come about. Among many other similar things, optics also explains the difference in the view of the moon at different latitudes.[667] Knowledge of the visibility of the new moon and of the occurrence of eclipses is based on that. There are many other such things.

Many Greeks wrote works on the subject. The most famous Muslim author on optics is Ibn al-Haytham.[668] Others, too, have written works on the subject. It is a branch of the mathematical sciences.

[21] *Astronomy.* III, *105*

This science studies the motions of the fixed stars and the planets. From the manner in which these motions take place, astronomy deduces by geometrical methods the existence of certain shapes and positions of the spheres requiring the occurrence of those motions which can be perceived by the senses. Astronomy thus proves, for instance, by the existence of the precession of the equinoxes, that the center of the earth is not identical with the center of the sphere of the sun. Furthermore, from the retrograde and direct motions of the stars, astronomy deduces the existence of small spheres (epicycles) carrying the (stars) and moving inside their great spheres. Through the motion of the fixed stars, astronomy then proves the existence of the eighth sphere. It also proves that a single star has a number of spheres, from the (observa-

[667] De Slane notes that Ibn Khaldûn should have said "longitudes."

[668] Al-Ḥasan (Ḥusayn) b. al-Ḥasan (Ḥusayn) b. al-Haytham (Alhazen), from *ca.* 354 [965] to 430 [1039]. Cf. *GAL*, I, 469 f.; *Suppl.*, I, 851 ff.

tion) that it has a number of declinations,[669] and similar things.

Only astronomical observation can show the existing motions and how they take place, and their various types. It is only by this means that we know the precession of the equinoxes and the order of the spheres in their different layers as well as the retrograde and direct motions (of the stars), and similar things. The Greeks occupied themselves very much with astronomical observation. They used instruments that were invented for the observation of the motion of a given star. They called them astrolabes. The technique and theory of how to make them, so that their motion conforms to the motion of the sphere, are a (living) tradition among the people.[670]

In Islam, only very little attention has been paid to astronomical observation. In the days of al-Ma'mûn, there was some interest in it. The construction of the instrument known as the astrolabe was begun but was not completed.[671]
III, *106* When al-Ma'mûn died, the institution of astronomical observation was lost and neglected. Later on, (scholars) based themselves upon the ancient observations. These were of no use because of the change in the motions (of the stars) over the course of time. The motion of the instrument used in astronomical observations conforms only approximately to the motion of the spheres and the stars and is not absolutely exact. When a certain amount of time has elapsed, the differences are revealed.

Astronomy is a noble craft. It does not, as is generally thought, teach the real form of the heavens nor the order of the spheres, but it teaches that the forms and shapes of the spheres are the result of those motions. As one knows, it is not improbable that one and the same thing may produce two different results. Therefore, when we say that the motions produce a result, we (merely) deduce from the (existence of)

[669] *Mayl.* Cf. al-Khuwârizmî, *Mafâtîḥ al-'ulûm*, p. 127: "*Mayl* is the distance of the sun or a given star from the equinoctial line." Cf. also al-Bîrûnî, *Kitâb at-tafhîm*, p. 59.

[670] Cf. Bombaci, p. 457.

[671] D: "but he died before it was completed."

what produces the result that the result exists, but the statement in no way teaches (us) the real character (of the resulting thing). Still, astronomy is an important science. It is one of the pillars of the mathematical disciplines.[672]

One of the best works on the subject is the *Majisṭî* (Almagest).[673] It is ascribed to Ptolemy, who, as the commentators of the work have established, was not one of the Greek rulers called Ptolemy. The leading Muslim philosophers have abridged Ptolemy's work. Avicenna, for instance, did that. He inserted his abridgment in the mathematical section of the *Shifâ'*. Ptolemy's work was also abbreviated by the Spanish philosopher Averroes, by Ibn as-Samḥ,[674] and by Ibn aṣ-Ṣalt,[675] in the *Kitâb al-Iqtiṣâr*. Ibn al-Farghânî[676] wrote an abridged astronomy. In it, he treated the subject along more easily understandable lines. He omitted the geometrical proofs.

"God taught man what he did not know."[677]

Astronomical tables[678]

III, *107*

A subdivision of astronomy is the science of astronomical tables. This is a craft based upon calculations according to

672 Cf. the translation of this passage by C. A. Nallino, *Raccolta di scritti editi e inediti*, V, 43 f.

673 I.e., Ptolemy's *Syntaxis Astronomica*. For the origin and vocalization of the Arabic term, cf. F. Rosenthal, "Al-Kindî and Ptolemy," in *Studi orientalistici in onore di Giorgio Levi Della Vida* (Rome, 1956), II, 438 f. Later Muslim scholars seem to have preferred the vocalization *Mijisṭî*.

674 Cf. p. 126, above.

675 Cf. p. 130, above.

676 Aḥmad b. Muḥammad (Alfraganus), d. after 247 [861/62]. Cf. *GAL*, I, 221; *Suppl.*, I, 392 f.

677 Qur'ân *96.5* (*5*).

678 *Zîj*, usually connected with Persian *zîk* "threads in the loom" > "lines in tables" > "tables." Cf. C. A. Nallino, *op. cit.*, V, 120. It may, however, be a distortion of *bizîdhaj*, the Middle Persian title of the *Anthology* of Vettius Valens. Intervocalic *dh* is known to change to *y* in Middle Persian (cf. W. Eilers, "Der Name des persischen Neujahrsfestes," in *Abhandlungen der Akademie der Wissenschaften und der Literatur, Geistes- und Sozialwissenschaftliche Klasse*, 1953, No. 2, p. 4), and *bi-* may have been lost, in the course of transmission, as preposition, as is known to happen.

Cf. now E. S. Kennedy, "A Survey of Islamic Astronomical Tables," in *Transactions of the American Philosophical Society*, N.S. XLVI (1956), 123–77.

arithmetical rules. It is concerned with the courses of motions peculiar to each star and with the character of that motion, fast, slow, direct, retrograde, and so on, as proven by astronomical means. This serves to show the positions of the stars in their spheres at any given time, by calculating their motions according to the rules evolved from astronomical works.

This craft follows certain norms. They constitute a sort of introductory and basic material for it. They deal with months and days and past eras.[679]

It (further) follows established basic principles. They deal with apogee and perigee, declinations,[680] the different kinds of motions, and how (these things) shed light upon each other. They are written down in well-arranged tables, in order to make it easy for students. These tables are called *zîj*. The determination of the positions of the stars at a given time by means of this craft is called "adjustment and tabulation." [681]

Both early and later scholars have written many works on the subject. Among such scholars, for instance, were al-Battânî [682] and Ibn al-Kammâd.[683]

Recent contemporary Maghribî scholars are using, as their reference work, the *zîj* that is ascribed to Ibn Isḥâq.[684]

[679] I.e., chronology, mathematical and historical.

[680] Cf. p. 134, above.

[681] *Ta'dîl* and *taqwîm*. The latter word became *tacuin* in Latin translations from the Arabic.

[682] Muḥammad b. Jâbir, *ca.* 244 [858] to 317 [929]. Cf. *GAL*, I, 222; *Suppl.* I, 397.

[683] Aḥmad b. Yûsuf b. al-Kammâd, d. 591 [1195]? Cf. *GAL*, *Suppl.*, I, 864. He is probably identical with Ibn al-Ḥammâd, an author of *zîjs* mentioned by al-Qifṭî, *Ta'rîkh al-ḥukamâ'*, p. 57, l. 15. Ḥâjjî Khalîfah, *Kashf aẓ-ẓunûn*, III, 569, seems to confuse him with Ibn Isḥâq and gives a wrong date (679 [1280/81]), which has caused considerable confusion to this day. Cf. R. Brunschvig, *La Berbérie orientale* (Publications de l'Institut d'Etudes Orientales d'Alger, Vols. VIII & XI) (Paris 1940–47), II, 369. The first to call attention to the situation seems to have been H. Suter, *Die Mathematiker und Astronomen der Araber und ihre Werke* (Abhandlungen zur Geschichte der mathematischen Wissenschaften, No. 10) (Leipzig, 1900), p. 196.

[684] Bulaq adds: "an astronomer in Tunis at the beginning of the seventh [thirteenth] century." He is Abû l-'Abbâs 'Alî b. Isḥâq, who made astronomical observations in 619 [1222]. Cf. H. P. J. Renaud in *Hespéris*, XXV (1938), 31; and *idem*, *Les Manuscrits arabes de l'Escurial* (Paris, 1941), II 3, 7, No. 909.

It is thought that Ibn Isḥâq based his work on astronomical observations. A Jew in Sicily who was skilled in astronomy and the mathematical sciences, and who occupied himself with astronomical observation, sent (Ibn Isḥâq) information on the conditions and motions of the stars he had ascertained. Thus, the Maghribîs have been using Ibn Isḥâq's work, be- III, *108*
cause they assume that it is based upon reliable information.

Ibn al-Bannâ'[685] wrote an abridgment (of Ibn Isḥâq's *Zîj*) which he entitled *al-Minhâj*. People have been very eager to use the *Minhâj*, because the operations described in it are easy.

(Knowledge of the) positions of the stars in the spheres is the necessary basis for astrological judgments, that is, knowledge of the various kinds of influence over the world of man that are exercised by the stars depending on their positions and that affect religious groups, dynasties, human activities, and all events. We shall explain this later on, and we shall clarify the evidence adduced by astrologers, if God, He is exalted, wills.

[22] *The science of logic.*[686]

(Logic concerns) the norms enabling a person to distinguish between right and wrong, both in definitions that give information about the essence of things, and in arguments that assure apperception.

This[687] comes about as follows: The basis of perception is the *sensibilia* that are perceived by the five senses. All living beings, those which are rational as well as the others, participate in this kind of perception. Man is distinguished from the animals by his ability to perceive universals, which are things abstracted from the *sensibilia*. Man is enabled to do this by virtue of the fact that his imagination obtains, from individual objects perceived by the senses and which agree with each other, a picture conforming to all these individual

[685] Cf. 1:238, and pp. 121, 123, 136 (n. 684), above.

[686] Cf. also pp. 246 ff. and 295 ff., below.

[687] Cf. Issawi, pp. 167 f.

objects. Such (a picture) is a universal. The mind then compares the individual objects that agree with each other, with other objects that (also) agree with them in some respects. It thus obtains a picture conforming to both of the two groups
III, *109* of objects compared), in as much as they agree with each other. In this way, abstraction continues to progress. Eventually, it reaches the universal (concept), which admits no other universal (concept) that would agree with it, and is, therefore, simple.

For instance, from the individual specimens of man, the picture of the species to which all the individual specimens conform is abstracted. Then, man (the human species) is compared with the animals, and the picture of the genus to which both men and animals conform is abstracted. Then, this is compared with the plants, until, eventually, the highest genus is reached, which is "substance." [688] There is no (other) universal (concept) that would in any way agree with it. Therefore, the intellect stops here and makes no further abstraction.

God created in man the ability to think. Through it, he perceives the sciences and crafts. Knowledge is either a perception (*taṣawwur*) of the essence of things—*taṣawwur* meaning a primitive kind of perception not accompanied by (the exercise of) judgment—or it is apperception (*taṣdîq*), that is, the judgment that a thing is so.

(Man's) ability to think may try to obtain the desired (information) by combining the universals with each other, with the result that the mind obtains a universal picture that conforms to details outside. Such a picture in the mind assures a knowledge of the quiddity of the individual objects. Or, (man's) ability to think may judge one thing by another and draw conclusions (from the one thing as to the other). Thus, (the other thing) is established in (the mind). This is apperception. In fact, (apperception) ultimately reverts to perception, because the only use of having (perception) is (to

[688] Cf. Bombaci, p. 457.

achieve) knowledge of the realities of things, which is the required goal of apperceptive [689] knowledge.

(Man's) ability to think may embark on this (process) in either the right or the wrong way. Selection of the way to be followed by man's ability to think in its effort to attain the knowledge desired, requires discernment, so that (man) can distinguish between right and wrong. This (process) became the canon of logic. III, *110*

When the ancients first began to discuss (logic), they did so in a sententious, disconnected manner by selecting certain stray propositions. Logical methods were unimproved. The problems of logic were not seen together. Eventually, Aristotle appeared among the Greeks. He improved the methods of logic and systematized its problems and details. He assigned to logic its proper place as the first philosophical discipline and the introduction to philosophy. Therefore (Aristotle) is called "the First Teacher." [690] His work on logic is called "the Text." [691] It comprises eight books, three [691a] on the forms of analogical reasoning, and five on the matter (to which analogical reasoning is applied).

This is because the objects of apperception are of different kinds. Some of them concern things that are certain by nature. Others concern things that are hypothetical in various

[689] *Ḥukmî* is added in C *supra lineam,* and in the text of D. Cf. p. 248, below.

[690] Cf. pp. 115 f., above; pp. 153 and 249, below.

[691] *Al-faṣṣ.* The word occurs in individual titles of Aristotle's works on logic in Arabic. Cf. Ibn an-Nadîm, *Fihrist* (Cairo, 1348/1929–30), pp. 368 and 370. However, it is not commonly used for the *Organon,* and I am not sure from which author (Averroes? cf. below, p. 254) Ibn Khaldûn derived it. Cf. also E. I. J. Rosenthal in *al-Andalus,* XX (1955), 80.

Among the most recent works concerned with Arabic translations of the so-called *Organon,* we may mention the work by ʿAbd-ar-Raḥmân Badawî, of which three volumes have appeared so far (Cairo, 1948——), and the publication of Porphyry's *Isagoge* by A. F. al-Ahwânî (Cairo, 1371/1952). Cf., in particular, R. Walzer, "New Light on the Arabic Translations of Aristotle," *Oriens,* VI (1953), 91–142.

[691a] "Three" appears in A, possibly as a correction of an erased word. B, C, and D have "four." This seems to be an error on the part of Ibn Khaldûn, who was thinking of the *Eisagoge* and included it in his count. Bulaq corrects the following "five" to "four," which is nonsensical.

degrees. Therefore, logic studies analogical reasoning from the point of view of the desired (information) it is expected to yield. It studies what the premises (of the desired information) ought to be, as seen in this light, and to which kind of certain or hypothetical knowledge the (desired information) belongs. Logic studies analogical reasoning (the syllogism), not with some particular object in mind but exclusively with regard to the way in which it is produced. Therefore, the first study, it is said, is undertaken with regard to matter, that is, the matter that produces some particular certain or hypothetical information. The second study, it is said, is undertaken with regard to the form and the manner in which analogical reasoning (the syllogism) in general is produced. Thus, the number of the books on logic came to be eight.

The first book deals with the highest genera that abstraction among the *sensibilia* may attain in the mind and that admit no (more universal) genera above them. It is called *Kitâb al-Maqûlât* (*Categories*).

The second book deals with the various kinds of apperceptive propositions. It is called *Kitâb al-'Ibârah* (*Hermeneutics*).

The third book deals with analogical reasoning (the syl-
III, *111* logism) and the form in which it is produced in general. It is called *Kitâb al-Qiyâs* (*Analytics*). Here ends the logical study from the point of view of (its) form.

The fourth book is the *Kitâb al-Burhân* (*Apodeictica*). It studies the kind of analogical reasoning (the syllogism) that produces certain (knowledge). It also studies (the problem of) why its premises must be certain ones. In particular, it mentions other conditions for yielding certain knowledge. For instance, the (premises) must be essential, primary, and so on. This book contains a discussion of determinatives [692] and definitions, because one wants them to be certain, since

---

[692] The Arabic word used here should probably be read *al-mu'arrifât*, and not, as might be thought at first glance, *al-ma'rifât* "various kinds of knowledge," even though Aristotle speaks about *gnosis* right at the beginning of the work.

it is necessary—nothing else is possible—that a definition conform to the thing defined. Therefore, (definitions) were treated by the ancients in this book.

The fifth book is the *Kitâb al-Jadl* (*Topics*). *Jadl* ("disputation") is the kind of analogical reasoning that shows how to cut off a troublesome adversary and silence one's opponent, and teaches the famous (methods) to be employed to this end. It is also concerned with other conditions required in this connection. They are mentioned here. The book deals with the "places" (*topoi*) from which the syllogism is evolved by using them to clarify the so-called middle term that brings the two ends of the desired information together.[693] It also deals with the conversion of terms.

The sixth book is the *Kitâb as-Safsaṭah* (*Sophistici Elenchi*). Sophistry is the kind of analogical reasoning that teaches the opposite of the truth and enables a disputant to confuse his opponent. The (book) is bad because of its purpose. It was written only so that one might know sophistical reasoning and be on guard against it.

The seventh book is the *Kitâb al-Khiṭâbah* (*Rhetoric*). Rhetoric is the kind of analogical reasoning that teaches how to influence the great mass and get them to do what one wants them to do. It also teaches the forms of speech to be employed in this connection.

The eighth book is the *Kitâb ash-Shi'r* (*Poetics*). Poetics is the kind of analogical reasoning that teaches the invention of parables and similes, especially for the purpose of (en- III, *112*
couraging oneself and others) to undertake something or avoid doing something. It also teaches the imaginary propositions [694] to be employed in this connection.

These are the eight books on logic according to the ancients.

After logic had been improved and systematized, the

[693] Cf. p. 145, below.

[694] In contrast to syllogisms based on logical judgment. Cf. F. Gabrieli, "Estetica e poesia araba nell'interpretazione della Poetica Aristotelica presso Avicenna e Averroè," *Rivista degli studi orientali*, XII (1929–30), 298.

Greek philosophers were of the opinion that it was necessary to discuss the five universals providing the perception that[695] conforms to the quiddities outside or to their parts or accidents. The (five) are genus, difference, species, property, and general accident.[696] Therefore, they took the subject up in a special book concerned with the (five universals), which serves as an introduction to the discipline. Thus, the books on (logic) came to be nine.

All of them were translated in Islam. The Muslim philosophers wrote commentaries and abridgments of them. Al-Fârâbî and Avicenna, for instance, did this, and, later on, the Spanish philosopher, Averroes. Avicenna wrote the *Kitâb ash-Shifâ'*,[697] which comprises all the seven philosophical disciplines.

Later on, more recent scholars have changed the terminology of logic. They added to the study of the five universals the (study of) its fruit, namely, the discussion of definitions and descriptions which they took over from the *Apodeictica*. They discarded the *Categories*, because (the logicians') study of the book is accidental and not essential. To the *Hermeneutics* they added the discussion of the conversion (of terms), whereas the ancient books included that subject in the *Topics*,[698] but, in some respects, it does fall under the discussion of propositions.

Then, they discussed analogical reasoning in as much as it produces the desired information in general, and without regard to any matter. They discarded study of the matter to which analogical reasoning (is applied). That concerned five
III, *113* books, the *Apodeictica*, the *Topics*, the *Rhetoric*, the *Poetics*,

[695] The remainder of this sentence and the next one are not found in Bulaq.

[696] The reference is to Porphyry's *Isagoge* and the πέντε φωναί (*quinque voces*): γένος (*genus*); διαφορά (*differentia*); εἶδος (*species*); ἴδιον (*proprium*); and συμβεβηκός (*accidens*). Cf. again, p. 145, below.

[697] The beginning of the section on logic from the *Shifâ'* has been published by I. Madkûr, M. al-Khudayrî, M.-M. Anawati, and A. F. al-Ahwânî (Cairo, 1371/1952), as the first volume of the planned publication of the whole *Shifâ'*. The section on *al-Burhân* (*Apodeictica*), published by 'Abd-ar-Raḥmân Badawî, appeared in Cairo in 1954.

[698] The "whereas" clause is not found in Bulaq.

and the *Sophistici Elenchi.* Some of them occasionally touched a little on those books. (But in general,) they neglected them, as if they had never been, whereas they are a very important basis of the discipline.

Then, they thoroughly discussed their writings on logic and studied them as a discipline in its own right, not as an instrument for the sciences. This resulted in a long and extensive discussion of the subject. The first to do this was the imam Fakhr-ad-dîn b. al-Khaṭîb.[699] He was followed by Afḍal-ad-dîn al-Khûnajî.[700] Al-Khûnajî's books are used by contemporary easterners as reference works. On logic, he wrote the long *Kitâb Kashf al-asrâr*, the *Mukhtaṣar al-mûjiz* which is good as a textbook, and the *Mukhtaṣar al-jumal.*[701] The last-mentioned work consists of four leaves and gives a synopsis of the discipline and its basic principles. Contemporary students use it and profit from it. The books and methods of the ancients are avoided, as if they had never been, although they are full of the results and useful aspects of logic, as we have stated.

God is the guide to that which is correct.

It [702] should be known that the early Muslims and the early speculative theologians greatly disapproved of the study of this discipline. They vehemently attacked it and warned against it. They forbade the study and teaching of it. Later on, ever since al-Ghazzâlî and the imam Ibn al-Khaṭîb, scholars have been somewhat more lenient in this respect. Since that time, they have gone on studying (logic), except

[699] Cf. 1:402, above.

[700] Muḥammad b. Nâmwar, 590–646 [1194–1248]. Cf. *GAL*, I, 463; *Suppl.*, I, 838. His *Jumal* were discussed in the circle of Ibn Khaldûn's friends, as we learn from Ibn al-Khaṭîb, *al-Iḥâṭah fî akhbâr Gharnâṭah* (Cairo, 1319/1901), II, 158 f. Ibn Khaldûn himself knew them by heart; cf. p. 396, below.

[701] The works I checked indicate the titles of the last two works as *al-Mûjiz* and *al-Jumal*, without *mukhtaṣar*. The word *mukhtaṣar*, as it is used here, cannot mean "brief work" (which would be correct), but only "abridgement of a work entitled *Mûjiz*, etc." (which would not be correct).

[702] The following discussion, to the end of the section (p. 147), is not found in Bulaq.

for a few who have recourse to the opinion of the ancients concerning it and shun it and vehemently disapprove of it.

Let us explain on what the acceptance or rejection of (logic) depends, so that it will be known what scholars have in mind with their different opinions. This comes about as follows:

III, *114* When the theologians invented the science of speculative theology, in order to support the articles of faith with rational evidence, their approach was to use some particular evidence, which they mentioned in their books. Thus, they proved the createdness of the world by affirming that accidents exist and are created, that bodies cannot possibly be free from accidents, and that something that cannot be free from created things must itself be created. Or, they affirmed the oneness of God by the argument of mutual antagonism.[703] They affirmed the existence of primeval attributes with reference to the four comprehensive (attributes),[704] in that they drew conclusions from the visible as to the supernatural. There are other such arguments mentioned in their books.

Then, they strengthened that evidence by inventing basic principles constituting a sort of premises for the evidence. Thus, they affirmed the existence of atomic matter and atomic time and the vacuum. They denied nature [705] and the intellectual combination of quiddities. They affirmed that an accident does not persist two moments.[706] They also affirmed the existence of the "state," that is, an attribute of something existing, that neither exists nor yet does not exist.[707] They have still other basic principles upon which they have built their particular arguments.

It then came to be the opinion of *Shaykh* Abû l-Ḥasan (al-Ash'arî), Judge Abû Bakr (al-Bâqillânî), and Professor

[703] Cf. 1:394, and pp. 44 and 63, above.

[704] Cf. pp. 48 f., above. The reference is to the four attributes of power, knowledge, life, and volition.

[705] Cf. p. 146, below, where Ibn Khaldûn speaks about the outside existence of natural quiddities and their universals. This appears to be meant here.

[706] Cf. p. 51, above.

[707] Cf. S. Munk, *Mélanges de philosophie juive et arabe* (Paris, 1859), pp. 327 ff.

Abû Isḥâq (al-Isfarâyinî), that the evidence for the articles of faith is reversible in the sense that if the arguments are wrong, the things proven (by them) are wrong.[708] Therefore, Judge Abû Bakr thought that the arguments for the articles of faith hold the same position as the articles of faith themselves and that an attack against them is an attack against the articles of faith, because they rest on those (arguments).

Now, if one considers logic, one will find that it all revolves around intellectual combination and the affirmation of the outside existence of a natural universal to which must correspond the mental universal that is divided into the five universals, namely, genus, species, difference, property, and III, *115*
general accident.[709] This is wrong in the opinion of the speculative theologians. The universal and essential is to them merely a mental concept having no correspondence outside (the mind), or—to those who believe in the theory of "states"—(it is merely) a "state." Thus, the five universals, the definitions based on them, and the ten categories are wrong, and the essential attribute is a wrong (concept and does not exist). This implies that the essential and necessary propositions on which argumentation is predicated are wrong and that the rational cause is a wrong (concept and does not exist). Thus, the *Apodeictica* is wrong, and the "places" (*topoi*) which are the central part of the *Topics* are a wrong (concept). They were the things from which one derives the middle term that brings the two ends together in analogical reasoning.[710]

The only thing that remains is formal analogical reasoning (the syllogism).[711] The only remaining definition is the one that is equally true for all details of the thing defined and

[708] Cf. p. 51, above. The reversed statement in this case would be: Since the articles of faith are correct, the arguments proving them must be correct.

[709] Cf. p. 142, above.

[710] Cf. p. 141, above.

[711] *Al-qiyâs aṣ-ṣûrî.* My limited knowledge of Arabic logic prevents me from stating whether, or where, this expression may occur as a technical term for some kind of syllogism. However, it may not be a technical term, in which case the above translation may render the thought perfectly well: the only thing that remains is studying the forms of syllogism, not their matter.

cannot be more general, because then other matters would enter it, nor can it be more restricted, because then part of those details would be left out. That is what the grammarians express by *jam'* and *man'*, and the speculative theologians by *ṭard* and *'aks* (complete identity of the definition and the thing defined, and reversibility of the definition).[712]

Thus, all the pillars of logic are destroyed. (On the other hand,) if we affirm their existence, as is done in logic, we (thereby) declare wrong many of the premises of the speculative theologians. This, then, leads to considering wrong their arguments for the articles of faith, as has been mentioned before. This is why the early theologians vehemently disapproved of the study of logic and considered it innovation or unbelief, depending on the particular argument declared wrong (by the use of logic). However, recent theologians since al-Ghazzâlî have disapproved of (the idea of the) reversibility of arguments and have not assumed that the fact that the arguments are wrong requires as its necessary consequence that the thing proven (by them) be wrong. They con-
III, *116* sidered correct the opinion of logicians concerning intellectual combination and the outside existence of natural quiddities and their universals. Therefore, they decided that logic is not in contradiction with the articles of faith, even though it is in contradiction to some of the arguments for them. In fact, they concluded that many of the premises of the speculative theologians were wrong. For instance, they deny the existence of atomic matter and the vacuum and (affirm) [713] the persistence of accidents, and so on. For the arguments of the theologians for the articles of faith, they substituted other arguments which they proved to be correct by means of speculation and analogical reasoning. They hold that this goes in no way against the orthodox articles of faith. This is the opinion of the imam (Fakhr-ad-dîn Ibn al-Khaṭîb),[714] al-Ghazzâlî, and their contemporary followers.

---

[712] Cf. at-Tahânawî, *Kashshâf iṣṭilâḥât al-funûn*, pp. 904 f.

[713] Cf. pp. 50 f., above.

[714] Cf. Bombaci, p. 458.

This should be considered. The methods and sources used by religious scholars to form their opinions should be understood.

God gives guidance and success to that which is correct.

[23] *Physics.*

This is a science that investigates bodies from the point of view of the motion and stationariness which attach to them. It studies the heavenly and the elementary bodies (substances), as well as the human beings, the animals, the plants, and the minerals created from them. It also studies the springs and earthquakes that come into being in the earth, as well as the clouds, vapors, thunder, lightning, and storms that are in the atmosphere, and other things. It further studies the beginning of motion in bodies — that is, the soul in the different forms in which it appears in human beings, animals, and plants.

The books of Aristotle on the subject are available to scholars. They were translated together with the other books on the philosophical sciences in the days of al-Ma'mûn. Scholars wrote books along the same lines and followed them III, *117*
up with explanation and comment.[715] The most comprehensive work written on the subject is Avicenna's *Kitâb ash-Shifâ'*. In it, Avicenna treats all the seven philosophical sciences, as we have mentioned before.[716] Avicenna later on abridged the *Kitâb ash-Shifâ'* in the *Kitâb an-Najâh* and the *Kitâb al-Ishârât*. In a way, he opposed Aristotle on most (physical) problems and expressed his own opinion on them. Averroes, on the other hand, abridged the books of Aristotle and commented on them, but followed him and did not oppose him. Scholars have written many works on the subject,[717] but these are the works that are famous at this time and to which

[715] The last half of the sentence is added in C and D.

[716] Cf. p. 142, above.

[717] C̆ and D add: "after him (i.e., Averroes)." This would mean that only the works of Averroes, and not those of Avicenna, were famous and studied in Ibn Khaldûn's time. Considering the repeated references to Avicenna in the *Muqaddimah*, Ibn Khaldûn hardly meant to say that.

attention is paid when one (studies) the craft (of physics).

The people of the East are concerned with Avicenna's *Kitâb al-Ishârât*. The imam Ibn al-Khaṭîb wrote a good commentary on it. The same was done by al-Âmidî.[718] Another commentary on the work was written by Naṣîr-ad-dîn aṭ-Ṭûsî,[719] who is known as Khawâjah (Khoja), an 'Iraqî scholar. He investigated many of the problems (of the *Ishârât*) and compared what the imam (Ibn al-Khaṭîb) had to say about them. He went beyond (Ibn al-Khaṭîb's) studies and investigations.

"And He knows more than any scholar." [720]

[24] *The science of medicine.*[721]

Medicine is a craft that studies the human body in its illness and health. The physician attempts to preserve health and to cure illness with the help of medicines and diets, but first he ascertains the illness(es) peculiar to each limb of the body, and the reasons causing them. He also ascertains the medicines existing for each illness. Physicians deduce the (effectiveness of) medicines from their composition and powers. They deduce (the stage of) an illness from signs indicating whether the illness is ripe and will accept the medicine or not. (These signs show themselves) in the color (of the patient), the excretions, and the pulse. The physicians in this
III, *118* imitate the power of nature, which is the controlling element in both health and illness. They imitate nature and help it a little, as the nature of the matter (underlying the illness), the season (of the year), and the age (of the patient) may require in each particular case. The science dealing with all these things is called medicine.

718 Al-Âmidî (cf. p. 29, above) wrote, in fact, against Fakhr-ad-dîn ar-Râzî's (Ibn al-Khaṭîb's) commentary on the *Ishârât*. His work is entitled *Kashf at-tamwîhât*.

719 Muḥammad b. Muḥammad, 597–672 [1201–1274]. Cf. *GAL*, I, 508 ff.; *Suppl.*, I, 924 ff. His commentary is entitled *Ḥall mushkilât al-Ishârât*. "'Irâqî" (corrected in Bulaq to "eastern") refers to what Ibn Khaldûn called "the non-Arab 'Irâq."

720 Qur'ân 12.76 (76).

721 Medicine was treated as a craft above, 2:373 ff.

Certain limbs are occasionally discussed as individual subjects and are considered to (form the subjects of) special sciences. This is the case, for instance, with the eye, the diseases of the eye, and the collyria (used in the treatment of eye diseases).

(Scholars) have also added to this discipline the (study of the) uses of the parts of the body, that is, the useful purpose for which each limb of the animal body was created. This is not a medical subject, but it has been made into an annex and subdivision of medicine. Galen has written an important and very useful work on this discipline.[722]

Galen is the leading ancient authority on medicine. His works have been translated (into Arabic). He is said to have been a contemporary of Jesus and to have died in Sicily on his wanderings while in voluntary exile.[723] His works on medicine are classics which have been models for all later physicians.

There have been leading physicians in Islam of surpassing skill, such as, for instance, ar-Râzî,[724] al-Majûsî,[725] and Avicenna. There have also been many Spanish physicians. Most famous among them was Ibn Zuhr.[726]

In contemporary Muslim cities, the (craft of medicine) seems to have deteriorated, because the civilization (population) has decreased and shrunk. (Medicine) is a craft required

---

722 This reference to Galen's *De usu partium* is added in C and D. Cf. also 1:90, above.

723 The Arabs had more historically accurate data on Galen's life, but the misinformation that Ibn Khaldûn presents was widely known, although usually rejected as wrong. Cf. R. Walzer, *Galen on Jews and Christians* (Oxford, 1949), pp. 92 ff.; G. Levi Della Vida in *Journal of the American Oriental Society*, LXX (1950), 184. Cf. also Sibṭ Ibn al-Jawzî, *Mir'ât az-zamân*, Pt. II (MS. Köprülü, photostat Cairo, Egyptian Library, *ta'rîkh* 551, pp. 41 f., 111, 114), who refers to Pseudo-Ghazzâlî, *Sirr al-ʽâlamayn*. Cf., further, *ʽIbar*, II, 188; and, most recently, G. Vajda in *Annuaire de l'Institut de Philologie et d'Histoire Orientales et Slaves*, XIII (1953), pp. 641–52.

724 Muḥammad b. Zakarîyâ' (Rhazes), 251–313 [865–925]. Cf. *GAL*, I, 233 ff.; *Suppl.*, I, 417 ff.

725 ʽAlî b. al-ʽAbbâs [tenth century]. Cf. *GAL*, I, 237; *Suppl.*, I, 423.

726 ʽAbd-al-Malik b. Zuhr (Avenzoar), d. 557 [1162]. Cf. *GAL*, I, 487; *Suppl.*, I, 890.

only by sedentary culture and luxury, as we shall explain later on.[727]

Civilized Bedouins have a kind of medicine which is
III, *119* mainly based upon individual experience. They inherit its use from the *shaykhs* and old women of the tribe. Some of it may occasionally be correct. However, (that kind of medicine) is not based upon any natural norm or upon any conformity (of the treatment) to the temper of the humors. Much of this sort of medicine existed among the Arabs. They had well-known physicians, such as al-Ḥârith b. Kaladah [728] and others.

The medicine mentioned in religious tradition [729] is of the (Bedouin) type. It is in no way part of the divine revelation. (Such medical matters) were merely (part of) Arab custom and happened to be mentioned in connection with the circumstances of the Prophet, like other things that were customary in his generation. They were not mentioned in order to imply that that particular way of practicing (medicine) is stipulated by the religious law. Muḥammad was sent to teach us the religious law. He was not sent to teach us medicine or any other ordinary matter. In connection with the story of the fecundation of the palms, he said: "You know more about your worldly affairs (than I)." [730]

None of the statements concerning medicine that occur in sound traditions should be considered to (have the force of) law. There is nothing to indicate that this is the case. The

[727] Actually, medicine is considered a basic craft (2:355 f., above), though one needed only in cities. See 2:376 f., above.

[728] For this legendary physician, whose lifetime is said to have spanned the period from Muḥammad to Mu'âwiyah, cf. Ibn Abî Uṣaybi'ah, I, 109–13; tr. B. R. Sanguinetti, *Journal asiatique*, V 5 (1855), 403–19. Ibn Khallikân, tr. W. M. de Slane, IV, 253 f. Some of the stories connected with him are reproduced in C. Elgood, *A Medical History of Persia* (Cambridge, 1951), pp. 66–68.

[729] C and D have: "traditions concerned with the medicine of the Prophet" (*an-nabawîyât* instead of *ash-shar'îyât*).

[730] Muḥammad had advised some people to try a different method of fecundation, but his method proved a failure. Cf. I. Goldziher, *Die Ẓâhiriten*, pp. 82 f.

only thing is that if that type of medicine is used for the sake of a divine blessing and [731] in true religious faith, it may be very useful. However, that would have nothing to do with humoral medicine but be the result of true faith. This happened in the case of the person who had a stomach-ache and was treated with honey,[732] and similar stories.

God guides to that which is correct.

[25] *The science of agriculture.*[733] III, *120*

This craft is a branch of physics. It concerns the study of the cultivation and growth of plants through irrigation, proper treatment, improvement of the soil,[734] (observance of) the suitable season, and the care for them by applying these things in a way that will benefit them and help them to grow.

The ancients were very much concerned with agriculture. Their study of agriculture was general. They considered the plants both from the point of view of planting and cultivation and from the point of view of their properties, their spirituality, and the relationship of (their spirituality) to the spiritualities of the stars and the great (heavenly) bodies, which is something (also) used in sorcery. Thus, they were very much concerned with the subject.

One of the Greek works, the *Kitâb al-Falâḥah an-Nabaṭîyah,*[735] was translated. It is ascribed to Nabataean scholars. It contains much information of the type (mentioned). The Muslims who studied the contents of the work

[731] "And" is not found in B.

[732] Cf. al-Bukhârî, *Ṣaḥîḥ,* IV, 57: "A person came to the Prophet and said: 'My brother has diarrhea.' The Prophet said: 'Give him honey to drink.' He did so. Then, he said: 'I gave him honey to drink, but it only made his diarrhea worse.' Whereupon Muḥammad said: 'God speaks the truth. Your brother's stomach lies.' " Cf. also *Concordance,* I, 191*b*. The story does not exactly illustrate the point Ibn Khaldûn wants to make.

[733] Agriculture was treated as a craft above, 2:356 f. Cf. [H. Pérès], in *Bulletin des études arabes* (Algiers), VII (1947), 14 f.

[734] The rest of the sentence appears in the above form in C and D. The earlier texts have: "and similar ways of taking care of them."

[735] The famous *Nabataean Agriculture* (*falâḥah* or *filâḥah*) which is ascribed to Abû Bakr Muḥammad b. 'Alî Ibn Waḥshîyah. Cf. *GAL,* I, 242 f.; *Suppl.,* I, 430 f. Cf. also p. 156, below.

(noticed that it belonged to) sorcery, which is barred (by the religious law) and the study of which is forbidden. Therefore, they restricted themselves to the part of the book dealing with plants from the point of view of their planting and treatment and the things connected with that. They completely banished all discussion of the other part of the book. Ibn al-'Awwâm[736] abridged the *Kitâb al-Falâḥah an-Nabaṭîyah* in this sense. The other part of it remained neglected. Some of the main problems of (that other part) were transmitted by Maslamah in his magical works. We shall mention that in connection with the discussion of sorcery, if God, He is exalted, wills.[737]

There are many books on agriculture by recent scholars. They do not go beyond discussion of the planting and treat-
III, *121* ment of plants, their preservation from things that might harm them or affect their growth, and all the things connected with that. (These works) are available.

[26] *The science of metaphysics.*

Metaphysics is a science that, (metaphysicians) assume, studies existence as such. First, (it studies) general matters affecting corporeal and spiritual things, such as the quiddities, oneness, plurality, necessity, possibility, and so on. Then, it studies the beginnings of existing things and (finds) that they are spiritual things. It goes on (to study) the way existing things issue from (spiritual things), and also (studies) their order. Then, (it studies) the conditions of the soul after its separation from the body and its return to (its) beginning.

The (metaphysicians) are of the opinion that (metaphysics) is a noble discipline. They assume that it gives them a knowledge of existence as it is. This, they think, is identical with happiness. They will be refuted later on.[738] In their arrangements, metaphysics comes after physics. Therefore,

[736] Yaḥyâ b. Muḥammad [first half of the twelfth century]. Cf. *GAL*, I, 494 f.; *Suppl.*, I, 903.

[737] Cf. pp. 157, 164, and 228 f., below.

[738] Cf. pp. 253 ff., below.

they called it "that which comes after physics" (metaphysics).[738a]

The books of the First Teacher[739] on the subject are available to scholars. They were abridged by Avicenna in the *Kitâb ash-Shifâ'* and the *Najâh*. They were also abridged by the Spanish philosopher, Averroes.

Recent scholars wrote systematic treatments of the sciences of the people (the Muslims). Al-Ghazzâli, at that time, refuted a good many of the (opinions of the metaphysicians). Recent speculative theologians, then, confused the problems of theology with those of philosophy, because the investigations of theology and philosophy go in the same direction, and the subject and problems of theology are similar to the subject and problems of metaphysics.[740] III, *122*
(Theology and metaphysics,) thus, in a way came to be one and the same discipline. (The recent theologians,) then, changed the order in which the philosophers (had treated) the problems of physics and metaphysics. They merged the two sciences in one and the same discipline. Now, in (that discipline), they first discussed general matters. This was followed, successively, by (the discussion of) the corporeal things and the matters that belong to them, the spiritual things and the matters that belong to them, and so on to the end of the discipline. The imam Ibn al-Khaṭîb,[741] for instance, proceeded in this manner in the *Mabâḥith al-mashriqîyah*, and so did all later theologians. The science of speculative theology thus merged with the problems of philosophy, and theological works were filled with the latter. It seemed as if the purpose which theology and philosophy followed in their respective subjects and problems was one and the same.

This confused people, but it is not correct. The problems with which the science of speculative theology deals are articles of faith derived from the religious law as transmitted

[738a] In this section, Ibn Khaldûn generally uses another Arabic term for "metaphysics," which, translated literally, means "science of divine matters."

[739] Cf. 3:115 (n. 591), above.

[740] For this discussion, cf. p. 52, above.

[741] Cf. 1:402, above.

by the early Muslims. They have no reference to the intellect and do not depend on it in the sense that they could not be established except through it. The intellect has nothing to do with the religious law and its views. Speculative theologians do not use the (rational) arguments they talk about as do the philosophers, in order to investigate the truth of the (articles of faith), to prove the truth of what had previously not been known, and to make it known. (Their use of rational arguments) merely expresses a desire to have rational arguments with which to bolster the articles of faith and the opinions of the early Muslims concerning them, and to refute the doubts of innovators who believe that their perceptions of (the articles of faith in their interpretation) are rational ones. (Rational arguments were used only) [742] after the correctness of the articles of faith, as they had been received and believed in by the early Muslims, had been stipulated by traditional evidence.

There is a great difference between the two positions. The perceptions which the Master of the religious law (Muḥammad) had are wider (than those of philosophers), because they go beyond rational views. They are above them and include them, because they draw their support from the
III, *123* divine light. Thus, they do not fall into the canon of weak speculation and circumscribed [743] perceptions. When the Lawgiver (Muḥammad) guides us toward some perception, we must prefer that (perception) to our own perceptions. We must have more confidence in it than in them. We must not seek to prove its correctness rationally, even if (rational intelligence) contradicts it. We must believe and know what we have been commanded (to believe and to know). We must be silent with regard to things of this sort that we do not understand. We must leave them to the Lawgiver (Muḥammad) and keep the intellect out of it.

The only thing that caused the theologians (to use

[742] Cf. Bombaci, p. 458.

[743] Lit., "perceptions which are included by (the higher perceptions of Muḥammad)." Cf. Bombaci, p. 458, and, for instance, p. 38, above.

rational arguments) was the discussions of heretics who opposed the early Muslim articles of faith with speculative innovations. Thus, they had to refute these heretics with the same kind of arguments. This (situation) called for using speculative arguments and checking on the early Muslim articles of faith with these arguments.

The verification or rejection of physical and metaphysical problems, on the other hand, is not part of the subject of speculative theology and does not belong to the same kind of speculations as those of the theologians. This should be known, so that one may be able to distinguish between the two disciplines, as they have been confused in the works of recent scholars. The truth is that they are different from each other in their respective subjects and problems. The confusion arose from the sameness of the topics discussed. The argumentation of the theologians thus came to look as though it were inaugurating a search for faith through (rational) evidence. This is not so. (Speculative theology) merely wants to refute heretics. The things it investigates are stipulated (by the religious law) and known to be true. Likewise, recent extremist Sufis, those who speak about ecstatic experiences, have confused the problems of (metaphysics and speculative theology) with their own discipline. They discussed all these things as part of one and the same subject. Thus, they discussed prophecy, union, incarnation, III, *124*
oneness, and other things. In fact, however, the perceptions of the three disciplines are distinct and different from each other. The Sufi perceptions are the ones that are least scientific. The Sufis claim intuitive[744] experience in connection with their perceptions and shun (rational) evidence. But intuitive experience is far removed from scientific perceptions and ways and the things that go with them, as we have explained above and as we shall (again) explain later on.[745]

God is the guide to that which is correct.

[744] Cf. p. 83 (n. 478), above.

[745] Cf. p. 89, above; pp. 253 f., below.

[27] *The sciences of sorcery and talismans.*

These are sciences showing how human souls may become prepared to exercise an influence upon the world of the elements, either without any aid or with the aid of celestial matters. The first kind is sorcery. The second kind is talismans.

These sciences are forbidden by the (various) religious laws, because they are harmful and require (their practitioners) to direct themselves to (beings) other than God, such as stars and other things. Therefore, books dealing with them are almost nonexistent among the people. The only exceptions are the books of the ancient nations from before the time of Moses' prophecy, such as the Nabataeans and the Chaldeans. None of the prophets who preceded (Moses) made or brought any laws. Their books were concerned with exhortations, with the recognition of the oneness of God, and with references to Paradise and Hell.[746]

The (magical) sciences were cultivated among the Syrian and Chaldean inhabitants of Babel and among the Copts of Egypt, and others. They composed books dealing with them and left information (concerning their occupation with them). Only very few of their books have been translated for us. (One book that was translated), for instance, is the *Falaḥâh an-*
III, *125* *Nabaṭîyah*,[747] a Babylonian work. People learned the science of sorcery from that work and developed its manifold branches. Later on, other works on sorcery were composed. Among such works were the *Books* (*Maṣâḥif*) *of the Seven Stars* and the book of Ṭumṭum the Indian [748] on the *Figures of the Degrees* (*of the Signs of the Zodiac*) *and the Stars*, and (works by) other (authors).

---

[746] Therefore, they did not say anything about the position of sorcery.

[747] C (in the margin) and D add: "by Ibn Waḥshîyah." Cf. p. 151, above.

[748] Cf. A. Hauber, "*Ṭomṭom* (*Ṭimṭim*) = Δάνδαμις = *Dindymus?*" in *Zeitschrift der Deutschen Morgenländischen Gesellschaft*, LXIII (1909), 457–72; (Pseudo-)Majrîṭî, *Ghâyah*, ed. H. Ritter (Leipzig & Berlin, 1933), p. 193; Carra de Vaux, in P. Tannery, *Mémoires scientifiques* (Toulouse & Paris, 1920), IV, 302 f. The title of the work mentioned by Ibn Khaldûn appears in slightly different forms.

Later on, Jâbir b. Ḥayyân,[749] the chief sorcerer of Islam, appeared in the East. He scrutinized the scholarly books and discovered the Art (the craft of sorcery and alchemy). He studied its essence and brought it out. He wrote a number of works on (sorcery). He lengthily discussed both sorcery and the craft of alchemy which goes together with sorcery, because the transformation of specific bodies (substances) from one form into another is effected by psychic powers, and not by a practical technique. Thus it is a sort of sorcery, as we shall mention in the proper place.[750]

Then, Maslamah b. Aḥmad al-Majrîṭî,[751] the leading Spanish scholar in the mathematical (scientific) and magical sciences, made his appearance. He abridged all these books and corrected them and collected all their different approaches in his *Ghâyat al-ḥakîm*. Nobody has written on this science since.

Let us present here some prefatory remarks that will explain the real meaning of sorcery. It is as follows. Human souls are one in species. However, they differ in view of their particular qualities.[752] They are of different kinds. Each kind is distinguished by a particular quality which does not exist in any other kind (of soul). These qualities come to constitute a natural disposition belonging (exclusively) to its particular kind (of soul).

The souls of the prophets have a particular quality through which they are prepared [753] to have divine knowl- III, *126*
edge, to be addressed by the angels in the name of God, as

[749] The legendary founder of Muslim alchemy. Cf. *GAL*, I, 240 f.; *Suppl.*, I, 426 ff.; P. Kraus, *Jâbir Ibn Ḥayyân*. Cf. also pp. 228 and 269, below.

[750] Cf. p. 245, below.

[751] Cf. 1:212, above.

[752] Cf. also pp. 393 f., below. For the basic theme, that the soul is one in species, different in powers, cf., for instance, Ibn Sînâ, *Kitâb an-Najâh* (Rome, 1593), p. 53.

[753] The Paris ed. adds: "to exchange human spirituality with angelic spirituality and to become an angel in the very moment the exchange takes place. This is the meaning of revelation, as has been mentioned in the proper place [1:199, above]. In this condition, the (prophetic souls) attain divine knowledge, are addressed .... " This addition is not found in Bulaq nor in the MSS. A, B, C, or D.

has been mentioned before,[754] and to exercise the influence upon created beings that goes with all that.

The souls of certain sorcerers also have the quality (of being able) to exercise influence upon created beings and to attract the spirituality of the stars, so that they can use it for being active (among created beings) and be able to exercise an influence through either a psychic or a Satanic power. Now, the prophets are able to exercise their influence with the help of God and by means of a divine quality. The souls of soothsayers, on the other hand, have a quality enabling them to observe supernatural things by means of Satanic powers. Thus, every kind (of soul) is distinguished by (its) particular quality, which does not exist in any other kind.

The souls that have magical ability are of three degrees. These three degrees will now be explained here.

The first (kind) exercises its influence merely through mental power, without any instrument or aid. This is what the philosophers call sorcery.

The second (kind) exercises its influence with the aid of the temper of the spheres and the elements, or with the aid of the properties of numbers. This is called talismans. It is weaker in degree than the first (kind).

The third (kind) exercises its influence upon the powers of imagination. The person who exercises this kind of influence relies upon the powers of imagination. He is somehow active in them. He plants among them different sorts of phantasms, images, and pictures, whichever he intends to use. Then, he brings them down to the level of the sensual perception of the observers with the help of the power of his soul that exercises an influence over that (sensual perception). As a result, the (phantasms, etc.) appear to the observers to exist in the external world, while, in fact, there is nothing (of the sort). For instance, a person is said to have seen gardens, rivers, and castles, while, in fact, there was nothing of the sort. This

[754] Cf. 1:184 f. and 199, above.

is what the philosophers call "prestidigitation" (*sha'wadhah* or *sha'badhah*).

Those are the different degrees of (sorcery).

Now, the sorcerer possesses his particular quality in potentiality, as is the case with all human powers. It is transformed (from potentiality) into actuality by exercise. III, *127*
All magical exercise consists of directing oneself to the spheres, the stars, the higher worlds, or to the devils by means of various kinds of veneration and worship and submissiveness and humiliation. Thus, magical exercise is devotion and adoration directed to (beings) other than God. Such devotion is unbelief. Therefore, sorcery is unbelief, or unbelief forms part of the substance and motives of sorcery, as has been seen. Consequently, (sorcerers must be killed). Jurists differ (only) as to whether they must be killed because of the unbelief which is antecedent to the practice (of sorcery), or because of their corrupting activity and the resulting corruption of created beings. All this comes from (sorcerers and sorcery).

Furthermore, since the first two degrees of sorcery are real and the third and last degree is not real, scholars differ as to whether sorcery is real or merely imaginary. Those who say that it is real have the first two degrees in mind. Those who say that it is not real have the third and last degree in mind. There is no difference of opinion among them about the matter itself, but (the difference of opinion) results from confusing the different degrees (of sorcery).

And God knows better.

It should be known that no intelligent person doubts the existence of sorcery, because of the influence mentioned, which sorcery exercises. The Qur'ân refers to it. It says, ". . . but the devils were unbelievers, teaching the people sorcery and that which had been revealed in Babel to the two angels, Hârût and Mârût. Those two always said before they taught anyone, 'We are a temptation. Do not be an unbeliever.' People learned from them how to cause discord

III, *128* between a man and his wife. (However,) they were not able to harm anyone except with God's permission." [755]

The Messenger of God, according to (the sound tradition of) the *Ṣaḥîḥ*,[756] was put under a magic spell, so that he imagined that he was doing a thing while, in fact, he was not doing it. The spell against him was placed in a comb, in flakes of wool, and in the spathe of a palm, and buried in the well of Dharwân.[757] Therefore, God revealed to him the following verses in the *Mu'awwidhatân:* "And (I take refuge in God) from the evil of the women who blow into knots." [758] 'Â'ishah said, "As soon as he recited the Qur'ân over one of those knots into which a spell against him had been placed, that particular knot became untied." [759]

There was much sorcery among the inhabitants of Babel, that is, the Nabataean and Syrian Chaldeans. The Qur'ân mentions much of it, and there are traditions about it. Sorcery was greatly cultivated in Babel and in Egypt at the time of Moses' prophetic mission. Therefore, the miracle Moses performed (as a proof of his prophecy) was of the kind claimed and bragged about (by sorcerers). The temples in Upper Egypt are remnants (of sorcery) attesting to the (cultivation of sorcery in ancient Egypt).[760]

We have seen with our own eyes (how a sorcerer) formed the picture of a person who was to be cast under a spell. He represented in it the characteristics of things he intended and planned (to make) that person adopt, as already existing in him in the shape of symbols of names and attri-

[755] Qur'ân 2.102 (96). For the dogma of the reality of sorcery in Islam and medieval Christianity, cf. E. Doutté, *Magie et religion dans l'Afrique du Nord* (Algiers, 1908), pp. 336 ff.

[756] The reference to the *Ṣaḥîḥ* is added in the margin of C and in the text of D.

[757] The well of Dharwân was located in Medina. References to the tradition of the spell cast over Muḥammad are found in *Handbook*, p. 161*b*. Cf. also the commentaries on the *Mu'awwidhatân*, the last two *sûrahs* of the Qur'ân.

[758] Qur'ân 113.4 (4). The verb translated as "blow" could also mean "spit." Cf. p. 168, below.

[759] Cf. p. 168, below.

[760] Cf. p. 113, above.

butes in homonym fashion[?].[761] Then he spoke (magic words) over the picture he had made to take the place of the person who was to be cast under a spell, concretely or symbolically.[762] During the repeated pronunciation of the evil words, he collected spittle in his mouth and spat upon (the picture). Then he tied a knot over the symbol in an object that he had prepared for the purpose,[763] since he considered tying knots and (making things) stick together to be auspicious (and effective in magical operations). He also entered into a pact with the jinn, asking them to participate in his spitting during the operation, intending to make the spell III, *129*
forceful. This (human) figure and the evil names have a harmful spirit. It issues from (the sorcerer) with his breath and attaches to the spittle he spits out. It produces (more) evil spirits. As a result, the things that the sorcerer intends (to happen to) the person who is cast under a spell, actually befall him.

We have also observed how people who practice sorcery point at a garment or a piece of leather and inwardly speak (magic words) over it, and behold! the object is torn to shreds. Others point in the same way at the bellies of sheep and goats at pasture with (a) ripping (gesture), and behold! the guts of the animals fall out of their bellies to the ground.[764]

We have also heard that in contemporary India, there still are (sorcerers) who point at a man, and his heart is extracted [765] and he falls dead. When someone looks for his heart, he cannot find it among his inner parts. Or, they point to a pomegranate. When someone opens it, no seeds are found in it.

We have likewise heard that in the Sudan and in the land

[761] It seems that Ibn Khaldûn used *ta'lîf* and *tafrîq* here in the sense of the terms *mu'talif* and *muftariq* of the science of tradition. Cf. 2:451 (n. 116), above. He may have wanted to say that the similarity between the real person and the picture of him made by the sorcerer was like that of homonyms.

[762] That is, either an actual picture of him or a symbolic representation.

[763] That is, he places the spell into some object (cf. the just-mentioned story of the spell cast over Muḥammad) and thus makes a magical "knot."

[764] Cf. p. 164, below.

[765] *Fa-yantajithu.*

of the Turks, there are (sorcerers) who cast a spell on a cloud, and rain falls upon a particular area.[766]

Also, we have observed remarkable things as to the efficacy of talismans that make use of "the loving numbers" 220 and 284. The sum of the aliquot parts of each of the loving numbers, such as one-half, one-fourth, one-sixth, one-fifth, and so on, is equal to the other number.[767] This is why the two numbers are called "loving numbers." It is a tradition among the people who know about talismans that these numbers may effect friendship and union between two lovers.
III, *130* Two effigies are made, one of them with Venus as the ascendant, when, either in her house or in her exaltation,[768] she looks at the moon lovingly and invitingly. As the ascendant of the other effigy, the seventh (house counting) from (that of) the first is taken. One of the loving numbers is placed upon the one effigy, and the other upon the other. The larger number is meant for the person whose friendship is sought, that is, the beloved. I do not know whether "larger number" means the higher number, or the one with the greater number of aliquot parts. The result (of the magical operation) is a close connection between the two lovers, so that the one is hardly able to break away from the other. This was reported by the author of the *Ghâyah*[769] and other authorities on magic, and it is attested by experience.[770]

[766] Cf. p. 245, below.

[767] $220 : 110 + 55 + 44 + 22 + 20 + 11 + 10 + 5 + 4 + 2 + 1 = 284$.

$284 : 142 + 71 + 4 + 2 + 1 = 220$.

For the theory of "loving numbers" among the Arabs, cf. M. Steinschneider in *Zeitschrift der Deutschen Morgenländischen Gesellschaft*, XXIV (1870), 367–69; S. Gandz in *Saadia Anniversary Volume* (New York, 1943), pp. 155–58. For a modern treatment of the problem, cf. E. B. Escott, "Amicable Numbers," *Scripta Mathematica*, XII (1946), 61–72.

[768] Cf. 2:213, above.

[769] (Pseudo-)Majrîṭî speaks of "loving numbers" in the *Ghâyah*, p. 278. A less complicated procedure was to eat cakes on which the loving numbers were inscribed; cf. T. Canaan in *Berytus*, IV (1937), 93. Cf. also Ṭâshköprüzâdeh, *Miftâḥ as-sa'âdah* (Hyderabad, 1329–56/1911–37), I, 332.

[770] Cf. Bombaci, p. 459.

Then, there is "the lion seal," [771] which is also called "the pebble seal." [772] On a steel thimble,[773] the sorcerer engraves the picture of a lion dragging its tail and biting on pebbles which it thus divides into two parts. A snake is represented in front of the lion. It is coiled at the lion's feet stretching upwards opposite the lion's head, so that its open mouth faces the lion's mouth. Upon the lion's back, a crawling scorpion is represented. In order to make the engraving, (the sorcerer) waits for a time when the sun enters the first or third decan [774] of Leo, provided (further) that the two luminaries (the sun and the moon) are well and out of their misfortune. When he finds and gets this (constellation), he makes an impression (of the engraving) upon a *mithqâl* or less of gold, which he then dips into saffron dissolved in rose water and preserves [775] in a yellow silk rag. (People) assume that the person who holds on to it has an indescribable power over rulers and is able to have close contact with them, to serve them, and to use them for his own ends. Likewise, the rulers themselves find in it strength and power over their subjects. This, too, was mentioned by authors on magic in the *Ghâyah* [776] and other works, III, *131*
and it is attested by experience.

Then, there is the magic square of thirty-six fields that belongs to the sun.[777] It has been said that it should be made when the sun enters its exaltation and is out of its misfortune,

[771] Cf. W. Ahrens in *Der Islam*, VII (1917), 215. Strangely enough, B and D (but not A or C) read *ṭâliʿ* "ascendant (of Leo)," instead of *ṭâbaʿ*.

[772] Cf. n. 776.

[773] Cf. R. Dozy in *Journal asiatique*, XIV 6 (1869), 164 f.

[774] Each sign of the zodiac is divided into three "faces" (*wajh*), Greek *prosôpon*, Latin *facies*, of ten degrees each. Cf. (Pseudo-)Majrîṭî, *Ghâyah*, pp. 126 ff. Cf. also p. 199, below, and A. Bouché-Leclerq, *L'Astrologie grecque* (Paris, 1899), pp. 215 ff.

[775] Cf. Dozy, *op. cit.*, pp. 165 f. Cf. German *aufheben* "to lift, to abolish, to preserve."

[776] The *Ghâyah*, pp. 35 f., mentions a simpler but rather similar talisman to be used against stones in the bladder, in Arabic designated by the same word as "pebbles."

[777] Cf. W. Ahrens, *op. cit.*, pp. 215 f., who states that this square is rather a combination of four nine-field squares.

and when the moon is well and under a royal ascendant in which the master of the tenth (house) is considered to look upon the master of the ascendant lovingly and invitingly and in which exalted indications concerning royal nativities prosper. It is preserved in a yellow silk rag, after having been dipped in perfume. (People) think that it influences one's friendship with rulers and one's (opportunity) to serve them and to be admitted into their company.

There are many similar things. The *Kitâb al-Ghâyah* by Maslamah b. Aḥmad al-Majrîṭî is the systematic treatment of this craft. It has it complete and presents its problems perfectly.

We have been told that the imam Fakhr-ad-dîn b. al-Khaṭîb wrote a book on the subject which he entitled *as-Sirr al-maktûm*. It is said to be in common use among the people in the East. We have not come across it. The imam (Fakhr-ad-dîn) is not considered an authority on magic, though the contrary might be the case (and he might have been an authority on magic).[778]

In the Maghrib, there is a type of magical practitioners who are known as "rippers" (*ba''âj*). They are the people to whom I referred above.[779] They point at a garment or a piece of leather, and it is torn to shreds. Or they point at the bellies of sheep and goats (with a) ripping (gesture), and they are ripped open. Such (sorcerers) nowadays are called "rippers," (in the Maghrib,) because most of their magical practice concerns ripping animals open. In that way, they frighten the owners of animals into giving them some (animal) they can spare. They keep their activities very much under cover,[780] because they are afraid of the authorities. I have
III, *132* met a number of them and witnessed their kind of magical

[778] Many MSS of the work are preserved; cf. *GAL*, I, 507; *Suppl.*, I, 923 f.; *GAL* (2d ed.), I, 669. Any doubt as to its authenticity was removed by H. Ritter, who found a reference to the *Sirr* in one of the works of Fakhr-ad-dîn ar-Râzî himself. See *Der Islam*, XXIV (1937), 285 (n. 2). The work as such speaks rather for, than against, the great philosopher's authorship.

[779] Cf. p. 161, above.

[780] Cf. Bombaci, p. 459.

practice. They informed me that they practice devotions and exercises. (Their devotions and exercises) consist, in particular, of heretical prayers and of association with the spiritualities of jinn and stars. These things are written down on a sheet (of paper) they possess, and called *al-Khinzîrîyah.*[781] They study it together. With the help of such exercises and devotions, they succeed in performing their magical actions. The influence they are able to exercise affects only objects other than free men. It affects, for instance, utensils, animals, and slaves. They express the (idea) by the words,[782] "things into which there goes money," [783] that is, all the things that are owned, sold, and bought. This is what they think. I questioned one of them, and he told me (what I have mentioned here). Their magical actions are plain fact. We have come across very much of it. We have observed them with our own eyes and have no doubt about it.

This is the situation with regard to sorcery and talismans and their influence in the world.

The philosophers made a distinction between sorcery and talismans. First, however, they affirmed that both (derive their effectiveness) from influences of the human soul. They deduced the existence of an influence of the human soul from the fact that the soul exercises an influence upon its own body that cannot be explained by the natural course of affairs or from corporeal reasons. At times, it results from the qualities of the spirits—such as heat, which originates from pleasure and joy—and at other times, it results from other psychic perceptions,[784] such as the things that result from imagination (*tawahhum*). Thus, a person who walks upon the ledge of

[781] The correctness of the reading seems to be certain. The meaning and derivation are uncertain. The word may refer to *khinzîr* "pig, boar." *Khinzîrîyah* "piggishness" occurs, for instance, in ar-Râghib al-Iṣfahânî, *Muḥâḍarât* (Cairo, 1287/1870), I, 431. However, it may be derived from a proper name, such as that of the Ibn Abî Khinzîr family, which provided governors for Sicily in the tenth century.

[782] Bulaq: "express that fact as follows: We act only upon

[783] "That have monetary value."

[784] Cf. Bombaci, p. 459.

a wall or upon a high tightrope [785] will certainly fall down if the idea of falling down is strongly present in his imagination.
III, *133* Therefore, there are many people who train themselves to get used to such things, so that they are not troubled by their imagination. They can walk upon the ledge of a wall or a high tightrope without fear of falling down. It is thus definite that we have here the result of an influence of the human soul and of the soul's imagining of the idea of falling down. If the soul can thus influence its own body without any natural corporeal causes, it is also possible that it can exercise a similar influence upon bodies other than its own. Its position with regard to its ability to exercise this type of influence is the same with regard to all bodies, since it is neither inherent nor firmly impressed in a (particular) body. Therefore, it is definite that the soul is able to exercise an influence upon other bodies.

Now, the distinction the (philosophers) make between sorcery and talismans is this. In sorcery, the sorcerer does not need any aid, while those who work with talismans seek the aid of the spiritualities of the stars, the secrets of numbers, the particular qualities of existing things, and the positions of the sphere that exercise an influence upon the world of the elements, as the astrologers maintain. The (philosophers, therefore,) say that sorcery is a union of spirit with spirit, while the talisman is a union of spirit with body (substance).[786] As they understand it, that means that the high celestial natures are tied together with the low (terrestrial) natures, the high natures being the spiritualities of the stars. Those

[785] C, at least, clearly indicates the reading *ḥabl* "rope," and not *jabal* "mountain." Ropedancers would certainly be a much more familiar picture in the medieval Muslim world than mountain climbers.

This example of the effects of imagination occurs in Avicenna and Averroes and in later Western literature, as shown by S. van den Bergh, "Pascal, Montaigne, et Avicenne," in *Millénaire d'Avicenne: Congrès de Bagdad* (Cairo, 1952), pp. 36–38; and *idem, Averroes' Tahafut al-Tahafut* (E. J. W. Gibb Memorial Series, N.S. No. 19) (Oxford & London, 1954), II, 174 f.

[786] Cf. p. 175, below.

who work with (talismans), therefore, as a rule, seek the aid of astrology.

(The philosophers) think that a sorcerer does not acquire his magical ability but has, by nature, the particular disposition needed for exercising that type of influence.

They think that the difference between miracles and sorcery is this. A miracle is a divine power that arouses in the III, *134* soul (the ability) to exercise influence. The (worker of miracles) is supported in his activity by the spirit of God. The sorcerer, on the other hand, does his work by himself and with the help of his own psychic power, and, under certain conditions, with the support of devils. The difference between the two actually concerns the idea, reality, and essence of the matter. We, however, (prefer to) deduce the differentiation merely from obvious signs. That is, miracles are found (to be wrought) by good persons for good purposes and by souls that are entirely devoted to good deeds. Moreover, (they include) the "advance challenge" (*taḥaddî*) [787] of the claim to prophecy. Sorcery, on the other hand, is found (practiced) only by evil persons and as a rule is used for evil actions,[788] such as causing discord between husband and wife, doing harm to enemies, and similar things. And it is found (practiced) by souls that are entirely devoted to evil deeds. This is the difference between (prophecy and sorcery) in the opinion of metaphysicians.

Among the Sufis some who are favored by acts of divine grace are also able to exercise an influence upon worldly conditions. This, however, is not counted as a kind of sorcery. It is effected with divine support, because the attitude and approach (of these men) result from prophecy and are a consequence of it. They enjoy divine support, as befits their state and faith and belief in the cause of God. Were someone among them capable of doing evil deeds, he would not do them, because he is bound by the divine command in whatever he may do or not do. Whatever he is not permitted to do,

[787] Cf. 1:188, and p. 100, above.
[788] Cf. 1:191, above.

he would certainly not do. Were he to, he would deviate from the path of truth and would in all likelihood lose his "state."

Miracles take place with the support of the spirit of God and the divine powers. Therefore, no piece of sorcery can
III, *135* match them. One may compare the affair of the sorcerers of Pharaoh with Moses and the miracle of the staff. Moses' staff devoured the phantoms the sorcerers produced, and their sorcery completely disappeared as if it had never been.[789]

Also, the following verse was revealed to the Prophet in the *Mu'awwidhatân*: "And (I take refuge in God) from the evil of the women who blow into knots." In this connection, 'Â'ishah said: "As soon as he recited the Qur'ân over one of the knots into which a spell against him had been placed, that particular knot became untied." [790] Sorcery cannot last whenever the name of God is mentioned in a believing state of mind.[791]

The historians report that the Darafsh-i-Kâviyân[792] — that is, the banner of the Persian emperor—had a magic square of a hundred fields [793] woven into it in gold. (That had been done) when there were certain astronomical positions that had been (especially) observed for the purpose of writing down the magic square. The banner was found on the day Rustum was killed at al-Qâdisîyah. It was lying on

[789] Cf. Qur'ân 7.117 (114); 26.45 (44). Cf. also p. 245, below.

[790] Cf. p. 160, above.

[791] "In a believing state of mind" is an addition of C and D. C has the words in the margin.

[792] Cf. A. Christensen, *L'Iran sous les Sassanides* (2d ed.; Copenhagen, 1944), pp. 502–4. The words mean "royal banner," but legend referred the word *kâvyân* to a mythical smith, Kâvagh by name, who tied his leather apron to a lance and led the revolt against the tyrant Dahâgh. The Arabic descriptions of the actual banner used at the end of the Sassanian empire, cited by Christensen, mentioned its great value but are not very clear or trustworthy. Ibn Khaldûn's description would certainly seem to reflect a fictional motif.
As the MSS show, Ibn Khaldûn read *Darqash Kâbiyân*.

[793] Apparently this is what is meant. Cf. E. Wiedemann in *Der Islam*, VIII (1918), 96 f., against W. Ahrens, *Der Islam*, VII (1917), 217. G. Bergsträsser refers to two such squares from al-Khalwatî, *an-Nûr as-sâṭi'*; cf. *Der Islam*, XIII (1923), 231. Cf. also al-Bûnî, in a work (or excerpt from a larger work, the *Shams al-ma'ârif*) which in two recent Cairo reprints, one undated, the other dated 1358/1939, goes under such titles as *Sharḥ ism Allâh al-a'ẓam* and *al-Lu'lu' al-manẓûm fî ṭ-ṭalâsim wa-n-nujûm*, p. 74.

the ground after the flight and dispersal of the Persians. The people who work with talismans and magic squares think that such (a magic square) means victory in war and that a banner containing it or accompanied by it could never be routed. However, (the spell) was counteracted by divine support, which resulted from the faith of the men around the Prophet and their belief in the cause of God. Through the presence of (faith), any magic spell was dissolved and did not last (this time, as it will always happen whenever faith is involved), "and what they did came to naught." [794]

The religious law makes no distinction between sorcery, talismans, and prestidigitation. It puts them all into the same class of forbidden things. The Lawgiver (Muḥammad) permitted us only those actions that are of relevance to us in our religion, which concerns the well-being of our life in the other world, and in our livelihood, which concerns the well-being of our life in this world. Things that are of no relevance in these two respects and that may cause harm or some kind of harm, are forbidden, (and the strictness of the prohibition is) in proportion to the harm they might do. Among such (irrelevant and harmful) things are sorcery, which causes III, *136*
harm when it is practiced. Talismans belong together with it, because the effect of sorcery and talismans is the same. There is also astrology, which causes a certain harm in that the belief in astral influences, referring as it does to (beings) other than God, corrupts the Muslim faith.

As to things that are of no relevance to us but cause no harm, nothing is easier than not to do them, in order to be close to God,[795] for "a good Muslim does not do what does not concern him." [796]

[794] Qur'ân 7.118 (115).

[795] Cf. Bombaci, p. 459.

[796] This is the famous, constantly quoted *ḥadîth* (cf. *Concordance*, I, 271*b*) that Abû Dâwûd, the author of one of the canonical *ḥadîth* collections, considered one of four traditions containing all the knowledge of traditions anyone needed. The other three are: "Actions (are judged) by intentions"; "a believer is a believer only when he wants for his brother the same things he wants for himself"; and "it is clear what is permitted, and it is clear what is forbidden. In between are ambiguous matters." Cf. al-Khaṭîb al-Baghdâdî, *Ta'rîkh Baghdâd*, IX, 57. Cf. pp. 251 and 299, below.

Thus, the religious law puts sorcery, talismans, and prestidigitation into one and the same class, because they may cause harm. It brands them as forbidden and illegal.

The speculative theologians said that the difference between miracles and sorcery lies in the "advance challenge" (*taḥaddî*),[797] that is, the claim that a (miracle) will occur just as it has been claimed (in advance that it would happen). It is not possible, they said, that a miracle could happen in agreement with the claim of a liar. Logic requires that a miracle indicate truthfulness. By definition, a miracle is something that can be verified. If it were performed with lying (intentions), it (could not be verified and thus) truth would have changed into falsehood, and that is absurd. Therefore, miracles never occur together with lying (intentions).[798]

As we have mentioned,[799] the philosophers assume that the difference between miracles and sorcery is the difference between the two extremes of good and evil. Nothing good issues from a sorcerer, and (sorcery) is not employed in good causes. Nothing evil issues from a worker of miracles, and (miracles) are not employed in evil causes. (Miracles and sorcery) are in a way contradictory by their very natures, as are good and evil.

"God guides whomever He wants to guide." [800]

The evil eye

III, *137* Another psychic influence is that of the eye—that is, an influence exercised by the soul of the person who has the evil eye.[801] A thing or situation appears pleasing to the eye of a person, and he likes it very much. This (circumstance) creates in him envy and the desire to take it away from its owner. Therefore, he prefers to destroy him.

It is a natural gift—I mean, the eye. The difference be-

[797] Cf. 1:188, and pp. 100 and 167, above.
[798] Cf. p. 100, above.
[799] Cf. p. 167, above.
[800] Qur'ân 2.142 (136), 213 (209), etc.
[801] Cf. E. Doutté, *Magie et religion dans l'Afrique du Nord*, p. 318.

tween it and the (other) [802] psychic influences is that it appears (and acts) as something natural and innate. It cannot be left alone. It does not depend on the free choice of its possessor. It is not acquired by him. Some of the other (psychic) influences may (also) not be acquired ones, but their appearance (in action) depends on the free choice of the person who exercises them. The thing that characterizes them as natural is their (possessors') potential ability to exercise them, not their (automatic) action.[803] Therefore it has been said: "A person who kills by means of sorcery or a miraculous act must be killed, but the person who kills with the eye must not be killed." The only reason for the (distinction) is that the (person who kills with the eye) did not want or intend to do so, nor could he have avoided doing so. The application (of the eye) was involuntary on his part.[804]

And God knows better.

[28] *The science of the secrets of letters.*

At the present time, this science is called *sîmiyâ'* "letter magic." [805] The word was transferred from talismans to this science and used in this conventional meaning in the technical terminology of Sufi practitioners of magic. Thus, a general (magical) term came to be used for some particular aspect (of magic).

This science originated in Islam after some time [806] of (its existence) had passed. When the extremist Sufis appeared, they turned to the removal of the veil of sense percep- III, *138*
tion, produced wonders, and were active in the world of the elements. At that time, they wrote systematic works on (Sufism) and (Sufi) terminology. They believed in the gradual descent of existence from the One. They believed that verbal perfection consists in helping the spirits of the

802 The following three lines are not in Bulaq.

803 Cf. Bombaci, p. 460.

804 Doutté, *op. cit.*, pp. 322 f., refers to different school opinions regarding the evil eye.

805 From Greek σημεῖα.

806 For *ṣadr*, cf. 1:373, and p. 53 (n. 361), above.

spheres and the stars (through words). The natures and secrets of the letters are alive in the words, while the words, in turn, are correspondingly alive in the created things. The created things have been moving in the different stages of (creation) and telling its secrets since the first creation. These (Sufi beliefs) caused the science of the secrets of the letters to originate. It is a subdivision of the science of *sîmiyâ'* "letter magic." It is an unfathomable subject with innumerable problems. Al-Bûnî,[807] Ibn al-'Arabî, and others in their wake wrote numerous works on it. These authors assume that the result and fruit of letter magic is that the divine souls are active in the world of nature by means of the beautiful names of God and the divine expressions that originate from the letters comprising the secrets that are alive in the created things.

The authorities on letter magic then differed as to the secret of the (magic) activity lying in the letters. Some of them assumed that it was due to inherent temper. They divided the letters into four groups corresponding to the elements. Each nature (element) had its own group of letters. Through this group (of letters), it can be active actively and passively. A technical procedure, which the (authorities on letter magic) call "breaking down" (*taksîr*),[808] classifies the letters as the elements are classified, as fiery, airy, watery, and earthy. The *alif* is fiery, *b* airy, *j* watery, and *d* earthy.
III, *139* Then, it starts again with the next letter, and so on, through the whole alphabet and the sequence of the elements. Thus, seven letters are fiery, namely, *alif*, *h*, *ṭ*, *m*, *f*, *s*, and *dh*.

[807] Aḥmad b. 'Alî. Cf. *GAL*, I, 497 f.; *Suppl.*, I, 910 f. For the date of death indicated in *GAL*, 622 [1225], there seems to be no better authority than Ḥâjjî Khalîfah, *Kashf aẓ-ẓunûn*, IV, 75. The printed edition of al-Bûnî's *Shams al-ma'ârif* (Cairo, 1321/1903), apparently a reproduction of the edition of 1291/1874, seems to refer to later dates such as 670 (I, 42), and to Ibn Sab'în, d. 669 (I, 51). The mystical pedigree of al-Bûnî (IV, 103) would also suggest a late seventh [thirteenth] century date for him. However, there is a MS of one of his works in Berlin, No. 4126, dated 669. Thus, he probably lived *ca.* A.D. 1200. The apparent lack of influence on al-Bûnî by Ibn 'Arabî would not, however, rule out his flourishing at a later period.

[808] Cf. pp. 183 and 225, below.

Seven are airy, namely, *b, w, y, n, ḍ, t, and ẓ*. Seven are watery, namely, *j, z, k, ṣ, q, th,* and *gh*. And seven are earthy, namely, *d, ḥ, l, 'ayn, r, kh,* and *sh*.[809]

The fiery letters serve to repel cold diseases and to increase the power of heat wherever desired, either in the sensual (physical) or in the astrological (sense). Thus, for instance, (one may want to) increase the power of Mars for warfare, the killing (of enemies), and aggressiveness.

In the same way, the watery letters serve to repel hot diseases, such as fevers and others, and to increase the cold powers, wherever desired, either in the sensual (physical) sense or in the astrological (sense). Thus, for instance, (one may want to) increase the power of the moon, and so on.

Other (authorities on letter magic) assumed that the secret of the (magic) activity that lies in the letters was their numerical proportion. The letters of the alphabet indicate numerical values which by convention and nature are generally accepted to be (inherent in) them. Thus, there exists a relationship between the letters themselves as a result of the relationship of their numerical values. For instance, there is a relationship between *b, k,* and *r,* because all three of them indicate two in its different positions. (The letter) *b* indicates two in the units, *k* indicates two in the tens (20), and *r* indicates two in the hundreds (200). Or, there is a special relationship between the letters mentioned and *d, m,* and *t*. The

[809] The order of the alphabet is according to the numerical values of the letters as employed in the West, which is:

alif	1	*y*	10	*q*	100
b	2	*k*	20	*r*	200
j	3	*l*	30	*s*	300
d	4	*m*	40	*t*	400
h	5	*n*	50	*th*	500
w	6	*ṣ*	60	*kh*	600
z	7	*'ayn*	70	*dh*	700
ḥ	8	*f*	80	*ẓ*	800
ṭ	9	*ḍ*	90	*gh*	900
				sh	1000

In the East, 60 is *s*; 90 is *ṣ*; 300 *sh*; 800 *ḍ*; 900 *ẓ*; and 1000 *gh*. Cf. also 1:236, 2:190, 194, above, and p. 220, below, as well as P. Kraus, *Jâbir Ibn Ḥayyân*, II, 223 ff.

(latter group of letters) indicates four, and the proportion of four to two is that of two to one. Then, there are magic
III, *140* squares for words as there are for numbers. Each group of letters has its particular kind of magic square which fits it in view either of the numerical value of the figure [810] or of the numerical value of the letters. (Magic) activity based on letter magic thus merges with that based on number magic, because there exists a relationship between letters and numbers.

The real significance of the relationship existing between letters and natural humors and between letters and numbers is difficult to understand. It is not a matter of science or reasoning. According to the (authorities on letter magic), it is based on mystical experience and the removal (of the veil). Al-Bûnî said, "One should not think that one can get at the secret of the letters with the help of logical reasoning. One gets to it with the help of vision and divine aid."

The fact that it is possible to be active in the world of nature with the help of the letters and the words composed of them, and that the created things can be influenced in this way, cannot be denied. It is confirmed by continuous tradition on the authority of many (practitioners of letter magic).

It has been thought that this activity and the activity of people who work with talismans are one and the same thing. This is not so. The people who work with talismans have made it clear that the influence of a talisman actually comes from spiritual powers derived from the substance of force. These powers exercise a powerful and forceful activity upon the things for which the (talisman) is composed, with the help of spherical secrets, numerical proportions, and vapors that attract the spirituality of the talisman and are mentally enclosed in it. The result is that the high natures come to be

[810] Possibly Ibn Khaldûn is thinking of squares designed so that the total of the numbers in the whole figure represents the numerical value of some word such as Allâh; cf. below, p. 177 (n. 816). Or, perhaps the word *'adad* in *'adad ash-shakl* is superfluous and a mistake, and *shakl* "figure" refers to entire words as they were used in constructing magic squares.

tied to the low ones. Talismans, they think, are like a ferment composed of and including earthy, airy, watery, and fiery (elements). Such ferment is instrumental in transforming and changing anything into which it might get, into its own essence and in turning it into its own form. The III, *141*
elixir[811] for metals, likewise, is a ferment that by transformation turns the mineral in which it is alive into itself. Therefore, it has been said that the subject of alchemy is body (substance) in body (substance), because all parts of an elixir are corporeal (substances). The subject of talismans, on the other hand, is spirit in body (substance),[812] because talismans tie the high natures to the low natures. The low natures are bodies (substances), while the high natures are spiritualities.[813]

One should realize that all (magic) activity in the world of nature comes from the human soul and the human mind, because the human soul essentially encompasses and governs nature. Consequently, the real difference between the activity of people who work with talismans and people who work with words is as follows. The activity of people who work with talismans consists in bringing down the spirituality of the spheres and tying it down with the help of pictures or numerical proportions. The result is a kind of composition that, through its nature, effects a transformation and change comparable to those effected by a ferment in the thing into which it gets. The activity of people who work with words, on the other hand, is the effect of the divine light and the support of the Lord which they obtain through exertion and the removal (of the veil). Thus, nature is forced to work (for them) and does so willingly with no attempt at disobedience. Their activity needs no support from the spherical powers or anything else, because the support it has is of a higher order than (all that).

811 Cf. pp. 268 f., below.
812 Cf. p. 166, above, and (Pseudo-)Majrîṭî, *Ghâyah*, p. 39.
813 For this paragraph, cf. *ibid.*, pp. 7 f.

People who work with talismans, therefore, need (only) a little exercise to give the soul the power to bring down the spirituality of the spheres. Devotions and exercises certainly
III, *142* play a very insignificant role in it. The opposite is the case with people who work with words. Their exercise is the most extensive that can be. It is not for the purpose of being active in the existing things, since that is a veil (standing between them and their real task). Such activity comes to them accidentally, as an act of divine grace.[814] A person who works with words may have no knowledge of the secrets of God and the realities of divinity, which is the result of vision and the removal (of the veil). He may restrict himself to the various relationships between words and the natures of letters and expressions, and he may become (magically) active with them in this capacity, and that is what people who practice letter magic are commonly supposed to do. But then, there is no difference between such a person and the people who work with talismans. In fact, a person who works with talismans is more reliable than he, because he has recourse to scientific natural principles and orderly norms. A person who works with the secrets of words but is not sincere in his devotion[815] and (in addition) has no technical norms of evidence on which he may rely and, therefore, lacks the removal (of the veil) that would show him the realities of expressions and the influence of relationships, is in a weaker position (than a person who works with talismans).

The person who works with words may mingle the powers of expressions and words with the powers of the stars. He may then set certain times for mentioning the beautiful names of God or the magic squares composed of them or, indeed, any word.[816] These times must be under the propi-

[814] Cf. Bombaci, p. 460.

[815] Cf. Bombaci, pp. 460 f.

[816] Such magic squares, for instance, as the *badûḥ* type, where letters take the place of numerals; cf. T. Canaan in *Berytus*, IV (1937), 100 ff. Or, the *Allâh* type, in which the squares may be filled with numerals equivalent in their total to the numerical value of the letters of the word Allâh (sixty-six). Cf. Canaan, *op. cit.*, p. 79:

tious influence of the star[817] that is related to a particular word. That was done, for instance, by al-Bûnî in his book entitled *al-Anmâṭ*.[818] The relationship (between star and magic word) is assumed to come from the nubilous (*'amâ-'îyah*) presence,[819] which is the purgatory station (*barzakhîyah*) of verbal perfection and which particularizes itself in the III, *143*
realities in accordance with the relationship they have (to the magic words [?]). They think that those expressions[820] depend on vision to be established. If a person who works with words lacks vision but knows about that relationship through

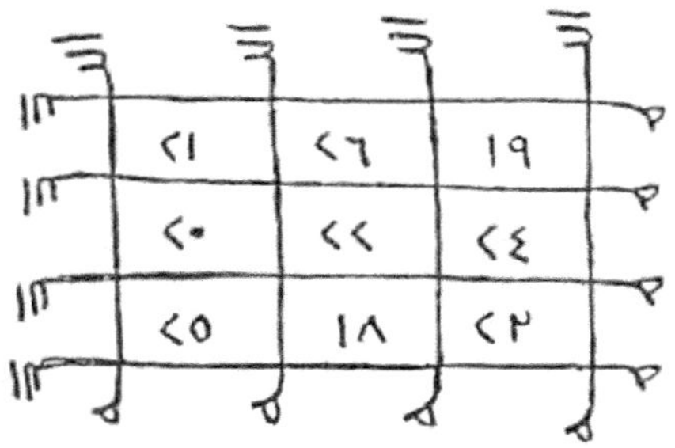

There is also a type of magic square consisting of phrases so arranged; cf., for instance, al-Bûnî, *Lum'ah* (Cairo, n.d.), where Qur'ân 2.37 (35) is thus distributed:

فتاب	كلمات	ربه	من	آدم	فتلقى
عليه	فتاب	كلمات	ربه	من	آدم
انه	عليه	فتاب	كلمات	ربه	من
هو	انه	عليه	فتاب	كلمات	ربه
التواب	هو	انه	عليه	فتاب	كلمات
الرحيم	التواب	هو	انه	عليه	فتاب

[817] *Al-kawkab,* as in C.

[818] *GAL,* I, 497 f.; *Suppl.,* I, 910, knows no such title, but it may be noted that the *Shams al-ma'ârif* has ten chapters (xxi–xxx) dealing with the beautiful names of God, arranged in *anmâṭ*.

[819] Cf. p. 88, above.

[820] Bulaq has "that relationship."

tradition, his actions correspond to those of the person who works with talismans. Indeed, as we have stated, the (latter) is more reliable than he.

In the same way, the person who works with talismans may mingle his actions and the powers of the stars which govern them, with the powers of prayers composed of special expressions indicating a relationship between those expressions and the stars. In his case, however, the relationship of expressions is not, as in the case of people who work with words, the result of direct observation in a state of vision. It is merely based upon the (general) basic requirement of the magic approach, namely, that the stars share in all the substances, accidents, essences, and ideas [821] existing in the world of created things. Letters and words belong to the things that exist in it. Thus, each star has its particular share in them. On this basis (magical practitioners) construct strange and disapproved theories. Namely, they divide the *sûrahs* and verses of the Qur'ân in this manner. That was what Maslamah al-Majrîṭî, for instance, did in the *Ghâyah*. It is also obvious from al-Bûnî's attitude in the *Anmâṭ* that he takes this method into consideration. A critical study of the *Anmâṭ* and of the prayers the work contains and their distribution among the hours of the seven stars, as well as a look at the *Ghâyah* and a critical study of the prayers (*qiyâmât*) of the stars contained in it [822] — "*qiyâmât* of the stars" is the name they give to the
III, *144* prayers that belong to each individual star, that is, the prayer performed (*yuqâmu bihâ*) for it — will show that this (procedure) belongs to the substance of (these works on letter magic) or that the relationship that came about in the original creation and in the purgatory (*barzakh*) of knowledge made all that necessary.

"And you were given but little knowledge." [823]

One cannot deny the actual existence of all the sciences

[821] Cf. Bombaci, p. 461.
[822] Cf. (Pseudo-)Majrîṭî, *Ghâyah*, pp. 195 ff., 225.
[823] Qur'ân 17.85 (87).

declared illegal by the religious law. It is definite that sorcery is true, although it is forbidden. But we are satisfied with the knowledge God taught us.

A few remarks (may help) to make things clear.[824]

Letter magic clearly is a kind of sorcery and, as such, attainable through various exercises which are legal according to the religious law. This comes about as follows. We have mentioned before [825] that two kinds of human beings are active in the world of created beings.[826] Prophets (are active) with the help of the divine power which God gave them by nature. Sorcerers (are active) with the help of the psychic power which is innate in them.

Saints may be active by acquiring the ability to be active through faith (*al-kalimah al-îmânîyah*). It is a result of detachment (from the *sensibilia*). They do not have it intentionally. It comes to them spontaneously. If it happens to mighty saints, they avoid it and take refuge in God against it and consider it a temptation.[827] There is, for instance, the story of Abû Yazîd al-Bisṭâmî.[828] One evening, when he reached the bank of the Tigris, he was in a hurry.[829] The two banks of the river came together (so that he would have been able to cross right over), but Abû Yazîd invoked

[824] The following remarks, down through p. 182, are not found in Bulaq. A and C have them on a special inserted sheet. The handwriting on the special sheet in A is quite remarkable in that it seems similar to that used for additions to C.

[825] Cf. p. 167, above.

[826] *Sic* C and D. The earlier texts have "nature."

[827] Cf. p. 102, above. "And consider it a temptation" appears in C and D.

[828] "Al-Bisṭâmî" is added in C and D. Cf. p. 102, above. The story is told in the name of Abû Yazîd in Ibn al-Jawzî, *Ṣifat aṣ-ṣafwah* (Hyderabad 1355–56/1936–37), IV, 91. In as-Sarrâj, *Luma'*, ed. Nicholson (E. J. W. Gibb Memorial Series, No. 22) (Leiden & London, 1914), pp. 324 f., Abû Yazîd is repeatedly quoted as being against *karâmât*, but the above story is told in the name of another famous Sufi, Abû l-Ḥusayn an-Nûrî. For Abû Yazîd's negative attitude toward *karâmât*, cf. also al-Qushayrî, *Risâlah*, p. 164.

[829] *Mutaḥaffizan?* or *munḥafizan*, as in A, and apparently also in B, C, and D?

God's protection and said, "I will not sell my share in God for a farthing (*dânaq*)." So, he boarded a boat and crossed over with the ferrymen.

An innate ability for sorcery requires exercise, in order to be capable of transformation from potentiality into actuality. Some (magical ability) which is not innate may be acquired, but such (acquired magical ability) is inferior to innate (magical ability). One (would, in any case, have to) exercise to (acquire magical ability), as one does on behalf of (innate
III, *145* magical ability). The (procedure of) such magical exercise is well known. Its various kinds and the ways in which it is executed[830] are mentioned by Maslamah al-Majrîṭî in the *Kitâb al-Ghâyah* and by Jâbir b. Ḥayyân in his *Treatises*, as well as by others. They are employed by many people who want to acquire magical ability and learn its norms and the conditions governing it.

However,[831] this magical exercise of early (practitioners) is full of matters of unbelief. For instance, it includes devotions directed to the stars and prayers to them, called *qiyâmât*,[832] for the purpose of attracting their spirituality. It also includes the belief in influences by (beings) other than God, in that (one's) actions are tied to magical horoscopes and the mutual aspects of the stars in the signs (of the zodiac), in order to obtain the desired results.

* Many people who wished to be (magically) active in the world of existing things were arrested by this (fact). They wanted to obtain the (ability to be magically active) in a way that would have nothing to do with any involvement in unbelief and the practice of it. They turned their exercise into one that was legal according to the religious law. It con-

Many people want to be (magically) active but want to avoid having anything to do with any involvement in sorcery and the name and technicalities of sorcery. Therefore, they

[830] *Wa-kayfîyâtihâ.*

[831] The upper text is that of C and D, the lower that of A and B.

[832] Cf. p. 178, above.

sisted of *dhikr* exercises and prayers (*subuḥât*) from the Qur'ân and the Prophetic traditions. They learned which of these things were appropriate for (their particular) need from the afore-mentioned division of the world with its essences, attributes, and actions according to the influences of the seven stars. In addition, they also selected the days and hours appropriate to the distribution of (the influences of the stars). They used this kind of legal exercise as a cover, in order to avoid having anything to do with ordinary sorcery, which is unbelief or calls for unbelief. They kept to a legal (kind of) devotion because of its general and honest character. That was done, for instance, by al-Bûnî in his *Kitâb al-Anmâṭ* and other works of his, and by others. They called this approach "letter magic," since they were very eager to avoid the name of sorcery. In fact, (however,) they fall under III, *146*
the idea of sorcery, even though they have a legal (kind of) devotion. They are not at all free from the belief in influences by (beings) other than God.

These people also want to be (magically) active in the world of existing things. That is something forbidden by

choose a special exercise consisting of prayers (subuḥât) *and* dhikr *exercises. They are legal according to the religious law and yet they correspond to magical exercise in the kind of devotion and the expressions used. They choose the time of certain ascendants, as is done by the people (the learned magicians). They refrain from having any harmful intentions in their devotion, so that, in this manner, they may have nothing to do with sorcery. But they are far off the mark in this (assumption). Any devotion in the intention of being (magically) active is the very same thing as sorcery. Moreover, if one looks at it carefully, the exercise of these people evokes (the idea of) magical exercise in view of the expressions used in it, as (one finds them) in the* Anmâṭ *and other works of al-Bûnî.*

Now, if the assumption is erroneous that this is a legal way of obtaining the ability to be (magically) active, it should be avoided. One should realize that (magical) activity from the

the Lawgiver (Muḥammad). The miracles performed by the prophets were performed at God's command. He gave the power to perform them. The miracles of the saints were performed, because by means of the creation [833] of a necessary knowledge, through inspiration or something else, they obtained (divine) permission to perform them. They did not intend to perform them without permission.

Thus, the trickery of the people who practice letter magic should not be trusted. As I have made it clear, letter magic is a subdivision and kind of sorcery.

God guides toward the truth through His kindness.*

The Zâ'irajah [834]

A branch of the science of letter magic, (practiced) among the (authorities on letter magic), is (the technique of) finding out answers from questions by means of connections existing between the letters of the expressions (used in the question). They imagine that these (connections) can form the basis for knowing the future happenings they want to know. Here we have something like puzzles and trick problems.[835] There are many discussions of the subject by them. The most compre-

very beginning is not legal and that the great saints keep away from it. The (great saints) who practiced it did so because they had permission, through inspiration or something else. Also, saints are (magically) active through faith (al-kalimah al-îmânîyah), *and not through psychic power.*

This is the true character of letter magic. As one can see, it is a subdivision and kind of sorcery.

God guides toward the truth through His kindness.

[833] *Bi-khalq.*

[834] Cf. the discussion of as-Sabtî's *Zâ'irajah of the World,* 1:238 ff., above.

[835] *Al-masâ'il as-sayyâlah.* The last word may be derived from the root *sa'ala* "to ask," or rather be connected with the ordinary word *sayyâl* "fluid, changeable" (cf. *Ghâyah,* p. 3, l. 6), but the precise meaning, though clear from the context, is not known.

hensive and most remarkable discussion of it is as-Sabtî's *Zâ'irajah of the World*. It has been mentioned before. Here, we shall explain what has been said about how to operate it. We shall quote the poem that, it is thought, as-Sabtî wrote on the subject.[836] Then, we shall give a description of the *Zâ'irajah* with its circle and the table written on the verso.[836a] Finally, we shall reveal the truth about it. It is nothing supernatural; (the indications derived from it) result from an agreement in the wording of question and answer. It is (just) one interesting way among others, and a curious one, for finding out the answer from the question with the help III, *147*
of the technique called the technique of "breaking down." [837] We have referred to all this before.

We have no authoritative tradition on which we might rely for the correctness of the poem and its attribution to as-Sabtî.[838] However, we have chosen (for our quotation) what gave the impression of being the best manuscript. This is the poem: [839]

There speaks a little Ceutian,[840] praising his Lord,
Praying for a guide who was God's messenger to mankind, (namely,)
Muḥammad who was sent as a prophet, the Seal of the Prophets,

[836] This sentence is not found in Bulaq.

[836a] The Arabic word used here, to be vocalized *muḥawwal,* must have acquired this meaning from its original meaning "changed (over)." For the *Zâ'irajah* table, see folding chart in pocket, end of this vol.

[837] Cf. p. 172, above, and p. 225, below. This sentence is not in Bulaq.

[838] "And its attribution to as-Sabtî" is found in the margin of C and in the text of D.

[839] As he says himself, Ibn Khaldûn did not quite understand the following poem, and our understanding of it cannot be expected to be much better. Probably only its author fully understood it, and even that is not entirely certain. A thorough study of the related literature and some bold interpretations will, I am sure, greatly improve upon the translation given here. The obvious flaws, it is hoped, will challenge some specialist on the history of magic to work on it successfully. At least, I feel that E. Doutté, *Magie et religion dans l'Afrique du Nord*, p. 381, was unduly pessimistic with regard to Ibn Khaldûn's section on the *Zâ'irajah.*

[840] I.e., as-Sabtî.

And expressing his satisfaction [841] with the men around him and those who followed them:
Behold, this is the *Zâ'irajah of the World* which
You [sing.] see revealed through your [pl.] senses, and through the intellect.
Whoever knows how to compose (the *zâ'irajah*) will know his body,
And will obtain laws given from on high.
Whoever knows how to tie (it down) will obtain power
And be noted for having obtained the fear of God and everything.[842]
He is seen taking on reality in the divine world.
This is the station of those who are perfected through *dhikr* exercises.
These are the secrets that you have to keep concealed.
III, *148* Set them up in circles and balance (them) with *ḥ*
And with *ṭ* which has a "throne" on which it is engraved,
In poetry and prose, or which one sees arranged as a table.
Set up circles corresponding to the relationship of their spheres
And draw stars for their highest degrees.
Come out for its strings (chords), and draw letters for them,
And repeat the same (letters) on the border of those that are free.
Set up the shape of their *zîr*,[843] and make its houses,
And verify with a *bamm* wherever their light is apparent.

[841] The "prayer for a guide" refers to the use of the formula *ṣallâ llâhu ʿalayhi wa-sallama*, and the "satisfaction" refers to the formula *raḍiya llâhu ʿanhum*.

[842] Bulaq has another verse which may have been left out of the later texts by mistake:

Whoever knows how to apply (it) will know his (own) reality
And understand his soul and become a true saint.

[843] *Zîr* is the treble string in musical terminology. *Bamm* is the bass string, and *mathnâ* and *mathlath*, mentioned later on, are the second and third strings, respectively. For identification of the strings of the lute with the elements, the humors, the planets, etc., cf., for instance, H. G. Farmer, *The Minstrelsy of "The Arabian Nights"* (Bearsden [Scot.], 1945), p. 14.

Present sciences as an engineer for the natures (elements),
And an established knowledge of figurations and the quadrants.
Work with music and the knowledge of their[844] letters
And the knowledge of an instrument. And verify and bring about
And make circles and set down their letters in the right relationship.
Set free their world and list the zones in a table.
We have an amir[845] who desires Bougie for a Zanâtah
Dynasty, which has appeared and which has manifestly seized power,
And a region of Spain, then [. . .][846]
The Banû Naṣr [?] came, and their victory followed.
Rulers, knights, and people of wisdom,
If you wish, write them down. Their region is empty. III, *149*
A Mahdî of the Almohads who rule in Tunis,
Rulers for an East set down in magic squares,[847]
Cast a spell over the region, and believe.
If you wish, represent (it) in Latin without linguistic error,
And (Al)fonso and Barcelona. *R* is the letter for it.
Their Franc(is) is *dh*,[848] and is perfected with *ṭ*.
Rulers of Kinâwah.[849] They have pointed to their *q*.[850]

844 Masculine plural, according to Bulaq and the MSS.

845 The reference seems to be to the Almohad ruler Ya'qûb al-Manşûr [1184–1199], under whom as-Sabtî is supposed to have lived.

846 "A son to their (the Spanish) Hûd [?]" looks like a reference to the Hudites of Saragossa, but such a reference would be very difficult to explain chronologically. If, in the following line, the Banû Naşr, the Naşrids of Granada, should actually be meant, the poem would have originated some decades after Ya'qûb al-Manşûr. But the Naşrids scarcely fit in the context, as far as it can be made out. The meter also seems to be disturbed.

847 *Sic* A, C, and D. B: "in the horizons."

848 Or "*d*," although the MSS seem to have *dhâka* "that."

849 According to Yâqût, *Mu'jam al-buldân*, IV, 307, Kinâwah is a Berber tribe and country adjacent to the Ghânah Negroes, which is identical with Qanâwah, Janâwah = Gnâwah "Sudan Negroes." Cf. G. Ferrand, "Le *Tuḥfat al-albâb* de Abû Ḥâmid al-Andalusî al-Ġarnâṭî," *Journal asiatique*, CCVII (1925), 285.

850 The MSS have *li-fâqihim* [?].

And the Arabs, our people, have been weakened.
Abyssinian India and Sind (Western India), then Hurmus [?]
And Tatar Persians, and what beyond them. . . .
Their Byzantine Emperor is a *ḥ*. Their (Persian) Yazdjard
Belongs to *k*. Their Copt was written with a long *l*,
And 'Abbâs, all of them noble and venerable.
But (they are) a Turk when the (magical) activity ceases.
If you want to know the rulers exactly and to find them out,
Seal fields, then bring (them) into relation and list (them) in a table
According to the norm and science of the letters
And the knowledge of their nature, and set up the whole of it.
Whoever knows the sciences will know our science.
III, *150* He will know the secrets of existence and become perfect.
He, then, has firmly rooted knowledge and knows His Lord,
And has a knowledge of predictions which is broken down through *ḥ-m*.
And whenever there comes a name, and the meter prefers it,[851]
A wise man will definitely decide that he must be killed.
Letters will come to you. Then, try to pick them.
The letters of Sîbawayh will come to you disconnected.
Then, strengthen with transformations and confront and exchange.
With your precious warble shake the parts.

Select a (star) rise. Figure out its signs.
Reverse its root [?]. Straighten (it) out with the cycle.

[851] *Yushiffuhû* seems a possible reading of the MSS.

Someone will perceive those things. He will achieve his purpose
And be given their letters in whose arrangement the evidence lies.
If it is lucky and the stars are lucky,
It should suffice you to have royal authority [?] and to have reached the dim star (δ) in Ursa Major on high [?]. III, *151*
The melody of their *d* with its bridled *bamm!*
Thus, sound harmonic chimes, and you will find the right place in it,
The strings of their *zîr*. To the *ḥ* belongs their *bamm*
And their *mathnâ*. The *mathlath* has appeared through its *j*.
Make entries with spheres. Straighten things out with a table.
Draw *a b c* and the remaining letters of the alphabet according to their numerical value
And permit the irregularity of the meter that occurs. Something similar
Has occurred in the prosody of a number of people.
A principle of our religion, a principle of our jurisprudence,
And some knowledge of grammar, keep and obtain!
Bring in the wall [?] for a large tent in harmony [?]!
Praise His name and say, "God is great," and "There is no God but God,"
And you will (succeed in) bringing out verses on any desired object
Through natural rhyme and a secret from on high.
If they are thus brought together, the judgment implied in their number will be acquired,[852]
And . . .
And you will bring out verses. Twenty multiplied

[852] *Leg. wa-yuqnâ bi-ḥaṣrihâ* [?].

III, *152* By one thousand by nature, O master of the Table,
Will show crafts of multiplication that are perfect.
Thus, (your) wishes will come out right for you, and the (world) on high will come out right for you.
And rhyme with their *zîr* and praise with a beat.
Set it up in circles for a *zîr*, and obtain (it).
Set it up with magic squares and a principle that you prepare
From the secrets of their letter, and bring it back in chain form.

[SIGNS] [853]

Discussion of how to discover the relationships and qualities of the weights,[854] the powers of their opposites, the power of the grade which is distinguished according to the relationship to the place of attached mixtures of natures (elements), and the science of medicine, or the craft of alchemy.

O student of medicine and of Jâbir's science (alchemy),[855]
And you who know the extent of the powers in succession,
If you want the science of medicine, there must exist a relationship
For the laws of scales, which [856] will hit upon a (possible) way.
III, *153* Your patient will be cured. The elixir will be right.
The soundness of the mixtures of your composition will be apparent.

[853] In this case, as also on the following pages, the "signs" are mainly *zimâm* numerals. See n. 882 to this chapter, below. Occasionally there are other numerals, letters, and magic signs. As far as I can see, these "signs" do not ever occur in the same combinations in the table.

[854] *Awzân* "weights" refers to *mîzân* "scale," which appears in the following verses and for which one may compare the chapter on the "Théorie de la balance" in P. Kraus, *Jâbir Ibn Ḥayyân*, II, 187 ff.

[855] Cf. p. 228, below.

[856] Or: "and you will hit." Cf. p. 191, l. 4, below.

Spiritual Medicine

And you want Îlâwush [857]—[SIGNS]—and his mind. . .
For Bahrâm-Birjîs [858] and seven, who is perfect,
For dissolving pains of cold diseases. Make it correct
This way, and (make) the composition (correct) wherever it has been handed down.

[SIGNS]

Appearances of rays that concern the nativities of rulers and their children.

The knowledge of rays cast is difficult.
The side of their bows shows itself in a belt [?].
But on a pilgrimage, there is the place where our imam stands.
He appears when the latitude of the stars is straightened out.
There are positions whose longitude is made clear,
And (also their) latitude. By reaching that, he becomes a junction [?].
Places where there is a quartile with its sign in the dejection,
Their sextile has the trine of the sign of the one that follows. III, *154*
One adds to the quartile. That is its analogy
In certainty, and its root [?]. With the *'ayn*, it is made to work.
From the relationship of the two quarters combine your rays
With a ṣ and double it. Its quartile will thus show itself.

[SIGNS]

857 Helios, the sun.
858 Bahrâm is Mars, and Birjîs Jupiter.

This operation here concerns rulers. The operation of the rule is consistent. Nothing more remarkable has ever been seen.

The position of rulers:

First position
Second position
Third position
Fourth position [*zimâm* NUMERALS FOR EACH POSITION]
Fifth position
Sixth position
Seventh position

The line of junction and separation:

[SIGNS]

The line of junction:

[SIGNS]

The line of separation:

[SIGNS]

The *zîr* for every(thing) and the complete follower of the root [?]:

[SIGNS]

Junction and separation:

[SIGNS]

The complete necessary (line) in junctions:

[SIGNS]

The establishments of lights:

[SIGNS]

The answering root [?] in the operation:

[SIGNS]

The establishment of questions concerning rulers:

[SIGNS]

The position of children:

The position of light:

[SIGNS]

The position of splendor:

[SIGNS]

(On) being spiritually influenced and divinely guided: III, *155*

O student of the secret of praising (the oneness) of God,
With the beautiful names of God [859] you will hit upon a (possible) way.
The Rabbis of mankind will obey you with their heart(s),
As well as [860] their chief. It is operated in the sun [??].
You will see all mankind tied to you

If you wish, you will live in (the world of) existence together with the fear of God
And solid religion, or you will be firmly rooted [861]
Like Dhû n-Nûn [862] and al-Junayd [863] together with the secret of an art.
I see you clothed in the secret of Bisṭâm.[864]
You will come into being created in the world on high,
As the Indians have said, and the Sufi crowd.
The path of the Messenger of God sparkles with the truth.
No work of a quality similar to (that of) Gabriel has yet been invented.
Your courage is saying, "There is no God but God," and your bow is the (East where the sun) rises [?].
Thursday is the beginning. Sunday appears.
On a Friday, too, the same (will be done [?]) with the names,
And on Monday, you will perfect the beautiful names of God. III, *156*

[859] The meter of the verse is in disorder.
[860] *Ka-dhâka:* C and D.
[861] *Mu'aṣṣalan.*
[862] The famous Sufi, d. 246 [861]. Cf. *GAL*, I, 198 f.; *Suppl.*, I, 353.
[863] Cf. 2:187, above.
[864] The reference is to Abû Yazîd al-Bisṭâmî. Cf. p. 102, above.

In its *ṭ*, there is a secret, as well as in its *h*.

At the end of the Resurrection, it is followed by a prayer
And sincere devotion, with the seven *mathânî*[865] being chanted.

The junction of the lights of the stars:

[SIGNS]

In your right hand, there is an iron (ring) and a seal
. . . but not in prayer.
Make (your) heart the tablet (to write on) the verse of Resurrection.
Recite and chant (it) when people are asleep.
It is the secret contained in the created beings; there is nothing but it.
It is the greatest verse. Therefore, make (it) accurate and get (it).
Through it, you will become a "pole" if you serve well.
You will perceive secrets from the world on high.
Sarî communicated them and, after him, Ma'rûf.[866]
Al-Ḥallâj[867] divulged them and was killed.
III, *157* Ash-Shiblî[868] always worked on them,
Until he went up higher than the (ordinary) Sufis and was exalted.
Therefore, clean your heart eagerly from impurities.
Practice *dhikr* exercises constantly. Fast. Do supererogatory devotions.

[865] Cf. Qur'ân 15.87 (87). The first *sûrah* is meant.

[866] The famous Sufis, Ma'rûf al-Karkhî, d. 200 or 204 [815/16 or 819/20], and as-Sarî as-Saqaṭî, d. 253 [867]. Cf. al-Khaṭîb al-Baghdâdî, *Ta'rîkh Baghdâd*, XII, 199–209; IX, 187–92.

Bulaq corrects "after" to "before."

[867] Cf. p. 102, above.

[868] Abû Bakr ash-Shiblî, d. 334 or 335 [946]. Cf. *GAL*, I, 199 f.; *Suppl.*, I, 357.

The secret of the people (the mystics) has been attained
only by thorough (devotees)
Who knew the secret of the sciences and were competent.

[SIGNS]

The position of love, of the inclination of the souls, of exertion, obedience, worship, love, infatuation, annihilation of annihilation (non-being), devotion, observance, and friendship [869] with permanent physical passivity.

Birjîs [870] has the magic square for love.
The mixture has been prepared with tin or copper which
were caused to work,
Or with silver. Correct I have seen it.
Your making its lucky position an ascendant is not improper.[871]
Try to get through it an increase of light for the moon.
Your making its sun ready to accept [872] is something
firmly grounded.
Put it to sleep with the incense being aloe wood belonging to their India,
And fix an hour. Its prayer is a benefit [?].
Its prayer is for a purpose. Thus, it is caused to work.
Its prayer from Ṭaysamân, which is ornamented, III, *158*
Is used, or a prayer for whose composition letters
Or problems are prepared with hot air.
You shall engrave letters with *d* and its *l*.
That is a magic square which consists of sixteen fields.
If their indication [?] does not please you,

Make good its *b*, and bring them away to [873]

[869] *Khullah* [?].
[870] I.e., Jupiter. Cf. p. 189, above.
[871] *Leg. ghalâ* [?].
[872] Or: "your making (it ready) to accept its sun."
[873] *Leg. wa-nâ'i bihim ilâ* [?].

That which pleases you. The small remainder of them is summarized.
Engrave certain shapes from some of them.
Whatever you add, make it proportionate, equal to your action
And the key of Maryam. For the actions of both of them are alike.
A call went out, and a Bisṭâmî recited her (Maryam's) *sûrah.*
Let your acting (be) with support. Search for
The proofs of a savage person who was set up for his text.
Turn over its [874] houses with a thousand and more.
Inside it, there is a secret. In the search for it, it has become apparent.

III, *159* On the stations for the end.

You have the supernatural, a picture from the world on high.
You make it find a house. Its clothing is jewelry.
Beautiful like Joseph—this one, similar to him,
Was sent down with . . . and a chant of reality.[875]
He is powerful and speaks about the supernatural.
He resembles a lute that competes with a nightingale.
Buhlûl [876] went crazy from love of her beauty.
When she appeared to Bisṭâm, he was forsaken
And died. . . . The love of her was instilled into
Junayd and Baṣrî.[877] They (he) neglected (their, his) body.
The ultimate in praise (of the oneness) of God is sought. Whoever has
God's beautiful names for himself without any relationship,
And whoever possesses them, succeeds with wisdom

[874] Referring to the *sûrah?* "Houses," of course, could be "fields."
[875] The MSS seem to read something like: *bytr wa-tartîli ḥaqîqatin*
[876] Or Bahlûl. Cf. *GAL, Suppl.*, I, 350.
[877] That is, al-Ḥasan al-Baṣrî. Cf. 2:184, above.

And attains nearness to the neighbors of (the world) on high.
You will be informed about the supernatural,[878] if you render good service,
Which will show you remarkable things, to Him who is a refuge.
This is true success. (It is) goodness that attains it. III, *160*
From (those things), there result additions for their interpretation which follows [?].

Testament, final statement, faith, Islam, prohibition, and suitability.

This is our poem. Ninety is its number
And the additional (verses) for introduction, end, and table.
I am surprised by verses, whose number is ninety,
Which produce (more) verses whose complete number is not apparent.
Whosoever understands the secret, let him understand himself,
And let him understand an ambiguous commentary which is difficult,
Forbidden and lawful, in order to show our secret
To people, even if they are a select group and have the suitable qualification.
If you want people suitable for it, place them under a strong oath.
Maltreat them[879] with manliness and extended religiosity.
Perhaps you will be saved, as well as the one who hears their secret,
From deciding to divulge (it), and you will become a chief on high.
A son of 'Abbâs keeps his secret hidden.
Thus, he obtained much happiness, and high rank followed him.

[878] The meter is corrupted.
[879] *Wa-buq-hum.*

III, 161 The Messenger of God rose among the people as preacher,

The spirits have boarded bodies to manifest themselves [?],
And have applied themselves, in order to kill them, by prolonged knocking
At the high world. Our nonexistence becomes nonexistent,
And we put on the garment of existence in succession.
Our rhyming is completed. Pray, our God,
For the seal of the messengers a prayer that will effect exaltation.
Pray, O God of the throne, Glorious and Exalted,
For a lord who ruled and perfected mankind,
Muḥammad, the guide, the intercessor, our leader,
And (pray for) the men around him, the noble, exalted people.

A rank that results from friendship.

[SIGNS]

The correct determination of sun and moon and the stars for every desired date:

[SIGNS]

III, 162 The *zâ'irajah* is completed.

The procedure of finding answers from questions through the *Zâ'irajah of the World* with the help of the might of God.[880]

A question may have three hundred and sixty answers, according to the degrees (of the firmament). The answers to

[880] Bulaq adds: "derived from people who work with the *zâ'irajah* and whom we have met." This seems quite a proper statement, in view of the fact that Ibn Khaldûn derived his knowledge of the problem discussed in the following pages from Jamâl-ad-dîn al-Marjânî, whom he had met in Biskra

one question under a given ascendant differ in accordance with different questions (forming part of the question asked), which are referred to the letters of the chords of the *zâ'irajah* and (in accordance with) the operation applied to finding out the letters from the verse of the poem.[881]

Note: The letters of the chords and the table are composed of three basic types. (1) Arabic letters, which are taken at their face value (as numerals). (2) *Ghubâr* letters.[882] They

in 1370/71. Cf. 1:xliii and 238 f., above. He mentions the question below, p. 199, and the answer is given below, p. 213.

The table constituting the *zâ'irajah* is not reproduced in all MSS and printed texts. It is found in A, E, and MS. Ragib Paşa (but not in B, C, and D), in the Turkish translation (Istanbul, 1277), and in the second Bulaq edition of 1284. Since the table requires a special sheet, it can, of course, easily become detached from the copy to which it originally belonged.

The letters evolved in the procedure described by Ibn Khaldûn are marked in this translation by boldface type. However, the rationale of their determination and the relationship of the description to the table are by no means clear to me. As in the case of the *zâ'irajah* poem, a translation—one might rather call it a transposition of Arabic into English words—is offered here in the hope that it may serve as a basis, however shaky, for future improvement.

881 The verse is quoted above, 1:240, and below, pp. 211 and 214.

882 *Ghubâr* means "dust," or rather, in this connection, "abacus," according to S. Gandz, "The Origin of the *ghubâr* Numerals, or The Arabian Abacus and the Articuli," *Isis*, XVI (1931), 393–424. The *ghubâr* letters are the numerals from one to nine, in a form practically identical with that in which the Arabic numerals are written in the West to this day. This is how they look in MS. B, fol. 224*a:*

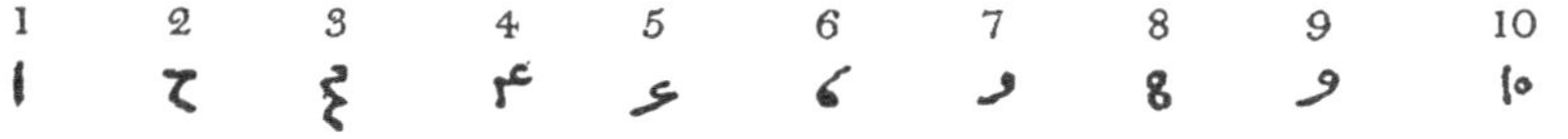

The *zimâm* letters are twenty-seven signs that have the numerical values from one to nine in the units, tens, and hundreds. They are supposed to be of Greek-Coptic origin. Cf. G. S. Colin, "De l'origine grecque des 'chiffres de Fès' et de nos 'chiffres arabes,' " *Journal asiatique*, CCXXII (1933), 193–215; G. Levi Della Vida, "Numerali Greci in documenti arabo-spagnoli," *Rivista degli studi orientali*, XIV (1934), 281–83; J. A. Sánchez Pérez, "Sobre las cifras Rūmíes," *al-Andalus*, III (1935), 97–125.

The *zimâm* letters have the following forms in MS. B, fol. 225*a:*

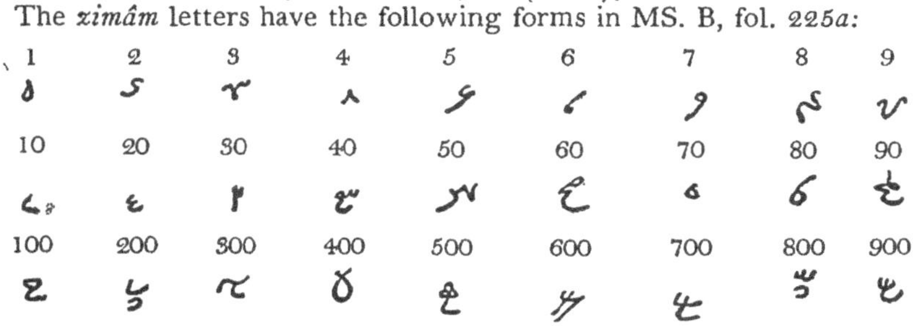

The sign  is apparently 1,000.

are treated differently. Some are taken at their face value, when there are no more than four cycles.[883] If there are more than four, they are used as tens as well as hundreds, as required by the operation, as we shall explain. (3) *Zimâm* letters. They are treated in the same way (as *ghubâr* letters). However, the *zimâm* letters offer another possibility. One may be used as one thousand and ten (as ten thousand), and they (may be used) in the proportion of five (to one) in relation to the Arabic letters [?]. One may place in (each) field of the table three letters of this type and two of the (other) type. Empty fields may be left in the table. If there are more than four basic cycles, (the empty fields) are counted in vertically.
III, *163* If there are no more than four, only the filled fields are counted.

The operation with the question requires seven principles. (1) The number of the letters of the chords. (2) The retention of their cycles after division by twelve. There are always eight cycles in the complete one, and six in the incomplete one. (3) The knowledge of the degree of the ascendant. (4) The ruler of the sign (of the zodiac). (5) The greatest principal cycle, which is always one. (6) The result of adding the ascendant to the principal cycle. And (7) the result of multiplying ascendant plus cycle by the ruler of the sign (of the zodiac), and (8) [884] of the ruler of the sign (of the zodiac) added to the ascendant.

The whole operation takes place in three cycles multiplied by four, thus making twelve cycles. The relationship of these three cycles, which are [. . .] [885] each growth having a beginning. Then, they are multiplied as quadruple cycles as

[883] *Dawr*, one of the technical terms of the Zâ'irajah, was introduced, though not explained, above, 1:242. It seems obvious that the term somehow refers to the circles of the *Zâ'irajah*, but the usual meaning of *dawr* is "cycle," not "circle."

Another frequently used technical term, "side of eight," is easily explained by reference to the reproduction of the *Zâ'irajah*.

[884] *Sic!* Cf. p. 211, below.

[885] The following words, which also introduce the term *nash'ah*, translated arbitrarily as "growth," are particularly obscure. Possibly the text is in disorder.

well as triple cycles [?]. Then, they may be the result of six multiplied by two, and thus have a(nother) growth. This is something apparent in the operation.

These cycles are followed by "results." They are in [?] the cycles. There may be one result, or more than one, up to six.

Now, to begin with, let us assume that someone asks, "Is the *zâ'irajah* a modern or an ancient science?" [886] The ascendant is in the first degree of Sagittarius.[887] Thus, we place the letters of the chord of the beginning of Sagittarius and the corresponding chord of the beginning of Gemini and, in the third place, the chord of the beginning of Aquarius up to the limit of the center. We add to it the letters of the questions.

We look at the number of (the letters). The smallest number there can be is eighty-eight,[888] and the largest ninety-six. This is the total of a complete cycle. Our question consists of ninety-three letters.[889] If the question contained more than ninety-six letters, it would be shortened by [890] dropping III, *164*
all twelve cycles. One keeps what comes out from them and what remains.[891] In our question, there are seven cycles. The remainder is nine.[892] They are set down among the letters, as long as the ascendant has not reached twelve degrees. If it has reached twelve degrees, no number or cycle is set down for them. But their numbers are again set down, when the ascendant has reached more than twenty-four degrees in the third decan.[893]

The ascendant is then set down as one, the ruler of the ascendant (the sign of the zodiac) as four, and the greatest cycle as one. The total of ascendant and cycle is added up,

[886] Cf. 1:238 (n. 364), above, and for the answer, p. 213, below.

[887] Bulaq adds: "among the letters of the chords, and then, the letters of the questions," which would seem to be out of place.

[888] One would expect a multiple of twelve: seventy-two or eighty-four?

[889] That is, the sum of the letters of the chords and the letters of the question. Cf. p. 211, below.

[890] *Sic* Bulaq.

[891] Apparently, the quotient and remainder after being divided by twelve.

[892] 93 ÷ 12 = 7, remainder 9.

[893] Cf. p. 163, above.

and, in this question, makes two. This total is multiplied by the ruler of the sign. This is eight. The ruler is added to the ascendant. This is five. These are (the) seven principles.

The result of multiplying the ascendant and the greatest cycle by the ruler of Sagittarius, when it is less than twelve, is entered at the "side of eight" from the bottom of the table upward. When it is more than twelve, it is divided in cycles. The remainder is entered at the side of eight. A mark is put upon the end of the number. The five that is the result of the addition of ruler and ascendant is what is entered [894] on the side of the uppermost large surface of the table. One counts, consecutively, groups of five cycles and keeps them until the number stops opposite the fields of the table that are filled. If it stops opposite one of the empty fields of the table, one should not pay any attention and go on with the cycles, until
III, *165* one reaches one of four letters, namely, *alif*, *b*, *j*, or *z*. In our operation, the number falls upon *alif* and leaves three cycles behind. Thus, we multiply three by three, which gives nine. That is the number of the first cycle. This must be set down. The total between the vertical and long sides must be added up. Then it will be in the field of eight.

The number in the first cycle, which is nine, must be entered in the front (recto) of the table adjacent to the field in which the two are brought together, going towards the left, which is (the field of) eight. It thus falls upon the letter *lâm-alif*, but no composite letter ever comes out of it. It thus is just the letter t—four hundred in *zimâm* letters.[895] A mark is put on it, after removing it, (indicating that it belongs) to the verse of the poem.[896]

---

[894] *Sic* C and D. The other texts have "is the ascendant."

[895] The *zimâm* numeral for 400 looks like the ligature *lâm-alif*, and the Arabic letter *t* ordinarily has the numerical value of 400.

[896] What is translated here and on the following pages as "indicating that it belongs to," or "belonging to," is the preposition *min*. It may mean that the mark is taken *from* the verse of the poem (by Mâlik b. Wuhayb; see p. 211, below), but this would not seem to make much sense. Without any connection with a letter belonging to the solution of the problem, this *min* occurs only p. 205 (n. 899*a*), below, and there it is doubtful whether the poem is meant and whether *bayt* means "verse" or something else.

Then, one adds up the numbers of the cycle of the ruler. One gets thirteen, which is entered among the letters of the chords. One sets down (the letter) upon which the number falls and puts a mark upon it, (indicating that it belongs to) the verse of the poem.

This rule shows how much the letters circulate according to the natural order. This is as follows. One adds the letter of the first cycle, which is nine, to the ruler of the sign (of the zodiac), which is four. Thus, one gets thirteen. This is doubled. Thus, one gets twenty-six. From this, one subtracts the degree of the ascendant, which, in this particular question, is one. Thus, there remains twenty-five. Accordingly, the first order of the letter <is twenty-five>, then twenty-three twice, then twenty-two twice, according to that subtraction, until the (procedure) reaches one at the end of the rhymed verse.[897] One does not stop at twenty-four, because the one (which would make twenty-four out of twenty-five) had originally been subtracted.

Then, one takes the second cycle and adds the letters of III, *166*
the first cycle to the eight resulting from the multiplication of ascendant and cycle by the ruler. This gives seventeen. The remainder is five. Thus, one goes up five on the side of eight from where one had stopped in the first cycle. One puts a mark on (that place). One enters seventeen on the front (recto) of the table, and then five. One does not count empty fields. The cycle is that of tens. We find the letter *th*—five hundred, but it (counts the same as) *n*, because our cycle represents the tens. Thus, five hundred is (counted as) fifty, because its cycle is seventeen. If it had been twenty-seven, it would have been in the hundreds. Thus, one sets down an **n.**

Then, one enters five, also from the beginning, and notes what (number of) the surface it confronts. It is found to be one. One reverses the number one. It falls upon five. One

[897] This refers to the method according to which the letters evolved by the procedure (and here marked in boldface) are later shuffled so as to produce the rhymed answer to the question. Cf. p. 213, below.

adds the one of the surface to five, and gets six. One sets down a **w** and marks it with four [?] (as belonging) to the verse of the poem. One adds them to the eight which was the result of the multiplication of ascendant and cycle by the ruler. Thus, one gets twelve. The remainder of the second cycle, namely five, is added to twelve. Thus, one gets seventeen. That is something that belongs to the second cycle. Thus, we enter seventeen among the letters of the chords. The number falls upon one. Thus, one sets down **alif** and puts a mark upon it (as belonging) to the verse of the poem. Of the letters of the chords, one drops three, the number of the result of the second cycle.

Then, one makes the third cycle. One adds five to eight and gets thirteen. The remainder is one. One moves the cycle at the side of eight by one. One enters thirteen into the verse of the poem. One takes the (letter) upon which the
III, *167* number falls. It is **q.** A mark is put upon it. Thirteen is entered among the letters of the chords. One sets down what comes out. It is **s.** A mark is put upon it (as belonging) to the verse of the poem. Then, the one which is the remainder of the cycle of thirteen is entered next to the resulting *s.* One takes the chord next to the letter *s.* It is **b.** It is set down, and a mark (indicating that it belongs) to the verse of the poem is put upon it. This is called the "leaning cycle." Its scale is correct. This is as follows. One doubles thirteen and adds to it the one which remains of the cycle. Thus, one gets twenty-seven. This is the letter *b*, which is derived from the chords (as belonging) to the verse of the poem. Thirteen is entered at the front part of the table. One notes what (part of) the surface confronts it. One doubles it and adds to it the one which is the remainder of thirteen. This is the letter *j.* The total, thus, is seven. This is the letter **z.** We set it down and put a mark upon it (indicating that it belongs) to the verse of the poem. The scale of it is that one doubles seven and adds to it the one which is the remainder of thirteen. Thus, one gets fifteen. It is the fifteenth of the verse of the poem. This is the end of the triple cycles.

Then, one makes the fourth cycle. It has the number nine, (obtained) by adding the remainder of the previous cycle. One then multiplies ascendant and cycle by the ruler. This cycle ends the operation in the first field of the quadruple (cycles).

Then, one picks two letters from the chords, goes up nine on the side of eight, and enters nine from the cycle of the letter which was taken last from the verse of the poem. The III, *168*
ninth is the letter **r.** It is set down, and a mark is put upon it. Then, nine is entered on the front (recto) of the table, and one notes what (letter of) the surface faces it. It is *j*. One reverses the number one. That is *alif*. This is the second after [?] the letter *r* (belonging) to the verse of the poem.

It is set down, and a mark is put upon it. One counts nine, starting next to the second. It again is an **alif.** It is set down, and a mark is put upon it. Then, one picks a letter from the chords and doubles nine. This gives eighteen. One enters it among the letters of the chords and comes to a stop at the letter *r*. It is set down and marked with eight and four, (indicating that it belongs) to the verse of the poem. Then, one enters eighteen among the letters of the chords and comes to a stop at the letter **s.** It is put down and marked with two. One adds two to nine, which is eleven, and enters eleven on the front (recto) of the table. It is confronted by an **alif** from the surface. It is set down and marked with six.

Then, one makes the fifth cycle. Its number is seventeen. The remainder is five. One goes up five on the side of eight. One picks two letters from the chords. One doubles five and adds the result to seventeen, the number of its cycle. The total is twenty-seven. It is entered among the letters of the chords. It falls upon **t.** It is set down and marked with thirty-two. One subtracts the two which is at the base of thirty-two,[898] from seventeen. The remainder is fifteen. One enters

[898] Since "exponent" is one of the meanings of *uss* in algebra (cf. n. 627 to this chapter, above), it might here be supposed that the relationship is $2^5 = 32$. However, here and on the following pages *uss* is also a special technical term in the *Zâ'irajah* procedure, and as such was mentioned above, 1:241. Possibly the two here is obtained by subtracting the full number of

it among the letters of the chords and comes to a stop at **q.** It is set down and marked with twenty-six. On the front part of the table one enters twenty-six. One comes to a stop at
III, *169* two in *ghubâr* letters. That is the letter **b.** It is entered and marked with fifty-four.

Then, one picks two letters from the chords and makes the sixth cycle. Its number is thirteen. The remainder is one. Thus, it becomes clear that the cycle of order (rhyming [?]) belongs to twenty-five. The cycles are ninety [?]-five, seventeen, five, thirteen, and one. One multiplies five by five which gives twenty-five. This is the cycle in the order of the verse. One removes the cycle on the side of eight by one. But, as we have mentioned before, thirteen is not entered in the verse of the poem, because it is a second cycle of a second compositional growth. But we add to one the four that belongs to the fifty-four which led to *b* (as belonging) to the verse of the poem. This gives five. One adds five to the thirteen that belongs to the cycle, and gets eighteen. One enters it on the front (recto) of the table and takes (the letter of) the surface that confronts it. It is **alif.** It is set down and marked with twelve, (as belonging) to the verse of the poem. One picks two letters from the chords.

At this point, one looks at the letters of the question. The (letters) that have come out (in the preceding operation) are paired with the verse of the poem, beginning at the end. One marks them with the letters of the question, so that it enters numerically into the verse of the poem. The same is done with every letter that comes out hereafter, in correspondence with the letters of the question. All the letters coming out are paired with the verse of the poem, beginning at the end, and a mark is put on them.

Then, one adds to eighteen the units with which one has
III, *170* marked the letter *alif*. They come to two. Thus, one gets a total of twenty. One enters it among the letters of the chords

degrees in the preceding sign from thirty-two. However, this is merely a guess. The original meaning of *uss* "base" has been retained in the translation, here and on the following pages.

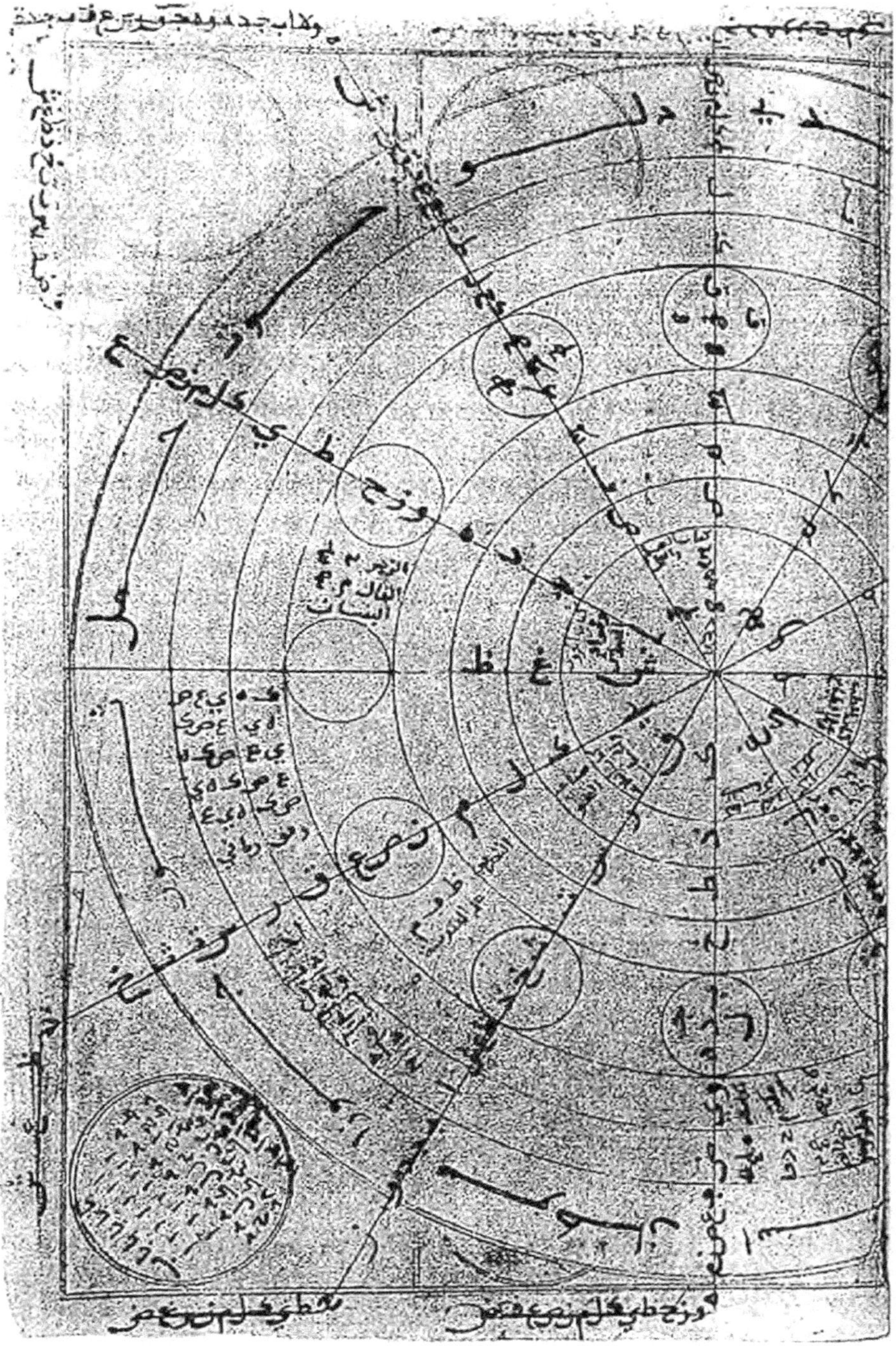

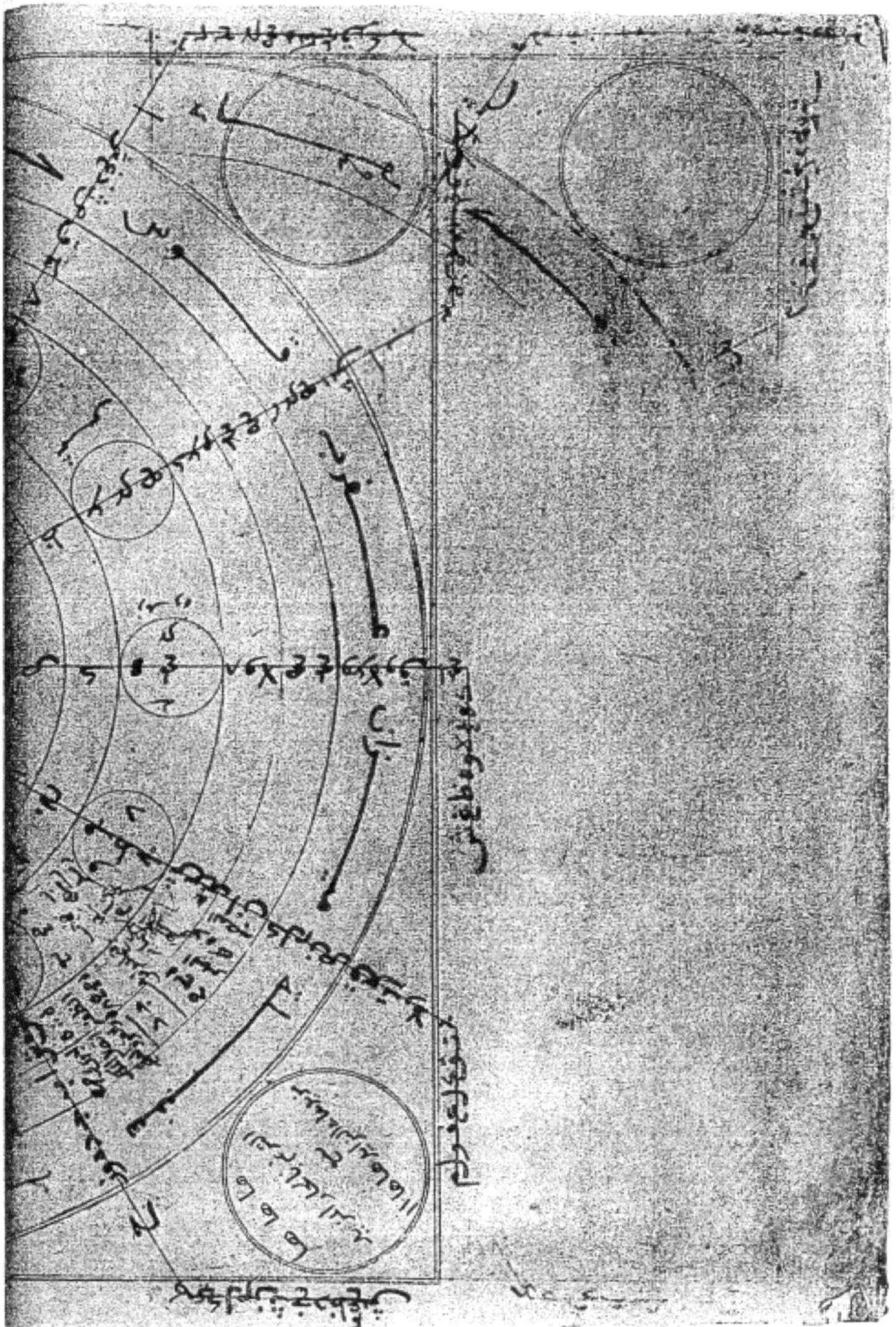

I. The *Zâ'irajah* (obverse) Cf. translation at end of volume

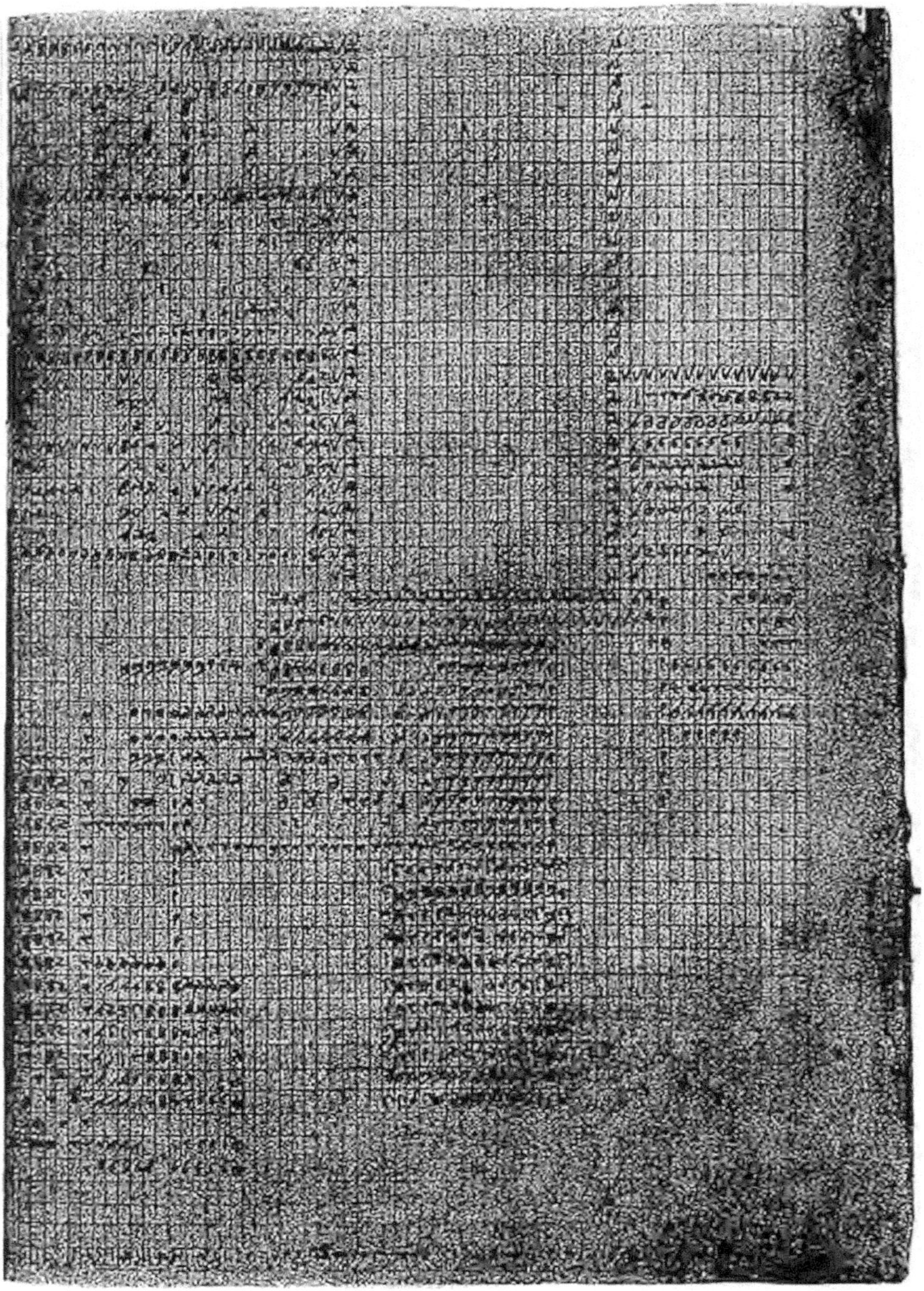

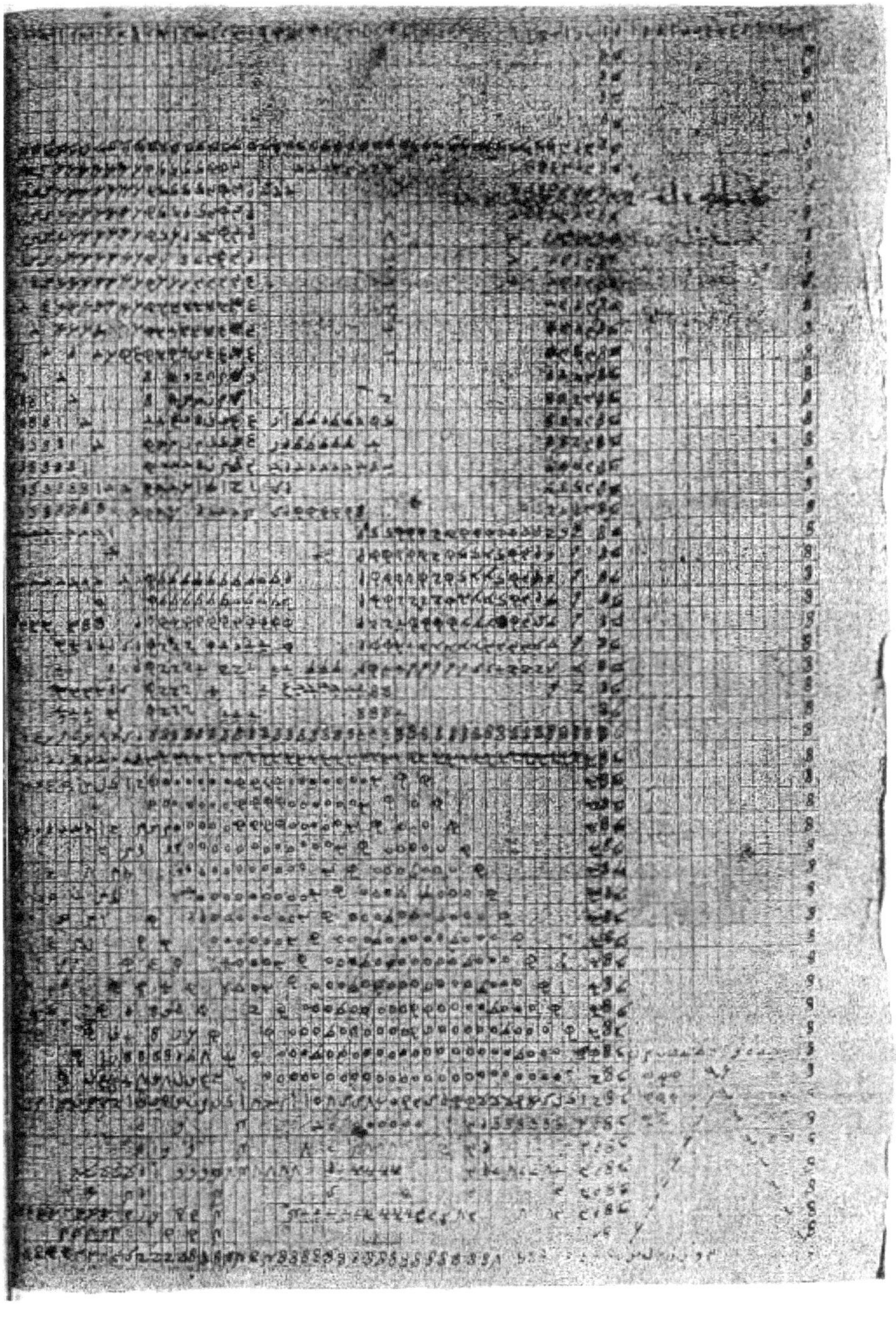

II. The *Zâ'irajah* (reverse)

and comes to a stop at the letter **r.** It is set down and marked with ninety-six, (as belonging) to the verse of the poem. This is the end of the cycle with regard to chord letters.

Then, one picks two letters from the chords and makes the seventh cycle. It is the beginning of the second of the two "inventions." This cycle contains the number nine. One adds one to it. Thus, one gets ten [899] for the second growth.

This one is added later on to twelve cycles, if it belongs to that proportion, or it is taken away from the principal (cycle). Thus, one gets a total of ten. One goes up on the side of ninety-eight, enters ten on the front (recto) of the table, and gets thus to stop at five hundred. It is, however, (counted) only as fifty, *n*. It is to be doubled. Thus, it is **q.** It is set down and marked with fifty-two (as belonging) to the verse of the poem. Two is dropped from fifty-two, and the nine which belongs to the cycle is dropped. The remainder is forty-one. One enters it among the letters of the chords and thus comes to a stop at one, which is set down. One also enters (forty-one) in the verse of the poem and thus finds one. This is the scale of the second growth.

It is marked with two signs (as belonging) to the verse of the poem, one (which is put) upon the last **alif** of the scale, and another upon the first **alif.** The second is twenty-four. Then, one picks two letters from the chords and makes the eighth cycle. Its number is seventeen. The remainder is five. One enters (it) on the side of fifty-eight, enters five in the III, *171*
verse of the poem, and thus comes to a stop at **'ayn,** seventy. It is set down, and a mark is put upon it. Five is entered in the table. One takes the (number) of the surface confronting it. It is one. It is set down and marked with forty-eight, (as belonging) to [?] [899a] the verse. One drops one from forty-eight for the second base and adds to it the five of the cycle. The total is fifty-two. That is entered on the front (recto) of the table. One thus comes to a stop at the *ghubâr* letter two. It is in the order of hundreds, because it should be a larger

[899] The MSS have "twenty," which is corrected to "ten" in Bulaq.
[899a] Cf. n. 896 to this chapter, above.

number. Thus, it is (counted as) two hundred, which is the letter **r.**[900] It is set down and marked with twenty-four, (as belonging) to the verse of the poem. Having reached ninety-six, the whole thing starts from the beginning, which is twenty-four. One adds the five of the cycle to twenty-four and drops one. The total is twenty-eight. One enters half of it in the verse of the poem and thus comes to a stop at eight. Thus, **ḥ** is set down, and a mark is put upon it.

One makes the ninth cycle. Its number is thirteen. The remainder is one. One goes up one on the side of eight. Here the operation does not follow the same procedure as in the sixth cycle, because the number should be many times larger. Also, the (cycle) belongs to the second growth and is the beginning of the third third of the quadruple (arrangement) of the signs of the zodiac and the end of the third fourth of the triple (arrangement).

Thus, one multiplies the thirteen of the cycle by the four that is (the number of) the preceding triple (arrangement) of the signs of the zodiac. The total is fifty-two. One enters it on the front (recto) of the table and thus comes to a stop at the *ghubâr* letter two. However, it is in the hundreds, having gone beyond the units and tens. Therefore, it is set
III, *172* down as two hundred, **r,** and marked with forty-eight, (as belonging) to the verse of the poem. One adds the one of the base to the thirteen of the cycle, enters fourteen in the verse of the poem, and thus comes to a stop at **ḥ.** It is marked with twenty-eight. Seven is subtracted from fourteen. There remains seven.

Then, one picks two letters from the chords. One enters seven and thus comes to a stop at the letter **l.** It is set down, and a mark (indicating that it belongs) to the verse is put on it.

Then, one makes the tenth cycle. Its number is nine. It is the beginning of the fourth triple (arrangement). One goes

[900] The listing of the letters on p. 213 shows an *m* between the *r* and the following *ḥ*. That *m*, however, is superfluous. Cf. also n. 904 to this chapter, below.

up nine on the side of eight. There is an empty (field). One goes up another nine and gets into the seventh (field) from the beginning. One multiplies nine by four, because we have gone up twice nine, so that (nine) was only multiplied by two. One enters thirty-six in the table and thus comes to a stop at the *zimâm* letter four. It should be in the tens, but we take is as a unit, because there are too few cycles. Thus, the letter **d** is set down. If one adds the one of the base to thirty-six, its limit [?] belongs to the verse of the poem. A mark is put upon it. If one had entered on the front (recto) of the table nine and nothing else, without multiplication, one would have come to a stop at eight. Thus, one divides forty-eight (by twelve).[901] The remainder is four. This is what one wants. If one had entered eighteen, which is nine multiplied by two, on the front (recto) of the table, one would have come to a stop at the *zimâm* letter one, which belongs to the tens. One subtracts two, which was used to double the nine. The remainder is eight, half of which is (four. Again, this is) what one looks for. If, by multiplying (nine) by three, one were to enter twenty-seven on the front (recto) of the table, one would come to a stop at the *zimâm* letter ten. The operation is the same. III, *173*

Then, nine is entered into the verse of the poem. (The letter) which comes out is set down. It is **alif.** Then, one multiplies nine with the three which is the component of the previous nine, drops one, and enters twenty-six in the front (recto) of the table. The number that comes out—two hundred—is set down with the letter **r.** It is marked with ninety-six, (as belonging) to the verse of the poem.

Then, one picks two letters from the chords and makes the eleventh cycle. It has (the number) seventeen. The remainder is five. One goes up five on the side of eight, corresponding to what had been undertaken in the first cycle. One enters four [902] on the front (recto) of the table and comes to a stop at

[901] The text is doubtful. Bulaq corrects it to read: "one subtracts four from eight."

[902] Bulaq: "five."

an empty (field). One takes (the number of) the surface which confronts it. It is one. Thus, one enters one into the verse of the poem. This is **r-s.**[903] It is set down and marked with four. If we had come to a stop at a filled field of the table, we would have set down the one as three. One doubles seventeen, drops the one, and adds four. Thus, one gets thirty-seven. One enters it in the chords and comes to a stop at **h.**[904] It is entered and marked with five. One doubles five, enters (ten) into the verse, and thus comes to a stop at **l.** It is set down and marked with twenty.

Then, one picks two letters from the chords and makes the twelfth cycle. It has (the number) thirteen. The remainder is one. One goes up one on the side of eight. This cycle is the last cycle, the end of the two inventions, the end of the three quadruple (arrangements), and the end of the four triple (arrangements).

The one on the front (recto) of the table falls upon the
III, *174* *zimâm* letter eight, which is just eight units. The only (number) we have in the cycles is one. Were there more than a four in the quadruple (arrangement) of the twelve, or more than a three in the triple (arrangement) of the twelve, there would be *ḥ* (eight). But it is just **d** (four). Therefore, it is set down and marked with seventy-four, (as belonging) to the verse of the poem. Then, one notes which (number) from the surface corresponds to it. It is five. The five which belongs to the base, is added to it. Thus, one gets ten. A **y** is set down, and a mark is put upon it. One notes in which rank it occurs. We find it in the seventh.[905] Thus, we enter seven among the letters of the chords. This entry is called the "letter birth."

[903] The appearance of two letters at the same time is strange, but, as shown on p. 213, this is what is needed.

[904] Bulaq has "six" and omits "with five" at the end of the next sentence. There is something wrong here. The listing on p. 213 shows an *alif* after the *h*. However, not an *alif* but a **w** is needed (unless the *w* has to be sought earlier in the discussion, p. 206 [n. 900], which seems unlikely). The "six" that appears in Bulaq may have something to do with the expected *w*.

[905] Bulaq: "fourth."

There is an **f.** One sets it down and adds the one of the cycle to seven. The total is eight. One enters it among the chords and gets to **s.** It is set down and marked with eight. One multiplies eight by the three that is in excess of the ten of the cycle—because it is the end of three quadruple (arrangements) of the cycles—and gets twenty-four. It is entered into the verse of the poem, and a mark is put upon (the number) which comes out from it. It is two hundred (**r**). Its sign is ninety-six, which is the end of the second [906] cycle of the letter cycles.

One picks two letters from the chords and writes down the first result. It has a nine. This number always corresponds to the remainder of the letters of the chords, after they have been divided into (twelve) cycles. It is nine.[907]

Then, one multiplies nine with the three which is in excess of the ninety letters of the chords, and adds to it the one which is the remainder in the twelfth cycle. Thus, one gets twenty-eight. One enters it among the letters of the chords and gets to an **alif.** It is set down and marked with ninety-six. If the seven [908]—which is the cycles of the ninety letters—is multiplied by four—which is the three that is in III, *175*
excess of ninety plus the one that is the remainder in the twelfth cycle—the result is the same.

One goes up nine on the side of eight and enters nine in the table. Thus, one gets to the *zimâm* letter two. One multiplies nine with the (number) of the surface corresponding to it, namely, three. Seven, the number of the chords with letters, is added to it, and the one which is the remainder in the twelfth cycle is subtracted. Thus, one gets thirty-three. One enters it into the verse and gets to five. One puts it down [909] (as **h**), doubles nine, and enters eighteen on the front (recto) of the table. One takes (the number) which is on the surface.

906 *Leg.* "twelfth"?
907 Cf. p. 199 (n. 892), above.
908 The MSS have nine, but apparently seven, as in Bulaq, is correct.
909 Bulaq has the required text. The other texts read: "one doubles it."

It is one. One enters it among the letters of the chords and gets to an **m.** It is set down, and a mark is put upon it.

Then, one picks two letters from the chords and writes down the second result. It has (the number) seventeen. The remainder is five. One goes up on the side of fifty-eight.[910] Five is multiplied by the three which is in excess of ninety. Thus, one gets fifteen. One adds to it the one which is the remainder in the twelfth cycle. This is nine.[911] One enters sixteen into the verse and gets to a **t.** It is set down and marked with sixty-four. One adds to five the three which is in excess of ninety, and one adds the one which is the remainder in the twelfth cycle. This is thirty-nine.[912] One enters it on the front (recto) of the table and gets to the *zimâm* letter thirty. One notes what (number) is on the surface. It is found to be one. It is set down (as **alif**), and a mark (indicating that it belongs) to the verse of the poem is put upon it. It also is the ninth from the verse. One enters nine on the front (recto) of the table and comes to a stop at a three in the tens. Therefore, an **l** (thirty) is set down, and a mark is put upon it.

III, *176* Then, one writes down the third result. Its number is thirteen. The remainder is one. One moves one on the side of eight. The three which is in excess of ninety, and the one which is the remainder in the twelfth cycle are added to thirteen. Thus, one gets seventeen, plus the one of the result, which gives eighteen. It is entered among the letters of the chords. It is an **l,** which is set down.

This is the end of the operation.

The example in the preceding question was this. We wanted to know whether the *zâ'irajah* was a modern or an ancient science.[913] The ascendant was in the first degree of Sagittarius. We set down:

[910] Bulaq corrects: "One goes up five on the side of eight."
[911] It should be sixteen, unless the sum $5 + 3 + 1$ is intended.
[912] Bulaq corrects to "nine."
[913] For the following eight principles, cf. p. 198, above.

The letters of the chords.
The letters of the question.
The principles, which are:

(1) The number of the letters — ninety-three.
(2) The cycles of (the letters) — seven, with the remainder of nine.
(3) The ascendant — one.
(4) The ruler of Sagittarius — four.
(5) The greatest cycle — one.
(6) The degrees of the ascendant plus the cycle — two.
(7) Ascendant plus cycle multiplied by the ruler — eight.
(8) The ruler added to the ascendant — five.

The verse of the poem: [914]

A weighty question you have got. Keep, then, to yourself
Remarkable doubts which have been raised and which can be straightened out with diligence.

The letters of the chords:

ṣ, ṭ, d,[915] *ṭ, h, n, th, k, h, m, ḍ, ṣ, w, n, th, h, s, alif, b, l, m, n, ṣ, 'ayn, f, ḍ, q, r, s, y, k, l, m, n, ṣ, 'ayn, f, q, r, s, t, th, kh, dh, ẓ, gh, sh, ṭ, k, n, 'ayn, ḥ, ṣ, z, w, ḥ, l, ṣ, k, l, m, n, ṣ, alif, b, j, d, h, w, z, ḥ, ṭ, y.*

The letters of the question:

alif, l, z,[915a] *y, r, j, t; 'ayn, l, m; m, ḥ, d, th; alif, m; q, d, y, m.*

914 Cf. 1:240, above, and pp. 214 and 224, below.
915 C and D: *k*.
915a The letter *alif*, which one would expect here, is not mentioned.

III, *177*

	358
561255	876
s	
w	2
alif	3
l	4
ayn	5
ẓ	6
y	7
m	8
alif	9
l	10
kh	11
l	12
q	13
ḥ	14
z	15
t	16
f	17
ṣ	18
n	19
alif	20
dh	21
n	22
gh	23
r	24
alif	25
y	26
b	27
sh	28
k	29
ḍ	30
b	31
ṭ	32
h	33
alif	34
l	35
j	36
d	37
	38

m th l alif
50
alif 41[916]

First Cycle:	9.	
Second Cycle:	17, remainder 5.	
Third Cycle:	13, remainder 1.	
Fourth Cycle:	9.	
Fifth Cycle:	17, remainder 5.	
Sixth Cycle:	13, remainder 1.	
Seventh Cycle:	9.	
Eighth Cycle:	17, remainder 5.	
Ninth Cycle:	13, remainder 1.	
Tenth Cycle:	9.	2652
Eleventh Cycle:	17, remainder 5.	28
Twelfth Cycle:	13, remainder 1.	3265
First Result:	9.	
Second Result:	17, remainder 5.	€355896
Third Result:	13, remainder 1.	58 65

t, w, n, alif, q, s, b, z, r, alif, alif, r, s, III, *178*
alif, t, q, b, alif, r, q, alif, 'ayn, alif, r,
[m [917]*], ḥ, r, ḥ,*[918] *l, d, alif, r, s, h, [alif* [919]*],*
l, d, y, f, s, r, alif, h, m, t, alif, l, l.

Their period is according to twenty-five, then twenty-three twice, then twenty-one twice, until one gets to the one at the end of the verse [?].[920] All the letters are moved. And God knows better.

t, r, w, ḥ, n; r, w, ḥ; alif, l, q, d, s; alif, b, r, z; s, r, h, alif;
l, alif, d, r, y, s; f, alif, s, t, r, q, alif; b, h, alif; m, r, t, q, alif; alif, l, 'ayn, l, alif.[921]

End of the discussion of how to find answers in rhymed form from the *Zâ'irajah of the World.*

People have methods other than the *zâ'irajah* for finding out answers from questions. (However,) those answers are not rhymed.

I think [922] that the secret of obtaining a rhymed answer III, *179*

[916] To the left, the letters of the verse are listed with consecutive numbering. At the end it seems that there was not enough room for the last four letters on the original table, so they were written to one side. Of course, it should be:

m	38
th	39
l	40
alif	41

[917] This letter is superfluous; cf. p. 206 (n. 900).

[918] The MSS have a wrong *j*.

[919] A *w* is required instead of *alif*. Cf. n. 904, above.

[920] Cf. p. 201, above.

[921] These letters, then, form the following verse, indicating that the *Zâ'irajah* was invented by Idrîs, the Qur'ânic sage who is identified with the Biblical Enoch. It reads:

Tarûḥanna rûḥu l-qudsî ubriza sirruhâ
Li-Idrîsa fa-starqâ bi-hâ murtaqâ l-'ulâ.
The Holy Spirit will depart, its secret having been brough forth
To Idrîs, and through it, he ascended the highest summit.

[922] Bulaq: "They think."

from the *zâ'irajah* lies in the fact that a verse, namely, that of Mâlik b. Wuhayb—"A weighty question, etc."—enters (into the operation). Thus, one gets an answer which rhymes on the rhyme letter of Mâlik's verse. In other methods, there is no rhymed answer.[923]

We are going to report this much about other methods of finding answers. A competent (practitioner of letter magic) said:

On learning hidden secrets from letter connections [924]

Let it be known to you—God guide us and you [925]—that the following letters are the basis for answers to any problem. They produce the answers through total division.[926] There are forty-three letters, as one can see:

alif, w, l, alif, 'ayn, ẓ, s, alif, l, m, kh, y, d, l, z, q, t, alif, f, dh, ṣ, r, n, gh, sh, r, alif, k, k, y, b, m, ḍ, b, j, ṭ, l, ḥ, h, d, th, l, th, alif.

Some excellent man has worked these letters into the form of a verse in which every double consonant stands for two letters. He called the (verse) the "pole." It runs:

A weighty question you have got. Keep, then, to yourself
Remarkable doubts which have been raised and which
can be straightened out with diligence.[927]

If one wants to produce the (answer from the) question,

[923] Cf. 1:243, above.

[924] This is the title of a treatise (or a section of a larger work). The author is not known.

[925] This formula, and even more so the one used below, p. 218, is characteristic of esoteric literature. Cf., for instance, the *Rasâ'il ikhwân aṣ-ṣafâ'* and Ibn 'Arabî's *Futûḥât*. Cf. also 1:194, above.

[926] The text appears to be: *bi-tajzi'atin bi-l-kullîyah.*

The following listing of the letters contains forty-four letters, and this is the number required, even though Ibn Khaldûn refers again to forty-three letters, p. 225, below. Instead of one of the *r*'s, an *n* should be read (for the last letter of *idhan*).

[927] The operation is described again below, pp. 224 f.

one must eliminate the letters of the question that are repeated and set down those that remain. Then, one eliminates one letter that is similar to (a letter of the question) from the basic (verse), the "pole," for each remaining letter of the question. One sets down what remains. Then, one mixes the III, *180*
two remainders together in one line. One begins by taking as the first (letter), one from the remainder from the basic (verse), and as the second, one from the remainder from the question, and so forth, until the two remainders are finished, or until one of them is finished before the other. (In the latter case,) one leaves the rest as it is. If the number of the letters that come out after the mixing agrees with the number of the letters in the basic (verse), before elimination, the operation is correct. Then, one adds to them five *n*'s, in order to have the musical scales balanced and to have a complete complement of forty-eight letters. With those letters, one fills a table of squares. The end of the first line is the beginning of the second, and the rest is moved as it is, and so forth, until the table is filled and the first line reoccurs. The letters in the "region" follow each other in proportion to the motion. Then, one finds out the chord of each letter through square division by the smallest aliquot part found in it,[927a] and one puts (each) chord opposite its letter. Then, one finds out the elemental relations for the letters of the table and indicates their natural power, their spiritual power, their spiritual scales, their psychic dispositions, and their principal bases from the table which has been composed for the purpose and which looks as follows: [928]

(*See next page*)

[927a] Cf. p. 222, below, for an explanation.

[928] The numerals appearing in the following table are all *zimâm* numerals. The letters appearing in the right-hand column represent the numerical values from one-to-seven.

III, *181*

Bases	Dispositions	Scales	Powers	'
300 60	80 7	1,000 900[?] 1	500 10 4	*b*
100 3	800 70 9	400 30 7	200 20 5	*j*
900 80 6	200 80 400	40 2	700[?]90 5	*d*
40 5	20 7	10 9	90 4	*h*
500 4	100 10 2			*w*
20 5	90 8			*z*

00	00	0	1
	200	20	2
		30	3
	300	40	4
	400	50	5
	500	60	6
		70	7
	600	80	8
	700	90	9
	800		
	900		

w Dispositions	Result
Scales	*t*
Principal Base	Powers *k*

Then,[929] one takes the chord of each letter after multiplying it by the bases of the four cardines of the (celestial) spheres. One should avoid what is adjacent to the cardines and also the *sawâqiṭ*,[930] because their relationship is confused. The result here is the first degree of diffusion.[931] Then, one takes the total of the elements and subtracts from it [?] the bases of the generated things. There remain the bases of the world of creation, after it has been exposed to the moments [?] of creation. Then, there are transferred to it some abstractions III, *182*
from matter—the elements that constitute matter. The result is the middle horizon of the soul. The first degree of diffusion is subtracted from the total of the elements. There remains [932] the world of mediation. It has to do with the world of simple beings, and not with (those of) composite ones.

The world of mediation is then multiplied by the middle horizon of the soul. The result is the most high horizon. To it, the first degree of diffusion is transferred. Then, the first of the elements basically constituting matter is subtracted from the fourth (degree of diffusion [?]). There remains the third degree of diffusion. The total of the particulars of the elements is always multiplied by the fourth degree of diffusion. The result is the first world of particularization. The result of the multiplication of the second (element) with the second (degree of diffusion) is the second world of particularization; that of the third with the third is the third; and that of the fourth with the fourth is the fourth world of particularization. The worlds of particularization are added up and subtracted from the world of totality. There remain the worlds of abstraction. They are divided by the most high horizon. The result is the first particular. The remainder is divided by the middle horizon. The result is the second particular. The re-

[929] For the following discussion, cf. p. 226, below.

[930] I.e., the seven letters (*th, j, kh, z, sh, ẓ,* and *f*) that do not occur in the first *sûrah* of the Qur'ân.

[931] *Sarayân*, which in Avicenna's terminology might be translated as diffusion, infiltration, circulation, according to A.-M. Goichon, *Lexique de la langue philosophique d'Ibn Sînâ*, p. 150.

[932] The correct text is found in Bulaq. Cf. p. 226, below.

mainder is the third. The fourth here is fixed for the fourth (division [?]). If one wants more than four (divisions [?]), one must increase the number of the worlds of particularization, that of the degrees of diffusion, and that of the magic squares containing letters in their numerical value. God guide us and you.

Likewise, if the world of abstraction is divided by the first degree of diffusion, the result is the first particular of the world of composition, and so forth to the end of the last degree of the world of existence.

This should be understood and contemplated. God is
III, *183* guide and helper.

Another method to find the answer is this. A competent (practitioner of letter magic) said:

Let it be known to you—God strengthen us and you with a spirit coming from Him—that the science of letters is an important science. The scholar who knows it comes to know things that he would not be able to know with the help of any other science in the world. The practice of the science of (letter magic) requires certain conditions. With its help, the scholar may discover the secrets of creation and the inner workings of nature. Thus, he learns the two results of philosophy, which are letter magic and its sister (alchemy). The veil of the unknown is lifted for him. He thus learns the contents of the secret recesses of the heart. A number of people in the Maghrib have been observed [933] to have a knowledge of the science (of letter magic). They have produced remarkable and extraordinary things and have been active in the world of existence with the help of God. It should be known that every virtue depends on exertion. A good habit, together with patience, is the key to everything good, just as a lack of skill and haste are the beginning of all failure.

I say: If one wants to know the power of each letter of the

[933] Bulaq may be translated as "I have observed . . ." and this may be the correct text.

alphabetos [934]—the alphabet—to the last number—and this is the beginning of the science of letters—one must look for the number that belongs to each letter. This degree, which means harmony for the letters [?], constitutes the power that a (particular letter) possesses with regard to the *corporealia.* The number is then multiplied by itself. The result is the power that a (particular letter) possesses with regard to the *spiritualia.* It is the "chord" (of the particular letter). This cannot be done with letters that have diacritical points. It can be done only with those that have no diacritical points, because the letters with diacritical points have degrees of meaning which will be explained later on.[935]

It should be known that the form of every letter has a III, *184*
(corresponding) form in the world on high, the (divine) throne. These (forms) may be moving or stationary, high or low, as is indicated in the proper places on the tables written down in (connection with) the *zâ'irajahs.*

It should be known that the powers of the letters fall into three categories. The first (category) is the least (important one). It is a power that becomes manifest after (the letters) have been written down. Such (a letter) is thus written down for a spiritual world which belongs to that particular letter. Whenever the letter produces a psychic power and concentration of mind, the powers of letters exercise an influence upon the world of the bodies.

The second (category) is the power of (the letters) in the realm of thought. It is the result of the activation of the *spiritualia* for (the letters). It is a power among the *spiritualia* on high, and a formal power in the world of *corporealia.*

The third (category) is what causes the inward—the psychic power—to concentrate upon bringing (the letter) into being. Before (a letter) is pronounced, it is a form in the soul. After it is pronounced, it is a form among the letters and a power in speech.

The natures of (the letters) are the same as those at-

[934] According to the MSS, Ibn Khaldûn pronounced the word *al-qâfîṭûs.*
[935] Ibn Khaldûn apparently did not quote this explanation.

tributed to (all) created things, namely, heat-and-dryness, heat-and-cold, cold-and-humidity, and cold-and-dryness. This is the secret of the ogdoad. Heat combines air and fire. The two are (represented by the letters) [936] *alif*, *h*, *ṭ*, *m*, *f*, *sh*, *dh*, *j*, *z*, *k*, *s*, *q*, *th*, and *ẓ*. Cold combines earth and water: *d*, *ḥ*, *l*, *ʿayn*, *r*, *kh*, *gh*, *b*, *w*, *y*, *n*, *ṣ*, *t*, and *ḍ*. Humidity combines air and water: *j*, *z*, *k*, *s*, *q*, *th*, *ẓ*, *d*, *ḥ*, *l*, *ʿayn*, *r*, *kh*, and *gh*. Dryness combines fire and earth: *alif*, *h*, *ṭ*, *m*, *f*, *sh*, *dh*, *b*, *w*, *y*, *n*, *ṣ*, *t*, and *ḍ*. This is the relationship and mutual interpenetration of the letters representing the natures and the interpenetration of the particulars of the world within (the letters) on high and here below, through the agency of
III, *185* the primary mothers, that is, the four individual natures (elements).

If one wants to find out the unknown from a given question, one must ascertain the ascendant of the questioner, or the ascendant of his question. Then, the letters of the four cardines of (the horoscope)—one, five,[937] seven, and ten—must be "spelled" (*istinṭâq*) [938] equally and according to order, and the numbers of the powers and the chords must be found out, as we shall explain. One adds up, establishes proportions, and tries to open up [?] the answer. Thus, one will find what one is looking for, either clearly expressed or implied.

The same is the case with any question one may happen to have to explain. If one wants to discover the powers of the letters of the ascendant, together with the name of the questioner and the object, one must add up the numerical values of

---

[936] Cf. pp. 172 f., above. Here, however, the sequence of the letters is that used in the East. Furthermore, according to the above-mentioned distribution of the letters among the elements, the letters mentioned here would indicate the combinations fiery-watery, earthy-airy, watery-earthy, and fiery-airy.

[937] "Four," as in Bulaq, may be a necessary correction.

[938] As explained by at-Tahânawî, *Kashshâf iṣṭilâḥât al-funûn*, pp. 127 f., *s.v.* "basṭ," *istinṭâq* means the retransformation of the numerical value of a word into letters. For instance, the numerical value of *M* (*u*) *ḥ* (*a*) *m* (*ma*) *d* is ninety-two. Thus, its *istinṭâq* is *ṣ-b*. Here, *istinṭâq* may refer to the method of the "great calculation," described hereafter.

(the letters) according to the "great calculation."[939] The ascendant, (let us assume,) is Aries, (and) the fourth (sign after Aries)[940] is Cancer, the seventh Libra, and the tenth Capricornus, which is the strongest of the cardines. The article that goes with the name of each sign is omitted. One notes which rational numbers placed in their circle belong to each house (of the zodiac). Then, all the parts of multiples [?] in the proportions resulting from *istinṭâq* are eliminated. Under each letter, (the number [?]) which belongs to it in this connection is written down. Then, one follows the same procedure with regard to the numerical values of the letters of the four elements and (the number [?]) that belongs to them. All these (numbers) are written as letters. The cardines, powers, and dispositions[941] are arranged in a mixed line. One spells the letters out and multiplies whatever must be multiplied, in order to find out the (various) scales. One sums up and tries to open up [?] the answer. Thus, the hidden thought and its answer will be found.

For instance, let us assume that the ascendant is Aries (*al-ḥamal*), as mentioned before. It is written down (in unconnected letters) *ḥ-m-l*. The numerical value of *ḥ* is eight, III, *186*
which can be divided by two, four, and eight. (It thus yields) *d* (four), *b* (two), and *alif* (one). The numerical value of *m* is forty, which can be divided by two, four, eight, ten, and twenty. (It thus yields,) to be precise, [*m* (forty),] *k* (twenty), *y* (ten), *h* (five), *d* (four), and *b* (two). The numerical value of *l* is thirty, which can be divided by two, two-thirds, three, five, six, and ten. (It thus yields) *k* (twenty), *y* (ten), *w* (six), *h* (five), and *j* (three). The same is done with all the letters of the question and the name in each word which happens to occur (in connection with the problem). The chords are found

---

[939] The "great calculation" consists of counting the numerical values of the letters of the *names* of the letters of a given word, disregarding the letters of the word as such. For instance, in the name Muḥammad, the numerical values of *mîm* (*m-y-m*), *ḥâ'* (*ḥ-'*), etc., are added up. Cf. C. A. Nallino, *Raccolta di scritti editi e inediti*, V, 368 (n. 3).

[940] Aries is counted in.

[941] Bulaq: *al-qarâ'in*.

by dividing the square of each letter by its smallest aliquot part.[942] For instance, the numerical value of *d* is four, the square of four is sixteen. This (number) is to be divided by its smallest aliquot part, namely, two. Thus, the chord of *d* is eight. Each chord, then, is placed opposite its letter. Then, the elemental relationships are found out, as has been mentioned before in connection with the explanation of the spelling (method of the great calculation). They have a foundation useful for finding them out from the nature of the letter and the nature of the field of the table in which the (letter) occurs, as was mentioned by the *shaykh* for (the benefit of) those who know the technical terminology.

Deductions that can be drawn with the help of letter systems as to deeply hidden thoughts.

This goes as follows: If someone asks what is the sickness of the patient, the cause of whose disease is not known, and what medicine will be appropriate for its cure, one orders the person who asks the question to name something that can be applied to the name of the unknown sickness, so that the word he names can be made the foundation of (the operation). The word is "spelled out" (*istinṭâq*) together with the name of the ascendant, the elements, the questioner, the day, and the hour, if one wants to go thoroughly into the question. If not, one restricts oneself to the word that the questioner
III, *187* says, and uses it, as we shall explain.

For instance, the questioner says "horse" (*faras*). The numerical value of the three letters (*f-r-s*) with their rational aliquot parts is set down. The numerical value of *f* is eighty,[943] which has the aliquot parts *m* (forty), *k* (twenty), *y* (ten), *ḥ* (eight), and *d* (four). The numerical value of *r* is two hundred, which has the aliquot parts *q* (one hundred), *n* (fifty),

[942] Lit., "largest fraction," that is, the fraction with the largest denominator

[943] A, C, and D have eight. In B, eighty seems to result from a correction of eight.

k-h (twenty-five), *k* (twenty), and *y* (ten). The numerical value of *s* is sixty,[944] which has the aliquot parts *m* (forty), *l* (thirty), *k* (twenty), *y* (ten), *w* (six), and *j* (three). *W* is a perfect number, having (the aliquot parts) four, three, and two, and so is *s*, having (the aliquot parts) forty, thirty, twenty, and ten.[945] If one simplifies [946] the letters of the words and then finds two elements equal, one assumes that the one that has more letters has superiority over the other. Then, one adds up the number of the letters of the elements in the name of the desired object, together with its letters, without simplification. One does the same with the name of the questioner. One assumes that the greater and stronger (number) has superiority.

Description of how to find out the powers of the elements.

FIRE	EARTH	AIR	WATER
	w	*j*	
hhh	*yyyy*	*kkkk*	*ḥ*
mm	*n*	*q*	*l*

The superiority here goes to the earth. Its nature, cold-and-dryness, is the nature of the black bile. Thus, one assumes that the sick person suffers from the black bile. After one has composed an appropriate statement from the letters resulting from the breakdown into aliquot parts, it turns out that the throat is the place where the pain is located. The appropriate medicine is a clyster, and the appropriate liquid lemon juice. This results from the powers of the numbers of the letters of the word "horse." The (preceding discussion) is a brief, appropriate example.

944 Again, according to the Eastern value. Forty as an aliquot part of sixty is two-thirds; cf. p. 221, above.

945 This sentence is not found in B. A "perfect number" is one that is equal to the sum of its aliquot parts (including one). Six, thus, is the sum of one, two, and three.

946 This might refer to the operation called *basṭ*.

III, *188* In order to find out the powers of the elements from proper names, one proceeds in the following way. For instance, one takes "Muḥammad" and writes it with unconnected letters (*m-ḥ-m-d*). Then, one writes down the names of the four elements according to the composition of the (celestial) sphere. The result will be the letters and number of each element. For instance:

FIRE	EARTH	AIR	WATER
Three kinds	Three kinds	Six kinds	Six kinds
'''	*bbb*	*JJ*	*dddd*
hh	*www*	*zz*	*ḥḥḥ*
		kkk	*lll*
mm	*nn*	*ss*	‘‘‘‘
		qq	*rrr*
		nn	*ḥḥḥ*

One will find that the strongest of the elements of the name mentioned is the element of water, because the number of its letters is twenty. Therefore, one gives it superiority over the other elements of the name mentioned. One proceeds in the same way with all names. They are then added to their chords, or to the chord attributed to the ascendant in the *zâ'irajah*, or to the chord of the verse ascribed to Mâlik b. Wuhayb which he made the basis for the mixture of questions and which runs:

> A weighty question you have got. Keep, then, to yourself
> Remarkable doubts which have been raised and which
> can be straightened out with diligence.[947]

This is a famous chord for finding out unknown things. It served as the basis for Ibn ar-Raqqâm [948] and his colleagues.
III, *189* It is a complete, self-sufficient operation (that works) in (all) arbitrary instances.

[947] Cf. p. 214, above.

[948] He might be identical with the mathematician Muḥammad b. Ibrâhîm, d. 715 [1315]. Cf. *GAL*, *Suppl.*, II, 378, though proof is needed for this identification.

The operation with this mentioned chord is as follows.[949] One writes it down with its letters unconnected and mixed with the word of the question according to the technique of "breaking down." [950] The number of the letters of this chord —that is, the verse—is forty-three, because every doubled letter counts as two. Then, the letters (of the questions), which are repeated in the mixing, are eliminated, and one letter which is similar to the letter of the question is eliminated from the basic (verse) for each remaining letter of the question. The two remainders are set down on one line, so mixed that the first letter is taken from the remainder of the "pole," and the second from the remainder of the question, (and so forth), until the two remainders are used up. This yields forty-three (letters). Five *n*'s are then added, so that there are forty-eight letters, and the musical scales are balanced through them. Then, one writes down the remainder in order. If the number of the letters that come out after the mixing, agrees with the original number before elimination, the operation is correct. Then, a table of squares is filled with the (letters) that have been mixed. The end of the first line is the beginning of the second, and so on, until the first line reoccurs. The letters in the "region" follow each other in proportion to the motion. Then, the chord of each letter is brought out, as was mentioned before. It is put opposite its letters. Then, the elemental relations of the letters of the table are found out, in order to indicate their natural power, their spiritual scales, their psychic dispositions, and their principal bases from the table that has been composed for that purpose.

The way to find out the elementary relations is to note III, *190*
what the nature of the first letter of the table is, and what the nature of the field in which it resides is. If the two agree, it is good. If not, a relation between the two letters must be found out. This rule extends to all the letters of the table. Those who know the rules as they have been established in the

[949] Cf. pp. 214 f., above.
[950] Cf. pp. 172 and 183, above.

musical circle can easily prove the correctness of this (procedure).

Then,[951] one takes the chord of each letter after multiplying it by the bases of the four cardines of the (celestial) sphere, as was mentioned before. One should avoid what is adjacent to the cardines, and also the *sawâqiṭ*, because their relationship is confused. The result here is the first degree of diffusion. Then, one takes the total of the elements and subtracts from it [?] the bases of the generated things. There remains the base of the world of creation after it has been exposed to the moments [?] of creation. Then, there are transferred to it some abstractions from matter—the elements that constitute matter. The result is the middle horizon of the soul. The first degree of diffusion is subtracted from the total of the elements. There remains the world of mediation. It has to do with the worlds of simple beings and not with (those of) composite ones.

The world of mediation is then multiplied by the middle horizon of the soul. The result is the most high horizon. To it, the first degree of diffusion is transferred. Then, the first of the elements basically constituting matter is subtracted from the fourth (degree of diffusion [?]). There remains the third degree of diffusion. The total of the particulars of the elements is always multiplied by the fourth degree of diffusion. The result is the first world of particularization. The result of the multiplication of the second (element) with the second (degree of diffusion) is the second world of particularization. The same is the case with the third and fourth.
III, *191* The worlds of particularization are added up and subtracted from the world of totality. There remain the worlds of abstraction. They are divided by the most high horizon. The result is the first particular.

From here, the operation is continued until its completion. There are preliminary remarks to it in the books of Ibn Waḥshîyah, al-Bûnî, and others. The procedure follows a

[951] For the following operation, cf. pp. 217 f., above.

natural and definite[951a] norm that applies to this and other metaphysical disciplines. The construction of letter *zâ'irajahs*, as well as the divine art and philosophical magic center around it.

It[952] should be known that all these operations lead only to getting an answer that corresponds to the idea of the question. They do not give information on anything supernatural. They are a sort of witty (game), as we mentioned at the beginning of the book.[953] Likewise, they do not belong to the science of letter magic (*sîmiyâ'*), as we have explained it.

God gives inspiration. He is asked for help. He is trusted. He suffices us. He is a good protector.

[29] *The science of alchemy.*[954]

This is a science that studies the substance through which the generation of gold and silver may be artificially accomplished, and comments on the operation leading to it. The (alchemists) acquire knowledge of the tempers and powers of all created things and investigate them critically. They hope that they may thus come upon the substance that is prepared to (produce gold and silver). They even investigate the waste matter of animals, such as bones, feathers, hair,[955] eggs, and excrements, not to mention minerals.[956]

Alchemy, then, comments on the operations through which such a substance may be transformed from potentiality into actuality, as, for instance, by the dissolution of bodies (substances) into their natural components through sublima- III, *192*
tion and distillation,[957] by the solidification of meltable (substances) through calcification, by the pulverization of solid materials with the help of pestles and mullers and similar

---

[951a] *Ḥukmî*, rather than *ḥikmî* "philosophical."

[952] This paragraph is not in Bulaq. C has it in the margin.

[953] The reference appears to be to 1:243 f., above.

[954] Cf. also pp. 267 ff., below.

[955] "Hair" is added in C and D.

[956] Cf. p. 268, below.

[957] *Taṣ'îd* and *taqṭîr* are differentiated by the material subjected to the chemical process. Cf. al-Khuwârizmî, *Mafâtîḥ al-'ulûm*, p. 149.

things. The (alchemists) assume that all these techniques lead to the production of a natural substance which they call "the elixir." [958] When some mineral substance, such as lead, tin, or copper, which is prepared, in a manner (and degree) that closely approaches (preparedness) in actuality, for receiving the form of gold or silver, is heated in the fire and some (quantity) of the elixir is added [959] to it, that substance turns into pure gold. In the technical terminology that the (alchemists) use for purposes of mystification, they give the cover name of "spirit" to the elixir and that of "body" to the substance to which the elixir is added.

The science that comments on this technical terminology and on the form of the technical operation by which predisposed substances are turned into the form of gold and silver, is the science of alchemy. In both ancient and modern times, people have written works on alchemy. Discussions of alchemy are occasionally ascribed to people who were not alchemists.

The chief systematic writer on alchemy, according to the alchemists, is Jâbir b. Ḥayyân. Alchemists even consider alchemy Jâbir's special preserve and call it "the science of Jâbir." He wrote seventy treatises on alchemy.[960] All of them read like puzzles. It is thought [961] that only those who know all that is in (Jâbir's treatises) can unlock the secrets of alchemy.[962]

Aṭ-Ṭughrâ'î,[963] a recent Eastern philosopher, wrote systematic works on alchemy and disputations with alchemists and other philosophers.

Maslamah al-Majrîṭî, a Spanish philosopher, wrote on alchemy the *Rutbat al-ḥakîm*. He wrote the *Rutbah* as a counterpart to his work on sorcery and talismans entitled

[958] *Al-iksîr*, from Greek ξήριον.

[959] Literally, "thrown," corresponding to Greek ἐπιβάλλειν.

[960] Cf. P. Kraus, *Jâbir Ibn Ḥayyân*, I, 41 ff. Cf. p. 157, above, and p. 269, below.

[961] Or rather: "He thought"?

[962] Cf. Bombaci, p. 461.

[963] Al-Ḥasan (al-Ḥusayn) b. ʿAlî, *ca.* 453 [1061] to 515 [1121]. Cf. *GAL*, I, 247 f.; *Suppl.*, I, 439 f.

Ghâyat al-ḥakîm. He thought that the two arts (alchemy and sorcery) were both results and fruits of philosophy and III, 193
science, and that those who were not acquainted with them would miss the fruit of scholarship and philosophy altogether.[964]

Maslamah's discussion in the *Rutbah* and the discussions of all the (alchemists) in their respective works employ puzzling means of expression which are difficult for those who have not familiarized themselves with the technical terminology of (alchemists), to understand. We shall mention the reason why the alchemists had recourse to these cover names and puzzling means of expression.[965]

Ibn al-Mughayribî,[966] a leading alchemist, has (written alchemical) maxims in verses the rhyme letter of which is each letter of the alphabet, taken up in turn. The verses belong among the most original poetry there is. All of them employ a puzzling manner of expression, (and they are) like elusive riddles. They can hardly be understood.

Works on alchemy are attributed to al-Ghazzâlî,[967] but this attribution is not correct, because al-Ghazzâlî's lofty perceptions would not have permitted him to study, or, eventually, to adopt the errors of alchemical theories.

Some alchemical theories and opinions are occasionally attributed to Khâlid b. Yazîd b. Mu'âwiyah,[968] a stepson of

[964] Cf. Ibn Khaldûn's opinion below, p. 246.

[965] Cf. p. 246, below.

[966] He is mentioned again as al-Mughayribî, p. 269, below. A Mughayribî family is mentioned, in the fifteenth century, in as-Sakhâwî, *aḍ-Ḍaw' al-lâmi'* (Cairo, 1353–55/1934–36), VIII, 164, but in spite of the rarity of the name, there is no information to connect the above-mentioned author with the later family. (He is Ibn Arfa' Ra'sahû [M. Ullmann].)

[967] Cf. the list of titles in *GAL*, I, 426; *Suppl.*, I, 755 f. The MS. Nuru Osmaniye, 3634, in Istanbul, also contains two short works on the elixir, ascribed to al-Ghazzâlî, one without a title, and the other entitled *at-Taqrîb fî ma'rifat at-tarkîb*.

[968] The legendary first Muslim scientist and translator of Greek literature into Arabic, who is said to have died between 84 and 90 [703 and 708/9]. Cf. *GAL*, I, 67; *Suppl.*, I, 106; Ibn an-Nadîm, *Fihrist*, pp. 242, 354 (ed. Flügel); pp. 338, 497 (Cairo, 1348/1929–30); al-Bukhârî, *Ta'rîkh*, II 1, 166; Ibn Ḥajar, *Tahdhîb*, III, 128 f. The historical Khâlid aspired to the caliphate for a short time. Marwân married his mother, Yazîd's wife, for political reasons.

Marwân b. al-Ḥakam. However, it is very well known that Khâlid was an Arab by race and close to the Bedouin attitude. Thus, he was not familiar with the sciences and crafts in general. How, then, could he have known an unusual craft based upon knowledge of the natures and tempers of composite things, when the physical and medical works of scholars who did research on those subjects had not yet appeared and had not yet been translated? The only possibility is that there existed another Khâlid b. Yazîd among persons versed in the various crafts, and that the mix-up was caused by identical names.

I shall pass on here an epistle on alchemy written by Abû
III, 194 Bakr b. Bishrûn [969] to Ibn as-Samḥ. Both were pupils of Maslamah. If considered as carefully as it deserves to be, the discussion of (Ibn Bishrûn) will show my [970] attitude toward alchemy. After some introductory (remarks) in the epistle, which have nothing to do with the subject, Ibn Bishrûn said:

"The premises of this noble craft were mentioned by the ancients. All of them were reported by the philosophers. Such premises are knowledge of the generation of minerals, of the creation of rocks and precious stones, and of the different natures of regions and localities. As they are well known, we shall not mention them. But I shall explain to you

---

[969] Ibn Bishrûn's lifetime is fixed at *ca.* A.D. 1000 through his relationship to Maslamah and Ibn as-Samḥ. Cf. pp. 126 f., above. On the title page of the *Rutbah* in the Istanbul MS. Ragib Paşa, 963, fol. 90*a*, there is a biography of Maslamah which mentions Abû Bakr Ibn Bishrûn among his pupils and as authority for the statement that an estrangement had taken place between Ibn as-Samḥ and Maslamah.

It may be mentioned that there is no information that Ibn as-Samḥ wrote works on alchemy, nor is the historical Maslamah considered an author on alchemy or magic. Thus, Ibn Bishrûn's treatise may be pseudepigraphical. Ḥâjjî Khalîfah, *Kashf aẓ-ẓunûn*, III, 595 f., refers to a work on alchemy, *Sirr al-kîmiyâ'*, by a certain Ibn Bishrûn al-Maghribî, who may be identical with our Ibn Bishrûn. Identification with the Sicilian poet 'Uthmân b. 'Abd-ar-Raḥîm b. Bashrûn, implied by E. Griffini in *Centenario della nascita di M. Amari* (Palermo, 1910), I, 445, is almost certainly wrong. * A different but related work by Ibn Bishrûn in MS. Beshir Agha 505, 86*a*–91*b* (Fuat Sezgin).

[970] The MSS read *adhhabu* (the vocalization is indicated in C). Bulaq corrects to *dhahaba*, which would mean "*his* attitude." At first glance this might appear the more natural idea, but the text as transmitted cannot be understood that way, since a reading *udhhiba* is not possible.

what one needs to know of this craft. Thus, let us start with that knowledge.

"It has been said: The students of this science must first know three things: (1) whether it exists, (2) what brings it into being, and (3) how it comes into being. If the student of alchemy knows these three things well, he achieves his object and knows as much as can be known about this science.

"As to the problem of the existence of alchemy and the proofs for the (forces) that bring alchemy into existence, the elixir that we have sent to you is a satisfying answer.

"The question of what brings alchemy into being implies, according to alchemists, search for the stone that makes the (alchemical) operation possible. Potentially, the operation may be performed with any (conceivable) thing, because the (potentiality to perform the operation) comes from the four natures (elements). It originated from their composition at the beginning and will revert to them at the end. However, there are things that might be used for the operation (only) potentially, not actually. This comes about as follows. There are some things that can be decomposed. There are others that cannot be decomposed. Those that can be decomposed III, *195*
can be processed and treated. They are the things that can be transformed from potentiality into actuality. On the other hand, the things that cannot be decomposed cannot be processed and treated, because they have nothing but potentiality in them. They cannot be decomposed, in order to give some of the elements they contain an advantage over the others and to have the power of the bigger (elements) predominate over the lesser ones.

"You—may God give you success—must therefore know the most suitable of the decomposable stones that can be used for the operation. You must know its genus, power, action, and which kind of dissolution or solidification, purification, calcification, absorption, or transformation it may be able to effect. People who do not know these basic principles of alchemy will never be successful or achieve any good results. You must know whether (the stone) can be aided by something else or is sufficient by itself, and whether it is one (thing by itself) at the beginning or is associated with something else and becomes one (thing by itself) during the treatment, and is therefore called 'stone.' You must also know how it works; how much its components must weigh and what times (are suitable) for it; how the spirit is inserted and the soul made to enter into it; whether fire can separate (the soul) from (the stone) after it has been inserted (in it); if not, why (not), and what makes it necessary that it be that way. This is what one wants (to know).

"It should be understood and realized that all philosophers have praised the soul and thought that it is the soul that governs, sustains, and defends the body and is active in it. For, when the soul leaves the body, the body dies and gets cold. It cannot move or defend itself, because there is no life in it and no light. I have mentioned the body and the soul only because this craft (alchemy) is similar to the body of man, which is built up by regular meals [971] and which persists and is perfected by the living, luminous soul, which enables
III, *196* the body to do the great and mutually contradictory things that only the living power of the soul can do. Man suffers from the disharmony of his component elements. If his elements were in complete harmony and (thus) not affected by accidents and (inner) contradictions, the soul would not be able to leave his body. Man would then live eternally. Praised be He who governs all things, He is exalted.

"It should be known that the natures (elements) producing the (alchemical) operation constitute a quality that pushes (forward) at the beginning, and a process of emanation requiring an end. When they have reached this limit, they cannot be transformed (back) into the (state) that (formed the starting point of) their composition, as we stated at the outset with regard to man.[972] The natures of the substance had been separate, but now they adhere to each other and have

[971] Lit., "luncheon and dinner."

[972] Referring to the statement that body and soul can be separated but not reunited after separation?

become one thing, similar to the soul in power and activity, and similar to the body in having composition and pulse.[973] There is a strange thing about the actions of the elements. It is the weak (element) that is powerful, since it has power over the decomposition, composition, and completion of things. It is in this sense that I use (the words) 'powerful' and 'weak.' Change and nonbeing in the first composition occur only as the result of disharmony (among the component elements). They do not occur in the second composition, because there then is harmony (among the component elements).

"An early (philosopher-alchemist) has said: 'Decomposition and division mean life and duration, as far as the alchemical operation is concerned, while composition means death and nonbeing.' This statement has a subtle meaning. The philosopher meant by 'life and duration' its [974] transformation from nonexistence into existence. As long as it remains in (the state of) its first composition, it is, no doubt, nonbeing. But when the second composition takes place, nonbeing no longer exists. Now, the second composition comes about only after decomposition and division. Thus, decomposition and division are peculiar to the (alchemical) III, *197*
operation. If it [975] is applied to the soluble body (substance), it spreads in it, because it has no form, since it has come to take in the body the place of the soul which has no form. This is because it has no weight as far as (the substance) is concerned. You will see this, if God—He is exalted—wills.

"You must realize that mixing a fine thing with another fine thing is easier than mixing a coarse thing with another coarse thing. I have in mind here the similarity in form among spirits (on the one hand) and bodies (substances, on the other), for it is the form of things that causes their union. I mention this to you, so that you may know that the (alchemical) operation is more agreeable and simpler if it is

[973] For "pulse" in alchemical literature, cf. P. Kraus, *Jâbir Ibn Ḥayyân, textes choisis* (Paris & Cairo, 1354/1935), pp. 51 ff., and *Jâbir Ibn Ḥayyân*, II, 236.

[974] That is, the transformation of the alchemical operation, or of the stone.

[975] That is, the operation, or the stone.

undertaken with fine spiritual elements than if it is undertaken with coarse corporeal (substances).

"It is logical that stones are stronger in their resistance to fire than spirits. Likewise, gold, iron, and copper are observed to offer more resistance to fire than sulphur, mercury, and other spirits. Therefore, I say: The substances were spirits at the beginning. When the heat of the natural process (*kiyân*) affects them, they are transformed by it into coarse, coherent substances. Fire is not able to consume them, because they are exceedingly coarse and coherent. When an exceedingly great amount of fire is applied to them, it turns them again into spirits, as they had been when they were first created. If fire (then again) affects the fine spirits, they flee and are not able to endure it. Thus, you must know what brought the substances to their particular condition and (what) brought the spirits to theirs. That is the most important knowledge you can have.

"I say: The spirits flee and are burned, because of their combustibility and fineness. They became combustible because of their great share of humidity. When fire notices
III, *198* humidity, it attaches itself to it, because (humidity) is airy [975a] and (thus) similar to fire. (The fire) does not stop eating it, until (the humidity) is consumed. The same applies to substances when, (noticing) the approach of fire, they flee,[976] because they have little coherence and are coarse. (But) they are not combustible, because they are composed of earth and water which offers resistance to fire, in that the fine (components of water) unite with its coarse (components) through a long (process of) cooking which softens and mixes things. For, anything that is annihilated through fire [977] is annihilated only because its fine (components) separate (under the influence of fire) from its coarse (components), and its parts

[975a] *Hawâ'îyah ?* The MSS have *hw'yh*. The meaning is doubtful. Perhaps, *huwîyah* is meant: "a substance similar to fire."

[976] Bulaq has a simpler, perhaps correct text: "when they notice the approach of fire."

[977] "Through fire" belongs here, rather than after the second "annihilated."

merge with each other without dissolution and adaptation. Thus, the resulting combination and interpenetration is (mere) aggregation, not (real) mixture. Therefore, (the fine and the coarse elements) are as easily separated (under the influence of fire) as water and oil (are), or similar things. I describe this merely so that you may learn from it (the facts) about composition and opposition with regard to the elements. If you have a sufficient knowledge of this, you know as much about the (elements) as can be known by you.

"You must (further) know that the mixtures, which are the elements of alchemy, agree with one another. They are derived from one substance. One order and one treatment unite them all. Nothing strange enters into either a (single) part or into the whole of it.[978] In this sense, the philosopher has said: 'If you have a good knowledge of the treatment and composition of the elements, and if you do not permit anything strange to enter into them, you [979] have a good knowledge of what you want to know well and definitely, since the (alchemical) element is one (element) and contains nothing that is strange to it. He who brings something strange into it falsifies it and commits an error.'

"It should be known that if a cognate substance is properly dissolved for this (alchemical) element, so that it becomes similar to it in respect of fineness and subtleness, the (alchemical) element expands in it and follows it wherever it goes. As long as substances remain coarse and rough, they cannot expand or be paired, and they can dissolve only with III, *199*
the help of spirits.

"You—may God guide you—should understand this statement in that sense. You—may God guide you—should know that such dissolution in the animal substance is the truth, which neither perishes nor decreases. It is the thing that transforms the elements, holds them, and produces for

[978] The suffix used in Arabic seems to refer to "treatment," but one would expect it to refer to "the mixtures." Cf. below. This, however, would require too much of a correction. Is the suffix meant to refer to "substance"?

[979] The complete text as translated, to the end of the paragraph, is found in Bulaq, and not in A, B, C, or D.

them marvelous colors and blossoms. Not every substance dissolves in this way,[980] which is (the way of) complete dissolution, because it is contrary to life. It dissolves only in so far as (the process of dissolution) is agreeable to it and serves to defend it against the burning action of fire, until it is no longer coarse and the elements are transformed to the degree of fineness or coarseness possible for them. When the substances have reached their limit of dissolution and refinement, they then obtain a power that holds, immerses,[981] transforms, and pervades. An (alchemical) operation, the test of whose truthfulness does not appear at the beginning, is no good.

"It should be known that the cold nature dries things out and ties down their humidity, while heat causes the humidity of things to appear and ties down their dryness. I have singled out heat and cold because they are active, and humidity and dryness (because they) are passive. The passivity of (the two opposites) toward each other creates and generates the substances. Heat, however, does so more actively than cold, because the cold cannot transport and move things, while heat is the cause of motion. When the heat that causes generation is weak, it never achieves anything. Correspondingly, if the heat affecting a thing is excessive, and there is no cold there, it burns the thing and destroys it. For this reason, some cold is needed in (alchemical) operations, so that the power of opposites may be balanced and there may be protection
III, 200 against the heat of fire.

"There is nothing the philosophers have warned against more insistently than burning fires. They have commanded (alchemists) to cleanse the elements and the breaths, to remove their dirt and humidity, and to keep away their harmful (actions) and uncleanliness from (fires). That is the sound basis of their doctrine and treatment. The (alchemical) operation begins with fire and ends with fire. Therefore, the philos-

[980] *Leg.: ḥallan <mithla hâdhâ l-ḥalli wa-> hâdhâ.*

[981] *Taghûṣu,* as in C and D, which would be intransitive, or perhaps, rather, transitive *tughawwiṣu.* Cf. p. 241, l. 7, below.

ophers have said, 'Beware of burning fires.' By that they meant that one should keep away the harmful (actions) that go with (fire). (Otherwise,) two kinds of harmful (actions) would combine against the substance and speed its destruction. Also, anything may suffer annihilation and corruption through itself,[982] because its elements are opposed to each other and there is disharmony in it. It thus stands in the middle between two things [983] and does not find anything to strengthen and aid it, but the harmful (actions) overpower and destroy it.

"It should be known that the sages have mentioned that spirits return repeatedly to bodies (substances), so that they may have greater coherence with them and greater strength to fight the fire, since they (the spirits) come into contact with (the fire) at the moment of union—I mean here elemental fire. This should be realized.

"We are now going to speak about the stone that makes the (alchemical) operation possible, as mentioned by the philosophers. They have held different opinions about it. Some have thought that it is (to be found) in animals; some have thought, in plants; some have thought, in minerals; and, according to some, in everything. We do not have to examine these claims and enter into a dispute concerning them with the people who make them, because that would be a very long discussion. I have already stated [984] that the (alchemical) operation might potentially be performed with anything, because the elements exist in every thing. This is so.

"We want to know what produces the (alchemical) operation (both) potentially and actually. Therefore, we turn to the statement of al-Ḥarrânî [985] that all dyeing [986] consists of

[982] "Through itself" (*min dhâtihî*) is the correct addition of Bulaq.

[983] I.e., its own tendency toward destruction and the destructive action of fire.

[984] Cf. p. 231, above.

[985] None of the many Ḥarrânîs of the ninth and tenth centuries is known as an outstanding authority on alchemy. He might possibly be Sâlim, the "Syrian" alchemical authority from Ḥarrân, mentioned by ar-Râzî. Cf. J. Ruska in *Der Islam*, XXII (1935), 289. * MS. Beshir Agha, *505*, 149*b*.

[986] From Greek βαφή.

III, 201 two kinds. One may use a substance such as saffron, which is used to dye a white garment. The (saffron) eventually changes in it, vanishing and being decomposed. The second kind of dyeing is transformation of the substance of one thing into the substance and color of something else. Thus trees, for instance, transform the soil into themselves, and animals the plants, so that eventually the soil becomes plants, and the plants animals. This can come about only with the help of the living spirit and the active nature (*kiyân*) which has the ability to generate substances and change essences.

"If this be so, I say that the (alchemical) operation must be either in animals or in plants. Proof of this is that both animals and plants need food by their very nature, in order to subsist and to materialize.

"Plants do not have the same fineness and power that animals have. Therefore, the sages rarely turned to them. Animals are the last and final stage of the three permutations. Minerals turn into plants, and plants into animals, but animals cannot turn into anything finer than themselves. They may, however, revert back to (greater) coarseness. Furthermore, animals are the only things in the world to which the living spirit attaches itself. Now, the spirit is the finest thing there is in the world. It attaches itself to animals only because it is similar to them. The spirit existing in plants is insignificant. It is coarse and thick. In addition, it is submerged and hidden in plants, because it is coarse itself and because the substance of plants is coarse. (Plants,) thus, cannot move, because they themselves are coarse and because their spirit is coarse. The mobile spirit is much finer than the hidden one.
III, 202 The former accepts food. It can be moved, and it can breathe. The latter can only accept food. As compared with the living spirit, it occupies no better position than that of earth as compared to water. This is how plants compare with animals. Therefore, it is much more advanced and much simpler to use animals for the (alchemical) operation. The intelligent person who knows this must try the (method) that is easy. He must not do what he fears might be difficult.

"It should be known that the sages have divided living beings into 'mothers'—the elements—and 'young ones'—the generated beings. That is well known and easy to understand. The sages thus divided the elements and the generated beings into living ones and dead ones. They assumed that anything that moves is active and living and that anything that is stationary is passive and dead. They made this division for all things, for the meltable substances and the mineral drugs. Anything that is meltable in fire and volatile and combustible, they called 'living.' Anything of the opposite qualities, they called 'dead.' The animals and plants that can be decomposed into the four elements, they called living. Those that cannot, they called dead.

"Then, they searched all the living groups. Among the things that can be decomposed into four components obvious to the eye, they did not find anything suitable for alchemy. The only (suitable) thing they found was 'the stone' which is in animals. They studied its genus. Eventually, they came to know it. They took it and treated it. As a result, they obtained the desired qualities from it.

"Similar qualities may be obtained in minerals and plants, after (various mineral or vegetable) drugs are combined, mixed, and then separated again. There are plants, such as III, 203
saltwort,[987] that can be decomposed into certain of the (four) components. Minerals contain substances, spirits, and breaths which, when they are mixed and treated, produce something that may exercise an influence. We have tried all that out.

"Animals are much more advanced. Their treatment is much simpler. Thus, one must know what is the stone that exists in animals, and how it can be found.

"We have made it clear that animals are the highest of generated things. In the same sense, whatever is composed from them (animals) is finer than (plants),[988] just as plants are finer than earth. Plants are finer than earth, because they are

[987] Used for the preparation of alkali.

[988] As it stands, the Arabic suffix has no antecedent except "animals."

created from its [989] pure essence and fine substance. Therefore, they are necessarily fine and subtle. The animal stone is in the same position (among animals) as plants are in the soil. In general, there is nothing in living beings that can be decomposed into four elements except (that stone). This statement must be understood. It can hardly remain concealed from anyone except an obviously stupid person who has no intelligence.

"I have thus informed you about the quiddity and genus of the stone. Now I am going to explain to you the different kinds of treatment. Thus, we shall give you your fair share (of information), as we have taken it upon ourselves to do, if God—praised be He—wills.

"With God's blessing, here is the treatment: Take the noble stone. Deposit it in the cucurbit and alembic. Separate its four elements, which are water, air, earth, and fire. They are substance, spirit, soul,[990] and dyeing. When you have separated the water from the earth and the air from the fire, keep each one apart in its own vessel. Take the dregs—the
III, *204* sediment—at the bottom of the vessel. Wash it with hot fire, until the fire has removed its blackness, and its coarseness and toughness have disappeared. Blanch it carefully and evaporate the superfluities of the humidities concealed [991] in it. It will thus become white water, which contains no darkeness, dirt, or disharmony. Then, turn to those primary elements that are distilled from it. Cleanse them, too, of blackness and disharmony. Wash them repeatedly and sublimate them, until they become fine, subtle, and pure. When you have done this, God has given you success.

"Then, start with the composition around which the operation centers. This is as follows. Composition comes about only through pairing (marriage) and putrefaction. Pairing (marriage) is the mixture of the fine with the coarse.

[989] I.e., the pure essence of earth. The text must be corrected in this sense. As it stands, the Arabic suffix can refer only to "plants."

[990] Here the reading *nafs*, and not *nafas* "breath," is indicated.

[991] *Mustajinnah*, as in Bulaq and the MSS.

Putrefaction is purgation [992] and pulverization undertaken so that the various parts may mix, as water does, with each other and form one thing containing no confusion [993] or deficiency in itself. In this condition, the coarse (components) have the strength to hold the fine ones back; the spirit has the strength to oppose the fire and can tolerate it; and the soul has the strength to immerse itself and slip into the substances.

"This (situation) exists only after composition. When the soluble substance is paired with the spirit, it mingles with it in all its parts, and the parts interpenetrate, because they are similar to each other. Thus, (the resulting mixture) becomes one thing. The fact that (the spirit) is mixed (with the body) makes it necessary for the spirit to be affected by well-being, corruption, duration [?],[994] and persistence, like the body. Likewise, when the soul mixes with (substance and spirit) and penetrates them through the services of the (alchemical) treatment, all the parts of the (soul) [995] mingle with all the parts of the two other (things), that is, spirit and III, 205
substance. Thus, the (soul) and the two become one thing that contains no disagreement and is in the position of the universal particular whose elements are intact and whose parts are in harmony with each other.

"When this compound meets the soluble substance, and fire is constantly applied to it, and the humidity in it is brought to the surface, it melts in the soluble substance. Humidity implies combustion and an attachment of the fire to itself. But when the fire wants to attach itself to it, its admixture of water prevents it from union with the soul, for fire does not unite with oil, until it is pure. Likewise, water implies aversion to fire. Thus, when fire is constantly applied

[992] This seems the most likely meaning of *tamshiyah* in this context, although the word is not known to me as a technical term of alchemy. It might have a meaning close to "digestion," which is always associated with putrefaction. (*Tamsiyah*, "decomposition" [M. Ullmann].)

[993] *Ikhtilâṭ* usually means "mixture," but this meaning would not seem to make sense in the context. Bulaq corrects to *ikhtilâf* "disagreement."

[994] One would expect, rather, "annihilation, nonbeing" (*al-fanâ'*), and possibly the text should be corrected in this sense.

[995] *Ajzâ'uhâ.*

to it and wants to evaporate it, the dry substance which is mixed with (the water) keeps it back inside and prevents it from evaporation. Thus, the substance is the cause of holding the water; the water is the cause of the duration of the oil; the oil is the cause of the persistence of the dyeing; and the dyeing is the cause of the appearance of color and the indication of oiliness in dark things that have no light and no life. This is the right substance. The (alchemical) operation comes about in this way.

"The 'egg' [996] about which you have inquired (is the thing) the sages call 'egg.' It is what they have in mind (when they speak about the 'egg'), and not the egg of the chicken. It should be known that the sages did not choose an inappropriate name by calling it 'egg.' They called it 'egg,' because it can be compared to an egg. I asked Maslamah about it one day when I was alone with him. I said to him, 'O excellent sage, tell me, why did the sages call the animal compound "egg"? Was that something arbitrary on their part, or was there some reason that caused them to do so?' He replied,
III, *206* 'Indeed, there is deep meaning in it.' I said, 'O sage, what advantage (did they see) and what indication of a connection with alchemy did they find in comparing it with an egg and calling it "egg"? ' He said, 'Because the egg is similar to and related to the compound. Think it over, and the meaning of it will appear to you.' I remained with him, thinking it over, but I could not get at the meaning of it. When he saw that I was deep in thought and my soul immersed in it, he grasped my arm, nudged me slightly, and said to me, 'O Abû Bakr, it is because of the relationship that exists between the two with regard to the quantity of colors at the time of the mixture and composition of the elements.' When he said that, the

[996] On the "egg" of the alchemists, originally intended to be an alloy of copper, lead, iron, and tin, but also considered as the alchemical "stone," cf., esp., M. Berthelot and C. E. Ruelle, *Collection des anciens alchimistes grecs* (Paris, 1888), pp. 18 ff. (text), pp. 18 ff. (tr.).

What follows is a characteristic device of esoteric literature, namely, the pupil asking the teacher for an explanation. Cf., for instance, P. Kraus, *Jâbir Ibn Ḥayyân, textes choisis*, p. 79; *Jâbir Ibn Ḥayyân*, I, XXXVI (n. 6).

darkness (that had enveloped my mind) left me. A light lit up my heart and gave my intellect the power to understand it. I stood up and went home, thanking God—He is exalted—for it. I constructed a geometrical figure to illustrate it. It proves the correctness of Maslamah's statement. I am writing it down for you in this book (epistle).

"For instance: when the compound is complete and perfect, the element of air in it is, to the element of air in the egg, in the same proportion as the element of fire in the former is to the element of fire in the latter. The same applies to the two other elements, earth and water. Now, I say: two things that in this manner are proportionate to each other are similar to each other. For example, assume that the plane of the egg is *HZWḤ*.[997] If we want that, we take the smallest element [998] of the compound, that of dryness, and add to it the same (amount) of the element of humidity. We treat the two, until the element of dryness absorbs the element of humidity and takes over its power. This discussion contains a certain secret hint which, however, will not remain con- III, 207
cealed from you. Then we add to the two the same (amount as theirs) of the spirit, that is, water. Thus, the whole consists of six equal (parts). Then we treat the whole and add to it the same (amount) of the element of air, which is the soul. That is three parts. Thus, the whole consists of nine parts equal in power to dryness. Under each of two sides of this compound whose nature (element) encloses the plane of the compound, we then put two elements. The first two sides that enclose the plane of the compound are assumed to be those of the elements of water and air. They are the two sides *AJD*.[999] The plane is *ABJD*. Correspondingly, the two sides that enclose the plane of the 'egg' (and) which represent water and air are two sides of the (plane) *HZWḤ*. Now, I

[997] In our letters, *EGFH*. The plane of the "egg" *EGFH* is said to be similar to the plane of the "stone" *AJBD* (in our letters, *ACBD*), and, therefore, the "stone" is called "egg."

[998] *Leg. ṭabâʾiʿ*, as in Bulaq, or, perhaps, *aṭ-ṭabâʾiʿ* <*fî*>.

[999] The MSS seem to have *AḤJ*, but apparently the sides *AJ* and *AD* of the plane *AJBD* are meant.

say: the plane *ABJD* is similar to the plane *HZWḤ* <. . .> the element of air which is called 'soul.' [1000] The same applies to (the side) *BJ* of the plane of the compound. The sages never called anything by the name of something (else), except when the first thing could be compared to the other.

"Words for an explanation of which you have asked (me) are 'holy land' [1001] – it means the combination of the higher and the lower elements; 'copper,' which is the (substance) the blackness of which has been removed and which was cut in pieces until it became an atom, and was then colored red with copperas, until it came to be copper.[1002] '*Maghnîsiyâ*' [1003] is the stone of the (alchemists) in which the spirits are frozen and which is brought forth by the higher nature in which the spirits are emprisoned, in order to fight the fire (and protect) them against it. '*Furfurah*' (purple) is a perishable red color that is produced by nature (*kiyân*). 'Lead' is a stone that has three powers of different individualities which, however, are similar to each other in form and genus. One of them is spiritual, luminous, and clear. It is the active power. The second is psychic. It moves and has sensual perception. How-
III, *208* ever, it is coarser than the first power. Its center is below that of the first (power). The third power is an earthy power. It is solid and astringent. It turns back toward the center of the earth because of its gravity. It is the power that holds the spiritual and psychic powers together and encloses them.

"All the remaining (words) are innovations created in order to confuse the ignorant. He who knows the (basic) premises can dispense with everything else.

"That is all you have asked me about. I have explained

[1000] Or "breath"?

[1001] For "Holy Land" as a cover name for mercury, cf. A. Siggel, *Decknamen in der arabischen alchemistischen Literatur* (Berlin, 1951), p. 34.

[1002] Bulaq: *nukhâsîyan* "like copper."

[1003] The "Magnesia" of the alchemists is some undetermined kind of alloy. Cf. E. O. von Lippmann, *Entstehung und Ausbreitung der Alchemie* (Berlin, 1919), Index, *s.v.* "Magnesia."

it to you in this epistle. We hope with God's help that you will achieve your wish. Farewell."

Here ends the discussion by Ibn Bishrûn, one of the great pupils of Maslamah al-Majrîṭî, the Spanish authority on alchemy, letter magic, and sorcery, for the third [ninth] century and later (times).

One can see how all the expressions used by (alchemists) tend to be secret hints and puzzles,[1004] scarcely to be explained or understood. This is proof of the fact that alchemy is not a natural craft.

The truth with regard to alchemy, which is to be believed and which is supported by actual fact, is that alchemy is one of the ways in which the spiritual souls exercise an influence and are active in the world of nature. (It may) belong among the (miraculous) acts of divine grace, if the souls are good. Or it may be a kind of sorcery, if the souls are bad and wicked.[1005] It is obvious that (alchemy may materialize) as a (miraculous) act of divine grace. It may be sorcery, because the sorcerer, as has been established in the proper place, may change the identity of matter by means of his magic power.[1006] (People) think that a (sorcerer) must use some substance (in order) for his magical activity to take place. Thus, certain animals may be created from the substance of earth, of hair, or of plants, or, in general, from substances other than their own. That, for instance, happened to the sorcerers of Pharaoh with their III, 209
ropes and sticks.[1007] It also is reported, for instance, of the Negro and Indian sorcerers in the far south and of the Turks in the far north, that by sorcery they force the air to produce rain, and other things.[1008]

Now, since alchemy is the creation of gold in a substance other than that of (gold), it is a kind of sorcery. The famous

[1004] According to the vocalization indicated in D, one would have to translate, "he has turned all the expressions into secret hints . . ."

[1005] Cf. p. 167, above.

[1006] Cf. p. 157, above.

[1007] Cf. p. 168, above.

[1008] Cf. pp. 161 f., above.

sages who discussed the subject, men such as Jâbir, Maslamah, and their non-Muslim predecessors, followed this line. Therefore, they used puzzling expressions. They wanted to protect alchemy from the disapproval that religious laws express for the various kinds of sorcery. It was not because they were reluctant to communicate it (to others), as was thought by people who did not investigate the matter thoroughly.

One may compare the fact that Maslamah called his book on alchemy *Rutbat al-ḥakîm*, while he called his book on sorcery and talismans *Ghâyat al-ḥakîm*. He wanted to intimate that the subject of the *Ghâyah* is a general one, whereas the subject of the *Rutbah* is a restricted one, for *ghâyah* "final goal" is a higher (stage in research) than *rutbah* "degree, rank." The problems of the *Rutbah* are in a way part of the problems of the *Ghâyah*, or deal with the same subjects. (Maslamah's) discussion of the two disciplines clarifies what we have said.

Later on, we shall explain that those who assume that the achievements of alchemy are the result of a natural craft are wrong.[1009]

God is "wise and knowing." [1010]

[30] *A refutation of philosophy. The corruption of the students of philosophy.*

This and the following (two) sections are important. The sciences (of philosophy, astrology, and alchemy) occur in
III, 210 civilization. They are much cultivated in the cities. The harm they (can) do to religion is great. Therefore, it is necessary that we make it clear what they are about and that we reveal what the right attitude concerning them (should be).

There are (certain) intelligent representatives of the human species who think that the essences and conditions of the whole of existence, both the part of it perceivable by the senses and that beyond sensual perception, as well as the reasons and causes of (those essences and conditions), can be

[1009] Cf. pp. 267 ff., below.
[1010] Qur'ân 66.3 (3).

perceived by mental speculation and intellectual reasoning. They also think that the articles of faith are established as correct through (intellectual) speculation and not through tradition, because they belong among the intellectual perceptions. Such people are called "philosophers"—*falâsifah*, plural of *faylasûf*—which is Greek and means "lover of wisdom." [1011]

They did research on the (problem of perception). With great energy, they tried to find the purpose of it. They laid down a norm enabling intellectual speculation to distinguish between true and false. They called (that norm) "logic." [1012] The quintessence of it is that the mental speculation which makes it possible to distinguish between true and false, concentrates on ideas abstracted from the individual *existentia*. From these (individual *existentia*), one first abstracts pictures that conform to all the individual (manifestations of the *existentia*), just as a seal conforms to all the impressions it makes in clay or wax. The abstractions derived from the *sensibilia* are called "primary *intelligibilia*." These universal ideas may be associated with other ideas, from which, however, they are distinguished in the mind. Then, other ideas, namely those that are associated (and have ideas in common) with (the primary *intelligibilia*), are abstracted from them. Then, if still other ideas are associated with them, a second and third abstraction is made, until the process of abstraction
reaches the simple universal ideas, which conform to all ideas III, *211*
and individual (manifestations of the *existentia*). No further abstraction is possible. They are the highest genera. All abstract (ideas) that are not derived from the *sensibilia* serve, if combined with each other, to produce the sciences. They are called "secondary *intelligibilia*."

(Man through his) ability to think studies these abstract *intelligibilia* and seeks through them to perceive existence as it is. For this purpose, the mind must combine some of them

[1011] This correct translation of *φιλόσοφος* was well known to the Arabs. Cf., for instance, Ṣâ'id al-Andalusî, *Ṭabaqât al-umam*, tr. Blachère, p. 58.

[1012] Cf. p. 137, above.

with others or keep them apart with the help of unequivocal rational argumentation. This should give (the mind) a correct and conformable perception of existence, if the (process) takes place according to a sound norm, as mentioned before.

The combination of (abstract *intelligibilia*) and the judgment (concerning them) is apperception (*taṣdîq*).[1013] At the end, philosophers give apperception precedence over perception (*taṣawwur*), but at the beginning and during the process of instruction, they give perception precedence over apperception, because they think that perfected perception is the goal of the search for understanding and that apperception is merely a means for (undertaking that search). In the books of the logicians, one finds a statement to the effect that perception has precedence and that apperception depends upon it. This statement must be understood in the sense of (arriving at) consciousness and not in the sense of (achieving) complete knowledge. This is the opinion of the greatest of them, Aristotle.

Then, philosophers think that happiness consists in arriving at perception of all existing things, both the *sensibilia* and the (things) beyond sensual perception, with the help of (rational) speculation and argumentation. The sum total of their perceptions of existence, the result to which (their perceptions) lead, that is, the detailed conclusions of their speculative propositions, is the following. First, they conclude from observation and sensual perception that there is a
III, *212* lower substance. Then, their perception progresses a little. (The existence of) motion and sensual perception in animals makes them conscious of the existence of the soul. The powers of the soul, then, make them aware of the dominant position of the intellect. Here, their perception stops. They draw their conclusions with regard to the most high celestial body in the same way they drew their conclusions with regard to the human essence. They (thus) consider it necessary that the (celestial) sphere must have a soul and an intellect, like

[1013] Cf. p. 138, above.

human beings. Then, they take as a limit for the (whole system), the number of units, which is ten. Nine are derived in essence and pluralistic. One, the tenth, is primary and singular.[1014]

They assume that happiness consists in the perception of existence with the help of such conclusions (if, at the same time, such perception is) combined with the improvement of the soul and the soul's acceptance of a virtuous character.[1015] Even if no religious law had been revealed (to help man to distinguish between virtue and vice), they think the (acquisition of virtue) possible by man because he is able to distinguish between vice and virtue in (his) actions by means of his intellect, his (ability to) speculate, and his natural inclination toward praiseworthy actions, his natural disinclination for blameworthy actions. They assume that when the soul becomes (virtuous), it attains joy and pleasure, and that ignorance of (moral qualities) means eternal pain. This, in their opinion, is the meaning of bliss or punishment in the other world. They go further in this manner, and by the words they use, they display their well-known obtuseness as far as details are concerned.

The leading representative of these doctrines, who presented the problems connected with them, wrote books on them as (the subject of) a systematic science, and penned the arguments in favor of them, as far as we presently know, was Aristotle the Macedonian, from Macedonia in Byzantine territory, a pupil of Plato and the teacher of Alexander. He is called "the First Teacher," [1016] with no further qualification. It means "teacher of logic," because logic did not exist in an improved form before Aristotle. He was the first to systematize the norms of logic and to deal with all its problems and to III, *213*
give a good and extensive treatment of it. He would, in fact,

[1014] This refers to the sphere of the earth, the seven spheres of the planets, the sphere of the fixed stars, and the tenth, the highest, divine sphere. Cf., for instance, the pseudo-Aristotelian *Secretum secretorum*, tr. from the Arabic in Roger Bacon, *Opera hactenus inedita* (Oxford, 1920), V, 228.

[1015] This refers to ethics as a part of philosophy.

[1016] Cf. 1:275 (n. 75), and pp. 115 f., 139, and 153, above.

have done very well with his norm of logic if (only) it had absolved him of responsibility for the philosophical tendencies that concern metaphysics.[1017]

Later, in Islam, there were men who adopted these doctrines and followed (Aristotle's) opinion with respect to them very closely [1018] except on a few points. This came about as follows.[1019] The 'Abbâsid caliphs had the works of the ancient (philosophers) translated from Greek into Arabic. Many Muslims investigated them critically. Scholars whom God led astray adopted their doctrines and defended them in disputations. They held different opinions on some points of detail. The most famous of these (Muslim philosophers) were Abû Naṣr al-Fârâbî in the fourth [tenth] century, at the time of Sayf-ad-dawlah, and Abû 'Alî Ibn Sînâ (Avicenna) in the fifth [eleventh] century, at the time of the Bûyids [1020] in Iṣfahân, and others.

It should be known that the (opinion) the (philosophers) hold is wrong in all its aspects. They refer all *existentia* to the first intellect and are satisfied with (the theory of the first intellect) in their progress toward the Necessary One (the Deity). This means that they disregard all the degrees of divine creation beyond the (first intellect). Existence, however, is too wide to (be explained by so narrow a view). "And He creates what you do not know." [1021] The philosophers, who restrict themselves to affirming the intellect and neglect everything beyond it, are in a way comparable to physicists who restrict themselves to affirming the body and who disregard (both) soul and intellect in the belief that there

[1017] Lit., "if the responsibility for . . . had been taken (*tukuffila*) for him by others." That is, while Aristotelian logic is acceptable, Aristotelian theological opinions are objectionable.

[1018] Lit., "as one shoe is fashioned after the other."

[1019] For the following remarks, cf. pp. 115 f., above.

[1020] Bulaq has the strange addition of "the Bûyid Niẓâm-al-mulk," which perhaps is a mistake of Ibn Khaldûn's first draft? The Bûyid he would have had in mind could be Tâj-al-mulk (Tâj-ad-dawlah), but the Kâkôyid 'Alâ'-ad-dawlah, ruler of Iṣfahân, who was Avicenna's patron in his later years, would be more likely.

[1021] Qur'ân 16.8 (8).

is nothing beyond the body in (God's) wise plan concerning (the world of) existence.

The arguments that (the philosophers) parade for their claims regarding the *existentia* and that they offer to the test of the norms of logic, are insufficient for the purpose. III, *214*

The arguments concerning the corporeal *existentia* constitute what they call the science of physics. The insufficiency lies in the fact [1022] that conformity between the results of thinking—which, as they assume, are produced by rational norms and reasoning—and the outside world, is not unequivocal. All the judgments of the mind are general ones,[1023] whereas the *existentia* of the outside world are individual in their substances. Perhaps, there is something in those substances that prevents conformity between the universal (judgments) of the mind and the individual (substances) of the outside world. At any rate, however, whatever (conformity) is attested by sensual perception has its proof in the fact that it is observable. (It does not have its proof) in (logical) arguments. Where, then, is the unequivocal character they find in (their arguments)?

The mind is also often applied to the primary *intelligibilia*, which conform to the individual (*existentia*), with the help of pictures of the imagination, but not to the secondary *intelligibilia*,[1024] which are abstractions of the second degree. In this case, judgment becomes unequivocal, comparable to (judgment in the case of) *sensibilia*, since the primary *intelligibilia* are more likely to agree with the outside world, because they conform perfectly (by definition, to the individual manifestations of the *existentia*). Therefore, in this case, one must concede (the philosophers') claims in this respect. However, we must refrain from studying these things, since such (restraint) falls under (the duty of) the Muslim not to do what does not concern him.[1025] The problems of physics are of no importance

[1022] Cf. Bombaci, p. 461.

[1023] Bulaq: "The judgments . . . are universal and general."

[1024] "But . . . *intelligibilia*" is found only in Bulaq, but, in view of pp. 137 f. and 247, above, and p. 310, below, appears to be the correct text.

[1025] Cf. p. 169, above.

for us in our religious affairs or our livelihoods. Therefore, we must leave them alone.

The arguments concerning the *existentia* beyond sensual perception—the *spiritualia*—constitute what the (philosophers) call "the divine science" or science of metaphysics. The essences of (the *spiritualia*) are completely unknown. One
III, *215* cannot get at them, nor can they be proven by logical arguments, because an abstraction of *intelligibilia* from the individual *existentia* of the outside world is possible only in the case of things we can perceive [1026] by the senses, from which the universals are thus derived. We cannot perceive the spiritual essences and abstract further quiddities from them, because the senses constitute a veil between us and them. We have, thus, no (logical) arguments for them, and we have no way whatever of affirming their existence. There are only available to us (in this connection) the situations in which perceptions of the human soul take place, and especially the dream visions which are within the intuitive experience of all.[1027] But beyond that, the reality and attributes of the (*spiritualia*) are an obscure matter, and there is no way to learn about them. Competent (philosophers) have clearly said so. They have expressed the opinion that whatever is immaterial cannot be proven by (logical) arguments, because it is a condition of (logical) arguments that their premises must be essential ones.[1028] The great philosopher Plato said that no certainty can be achieved with regard to the Divine, and one can state about the Divine only what is most suitable and proper [1029]—

[1026] The remainder of the sentence is not found in Bulaq.

[1027] Cf. 1:207 ff., and pp. 103 ff., above. For *wijdânî* in this passage, cf. the remark made in n. 277 to Ch. 1, above.

[1028] Cf. p. 140, above.

[1029] S. van den Bergh, *Umriss der Muḥammedanischen Wissenschaften nach Ibn Ḫaldûn* (Leiden, 1912), p. 26, suggests Plato's *Timaeus* as the source of this quotation, apparently referring to *Timaeus* 28 C: "It is difficult to find out about the maker and father of this universe, and it is impossible for anyone who has found out about him, to tell everybody else." Clement of Alexandria, after quoting this passage, adds: "For he cannot be named like all the other things that can be known." Cf. *Stromateis*, ed. Stählin, II, 377. Porphyry, in his *Philosophus Historia*, ascribes to Plato the belief that "one cannot give (the one God) a fitting name, nor can human understanding en-

that is, conjectures. If, after all the toil and trouble, we find only conjectures, the (conjectures) that we had at the beginning may as well suffice us. What use, then, do these sciences and the pursuit of them have? We want certainty about the *existentia* that are beyond sensual perception,[1030] while, in their (philosophy), (those conjectures) are the limit that human thinking can reach.

The (philosophers) say that happiness consists in coming to perceive existence as it is, by means of (logical) arguments. This is a fraudulent statement that must be rejected. The matter is as follows. Man [1031] is composed of two parts. III, *216*
One is corporeal. The other is spiritual, and mixed with the former. Each one of these parts has its own perceptions, though the (part) that perceives is the same in both cases, namely, the spiritual part. At times, it perceives spiritual perceptions. At other times, it perceives corporeal perceptions. However, it perceives the spiritual perceptions through its own essence without any intermediary, while it perceives the corporeal perceptions through the intermediary of organs of the body, such as the brain and the senses.

Now, anybody who has perceptions greatly enjoys whatever he perceives. For example, a child having its first corporeal perceptions, which (like all corporeal perceptions) come through an intermediary, greatly enjoys the light it sees and the sounds it hears. Thus, there can be no doubt that the soul finds even greater joy and pleasure in perceptions that come from its own essence without an intermediary. When the spiritual soul becomes conscious of the perception coming to it from its own essence without an intermediary, it derives from it inexpressible joy and pleasure. Such percep-

compass Him, and the names by which the moderns address Him are metaphorical expressions (*katachrêstikôs katêgorein*)." Cf. Cyrillus *Contra Julianum* xxxi (p. 549 A of the ed. Migne); F. Jacoby, *Die Fragmente der griechischen Historiker*, II, 1211. The passage from Porphyry seems to be the ultimate source of Ibn Khaldûn. (Cf., in general, H. A. Wolfson, "The Knowability and Describability of God in Plato and Aristotle," *Harvard Studies in Classical Philology*, LVI–LVII [1947], 233–49.)

1030 Cf. Bombaci, p. 462.

1031 Cf. Issawi, pp. 176–79.

tion cannot be achieved by (intellectual) speculation and science. It is achieved by the removal of the veil of sensual perception and by forgetting all corporeal perceptions. The Sufis are very much concerned with achieving this great joy through having the soul achieve that kind of perception. They attempt to kill the bodily powers and perceptions through exercise, and even the thinking power of the brain. In this way, the soul is to achieve the perception that comes to it from its own essence, when all the disturbances and hindrances caused by the body are removed. (The Sufis,) thus, achieve inexpressible joy and pleasure.[1032] This, (the philosophers) imply, is a correct assumption, and must be conceded
III, *217* them; yet it does not account for (the idea) they had in mind.[1033]

(At any rate,) their statement that logical arguments and proofs produce this kind of perception and the resulting great joy is false, as one can see. The arguments and proofs belong in the category of corporeal perceptions, because they are produced by the powers of the brain, which are imagination, thinking, and memory. The first thing we are concerned with when we want to attain this kind of perception is to kill all these powers of the brain, because they object to such (perception) and work against it. One finds able (philosophers) poring over the *Kitâb ash-Shifâ'*, the *Ishârât*, the *Najâh* (of Avicenna), and over Averroes' abridgements of the "Text" (*Organon*) [1034] and other works by Aristotle. They wear out the pages of these works. They firmly ground themselves in the arguments they contain, and they desire to find in them that portion of happiness (they believe they contain). They do not realize that in this way they (only) add to the obstacles on (the road to happiness). They base themselves on statements reported on the authority of Aristotle, al-Fârâbî, and Avicenna, to the effect that those who have attained perception of the active intellect and are united with it in their life

1032 Cf., for instance, pp. 81 f., above.
1033 Cf. Bombaci, p. 462.
1034 Cf. p. 139, above.

in this world[1035] have attained their share of happiness. To them, the active intellect means the first (highest) of the degrees of the *spiritualia* from which (the veil of) sensual perception is removed. They assume union with the active intellect to be (the result of) scientific perception. One has seen that this is wrong. When Aristotle and his colleagues speak about union and perception in this way, they mean the perception of the soul that comes to it from its own essence and without an intermediary, but such (perception) is attained only by the removal of the veil of sensual perception.

Furthermore, (philosophers) state that the great joy originating in that kind of perception is identical with the promised[1036] happiness. This, too, is wrong. The things that III, *218*
have been established by the (philosophers) make it clear to us that, beyond sensual perception, there is something else perceived by the soul without an intermediary. This causes very great joy to the soul, but we do not think that this makes it definite that it is identical with the happiness of the other world, although it must be one of the pleasures that constitute that happiness. (At any rate,) their statement that happiness consists in coming to perceive the *existentia* as they are, is wrong. It is based upon the erroneous supposition, which we mentioned before in connection with the principle of divine oneness,[1037] that anybody who has perception comprises (the whole) of existence in his perceptions. We explained that this (assumption) is wrong, and that existence is too vast to be completely encompassed or perceived, either spiritually or corporeally.

The sum total of all the (philosophical) doctrines we have set down (here) is that the spiritual part (of man), when it separates from the powers of the body, has an essential perception belonging to a special kind of perceptions, namely, the *existentia* that are encompassed by our knowledge. It does

---

1035 "In this world" is not found in Bulaq.

1036 I.e., promised by Islam as the reward of the believer in the other world.

1037 Cf. p. 37, above.

not have a general perception of all the *existentia*, since they cannot be encompassed in their totality. It greatly enjoys this kind of perception, exactly as a child is pleased with its sensual perceptions when it begins to grow up. Nobody, then, (should try to tell) us that it is possible to perceive all the *existentia* or to achieve the happiness the Lawgiver (Muḥammad) promised us, if we do not work for it. "Away, away with what you are promised." [1038]

(Philosophers) further state that man is able, by himself, to refine and improve his soul by adopting praiseworthy
III, *219* character qualities and avoiding blameworthy ones. This is connected with the assumption that the great joy that the soul has through the perception coming to it from its own essence, is identical with the promised happiness. For the vices give the soul corporeal habits and the resulting coloring. Thus, they impede it in the realization of that perception.

Now, we have already explained that happiness and unhappiness are found beyond corporeal and spiritual perceptions. The improvement (of the soul that the philosophers) have come to know is useful only in that it (produces) great joy, originating from the spiritual perception that takes place according to rational and established norms. But the happiness beyond such (joy), which the Lawgiver (Muḥammad) promised us if we would act and behave as he commanded us, is something that cannot be encompassed by anybody's perceptions.

The leading philosopher, Abû 'Alî Ibn Sînâ (Avicenna), was aware of this. He expressed himself in the following sense in his *Kitâb al-Mabda' wa-l-ma'âd:* [1039] "The spiritual resurrection and its circumstances are something that we may come to know by means of rational arguments and reasoning, because it proceeds in a safely natural and uniform

[1038] Qur'ân 23.36 (38). The verse is meant to apply here to the false promises of the philosophers.

[1039] This quotation has been traced by E. I. J. Rosenthal to *Avicenna De Almahad* (Venice, 1546). Cf. *al-Andalus*, XX (1955), p. 80. The *Risâlah aḍḥawîyah fî amr al-ma'âd* (Cairo, 1368/1949) contains nothing that could properly be compared to Ibn Khaldûn's summary.

manner. Thus, we can use (logical) arguments for it. But the bodily resurrection and its circumstances cannot be perceived by means of (logical arguments), because it does not proceed in a uniform manner. It has been explained to us by the true Muḥammadan religious law. The religious law should, therefore, be considered and consulted with regard to the circumstances of (the bodily resurrection)."

Thus, as one has seen, the science (of logic) is not adequate to achieve the avowed intentions (of the philosophers). In addition, it contains things that are contrary to the religious laws and their obvious meaning. As far as we know, this science has only a single fruit, namely, it sharpens the mind in the orderly presentation of proofs and arguments, III, 220
so that the habit of excellent and correct arguing is obtained. This is because the orderly process and the solid and exact method of reasoning are as the philosophers have prescribed them in their science of logic. They employ (logic) a good deal in the physical and mathematical sciences as well as in the science that comes after them (metaphysics). Since (logical) arguments are much employed in those sciences in the way they should be employed, the student of them is able to master the habit of exact and correct arguing and deducing. Even if (those sciences) are not adequate to achieve the intentions of the (philosophers), they constitute the soundest norm of (philosophical) speculation that we know of.

Such is the fruit of this craft (of logic). It also affords acquaintance with the doctrines and opinions of the people of the world.[1040] One knows what harm it [1041] can do. Therefore, the student of it should beware of its pernicious aspects as much as he can. Whoever studies it should do so (only) after he is saturated with the religious law and has studied the interpretation of the Qur'ân and jurisprudence. No one who has no knowledge of the Muslim religious sciences should

[1040] Bulaq corrects "people of the world" to "scholars."

[1041] I.e., the craft of logic or philosophy, and not "they" referring to "doctrines and opinions."

apply himself to it. Without that knowledge, he can hardly remain safe from its pernicious aspects.[1042]

God gives success and guidance to the truth. "We would not be persons who are guided aright, had God not guided us." [1043]

[31] *A refutation of astrology. The weakness of its achievements. The harmfulness of its goal.*

Astrologers think that astrology, with the knowledge it
III, *221* gives of astral powers, individually or in combination, and of astral influences upon elemental creations, enables them to know the things that are going to be in the world of the elements, before they are created. The positions of the spheres and the stars (are) thus (taken to) indicate every single kind of future event, both universal and individual.

The ancient (astrologers) were of the opinion that the knowledge of astral powers and influence is acquired through experience. It (thus) is something that all (human) lives combined would not be able to achieve, because experience is obtained through numerous repetitions which make the obtainment of (empirical) knowledge or conjectures possible. Astral revolutions may be very long. Greatly extended periods of time are required for their repetition. Even (all) the lives [1044] in the world (combined) would be too short for (observing) them.

Some weak-minded (astrologers) take the attitude that the knowledge of astral powers and influences comes through revelation. This is a fallacy. They themselves have furnished us arguments sufficient to refute it. The clearest proof is that, as one knows, of all people, the prophets are least familiar with the crafts.[1045] They do not undertake to give information

[1042] Cf. R. Dozy in *Journal asiatique*, XIV 6 (1869), 166 f. Ibn Khaldûn expressed himself in a similar vein with regard to the Qur'ân commentary by az-Zamakhsharî; cf. 2:447, above.

[1043] Qur'ân 7.43 (41).

[1044] Bulaq: "the longest lives." For the argument against astrology presented in this paragraph, cf. S. van den Bergh, *Die Epitome der Metaphysik des Averroes* (Leiden, 1924), pp. 269 f.

[1045] Cf. 2:383, above.

about the supernatural, unless (such information) comes (to them) from God. Why, then, should they claim to produce (supernatural information) through a craft (such as astrology) and make it the law for their followers to do so?

Ptolemy and his followers were of the opinion that the stars are able to indicate (the future) as the natural result of a temper they produce in the elemental existing things. He said:[1046] "(This must be so,) because the activity of sun and moon and their influence upon elemental things are so obvious that no one can deny them. For instance, the sun influences the changes and tempers of the seasons, the ripening of fruits and grains, and so on. The moon influences humidity, the water, the (process) of ripening (putrefaction) III, 222
in putrescent substances and cucumbers, and so on." Ptolemy continued: "With regard to the stars that come after sun and moon, we have two approaches. One—which, however, is unsatisfactory—is to follow the tradition of the astrological authorities. The other is (to rely upon) conjecture and empirical knowledge gained through comparing each star to the sun, whose nature and influence is clearly known to us. We thus note whether a given star increases the power and temper of (the sun) at (its) conjunction (with it). If this is the case, we know that the nature of that particular star agrees with that of the sun. If, on the other hand, (the star) diminishes (the power and temper of the sun), we know that its nature is opposite to that of (the sun).[1047] Then, when we know the individual powers of the stars, we (can also) know them in combination. That happens when they look upon each other in the trine, the quartile, or other aspects. The knowledge here is derived from the natures of the signs (of the zodiac), which similarly (are known) through comparison with the sun.

"Thus, we get to know all the astral powers. They exer-

[1046] As Ibn Khaldûn himself says at the end of the quotation, this is not a literal quotation from the *Quadripartitum* alone, but goes back to "the *Quadripartitum* and other works." Cf. also 1:226, above.

[1047] Cf. Bombaci, pp. 462 f.

cise an influence upon the air. This is obvious. The resulting temper of the air communicates itself to the created things below the air, and shapes sperm and seeds. Thus, (this temper) comes to underlie the body created from (sperm or seed), the soul which attaches itself to the body, pours itself into the body, and acquires its perfection from the body, and all the conditions depending on soul and body. The qualities of sperm and seed are the qualities of the things that are created and produced from (sperm and seed)." [1048]

(Ptolemy) continued: "Still, (astrology) remains conjectural and is not certain in any respect. It also forms no part of the divine decree—that is, predestination. It is just one of the natural causes common to all existing things, whereas the divine decree is prior to everything." This is the
III, 223 sum total of the discussion by Ptolemy and his colleagues. (This discussion) is found in the *Quadripartitum* and other works.

It makes the weakness of the achievements of astrology clear. Knowledge of, or conjectures about, things that come into being can only result from knowledge of all their causes, that is, agent, recipient, form, and end, as has been explained in the proper place. According to (the astrologers), the astral powers are merely agents. The elemental part is the recipient. Furthermore, the astral powers are not the sole agents. There are other powers that act together with (the astral powers) upon the material element (involved), such as the generative power of father and species contained in the sperm, the powers of the particular quality distinguishing each variety within the species, and other things. When the astral powers reach perfection and are known, they (still) are only one among many causes that go into the making of a thing that comes into being.

Furthermore,[1049] in addition to a knowledge of astral powers and influences, a great amount of conjecturing and guesswork is required. Only then is (the astrologer) able

[1048] Cf. Bombaci, pp. 463 f.
[1049] Cf. Bombaci, p. 464.

to guess that a thing might happen. Now, conjecturing and guesswork are powers in the mind of the student. They are not causes or reasons [1050] of the things that come into being. Without conjectures and guesswork, (astrology) steps down from conjecture to doubtfulness.[1050a]

Such is the situation (even) if one's knowledge of the astral powers is accurate and without defect. Now, that is difficult. The ability to calculate the courses of the stars is required in order to know their positions. Moreover, it is not proven that every star has its own particular power. The method Ptolemy used in establishing the powers of the five planets, that is, comparison with the sun, is a weak one, be- III, 224
cause the power of the sun is superior to all (other) astral powers and dominates them. Thus, one hardly ever becomes aware of an increase or decrease in the (powers of the sun) at its conjunction (with a given star),[1051] as Ptolemy said. All this speaks against the assumption that it is possible to predict things that will happen in the world of the elements with the help of astrology.

Furthermore, it is wrong to assume that the stars exercise an influence on (the world) below them. It has been proven deductively in the chapter on the Oneness of God, as one has seen,[1052] that there is no agent but God. In this connection, speculative theologians use the self-evident argument that how causes are related to the things caused is not known, and suspicion attaches to the conclusions of the intellect regarding what appears superficially to be (due to some definite) influence. Perhaps, the relationship of (the causes to the things

[1050] Bulaq: "causes of the things that come into being, nor are they basic principles of astrology." This, at least, provides a suitable antecedent for the Arabic suffix used in the following sentence and explained here by "(astrology)." As the text stands, the only possible antecedent would be "causes or reasons," which makes no sense. Though the Bulaq text probably is the result of an arbitrary correction, "astrology" seems indeed to have been in Ibn Ḵhaldûn's mind as the antecedent of the suffix.

[1050a] The lowest of the three kinds of knowledge, as mentioned p. 86, above.

[1051] Cf. Bombaci, p. 464, and above, p. 259.

[1052] Cf. pp. 36 f., above.

caused) is effected by some other than the ordinary form of influence. The divine power (would seem to) tie the two together, as it does with all created things, (both) high and low, especially since the religious law attributes all happenings to the power of God and does not want to have anything to do with anything else.

Prophecy also denies the importance and influence of the stars. A perusal of the legal material also attests this fact. For instance, (Muḥammad) said: "No eclipse of either sun or moon takes place to indicate the death or life of anybody." [1053] And (God) said: "Some of My servants believe in Me. Others do not. Those who say, 'We had rain through the kindness and mercy of God,' believe in Me and do not believe in the stars. Whereas those who say, 'We had rain through such and such a constellation,' do not believe in Me, but believe in the stars," (as) the sound tradition (goes).[1054]

III, 225 Thus, the worthlessness of astrology from the point of view of the religious law, as well as the weakness of its achievements from the rational point of view, are evident. In addition, astrology does harm to human civilization. It hurts the faith of the common people when an astrological judgment occasionally happens to come true in some unexplainable and unverifiable manner. Ignorant people are taken in by that and suppose that all the other (astrological) judgments must be true, which is not the case. Thus, they are led to attribute things to some (being) other than their Creator.

Further, astrology often produces the expectation that signs of crisis [1055] will appear in a dynasty. This encourages the enemies and rivals of the dynasty to attack (it) and revolt (against it). We have (personally) observed much of the sort. It is, therefore, necessary that astrology be forbidden to

[1053] Cf. al-Bukhârî, *Ṣaḥîḥ*, I, 264 ff., and, for further references, *Concordance*, II, 30*a*.

[1054] Cf. al-Bukhârî, *Ṣaḥîḥ*, I, 217, and, for further references, *Concordance*, I, 112*b*, I. 3. The concluding words would usually mean that the tradition is not quoted in full, but here the complete text is quoted.

[1055] For *qawâṭiʿ*, cf. C. A. Nallino in *Rivista degli studi orientali*, VIII (1919–21), 739–43, repeated in *Raccolta di scritti editi e inediti*, V, 372–75.

all civilized people, because it may cause harm to religion and dynasty. The fact that it exists as a natural part of human perceptions and knowledge does not speak against (the need to forbid it). God and evil exist side by side in the world and cannot be removed. Responsibility comes in connection with the things that cause good and evil. It is (our) duty to try to acquire goodness with the help of the things that cause it, and to avoid the causes of evil and harm. That is what those who realize the corruption and harmfulness of this science must do.

This (situation) should make one realize that even if astrology were in itself sound, no Muslim could acquire the knowledge and habit of it. He who studies it and thinks that
he knows it fully, is most ignorant of the actual situation. III, *226*
Since the religious law forbids the study of astrology, civilized people no longer gather to study it and to form classes [1056] for the study of astrology. Those who are eager to learn it—and they are very, very few—have to read the books and treatises on astrology in a secluded corner of their houses. They have to hide from the people and are under the watchful eye of the great mass. And then, astrology is a very complicated subject with many branches and subdivisions and is difficult to understand. How could people under such conditions acquire a mastery of it? Jurisprudence is of general usefulness in both religious and worldly affairs; its sources are easily available in the Qur'ân and the accepted Sunnah, and it has been studied and taught by the great mass of Muslims. There have been classes and seminars (on jurisprudence). There has been much instruction (in it) and a great many lectures. Still, only an occasional individual in each age and generation (race) has been able to master it. How, then, can anyone learn a subject (such as astrology) that is discarded by the religious law, banned as forbidden and illegal, concealed from the great mass, its sources difficult of access, and that, after the study and acquisition of its basic principles and details, requires a great amount of support

Cf. R. Dozy, *Journal asiatique*, XIV^{6} (1869), 167.

from conjecture and guesswork on the part of the student? [1057] How could anyone acquire and become skilled in such a subject in the face of all (these difficulties)? Anybody who claims (such astrological skill) is frustrated and has no witness to attest (to his claim), because the discipline (of astrology) is unusual in Islam and few people cultivate it. When all this is taken into consideration, the soundness of our opinion (with regard to astrology) will become clear. God "knows the supernatural (secrets), and He does not disclose to anyone His supernatural (secrets)." [1058]

Some of our contemporaries had an experience of the (futility of astrology) when the Arabs overpowered the army of Sultan Abû l-Ḥasan.[1059] They laid siege to him in al-Qayrawân. There was much unrest among the two parties,
III, *227* both friends and foes. On that occasion, the Tunisian poet Abû l-Qâsim ar-Rahawî, said:

Constantly, I ask God for forgiveness.
Gone is life and ease.
In Tunis, both in the morning and in the evening—
And the morning belongs to God as does the evening—
There is fear and hunger and death,
Stirred up by tumult and pestilence.
People are in rebellion and at war—
Rarely does anything good come out of rebellion.
The partisans of Aḥmad think that perdition
And ruin have descended upon 'Alî.[1060]
And the others say: He ('Alî) will be brought (back)
To you by a mild zephyr.

[1057] Cf. Bombaci, pp. 464 f., who suggests: ". . . and a great amount of conjecture and guesswork that precludes (acquisition of) this (science) by the student."

[1058] Qur'ân 72.26 (26).

[1059] The famous event of 1348, that played such a momentous role in Ibn Khaldûn's life. Cf. 1:xxxix, above. Poems by ar-Raḥawî are quoted in *'Ibar*, VII, 270 ff., and in the *Autobiography*, pp. 23 ff.

[1060] The rebellious Arabs had appointed a certain Aḥmad b. 'Abd-as-Salâm as their ruler. Cf. R. Brunschvig, *La Berbérie orientale*, I, 169. Sultan Abû l-Ḥasan's name was 'Alî.

God is above this one and that one.
He destines for His two servants whatever He wishes.
O you observer of the retreating, running[1061] (stars)!
What did these heaven(ly bodies) do?
You have been putting us off while you pretended (each day)
That today you would pay off.[1062]
One Thursday went by after the other.
Saturday came, and Wednesday.
Half a month, and a second decade,
And a third came to an end,
And we see nothing but false statements.
Is this stupidity or contempt?
We belong to God. We know
That destiny cannot be repulsed.
I am pleased to have Allah as my God.
You are satisfied with the moon or the sun.
Those roving stars are nothing but
Slaves, male or female.
Their fate is destined. They do not destine (anybody's fate).
They have no power over mankind.
Intellects[1063] erred in considering primeval
What is subject to death[1064] and nonexistence.
They appointed as judge over (the world of) existence an element III, 228
Created from water and air,
Not considering sweet versus bitter,
Both being nourished by soil and water.[1064a]

1061 Cf. Qur'ân 81.15 (15 f.).

1062 That is, your prediction would come true. Cf. R. Dozy in *Journal asiatique*, XIV 6 (1869), 168–70.

1063 The rest of the poem is directed against the speculative theologians.

1064 C and D (and possibly A) read *al-kharmu*, which might possibly have the sense indicated. B seems to have a meaningless *al-ḥazm*. Possibly, we should read *al-jazmu* "fate, death."

1064a That is, things that the poet believes speculative theologians consider essentially different, such as the intellect and the world of the senses, may have the same origin, even as the opposites sweet and bitter originate from

God is my Lord. I do not know
What atom and vacuum are;
Nor what the hyle is which proclaims:
"I cannot be without form";
Nor what existence is or nonexistence,
Nor persistence and annihilation.
I do not know what acquisition [1065] is except
Something resulting from buying and selling.
My dogma and religion are
What (dogma and religion) were when the people were saints,
Since there are no details, no basic principles,
No dispute, and no doubting,
As long as one follows early Islam and the remainder.[1066]
What a good thing it is to take (early Islam) as model!
(The early Muslims) were as one knows them to have been.
(In their time,) the babble (of the theologians) did not exist.
O you contemporary Ash'arîs! I
Have been taught by summer and winter: [1067]
I am requited for evil with evil,
And good is the reward for good.
If I am obedient (to God), I shall be saved.
If I am disobedient, still, I have hope.
I am under the control of a Creator [1068]
Who is obeyed by the (divine) throne and the earth.[1069]

the same elements. While the intellect and the world of the senses are seemingly opposites, both are created.

[1065] Cf. D. B. Macdonald in *EI*, *s.v.* "Kasb."

[1066] *Wa-l-baqâyâ* "and the remainder" has been corrected in Bulaq: "and it is taken by us as our model." However, the word would seem to refer to the remaining second generation, after the first generation of early Islam (*ṣadr*) had gone.

[1067] I.e., by long experience. The Arabic text has here a play on words.

[1068] *Bârin*, for *bâri'in*. Or, perhaps we should read *bârrin*, one of the names of God, meaning "a pious (God)."

[1069] The MSS have *al-barâ'u* = *al-barâ*, as *ath-tharâ'u* = *ath-tharâ*, but the latter word, having the same meaning, is not the one intended here.

It[1070] is not in your writings, but
The (divine) judgment and fate have predestined it:
If al-Ash'arî were told who
The (present-day) followers of his opinions are,
He would say, "Tell them that I
Have nothing to do with what they say."

[32] *A denial of the effectiveness of alchemy. The impossibility of its existence. The harm that arises from practicing it.*[1071] III, 229

Many people who are unable to earn their living[1072] are led by greed to cultivate alchemy. They are of the opinion that it is a (proper) means and method of making a living and that the practitioners of (alchemy) find it easier and simpler (than other people) to acquire property. In fact, however, they have to pay for (their efforts) in the form of trouble, hardship, and difficulties, and in the form of persecution by the authorities and loss of property through expenditures. In addition, he[1073] loses standing and, eventually, when his secret[1074] is discovered, faces ruin.

They think that (in practicing alchemy) they know some gainful craft. However, they have been stimulated (to practice alchemy) solely by the thought that some minerals may be changed and transformed artificially into others, because of the matter common (to all minerals). Thus, they try to treat silver and transform it into gold; copper and tin (they try to transform) into silver. They think that it is possible in the realm of nature to do this.

There are different procedures followed by (the alchemists). These depend on the different opinions held concern-

[1070] Namely, the following statement, which gives the poem a rather biting, humorous conclusion. De Slane translates: "It is not by your writings (that events are determined), but the (divine) judgment . . . ."

[1071] Cf. pp. 227 ff., above.

[1072] Cf. 1:228 f. and 2:320, above.

[1073] *Sic!* One would expect "they."

[1074] C: *ẓuhira 'alâ khab'ihî*. D has *khabîyatin*. B seems to have *khaybatin* "if failure becomes apparent."

ing the character and form of the (alchemical) treatment and concerning the substance invented [1075] for the treatment and which they call "the Noble Stone." This may be excrements, or blood, or hair, or eggs, or anything else.[1076]

After the substance has been specified, it is treated by them along the following lines. The (substance) is pulverized with a pestle, on a solid and smooth stone. During the pulverization it is macerated in water, after drugs have been
III, 230 added, suitable for the purpose (the substance) is to achieve and able to effect its transformation into the desired mineral. After having been macerated, (the substance) is dried in the sun, or cooked in a fire, or sublimated, or calcified, in order to eliminate the water or earth it contains. If this process and treatment are completed to the satisfaction of the (alchemist) and in accordance with the requirements of the basic principles of alchemy, the result is an earthen or fluid (substance) which is called "the elixir." (Alchemists) think that if the elixir is added to silver which has been heated in a fire, the silver turns into gold. If added to copper which has been heated in a fire, the copper turns into silver, just as (the alchemists), by means of the (alchemical) operation, intend it to be.

Competent (alchemists) think that the elixir is a substance composed of the four elements.[1077] The special (alchemical) processing and treatment give the substance a certain temper and [1078] certain natural powers. These powers assimilate to themselves everything with which they come into contact, and transform it into their own form and temper. They transmit their own qualities and powers to it, just as yeast in bread assimilates the dough to its own essence and produces in the bread its own looseness and fluffiness, so that the bread will be easily digestible in the stomach and quickly transformed into nourishment.[1079] In the same way,

[1075] Or "used as the basis."
[1076] Cf. p. 227, above.
[1077] Cf. (Pseudo-)Majrîṭî, *Ghâyah*, pp. 7 f.
[1078] Bulaq: "which includes."
[1079] Cf. p. 175, above, and p. 278, below.

the elixir of gold and silver assimilates the minerals with which it comes into contact to (gold and silver) and transforms them into the forms of (gold and silver).

This, in general, is the sum total of the theory (of alchemists).

We find that the (alchemists) constantly experiment with the (alchemical) process and hope to find their sustenance and livelihood in it. They transmit to each other the rules and basic principles (of the treatment as derived) from the books of the leading earlier alchemists. They pass these books around among themselves and discuss the meaning and interpretation of the puzzling expressions and secrets in them. For the most part, they are like riddles. Such books are the
Seventy Treatises of Jâbir b. Ḥayyân, the *Rutbat al-ḥakîm* of III, 231
Maslamah al-Majrîṭî, (the works) of aṭ-Ṭughrâ'î, and the very well-composed poem of al-Mughayribî,[1080] and similar works. However, after all (these efforts), the (alchemists) do not get anywhere.

I once discussed something of the sort with our teacher, the leading Spanish scholar, Abû l-Barakât al-Ballafîqî.[1081] I called his attention to a certain work on (alchemy). He examined it for a long time, then returned it to me and said: "I guarantee it to (the author) that he will come home a failure."

Certain (alchemists) restricted themselves to mere forgery. It may be of an obvious type, such as covering silver with gold, or copper with silver, or mixing the (two metals) in the ratio of one to two, or one to three. Or it may be a concealed type of forgery, such as treating a mineral to make it look like another similar one. Copper, for instance, may be blanched and softened with sublimate of mercury. Thus, it turns into a mineral that looks like silver to anyone but an expert assayer.[1082]

Such forgers use their product to coin money with the

[1080] Cf. p. 229, above, where al-Mughayribî is called Ibn al-Mughayribî.

[1081] Cf. 1:xlii, above.

[1082] Cf. E. O. von Lippmann, *Enstehung und Ausbreitung der Alchemie*, pp. 3 ff.

official imprint, which they circulate among the people. Thus, they cheat the great mass with impunity. Theirs is the most contemptible and pernicious profession (there could be). The forgers conspire to steal the property of the people, for they give copper for silver, and silver for gold, so as to get exclusive possession of (other people's property). They are thieves, or worse than thieves.

Most of that sort of people here in the Maghrib are
III, *232* Berber "students"[1083] who choose for their territory remote regions and the homes of stupid people. They visit the mosques of the Bedouins and convince rich[1084] (Bedouins) that they know how to make gold and silver. People are very much in love with (gold and silver). They are eager to spend all (their money) to search for them. This (attitude) enables the (Berber students) to make a living. They must go about their activity fearfully and under the watchful eye (of the authorities). Eventually, (their) inability (to produce gold and silver) becomes evident and they are disgraced. Then, they flee to another place and start the whole business anew.[1085] They cause wealthy people to succumb to the desire of obtaining what they have to offer. In this way, they constantly work hard trying to make a living.

There is no point talking with that sort of people, because they have reached the limit in ignorance and viciousness and make a business out of thievery. The only way to cure them is for the government to take energetic measures against them, to seize them wherever they are, and to cut off their hands (as thieves) whenever their activities are discovered, for those activities mean deterioration of the currency, a matter of general concern. The currency (in circulation) is the very backbone of everyone's wealth. The ruler has the obligation to keep it intact, to watch over it, and to take energetic measures against those who corrupt it.

[1083] Cf. 2:320 f., above.

[1084] *Sic* B (*al-aghniyâ'*). C and D have "stupid" (*al-aghbiyâ'*). The latter may actually be more in keeping with Ibn Khaldûn's thinking, because "rich" farmers would be most unusual.

[1085] Cf. Bombaci, p. 465, who suggests: "and invent new tricks."

However, it is possible for us to talk with alchemists who do not like such forgeries, but avoid them and refrain from corrupting the currency and coinage of the Muslims. They merely seek to transform silver into gold, or lead and copper and tin into silver, with the help of a particular alchemical process and the elixir which results from it. We can discuss with them and investigate their achievements in this respect. Yet, we know of not one in the world who has attained the III, 233
goal (of alchemy) or got any desirable result out of it. Alchemists spend their lives on the (alchemical) treatment, (using the) pestle and muller, subliming and calcifying, and running risks in collecting drugs and searching for them. They tell stories about other (alchemists) who attained the goal (of alchemy) or were successful. They are satisfied with listening to these stories and discussing them. They have no suspicions as to whether (or not) they can be considered true. They are like people who are infatuated with something and taken in by fanciful stories about the subject of their infatuation. When they are asked whether the (story) has been verified by actual observation, they do not know. They say, "We have heard (about it), but have not seen it." This has been the case with (alchemists) in every age and of every race (generation).

It should be known that the practice of this art is something very ancient in the world. Ancient and modern (scholars) have discussed it. We shall report their opinions in this connection and then state what seems to us the actual truth of the matter. God gives success to that which is correct.

We say: The philosophers base their discussion of alchemy on the condition of the seven malleable[1086] minerals: gold, silver, lead, tin, copper, iron, and *khârṣînî*.[1087] The question is whether these (seven metals) are different in their

[1086] Cf. Bombaci, p. 465.

[1087] An alloy, considered to be of Chinese provenience, the exact composition of which is not known. Cf. P. Kraus, *Jâbir Ibn Ḥayyân*, II, 22; A. Siggel, *Arabisch-Deutsches Wörterbuch der Stoffe* (Berlin, 1950), p. 79.

(specific) differences,[1088] each constituting a distinct species, or whether they differ in certain properties and constitute different kinds of one and the same species.

Abû Naṣr al-Fârâbî and the Spanish philosophers who followed him held the opinion that all (the metals) are of one and the same species and that their difference is caused by qualities, such as humidity and dryness, softness and hardness, and colors, such as yellow, white, and black. All of them are different kinds of one and the same species.

III, *234* On the other hand, Avicenna and the eastern philosophers who followed him were of the opinion that the (metals) differ in (specific) difference and constitute different species of their own, each of which exists in its own right and has its own (specific) difference and genus, like all other species.

On the strength of his opinion that all (the metals) are of one and the same species, Abû Naṣr al-Fârâbî assumed that it is possible for one metal to be transformed into another, because it is possible to transform accidents and treat them artificially. From this point of view, he considered alchemy possible and easy.[1089]

Avicenna, on the other hand, on the strength of his opinion that (all the metals) belong to different species, assumed that the existence of alchemy must be denied and is impossible.[1090] His assumption is based on the fact that (specific) differences cannot be influenced by artificial means. They are

[1088] *Faṣl*, *διαφορά*, a term of Aristotelian logic (cf. p. 142, above), could here and in the following discussion be rendered approximately by "structure."

[1089] Cf. al-Fârâbî, *Fî wujûb ṣinâʿat al-kîmiyâʾ*, ed. Aydın Sayılı in *Belleten*, XV (1951), 65–79; tr. E. Wiedemann in *Journal für praktische Chemie*, N.F. LXXVI (1907), 115–23. The brief treatise deals mainly with the problem of why works on alchemy are written so as to be comprehensible only to the initiated. (Cf. n. 1099, below.) Only very briefly at the end is reference made to (pseudo-) Aristotle's opinion that all noncombustible metals are of one species and differentiated only by their accidents. Cf. also Ḥâjjî Khalîfah, *Kashf aẓ-ẓunûn*, ed. Flügel, V, 272 f., where al-Fârâbî is quoted following Ibn Bâjjah, and reference is also made to Avicenna's theory.

[1090] The relevant passages from Avicenna's *Shifâʾ* are dealt with by E. J. Holmyard and D. C. Mandeville, *Avicennae de congelatione et conglutinatione lapidum, being sections of the Kitâb al-Shifâʾ* (Paris, 1927), pp. 5 ff., 41 f.,

created by the Creator and Determiner of things, God Almighty. Their real character is utterly unknown and cannot be perceived (*taṣawwur*). How, then, could one attempt to transform them by artificial means?

Aṭ-Ṭughrâ'î, one of the great alchemists, considered Avicenna's statement erroneous. He objected that (alchemical) treatment and processing does not mean a new creation of a (specific) difference, but merely the conditioning of a substance for the acceptance of a particular (specific difference). After (a given substance) is conditioned, it gets (its new specific) difference from its Creator and Originator. This might be compared to the way light pours upon bodies as the result of polishing and giving (them) luster. We do not have to perceive (*taṣawwur*) or know (how) this (comes about).

Aṭ-Ṭughrâ'î continued: "In fact, we know about the (spontaneous) generation of certain animals, even though we are ignorant of their (specific) differences. For instance,[1091] scorpions are created from earth and straw. Snakes are created from hair. Agricultural scholars [1092] mention that bees, when they no longer exist, are created (again) from calves, and that reeds come out of the horns of cloven-hoofed animals III, 235
and are transformed into sugar cane, when the horns are filled with honey while the soil is being prepared for them (to be planted). Why, then, should it be impossible for us to make similar observations in the case of [1093] minerals? All that comes about by artificial means applied to a given sub-

54 f., 85 f. In his "Refutation of the Astrologers," Avicenna also briefly condemned alchemy. Cf. A. F. Mehren in *Homenaje á D. Francisco Codera* (Saragossa, 1904), p. 238. A recent publication by A. Ateş, "Ibn Sina ve Elkimya," in *Ilahiyat Fakültesi Dergisi*, I^{4} (1952), 47–71, probably contains important material on Avicenna's attitude toward alchemy. A recent article by Adnan Adıvar, in the *M. Shafi Presentation Volume*, is also said to deal with the same subject.

[1091] For the problem of spontaneous and artificial generation in Muslim alchemy, see the important third chapter in P. Kraus, *Jâbir Ibn Ḥayyân*, II, 97 ff. For the *generatio aequivoca* of snakes, scorpions, and bees (*bugonia*), cf., esp., II, 106 f. Cf. also E. O. von Lippmann, *Urzeugung und Lebenskraft* (Berlin, 1933).

[1092] In the sense of "experts in works such as the *Nabataean Agriculture*."

[1093] The following five lines are omitted by Bulaq.

stance. Treatment and processing conditions the substance for the acceptance of (specific) differences, no more."

(Aṭ-Ṭughrâ'î) continued: "We attempt something similar with regard to gold and silver. We take a certain matter possessing primary preparedness for the acceptance of the *form* of gold and silver. We treat it and then we attempt to process it until it possesses fully the preparedness to accept the (*specific*) *difference* of (gold and silver)."

This is the gist of aṭ-Ṭughrâ'î's discussion. He is right in his refutation of Avicenna.

We, however, have another starting point for refuting the alchemists. It shows that the existence of alchemy is impossible and that the assumptions of all (who defend alchemy), not only those of aṭ-Ṭughrâ'î and Avicenna,[1094] are wrong. (Our argument) is as follows:

The (alchemical) process follows these lines: The (alchemists) take a substance possessing primary preparedness. They use it as the basis. In treating and processing it, they imitate the way nature processes substances in mines and, eventually, transforms them into gold or silver. They (try) hard to increase the active and passive powers (in the process), so that it will be completed in a shorter time (than required by nature). It has been explained in the proper place that an increase in the power of the agent shortens the time needed for his activity. (Now,) it is clear that the generation of gold in the mine is completed only after 1,080 years, which is the period of the great revolution of the sun.[1095] If the powers and qualities used in the process are greatly increased,
III, 236 the time needed for the generation of (gold) will necessarily be shorter than (1,080 years), as we have stated.

[1094] One would expect al-Fârâbî instead of Avicenna.

[1095] Above, 2:212, we find a discussion of the "great conjunction," which is said to reoccur in cycles of 960 years and which must be something different from the great solar revolution mentioned here. The figures for the "great year" that are mentioned by Pseudo-Plutarch, *Placita philosophorum* 892 C, are different from Ibn Khaldûn's figure. The *Placita* were well known to the Arabs. Cf. the edition of the Arabic translation by 'Abd-ar-Raḥmân Badawî, *Aristotelis De anima* (Cairo, 1954), p. 141.

Or, through processing, the (alchemists) choose to give the (basic) substance a form of composition to make it like yeast, and thus capable of producing the desired transformation in the processed matter. That is "the elixir," mentioned before.

(Now,) it should be known that every generated elemental thing must contain a combination of the four elements in different proportions. If they were all alike in proportion, no mixture would take place. Therefore, there must always be a part that is superior to all the (others). Likewise, everything generated through mixture must contain some natural heat which is active in creating it and preserves its form. Furthermore, everything that is created in time must go through different stages and pass from one stage to another during the time of its creation, until it reaches its goal. For instance, man goes through the successive stages of semen, blood clot, and lump of flesh.[1096] Next, he receives his form, becomes an embryo, a (newborn) child, a suckling, and so on, until he reaches the end of his (development). The proportion of the parts varies in quantity and quality at every stage. Were that not the case, the first stage would be identical with the last. The natural heat, too, is different at each stage.

One may now consider through how many stages and conditions gold (must have) passed in the mine over (a period of) 1,080 years. The alchemist has to follow the action of nature in the mine and imitate it in his treatment and processing, until it is completed. (Now,) it is a condition of (every) craft that (its practitioner) perceive (and know, III, 237
taṣawwur) the goals he intends to reach with the help of that particular craft. A current saying of the sages to this effect runs: "The beginning of action is the end of thinking, and the end of thinking is the beginning of action." [1097] Thus, (the alchemist) must perceive (and know) the different conditions

[1096] As indicated in the Qur'ân. Cf. 2:368 and 425, above.

[1097] Cf. 2:415, above, where the statement is cited according to its correct form.

of gold in the numerous stages of its (development), the different proportions (of its component elements) belonging to the different stages, the resulting differences in natural heat, how much time is spent at each stage, and how much of an increase in power (is needed) to substitute for and supplant (the natural development). All this should finally enable him to imitate the action of nature in the mine or to prepare for a certain substance a form of composition that would be what the form of yeast is for bread, active in the particular substance in proportion to its powers and quantity.

All this is known only to the all-comprehensive knowledge (of God). Human science is unable to achieve it. Those who claim to have made gold with the help of alchemy are like those who might claim the artificial creation of man from semen. If we (could) grant to someone an all-comprehensive knowledge of the parts of man, his proportions, the stages of his (development), the way he is created in the womb, if he could know all this in all its details, so that nothing escapes his knowledge, then we (would) grant him the (ability to) create a human being. But where does anyone possess such (knowledge)?

Let us present here a short restatement of the argument, so that it can be easily understood. We say: The general lines followed in alchemy and the sum total of the claims (alchemists) make for the (alchemical) treatment are that it follows and imitates mineral nature by artificial action, until a particular mineral substance is generated, or until a substance is created that has certain powers, a (capacity to) act, and a form of composition acting upon a given substance
III, 238 as nature does, thus changing and transforming it into its own form. The technical action must be preceded by detailed, consecutive perceptions (*taṣawwur*) of the various stages of the mineral nature one intends to follow and imitate, or in which one intends the powerful substance to be active. Now, there is an unlimited number of such stages. Human knowledge is not able to comprehend even a lesser number. It is

comparable to wanting to create human beings or animals or plants.

This is the sum total of the argument. It is the most reliable argument I know of. It proves the impossibility (of alchemy), but neither from the point of view of the (specific) differences (of the metals), as above,[1098] nor from that of nature. It proves it from the point of view of the impossibility of complete comprehension and the inability of human beings to have (an all-comprehensive knowledge). Avicenna's remarks say nothing of the sort.

There is another aspect to alchemy proving its impossibility. It concerns the result of alchemy. This is as follows. It was God's wise plan that gold and silver, being rare, should be the standard of value by which the profits and capital accumulation of human beings are measured. (Now,) if it were possible to obtain (gold and silver) artificially, God's wise plan in this respect would be foiled. Gold and silver would exist in such large quantities that it would be no use to acquire them.[1099]

There is still another aspect (to alchemy) proving its impossibility. Nature always takes the shortest way in what it does. It does not take the longest and most complicated one. (Now) if, as (the alchemists) suppose, the artificial method were sound, shorter, and took less time than that which nature follows in the mine, nature would not have abandoned it in favor of the method it has chosen for the generation and creation of gold and silver.

Aṭ-Ṭughrâ'î's comparison of the (alchemical) process with individual similar instances noticed in nature, such as the (spontaneous) generation of scorpions, bees, and snakes, is sound, in as much as those things, as he assumes, have been III, 239
(actually) observed (and thus proven). But nowhere in the

[1098] Cf. pp. 272 f., above.

[1099] According to al-Fârâbî, *op. cit.* (n. 1089, above), the alchemists reserved their writings for the initiated because a mass production of gold and silver would make "social organization" impossible and deprive gold and silver of their "necessary role in mutual business dealings."

world is there a report stating that anybody ever observed (the soundness of) alchemy and its method. The practitioners of (alchemy) have constantly been groping in the dark. They have found nothing but lying stories. Had any (alchemist) found a correct method, his children, his pupils, or his colleagues would have preserved it. It would have been handed down among friends. Its correctness would have been guaranteed by its later successful application. (Knowledge of) it would eventually have spread. Ourselves or others would have learned about it.

The (alchemists also) state that the elixir is similar to yeast [1100] and that it is a compound for transmuting and transforming everything with which it comes in contact into its own essence. However, it should be realized that yeast transforms the dough and conditions it for digestion. This is (a process of) corruption, and material destruction is an easy process which may be produced by the slightest of actions and of elemental (influences). However, the purpose of the elixir is to transform one mineral into a nobler and higher one. That is something creative and constructive. Creation is more difficult than destruction.[1101] Thus, the elixir cannot be compared with yeast.

The truth of the matter is that if it is correct that alchemy exists, as the philosophers who discuss alchemy, such as Jâbir b. Ḥayyân, Maslamah b. Aḥmad al-Majrîṭî, and others, think, it does not (at any rate) fall under the category of natural crafts, and it does not come about by any technical process. The discussion of alchemy by (alchemists) is not like that of physics (by physicists). It is like the discussion of magical and other extraordinary matters or the wonders performed by al-Ḥallâj [1102] and others. Maslamah mentioned something of the sort in the *Kitâb al-Ghâyah.* His discussion of alchemy in the *Kitâb Rutbat al-ḥakîm* points in the same

[1100] Cf. p. 268, above.
[1101] Cf. 1:356 and 2:242, above.
[1102] Cf. p. 102, above.

direction. Jâbir's discussion in his treatises is also of the same type. This tendency of (alchemical) discussion is well known. We do not have to comment on it. III, 240

In general, (alchemy) as they understand it, has to do with universal creations [1103] which are outside the (sphere of) effectiveness of the crafts. Wood and animals cannot be developed from their (respective matters) in a day or a month, if such is not the (ordinary) course of their creation. In the same way, gold cannot be developed from its matter in a day or a month. Its customary course (of development) can be changed only with the help of something beyond the world of nature and the activity of the crafts. Thus, those who try to practice alchemy as a craft lose their money and labor. The alchemical treatment is, therefore, called a "sterile treatment." In so far as it is sound, it is the result of (powers) beyond those of nature and the crafts. It is comparable to walking upon water, riding in the air, passing through solid substances,[1104] and similar acts of divine grace that are performed by saints and break through the customary course of nature. Or, it may be compared to the creation of birds and similar miracles of the prophets. God says: "And when you created something like the form of a bird from clay with my permission, and you blew into it, and the form thus became a bird with the permission of God." [1105]

The way in which (miracles of an alchemical nature) are performed depends on the condition of the person to whom (such miracles) are granted. They may be granted to a pious person who passes them on to someone else. They are in this case loaned to the other person, (but he, at any rate, is able to perform them). Or, they may be granted to a worthless person who cannot pass them on. In this case, they cannot be

[1103] The strange *al-mawâlid* is attested by the MSS. Bulaq corrects it to *al-mawâdd* "matters." This might be a necessary correction (?).

[1104] Cf. 1:191, above.

[1105] Cf. Qur'ân 5.110 (110), where the last words read: "with my permission." The phrase "with the permission of God" is found in the parallel passage, Qur'ân 3.49 (43).

performed by someone else. It is in this sense that the performance (of alchemical miracles) is magical.

Thus, it is clear that (alchemical miracles) are the result of psychic influences and extraordinary wonders, either as miracles or acts of divine grace, or as sorcery. Therefore, all
III, *241* the sages who have discussed (alchemy) use puzzling expressions whose real meaning is known only to those who have delved deeply into sorcery and are acquainted with the (magic) activities of the soul in the world of nature. (But) matters breaking through the ordinary course (of nature) are unlimited, and no one could get to know them (all). God "comprehends all you do." [1106]

The most common cause of the desire to practice alchemy is, as we have stated, a person's inability to make his living in a natural way and the wish to make a living in some way that, unlike agriculture, commerce, and (handi)craft, is not natural.[1107] A person without ability finds it difficult to make his living in such (legitimate occupations). He wants to get rich all at once through some (occupation) that is not natural, such as alchemy and other things. Alchemy is cultivated mostly by the poor among civilized people. (The fact that economic status is decisive for the recognition or nonrecognition of alchemy) applies even to the philosophers who discuss the possibility [1108] or impossibility of (alchemy). Avicenna, who states that alchemy is impossible, was a great wazir and a very wealthy person, while al-Fârâbî, who states that it is possible, was one of those poor persons who have not the slightest success in making a living by any means. This is an obvious suspicion as to the attitude of people who are eager to try (alchemy) out and practice it.[1109]

God "gives sustenance. He is strong and solid." [1110]

[1106] Qur'ân 11.92 (94).

[1107] Cf. 2:316, above.

[1108] Bulaq: "nonexistence."

[1109] Cf. Bombaci, p. 465, who translates: ". . . motive of suspicion that invalidates the theories of the people who

[1110] Qur'ân 51.58 (58).

[33] *The purposes that must be kept in mind in literary composition and that alone are to be considered valid.*[1111]

It should be known that the storehouse of human science is the soul of man. In it, God has implanted perception III, 242 (*idrâk*) enabling it to think and, thus, to acquire (scientific knowledge). (The process) starts with perception (*taṣawwur*) of the realities and is then continued by affirmation or negation of the essential attributes of the (realities), either directly or through an intermediary.

(Man's) ability to think thus eventually produces a problematic situation which it tries to solve affirmatively or negatively. When a scientific picture has been established in the mind (of one person) through these (efforts), it must, of necessity, be communicated to someone else, either through instruction or through discussion, in order to polish the mind by trying to show its soundness.

Such communication takes place through "verbal expression,"[1112] that is, speech composed of spoken words which God created in a limb (of the human body), the tongue, as combinations of "letters (sounds)"—that is, the various qualities of sound as broken by uvula and tongue—so that the thoughts of people can be communicated in speech. This is the first step in the communication of thoughts. As its most important and noble part, it includes the sciences. However, it comprises every statement or wish (command) that in general enters the mind.

After this first step in communication, there is a second. It is the communication of one's thoughts to persons who are out of sight or bodily far away, or to persons who live later and whom one has not met, since they are not contemporaries.

[1111] This section is not found in the earlier texts. C continues with the next section for one page, then starts on a left-hand page with this section, which is thus characterized as a later insertion. The section is incorporated in the text of D. Cf. also pp. 406 f., above.

[1112] Or "hermeneutics."

This kind of communication is written communication. Writing is figures made by the hand, whose shapes and forms, by convention, indicate the individual letters (sounds) and
III, 243 words of speech. Thus, they communicate thought through the medium of speech. Writing, therefore, constitutes the second step of communication and is one of its two parts. It gives information about the noblest part of thinking, namely, science and knowledge. Scholars take care to deposit all their scientific thoughts in books by means of writing, so that all those who are absent and live at a later time may have the benefit of them. People who do that are authors. Everywhere in the world, written works are numerous. They are handed down among all races and in all ages. They differ as the result of differences in religious laws and organizations and in the information available about nations and dynasties. The philosophical sciences do not show (such) differences. They have developed uniformly, as required by the very nature of thinking, which is concerned with the perception (*taṣawwur*) of existing things as they are, whether corporeal, spiritual, celestial, elemental, abstract, or material. These sciences show no differences. Differences occur in the religious sciences because of differences among the various religions, and in the historical sciences because of differences in the outward character of historical information.

Writing differs in that human beings have come to use different forms and shapes of it. (These differences) are called "pen" and script.[1113] There is the Ḥimyarite script, which is called *musnad*. It is the script of the Ḥimyar and the ancient inhabitants of the Yemen. It differs from the writing of the later Muḍar Arabs, exactly as the (language written in the Ḥimyarite script) is different from the language of (the Muḍar Arabs), though all of them are Arabs. However, the habit of linguistic expression among (the Ḥimyar) differed

[1113] As a very detailed discussion of foreign scripts by a Muslim author, one may compare the opening pages of Ibn an-Nadîm's *Fihrist*. Like the discussion of the origin and development of languages, the subject of writing may have been of some interest to jurists. Cf. also 2:378 ff., above.

from that of (the Muḍar Arabs). Both have their own general norms, which are evolved inductively from their (ways of linguistic) expression, and are different from the norms of the III, *244*
other (group). Those who do not know the habits of (linguistic) expression often are mistaken (about the relationship between the language of the Ḥimyar and that of the other Arabs).

Another script is the Syrian script. This is the writing of the Nabataeans and Chaldeans. Ignorant people often think that because the (Nabataeans and Chaldeans) were the most powerful [1114] nations (in antiquity), and the (Syrian script) is of great antiquity, it is the natural script (whereas all other scripts are conventional ones). This is a fanciful, vulgar idea. No action resulting from choice is a natural one. The fact is simply that (the Syrian script [1115] is) so old and was used for so long that it became a firmly rooted habit, thought by the observer to be a natural one. Many simpletons have the same idea [1116] about the Arabic language. They say that the Arabs express themselves in good Arabic and speak (it) by nature. This is a fanciful (idea).[1117]

Another script is the Hebrew script. It is the writing of the children of Eber, the son of Shelah, who are Israelites, and of other (people).

Another script is the Latin script, the script of the Latin Byzantines (Romans). They also have their own language.

Each nation has its own particular form of writing, which is attributed to it in particular. (This applies,) for instance, to the Turks, the European Christians, the Indians, and others. (However,) only three scripts are of interest. First, Syrian, because of its antiquity, as we have mentioned. Then, there are Arabic <and Hebrew>,[1118] since the Qur'ân

[1114] C and D: *aqdar*. This may be the more original text as compared with *aqdam* "most ancient," which appears in the Paris edition, but C and D have unusually many mistakes in this section.

[1115] It may, however, be that Ibn Khaldûn is thinking here in general terms rather than singling out the example of the "Syrian script."

[1116] The MSS. C and D have a meaningless *r's kabîr*.

[1117] Cf. pp. 343 and 359, below.

[1118] C and D omit "and Hebrew."

and the Torah were revealed in the Arabic and Hebrew scripts and languages, respectively. These two scripts came to be (the medium of) communication for the texts (written in them, that is, the Qur'ân and the Torah).[1119] There arose very early an interest in works composed in them, and norms for expressing oneself in that language [1120] according to its particular method (*uslûb*) [1121] were set forth, so that the obligations of the religious law might be properly deduced from the divine speech of (the Qur'ân).

Then, (thirdly) there is Latin, the language of the Byzan-
III, *245* tine (Romans). When they adopted Christianity, which, as mentioned at the beginning of this book,[1122] is entirely based upon the Torah, they translated the Torah and the books of the Israelite prophets into their language, in order to be able to derive the law from (Scripture) as easily as possible. Thus, they came to be more interested in their own language and writing than (in) any other.

The other scripts are of no interest. Every people employs its own particular kind of script.

Now, the purposes that must be kept in mind in literary composition and that alone are to be considered valid were restricted to seven.[1123]

[1119] For *matlûw*, cf. 1:192 (n. 261), above.

[1120] Ibn Khaldûn now thinks only of Arabic and the Qur'ân, paying no more attention to Hebrew and the Torah.

[1121] Cf. pp. 375 ff., below.

[1122] Cf. 1:476 ff., above, or *'Ibar*, II, 148? C and D have a meaningless *al-kitâbah*.

[1123] According to p. 287, below, the following statement goes back to Aristotle. Parallels to it are found quoted in F. Rosenthal, *The Technique and Approach of Muslim Scholarship* (Analecta Orientalia, No. 24) (Rome, 1947), pp. 64 ff. It may be noted that the statement of al-'Almawî quoted there goes back to the *'Âriḍat al-aḥwadhî* of Abû Bakr b. al-'Arabî, with whose work Ibn Khaldûn was very familiar. (Cf. 1:446, above, and p. 303, below.) Discussions of this sort can be found as early as the ninth century. Cf. al-Khuwârizmî, *Algebra*, ed. F. Rosen (London, 1831), p. 2; L. C. Karpinski, "Robert of Chester's Translation of the Algebra of al-Khowarizmi" in *Contributions to the History of Science*, p. 46. No explanation seems readily available for the ascription of the passage to Aristotle. The introductions to Aristotelian philosophy, which would seem to be the most likely source, do not discuss the subject.

(1) The invention of a science with its subject, its division into chapters and sections, and the discussion of its problems. Or the invention of problems and topics of research which occur to a competent scholar and which he wants to communicate to someone else, so that they may become generally known and useful. This, then, is deposited in a written volume, so that a later (generation) may have the benefit of it. This is what happened, for instance, with the principles of jurisprudence. Ash-Shâfi'î was the first to discuss, and briefly to describe, the legal arguments based on the wording (of the traditions). Then, the Ḥanafites appeared and invented the problems of analogical reasoning and presented them fully. This (material) has been used by subsequent generations down to the present time.

(2) (A scholar) may find the discussion and works of ancient (scholars) difficult to understand. God may open understanding of them to him. He will then wish to communicate his (knowledge) to someone else who may perhaps have difficulties with (the same problems), so that all those who are worthy may have the benefit of (his knowledge). This is the interpretational approach to books on the intellectual and traditional (sciences). It is a noble chapter.

(3) Some later (scholar) may come across an error or mistake in discussions by ancient (scholars) of renowned merit and famous authority as teachers. He may have clear proof III, 246
for it, admitting of no doubt. He will then wish to communicate this (discovery) to those after him, since it is impossible to eradicate a mistake (in the work in question) in view of its wide dissemination in space and time, the fame of (its) author, and the reliance people place in his learning. Therefore, he deposits this (discovery of the mistake) in writing, so that (future) students may learn the explanation of it.

(4) A particular discipline may be incomplete, certain problems or details indicated by the division of the subject of the discipline requiring treatment. The (scholar) who becomes aware of the fact will want to supply these lacking problems, in order to perfect the discipline by having all its

problems and details treated and leaving no room for deficiency in it.

(5) The problems of a particular science may have been treated without (the proper) arrangement into chapters and without order. The (scholar) who becomes aware of that (situation) will arrange and improve on the problems and put every problem in the chapter where it belongs. This happened to the *Mudawwanah*, as transmitted by Saḥnûn on the authority of Ibn al-Qâsim, and to the *'Utbîyah*, as transmitted by al-'Utbî on the authority of the companions of Mâlik. In these works, many problems of jurisprudence were not mentioned in the proper chapters. Therefore, Ibn Abî Zayd improved upon the *Mudawwanah*, while the *'Utbîyah* remained unimproved. Thus, in every chapter (of the *'Utbîyah*), we find problems that belong in another, and (scholars) restricted themselves to the *Mudawwanah* and the (improvements) made on it by Ibn Abî Zayd and, after him, by al-Barâdhi'î.[1124]

(6) The problems of a certain science might (only) exist scattered among the proper chapters of other sciences. Some excellent (scholar) will then become aware of the subject of that particular discipline (as a subject in its own right) and of (the need of) collecting [1125] its problems. He will do that, and a (new) discipline will make its appearance. He will give it its
III, *247* place among the sciences that mankind, with its ability to think, cultivates. This happened with the science of literary criticism (*bayân*).[1126] 'Abd-al-Qâhir al-Jurjânî [1127] and Abû (Ya'qûb) Yûsuf as-Sakkâkî [1128] found its problems mentioned more or less correctly [1129] in the books on grammar. In his

[1124] Cf. pp. 14 f., above.

[1125] C and D: *wa-jam'*.

[1126] Cf. pp. 335 ff., below.

[1127] 'Abd-al-Qâhir b. 'Abd-ar-Raḥmân [eleventh century]. Cf. *GAL*, I, 287; *Suppl.*, I, 503 f. Cf. also n. 1286 to this chapter, below.

[1128] Yûsuf b. Abî Bakr, 555–626 [1160–1228/29]. Cf. *GAL*, I, 294 ff.; *Suppl.*, I, 515 ff. Cf. also n. 4 to Ch. II, above.

[1129] The consonants of the MSS ought possibly to be read *mustaqrabatan* and translated as suggested above.

Kitâb al-Bayân wa-t-tabyîn,[1130] al-Jâḥiẓ had already brought together many of the problems of this science. In (dealing with) them, people became aware [1131] of the subject of (this science) and the fact that it constitutes a science in its own right. (Later,) the famous works (by the literary critics mentioned) were written on the subject. They became the basic works of the discipline of literary criticism. Later (scholars) studied (those works) and exceeded all their predecessors in (improving upon) them.

(7) Something in the main scholarly works may be too long and prolix. One will then try to compose a brief and succinct abridgment, omitting all repetitions. However, one has to be careful not to eliminate anything essential, so that the purpose of the first author will not be vitiated.

These are the purposes that must be kept in mind and not lost sight of in literary composition. All else is unnecessary, a mistake (or deviation) from the road that (all) intelligent (scholars) think must be followed. For instance, (someone may try) to ascribe the work of an earlier author to himself with the aid of certain tricks, such as changing the wording and the arrangement of the contents. Or, someone may eliminate material essential to a particular discipline, or mention unnecessary material, or replace correct (statements) with wrong ones, or mention useless material. All this shows ignorance and impudence.

Aristotle, when he enumerated the purposes (by which an author must be guided) and had come to the last one, therefore said: "Everything else is either superfluousness or greed," by which he meant ignorance and insolence. III, 248

We take refuge in God from doing what an intelligent

[1130] C and D read *at-tabayyun*, a mistake by Ibn Khaldûn. Judging by the situation below, p. 340, where *at-tabyîn* is found in A and B, *at-tabayyun* in C and D, he had the correct reading first and later changed it to the wrong one (possibly misled by the mistake of some copyist).

[1131] C and D: *tanabbaha*. *Leg.*, perhaps, *yunabbihu* "he (al-Jâḥiẓ) called the attention of people to . . ."

person ought not to do. God "guides to the things that are most correct." [1132]

[34] *The great number of scholarly works (available) is an obstacle on the path to attaining scholarship.*

It should be known that among the things that are harmful to the human quest for knowledge and to the attainment of a thorough scholarship are the great number of works (available), the large variety in technical terminology (needed for purposes) of instruction, and the numerous (different) methods (used in those works).[1133] The student is required to have a ready knowledge of (all) that. Only then is he considered an accomplished scholar.

Thus, the student must know all the (works), or most of them, and observe the methods used in them.[1134] His whole lifetime would not suffice to know all the literature that exists in a single discipline, (even) if he were to devote himself entirely to it. Thus, he must of necessity fall short of attaining scholarship.

For the Mâlikite school of jurisprudence, this (situation) may be exemplified, for instance, by the *Mudawwanah*, its legal commentaries, such as the books of Ibn Yûnus, al-Lakhmî, and Ibn Bashîr, and the notes and introductions (to it).[1135] Or (one may take) the sister work of the *Mudawwanah*, the *'Utbîyah* and the work written on it (by Ibn Rushd under the title of) *al-Bayân wa-t-taḥṣîl;* [1136] or the book of Ibn al-Ḥâjib and the works written on it. Furthermore, the student must be able to distinguish between the Qayrawânî method (of the Mâlikite school) and the methods of Cordo-

[1132] Qur'ân 17.9 (9).

[1133] Though "terminology" is a closer antecedent for the Arabic suffix than "works," the above translation seems justified. "Method," in this context, is most likely to mean "school system," as shown by the reference to the Qayrawânî, etc., "method" of Mâlikism.

[1134] Cf. Bombaci, p. 466, who here as above (n. 1133) refers the suffix to "terminology."

[1135] Cf. p. 15, above.

[1136] Cf. *GAL*, *Suppl.*, I, 662.

van, Baghdâdî, and Egyptian (Mâlikites) and those of their more recent successors. He must know all that. Only then is a person considered able to give juridical decisions.

All of (these things) are variations of one and the same subject. The student is required to have a ready knowledge of all of them and to be able to distinguish between them. (Yet,) a whole lifetime could be spent on (but) one of them. If teachers and students were to restrict themselves to the III, 249
school problems, (the task) would be much easier and (scholarly) instruction would be simple and easily accessible. However, this is an evil that cannot be cured, because it has become firmly ingrained through custom. In a way, it has become something natural, which cannot be moved or transformed.

Another example is Arabic philology.[1137] There is the *Book* of Sîbawayh and all the literature on it; (there are) the methods of the Baṣrians, the Kûfians, the Baghdâdîs, and, later on, the Spaniards; and (there are) the methods of the ancient and modern philologists, such as Ibn al-Ḥâjib and Ibn Mâlik, and all the literature on that. This (wealth of material) requires a great deal from the student. He could spend his (whole) life on less (material). No one would aspire to complete knowledge of it, though there are a few, rare exceptions (of men who have a complete knowledge of philology). For instance, we modern Maghribîs have received the works of an Egyptian philologist whose name is Ibn Hishâm. The contents show that Ibn Hishâm has completely mastered the habit of philology as it had not been mastered (before) save by Sîbawayh, Ibn Jinnî, and people of their class, so greatly developed is his philological habit and so comprehensive is his knowledge and experience as regards the principles and details of philology. This proves that excellence (in scholarship) is not restricted to the ancients,[1138] especially if (one considers) our remarks about the many

[1137] Cf. pp. 323 f., below.

[1138] Muslim scholars considered it necessary to stress the idea that there was constant progress, that the ancients left much for later scholars to do. Cf., for instance, F. Rosenthal in *Osiris*, IX (1950), 559.

obstacles (on the path to mastery of a science in modern times), which the great number of schools, methods, and works presents. No! "His excellence God bestows upon whomever He wants to." [1139] (Ibn Hishâm) is one of the rare wonders of the world. Otherwise, it is obvious that were the student to spend his entire lifetime on all these things, it would not be long enough for him to acquire, for instance, (a
III, 250 complete knowledge of) Arabic philology, which is (but) an instrument and means (for further studies). How, then, is it with the intended fruit (of study, the acquisition of thorough and comprehensive scholarship)? But "God guides whomever He wants to guide." [1140]

[35] *The great number of brief handbooks (available) on scholarly subjects is detrimental to (the process of) instruction.*

Many [1141] recent scholars have turned to brief presentations of the methods and contents of the sciences. They want to know (the methods and contents), and they present them systematically in the form of brief programs for each science. (These) brief handbooks express all the problems of a given discipline and the evidence for them in a few brief words that are full of meaning. This (procedure) is detrimental to good style and makes difficulties for the understanding.

(Scholars) often approach the main scholarly works on the various disciplines, which are very lengthy, intending to interpret [1142] and explain (them). They abridge them, in order to make it easier (for students) to acquire expert knowledge of them. Such, for instance, was done by Ibn al-Ḥâjib in

[1139] Qur'ân 5.54 (59); 57.21 (21); 62.4 (4). Needless to say, the word "excellence" does not have the meaning in the Qur'ânic context that it is given here by Ibn Khaldûn.

[1140] Qur'ân 2.142 (136), 213 (209), etc.

[1141] Cf. Issawi, pp. 160 f.

[1142] The word *li-t-tafsîr*, which in this context cannot refer to Qur'ân commentaries, is omitted in A and B, cut off in the margin of C, and missing in D. *Li-t-tafassur*, in the Paris ed., may be a misprint.

It may be added here that the word translated "expert knowledge" in the following sentence also has the equivalent meaning of "knowing by heart." Cf. n. 1362, below.

jurisprudence and the principles of jurisprudence,[1143] by Ibn Mâlik in Arabic philology,[1144] by al-Khûnajî in logic,[1145] and so on. This (procedure) has a corrupting influence upon the process of instruction and is detrimental to the attainment of scholarship. For it confuses the beginner by presenting the final results of a discipline to him before he is prepared for them. This is a bad method of instruction, as will be mentioned.[1146]

(The procedure) also involves a great deal of work for the student. He must study carefully the words of the abridgment, which are complicated to understand because they are crowded with ideas, and [1147] try to find out from them what the problems of (the given discipline) are. Thus, the texts of such brief handbooks are found to be difficult and complicated (to understand). A good deal of time must be spent on (the attempt to) understand them.

Moreover, after all these (difficulties), the (scholarly) III, *251*
habit that results from receiving instruction from brief handbooks, (even) when (such instruction) is at its best and is not accompanied by any flaw, is inferior to the habits resulting from (the study of) more extensive and lengthy works. The latter contain a great amount of repetition and lengthiness, but both are useful for the acquisition of a perfect habit. When there is little repetition, an inferior habit is the result. This is the case with the abridgments. The intention was to make it easy for students to acquire expert knowledge (of scholarly subjects), but the result is that it has become (more) difficult for them, because they are prevented from acquiring useful and firmly established habits.

Those whom God guides, no one can lead astray, and "those whom God leads astray have no one to guide them." [1148]

[1143] Cf. pp. 18 f. and 29 f., above.

[1144] Cf. p. 323, below.

[1145] Cf. p. 143, above.

[1146] Cf. p. 293, below.

[1147] Bulaq adds: "with great difficulty."

[1148] Qur'ân 7.185 (185).

[36] *The right attitude in scientific instruction and toward the method of giving such instruction.*[1149]

It [1150] should be known that the teaching of scientific subjects to students is effective only when it proceeds gradually and little by little. At first, (the teacher) presents (the student) with the principal problems within each chapter of a given discipline. He acquaints him with them by commenting on them in a summary fashion. In the course of doing so, he observes the student's intellectual potential and his preparedness for understanding the material that will come his way until the end of the discipline under consideration (is reached). In the process, (the student) acquires the habit of the science (he studies). However, that habit will be an approximate [1151] and weak one. The most it can do is to enable the student to understand the discipline (he studies) and to know its problems.

(The teacher,) then, leads (the student) back over the discipline a second time. He gives him instruction in it on a higher level. He no longer gives a summary but full com-
III, 252 mentaries and explanations. He mentions to him the existing differences of opinion and the form these differences take all the way through to the end of the discipline under consideration. Thus, the student's (scholarly) habit is improved. Then, (the teacher) leads (the student) back again, now that he is solidly grounded. He leaves nothing (that is) complicated, vague, or obscure, unexplained. He bares all the secrets (of the discipline) to him. As a result, the student, when he finishes with the discipline, has acquired the habit of it.

This is the effective method of instruction. As one can see, it requires a threefold repetition. Some students can get

[1149] For the following discussion of education, cf. L. Buret, "Notes marginales sur les Prolégomènes: Un Pédagogue arabe du XIVe siècle: Ibn Khaldoun," *Revue Tunisienne*, N.S. LV (1934), 23–33, and Jamâl al-Muḥâsib, "Ibn Khaldûn's Theory of Education" (in Arabic), *al-Machriq*, XLIII (1949), 365–98. Cf. also above, pp. 426 ff.

[1150] Cf. Issawi, pp. 157–59.

[1151] Bulaq: "partial."

through it with less than that, depending on their natural dispositions and qualifications.

We have observed that many teachers [1152] of the time in which we are living are ignorant of this effective method of instruction. They begin their instruction by confronting the student with obscure scientific problems. They require him to concentrate on solving them. They think that that is experienced and correct teaching, and they make it the task of the student to comprehend and know such things. In actual fact, they (merely) confuse him by exposing him to the final results of a discipline at the beginning (of his studies) and before he is prepared to understand them. Preparedness for and receptivity to scientific knowledge and understanding grow gradually. At the beginning, the student is completely unable to understand any but a very few (points). (His understanding is) only approximate and general and (can be achieved only) with the help of pictures (*muthul*) derived from sensual perception. His preparedness, then, keeps growing gradually and little by little when he faces the problems of the discipline under consideration and has them repeated (to him) and advances from approximate understanding of them to a complete, higher knowledge. Thus the habit of preparedness and, eventually, that of attainment materialize in the student, until he has a comprehensive knowledge of the problems of the discipline (he studies). But if a student is
exposed to the final results at the beginning, while he is still III, 253
unable to understand and comprehend (anything) and is still far from being prepared to (understand), his mind is not acute enough to (grasp them). He gets the impression that scholarship is difficult and becomes loath to occupy himself with it. He constantly dodges and avoids it. That is the result of poor instruction, and nothing else.

The teacher should not ask more from a student than that he understand the book he is engaged in studying, in accord-

[1152] MSS. A, B, C, and D have "students," but one must read "teachers," with Bulaq.

ance with his class (age group)[1153] and his receptivity to instruction, whether he is at the start or at the end (of his studies). (The teacher) should not bring in problems other than those found in that particular book, until the student knows the whole (book) from beginning to end, is acquainted with its purpose, and has gained a habit from it, which he then can apply to other (books). When the student has acquired (the scholarly) habit in one discipline, he is prepared for learning all the others. He also has become interested in looking for more and in advancing to higher (learning). Thus, he eventually acquires a complete mastery of scholarship. But if one confuses a student, he will be unable to understand (anything). He becomes indolent. He stops thinking. He despairs of becoming a scholar and avoids scholarship and instruction.

"God guides whomever He wants to guide."[1154]

It is also necessary (for the teacher) to avoid prolonging the period of instruction in a single discipline or book, by breaks in the sessions and long intervals between them. This causes (the student) to forget and disrupts the nexus between the different problems (of the discipline being studied). The result of such interruptions is that attainment of the (scholarly) habit becomes difficult. If the first and last things of a discipline are present in the mind and prevent the effects of forgetfulness, the (scholarly) habit is more easily acquired, more firmly established, and closer to becoming a (true) coloring. For habits are acquired by continuous and repeated
III, *254* activity. When one forgets to act, one forgets the habit that results from that particular action.

God "taught you what you did not know."[1155]

A good and necessary method and approach in instruction is not to expose the student to two disciplines at the same time.[1156] Otherwise, he will rarely master one of them, since

[1153] Bulaq corrects to "ability."
[1154] Qur'ân 2.142 (136), 213 (209), etc.
[1155] Qur'ân 2.239 (240).
[1156] Cf. p. 304, below.

he has to divide his attention and is diverted from each of them by his attempt to understand the other. Thus, he will consider both of them obscure and difficult, and be unsuccessful in both. But if the (student's) mind is free to study the subject that he is out (to study) and can restrict himself to it, that (fact) often makes it simpler (for the student) to learn (the subject in question).

God gives success to that which is correct.

You,[1157] student, should realize that I am here giving you useful (hints) for your study. If you accept them and follow them assiduously, you will find a great and noble treasure. As an introduction that will help you to understand these (hints), I shall tell you the following:

Man's ability to think is a special natural gift which God created exactly as He created all His other creations. It is an action and motion[1158] in the soul by means of a power (located) in the middle cavity of the brain.[1159] At times, (thinking) means the beginning of orderly and well-arranged human actions. At other times, it means the beginning of the knowledge of something that had not been available (before). The (ability to think) is directed toward some objective whose two extremes[1160] it has perceived (*taṣawwur*), and (now) it desires to affirm or deny it. In almost no time, it recognizes the middle term which combines the two (extremes), if (the objective) is uniform. Or, it goes on to obtain another middle term, if (the objective) is manifold. It thus finds its objective. It is in this way that the ability to think, by III, *255*
which man is distinguished from all the other animals, works.

Now, the craft of logic is (knowledge of the) way in which the natural ability to think and speculate operates. Logic describes it, so that correct operation can be distinguished from erroneous. To be right, though, is in the essence of the

[1157] The remainder of this section, and the following section down to p. 300, are missing in C.

[1158] Bulaq: "It is the existence (*wijdân*) of a motion." Cf. 1:198, above.

[1159] Cf. 1:197, 210, and 2:412, above.

[1160] I.e., the major and minor terms.

ability to think. However, in very rare cases, it is affected by error. This comes from perceiving (*taṣawwur*) the two extremes in forms other than are properly theirs, as the result of confusion in the order and arrangement of the propositions from which the conclusion is drawn. Logic helps to avoid such traps. Thus,[1161] it is a technical procedure which parallels (man's) natural ability to think and conforms to the way in which it functions. Since it is a technical procedure, it can be dispensed with in most cases. Therefore, one finds that many of the world's most excellent thinkers have achieved scholarly results without employing the craft of logic, especially when their intention was sincere and they entrusted themselves to the mercy of God, which is the greatest help (anyone may hope to find). They proceeded with the aid of the natural ability to think at its best, and this (ability), as it was created by God, permitted them by (its very) nature to find the middle term and knowledge of their objective.

Besides the technical procedure called logic, the (process of) study involves another introductory (discipline), namely, the knowledge of words and the way in which they indicate ideas in the mind by deriving them from what the forms (of the letters) say, in the case of writing, and from what the tongue—speech—says in the case of spoken utterances.[1162] You, the student, must pass through all these veils, in order to reach (the state where you can) think about your objective.

III, *256* First, there is the way in which writing indicates spoken words.[1163] This is the easiest part of it. Then, there is the way in which the spoken words indicate the ideas one is seeking. Further, there are the rules for arranging the ideas in their proper molds, as they are known from the craft of logic, in order to (be able to) make deductions. Then, there are those ideas in the mind that are abstract and (used) as nets with which one goes hunting for the (desired) objective with the

[1161] Cf. Issawi, pp. 168 f.
[1162] Cf. pp. 316 f., below. Cf. also 2:406 f., above.
[1163] Cf. pp. 281 f., above.

help of one's natural ability to think (and) entrusting oneself to the mercy and generosity of God.[1164]

Not everyone is able to pass through all these stages quickly and to cut through all these veils easily during the (process of) instruction.[1165] Disputes often cause the mind to stop at the veils of words. Disturbing quarrels and doubts cause it to fall into the nets of argument, so that the mind is prevented from attaining its objective. Rarely do more than a few (individuals), who are guided by God, succeed in extricating themselves from this abyss.

If you are afflicted by such (difficulties) and hampered in your understanding (of the problems) by misgivings or disturbing doubts in your mind, cast them off! Discard the veils of words and the obstacles of doubt! Leave all the technical procedures and take refuge in the realm of the natural ability to think given to you by nature! Let your speculation roam in it and let your mind freely delve in it, according to whatever you desire (to obtain) from it! Set foot in the places where the greatest thinkers before you did! Entrust yourself to God's aid, as in His mercy He aided them and taught them what they did not know! [1166] If you do that, God's helpful light will shine upon you and show you your objective. Inspiration will
indicate (to you) the middle term which God made a natural III, *257*
requirement of the (process of) thinking, as we have stated.[1167] At that particular moment, return with (the middle term) to the molds and forms (to be used) for the arguments, dip it into them, and give it its due of the technical norm (of logic)! Then, clothe it with the forms of words and bring it forth into the world of spoken utterances, firmly girt and soundly constructed!

Verbal disputes and doubts concerning the distinction between right and wrong logical evidence are all technical and conventional matters. Their numerous aspects are all alike or

[1164] Cf. Bombaci, pp. 466 f.
[1165] D: "study."
[1166] Cf. Qur'ân 2.239 (240).
[1167] Cf. p. 295, above.

similar, because of their conventional and technical character. If they stop you, (you [1168] will not be able) to distinguish the truth in them, for the truth becomes distinguishable only if it exists by nature. All the doubts and uncertainties will remain. The veils will cover the objective sought and prevent the thinker from attaining it. That has been the case with most recent thinkers, especially with those who formerly spoke a language other than Arabic, which was a mental handicap,[1169] or those who were enamored with logic and partial to it.[1170] They believe that logic is a natural means for the perception of the truth. They become confused when doubts and misgivings arise concerning the evidence, and they are scarcely able to free themselves from (such doubts).

As a matter of fact, the natural means for the perception of the truth is, as we have stated, (man's) natural ability to think, when it is free from all imaginings and when the thinker entrusts himself to the mercy of God. Logic merely describes the process of thinking and mostly parallels it.
III, 258 Take that into consideration and ask for God's mercy when you have difficulty in understanding problems! Then, the divine light will shine upon you and give you the right inspiration.

God guides in His mercy. Knowledge comes only from God.

[37] *Study of the auxiliary sciences should not be prolonged, and their problems should not be treated in detail.*[1171]

It [1172] should be known that the sciences customarily known among civilized people are of two kinds. There are the sciences that are wanted *per se*, such as the religious sciences

[1168] Notwithstanding the tense used by Ibn Khaldûn, the apodosis would seem to start here (against Bombaci, p. 467).

[1169] Cf. pp. 315 ff., below.

[1170] Cf., for instance, pp. 142 ff., above.

[1171] This section is missing in C. Cf. n. 1157 to this chapter, above.

[1172] Cf. Issawi, pp. 162 f.

of Qur'ân interpretation, Prophetic traditions, jurisprudence, and speculative theology, and the physical and metaphysical sciences of philosophy. In addition, there are sciences that are instrumental and auxiliary to the sciences mentioned. Among such auxiliary sciences are Arabic philology, arithmetic, and others, which are auxiliary to the religious sciences, and logic which is auxiliary to philosophy and often also to speculative theology and the science of the principles of jurisprudence (when treated) according to the method of recent scholars.[1173]

In the case of the sciences that are wanted (*per se*), it does no harm to extend their discussion, to treat their problems in detail, and to present all the evidence and (all the different) views (which exist concerning them). It gives the student of them a firmer habit and clarifies the ideas they contain which one wants to know. But the sciences that are auxiliary to other sciences, such as Arabic philology, logic, and the like, should be studied only in so far as they are aids to the other (sciences). Discussion of them should not be prolonged, and the problems should not be treated in detail, as this would lead away from their purpose, and their purpose is (to facilitate understanding of) the sciences to which they are auxiliary, nothing else. Whenever the (auxiliary sciences) cease to be (auxiliary to other sciences), they abandon their purpose, and occupation with them becomes an idle pastime.

Moreover,[1174] it is (also) difficult to acquire the habit of them, because they are large subjects with many details. III, *259*
Their (difficulty) is often an obstacle to acquiring the sciences wanted *per se*, because it takes so long to get to them. However, they are more important, and life is too short to acquire a knowledge of everything in this (thorough) form. Thus, occupation with the auxiliary sciences constitutes a waste of one's life, occupation with something that is of no concern.[1175]

Recent scholars have done this with grammar and logic and even with the principles of jurisprudence. They have pro-

[1173] Cf., for instance, pp. 28 and 49, above.
[1174] Or: "In spite of that." But "moreover" seems preferable.
[1175] Cf. n. 796 to this chapter, above.

longed the discussion of these disciplines both [1176] by transmitting (more material) and (by adding to the material) through deductive reasoning. They have increased the number of details and problems,[1177] causing them to be no longer auxiliary sciences, but disciplines that are wanted *per se*. In consequence, (the auxiliary sciences) often deal with views and problems for which there is no need in the disciplines that are wanted *per se* (and are the sole *raison d'être* of the auxiliary sciences). Thus, they are a sort of idle pastime and also do outright harm to students, because the sciences that are wanted (*per se*) are more important for them than the auxiliary and instrumental sciences. (Now,) if they spend all their lives on the auxiliary (sciences), when will they get around to (the sciences) that are wanted (*per se*)? Therefore, teachers of the auxiliary sciences ought not to delve too deeply in them [1178] and increase the number of their problems. They must advise the student concerning their purpose and have him stop there. Those who have the mind to go more deeply (into them) and [1178] consider themselves capable and able to do so, may choose (such a course) for themselves. Everyone is successful at the things for which he was created.[1179]

III, 260

[38] *The instruction of children and the different methods employed in the Muslim cities.*

It should be known that instructing children in the Qur'ân is a symbol of Islam. Muslims have, and practice, such instruction in all their cities, because it imbues hearts with a firm belief (in Islam) and its articles of faith, which are (derived) from the verses of the Qur'ân and certain Prophetic traditions. The Qur'ân has become the basis of instruction, the foundation for all habits that may be acquired later on. The reason for this is that the things one is taught in one's

[1176] Bulaq omits the rest of the sentence. It may be noted that the science of the principles of jurisprudence is not an auxiliary science, and Ibn Khaldûn said so at the beginning of the section.

[1177] Bulaq: "deductions."

[1178] The rest of the sentence is not found in Bulaq.

[1179] Cf. 2:332, and p. 109, above.

youth take root more deeply (than anything else). They are the basis of all later (knowledge). The first impression the heart receives is, in a way, the foundation of (all scholarly) habits. The character of the foundation determines the condition of the building. The methods of instructing children in the Qur'ân differ according to differences of opinion as to the habits that are to result from that instruction.

The Maghribî method is to restrict the education of children to instruction in the Qur'ân and to practice, during the course (of instruction), in Qur'ân orthography and its problems and the differences among Qur'ân experts on this score. The (Maghribîs) do not bring up any other subjects in their classes, such as traditions, jurisprudence, poetry, or Arabic philology, until the pupil is skilled in (the Qur'ân), or drops out before becoming skilled in it. In the latter case, it means, as a rule, that he will not learn anything. This is the method the urban population in the Maghrib and the native Berber Qur'ân teachers who follow their (urban compatriots), use in educating their children up to the age of manhood. III, *261*
They use it also with old people who study the Qur'ân after part of their life has passed. Consequently, (Maghribîs) know the orthography of the Qur'ân, and know it by heart, better than any other (Muslim group).

The Spanish method is instruction in reading and writing as such. That is what they pay attention to in the instruction (of children). However, since the Qur'ân is the basis and foundation of (all) that and the source of Islam and (all) the sciences, they make it the basis of instruction, but they do not restrict their instruction of children exclusively to (the Qur'ân). They also bring in (other subjects), mainly poetry and composition, and they give the children an expert knowledge of Arabic and teach them a good handwriting. They do not stress teaching of the Qur'ân more than the other subjects. In fact, they are more concerned with teaching handwriting than any other subject, until the child reaches manhood. He then has some experience and knowledge of the Arabic language and poetry. He has an excellent knowledge of handwriting, and he would have a thorough acquaintance with scholarship in general, if the tradition of scholarly instruction (still) existed in (Spain), but he does not, because the tradition no longer exists there.[1180] Thus, (present-day Spanish children) obtain no further (knowledge) than what their primary instruction provides. It is enough for those whom God guides. It prepares (them for further studies), in the event that a teacher (of them) can be found.

The people of Ifrîqiyah combine the instruction of children in the Qur'ân, usually, with the teaching of traditions. They also teach basic scientific norms and certain scientific problems. However, they stress giving their children a good knowledge of the Qur'ân and acquainting them with its
III, *262* various recensions and readings more than anything else. Next they stress handwriting. In general, their method of instruction in the Qur'ân is closer to the Spanish method (than to Maghribî or Eastern methods), because their (educational tradition) derives from the Spanish *shaykhs* who crossed over when the Christians conquered Spain, and asked for hospitality in Tunis.[1181] From that time on, they were the teachers of (Tunisian) children.

The people of the East, as far as we know, likewise have a mixed curriculum. I do not know what (subjects) they stress (primarily). We have been told that they are concerned with teaching the Qur'ân and the works and basic norms of (religious) scholarship once (the children) are grown up. They do not combine (instruction in the Qur'ân) with instruction in handwriting. They have (special) rule(s) for teaching it, and there are special teachers for it,[1182] just like any other craft which is taught (separately) and not included in the school curriculum for children. The children's slates (on which they practice) exhibit an inferior form of handwriting. Those who want to learn a (good) handwriting may do so later on (in their lives) from professional (calligraphers), to the extent of their interest in it and desire.

[1180] Cf. 2:430, above.
[1181] Cf. 1:xxxv f., above.
[1182] Cf. 2:378, above.

The fact that the people of Ifrîqiyah and the Maghrib restrict themselves to the Qur'ân makes them altogether incapable of mastering the linguistic habit. For as a rule, no (scholarly) habit can originate from the (study of the) Qur'ân, because no human being can produce anything like it. Thus, human beings are unable to employ or imitate its ways (*uslûb*), and they also can form no habit in any other respect. Consequently, a person who knows (the Qur'ân) does not acquire the habit of the Arabic language. It will be his lot to be awkward in expression and to have little fluency in speaking. This situation is not quite so pronounced among the people of Ifrîqiyah as among the Maghribîs, because, as we III, 263
have stated, the former combine instruction in the Qur'ân with instruction in the terminology of scientific norms. Thus, they get some practice and have some examples to imitate. However, their habit in this respect does not amount to a good style (eloquence), because their knowledge mostly consists of scholarly terminology which falls short of good style, as will be mentioned in the proper section.[1183]

As for the Spaniards, their varied curriculum with its great amount of instruction in poetry, composition, and Arabic philology gave them, from their early years on, a habit providing for a better acquaintance with the Arabic language. They were less proficient in all the other (religious) sciences, because they were little familiar with study of the Qur'ân and the traditions that are the basis and foundation of the (religious) sciences. Thus, they were people who knew how to write and who had a literary education that was either excellent or deficient, depending on the secondary education they received after their childhood education.

In his *Riḥlah*, Judge Abû Bakr b. al-'Arabî [1184] made a remarkable statement about instruction, which retains (the

[1183] Cf. pp. 394 f., below.

[1184] Cf. 1:446, and p. 285 (n. 1123), above. His views on education, from his *Marâqî az-zulfâ*, are quoted by I. Goldziher in his article, "Education," in Hastings' *Encyclopedia of Religion and Ethics*, V, 206a. Progressive views on education comparable to those quoted here, are found expressed in the early period of Muslim civilization in the *Nawâdir al-falâsifah* by the famous Ḥunayn b. Isḥâq, where he described what he considered to be the curriculum of Greek education.

best of) the old, and presents (some good) new features.[1185] He placed instruction in Arabic and poetry ahead of all the other sciences, as in the Spanish method, since, he said, "poetry is the archive of the Arabs.[1186] Poetry and Arabic philology should be taught first because of the (existing) corruption of the language.[1187] From there, the (student) should go on to arithmetic and study it assiduously, until he knows its basic norms. He should then go on to the study of the Qur'ân, because with his (previous) preparation, it will be easy for him." (Ibn al-'Arabî) continued: "How thoughtless are our compatriots in that they teach children the Qur'ân when they are first starting out. They read things they do not understand and work hard at something that is not as important for them as other matters." He concluded: "The student
III, 264 should study successively the principles of Islam, the principles of jurisprudence, disputation, and then the Prophetic traditions and the sciences connected with them." He also forbade teaching two disciplines at the same time, save to the student with a good mind and sufficient energy.[1188]

This is Judge Abû Bakr's advice. It is a good method indeed. However, accepted custom is not favorable to it, and custom has greater power over conditions (than anything else). Accepted custom gives preference to the teaching of the Qur'ân. The reason is the desire for the blessing and reward (in the other world resulting from knowledge of the Qur'ân) and a fear of the things that might affect children in "the folly of youth" [1189] and harm them and keep them from acquiring knowledge. They might miss the chance to learn the

[1185] Lit., "he repeated (old things) and brought forth new (original ideas)." Thus, one might translate: "which says everything." Cf. also R. Dozy, *Supplément aux dictionnaires arabes*, II, 186*a*.

[1186] Cf. 2:402, above, and pp. 341, 367, 374, and 410, below.

[1187] Cf. pp. 345 f., below, and elsewhere.

[1188] Cf. p. 294, above.

[1189] For this often-used phrase, cf., for instance, F. Rosenthal, *A History of Muslim Historiography*, p. 297. Cf. also the rather different application of the idea in the verse:

Only the folly of youth is life,
And when it is gone, the folly of wine.

Cf. at-Tawḥîdî, *al-Imtâ' wa-l-mu'ânasah* (Cairo, 1939–44), II, 180.

Qur'ân. As long as they remain at home, they are amenable to authority. When they have grown up and shaken off the yoke of authority, the tempests of young manhood often cast them upon the shores of wrongdoing. Therefore, while the children are still at home and under the yoke of authority, one seizes the opportunity to teach them the Qur'ân, so that they will not remain without knowledge of it. If one could be certain that a child would continue to study and accept instruction (when he has grown up), the method mentioned by the Judge would be the most suitable one ever devised in East or West.

"God decides, and no one can change His decision." [1190]

[39] *Severity to students does them harm.*

This comes about as follows. Severe punishment in the course of instruction does harm to the student, especially to little children, because it belongs among (the things that make for a) bad habit. Students,[1191] slaves, and servants who are brought up with injustice and (tyrannical) force are overcome by it. It makes them feel oppressed and causes them to III, 265
lose their energy. It makes them lazy and induces them to lie and be insincere. That is, their outward behavior differs from what they are thinking, because they are afraid that they will have to suffer tyrannical treatment (if they tell the truth). Thus, they are taught deceit and trickery. This becomes their custom and character. They lose the quality that goes with social and political organization and makes people human, namely, (the desire to) protect and defend themselves and their homes, and they become dependent on others.[1192] Indeed, their souls become too indolent to (attempt to) acquire the virtues and good character qualities. Thus, they fall short of their potentialities and do not reach the limit of their humanity. As a result, they revert to the stage of "the lowest of the low." [1193]

[1190] Qur'ân 13.41 (41).
[1191] Cf. Issawi, p. 161.
[1192] Cf., for instance, 1:257, above.
[1193] Cf. Qur'ân 95.5 (5).

That [1194] is what happened to every nation that fell under the yoke of tyranny and learned through it the meaning of injustice. One may check this by (observing) any person who is not in control of his own affairs and has no authority on his side to guarantee his (safety). One will thus be able to infer (from the observable facts) that things are (as I have stated). One may look at the Jews and the bad character they have acquired,[1195] such that they are described in every region and period as having the quality of *khurj*,[1196] which, according to well-known technical terminology, means "insincerity and trickery." The reason is what we have (just) said.

Thus, a teacher must not be too severe toward his pupil, nor a father toward his son, in educating them. In the book that Abû Muḥammad b. Abî Zayd wrote on the laws governing teachers and pupils, he said: "If children must be
III, 266 beaten, their educator must not strike them more than three times." [1197] 'Umar said: "Those who are not educated (disciplined) by the religious law are not educated (disciplined) by God." [1198] He spoke out of a desire to preserve the souls from the humiliation of disciplinary punishment and in the knowledge that the amount (of disciplinary punishment) that the religious law has stipulated is fully adequate to keep (a person) under control, because the (religious law) knows best what is good for him.

One of the best methods of education was suggested by ar-Rashîd to Khalaf b. Aḥmar, the teacher of his son Muḥam-

[1194] Cf. Issawi, p. 61.

[1195] Cf. 1:275 and 288, above.

[1196] This vocalization is indicated in B, C, and D. However, no such word in the meaning required seems to exist in Arabic dictionaries. Is it, perhaps, a dialectical variant of Arabic *khurq* "charlatanry, foolishness," or a Spanish or Northwest African dialectical expression?

[1197] Cf. 1:261, above.

[1198] Apparently, Ibn Khaldûn interprets this statement to demand that "discipline" (which may mean "education" or "corporal punishment") should be applied only where it is stipulated by the religious law, and not freely meted out by teachers. Actually, it seems to mean that where the religious law prescribes no punishment, none will result in the other world for the individual involved.

Cf. 1:260, above.

mad al-Amîn. Khalaf b. Aḥmar [1199] said: "Ar-Rashîd told me to come and educate his son Muḥammad al-Amîn, and he said to me: 'O Aḥmar, the Commander of the Faithful is entrusting (his son) to you, the life of his soul and the fruit of his heart. Take firm hold of him and make him obey you. Occupy in relation to him the place that the Commander of the Faithful has given you. Teach him to read the Qur'ân. Instruct him in history. Let him transmit poems and teach him the Sunnah of the Prophet. Give him insight into the proper occasions for speech and how to begin a (speech). Forbid him to laugh, save at times when it is proper. Accustom him to honor the Hâshimite dignitaries [1200] when they come to him, and to give the military leaders places of honor when they come to his salon. Let no hour pass in which you do not seize the opportunity to teach him something useful. But do so without vexing him, which would kill his mind. Do not always be too lenient with him, or he will get to like leisure and become used to it. As much as possible, correct him kindly and gently. If he does not want it that way, you must then use severity and harshness.' "

[40] *A scholar's education is greatly improved by traveling in quest of knowledge and meeting the authoritative teachers (of his time).*

The [1201] reason for this is that human beings obtain their knowledge and character qualities and all their opinions and III, 267
virtues either through study, instruction, and lectures, or through imitation of a teacher and personal contact with him. The only difference here is that habits acquired through personal contact with a teacher are more strongly and firmly rooted. Thus, the greater the number of authoritative teach-

[1199] Khalaf died between 796 and 805; cf. *GAL, Suppl.*, I, 111. Ibn Khaldûn's quotation is derived from al-Mas'ûdî, *Murûj adh-dhahab* (Paris, 1861–77), VI, 321 f. Cf. also al-Bayhaqî, *al-Maḥâsin wa-l-masâwî*, ed. Schwally (Giessen, 1902), p. 617, and ash-Sharîshî, *Sharḥ al-Maqâmât* (Cairo, 1306/1889), II, 300.

[1200] That is, his 'Abbâsid relatives.

[1201] Cf. Issawi, p. 162.

ers (*shaykhs*), the more deeply rooted is the habit one acquires.

Furthermore, the technical terminologies used in scientific instruction are confusing to the student. Many students even suppose them to be part of a given science. The only way to deliver them from that (wrong notion) is by personal contact with teachers, for different teachers employ different terminologies. Thus, meeting scholars and having many authoritative teachers (*shaykhs*) enables the student to notice the difference in the terminologies used by different teachers and to distinguish among them. He will thus be able to recognize the science itself behind the (technical terminology it uses). He will realize that (terminologies) are (merely) means and methods for imparting (knowledge). His powers will work toward acquiring strongly and firmly rooted habits. He will improve the knowledge he has and be able to distinguish it from other (knowledge). In addition, his habits will be strengthened through his intensive personal contact with teachers, when they are many and of various types. This is for those for whom God facilitated the ways of scholarship and right guidance. Thus, traveling in quest of knowledge is absolutely necessary for the acquisition of useful knowledge and perfection through meeting authoritative teachers (*shaykhs*) and having contact with (scholarly) personalities.

God "guides whomever He wants to guide to a straight path."[1202]

III, 268

[41] *Scholars are, of all people, those least familiar with the ways of politics.*

The[1203] reason for this is that (scholars) are used to mental speculation and to a searching study of ideas which they abstract from the *sensibilia* and conceive in their minds as general universals, so that they may be applicable to some matter in general but not to any particular matter, individual,

[1202] Qur'ân 2.142 (136), etc.
[1203] Cf. Issawi, pp. 64–66.

race, nation, or group of people. (Scholars,) then, make such universal ideas conform (in their minds) to facts of the outside world. They also compare things with others that are similar to or like them, with the help of analogical reasoning as used in jurisprudence, which is something familiar to them. All their conclusions and views continue to be something in the mind. They come to conform (to the facts of the outside world) only after research and speculation has come to an end, or they may never come to conform (to them). The facts of the outside world are merely special cases of the (ideas) that are in the mind. For instance, the religious laws are special cases derived from the well-known (texts) of the Qur'ân and the Sunnah. In their case, one expects the facts of the outside world to conform to them, in contrast with the intellectual sciences, where, in order to (prove) the soundness of views, one expects those views to conform to the facts of the outside world.

Thus, in all their intellectual activity, scholars are accustomed to dealing with matters of the mind and with thoughts. They do not know anything else. Politicians, on the other hand, must pay attention to the facts of the outside world and the conditions attaching to and depending on (politics). (These facts and conditions) are obscure. They may contain some (element) making it impossible to refer them to some- III, 269
thing like and similar, or contradicting the universal (idea) to which one would like them to conform. The conditions existing in civilization cannot (always) be compared with each other. They may be alike in one respect, but they may differ in other respects.

(Now,) scholars are accustomed to generalizations and analogical conclusions. When they look at politics, they press (their observations) into the mold of their views and their way of making deductions. Thus, they commit many errors, or (at least) they cannot be trusted (not to commit errors). The intelligent and alert (segment) of civilized people falls into the same category as (scholars). Their penetrating minds drive them toward a searching occupation with ideas, analogy, and comparison, as is the case with jurists. Thus, they (too) commit errors.

The average person of a healthy disposition and a mediocre intelligence has not got the mind for (such speculation) and does not think of it. Therefore, he restricts himself to considering every matter as it is, and to judging every kind of situation and every type of individual by its particular (circumstances). His judgment is not infected with analogy and generalization. Most of his speculation stops at matters perceivable by the senses, and he does not go beyond them in his mind, like a swimmer who stays in the water near the shore, as the poet says:

> Do not go out too deep when swimming.
> Safety lies near the shore.

Such a man, therefore, can be trusted when he reflects
III, 270 upon his political activities. He has the right outlook in dealing with his fellow men. Thus, he makes a good living and suffers no damage or harm in the (process of making a living), because he has the right outlook.

"And He knows more than any scholar." [1204]

This (situation) makes one realize that logic cannot be trusted to prevent the commission of errors, because it is too abstract and remote from the *sensibilia*. (Logic) considers the secondary *intelligibilia*. It is possible that material things contain something that does not admit of (logical) conclusions and contradicts them, when one looks for unequivocal conformity (between them and the facts of the outside world). It is different with speculation about the primary *intelligibilia*, which are less abstract. They are matters of the imagination and pictures of the *sensibilia*. They retain (certain features of the *sensibilia*) and permit verification of the conformity of (the *sensibilia* to the primary *intelligibilia*).[1205]

[1204] Qur'ân 12.76 (76).
[1205] Cf. p. 251, above.

[42] *Most of the scholars in Islam have been non-Arabs (Persians).*[1206]

It[1207] is a remarkable fact that, with few exceptions, most Muslim scholars both in the religious and in the intellectual sciences have been non-Arabs. When a scholar is of Arab origin, he is non-Arab in language and upbringing and has non-Arab teachers. This is so in spite of the fact that Islam is an Arabic religion, and its founder was an Arab.

The reason for it is that at the beginning Islam had no sciences or crafts. That was due to the simple conditions (that prevailed) and the desert attitude. The religious laws, which are the commands and prohibitions of God, were in the breasts of the authorities. They knew their sources, the Qur'ân and the Sunnah, from information they had received directly from the Lawgiver (Muḥammad) himself and from the men around him. The people at that time were Arabs. They did not know anything about scientific instruction or the writing of books and systematic works. There was no III, *271*
incentive or need for that. This was the situation during the time of the men around Muḥammad and the men of the second generation. The persons who were concerned with knowing and transmitting the (religious laws) were called "Qur'ân readers," that is, people who were able to read the Qur'ân and were not illiterate. Illiteracy was general at that time among the men around Muḥammad, since they were (Arab) Bedouins.[1208] People who knew the Qur'ân were at that time called "Qur'ân readers" with reference to the fact (that they were literate). They read the Qur'ân and the Sunnah, which were transmitted from God, (in order to know the religious

[1206] In Arabic linguistic usage, the non-Arabs designated by the term *'ajam* are primarily Persians. From the title of Ibn Khaldûn's *History* (see 1:13, above), one may perhaps conclude that in his mind *'Ajam* were mainly eastern non-Arabs, whereas the word Berber, as the most prominent group of western non-Arabs, stands for the latter. But cf. also 1:57, above.

[1207] Cf. Issawi, pp. 61–64.

[1208] Cf. 2:378 and 382 f., above.

laws,) because the religious laws were known only from the (Qur'ân) and from the traditions which are mostly explanations of and commentaries upon, the (Qur'ân). Muḥammad said: "I left among you two things. You will not go astray as long as you hold on to them: the Qur'ân and my Sunnah." [1209]

By the time of the reign of ar-Rashîd, (oral) tradition had become far removed (from its starting point). It was thus necessary to write commentaries on the Qur'ân and to fix the traditions in writing, because it was feared that they might be lost.[1210] It was also necessary to know the chains of transmitters and to assess their reliability, in order to be able to distinguish sound chains of transmitters from inferior ones.[1211] Then, more and more laws concerning actual cases were derived from the Qur'ân and the Sunnah. Moreover, the (Arabic) language became corrupt,[1212] and it was necessary to lay down grammatical rules.

All the religious sciences had (thus) become habits connected with producing and deriving (laws and norms) and with comparison and analogical reasoning. Other, auxiliary sciences became necessary, such as knowledge of the rules of the Arabic language, (knowledge of) the rules that govern the derivation (of laws) and analogical reasoning, and defense of the articles of faith by means of arguments, because a great number of innovations and heresies (had come into existence). All these things developed into sciences with their own
III, 272 habits, requiring instruction (for their acquisition). Thus, they came to fall under the category of crafts.

We have mentioned before that the crafts are cultivated by sedentary people and that of all peoples the Arab (Bed-

[1209] The references given in *Concordance*, I, 270*a*, l. 24, refer to different elaborations of the same theme.

[1210] The expression of this fear is ascribed to as early a figure as the caliph 'Umar b. 'Abd-al-'Azîz. Cf. F. Rosenthal, *A History of Muslim Historiography*, p. 226. Ibn Khaldûn may have in mind the story about Mâlik and al-Manṣûr. Cf. 1:34, above; also p. 325, below.

[1211] Cf. 2:448 f., above.

[1212] Cf. pp. 345 f., below.

ouins) are least familiar with the crafts.[1213] Thus, the sciences came to belong to sedentary culture, and the Arabs were not familiar with them or with their cultivation. Now, the (only) sedentary people at that time were non-Arabs and, what amounts to the same thing, the clients and sedentary people who followed the non-Arabs at that time in all matters of sedentary culture, including the crafts and professions. They were most versed in those things, because sedentary culture had been firmly rooted among them from the time of the Persian Empire.

Thus, the founders of grammar were Sîbawayh and, after him, al-Fârisî and az-Zajjâj.[1214] All of them were of non-Arab (Persian) descent. They were brought up in the Arabic language and acquired the knowledge of it through their upbringing and through contact with Arabs. They invented the rules of (grammar) and made (grammar) into a discipline (in its own right) for later (generations to use).

Most of the *ḥadîth* scholars who preserved traditions for the Muslims also were non-Arabs (Persians), or Persian in language and upbringing, because[1215] the discipline was widely cultivated in the 'Irâq and the regions beyond. (Furthermore,) all the scholars who worked in the science of the principles of jurisprudence were non-Arabs (Persians), as is well known. The same applies to speculative theologians and to most Qur'ân commentators. Only the non-Arabs (Persians) engaged in the task of preserving knowledge and writing systematic scholarly works. Thus, the truth of the following statement by the Prophet becomes apparent: "If scholarship hung suspended at the highest parts of heaven, the Persians[1216] would (reach it and) take it."

The Arabs who came into contact with that flourishing sedentary culture and exchanged their Bedouin attitude for

[1213] Cf. 2:353 f., above.

[1214] Abû Isḥâq Ibrâhîm b. as-Sarî, who died *ca.* 311 [923]. Cf. *GAL,* I, 110; *Suppl.*, I, 170. For the other two scholars, cf. pp. 323 and 361, below.

[1215] The remainder of the sentence appears only in C and D. D omits: "and the regions beyond."

[1216] Lit., "people of Fârs." * Cf. Ibn Ḥanbal, *Musnad,* II, 297, 420, 422, 469.

it, were diverted from occupying themselves with scholarship and study by their leading position in the ʿAbbâsid dynasty and the tasks that confronted them in government.
III, *273* They were the men of the dynasty, at once its protectors and the executors of its policy. In addition, at that time, they considered it a contemptible thing to be a scholar, because scholarship is a craft, and political leaders are always contemptuous of the crafts and professions and everything that leads to them.[1217] Thus, they left such things to non-Arabs and persons of mixed Arab and non-Arab parentage (*muwallad*). The latter cultivated them, and (the Arabs) always considered it their right to cultivate them, as they were their custom (*dîn*) and their sciences, and never felt complete contempt for the men learned in them. The final result, (however,) was that when the Arabs lost power and the non-Arabs took over, the religious sciences had no place with the men in power, because the latter had no relations with (scholarship). Scholars were viewed with contempt,[1218] because the (men in power) saw that (scholars) had no contact with them and were occupying themselves with things that were of no interest to the (men in power) in governmental and political matters, as we mentioned in connection with the religious ranks.[1219] The fact established here is the reason why (all) scholars in the religious sciences, or most of them, are non-Arabs.

The intellectual sciences, as well, made their appearance in Islam only after scholars and authors had become a distinct group of people and all scholarship had become a craft. (The intellectual sciences) were then the special preserve of non-Arabs, left alone by the Arabs, who did not cultivate them. They were cultivated only by Arabicized non-Arabs (Persians) [1220] as was the case with all the crafts, as we stated at the beginning.

[1217] The reference may be to 1:60, above. Cf. also pp. 410 f., below.
[1218] Cf. R. Dozy in *Journal asiatique*, XIV 6 (1869), 170 f.
[1219] Cf. 1:459 f., above.
[1220] Cf. R. Dozy, *loc. cit.*

This situation continued in the cities as long as the Persians and the Persian countries, the ʿIrâq, Khurâsân, and Transoxania, retained their sedentary culture. But when those cities fell into ruins, sedentary culture, which God has devised for the attainment of sciences and crafts, disappeared from them. Along with it, scholarship altogether disappeared from among the non-Arabs (Persians), who were III, 274
(now) engulfed by the desert attitude. Scholarship was restricted to cities with an abundant sedentary culture. Today, no (city) has a more abundant sedentary culture than Cairo (Egypt). It is the mother of the world, the great center (*îwân*) of Islam, and the mainspring of the sciences and the crafts.[1221]

Some sedentary culture has also survived in Transoxania, because the dynasty there provides some sedentary culture. Therefore, they have there a certain number of the sciences and the crafts, which cannot be denied. Our attention was called to this fact by the contents of the writings of a (Transoxanian) scholar, which have reached us in this country. He is Saʿd-ad-dîn at-Taftazânî.[1222] As far as the other non-Arabs (Persians) are concerned, we have not seen, since [1223] the imam Ibn al-Khaṭîb and Naṣîr-ad-dîn aṭ-Ṭûsî, any discussions that could be referred to as indicating their ultimate excellence.

When one considers and ponders this fact, one will observe (in it) one of the wondrous circumstances of this world. "God creates whatever He wishes." "There is no God but Him." [1224]

[43] *A person whose first language was not Arabic finds it harder than the (native) speaker of Arabic to acquire the sciences.*[1225]

This is explained by the fact that all scientific research deals with ideas of the mind and the imagination. This applies

1221 Cf. *Autobiography*, p. 246; above, 1:lviii.
1222 Cf. p. 117, above.
1223 Cf. Bombaci, p. 467, and above, p. 148.
1224 Qur'ân 3.47 (42), etc., and Qur'ân 2.163 (158), etc.
1225 This section is not found in Bulaq.

to the religious sciences in which research is mostly concerned with words and the substance of which is the laws derived from the Qur'ân, the Sunnah, and the language used in (both the Qur'ân and the Sunnah) that leads to (the formulation of) these (laws). These are all matters of the imagination. The same fact also applies to the intellectual sciences, which are matters of the mind.

Linguistic expression is merely the interpreter of ideas
III, *275* that are in the mind. One (person) conveys them to another in oral discussion, instruction, and constant scientific research. His purpose is to obtain the (various) habits of (all these things [1225a]) through constant application. Words and expressions are media and veils between the ideas. They constitute the bonds between them and give them their final imprint. The student of ideas must extract them from the words that express them. For this he needs a knowledge of their linguistic meaning and a good (linguistic) habit. Otherwise, it is difficult for him to get (the ideas), apart from the (usual) difficulties inherent in mental investigation of them. When he has a firmly rooted habit as far as semantics is concerned, so that the (correct) ideas present themselves to his mind when he (hears) certain words used, spontaneously and naturally, the veil between the ideas and the understanding is either totally removed, or becomes less heavy, and the only task that remains is to investigate the problems inherent in the ideas.

All this applies to instruction by personal contact in the form of oral address and explanation. But when the student has to rely upon the study of books and written material and must understand scientific problems from the forms of written letters in books,[1226] he is confronted with another veil, (namely, the veil) that separates handwriting and the form of letters (found) in writing from the spoken words (found) in

[1225a] The reference is to discussion, instruction, and the sciences, not merely to the sciences alone. "Linguistic expression" can hardly be meant, and the use of the plural "habits" would not go well with it.

[1226] Cf. p. 296, above.

the imagination. The written letters have their own way of indicating the spoken words. As long as that way is not known, it is impossible to know what they express. If it is known imperfectly, (the meaning) expressed (by the letters) is known imperfectly. Thus, the student is confronted with another veil standing between him and his objective of at- III, *276*
taining scientific habits, one that is more difficult to cope with than the first one. (Now,) if his habit, as far as the meaning of words and writing goes, is firmly established, the veils between him and the ideas are lifted. He has merely to occupy himself with understanding the problems inherent in the (ideas). The same relationship of ideas with words and writing exists in every language. The habits of students who learn these things while they are young, are more firmly established (than those of other people).

Furthermore, the Muslim realm was far-flung and included many nations. The sciences of the ancients were wiped out through the prophecy of (Islam) and its (holy) book. Illiteracy was the proper thing and symbol (of Islam). Islam then gained royal authority and power. (Foreign) nations served the (Muslims) with their sedentary culture and refinement. The religious sciences, which had been traditional, were turned by the (Muslims) into crafts. Thus, (scholarly) habits originated among them. Many systematic works and books were written. (The Muslims) desired to learn the sciences of the (foreign) nations. They made them their own through translations. They pressed them into the mold of their own views. They took them over into their own language from the non-Arab languages and surpassed the achievements of (the non-Arabs) in them. The manuscripts in the non-Arabic language were forgotten, abandoned, and scattered.[1227] All the sciences came to exist in Arabic. The systematic works on them were written in (Arabic) writing. Thus, students of the sciences needed a knowledge of the meaning of (Arabic) words and (Arabic) writing. They could

[1227] Lit., "a forgotten object, a deserted ruin, and a scattered particle of dust." Cf. Qur'ân 25.23 (25).

dispense with all other languages, because they had been wiped out and there was no longer any interest in them.

We have mentioned before that language is a habit of the tongue.[1228] Likewise, handwriting is a craft, the habit of which is located in the hand.[1229] The tongue which had at first the
III, 277 habit of speaking another language than Arabic, becomes deficient in (its mastery of) Arabic, because, as we have mentioned before,[1230] the person whose habit has advanced to a certain point in a particular craft is rarely able to master another one. This is obvious. (Now,) if (a person) is deficient in (his mastery of) Arabic, in (his knowledge of) the meaning of its words and its writing, it is difficult for him to derive the ideas from (Arabic words and Arabic writing), as has been mentioned before. Only if the early habit of speaking a non-Arab language is not yet firmly established in a person when he makes the transition from it to Arabic, as is the case with small non-Arab children who grow up with Arabs before their (habit) of speaking a non-Arab language is firmly established, only then does the Arabic language come to be like a first (native) language, and his ability to derive the ideas from (the words of) the Arabic language is not deficient.[1231] The same applies to persons who learned non-Arabic writing before Arabic writing.

This is why we find that most non-Arab scholars in their research and classes do not copy comments (directly) from books but read them aloud. In this way they are less disturbed by the veils (between words and ideas), so that they can get more easily at the ideas. When a person possesses the perfect habit as far as verbal and written expression is concerned, he does not have to (read aloud). For him, it has become like a firmly ingrained natural disposition to derive an understanding of words from writing and of ideas from words. The veils between him and the ideas are lifted.

[1228] Cf. pp. 282 f., above (?), and pp. 321, 342, and 371, below.
[1229] Cf. p. 378, above.
[1230] Cf. 2:354 f., above.
[1231] Cf. pp. 342 f., 353, 358, 360 ff., and 391, below.

Intensive study and constant practice of the language and of writing may lead a person to a firmly rooted habit, as we find in most non-Arab scholars. However, this occurs rarely. When one compares such a person with an Arabic III, 278 scholar of equal merit, the latter is the more efficient, and his habit the stronger. The non-Arab has trouble because his early use of a non-Arab language necessarily makes him inferior.

This is not in contradiction with the afore-mentioned fact [1232] that most Muslim scholars are non-Arabs. In that connection, "non-Arab" meant non-Arab by descent. Such non-Arabs had a long (history of) sedentary culture which, as we have established, causes cultivation of the crafts and habits, including the sciences. Being non-Arab in language is something quite different, and this is what is meant here.

It is also not in contradiction with the fact that the Greeks were highly accomplished scholars. They learned their sciences in their own first (native) language and in their own writing, such as was customarily used among them. The non-Arab Muslim who studies to become a scholar learns his subject in a language other than his first (native) one and from a writing other than the one whose habit he has mastered. This, then, becomes a veil for him, as we have stated.

This applies quite generally to all kinds of speakers of non-Arab languages, such as the Persians, the Turks, the Berbers, the European Christians, and all others whose language is not Arabic.[1233]

"Here are signs for people who understand signs." [1234]

[44] *The sciences concerned with the Arabic language.*

The pillars of the Arabic language are four: lexicography, grammar, syntax and style (*bayân*), and literature. Knowledge of them all is necessary for religious scholars, since the III, 279 source of all religious laws is the Qur'ân and the Sunnah,

[1232] Cf. the preceding section.
[1233] Cf. also p. 372, below.
[1234] Qur'ân 15.75 (75).

which are in Arabic. Their transmitters, the men around Muḥammad and the men of the second generation, were Arabs. Their difficulties are to be explained from the language they used. Thus, those who want to be religious scholars must know the sciences connected with the Arabic language.

These sciences differ in emphasis (as to their importance) according to the different degrees (of usefulness) they possess for conveying the intended meaning of speech, as will become clear when they are discussed one by one. The conclusion will be that the first and most important of them is grammar, since it gives a clear indication of the basic principles (used in expressing) the various intended meanings. Thus, one can distinguish between subject and object, as well as between the subject of a nominal sentence and its predicate. Without grammar, one would not know on what to base giving information (about anything).

Lexicography would deserve to be first, were not most of its data constant (and restricted) to their (conventional) meanings, incapable of changing, in contrast to the case endings (in grammar) which indicate dependence, the (person or thing) that is dependent, and the (person or thing) on which (something else) depends.[1235] They always change completely and leave no trace. Thus, grammar is more important than lexicography, since ignorance of (grammar) is very harmful to mutual understanding. This is not the case with lexicography.

And God knows better.

Grammar

It should be known that language, as the term is customarily used, is the expression by a speaker of his intention. Such expression is an act of the tongue which originates in an intention to convey the meaning of speech.[1236] Therefore,

[1235] Cf. p. 332, below.

[1236] The relative clause appears in C in the margin and is incorporated in the text of D.

(language) must become an established habit (located) in the part of the body that produces it, namely, the tongue.[1237]

In every nation, the (formation of language takes place) according to their own terminology. The linguistic habit that the Arabs obtained in that way is the best there is. It is the III, 280
one most clearly expressing the intended meaning, since many ideas are indicated in it by something else than words. There are, for instance, vowels to distinguish the subject from object and *i*-case—that is, the genitive—and (there are) letters to transform actions (verbs)—that is, motions—into essences,[1238] without need of other words. These (features) are found in no other language but Arabic. All other languages need special words to indicate a particular idea or situation. Therefore, we find non-Arabs lengthier in their speech than we would consider necessary in Arabic. This is what was meant in the following remark by Muḥammad: "I was given the most comprehensive words, and speech was made short for me."[1239]

The consonants, vowels, and positions (of letters [sounds]), that is, the forms of the Arabic language, came to indicate the intended meaning in a definite manner. The (Arabs) did not need a craft to teach them their meaning. It was a habit in their tongues that one generation learned from the other, as our children nowadays learn our languages.

Then Islam came. The Arabs left the Ḥijâz to seek the royal authority that was in the hands of (foreign) nations and dynasties. They came into contact with non-Arabs. As a result, their linguistic habit changed under the influence of

1237 Cf. p. 318 (n. 1228), above.

1238 It seems that *af'âl* "actions, verbs," is used here to indicate the fluid, "movable" roots, while *dhawât* "essences," refers to the static, definite categories of nouns, adjectives, and verbal forms that are meaningful by themselves and produced by prefixes, infixes, and suffixes. The statement does not refer merely to the transformation of verbs by means of prefixes, infixes, and suffixes, into particular verbal forms.

1239 For the first half of the tradition, cf. the references in *Concordance*, I, 365*a*. Cf. also Ibn Rashîq, *'Umdah* (Cairo, 1353/1934), I, 224, and al-Mas'ûdî, *Murûj adh-dhahab*, IV, 165. Cf. also below, pp. 345 and 415.

the solecisms they heard non-Arab speakers of Arabic make, and it is hearing that begets the linguistic habit. Thus, the (Arab linguistic habit began to) incline toward adopting forms of speech at variance with it, because (the Arabs) became used to hearing them spoken, and (their linguistic habit) became corrupted.[1240]

III, *281* Cultured people feared that the (Arab linguistic) habit would become entirely corrupted and that, if the (process of corruption) went on for a long time, the Qur'ân and the traditions would no longer be understood. Therefore, they derived certain norms for the (Arab linguistic) habit from their way of speaking. (These norms are) of general applicability, like universals and basic principles. They checked all the other parts of speech with them and combined like with like. (Among such norms,) for instance, are these:

The agent has the *u*-ending.

The object has the *a*-ending.

The subject of a nominal sentence has the *u*-ending.

Then, they considered (the fact) that the meaning changes with the change of vowel (endings). For this (phenomenon), they used the technical term of *i'râb*. For the thing that necessitates the change (in meaning), they used the technical term "agent," (*'âmil*), and so on. All these things came to be technical terms peculiar to the (grammarians) who set them down in writing and made a particular [1241] craft of them. The technical term they used for that (craft) is "grammar" (*naḥw*).

The first to write on (grammar) was Abû l-Aswad ad-Du'alî, of the Banû Kinânah.[1242] It is said that he did so upon the advice of 'Alî, who noticed that the (linguistic) habit was changing. Therefore he advised (ad-Du'alî) to protect it, and

[1240] Cf. p. 346, below.

[1241] An additional "of their own," which appears in the earlier texts, is omitted in C and D.

[1242] The legend that makes 'Alî the driving force behind the creation of Arabic grammar is often mentioned but is, of course, unhistorical, as is the role of ad-Du'alî. Cf. *GAL*, I, 42 and 96; *Suppl.*, I, 72 and 155; Ibn an-Nadîm, *Fihrist*, pp. 40 f. (ed. Flügel); pp. 59 ff. (Cairo, 1348/1929-30). Cf. also F. Rosenthal, *A History of Muslim Historiography*, p. 262.

(ad-Du'alî) anxiously went about the task of fixing it accurately by means of comprehensive, inductively evolved rules.

Later on, scholars wrote books on (grammar). Eventually, in the time of al-Khalîl b. Aḥmad al-Farâhîdî,[1243] in the days of ar-Rashîd, people were more in need of (grammatical rules than ever before), because the (linguistic) habit was disappearing from among the Arabs. (Al-Khalîl) improved the craft (of grammar) and perfected its various chapters. Sîbawayh [1244] learned (grammar) from him. He perfected its details and increased the number of proofs and examples used in connection with it. He wrote on it his famous *Book* which became the model for everything subsequently written on (grammar).[1245] Short books for students were later written III, 282
by Abû 'Alî al-Fârisî [1246] and Abû l-Qâsim az-Zajjâjî.[1247] In them, they followed the model of (Sîbawayh's) *Book*.

Then, there was much grammatical discussion. Divergent opinions originated among the grammarians of al-Kûfah and al-Baṣrah, the two old cities of the Arabs. They used an increasing number of proofs and arguments. The methods of (grammatical) instruction also became different. There was much difference of opinion with regard to vowel endings in many verses of the Qur'ân, since the grammarians held different opinions as to the basic rules of (grammar). This became a lengthy subject for students (to study). Then recent scholars came, with their method of being brief. They cut short a good deal of the long discussion, though they included everything that had been transmitted. That, for instance, was what Ibn Mâlik [1248] did in the *Kitâb at-Tashîl*, and

[1243] He lived through most of the eighth century. Cf. *GAL*, I, 100; *Suppl.*, I, 159 f. Cf. pp. 325 ff., below.

[1244] Sîbawayh died *ca.* 800. Cf. *GAL*, I, 100 ff.; *Suppl.*, I, 160.

[1245] Cf. also p. 356, below.

[1246] Al-Ḥasan b. Aḥmad (Muḥammad), 288–377 [901–987]. Cf. *GAL*, I, 113 f.; *Suppl.*, I, 175 f. Cf. p. 313, above.

[1247] 'Abd-ar-Raḥmân b. Isḥâq, who died *ca.* 337 [949]. Cf. *GAL*, I, 110; *Suppl.*, I, 170 f.

[1248] Muḥammad b. 'Abdallâh, d. 672 [1274]. Cf. *GAL*, I, 298 ff.; *Suppl.*, I, 521 ff.

others. Or, they restricted themselves to elementary rules for (beginning) students. That, for instance, was what az-Zamakhsharî did in the *Mufaṣṣal* and Ibn al-Ḥâjib in the *Muqaddimah.*[1249] They also frequently versified the subject. That was done, for instance, by Ibn Mâlik in two *rajaz* poems, the large and the small one, and by Ibn Mu'ṭî [1250] in a *rajaz* poem of a thousand verses (*alfîyah*).

In general, the works on this subject are innumerable and cannot all be known, and the methods of (grammatical) instruction are varied. The method of the ancients is different from that of recent (grammarians). The methods of the Kûfians, the Baṣrians, the Baghdâdîs, and the Spaniards also, are all different.

Grammar has come to the point of being allowed to disappear, along with the decrease in the other sciences and crafts which we have noted and which is the result of a decrease in civilization. At the present time, there has reached us in the Maghrib a systematic work (*dîwân*) from Egypt attributed to
III, 283 the Egyptian scholar, Jamâl-ad-dîn b. Hishâm.[1251] He treats in it all the rules governing vowel endings, both in general and in detail. He discusses the letters (sounds) and the individual words and sentences. He omits the repetitions found in most chapters of grammar. He called his work *al-Mughnî fî l-i'râb.*[1252] He indicates all the fine points of the vowel endings in the Qur'ân and sets them down accurately in chapters and sections and according to basic norms all of which are very orderly. We have found in (the work) much information attesting to (the author's) great ability and abundant knowl-

[1249] Cf. 2:446, and p. 18, above.

[1250] Yaḥyâ b. 'Abd-al-Mu'ṭî az-Zawâwî, d. 628 [1231]. Cf. *GAL*, I, 302 f.; *Suppl.*, I, 530 f. His *Durrah al-alfîyah* was the model of Ibn Mâlik's famous *Alfîyah*. Cf. *GAL, Suppl.*, I, 522.

[1251] 'Abdallâh b. Yûsuf, 708–761 [1309–1360]. Cf. *GAL*, II, 23 ff.; *Suppl.*, II, 16 ff. Ibn Khaldûn mentioned this passage concerning Ibn Hishâm to Ibn Ḥajar, *ad-Durar al-kâminah*, II, 309. Cf. p. 289, above.

[1252] The full title of the work, of which there exist many editions, is *Mughnî al-labîb 'an kutub al-a'ârîb*. There is no need to assume, with de Slane, that Ibn Khaldûn here combined the titles of two works by Ibn Hishâm, the *Mughnî* and the *I'râb* (*'an qawâ'id al-i'râb*).

edge of grammar. In a way, his approach follows the method of the Mosul grammarians who followed in the footsteps of Ibn Jinnî and adopted his technical terminology for (grammatical) instruction. In this way, he has produced a remarkable work that shows his powerful (linguistic) habit and his acquaintance with the subject.

God "gives in addition to the creatures whatever He wishes to give to them." [1253]

The science of lexicography

This science is concerned with explaining the (conventional) meanings of the (words of the) language. This comes about as follows. The habit of the Arabic language, as far as the vowels called *i'râb* by the grammarians are concerned, became corrupted.[1254] Rules for protecting the (vowel endings) were developed, as we have stated. However, the (process of) corruption continued on account of the close contact (of the Muslims) with non-Arabs. Eventually, it affected the (conventional) meanings of words. Many Arabic words were no (longer) used in their proper meaning. This was the result of indulgence shown to the incorrect language used by non-Arab speakers of Arabic in their terminologies, in contradiction to the pure Arabic language. It was, therefore, necessary to protect the (conventional) meanings of the (words of the) language with the help of writing and systematic works, because it was to be feared that (otherwise) they might be wiped out and that ignorance of the Qur'ân and the III, 284
traditions would result.[1255]

Many leading philologists set out eagerly on this task and dictated systematic works on the subject. The champion in this respect was al-Khalîl b. Aḥmad al-Farâhîdî.[1256] He wrote

[1253] Qur'ân 35.1 (1).

[1254] Cf. p. 346, below.

[1255] Cf. p. 312, above.

[1256] Cf. p. 323, above. For him and the other lexicographers mentioned in this chapter, cf. also J. Kraemer, "Studien zur altarabischen Lexikographie," *Oriens*, VI (1953), 201–38.

the *Kitâb al-ʿAyn* on lexicography. In it, he dealt with all (possible) combinations of the letters of the alphabet, that is, with words of two, three, four, and five consonants. (Five-consonant words) are the longest letter combinations found in Arabic.

It was possible for al-Khalîl to calculate arithmetically the total number of such combinations. This goes as follows. The total number of two-consonant words is the sum of the arithmetical progression from one to twenty-seven. Twenty-seven is one letter less than the number of letters in the alphabet. For the first consonant (of the alphabet) is combined with the remaining twenty-seven letters. This results in twenty-seven two-consonant words. Then, the second letter is combined with the remaining twenty-six consonants, then the third and the fourth, and so on, to the twenty-seventh consonant, which is combined (only) with the twenty-eighth consonant. This results in one two-consonant word. Thus, the number of two-consonant words is the arithmetical progression from one to twenty-seven. The total can be figured out with the help of a well-known arithmetical operation—that is,[1257] one adds up the first and last (numbers of the progression) and multiplies the total by one-half of the number (of numbers in the progression). The resulting number is then doubled, because the position of the consonants can be inverted. The position of consonants must be taken into consideration in combining them. The result is the total number of two-consonant words.[1258]

The number of three-consonant words is the result of
III, 285 multiplying the number of two-consonant words by the sum of the arithmetical progression from one to twenty-six. For every two-consonant word becomes a three-consonant word through the addition of one consonant. Thus, the two-consonant words may take the place of one consonant to be

[1257] The explanation of the calculation was added by C in the margin and is found in the text of D. The number 756 for two-consonant words is also indicated in A in a marginal note.

[1258] I.e., $\frac{(1 + 27) \cdot 27}{2} \cdot 2 = 756$.

combined with each of the remaining consonants of the alphabet, which number twenty-six. Thus, the sum of the arithmetical progression from one to twenty-six is calculated and multiplied by the number of two-consonant words. The result, then, is multiplied by six, which is the possible number of combinations of three consonants. The result is the total number (of words of three consonants that can be made) from the consonants of the alphabet.[1259] The same is done with four-consonant and five-consonant words. In this way, the total number of (possible) letter combinations was calculated (by al-Khalîl).[1260]

Al-Khalîl did <not?> arrange the chapters of the book according to the customary sequence of the letters of the alphabet. (Instead,) he used the sequence of the positions (in throat and mouth) in which the various sounds are produced. Thus, he started with the laryngeals. They were followed, successively, by velars, dentals, and labials. Al-Khalîl put the weak consonants, which are the (so-called) airy consonants (*alif*, *w*, *y*), in the last place. Among the laryngeals, he started with *'ayn*, because it is the (sound produced) farthest

1259 That would be $\frac{(1+26)\cdot 26}{2}\cdot 756\cdot 6 = 1{,}592{,}136$, which, however, is much too high. Including combinations containing the same letter twice (but excluding combinations consisting of the same letter repeated three times, which do not occur), the number of three-consonant combinations would be $28^3 - 28 = 21{,}924$. This, of course, includes many impossible combinations.

1260 Actually, as far as we know, al-Khalîl did not indulge in these calculations in the *Kitâb al-'Ayn*, but they were undertaken by later scholars. Cf. E. Bräunlich in *Islamica*, II (1926), 74. As-Suyûṭî, *Muzhir* (I, 74 f., in a recent, undated, and unreliable Cairo edition), sums up the discussion as follows. According to the *Muwâzanah* of Ḥamzah al-Iṣfahânî (*GAL*, I, 145; *Suppl.*, I, 221 f.), al-Khalîl stated in the *Kitâb al-'Ayn* that the number of possible words of two, three, four, and five consonants is 12,305,412. There are 756 two-consonant words, 19,650 (*sic leg.*) three-consonant words, 491,400 four-consonant words, and 11,793,600 five-consonant words (the sum of these figures would be smaller by six than the total given before).

According to the abridgment of the *Kitâb al-'Ayn* by az-Zubaydî (cf. p. 328, below), there are, as-Suyûṭî says, 6,659,400 possible combinations, of which 5,620 are in actual use. There are 756 (*sic leg.*) two-consonant words, of which 489 are in use. There are 19,650 three-consonant words, of which 4,269 are in use.

(back in the throat). Therefore, his book was called *Kitâb al-'Ayn*. The ancient (scholars) did such things when they selected titles for their works. They called them after the first words or phrases that occurred in them.

(Al-Khalîl) then made a distinction between (letter combinations) that are not used and those that are. The largest number of (letter combinations) that are not used are among words of four or five consonants. The Arabs rarely use them because of their heaviness. Next come the two-consonant words. They have little circulation. The three-consonant words are the ones used most. Thus, they possess the greatest number of (conventional) meanings, because they are (so much) in circulation.

All this was included by (al-Khalîl) in the *Kitâb al-'Ayn* and treated very well and exhaustively.

III, *286* Abû Bakr az-Zubaydî,[1261] the writing teacher of Hishâm al-Mu'ayyad in Spain in the fourth [tenth] century, abridged the (*Kitâb al-'Ayn*) but preserved its complete character. He omitted all the words that are not used. He also omitted many of the examples clarifying words in use. Thus, he produced a very good abridgment for memorizing.

Among eastern scholars, al-Jawharî [1262] composed the *Kitâb aṣ-Ṣiḥâḥ*, which follows the ordinary alphabetical sequence. He started with *hamzah* (*alif*). He arranged the words according to their last letter, since people have mostly to do with the last consonants of words. He made a special chapter (of each last letter), and within each chapter he also proceeded alphabetically by the first (letters) of the words and listed all of them as separate entries to the end.[1263] He gave a comprehensive presentation of the (lexicographical facts of the Arabic) language in imitation of the work of al-Khalîl.

[1261] Muḥammad b. al-Ḥasan, d. 379 [989]. Cf. *GAL*, I, 100, 132 f.; *Suppl.*, I, 203.

[1262] Ismâ'îl b. Ḥammâd, who died at the beginning of the eleventh century. Cf. *GAL*, I, 128 f.; *Suppl.*, I, 196 f. The title of the work is also vocalized *aṣ-Ṣaḥâḥ*.

[1263] The last sentence appears in the margin of C and in the text of D.

Among Spanish scholars, Ibn Sîdah, of Denia,[1264] wrote the *Kitâb al-Muḥkam*, a similarly comprehensive work following the arrangement of the *Kitâb al-'Ayn*. He wrote during the reign of 'Alî b. Mujâhid. Ibn Sîdah's own contribution was an attempt to give the etymologies and grammatical forms of the words. Thus, his work turned out to be one of the best systematic works (on lexicography). An abridgment of it was written by Muḥammad b. Abî l-Ḥusayn,[1265] a companion of the Ḥafṣid ruler al-Mustanṣir in Tunis. He changed the (alphabetical) sequence to that of the *Kitâb aṣ-Ṣiḥâḥ*, in that he considered the last consonants of the words and arranged the entries according to them. The two (works) [1266] are thus like real twins. Kurâ',[1267] a leading philologist, wrote the *Kitâb al-Munajjad*, Ibn Durayd [1268] the *Kitâb al-Jamharah*, and Ibn al-Anbârî [1269] the *Kitâb az-Zâhir*. III, 287

These are the principal works on lexicography, as far as we know. There are other brief works restricted to particular kinds of words. They contain some chapters, or they may contain all of them, but, still, they are obviously not comprehensive, while comprehensiveness is an obvious feature in the works (mentioned), dealing with all (the possible letter) combinations, as one has seen. Another work on lexicography is the one by az-Zamakhsharî on metaphoric usage, entitled *Asâs al-balâghah*.[1270] Az-Zamakhsharî explains in it all the words used metaphorically by the Arabs, (and he explains) what meanings are used metaphorically by them. It is a highly useful work.

Furthermore, the Arabs may use a general term for one

[1264] 'Alî b. Ismâ'îl (Aḥmad), *ca.* 398 [1007/8] to 458 [1066]. Cf. *GAL*, I, 308 f.; *Suppl.*, I, 542.

[1265] He died in 671 [1272/73]. Cf. *'Ibar*, VI, 294 f.; de Slane (tr.), II, 369 ff.

[1266] I.e., the works of al-Jawharî and Ibn Abî l-Ḥusayn.

[1267] This sentence is added in C and D. Kurâ''s name was 'Alî b. al-Ḥusayn, and he lived in the tenth century. Cf. *GAL*, *Suppl.*, I, 201.

[1268] Muḥammad b. al-Ḥasan, d. 321 [933]. Cf. *GAL*, I, 111 f.; *Suppl.*, I, 172 ff.

[1269] Muḥammad b. al-Qâsim, 271–328 [885–940]. Cf. *GAL*, I, 119; *Suppl.*, I, 182 f.

[1270] Cf. n. 104 to this chapter, above.

(particular) meaning, but (for the expression of the same idea) in connection with particular objects, they may employ other words that can be used (in this particular meaning) only with those particular objects. Thus, we have a distinction between (conventional) meaning and usage. This (situation) requires a lexicographical "jurisprudence." It is something difficult to develop. For instance, "white" [1271] is used for anything that contains whiteness. However, the whiteness of horses is indicated by the special word *ashhab*, that of men by the word *azhar*, and that of sheep by the word *amlaḥ*. Eventually, the use of the ordinary word for "white" in all these cases came to be (considered) a solecism and deviation from the Arabic language. Ath-Tha'âlibî,[1272] in particular, wrote in this sense. He composed a monograph on the subject entitled *Fiqh al-lughah* "Jurisprudence of Lexicography." It is the best control a philologist has, in order to keep himself from deviating from (proper) Arabic usage. A knowledge of the primary (conventional) meaning is not enough for (the use of proper) word combinations. It must be attested by (actual) Arabic usage. This (knowledge) is needed most by poets and prose writers, in order to avoid committing frequent solecisms in connection with the (conventional) meanings of words, whether they are used in individual words or
III, *288* in combinations. (Improper use in this respect) is worse than solecisms in (use of the) vowel endings. Likewise, a recent scholar wrote on homonyms and undertook to give a comprehensive presentation of them. However, he did not fully succeed, though his work contains most of the (material).

There are many brief works on the subject. They are particularly concerned with widespread and much used lexicographical materials. Their purpose is to make it easy for the student to memorize them. For instance, there are the

[1271] Bulaq adds: "in its general (conventional) meaning."

[1272] 'Abd-al-Malik b. Muḥammad, 350 [961/62] to 429 or 430 [1037–39]. Cf. *GAL*, I, 284 ff.; *Suppl.*, I, 499 ff.

Alfâẓ of Ibn as-Sikkît,[1273] the *Faṣîḥ* of Tha'lab,[1274] and others. Some contain less lexicographical material than others, depending on the different views of their authors as to what is most important for the student to know.

God is "the Creator, the Knowing One." [1275]

It [1276] should be known that the tradition through which (any particular) lexicographical (usage) is confirmed is a tradition indicating that the Arabs used certain words in certain meanings. It does not indicate that they invented their (conventional meanings). This is impossible and improbable. It is not known (for certain) that any one of them ever did that.

Likewise, the meanings of words cannot be established by analogy,[1277] if their usage is not known, although,[1277a] for jurists, their usage may be known by virtue of (the existence of) an inclusive (concept) that attests to the applicability of (a wider meaning) to the first (word).[1278] (The use of the word) *khamr* "grape wine" for *nabîdh* "date wine" is established by its use for "juice of grapes" and by application of the inclusive (concept) of "causing intoxication." (This is so) only because the use of analogy (in this case) is attested by the religious law, which deduces the soundness of (the application of)

[1273] Ya'qûb b. Isḥâq, who died in or after 243 [857]. Cf. *GAL*, I, 117 f.; *Suppl.*, I, 180 f.

[1274] Aḥmad b. Yaḥyâ, 200–291 [815/16–904]. Cf. *GAL*, I, 118; *Suppl.*, I, 181 f.

[1275] Qur'ân 15.86 (86); 36.81 (81).

[1276] The remainder of the section is added in C and D.

[1277] Cf. p. 26, above.

[1277a] Lit., "in the way in which, in the reasoning of jurists

[1278] That is, in jurisprudence, for legal purposes, a word may be given a certain meaning by analogical reasoning of some sort or other and be used in that meaning. However, this could not be done in lexicography, and no meaning gained by a process of analogical reasoning would be recognized as firmly established. A jurist might consider *nabîdh* as having the meaning of *khamr*, because, like *khamr*, it can be used for something somehow connected with grapes. On this basis, a jurist might treat *nabîdh* as forbidden, just as *khamr* is forbidden. But it would be improper for a lexicographer to identify the two words *khamr* and *nabîdh* in this way.

analogy (in this case) from the (general norms) on which it is based. We do not have anything like it in lexicography. There, only the intellect can be used, which means (relying on) judgment. This is the opinion of most authorities, even though the Judge (al-Bâqillânî) [1279] and Ibn Surayj [1280] and others are inclined to (use) analogy in connection with (the meaning of words). However, it is preferable to deny its (applicability). It should not be thought that the establish-
III, *289* ment of word meanings falls under the category of word definitions. A definition indicates (the meaning of) a given idea by showing that the meaning of an unknown and obscure word is identical with the meaning of a clear and well-known word. Lexicography, on the other hand, affirms that such-and-such a word is used to express such-and-such an idea. The difference here is very clear.

The science of syntax and style and literary criticism [1281]

This is a science which originated in Islam after Arabic philology and lexicography. It belongs among the philological sciences, because it is concerned with words and the ideas they convey and are intended to indicate. This is as follows:

The thing that the speaker intends to convey to the listener through speech may be a perception (*taṣawwur*) regarding individual words which are dependent and on which (something else) depends [1282] and of which one leads to the other. These (concepts) are indicated by individual nouns, verbs, and particles. Or, (what the speaker intends to convey) may be the distinction between the things that are dependent and those that depend on them and (the distinction between)

[1279] Cf. 1:43, above.

[1280] He seems to be the famous Shâfi'ite Aḥmad b. 'Umar, 248–306 [863–918]. Cf. *GAL, Suppl.*, I, 306 f.; al-Khaṭîb al-Baghdâdî, *Ta'rîkh Baghdâd*, IV, 287 ff.

[1281] *'Ilm al-bayân*. Cf. pp. 335 f., below, where we find an explanation of the difficulties the word *bayân* presents to the translator. Cf. also pp. 398 ff., below.

[1282] Cf. p. 320, above.

tenses. These (concepts) are indicated by the change of vowel endings and the forms of the words. All this belongs to grammar.

Among the things that are part of the facts and need to be indicated, there still remain the conditions of speakers and agents and the requirements of the situation under which the action takes place.[1283] This needs to be indicated, because it completes (the information) to be conveyed. If the speaker is able to bring out these (facts), his speech conveys everything that it can possibly convey. If his speech does not have any- III, 290
thing of that, it is not real Arabic speech. The Arabic language is vast. The Arabs have a particular expression for each situation, in addition to a perfect use of vowel endings and clarity.

It is known that "Zayd came to me" does not mean the same as "There came to me Zayd." Something mentioned in the first place (such as "Zayd" in the first example) has greater importance in the mind of the speaker. The person who says: "There came to me Zayd," indicates that [1284] he is more concerned with the coming than with the person who comes. (On the other hand,) the person who says: "Zayd came to me," indicates that he is more concerned with the person than with his coming, which (grammatically) depends on (the person who comes).

The same applies to the indication of the parts of a sentence by relative pronouns, demonstrative pronouns, or determinations appropriate to the situation. It also applies to "emphatic" [1285] connection in general. For instance, (the three sentences): "Zayd is standing," "Behold, Zayd is standing," and "Behold, Zayd is indeed standing," all mean something different, even if they are alike as far as vowel endings are concerned. The first (sentence), without the emphatic particle, informs a person who has no previous knowledge as to (whether Zayd is standing or not). The second

[1283] Cf. p. 399, below.
[1284] The following three lines are found only in Bulaq.
[1285] That is, use of the particle *inna* "behold."

(sentence), with the emphatic particle "behold," informs a person who hesitates (whether he should acknowledge the fact of Zayd's standing or not). And the third (sentence) informs a person who (persists in) denying (the fact of Zayd's standing). Thus, they are all different.[1286]

The same applies to a statement such as: "There came to me *the* man," which is then replaced by the statement: "There came to me *a* man." The use of the form without the article may be intended as an honor (for the man in question) and as an indication that he is a man who has no equal.

Furthermore, a sentence may have the structure of a statement and thus be a sentence that conforms, originally (at least), to something in the outside world. Or, it may have the structure of a command [1287] and thus be a sentence that has no correspondence in the outside world, as, for example, requests and the different ways they (can be expressed).

Furthermore, the copula between two (parts of a) sentence must be omitted, if the second (part) has an integral place in the sentence structure.[1288] In this way, the (second part) takes the place of an individual apposition and is either attribute, or emphasis,[1289] or substitute [1290] (attached to the
III, *291* part of the sentence to which it belongs), without copula. Or, if the second (part of the) sentence has no such integral place in the sentence structure, the copula must be used.

Also, the given situation may require either lengthiness or brevity. (The speaker) will express himself accordingly.

[1286] Cf. p. 345, below, where the same argument is reported in the name of Khalîl's teacher, ʿÎsâ b. ʿUmar ath-Thaqafî. Al-Jurjânî, *Dalâʾil al-iʿjâz* (Cairo, 1331/1913), p. 242, uses it in connection with an anecdote concerning the philosopher al-Kindî, who doubted the perfection of the Arabic language and was convinced by the above story. Cf. F. Rosenthal in *Orientalia*, N.S. IX (1942), 273. Al-Jurjânî is quoted by al-Qalqashandî, *Ṣubḥ al-aʿshâ* (Cairo, 1331–38/1913–19), I, 184.

[1287] Cf. 1:76 (n. 14), 3:281 (l. 26), above; p. 378 (l. 25), below.

[1288] *Maḥall min al-iʿrâb* means "to form an integral part of the sentence structure." Cf. Silvestre de Sacy, *Grammaire arabe* (2d ed.; Paris, 1831), II, 596.

[1289] The grammatical term for expressions such as "all" or "(him)self."

[1290] The grammatical term for a corrected statement, e.g., "I ate a loaf—one-third of it."

Then, an expression may be used other than in its literal meaning. It may be intended to indicate some implication of it. This may apply to an individual word. For instance, in the statement: "Zayd is a lion," no actual lion, but the bravery implicit in lions, is meant and referred to Zayd. This is called metaphorical usage. It also may be a combination of words intended to express some implication that results from it. The statement: "Zayd has a great deal of ash on his pots," [1291] is intended to indicate the implied (qualities) of generosity and hospitality, because a great deal of ash is the result (of generosity and hospitality). Thus, it indicates those (qualities). All these things are meanings in addition to the (original) meaning of the individual word or combination of words. They are forms and conditions that the facts may take and that can be expressed by conditions and forms of speech that have been invented for that purpose, as required by the particular situation in each case.

The discipline called syntax and style (*bayân*) expresses the meaning that the forms and conditions of speech have in various situations. It has been divided into three subdivisions.

The first subdivision has as its subject the investigation of forms and conditions of speech, in order to achieve conformity with all the requirements of a given situation. This is called "the science of rhetoric" (*balâghah*).[1292]

The second subdivision has as its subject the investigation of what a word implies or is implied by it—that is, metaphor and metonymy,[1293] as we have just stated. This is called "the science of style" (*bayân*).

(Scholars) have added a (third) subdivision, the study of the artistic embellishment of speech.[1294] Such embellishment III, *292*
may be achieved through the ornamental use of rhymed prose (*saj'*), which divides (speech) into sections; or through the

[1291] Cf. Lane's *Arabic-English Dictionary*, p. 1154c, *s. radice* "rmd."

[1292] *Balâghah* means both eloquence in oral expression and good style in written expression.

[1293] Cf. p. 400, below.

[1294] Cf. pp. 401 f., below.

use of paronomasia (*tajnîs*),[1295] which establishes a similarity among the words used; or through the use of internal rhyme (*tarṣî'*), which cuts down the units of rhythmic speech (into smaller units); or through the use of allusion (*tawriyah*) to the intended meaning by suggesting an even more cryptic idea which is expressed by the same words; [1296] or through the use of antithesis (*ṭibâq*); [1297] and similar things. They called this "the science of rhetorical figures" (*'ilm al-badî'*).

Recent scholars have used the name of the second subdivision, *bayân* (syntax and style), for all three subdivisions,[1298] because the ancient scholars had discussed it first.

The problems of the discipline, then, made their appearance one after the other. Insufficient works on the subject were dictated by Ja'far b. Yaḥyâ,[1299] al-Jâḥiẓ,[1300] Qudâmah,[1301] and others. The problems continued to be perfected one by one. Eventually, as-Sakkâkî [1302] sifted out the best part of the discipline, refined its problems, and arranged its chapters in the manner mentioned by us at the start. He composed the book entitled *al-Miftâḥ fî n-naḥw wa-t-taṣrîf wa-l-bayân* "On Grammar, Inflection, and Syntax and Style." He made the discipline of *bayân* one of the parts (of the book). Later scholars took the subject over from (as-Sakkâkî's) work.

[1295] For this and the following terms of the *'ilm al-badî'*, one may, for instance, compare G. E. von Grunebaum, *A Tenth-Century Document of Arabic Literary Criticism* (Chicago, 1950), pp. 20 f. (*tajnîs*); 35 (*tarṣî'*); 17 ff. (*ṭibâq*); and 2 (*'ilm al-badî'*).

[1296] The idea of *tawriyah* is more simply expressed below, p. 401. For the very common term *tawriyah*, cf. A. F. Mehren, *Die Rhetorik der Araber* (Copenhagen & Vienna, 1853), pp. 105 ff.

[1297] Not in Bulaq.

[1298] In this case, the word usually corresponds to "literary criticism."

[1299] He seems to be the Barmecide who is credited with some poetical composition in Ibn an-Nadîm, *Fihrist*, p. 166, l. 7 (ed. Flügel); p. 236 (Cairo, 1348/1929–30). He is occasionally quoted as an authority on eloquence; cf. Ibn Rashîq, *'Umdah*, I, 214 and 220. However, he is not known to have had any particular significance in the sense indicated. Perhaps Ibn Khaldûn made a mistake here, caused by the reference to Ja'far b. Qudâmah, or Qudâmah b. Ja'far?

[1300] Cf. p. 62, above.

[1301] Qudâmah b. Ja'far, who lived *ca.* 900. Cf. *GAL*, I, 228; *Suppl.*, I, 406 f.

[1302] Cf. p. 286, above.

They abridged it in authoritative works which are in circulation at this time. That was done, for instance, by as-Sakkâkî (himself) in the *Kitâb at-Tibyân*, by Ibn Mâlik[1303] in the *Kitâb al-Miṣbâḥ*, and by Jalâl-ad-dîn al-Qazwînî[1304] in the *Kitâb al-Îḍâḥ* and the *Kitâb at-Talkhîṣ*, which is shorter than the *Îḍâḥ*. Contemporary Easterners are more concerned with commenting on and teaching (the *Miftâḥ*) than any other (work).

In general, the people of the East cultivate this discipline more than the Maghribîs. The reason is perhaps that it is a III, *293*
luxury,[1305] as far as the linguistic sciences are concerned, and luxury crafts exist (only) where civilization is abundant, and civilization is (today) more abundant in the East than in the West, as we have mentioned.[1306] Or, we might say (the reason is that) the non-Arabs (Persians) who constitute the majority of the population of the East occupy themselves with the Qur'ân commentary of az-Zamakhsharî, which is wholly based upon this discipline.[1307]

The people of the West chose as their own field the (third) subdivision of this discipline, the science of rhetorical figures (*'ilm al-badî'*). They made it a part of poetical literature. They invented a detailed (nomenclature of rhetorical) figures[1308] for it and divided it into many chapters and subdivisions. They thought that they could consider all that part of the Arabic language. However, the reason (why they cultivated the subject) was that they liked to express themselves artistically. (Furthermore,) the science of rhetorical figures is easy to learn, while it was difficult for them to learn rhetoric and style,[1309] because the theories and ideas of (rhetoric and style) are subtle and intricate. Therefore, they

[1303] Cf. p. 323, above.
[1304] Muḥammad b. 'Abd-ar-Raḥmân, 666–739 [1267–1338]. Cf. *GAL*, I, 295; II, 22; *Suppl.*, I, 516; II, 15 f.
[1305] Cf. Bombaci, p. 467.
[1306] Cf., for instance, 2:348 f. and 431 f., above.
[1307] Cf. 2:446 f., above, and pp. 338 f., below.
[1308] *Alqâb* is used again, pp. 371, 401, 405 f., and 409, below.
[1309] The first two kinds of the discipline, p. 335, above.

kept away from those two subjects. One of the authors in Ifrîqiyah who wrote on rhetorical figures was Ibn Rashîq.[1310] His *Kitâb al-'Umdah* is famous. Many of the people of Ifrîqiyah and Spain wrote along the lines of (the *'Umdah*).

It should be known that the fruit of this discipline is understanding of the inimitability of the Qur'ân.[1311] The inimitability of (the Qur'ân) consists in the fact that the (language of the Qur'ân) indicates all the requirements of the situations (referred to), whether they are stated or understood. This is the highest stage of speech. In addition, (the Qur'ân) is perfect [1312] in choice of words and excellence of arrangement and combination. This is (its) inimitability, (a quality) that surpasses comprehension. Something of it may be understood by those who have a taste [1313] for it as the result of their contact with the (Arabic) language and their posses-
III, 294 sion of the habit of it. They may thus understand as much of the inimitability of the Qur'ân as their taste permits. Therefore, the Arabs who heard the Qur'ân directly from (the Prophet) who brought it (to them) had a better understanding of its (inimitability than later Muslims). They were the champions and arbiters of speech, and they possessed the greatest and best taste (for the language) that anyone could possibly have.

This discipline is needed most by Qur'ân commentators. Most ancient commentators disregarded it, until Jâr-Allâh az-Zamakhsharî appeared.[1314] When he wrote his Qur'ân commentary, he investigated each verse of the Qur'ân according to the rules of this discipline. This brings out, in part,

[1310] Cf. 1:10 and 2:403, above, and pp. 384, 387, and 405 f., below.

[1311] For the significance of literary criticism for the problem of the inimitability of the Qur'ân, cf. the work by G. E. von Grunebaum cited above, n. 1295.

[1312] The translation follows the reading suggested by Bulaq: *marâtib al-kalâm ma'a l-kamâl*, which might be a necessary correction of *marâtib al-kamâl ma'a l-kalâm*, found in the MSS. (B has *marâtib al-kalâm* and supplies the rest in the margin.) Perhaps we should read: *marâtib al-kamâl fî l-kalâm ma'a l-kamâl* . . .

[1313] Cf. pp. 358 ff., below.

[1314] For the following remarks, cf. 2:446 f., above.

its inimitability. It gives his commentary greater distinction than is possessed by any other commentary. However, he tried to confirm the articles of faith of the (Mu'tazilah) innovators by deriving them from the Qur'ân by means of different aspects of rhetoric (*balâghah*). Therefore, many orthodox Muslims have been on their guard against his (commentary), despite his abundant knowledge of rhetoric (*balâghah*). However, there are people who have a good knowledge of the orthodox articles of faith and who have some experience in this discipline. They are able to refute him with his own weapons, or (at least) they know that (his work) contains innovations. They can avoid them, so that no harm is done to their religious beliefs. Such persons do not risk being affected by the innovations and sectarian beliefs. They should study (as-Zamakhsharî's commentary), in order to find out about certain (aspects of) the inimitability of the Qur'ân.

God guides whomever He wants to guide to "an even road." [1315]

The science of literature

This science has no object the accidents of which may be studied and thus be affirmed or denied. Philologists consider its purpose identical with its fruit, which is (the acquisition of) a good ability to handle prose and poetry according to the III, 295
methods and ways of the Arabs. Therefore, they collect and memorize (documents) of Arabic speech that are likely to aid in acquiring the (proper linguistic) habit. (Such documents include) high-class poetry, rhymed prose of an even quality, and (certain) problems of lexicography and grammar, found scattered among (documents of Arabic poetry and prose) and from which the student is, as a rule, able to derive inductively most of the rules of Arabic. In addition, they mention certain of the battle-day narratives of the Arabs, which serve to

[1315] Cf. Qur'ân 5.60 (65), 77 (81).

explain the references to (battle days) occurring in the poems. Likewise, they mention famous pedigrees and general historical information of importance. The purpose of all this is not to leave the students investigating such things in the dark about any (of the documents of) Arabic speech, about any of the (literary) methods used, or about any of the methods of Arab eloquence. Merely memorizing them does not give (a student the proper linguistic) habit, unless he first understands them. Therefore, he must give preference to everything upon which understanding of (Arabic literature) depends.

(Philologists) who wanted to define this discipline said: "Literature is expert knowledge of the poetry and history of the Arabs as well as the possession of some knowledge regarding every science." They meant (knowledge) of the linguistic sciences and the religious sciences, but only the contents (of the latter)—that is, the Qur'ân and the traditions. No other science has anything to do with Arab speech, save in as much as recent scholars who have occupied themselves with the craft of rhetorical figures (*'ilm al-badî'*) have come to use allusion (*tawriyah*)[1316] by means of (references to terms of) scientific terminologies, in their poetry and their straight prose (*tarsîl*).[1317] Therefore, littérateurs need to know scientific terminologies, in order to be able to understand (such allusions).

III, *296* We heard our *shaykhs* say in class that the basic principles and pillars of this discipline are four works: the *Adab al-kâtib* by Ibn Qutaybah,[1318] the *Kitâb al-Kâmil* by al-Mubarrad,[1319] the *Kitâb al-Bayân wa-t-tabyîn* by al-Jâḥiẓ,[1320] and the

[1316] Cf. p. 336, above, and p. 401, below.

[1317] Cf. Bombaci, p. 467, and below, p. 370. Ibn Khaldûn uses the term also in connection with the prose of government correspondence, the type of prose composition cultivated by government officials. Cf. pp. 393 f., below.

[1318] 'Abdallâh b. Muslim, who was born in 213 [828/29] and died between 270 and 276 [884–89]. Cf. *GAL*, I, 120 ff.; *Suppl.*, I, 184 ff.

[1319] Muḥammad b. Yazîd, 210–285 [825/26–898]. Cf. *GAL*, I, 108 f.; *Suppl.*, I, 168 f.

[1320] Cf. p. 287, above.

Kitâb an-Nawâdir by Abû 'Alî al-Qâlî al-Baghdâdî.[1321] All other books depend on these four and are derived from them. The works of recent writers on the subject are numerous.

At the beginning of (Islam) singing (music) belonged to this discipline. (Singing) depends on poetry, because it is the setting of poetry to music.[1322] Secretaries and outstanding persons in the 'Abbâsid dynasty occupied themselves with it, because they were desirous of becoming acquainted with the methods and (literary) disciplines of the Arabs.[1323] Its cultivation was no blemish on probity or manliness. The early Ḥijâzî Muslims in Medina and elsewhere, who are models for everybody else to follow, cultivated it.[1324] Such a great (scholar) as Judge Abû l-Faraj al-Iṣfahânî [1325] wrote a book on songs, the *Kitâb al-Aghânî*. In it, he dealt with the whole of the history, poetry, genealogy, battle days, and ruling dynasties of the Arabs. The basis for the work were one hundred songs which the singers had selected for ar-Rashîd. His work is the most complete and comprehensive one there is. Indeed, it constitutes an archive of the Arabs.[1326] It is a collection of the *disjecta membra* of all the good things in Arab poetry, history, song, and all the other conditions (of the Arabs). There exists no book comparable to it, as far as we know. It is the ultimate goal to which a littérateur can aspire and where he must stop—as though he could ever get so far! [1327]

Let us now return to the verification of our remarks about the linguistic sciences in general (terms).

God is the guide to that which is correct.

[1321] Ismâ'îl b. al-Qâsim, 280–356 [893/94–967]. Cf. *GAL*, I, 132; *Suppl.*, I, 202 f. For the date of his birth, 280 seems to be more likely than 288, which is also given. The *Nawâdir* are also known under the title of *Amâlî*.

[1322] Cf. 2:395, above.

[1323] Bulaq and Paris have "the methods and disciplines of poetry."

[1324] This sentence is added in C and D.

[1325] 'Alî b. al-Ḥusayn, 284–356 [897/98–967]. Cf. *GAL*, I, 146; *Suppl.*, I, 225 f.

[1326] Cf. 3:304 (n. 1186), above.

[1327] Cf. R. Dozy in *Journal asiatique*, XIV 6 (1869), 171; Bombaci, p. 467. On the *Aghânî*, cf. also pp. 366 f. and 383, below.

III, 297 [45] *Language is a technical habit.*

It[1328] should be known that all languages are habits similar to crafts (techniques). They are habits (located) in the tongue and serve the purpose of expressing ideas. The good or inadequate (character of such expression) depends on the perfection or deficiency of the habit. This does not apply to individual words but to word combinations. A speaker who possesses a perfect (linguistic) habit and is thus able to combine individual words so as to express the ideas he wants to express, and who is able to observe the form of composition that makes his speech conform to the requirements of the situation, is as well qualified as is (humanly) possible to convey to the listener what he wants to convey. This is what is meant by eloquence.

Habits result only from repeated action.[1329] An action is done first (once). Thus, it contributes an attribute to the essence. With repetition it becomes a condition, which is an attribute that is not firmly established. After more repetition it becomes a habit, that is, a firmly established attribute.

As long as the habit of the Arabic language existed among the Arabs, an Arab speaker always heard the people of his generation (race) speak (Arabic). He hears their ways of address and how they express what they want to express. He is like a child hearing individual words employed in their proper meanings.[1330] He learns them first.[1331] Afterwards, he hears word combinations and learns them likewise. He hears something new each moment from every speaker,[1331a] and his own practice is constantly repeated, until (use of proper
III, 298 speech) becomes a habit and a firmly established attribute. Thus, (the child) becomes like one of (the Arabs). In this

1328 Cf. Issawi, pp. 149 f.

1329 Cf. 2:346, and p. 292 f., above.

1330 "In their proper meanings" is found in Bulaq, C *in marg.*, and D.

1331 "First" is found in Bulaq, C *in marg.*, and D.

1331a The correct reading may be *samā'uhū*, instead of *samā'uhum* which can be explained only with some difficulty. The meaning is hardly affected by the correction.

way, (Arab) languages and dialects have passed from generation to generation, and both non-Arabs and children have learned them.[1332]

This is (what is) meant by the common saying: "The Arabs have (their) language from nature." [1333] That is, they have it from (their own) original habit, and while (others) learned it from them, they themselves did not learn it from anyone else.

The (linguistic) habit of the Muḍar became corrupt when they came into contact with non-Arabs. The reason for that corruption was that the generation growing up heard other ways of expressing the things they wanted to express than the Arab (ways). They used them to express what they wanted to express, because there were so many non-Arabs coming into contact with the Arabs. They also heard the ways in which the Arabs expressed themselves. As a result, matters became confused for them. They adopted (ways of expressing themselves) from both sides. Thus, there originated a new habit which was inferior to the first one. This is what is meant by "corruption of the Arabic language." [1334]

Therefore, the dialect of the Quraysh was the most correct and purest Arabic dialect, because the Quraysh were on all sides far removed from the lands of the non-Arabs. Next came (the tribes) around the Quraysh, the Thaqîf, the Hudhayl, the Khuzâʻah, the Banû Kinânah, the Ghaṭafân, the Banû Asad, and the Banû Tamîm. The Rabîʻah, the Lakhm, the Judhâm, the Ghassân, the Iyâd, the Quḍâʻah, and the Arabs of the Yemen lived farther away from the Quraysh, and were (variously) neighbors of the Persians, the Byzantines, and the Abyssinians. Because they had contact with non-Arabs, their linguistic habit was not perfect. The Arabic dialects were used by Arab philologists as arguments for (linguistic) soundness or corruption according to the (degree

[1332] Cf. p. 318 (n. 1231), above.
[1333] Cf. p. 283, above, and p. 359, below.
[1334] Cf. p. 346, below.

of) remoteness of (the tribes speaking them) from the Quraysh.

And God knows better.

III, 299 [46] *Contemporary Arabic*[1335] *is an independent language different from the languages of the Muḍar and the Ḥimyar.*

This is as follows. We find that with regard to clear indication of what one wants to express and full expression of meaning, Arabic (as it is spoken today) follows the ways of the Muḍar language. The only loss is that of the vowels indicating the distinction between subject and object. Instead, one uses position within the sentence and syntactic combinations (*qarâ'in*)[1336] to indicate certain special meanings one wants to express. However, the clarity and eloquence of the Muḍar language are greater and more firmly rooted (than those of present-day Arabic). The words themselves indicate the ideas. What still requires indication are the requirements of a particular situation, called "the spread of the situation."[1337] Of necessity, every idea is surrounded by situations peculiar to it. Therefore, it is necessary to indicate those situations in conveying the meaning one wants to convey, because they belong to it as attributes. In all (other) languages, the situations are as a rule indicated by expressions restricted, by convention, to (those situations). But in the Arabic language, they are indicated by the conditions and possibilities of combining words (in a sentence), such as earlier or later position (of words in a sentence), ellipsis, or vowel endings. They are (also) indicated by letters that are not used independently. Hence, the classes of speech in the Arabic language differ according to the dif-
III, 300 ferent ways of indicating the possibilities, as we have stated before. Therefore, Arabic speech is more concise and uses fewer words and expressions than any other language. This is

1335 Ibn Khaldûn is thinking here of Bedouin Arabic.

1336 Cf. p. 415, below.

1337 *Bisâṭ al-ḥâl* "the circumstances."

what was meant in the following remark by Muḥammad: "I was given the most comprehensive words, and speech was made short for me." [1338]

One may compare the story of 'Îsâ b. 'Umar.[1339] A grammarian said to him: "I find duplications in Arabic speech. The (three) sentences, 'Zayd is standing,' 'Behold, Zayd is standing,' and 'Behold, Zayd is indeed standing,' all mean the same." 'Îsâ replied: "(No! All three) mean something different. The first (sentence) gives information to a person who has no previous knowledge as to whether Zayd is standing (or not). The second (sentence) gives information to a person who has heard about it but denies it. And the third (sentence) gives information to a person who knows it but persists in denying it. Thus, the meaning differs according to the different situations (one wants to express)."

Such eloquence and stylistic (precision) has continued to this day to be a part of Arab custom and method. No attention should be paid to the nonsensical talk of certain professional grammarians who are not capable of understanding the situation correctly and who think that eloquence no longer exists and that the Arabic language is corrupt. They draw this conclusion from the corruption of the vowel endings, the rules for which are their (particular) subject of study. But such a statement is inspired by both partisan attitude and lack of ability. Actually, we find that most Arabic words are still used today in their original meanings. Arabic speech can still today express what one wants to express with different degrees of clarity. In their speeches (the Arabs) still employ the methods and the different branches [1340] of the (old language of) prose and poetry. There still exist eloquent speak- III, *301*
ers at (Arab) parties and gatherings. There are poets who are gifted in all the ways of the Arabic language. (The existence of) a sound taste and healthy disposition (as far as linguistic

[1338] Cf. p. 321, above.

[1339] He died in 149 [766/67]. Cf. *GAL*, I, 98 f.; *Suppl.*, I, 158. For the story, cf. pp. 333 f., above.

[1340] A and B have "methods and power."

matters are concerned) attests to the fact that (the Arabic language is still intact).[1341] The only part of the codified language that no longer exists is the *i'râb*, the vowel endings that were used in the language of the Muḍar in a uniform and definite manner and that form part of the laws of (the Arabic) language.

Concern [1342] for the Muḍar language was only felt when that language became corrupt through the contact of (Arabs) with non-Arabs, at the time when (the Arabs) gained control of the provinces of the 'Irâq, Syria, Egypt, and the Maghrib. (At that time) the (Arabic linguistic) habit took on a form different from the one it had had originally. The (Muḍar language) was thus transformed into another language. (Now,) the Qur'ân was revealed in (the language of the Muḍar), and the Prophetical traditions were transmitted in it, and both the Qur'ân and the traditions are the basis of Islam. It was feared that, as a result of the disappearance of the language in which they were revealed, they themselves might be forgotten and no longer be understood. Therefore, a systematic treatment of its laws, a presentation of the analogical formations used in it, and the derivation of its rules

1341 Cf. pp. 397 f., below.

1342 Cf. Issawi, pp. 150 f. For the traditional picture of the corruption of the Arabic language, to which Ibn Khaldûn has already alluded many times in the preceding pages, see, for instance, Majd-ad-dîn Ibn al-Athîr, *Nihâyah*, I, 4: "Among (the early Muslims,) the Arabic language was preserved in a form that was correct and unaffected by defects and errors. Then, the great cities were conquered. The Arabs mixed with peoples of other races, such as the Byzantines, the Persians, the Abyssinians, the Nabataeans [Aramaic-speaking 'Irâqîs], and other peoples whose countries were conquered by the Muslims with the help of God and whose property and persons fell to them as the prize of conquest. In consequence, the different parties intermingled, the languages became mixed, and the idioms interpenetrated. A new generation grew up. They learned as much Arabic and Arabic idiom as they needed for conversation and as was indispensable to them in discussion. They had no need for anything else. They had little interest in anything that would call for a (deeper study of Arabic). Therefore they neglected it completely. Thus (the Arabic language,) which had been one of the most important subjects of study and an obligatory necessity, was rejected and avoided and came to be considered as of no account. . . . (By the time a second generation appeared) the Arabic language had become un-Arabic, or nearly so. "

were needed. (Knowledge of Arabic) thus became a science with subdivisions, chapters, premises, and problems. The scholars who cultivated that science called it grammar and Arabic philology. It became a discipline known by heart and fixed in writing, a ladder leading up to the understanding of the Book of God and the Sunnah of His Prophet.

Perhaps, if we were to concern ourselves with the present-day Arabic language and evolve its laws inductively, we would find other things and possibilities indicating what the vowel endings, which no longer exist, (used to) indicate, things that exist in the (present-day language) and that have their own peculiar rules.[1343] Perhaps, (certain rules) apply to III, *302*
the endings of (the words of the present-day Arabic language, only) in a manner different from that which existed originally in the language of the Muḍar. Languages and (linguistic) habits are not matters of chance.

The relationship of the Muḍar language to the Ḥimyarite language was of the same type. Many of the meanings and inflections of the words of the Ḥimyarite language were changed in Muḍar usage. This fact is attested by the transmitted material available to us. It is contrary to the opinions of those whose deficient (knowledge) leads them to assume that the Muḍar and Ḥimyar languages are one and the same, and who want to interpret the Ḥimyarite language according to the formations and rules of the Muḍar language. For instance, certain of these persons assume that the Ḥimyarite word *qayl* "leader" is derived from *qawl* "speaking," [1344] and so on. This is not correct. The Ḥimyarite language is another language and differs from the Muḍar language in most of its (conventional) meanings, inflections, and vowels, (and has) the same relationship (to it) that the Muḍar language has to present-day Arabic. The only difference is that the interest in the Muḍar language which, we have stated, exists on account of (the connection of that language with) the religious law,

[1343] Bulaq does not have the relative clause.

[1344] Modern scholarship, in fact, assumes that South Arabic *qayl* is derived from the same root as *qawl*.

caused [1345] (scholars) to evolve and derive (its rules). There is nothing nowadays to move us to do the same (for present-day Arabic).

A characteristic feature of the language of present-day Arab (Bedouins), wherever they may live, is the pronunciation of *q*. They do not pronounce it as the urban population pronounces it and as it is indicated in works on Arabic philology, namely, where the hindmost part of the tongue meets the soft palate above it. Neither [1346] is it pronounced as *k* is pronounced, even though *k* is articulated in a place below that where *q* is articulated in the vicinity of the soft palate, as it is (when properly articulated). It is pronounced some-
III, *303* where between *k* [1347] and *q*. This is the case with all Arab Bedouins, wherever they are, in the West or the East. It has eventually become their distinguishing mark among the nations and races. It is a characteristic of theirs that no one else shares with them. This goes so far that those who want to Arabicize themselves and to affiliate themselves with the Arabs imitate the Arab pronunciation of (*q*). (Arabs) think that a pure Arab can be distinguished from Arabicized and sedentary people by this pronunciation of *q*. It is thus obvious that this is the (pronunciation of *q* found in) the Muḍar language. The largest and leading group of Arab Bedouins who still live in the East and the West consists of descendants of Manṣûr b. ʿIkrimah b. Khaṣafah b. Qays b. ʿAylân [1348] through Sulaym b. Manṣûr and through the Banû ʿÂmir b. Ṣaʿṣaʿah b. Muʿâwiyah b. Bakr b. Hawâzin b. Manṣûr. Now-

[1345] The text should probably be corrected to *ḥamala⟨t⟩ ʿalâ dhâlika*. Bulaq suggests: *ḥamala dhâlika ʿalâ*. A has *wa-ḥamala . . .*

[1346] The following reference to the pronunciation of *k* is found in Bulaq, and in the margins of C and D. The clause at the end ("as it is . . .") also appears in the other text, where it belongs to the preceding sentence, and this may be its original and correct position.

[1347] The MSS usually do not have a dot under the *k*, which would indicate a sound like *g*. Such a dot under the *k* is, however, found in C in the passage below, p. 349, l. 32, which appears in C on a separately inserted sheet.

[1348] The Arab authorities disagree as to whether ʿAylân was the father of Qays, or whether ʿAylân was added to the name of Qays as an epithet. Cf., for instance, Ibn Ḥazm, *Jamharat ansâb al-ʿArab* (Cairo, 1368/1948), pp. 232 ff.; *Lisân al-ʿArab*, XIII, 519.

adays, they constitute the most numerous and powerful nation of the inhabited part of the earth. They are descendants of the Muḍar.[1349] They and all the other (Arab Bedouins) of the Banû Kahlân [1350] are the model for the pronunciation of *q* mentioned. It was not invented by these Arab Bedouins but inherited by them over the generations. This makes it obvious that it was the pronunciation of the ancient Muḍar. Perhaps it is the very pronunciation that was used by the Prophet. ʿAlid jurists made that claim. They thought that he who reads in the first *sûrah* the words "the straight path" (*aṣ-ṣirâṭa l-mustaqîma*) [1351] without pronouncing the *q* (in *al-mustaqîm*) as is done by (present-day) Arab Bedouins, commits an error, and his prayer is not valid.

I do not know how this (differentiation in the pronunciation of *q*) came about. The language of the urban population was not invented by the urban population itself, either. It was transmitted to them from their ancestors, most of whom belonged to the Muḍar, when they settled in the cities at the III, *304*
time of the (Muslim) conquest and later. The Arab Bedouins did not invent (their pronunciation of *q*), either. However, they had less contact with the non-Arab urban population. Therefore, the linguistic features found in their (speech) can preferably be assumed to belong to the language of their ancestors. In addition, all Arab Bedouins in the East and the West agree upon that (pronunciation of *q*). It is the peculiar characteristic that distinguishes the Arabs from half-breeds and sedentary people.

It [1352] is obvious that the pronunciation of *q* as practiced by (present-day) Arab Bedouins is the same as that of the ancient speakers (of Arabic). The place (where the sound) of *q* may be produced is wide, ranging from the soft palate to the place next to where *k* is articulated. The velar pronuncia-

1349 Cf. Bombaci, p. 468.

1350 The express reference to the Banû Kahlân is not found in Bulaq.

1351 Qur'ân 1.6 (5).

1352 The remainder of the section is not found in Bulaq. C has it on an inserted sheet.

tion is the urban one. The pronunciation close to *k* is that of (present-day) Arab Bedouins.

This fact refutes the statement of the 'Alids that failure to pronounce the *q* in the first *sûrah* (as it is pronounced by present-day Bedouins) invalidates one's prayer. All the jurists of the (great) cities hold the contrary opinion. It is improbable that all of them would have overlooked this (point). The matter is to be explained as we have stated it.

We do say (however) that the Arab Bedouins' pronunciation (of *q*) is preferable and more proper, because, as we have mentioned before, its continuity among them shows that it was the pronunciation of their early Arab-Bedouin ancestors and the pronunciation of the Prophet. The fact that they assimilate *q* to *k* (in pronunciation) because of the proximity of the places where the two sounds are articulated, also makes this (assumption) appear preferable. If it were pronounced far back, as a velar, as is done by the urban population, it
III, *305* would not be close to *k* in its place of articulation and would not be assimilated (to it).

Arab philologists have mentioned this *q* which is close to *k*, as pronounced by present-day Arab Bedouins. They consider it a sound intermediary between *q* and *k*, and an independent sound (phoneme). This is improbable. It is obvious that it is a *q* pronounced at the end of the wide range of articulation available for *q*, as we have stated. The (philologists) then openly denounced (that *q*) as an ugly, un-Arabic sound, as if they did not recognize that (the way in which it was pronounced) was the pronunciation of the early Arabs. As we have mentioned, it belonged to (Arab) linguistic tradition, because (the Arabs) inherited it from their ancestors, generation after generation, and it was their particular symbol. That is proof that (the way in which it is pronounced) was the pronunciation of the early Arabs and the pronunciation of the Prophet, as has all been mentioned before.

There is a theory that *q* as pronounced by the urban population does not belong to the (original) *q*-sound, but is the result of their contact with non-Arabs. They pronounce it as they do, but it is not an Arabic sound. However, our afore-mentioned statement that it is (all) one sound with a wide (range of) articulation is more appropriate.

This should be understood. God is the clear guide.

[47] *The language of the sedentary and urban population is an independent language different from the language of the Muḍar.*

It should be known that the usual form of address used among the urban and sedentary population is not the old Muḍar language nor the language of the (present-day) Arab Bedouins. It is another independent language, remote from the language of the Muḍar and from the language of present-day Arab Bedouins. It is more remote from the former (than from the latter). III, *306*

It is obvious that it is an independent language by itself. The fact is attested by the changes it shows, which grammatical scholarship[1353] considers solecisms. Moreover, it is different in the various cities depending on the differences in terminologies used by their (inhabitants).[1354] The language of the inhabitants of the East differs somewhat from that of the inhabitants of the West. The same applies to the relationship of the language of the Spaniards to either of them. All these people are able to express in their own language whatever they want to express, and to explain their ideas. That is what languages and dialects are for. Loss of the vowel endings does not disturb them, as we have stated in connection with the language of present-day Arab (Bedouins).[1355]

The fact that (the language spoken in present-day cities) is more remote from the ancient (Arabic) language than the language of present-day Arab Bedouins is conditioned by the fact that remoteness from the (ancient Arabic) language is due to contact with non-Arabs. More contact with non-Arabs

[1353] Bulaq, C, and D correct *'inda ṣinâ'at ahl an-naḥw* to the simpler *'inda ahl ṣinâ'at an-naḥw* "grammatical scholars."

[1354] Cf. p. 413, below.

[1355] Cf. pp. 344 and 347, above.

means greater remoteness from the original language. For, as we have stated, a (linguistic) habit results only from instruction, and the (new) habit is a mixture of the ancient (linguistic) habit of the Arabs and the later (acquired linguistic) habit of the non-Arabs.[1356] The longer people listen to non-Arab (speech) and the longer they are brought up in such a condition, the more remote from the ancient habit do they become.

In this connection, one may compare the cities of Ifrîqiyah, the Maghrib, Spain, and the East. In Ifrîqiyah and the Maghrib, the Arabs had contact with the non-Arab Berbers who constitute the bulk of the population (*'umrân*) of (those
III, *307* countries). Hardly any city or group was without (Berbers). Therefore, the non-Arab (element) there gained preponderance over the language of the Arabs. Thus, there originated another, mixed language in which the non-Arab (element) was preponderant, for the reasons mentioned. (The language spoken there) is more remote from the ancient language (than other dialects).

Likewise, in the East, the Arabs gained superiority over the Persian and Turkish nations there. They had contact with them. These languages circulated among them in (the speech of) farmers, peasants, and captives whom they used as servants, wet nurses, and foster mothers. Thus, their (linguistic) habit was corrupted. With that, their language (also was corrupted, and) eventually it came to be another language.

The same (happened to) the Spaniards in their relations with the non-Arab Galicians and European Christians. The entire urban population of those zones came to speak another language, one peculiar to them and different from the language of the Muḍar. It also showed (dialectical) differences within itself, as we are going to mention.[1357] In a way, it was another language (and no longer Arabic), in as much as the

[1356] Cf. p. 342, above.
[1357] Cf. p. 413, below.

habit of it became firmly rooted among those people (in Spain).

"God creates whatever He wishes." [1358]

[48] *Instruction in the Muḍar language.*

It should be known that the habit of the Muḍar language has disappeared and become corrupted at this time. All Arab Bedouins speak a language that differs from the Muḍar language in which the Qur'ân was revealed. It has become another language through the admixture of non-Arab elements, as we have stated before.[1359]

However, since languages are habits, as mentioned before,[1360] it is possible to learn them like any other habit. The [1361] obvious method of instruction for those who desire to obtain the habit of the ancient (Muḍar) language is to acquire III, 308
expert [1362] knowledge of the linguistic documents (written) in it, such as the Qur'ân, the traditions, the speeches in rhymed prose and verse of the ancients and of outstanding Arabs, as well as the statements of (early) men of mixed Arab and non-Arab parentage (*muwallad*) in all disciplines. Eventually, the student obtains expert knowledge of a great amount of such poetical and prose material. As a result, he is like a person who grew up among the (old speakers of Arabic) and learned from them how to express what he wants to express.[1363]

After that, he may try to express his own thoughts with the expressions and in the style they would have used and to follow their ways and word arrangement, of which he has, by now, an expert knowledge. His expert and practical use (of the material) gives him the habit of (the old language).

[1358] Qur'ân 3.47 (42); 5.17 (20); 24.45 (44); 28.68 (68); 30.54 (53); 42.49 (48).

[1359] Cf. the preceding section.

[1360] Cf. pp. 342 ff., above.

[1361] Cf. Issawi, p. 153.

[1362] *Ḥfẓ* "to memorize, to know by heart, to be an expert in."

[1363] Cf. p. 318 (n. 1231), above.

With the increase in (his knowledge and practical use of the material,[1364] his habit) becomes more firmly rooted and stronger.

In addition, the student needs a healthy disposition and a good understanding of the aspirations and ways of the Arabs in (their) word combinations and in (their) efforts that those word combinations should conform to the requirements of the given situation.[1365] Taste attests to the fact that (these things are needed by the student), for it originates as the result of the (existence of the proper linguistic)[1366] habit and of a healthy disposition, as we shall mention later on. The more the student knows by heart and the more he uses (the material), the better will his utterances in prose and verse turn out to be. The (student) who has obtained these (linguistic) habits knows the Muḍar language. He has a critical understanding of what constitutes good style (eloquence) in it.

This is how the (Muḍar language) must be studied. God "guides whomever He wants to guide."[1367]

III, 309 [49] *The habit of the (Muḍar) language is different from Arabic philology and can dispense with it in (the process of) instruction.*

The[1368] reason for this is that Arabic philology is merely a knowledge of the rules and forms of this habit. It is the knowledge of a quality,[1369] and not a quality itself. It is not the habit itself. Rather, it is comparable to a person who has a theoretical knowledge of a craft but does not know how to exercise it in practice. For instance, someone may know all about tailoring but not possess the habit of it. Such a person might explain some of the aspects of tailoring as follows: One introduces the thread into the eye of the needle; one inserts the needle into two pieces of material held together; one

[1364] *Wa-tazdâdu bi-kathratihâ* (= *bi-kathratihimâ*).
[1365] Cf., for instance, p. 333, above.
[1366] Cf. pp. 358 ff., below.
[1367] Qur'ân 2.142 (136), etc.
[1368] Cf. Issawi, pp. 151–53.
[1369] *Kayfîyah* "know-how."

brings it out on the other side at such-and-such a distance; returns it to (the side) where he started; brings it out in front of the place where it first went in, so that there is some room between the first two holes. In this way, the person might go on and describe the whole operation and give a description of how to use bands, to quilt, and to cut openings,[1370] along with all the other aspects and operations of tailoring. But if he were challenged to do something like the (things he talks about) with his own hands, he would in no way be able to.

Likewise, a person who knows about carpentry might be asked about splitting wood.[1371] He would say: One places the saw on top of a piece of wood; one person holds one end of the saw, and another person opposite him the other; the two alternately push and pull, and the sharp teeth of the saw cut the part of the piece of wood over which they pass back and
forth, until one gets through the bottom of the wood. If such III, *310*
a person were challenged actually to do it, or some part of it, he might not be able to.

The same applies to the relationship between knowledge of the rules governing the vowel endings and the (linguistic) habit itself. Knowledge of the rules is a knowledge of how to use them, but it is not the actual use of them. Therefore, we find that many outstanding grammarians and skilled Arab philologists who have a comprehensive knowledge of those rules make many mistakes and commit many solecisms when they are asked to write one or two lines to a colleague or friend, or to write a complaint concerning some injustice or anything else they might want to say. They cannot put (the words) together and express what they want to say in a way that corresponds to the ways of the Arabic language.

Likewise, we find many people who have a good (linguistic) habit and a good (ability to express themselves in) both prose and poetry, but cannot distinguish between the

[1370] Cf. 2:367, above.
[1371] Cf. 2:364, above.

vowel endings of subject and object, or nominative and genitive, and know nothing about the rules of Arabic philology. This shows that the (linguistic) habit is different from Arabic philology and can completely dispense with it.

We find that some scholars who are skilled in the vowel endings have a good knowledge of how it is with the (linguistic) habit. This, however, is rare and a matter of chance. It happens mostly to those (students) who have close contact with the *Book* of Sîbawayh.[1372] For Sîbawayh did not restrict himself to the rules governing the vowel endings, but filled his work with Arab proverbs and evidential Arab verses [1373] and expressions. Thus, his work contains a good deal of (the things that go with) teaching the (linguistic habit). Therefore, we find that the (students) who apply themselves diligently to (Sîbawayh's *Book*) and come to know it, learn a good deal of Arab speech (from it). Where, and according to what arrangement, (Arab speech) is prop-
III, *311* erly used becomes impressed in the (student's) memory and makes him aware of the importance of the (linguistic) habit, with the result that he is taught the habit in its entirety. Therefore, (Sîbawayh's *Book*) is more instructive (than any other work).[1374] (However,) some of the (students) who have contact with the *Book* of Sibawayh fail to realize this. Thus, they learn philology as a craft but do not obtain a (linguistic) habit.

Students who have close contact with the books of recent scholars that have nothing of the sort but deal only with grammatical rules and contain no Arab poems or (documents of) Arab speech, for this very reason are rarely conscious of (linguistic) habit or aware of its importance. One finds that they think they have gotten somewhere in knowledge of the

[1372] Cf. p. 323, above.

[1373] *Shawâhid* "evidential verses," usually by pre-Islamic or early Islamic poets, were used to illustrate a point of grammar or lexicography.

[1374] Bombaci, p. 468, follows a translation by Silvestre de Sacy: "They (the students) have tried to acquire it completely through study. Thus they have succeeded in being able to express better that which they want to express."

Arabic language. In fact, they are farther from it than anyone else.

The Arabic philologists and teachers of Arabic in Spain are closer to acquiring and teaching the (linguistic) habit than others. They use evidential Arab verses and proverbs in this connection and investigate a good deal of (Arabic) word combinations in the classroom. Thus, a good deal of (linguistic) habit comes to the beginners early in (their) instruction. (Their) souls are impressed by it and are prepared to obtain and accept it.

Other people, such as the inhabitants of the Maghrib and Ifrîqiyah and others, treated Arabic philology like any other research discipline. They did not tolerate investigations of the word combinations of Arab speech. They merely provided an evidential verse with the ending vowels, or decided in favor of one rule (against another), in accordance with theoretical requirements, and not in accordance with the usage and word combinations of the (Arabic) language. With them,[1375] Arabic philology thus came to be, in a way, one of the intellectual norms of logic and dialectics and (thereby) remote from the ways and habit of language.

Arabic philologists in these cities and their adjacent re- III, *312*
gions [1376] thus became totally estranged from the (linguistic) habit, and it was as if they had not studied the Arabic language (at all).[1377] The only reason was their aversion to investigating the evidential verses and word combinations and to making a discerning study of the methods of the (Arabic) language, as well as their disregard for the (necessity of) constant practice of those things by the student. In fact, (to investigate these things) is the best way to teach the habit of the (Arabic) language. The (grammatical) rules are merely means for purposes of instruction. However, (scholars) employed them as they were not intended to be employed, and caused them to become a purely scholarly disci-

1375 Added in C and D.
1376 C and D: "in those regions and the cities belonging to it."
1377 This sentence is not found in Bulaq.

pline.[1378] (Thus,) they were deprived of their (real) fruit.

Our remarks in this chapter show that the habit of the Arabic language can be obtained only through expert knowledge of the (documents of) Arab speech. Thereby, the imagination of (the student) will eventually have a picture of the loom on which the Arabs wove their word combinations, so that he can use it himself. Thus, he achieves the position of one who grew up with them and had close personal contact with the ways they expressed themselves in their speech and who, thus, eventually obtains the firm habit of expressing what he wants to express in the manner in which they would have said it.[1379]

God determines all affairs.

[50] *The interpretation and real meaning of the word "taste" according to the technical terminology of literary critics. An explanation of why Arabicized non-Arabs as a rule do not have it.*

It should be known that the word "taste" is in current use among those who are concerned with the various branches of
III, 313 literary criticism (*bayân*). It means the tongue's possession of the habit of eloquence. What eloquence is [1380] was explained above. It is the conformity of speech to the meaning (intended), in every aspect, (and this is achieved) by means of certain qualities that give this (conformity) to the word combinations. An eloquent speaker of the Arabic language chooses the form (of expression) that affords such (conformity) according to the methods and ways of Arab address. He arranges (his) speech along such lines so far as he is able. When he does this constantly in his use of Arabic speech, he gets the habit of arranging (his) speech along those lines. (The use of proper) word combinations becomes a simple

1378 Cf. Bombaci, p. 468.

1379 Cf. p. 318 (n. 1231), above.

1380 For *bayân* and *balâghah*, cf. pp. 335 f., above. For "taste" as a term of mysticism, cf. p. 79, above.

matter for him. In this respect he hardly ever swerves from the way of Arab eloquence. If he hears a word combination that is not along those lines, he spits it out, and his ear recoils from it upon the slightest reflection. Indeed, no reflection whatever (is needed, for his reaction is) the consequence of the (linguistic) habit he has obtained.

Habits [1381] that are firmly established and rooted in their proper places appear to be natural and innate in those places. Therefore, many ignorant people who are not acquainted with the importance of habits, think that the correct use of vowel endings and the proper eloquence of Arabs in their language are natural things. They say that "the Arabs speak (correct Arabic) by nature." [1382] This is not so. (Correct Arabic speech) is a linguistic habit of (proper) speech arrangement that has become firmly established and rooted (in speakers of Arabic), so that, superficially, it appears to be something natural and innate. However, as mentioned before,[1383] this habit results from the constant practice of Arabic speech and from repeated listening to it and from understanding the peculiar qualities of its word combinations. It is not obtained through knowledge of the scientific rules evolved by literary critics.[1384] Those rules merely afford a III, 314
knowledge of the (Arabic) language. They do not give (a person) possession of the actual habit in its proper place. This was mentioned before.

(Now,) if this is established, (we may say that it is) the tongue's habit of eloquence that guides an eloquent person toward the various aspects of (word) arrangement and toward use of the correct combinations (of words) corresponding to the word combinations and arrangement used by Arabs when they speak Arabic. When a person who possesses the (Arabic linguistic) habit attempts to deviate from the specific ways and the word combinations peculiar (to Arabic speech),

[1381] Cf. Issawi, pp. 154 f.
[1382] Cf. p. 343, above.
[1383] Cf. p. 342, above.
[1384] Bulaq: "philologists."

he is not able to do so. His tongue will not go along with him, because it is not used to (improper speech), and its firmly rooted habit will not let it use it. Should any (form of) speech that deviates from the method of the Arabs and the eloquence they use in arranging their speech occur to him, he would avoid it, spit it out, and know that it does not belong to the Arabic speech that he has assiduously practiced. He may often be unable to support his attitude by arguments, as the people who know the grammatical and stylistic rules can do. But such is a matter of argumentation with the help of inductively derived rules, whereas (correct use of the language) is something intuitive,[1385] resulting from the constant practice of Arabic speech until such time as (the person who practices it) comes to be like one of (the Arabs).

For comparison, let us assume an Arab child who grows up and is reared among Arab Bedouins.[1386] He learns their language and has a good knowledge of the vowel endings and of eloquent (Arabic) expression. He masters (all) that completely, but he does not have any knowledge whatever of grammatical rules. His (correctness and eloquence of speech) is purely the result of the linguistic habit he has obtained. In the same way, the (linguistic) habit may be acquired by those who live after the time of the (ancient) Arab Bedouins, with the help of expert knowledge of, and constant occupation with, (the documents of) their speech, their poems, and addresses. This will eventually give them the (linguistic)
III, *315* habit and make them like persons who grew up and were reared among them. The (grammatical) rules cannot do that.

This habit, if firmly rooted and established, is metaphorically called "taste," a technical term of literary criticism. "Taste" is (conventionally) used for the sensation caused by food. But, since the (linguistic) habit is located in the tongue, which is the seat of speech as it is the seat of the sensation caused by food, the name of "taste" is metaphorically used for it. Furthermore, it is something intuitively observed by

[1385] Cf. 1:198 (n. 277), above.
[1386] Cf. p. 318 (n. 1231), above.

the tongue, just as food is something sensually perceived by it. Therefore, it is called "taste."

If this is clear, it will make one realize that non-Arabs, such as Persians, Byzantines, and Turks in the East, and Berbers in the West, who are strangers to the Arabic language and adopt it and are forced to speak it as the result of contact with the Arabs, do not possess such taste. They have too small a share in the (linguistic) habit the significance of which we have established. They formerly had another linguistic habit—their own language—and part of their lives had gone by (before they got to know Arabic). Now, the most they can do is to occupy themselves with the individual words and word combinations in current use in the conversation of the (Muslim) urban population in their midst and which they are forced to use.

The (ancient Arabic linguistic) habit is lost to the urban population, and they are strangers to it, as mentioned before.[1387] They have another linguistic habit, which is not the desired linguistic habit (of the Arabs). Those who know the (Arabic linguistic) habit (merely) from rules codified in
books are in no way in the possession of (that) habit. They III, *316*
merely know the laws governing it, as one knows (now after our preceding discussion). The (linguistic) habit can be obtained only through constant practice, becoming accustomed to Arab speech, and repeatedly (using and listening to) it.

One may hear it said that Sîbawayh, al-Fârisî, az-Zamakhsharî, and other authorities on Arab speech were non-Arabs and yet possessed the (Arab linguistic) habit.[1388] Then one should realize that these people one hears about were non-Arab only by descent. They grew up and were reared among Arabs who possessed the (Arabic linguistic) habit, or among people who had learned it from them. Thus, they were able to master (Arabic) speech to a degree that cannot be surpassed. In a way, in their early childhoods they were in the position of Arab children who grow up among Arab

[1387] Cf. pp. 351 f., above.
[1388] Cf. pp. 313 and 319, above.

Bedouins and thus achieve a knowledge of all the finesses of the language and become speakers of (pure) Arabic.[1389] Although these (scholars) were non-Arab by descent, they were not non-Arabs as far as language and speech are concerned, because they lived in a time when Islam was in its prime and the Arabic language in its young manhood. The (linguistic) habit had not yet entirely disappeared, not even among the urban population. They assiduously devoted themselves to the constant study and practice of Arab speech. Eventually, they mastered it completely.

(However,) nowadays, when a non-Arab has contact with Arabic speakers in the cities, the first thing he finds is that the desired Arabic linguistic habit is completely gone, and he finds that the (linguistic) habit peculiar to them is another one and different from the Arabic linguistic habit. Assuming
III, *317* that he proceeds with persistence to study and memorize the speech and poems of the Arabs, in order to obtain the (linguistic habit), still, he will rarely be successful, because, as mentioned before,[1390] a habit the place of which was originally taken by another habit, will be defective and mutilated. Assuming (further) that he is non-Arab by descent but has had no contact whatever with a non-Arabic language, and that he now sets out to learn the (Arabic linguistic) habit through memorizing and studying, he may occasionally be successful. This, however, is rare, a fact about which the previous remarks will have left no doubt.

Those who have studied the stylistic norms (of Arabic) occasionally claim that they have given them the "taste" (of the Arabic language). This, (however,) is an error and a deception. If they have obtained any habit, it is the habit of the stylistic norms. That habit has nothing whatever to do with the habit of (linguistic) expression.

God "guides whomever He wants to guide to a straight path." [1391]

[1389] Cf. p. 318 (n. 1231), above.
[1390] Cf. 2:354 f., above.
[1391] Qur'ân 2.142 (136), etc.

[51] *The urban population is in general deficient in obtaining the linguistic habit that results from instruction. The more remote urban people are from the Arabic language, the more difficult*[1392] *it is for them to obtain it.*

The reason for this is that the student has previously obtained a habit incompatible with the desired (Arabic linguistic) habit, since he has grown up speaking the sedentary language, which was influenced by non-Arab (speech) to such a degree that, eventually, the original habit of the (Arabic) language was replaced by another. This (other habit) is the language of the present-day sedentary population.

Therefore, we find that teachers (attempt to) teach chil- III, *318*
dren the (Arabic) language[1393] first. The grammarians think that this is done through grammar. But this is not so. It is done through teaching them the (linguistic) habit through direct contact with the (Arabic) language and Arab speech. It is true that grammar comes closer (than anything else) to bringing about contact with those (things).

The more firmly rooted in non-Arab (speech habits) an urban language is and the more remote it is from the language of the Muḍar, the less able are its speakers to learn the language of the Muḍar and to obtain the habit of it. In such cases, the forces that are incompatible with (acquisition of the habit of the Muḍar language) are firmly entrenched.

One may compare the inhabitants of the various regions. The inhabitants of Ifrîqiyah and the Maghrib were more firmly rooted in non-Arab (speech habits) and more remote from the ancient language (than other Arabic speakers). Thus, they were altogether deficient in obtaining the habit of (the ancient language) through instruction. Ibn ar-Raqîq[1394] tells the story of a secretary in al-Qayrawân who wrote to a colleague of his: "O my friend and whose loss I may indeed

[1392] Bulaq adds: "and the harder."
[1393] The correct text in Bulaq, C, and D.
[1394] Cf. 1:9, above.

be denied, Abû Sa'îd taught me word that you had been mentioning that we was to be with those who was to come,[1395] but it hindered us today, and it was not possible for us to go out. The people of (my) house, those dogs, concerning the straw [1396] lied this falsely; there is not a single letter of that (true). I am writing to you. I am missing you."

Such was the habit of the Muḍar language that those (people possessed). The facts we have mentioned explain why.

Likewise, their poems did not show the (correct lin-
III, 319 guistic) habit and were inferior. This has continued to be so to this time. There have been no famous poets in Ifrîqiyah, except for Ibn Rashîq and Ibn Sharaf.[1397] Most of the poets there have been recent immigrants. Down to this day, their eloquence has inclined to the inferior.

The Spaniards came closer to obtaining the (linguistic) habit (than the people of Ifrîqiyah), because they were greatly interested in it and saturated with poetry and prose they had memorized. They had the historian Ibn Ḥayyân [1398] as their leading craftsman in matters of language and standard-bearer of the (Arabic linguistic) habit. They also had Ibn 'Abdrabbih,[1399] al-Qasṭallî,[1400] and other poets in the (time of the) *reyes de taïfas*. Language and literature flourished in (Spain). They were cultivated there for hundreds of years, down to the time of the dispersion and exile when the Christians gained the upper hand. Thereafter, the (Spaniards) had no leisure to occupy themselves with such things. Civili-

1395 Ibn Khaldûn read: "that you were to come with the oil." But, utilizing a slight correction suggested in Bulaq, we might perhaps read: *annak nakun ma'a lladhîn na'tî*. This would make much better sense and be quite in keeping with the barbaric distortion of Arabic that the author invented for the entertainment of his readers.

1396 Again, Bulaq may be justified in correcting *at-tibn* to *ash-shayn*, which would mean "those dogs of nastiness," or something of the sort.

1397 Cf. 1:10 and 316, above.

1398 Cf. 1:8 f., above.

1399 Cf. 1:32, above.

1400 Aḥmad b. Muḥammad, Ibn Darrâj, from Qasṭallat Darrâj (Cacella in Portugal), who died *ca.* 1030. Cf. *GAL, Suppl.*, I, 478; E. Lévi-Provençal, *La Péninsule Ibérique* (Leiden, 1938), p. 192; Ibn Bassâm, *Dhakhîrah* (Cairo, 1358/1939), I 1, 43 ff.

zation decreased. As a result, (language and literature) decreased, as is the case with all crafts (under such conditions). The (linguistic) habit among (Spaniards) was then no longer adequate to its purpose. Eventually, it sank to the lowest point. Among the last (of the Spanish littérateurs) were Ṣâliḥ b. Sharîf [1401] and Mâlik b. al-Muraḥḥal [1402] (who was) a pupil of the Sevillian community in Ceuta, when [1403] the dynasty of the Banû al-Aḥmar (the Naṣrids of Granada) was just beginning. Spain (at that time) sent its most treasured (children and best) speakers of Arabic into exile on the (African) shore. From Sevilla, they went to Ceuta, and from eastern Spain to Ifrîqiyah. But soon, their time was up. The tradition of teaching Arabic philology as cultivated by them, came to an end. (Arabic) was too hard and difficult for (the people of) the (African) shore to learn. Their tongues were III, 320 too twisted, and they were too firmly rooted in non-Arabic Berber (speech habits), which are incompatible with (the Arabic linguistic habit) for the reasons we have stated.

Afterwards, the (Arabic linguistic) habit came to exist again in Spain, as it had been before. There appeared there Ibn Shibrîn,[1404] Ibn Jâbir,[1405] Ibn al-Jayyâb,[1406] and (other men

[1401] Ṣâliḥ b. Yazîd, 601–684 [1204–1285/86]. Cf. Ibn al-Khaṭîb, *al-Iḥâṭah*, as quoted by M. Casiri, *Bibliotheca Arabico-Hispana Escurialensis* (Madrid, 1760–70), II, 97.

[1402] Mâlik b. ʻAbd-ar-Raḥmân, 604–699 [1207/8–1299/1300]. Cf. *GAL*, I, 274; *Suppl.*, I, 484; 2d ed., I, 323 f.

[1403] Bulaq, A, and B have *wa-kuttâb* instead of *wa-kânat*, which we find in C (by correction?) and D. Actually, Ibn Khaldûn's earlier text may have been the more correct one. It would mean: "who were pupils of the Sevillian community in Ceuta and who had been secretaries [pl. used instead of the dual] at the beginning of the dynasty of Ibn al-Aḥmar." It depends on whether this statement is factually correct, something I am not prepared definitely to assert. "Community," lit. "class," means, specifically, the community of poets and littérateurs.

[1404] Muḥammad b. Aḥmad, 674–747 [1276–1346]. Cf. Ibn al-Khaṭîb, *al-Iḥâṭah*, II, 174 ff.; Ibn Ḥajar, *ad-Durar al-kâminah*, III, 349 f. The form Shibrîn is thus indicated in C. The sources quoted print Shîrin. The edition by an-Nubâhî, *Kitâb al-Marqabah al-ʻulyâ* (Cairo, 1948), p. 153, vocalizes Shabrîn.

[1405] He would seem to be Muḥammad b. Aḥmad b. ʻAlî, 698–780 [1298/99–1378]. Cf. *GAL*, II, 13 f.; *Suppl.*, II, 6, although he is younger than the men with whom he is mentioned.

[1406] ʻAlî b. Muḥammad, 673–749 [1274–1349]. Cf. *GAL*, *Suppl.*, II, 369.

of) their class. After them came Ibrâhîm as-Sâḥilî aṭ-Ṭuwayjin[1407] and (other men of) his class. They were followed by Ibn al-Khaṭîb,[1408] who recently died a martyr's death as the result of denunciation by his enemies. He possessed an unequaled linguistic habit. His pupils followed in his footsteps.

In general, the (Arabic linguistic) habit plays a greater role in Spain, and instruction in it is simpler and easier (there than elsewhere), because the (Spaniards) are nowadays greatly interested in, and concerned with, philology and literature and the teaching tradition in those (subjects), as we have mentioned before.[1409] Also, non-Arabic speakers with a corrupt (linguistic) habit are only recent immigrants in (Spain), and non-Arabic (speech habits) are not the basis of the language of the Spaniards.

(On the other hand,) the Berbers on the (African) shore constitute the (native) inhabitants of the region. Their language is the language (of the country), except in the cities. (The language there) is entirely submerged in the non-Arab native idiom of the Berbers. It is difficult for them, therefore, in contrast to the Spaniards, to obtain the (Arabic) linguistic habit through instruction.

The situation (of the people) of the East at the time of the Umayyad and 'Abbâsid dynasties was the same as we find it in Spain, with reference to the perfection and refinement of their (linguistic) habit. At that time, apart from rare cases, they were remote from contact with non-Arabs. Therefore, the (linguistic) habit was at that time more firmly entrenched (than at any other time). Excellent poets and secretaries existed in abundant numbers, because the number of Arabs
III, *321* and their descendants was abundant in the East. Glance (in this connection) at the poems and prose texts of the *Kitâb al-*

1407 Ibrâhîm b. Muḥammad, d. 747 [1346]. Cf. Ibn Ḥajar, *ad-Durar al-kâminah*, I, 54, who has the wrong date 739 [1338/39]; al-Maqqarî, *Analectes*, ed. R. Dozy *et al.* (Leiden, 1855–61), I, 589 f., 910 f.; as-Suyûṭî, *Bughyah* (Cairo, 1326/1908), p. 189.

1408 Cf. 1:xliv and xlix, above.

1409 Cf. p. 303, above.

Aghânî. It is the book and archive of the Arabs.[1410] It deals with their language, their history, their battle days, the Arab religious organization and the biography of their Prophet,[1411] the remarkable deeds of their caliphs and rulers, their poems and songs, and all the other conditions (of the Arabs).[1412] There is no book that gives more complete information about the conditions of the Arabs.[1413]

During the rule of the (Umayyaḍ and 'Abbâsid) dynasties, the (linguistic) habit remained firmly established in the East. (Poets and littérateurs of that period) were often superior to the pre-Islamic (poets and littérateurs) with regard to (their linguistic habit), as we shall mention later on.[1414] Eventually, however, the Arabs lost power. Their language was wiped out. Their speech was corrupted. Their power and dynasties came to an end. The non-Arabs seized power. They gained royal authority and superiority. This happened under the dynasty of the Daylam and the Saljûqs. They had contact with the urban population and [1415] exceeded them in number. The earth came to be full of their languages, and non-Arab (speech habits) gained power over the urban and sedentary population. Eventually, people came to be remote from the Arabic language and the habit of it. Those who studied it were not able to obtain it. This we find to be the condition in which their language finds itself today. It affects both their prose and poetry, even if much is being produced by them in (both fields).

God "creates whatever He wishes, and His is the choice." [1416]

[1410] Cf. p. 304 (n. 1186), above.

[1411] Bulaq corrects "the biography of their Prophet" to "their ways of life," in order to be closer to the actual situation.

[1412] The older texts have *ma'ânîhim lahum* (Bulaq *maghânîhim lahû*), which seems to mean "and all their other interests."

[1413] Cf. p. 341, above, and p. 383, below.

[1414] Cf. pp. 396 f., below.

[1415] The text from here to "urban and" (l. 21) is found in C in the margin and in the text of D. We have here an interesting example, not of homoeoteleuton omission (in the older texts), but of a homoeoteleuton addition by the author at a later stage.

[1416] Qur'ân 28.68 (68).

III, 322 [52] *The division of speech into poetry and prose.*

It should be known that the Arabic language and Arab speech are divided into two branches. (One of them) is rhymed poetry. It is speech with meter and rhyme, which means that every line of it ends upon a definite letter, which is called the "rhyme." The other branch is prose, that is, non-metrical speech.

Each of the two branches comprises various subbranches and ways of speech. Poetry comprises laudatory and heroic [1417] poems and elegies (upon the dead). Prose may be rhymed prose. Rhymed prose consists of cola ending on the same rhyme throughout,[1418] or of sentences rhymed in pairs. This is called "rhymed prose" (*saj'*). Prose may also be "straight prose" (*murassal*). In (straight prose), the speech goes on and is not divided into cola, but is continued straight through without any divisions, either of rhyme or of anything else. (Prose) is employed in sermons and prayers and in speeches intended to encourage or frighten the masses.[1419]

The Qur'ân is in prose. However, it does not belong in either of the two categories. It can neither be called straight prose nor rhymed prose. It is divided into verses. One reaches breaks where taste tells one that the speech stops. It is then resumed and "repeated" in the next verse. (Rhyme) letters which would make that (type of speech) rhymed prose are not obligatory, nor do rhymes (as used in poetry) occur. This (situation) is what is meant by the verse of the Qur'ân: "God revealed the best story, a book harmoniously arranged with repeated verses (*mathâniya*). It raises goose pimples on the skin of those who fear their Lord." [1420] God
III, 323 also said: "We have divided the verses." [1421] That is why the

[1417] Bulaq: "satirical." Cf. Bombaci, p. 468.

[1418] "On the same . . . or" is added in the margin of C, and in D.

[1419] This is one of the purposes of rhetoric as defined in Aristotelian tradition. Cf. 1:78, above, and p. 370, below.

[1420] Qur'ân 39.23 (24).

[1421] Qur'ân 6.97 (97), 98 (98), 126 (126). In the context, the verse means: "We have explained the signs."

ends of the individual verses are called "dividers" (*fawâṣil*). They are not really rhymed prose, since the (rhyme) which is obligatory in rhymed prose is not obligatory in them, nor are there rhymes as in poetry. The name "repeated verses" (*mathânî*) is generally used for all the verses of the Qur'ân, for the reasons mentioned. It is used in particular for the first *sûrah*, because of the prominence (of repeated verses) in it, just as the (general) word "star" is used for the Pleiades. Therefore, the (first *sûrah*) was called "the seven repeated (verses)." [1422] One may compare what the Qur'ân commentators have said in explanation of the fact that the first *sûrah* is called "the repeated (verses)." One will find that our explanation deserves the preference.

It should be known that each of these branches of poetry [1423] has its own particular methods, which are considered peculiar to it by the people who cultivate that branch and which do not apply to any other (branch) and cannot be employed for it. For instance, there is the *nasîb*,[1424] which is restricted to poetry. There are the praise of God and prayer (*du'â'*), which are restricted to sermons, and there are the formulas of blessing (*du'â'*), which are restricted to addresses, and so on.

Recent authors employ the methods and ways [1425] of poetry in writing prose. (Their writing) contains a great deal of rhymed prose and obligatory rhymes as well as the use of the *nasîb* before the authors say what they want to say. When one examines such prose, (one gets the impression that) it has actually become a kind of poetry. It differs from poetry only through the absence of meter. In recent times, secretaries took this up and employed it in government correspondence. They restricted all prose writing to this type, which they liked. They mixed up (all the different)

[1422] Cf. Qur'ân 15.87 (87). Cf. J. Horovitz, *Koranische Untersuchungen* (Berlin & Leipzig, 1926), pp. 26 f.

[1423] "Of poetry" is added in C and D.

[1424] The erotic part at the beginning of a poem. Cf. I. Lichtenstädter, "Das Nasîb der altarabischen Qaṣîde," *Islamica*, V (1931), 17 ff., and in *EI*, *s.v.*

[1425] Bulaq corrects to "meters."

methods in it. They avoided straight prose and affected to forget it, especially the people of the East. At the hand of stupid secretaries, present-day government correspondence
III, 324 is handled in the way described. From the point of view of good style (*balâghah*), it is not correct, since (in good style) one looks for conformity between what is said and the requirements of the given situations in which the speaker and the person addressed find themselves.[1426] In recent times, secretaries introduced the methods of poetry into this type of prose-with-rhyme. However, it is necessary that government correspondence be kept free from it. The methods of poetry admit wittiness, the mixture of humor with seriousness, long descriptions, and the free use of proverbs, as well as frequent similes and metaphoric expressions, (even) where none of these are required in (ordinary) address. The (constant) obligatory use of rhyme is also something witty and ornamental. All of this is quite incompatible with the dignity of royal and governmental authority and with the task of encouraging or frightening the masses [1427] in the name of the ruler. In government correspondence, what deserves praise is the use of straight prose—that is, straightforward speech with only a very occasional use of rhymed prose in places where (sound linguistic) habit can use rhymed prose in an unforced manner—and (forms of) speech that conform properly to the requirements of a given situation.[1428] The (existing) situations are always different. Each situation has its peculiar method (of expression. A situation may require) lengthiness or brevity, ellipsis or assertion, directness or allusion, the use of metonymy or metaphors.

Government correspondence done in the (aforementioned) way, that is, in a method proper to poetry, deserves censure. The only reason why (our) contemporaries do it is the fact that non-Arab (speech habits) exercise a firm hold
III, 325 over their tongues, and, as a result, they are unable to give

[1426] Cf., for instance, pp. 333 and 354, above.
[1427] Cf. p. 368, above.
[1428] Cf. p. 340 (n. 1317), above.

their speech its proper measure of conformity with the requirements of a given situation. Thus, they are unable to use straight speech. It is a difficult task and (takes) long effort to achieve eloquence in it. They eagerly use the type of rhymed prose (mentioned), in this way covering up their inability to make their speech conform to the things they want to say and to the requirements of the particular situation (with which they deal). They make up for their (inability in this respect) by greatly embellishing (their speech) with rhymed prose and rhetorical figures (*alqâb*).[1429] They neglect everything else.

Present-day secretaries and poets in the East use this method most and apply it in an exaggerated manner to all kinds of speech. They go so far as to tamper with the vowel endings and inflections of words when it happens to them that these conflict [1430] with some paronomasia or antithesis (that they want to use). In such a case, they give preference to the paronomasia and pay no attention to the (correct) vowel ending, (preferring to) corrupt the form of the word so that it might fit the paronomasia.

When this matter is studied critically from the point of view of our preceding remarks, it will be seen that our remarks are correct.

God gives success.

[53] *The ability to write both good poetry and good prose is only very rarely found together in one person.*

The reason for this is that, as we have explained, it [1431] is a habit (located) in the tongue. If another habit previously occupied the place of (that habit), the subsequent habit has

[1429] Cf. n. 1308 to this chapter, above.

[1430] *Yasa'âni*, as clearly indicated in B and C.

[1431] "It" means, literally, "the problem under consideration," and refers to speech in general. Cf. pp. 318, 321, and 342, above. Though Ibn Khaldûn may occasionally use the expression "poetical habit," he does not distinguish between the habits of poetry and prose in this section. Indeed, the thesis announced in the heading is not discussed at all.

III, *326* not enough room to develop, because the acceptance and obtainment of habits is simpler and easier for natures in their original state. If there are other previous habits, they resist the (new habit) in the substance that is to receive the (new habit). They prevent it from being quickly accepted. Thus, there arises incompatibility. It becomes impossible for the (new) habit to develop (to perfection). This is, in general, the case with all technical habits. We have proved that fact in the proper place with an argument similar to the one used here.[1432]

The same applies to languages. They are habits of the tongue which are in the same position as the crafts. It can be observed how persons with some previous non-Arab (speech habits) are always deficient in (their knowledge of) the Arabic language.[1433] Non-Arabs who previously spoke Persian cannot master the Arabic linguistic habit and will always be deficient in Arabic, even though they may study and (come to) know it. The same is the case with Berbers, Byzantines, and European Christians. One rarely finds among them any one who possesses a good Arabic linguistic habit. The only reason here is that their tongues previously had the habit of another language. This goes so far that a student whose native language is one of the (non-Arabic) languages, but who studies (his subjects) among Arabic speaking people and from Arabic books,[1434] will never be perfect in his knowledge and attainments. The only reason is the language.

It was mentioned before that languages and dialects are similar to the crafts.[1435] It was also mentioned before that the crafts and the habits of them do not come together in groups.
III, *327* Persons who previously had some good habit [1436] are rarely able to become skilled in another or to master it completely.

"God created you and whatever you do." [1437]

[1432] Cf. 2:354 f., above.
[1433] Cf. pp. 315 ff., above.
[1434] Not in Bulaq.
[1435] Cf. p. 342, above.
[1436] Bulaq: "craft."
[1437] Qur'ân 37.96 (94).

[54] *The craft of poetry and the way of learning it.*

This discipline is one of the disciplines connected with Arab speech. (The Arabs) call it "poetry" (*shi'r*). It exists in all the other languages. Here, however, we speak only about Arabic poetry. It is possible that the speakers of other languages, too, find in (poetry) the things they desire to express in their speech.[1438] However, each language has its own particular laws concerning eloquence.[1439]

(Poetry) in the Arabic language is remarkable in (its) manner and powerful in (its) way. It is speech that is divided into cola having the same meter and held together by the last letter of each colon. Each of those cola is called a "verse." The last letter, which all the verses (of a poem) have in common, is called the "rhyme letter." The whole complex is called a "poem" (*qaṣîdah* or *kalimah*). Each verse, with its combinations of words, is by itself a meaningful unit. In a way, it is a statement by itself, and independent of what precedes and what follows. By itself it makes perfect sense, either as a laudatory or an erotic (statement), or as an elegy. It is the intention of the poet to give each verse an independent meaning. Then, in the next verse, he starts anew, in the same way, with some other (matter). He changes over from one (poetical) type to another, and from one topic to another, by preparing the first topic and the ideas expressing it in such a way that it becomes related to the next topic. Sharp contrasts III, *328*
are kept out of the poem. The poet thus continuously changes over from the erotic to the laudatory (verses). From a description of the desert and the traces of abandoned camps, he changes over to a description of camels on the march, or

[1438] The text found in Bulaq, A, and B (*fîhi . . . maqṣûdahum min kalâmihim*) is better than that in C and D, which has *fîhi* crossed out and reads *kalâminâ* instead of *kalâmihim*, which makes no sense.

[1439] Thus, as some people really believe (cf. p. 382, below), poetry may not exist in other languages than Arabic. Ibn Khaldûn does not himself believe this; cf. p. 382 and, especially, pp. 412 f. Still, it is hardly correct to suggest, as Bombaci does (p. 469), that Ibn Khaldûn is here saying that he is justified in restricting the discussion to Arabic poetry because of the different character of poetic expression in other languages.

horses, or apparitions (of the beloved in a dream). From a description of the person to be praised, he changes over to a description of his people and his army. From (an expression of) grief and condolence in elegies, he changes over to praise of the deceased, and so on. Attention is paid to retaining the same meter throughout the whole poem, in order to avoid one's natural inclination to pass from one meter to another, similar one. Since (the meters) are similar (to each other), many people do not notice (the need to retain the same meter).

The meters are governed by certain conditions and rules. They are the subject of the science of prosody. Not every meter that may occur in nature was used by the Arabs in poetry. The (meters used) are special ones called meters (*buḥûr*) by the prosodists, who restricted their number to fifteen, indicating that they did not find the Arabs using other natural meters in poetry.

It should be known that the Arabs thought highly of poetry as a form of speech. Therefore, they made it the archive of their sciences and their history,[1440] the evidence for what they considered right and wrong, and the principle basis of reference for most of their sciences and wisdom. The poetical habit was firmly established in them, like all their other habits. The (Arabic) linguistic habits can be acquired only through technical (skill) and (constant) practice of (Arab) speech. Eventually, some sign [1441] of the (poetical) habit may be obtained.

Of the forms of speech, poetry is a difficult thing for
III, 329 modern people to learn, if they want to acquire the habit of it through (study of it as) a technique. Each verse is an independent statement of meaning suitable for (quotation) by

[1440] Cf. p. 304 (n. 1186), above.

[1441] De Slane thinks of *shubah* "doubts (as to the technical character of the Arab poet's poetical habits)," and Bombaci, p. 469, suggests *shibh* "a semblance." C and D suggest the reading *shabahun*. However, a derivation from the root *sh-b-h* seems hardly possible. Therefore it may be suggested that Ibn Khaldûn originally wrote *shiyatun* "mark, marking, detail." He used the word also above, 1:371, l. 10, and 2:73 (n. 611).

itself. It requires a kind of refinement of the (poetical) habit, for the (poet) to be able to pour poetical speech into molds suitable to this tendency of Arabic poetry (to have verses that are units by themselves). A poet must produce (a verse that) stands alone, and then make another verse in the same way, and again another, and thus go through all the different topics suitable to the thing he wants to express. Then, he establishes harmony among the verses as they follow upon each other in accordance with the different topics occurring in the poem.

(Poetry) is difficult in its tendency and strange in its subject matter. Therefore, it constitutes a severe test of a person's natural talent, if he wants to have a good knowledge of (poetical) methods.[1442] (The desire) to press speech into the molds of (poetry) sharpens the mind. (Possession of) the Arabic linguistic habit in general does not suffice. In particular, a certain refinement is needed, as well as the exercise of a certain skill in observing the special poetic methods which the Arabs used.

Let us mention the significance of (the word) "method" (*uslûb*) as used by (poets), and what they mean by it.[1443]

It should be known that they use it to express the loom on which word combinations are woven, or the mold into which they are packed.[1444] It is not used to express the basis (upon which) the meaning (of a statement rests). That is the task of the vowel endings. It also is not used for perfect expression of the idea resulting from the particular word combination used. That is the task of eloquence and style (*bayân*).[1445] It also is not used in the sense of meter, as em- III, *330*
ployed by the Arabs in (connection with poetry). That is the task of prosody. These three sciences fall outside the craft of poetry.

[1442] Cf. Bombaci, p. 469.

[1443] The discussion of *uslûb* continues down to p. 381.

[1444] The metaphors of mold and loom are repeated again and again in the following pages. The metaphor of the loom, in particular, is common in Arabic.

[1445] Cf. p. 335, above.

(Poetical method) is used to refer to a mental form for metrical word combinations which is universal in the sense of conforming with any [1446] particular word combination. This form is abstracted by the mind from the most prominent individual word combinations and given a place in the imagination comparable to a mold or loom. Word combinations that the Arabs consider sound, in the sense of having the (correct) vowel endings and the (proper) style, are then selected and packed by (the mind) into (that form), just as the builder does with the mold, or the weaver with the loom. Eventually, the mold is sufficiently widened to admit the word combinations that fully express what one wants to express. It takes on the form that is sound in the sense (that it corresponds to) the Arabic linguistic habit.

Each branch of (poetical) speech has methods peculiar to it and existing in it in different ways. Thus, in poetry the subject of inquiring after the traces of abandoned camps is treated in the form of direct address. For instance:

O house of Mayyah on the height, and the cliff.[1447]

Or, it is treated in the form of inviting one's (traveling) companions to stop and inquire. For instance:

Stop you two, and let us inquire about the house whose inhabitants left so suddenly.[1448]

Or, it is treated in the form of asking one's (traveling) companions to weep for the abandoned camp. For instance:

Stop you two, and let us weep in remembrance of a beloved and an encampment.[1449]

[1446] "Any" (*kull*) is added in the margin of C and in the text of D.

[1447] A verse by an-Nâbighah adh-Dhubyânî. Cf. pp. 397 and 410, below. Cf. H. Derenbourg in *Journal asiatique*, XII6 (1868), 301. Ibn Khaldûn certainly did not collect these verses by himself but derived them from an older work that remains to be determined.

[1448] I have not so far succeeded in identifying the author of this verse. Doubtless he is a very famous poet, like the others quoted here.

[1449] A verse by Imru'u-l-Qays, from the beginning of his famous *mu'allaqah*. Cf. p. 410, below.

Or, it is treated in the form of asking about the answer given to an unspecified addressee. For instance:

Did you not ask, and the traces informed you?[1450] III, *331*

Or, for instance, the traces of abandoned camps are greeted by commanding an unspecified addressee to greet them. For instance:

Greet the houses near al-'Azl.[1451]

Or, (they are greeted) in the form of praying for rain for them. For instance:

Let a pouring rain water the traces of their abandoned camps,
And let them be covered by luxuriant verdure.[1452]

Or, (they are greeted) in the form of asking the lightning to give them rain. For instance:

O lightning, look out over an encampment in al-Abraq
And drive the clouds there, just as she-camels are driven.[1453]

Or, for instance, in an elegy grief is expressed in the form of asking (people) to weep. For instance:

So be it. Let the matter be described and treated as an odious one.
There is no excuse for an eye whose tears are not shed.[1454]

Or, (it is expressed) in the form of stressing the importance of the happening. For instance:

1450 The author of this verse is still unidentified. Cf. n. 1448, above.

1451 Another verse by Imru'u-l-Qays, which is quoted by the geographers under *al-'Azl.*

The word "houses" does not fit the meter. The original text has "litters." Cf. the poet's *Dîwân*, ed. and tr. W. M. de Slane (Paris, 1837), p. 47 (text), p. 70 (tr.).

1452 A verse by Abû Tammâm. Cf. *Kitâb al-Aghânî* (Bulaq, 1285/1868), XV, 105.

1453 Another verse by Abû Tammâm. Cf. his *Dîwân* (Beirut, n.d.), p. 211.

1454 Another verse by Abû Tammâm. Cf. *Kitâb al-Aghânî,* IX, 98; XV, 107.

Did you see whom they carried by on wooden boards?
Did you see how the light of the (tribal) council went out?[1455]

Or, (it is expressed) in the form of stating that (all) created things are destined to misfortune because of the loss (of the mourned person). For instance:

Verdant pastures! (You have) no protector and guardian.
Death took away the (warrior) with the long lance and the great power.[1456]

Or, (it is expressed) in the form of expressing disapproval of the lifeless objects that show no grief, as in the verse of the Khârijite (poetess):

III, *332* O trees of the Khâbûr! What is the matter with you that you are green,
As if you were feeling no grief for Ibn Ṭarîf.[1457]

Or, (it is expressed) in the form of congratulating the adversary of (the deceased), that he can now rest from the force of (the deceased's) onslaught. For instance:

Rabî'ah b. Nizâr, lay down (your) lances.
Death took away your adversary, who was always going on raids.[1458]

There are many similar things in all branches and ways of (poetical) speech.

Word combinations in (poetry) may or may not be sentences. They may be commands or statements, nominal sentences or verbal sentences, followed by appositions or not fol-

[1455] This is a verse by ash-Sharîf ar-Raḍî. Cf. his *Dîwân* (Baghdad, 1306/1889), p. 155.

[1456] *Ibid.*, p. 267.

[1457] A frequently quoted verse by al-Fâri'ah bint Ṭarîf, from the elegy in which she mourned her brother al-Walîd b. Ṭarîf, who was killed by Yazîd b. Mazyad, a general under Hârûn ar-Rashîd. Cf. Ibn 'Abdrabbih, *'Iqd* (Cairo, 1305/1887), II, 19; *Kitâb al-Aghânî*, XI, 8 ff., quoted in T. Nöldeke and A. Müller, *Delectus carminum Arabicorum* (Berlin, 1890; repr. 1933), p. 93; ad-Dimashqî, *al-Ishârah ilâ maḥâsin at-tijârah*, tr. H. Ritter in *Der Islam*, VII (1917), 61. Ibn Khaldûn quotes the verse again, *'Ibar*, III, 169.

[1458] Ash-Sharîf ar-Raḍî, *Dîwân*, p. 207.

lowed by appositions, separate or connected, as is the case with the word combinations of Arabic speech and [1459] the position of individual words in respect to each other. This teaches a person the universal mold which he can learn through (constant) practice in Arabic poetry. (This universal mold) is an abstraction in the mind derived from specific word combinations, to all of which the (universal) mold conforms. The [1460] author of a spoken utterance is like a builder or weaver. The proper mental form is like the mold used in building, or the loom used in weaving. The builder who abandons his mold, or the weaver who abandons his loom, is unsuccessful.

It should not be said that knowledge of the rules of eloquence suffices in this respect. We say: They are merely basic scientific rules which are the result of analogical reasoning and which indicate by means of analogical reasoning that the word combinations may be used in their particular forms. We have here scientific analogical reasoning that is sound and coherent, as is the analogical reasoning that establishes the rules concerning the vowel endings. (But) the (poetical) methods which we try to establish here have nothing to do with analogical reasoning. They are a form that is III, *333*
firmly rooted in the soul. It is the result of the continuity of word combinations in Arabic poetry when the tongue uses them. Eventually, the form of (those word combinations) becomes firmly established. It teaches (the poet) the use of similar (word combinations). (It teaches him) to imitate them for each word combination (that he may use) in the poetry (he produces), just as we have mentioned before in connection with speech in general.[1461]

The scientific rules that govern the word endings or [1462] syntax and style (*bayân*) do not teach (poetry). Not everything that is correct according to analogical reasoning, as

[1459] Bulaq, A, and B have *fî:* "with regard to."
[1460] Cf. Issawi, p. 154.
[1461] Cf. Bombaci, p. 470. The reference is apparently to pp. 358 ff., above.
[1462] Bulaq has "Arabic philology" instead of "word endings (grammar)." In C and D, "or" replaces an earlier "and."

used in connection with Arabic speech and the scientific (grammatical) rules, is used by (poets). They use certain ways (of expressing themselves) which are known and studied by those who have expert knowledge of (poetical) speech and the forms of which fall (automatically) under those analogical rules. If Arabic poetry is to be studied under this aspect and under the aspect of the methods in the mind that are like molds (for poetical expression), it means studying word combinations as they are used by the (Arabs). It does not mean studying the things required by analogical reasoning.

Therefore, we have stated that the molds in the mind are the result of expert knowledge of Arab poetry and speech. Such molds exist not only for poetry but also for prose. The Arabs used their speech for both (poetry and prose), and they used certain types of divisions for both kinds of speech. In poetry, these are metrical cola, fixed rhymes, and the fact that each colon constitutes a statement by itself. In prose, as a rule, (the Arabs) observed symmetry and parallelism between the cola. Sometimes, they used prose rhymes, and sometimes straight prose.[1463] The molds for each kind of
III, *334* (expression) are well known in Arabic.

The author of a spoken utterance builds his utterance in (the molds) used by (the Arabs). They are known only to those who have expert knowledge of (Arabic) speech, such that in their minds they have an absolute universal mold, which is the result of abstraction from specific individual molds. They use (that universal mold) as their model in composing utterances, just as builders use the mold as their model, and weavers the loom. The discipline of speech composition, therefore, differs from the studies of the grammarian, the stylist (literary critic), and the prosodist. It is true, though, that observance of the rules of those sciences is obligatory for and indispensable to (the poet).

When all these qualities together are found to apply to a spoken utterance, it is distinguished by a subtle kind of in-

[1463] Cf. pp. 368 ff., above.

sight into those molds which are called "methods." Only expert knowledge of both Arab poetry and Arab prose gives (that insight).

Now that the meaning of "method" is clear, let us give a definition or description of poetry that will make its real meaning clear to us.[1464] This is a difficult task, for, as far as we can see, there is no such definition by any older (scholar). The definition of the prosodists, according to whom (poetry) is metrical rhymed speech,[1465] is no definition or description of the kind of poetry we have in mind. Prosody considers poetry only [1466] under the aspect of the agreement of the verses (of a poem), with respect to the number of successive syllables with and without vowels,[1467] as well as with respect to the similarity of the last foot of the first hemistich of the verses of a poem to the last foot of the second hemistich. This concerns meter alone and has nothing to do with the words and their meaning. (The definition of the prosodists mentioned) can serve as a definition (of poetry) for them. But as we look at poetry, as including vowel endings, eloquence, meter, and special molds (of expression peculiar to poetry), there can be no doubt that the definition of (the prosodists) is not a valid (definition of poetry) for us. We III, *335*
must have a definition that will give us the real meaning of poetry in our sense.

We say: Poetry is eloquent speech built upon metaphoric usage and descriptions; divided into cola agreeing in meter and rhyme letter, each colon being independent in purpose and meaning from what comes before and after it; and using the methods of the Arabs peculiar to it.

The phrase "eloquent speech" in our definition takes the place of genus. (The phrase) "built upon metaphoric usage and descriptions" differentiates (poetry) from (eloquent

[1464] "To us" is not found in Bulaq.

[1465] Cf. Ibn Rashîq, *'Umdah*, I, 99 (Ch. XVIII).

[1466] The lines following, down to "poetry" (l. 19), are not in Bulaq.

[1467] This refers to meter, while the following phrase refers to the internal rhyme of the first verse of a poem, and to rhyme in general.

speech), which does not have that (and which must be differentiated) because it is mostly not poetry. The phrase "divided into cola agreeing in meter and rhyme letter" differentiates (poetry) from the (kind of) prose speech that nobody would consider poetry. The phrase "each colon being independent in purpose and meaning from what comes before and after it" explains the real character of (poetry), because the verses of poetry can be only this way. This does not differentiate (poetry) from other things.[1468] The phrase "using the methods . . . peculiar to it" differentiates (poetry) from (speech) that does not use the well-known methods of poetry.[1469] Without them, it would not be poetry but merely poetical speech, because poetry has special methods which prose does not have. Likewise, prose has methods which do not apply to poetry. Rhymed speech that does not use those methods is not poetry. It was in this sense that most of the professors of literature whom we have met were of the opinion that the rhymes of al-Mutanabbi' and al-Ma'arrî are by no means poetry, because these (two men)
III, *336* did not follow Arab poetical methods.[1470]

The phrase in (our) definition, "using the methods of the Arabs . . ." differentiates it from the poetry of non-Arab nations. (This is) for those who are of the opinion that poetry exists both among Arabs and among other (people).[1471] (On the other hand,) those who are of the opinion that poetry exists only among the Arabs would not need the phrase. They might say instead: "using the methods peculiar to it" (omitting the words "of the Arabs").

Having finished with the discussion of the real character of poetry, we shall now return to the discussion of how poetry is produced. We say: It should be known that the production

[1468] Cf. Bombaci, p. 470, who stresses the fact that Ibn Khaldûn explains his definition in logical terminology.

[1469] Bulaq: "the Arabs" (instead of "poetry").

[1470] For al-Mutanabbi', cf. *GAL*, I, 86 ff.; *Suppl.*, I, 138 ff. For Abû l-'Alâ' al-Ma'arrî, cf. *GAL*, I, 254 ff.; *Suppl.*, I, 449. The latter's millenary celebration in 1944 inspired an especially large amount of literature on him, and some of his works were published. Cf. also p. 386, below.

[1471] Cf. p. 373, above, and pp. 412 f., below.

of poetry and the laws governing the (poetical) craft are subject to a number of conditions. The first condition is to have an expert knowledge of its genus—that is, the genus of Arabic poetry. (This is the thing) that eventually creates a habit in the soul upon which, as on a loom, (the poet is able) to weave. The material for memorizing should be selected from the most genuine and purest and most varied (poetry).[1472] The selection, at the least, should comprise the poetry of outstanding Muslim poets such as Ibn Abî Rabî'ah,[1473] Kuthayyir,[1474] Dhû r-Rummah,[1475] Jarîr,[1476] Abû Nuwâs,[1477] Ḥabîb (Abû Tammâm),[1478] al-Buḥturî,[1479] ar-Raḍî,[1480] and Abû Firâs.[1481] Most of the material would come from the *Kitâb al-Aghânî*, because it is a collection of all Muslim poetry and the choicest pre-Islamic poetry.[1482]

The poetry of poets who have no expert knowledge of (the old poetical material) is inferior and bad. Brilliance and sweetness is given to poetry only with the help of memorized knowledge of much (old poetical material). Those who know little or nothing of it cannot (produce) any (real) poetry. They merely produce bad rhymes. They would do better to keep away from poetry.

After the poet is saturated with memorized (poetical material) and has sharpened his talent, in order to be able to follow the great examples,[1483] he proceeds to make rhymes himself. Through more and more (practice), the habit of (rhyme making) becomes firmly established and rooted (in III, *337*
him).

[1472] Cf. pp. 392 ff., below.
[1473] 'Umar b. Abî Rabî'ah. Cf. *GAL*, I, 45 ff.; *Suppl.*, I, 76 ff.
[1474] Cf. *GAL*, I, 48; *Suppl.*, I, 79. Cf. also 1:407, above, and p. 404, below.
[1475] Cf. *GAL*, I, 58 f.; *Suppl.*, I, 87 ff.
[1476] Cf. *GAL*, I, 56 ff.; *Suppl.*, I, 86 f.
[1477] Cf. 1:36, above.
[1478] Cf. *GAL*, I, 84 f.; *Suppl.*, I, 134 ff.
[1479] Cf. *GAL*, I, 80; *Suppl.*, I, 125 ff.
[1480] Cf. *GAL*, I, 82; *Suppl.*, I, 131 f.
[1481] Cf. *GAL*, I, 89; *Suppl.*, I, 142 ff.
[1482] Cf. pp. 341 and 366 f., above.
[1483] Lit., "to weave on the loom."

It is often said that one of the conditions governing (poetical production) is to forget the memorized material, so that its external literal forms will be wiped out (of the memory), since they prevent the real use of (the poetical habit).[1484] After the soul has been conditioned by them, and they are forgotten, the method (of poetry) is engraved upon the (soul), as though it were a loom upon which similar such words can be woven as a matter of course.

The poet, then, needs solitude. The place he looks at should be a beautiful one with water and flowers. He likewise needs music. He must stir up [1485] his talent by refreshing it [1486] and stimulate it through pleasurable joy.[1487]

In addition to the (afore-mentioned) conditions, there is another. The (poet) must be rested and energetic. This makes him more collected and is better for his talent, so that he is able to create a loom similar to that which is in his memory. It has been said: "The best time for it is in the morning right after waking up, when the stomach is empty and the mind energetic, and in the atmosphere of the bath." [1488] It has (also) often been said: "Stimuli to poetry are love and drunkenness." This was mentioned by Ibn Rashîq in the *Kitâb al-'Umdah*.[1489] The *'Umdah* is especially devoted to poetry and has given it its due. No work on poetry like it [1490] has been written either before or since. (Then too,) it has been said: "If (the poet) finds it difficult (to make a poem) after

[1484] The Arabic suffix (unless it should be corrected to refer to "memorized material") has as its nearest antecedent "external literal forms." However, Ibn Khaldûn could scarcely have meant it to refer to that.

[1485] Bulaq, Paris, and A read *istinârah* "set afire," against *istithârah* in B, C, and D.

[1486] Through music, or rather, through all the stimulants mentioned here.

[1487] Cf. 2:397 ff., above.

[1488] "Bath" and not "restfulness" (*jamâm*), as suggested by Bulaq, is confirmed by the MSS and by references to the bath in Ibn Rashîq, *'Umdah*, I, 185 f.

[1489] This statement is derived from the quotations in the *'Umdah*, Ch. XXVIII, but is not there to be found as such. In general, the impression prevails that Ibn Khaldûn did not have a copy of the *'Umdah* at hand when he wrote the *Muqaddimah*. Cf., in particular, p. 387 (n. 1502), below.

[1490] "Like it" is added by Bulaq. Cf. also Bombaci, p. 470. For Ibn Rashîq, see p. 338 (n. 1310), above.

all that, he should leave it for another time. He should not force himself to do it."

(The poet) should have the rhyme (in mind), when the verse is first given shape and form. He should set it down and build (his) speech on it all the way through to the end, because, if the poet neglects to have the rhyme (in mind) when he makes a verse, it may be difficult for him to get the rhyme into its proper place, for it often is loose and unstable. If a verse is satisfactory but does not fit in its context, (the poet) III, *338*
should save it for a place more fitting to it. Every verse is an independent unit, and all that is to be done is to fit (the verse into the context of the poem). Therefore, (the poet) may choose to do in this respect whatever he wishes.

After a poem is finished, (the poet) should revise it carefully and critically. He should not hesitate to throw it away, if it is not good enough. Every man is fond of his own poetry, since it is a product of his mind and a creation of his talent.

(The poet) should use only the most correct word combinations and a language free from all (poetic) license, since [1491] the (use of it) is a defect as far as the linguistic habit is concerned. He should avoid it, because it might deprive (his) speech of eloquence. The leading authorities forbade the later-born (poets) [1492] to use (poetic) license, since by avoiding it they might be able to obtain the most exemplary (linguistic) habit. (The poet) should also keep away, as much as he can, from involved word combinations. He should try to use only those whose meaning can be understood more quickly than the (individual) words they contain.[1493] The same applies to putting too many ideas into one verse, which make it somewhat complicated to understand. The choicest (verse)

[1491] The remainder of the sentence is added in the margin of C and incorporated in the text of D.

[1492] *Muwallad,* used as a technical term for persons of mixed Arab and non-Arab parentage, is applied in literary criticism to designate the early poets who were born after the coming of Islam, and, more generally, all the older Islamic poets.

[1493] Cf. Ibn Rashîq, *'Umdah,* I, 216.

is the one whose words conform to the ideas (it contains) or are more copious (than the ideas). If there are many ideas, the verse becomes crowded. The mind examines the (ideas) and is distracted. As a result, (the listener's literary) taste is prevented from fully understanding, as it should, the eloquence (of the verse).[1494] A poem is easy only when its ideas are more quickly grasped by the mind than its words. Thus, our *shaykhs* used to criticize the poetry of the poet of eastern Spain, [Abû Bakr] b. Khafâjah,[1495] for crowding too many
III, *339* ideas into one verse. They used also to criticize the poetry of al-Mutanabbi' and al-Ma'arrî, because it does not follow the methods of the Arabs, as was mentioned before.[1496] Thus, the poetry of the (two men) was rhymed speech inferior to poetry. The judge in such matters is (one's) taste.[1497]

The poet should also keep away from farfetched and pretentious words.[1498] (He should) also (keep away) from vulgar words that become hackneyed through usage. (The use of such words) deprives the poem of eloquence. (He [1499] should) also (keep away) from ideas that have become hackneyed by being generally known. (Their use,) too, deprives the speech of eloquence. It becomes hackneyed and almost meaningless. For instance, such phrases as "The fire is hot" and "The heaven above us" (belong in this category). The closer a poem gets to being meaningless, the less can it claim to be eloquent, since (meaninglessness and eloquence) are (opposing) extremes. For this reason, poetry on mystical [1500] and prophetical subjects is not, as a rule, very good. Only the best poets are good in it, and (even they) only in small (por-

[1494] Cf. Bombaci, p. 470.

[1495] Ibrâhîm b. Abî l-Fatḥ, *ca.* 451 [1059/60] to 533 [1139]. Cf. *GAL*, I, 272; *Suppl.*, I, 480 f. Abû Bakr is found in A and B, whereas the words are deleted in C and D. According to a marginal note in Bulaq, its MSS seem to vacillate between Abû Bakr and Abû Isḥâq, the latter being the usual patronymic of Ibn Khafâjah.

[1496] Cf. p. 382, above.

[1497] Cf. p. 409, below.

[1498] Cf. R. Dozy in *Journal asiatique*, XIV⁶ (1869), 172 ff.

[1499] This and the following sentence not in Bulaq.

[1500] Cf. pp. 394 f., below.

tions of such poetry) and with great difficulty, because the ideas with which such poetry deals are generally known to the great mass and, thus, have become hackneyed.

If a person, after (observing) all (these conditions), (still) finds it impossible to produce poetry, he should (try and) practice it again and again, since talent is like an udder, giving milk only when it is milked, drying up and giving little milk [1501] when it is left alone and neglected.

In general, (the subject of) poetry and how to learn it is exhaustively treated in the *Kitâb al-'Umdah* by Ibn Rashîq. We have mentioned (such information) on poetry available to us, as far as we were able. Those who would like to study the subject exhaustively must turn to the (*'Umdah*). It contains all one could wish. (Our remarks) should suffice to give an III, *340*
idea. God gives support.

People have written poems dealing with poetry and its requirements. The following poem, which, I believe, is by Ibn Rashîq, is among the best statements made on the subject: [1502]

God curse poetry! How many
Kinds of stupid poets have we met!
They prefer strange (expressions) to what
Would be easy and clear to the listener.
They consider the absurd a sound idea,
And vile speech something precious.
They ignore what is right in (poetry).
On account of (their) ignorance, they do not know that
    they are ignorant.
Not we, but others, blame them.
We, in fact, find them excusable.
Poetry is that which is harmonious in its rhymes,

[1501] *Wa-yaghzíru* (thus vocalized) is added in C and D. Cf. Lane's *Arabic-English Dictionary*, p. 2246*a*.

[1502] Actually, the following poem is quoted in Ibn Rashîq, *'Umdah*, II, 108 f., and there attributed to the same Nâshî who wrote the very similar poem quoted below, p. 389 (n. 1506).

Even if in (its) descriptions, it is varied.
Each part of it has the same form as the other parts.
Front and back have come to be alike in it.
Every idea in a (poem) comes to you as you
Wish it would be, if it were not.
III, *341* It has attained such great beauty of style that
Its beauty comes close to being clear to those who look (at it).
Its words are like faces,
And the ideas contained in it are (their) eyes.
It fulfills all the wishes one might have.
Those who recite it are adorned [1503] with its beauty.
When you praise a noble free man in a poem,
You should set out to be as profuse as anyone.
You should make the *nasîb* easy and to the point.
You should make the laudatory (part) truthful and clear.
You should avoid whatever might not be nice to hear,
Even if it is properly put metrically.
When you satirize him,
You should consider the ways of those who use gross language blameworthy.[1504]
You should consider frank statement in (satire) medicine.
Recourse to allusions you should consider a hidden illness.
Whenever in (a poem) you lament those who will one day soon
Depart, and the women who are carried away (in their litters),
III, *342* You should suppress (your) grief. You should subdue
The tears that are stored up in (your) eyes.[1504a]

[1503] *Yataḥallâ,* as expressly indicated in C. The reading *yatajallâ* (cf. Ibn Rashîq, *'Umdah, loc. cit.*) is possible theoretically but not, apparently, intended here. The latter would mean: "its beauty is revealed by those who recite it."

[1504] Ibn Rashîq reads *'ifta* "you should loathe."

[1504a] However, since the idea expressed here is unusual and does not agree with what the following poem says in connection with the same topic, one may try this, admittedly difficult, rendering:

You should admit no consolation whatever. You should cause
The tears that are stored up in (your) eyes (to run) smoothly.

And when you express censure (of a friend), you should mingle promises
With threats, and harshness with gentleness.
Thus you will leave the person whom you censure
Wary as well as assured, strong as well as weak.
The soundest poetry is that which is outstanding in [1505] poetical
(Form), clear and transparent.
When recited, it must make everyone desirous (of producing something similar),
And when one wishes to make a (poem like it), this must be found impossible.

The same subject is also dealt with in the following verses of a poet—an-Nâshî: [1506]

Poetry is (a thing) the crookedness of whose front you have straightened out,
And the belt of whose back you have tightened through careful revision,
The cracks in which you have repaired [1507] through profuseness,
And whose half-blind eyes you have opened through conciseness,
The near and remote parts of which you have gathered together,
And whose stagnant (well water) and spring water you have united,

[1505] Bulaq: "close to."

[1506] The name of the poet is added in C and D. According to Ibn Rashîq, *'Umdah,* he is identical with the author of the preceding poem, the elder Nâshî, Abû l-'Abbâs 'Abdallâh b. Muḥammad, who died in 293 [905/6]. Cf. *GAL,* I, 123 f.; *Suppl.,* I, 188. The verses were quoted by an-Nâshî in his book on poetry. Cf. al-Ḥuṣrî, *Zahr al-âdâb* (Cairo, 1293/1876), II, 249 f.; (Cairo, 1305/1887, in the margin of Ibn 'Abdrabbih, *'Iqd*), II, 240 f. Al-Ḥuṣrî has two verses not found in our text and, in one place, has the verses in a different order. Ibn Rashîq, *'Umdah,* II, 109 f., has the same transposition found in al-Ḥuṣrî but has no additional verses. He omits the fourth verse and the last. In this connection, it should be noted that the fourth, and the last six, verses were added in the margin of C and incorporated in the text of D.

[1507] *Wa-ra'abta.* Al-Ḥuṣrî uses *la'amta,* with the same meaning.

And in which you have provided, wherever required,[1508]
(Like with) like, and counterpart with counterpart.
III, *343* If you praise in a (poem) a noble, generous person,
And repay with gratitude all the debts due him,
You should present him with what is (most) precious and grave (in poetry)
And distinguish him with what is important and valuable (in it).
Thus, (poetry) should be generous in the use of its various types,
And easy (to understand) in the (general) agreement of its various branches.
If in (a poem) you lament dwelling places and the people who lived there,
You should make the grieved person to shed the water of the sutures of his (skull).[1509]
If you want to hint at something dubious,
You should leave the matter midway between clear and cryptic.
Thus you make the person who hears it mingle his doubts
With clarity, and his conjectures with certainty.
If you censure a friend because of a slip,
You should cover the severity of censure with gentleness.
Thus, you will leave him civilized by mildness,
Reassured in the face of[1510] his sadness and grievances.
(But) if you want to attack the (girl) you love,
When she breaks with you, with seductive (poetry),[1511]
III, *344* You should (try to) enslave her with fine and subtle (verses)

[1508] This verse, which is found only in C and D, seems to have been read by Ibn Khaldûn: *wa-ʿamadta minhu munajjidan man yqtḍy*, but *man* makes no sense and should, at least, be corrected to *mâ*. Al-Ḥuṣrî has *wa-ʿahidta minhu li-kulli amrin yaqtaḍî*, which seems to be the correct text.

[1509] For *shuʾûn* and its use in the meaning of "tear (ducts)," cf. J. M. Peñuela, "*Die Goldene*" *des Ibn al-Munâṣif* (Rome, 1941), pp. 77 ff.

[1510] Instead of *mustaʾmanan*, Ibn Rashîq has *mustayʾisan* (distorted in al-Ḥuṣrî to *mustasbiyan*): "In despair because of," which seems to be the better text.

[1511] Cf. R. Dozy in *Journal asiatique*, XIV 6 (1869), 174.

And inflame her with (their) concealed and hidden (meanings).
If you would apologize for a mistake you (yourself) have made,
You should go at it (with verses somewhere) between fanciful and clear.
Thus, your sin will turn out in the eyes of him who is affected by (your poetry),
To be a censure of himself obliging him to swear (that he did nothing wrong).[1512]

[55] *Poetry and prose work with words, and not with ideas.*[1512a]

It should be known that both poetry and prose work with words, and not with ideas. The ideas are secondary to the (words). The (words) are basic.

The craftsman who tries to acquire the habit of poetry and prose uses words for that purpose. He memorizes appropriate words from Arab speech, so as to be able to employ it frequently and have it on his tongue. Eventually, the habit of the Muḍar language becomes firmly established in him. He becomes free from the non-Arab (linguistic habits) in which he was reared among the people of his race. He considers himself like a (half-breed) child who grows up among Arab Bedouins and learns their language as a child learns it. Thus, eventually, he becomes like one of them, as far as their language is concerned.[1513]

As we have mentioned before,[1514] this comes about as follows. Language is a habit concerned with speech. One tries to acquire it by repeated practice with the tongue, until one has acquired it, as is the case with (all other) habits.[1515] III, *345*

[1512] The difficult last verse is reproduced in a rather different, and apparently quite meaningless, form in al-Ḥuṣrî, and is not found in Ibn Rashîq.

[1512a] This chapter is quoted by E. G. Browne, *A Literary History of Persia* (London, 1902–24), II, 86 f.

[1513] Cf. p. 318 (n. 1231), above.

[1514] Cf. p. 342, above.

[1515] "As . . . habits" is added in the margin of C and found in the text of D.

Now, tongue and speech deal only with words. Ideas are in the mind. Furthermore, everyone may have ideas. Everyone has the capacity to grasp with his mind whatever (ideas) his mind wants and likes. No technique is required for their composition.[1516] But the composition of speech, for the purpose of expressing (ideas), requires a technique, as we have stated.[1517] (Speech) is like a mold for ideas. The vessels in which water is drawn from the sea may be of gold, silver, shells (mother-of-pearl), glass, or clay. But the water is one and the same. The quality of the vessels filled with water differs according to the material from which they are made, and not according to the water (in them). In the same way, the quality of language, and eloquence in its use, differ according to different levels (of attainment) in the composition of speech, depending on the manner in which an utterance conforms to (the situation) that it wants to express. But the ideas are one and the same.

A person who is ignorant of the composition of speech and its methods, as required by the (Arabic) linguistic habit, and who unsuccessfully attempts to express what he wants to express, is like an invalid who attempts to get up but cannot, because he lacks the power to do so.

God "teaches you what you did not know." [1518]

[56] *The (linguistic) habit is obtained by much memorizing. The good quality of (the linguistic habit is the result of) the good quality of the memorized material.*

We have mentioned before [1519] that those who desire to learn the Arabic language must memorize much material.
III, 346 The quality of the resulting habit depends on the quality, type, and amount of the memorized material. Those who

[1516] "For their composition" is added in the margin of C and found in the text of D.

[1517] Cf. pp. 342 ff., above.

[1518] Qur'ân 2.151 (146).

[1519] Cf. p. 383, above.

memorize the poetry of Arab Muslims or [1520] the poetry of Ḥabîb (Abû Tammâm), al-'Attâbî,[1521] Ibn al-Mu'tazz,[1522] Ibn Hâni',[1523] or ash-Sharîf ar-Raḍî,[1524] or the *Rasâ'il* (prose letters) of Ibn al-Muqaffa',[1525] Sahl b. Hârûn,[1526] Ibn az-Zayyât,[1527] al-Badî',[1528] or aṣ-Ṣâbi' [1529] will acquire a better habit, of a higher order of eloquence, than those who memorize the poetry of such recent poets as Ibn Sahl [1530] or Ibn an-Nabîh,[1531] or the prose correspondence of al-Baysânî [1532] or the 'Imâd al-Iṣfahânî,[1533] because they are inferior to the (older writers). This is obvious to the intelligent critic who has (literary) taste.

The quality of a person's own later use (of the language) depends on the quality of the material learned or memorized. After (a person has improved his material and his use of it), he can improve his habit.[1534] By raising the level of the memorized literary material, the resulting level (of one's habit) [1535] becomes higher, since nature takes (habit) as its model,[1536] and the powers of a habit grow through nourishing it. This comes about as follows. The soul is one in species according to its natural disposition. It differs in human beings depend-

[1520] "The poetry of Arab Muslims or" is added in the margin of C and incorporated in the text of D. It appears to refer to the earlier Umayyad poets.

[1521] Cf. *GAL*, *Suppl.*, I, 120.

[1522] Cf. *GAL*, I, 80 f.; *Suppl.*, I, 128 ff.

[1523] Cf. *GAL*, I, 91; *Suppl.*, I, 146 f.

[1524] Cf. p. 383, above.

[1525] Cf. *GAL*, I, 151 f.; *Suppl.*, I, 233 ff. Cf. also above, 1:82. His *rasâ'il* are literary essays, but Ibn Khaldûn is thinking of government correspondence.

[1526] Cf. *GAL*, *Suppl.*, I, 213.

[1527] Muḥammad b. 'Abd-al-Malik. Cf. *GAL*, *Suppl.*, I, 121.

[1528] Al-Hamadhânî. Cf. *GAL*, I, 93 ff.; *Suppl.*, I, 150 f.

[1529] Ibrâhîm b. Hilâl, 313–384 [925–994]. Cf. *GAL*, I, 95 f.; *Suppl.*, I, 153 f.

[1530] Ibrâhîm b. Sahl al-Isrâ'îlî, who died in 658 [1260]. Cf. *GAL*, I, 273 f.; *Suppl.*, I, 483. Cf. also below, p. 450.

[1531] 'Alî b. Muḥammad, d. 619 [1222]. Cf. *GAL*, I, 261 f.; *Suppl.*, I, 462.

[1532] Cf. 2:44, above.

[1533] Cf. 2:45, above.

[1534] Cf. Bombaci, p. 471.

[1535] Bulaq corrects to "the resulting habit."

[1536] Lit., "weaves on its loom."

ing on (its) greater or lesser intensity in connection with perceptions.[1537] This difference of the (soul) is the result of the differing perceptions, habits, and colorings that condition the soul from the outside. (Such conditioning) causes its existence to materialize and transforms its form from potentiality into actuality.

III, *347* (Now,) the habits obtained by the soul are obtained only gradually, as we have mentioned before.[1538] The poetical habit originates with the memorizing of poetry. The habit of secretaryship originates with the memorizing of rhymed prose and prose correspondence. The scientific habit originates in contact with the sciences and with various perceptions, research, and speculation. The juridical habit originates in contact with jurisprudence and through comparing the problems and considering them in detail and through deriving special cases from general principles. The mystical habit originates through worship and *dhikr* exercises [1539] and through inactivation of the outward senses by means of solitude and as much isolation from human beings as possible, until (the person who does that) acquires the habit of retiring to his inner sense and his spirit and thus becomes a mystic. The same is the case with all the other (habits). Each one of them gives the soul a special coloring that conditions it.

The good or bad quality of a particular habit depends on the (condition) under which the habit originated. A high-class habit of eloquence results only from the memorizing of high-class language material. This is why all jurists and scholars are deficient in eloquence. The sole reason is in the original character of the material they memorize, in the scientific rules and juridical expressions of which (their material) is full and which deviate from the proper method of eloquence and are inferior (to it). The expressions used for rules and sciences have nothing to do with eloquence. (Now,) when such memorized material is the first to occupy the mind

[1537] Cf. p. 157, above.

[1538] Cf. 2:346, and pp. 292 f., 342, above.

[1539] Cf. p. 81 (n. 471), above.

and is large and colors the soul, the resulting habit comes to be very deficient and the expressions connected with (that material) deviate from the methods of Arab speech. This, we find, applies to the poetry of jurists, grammarians, speculative theologians, philosophers, and others who are not saturated with memorized knowledge of the purest and noblest (most genuine) Arabic speech.[1540] III, 348

Our excellent colleague, Abû l-Qâsim b. Riḍwân,[1541] the writer of the *'alâmah*[1542] of the Merinid dynasty, told me the following story. "One day, I had a conversation with our colleague Abû l-'Abbâs b. Shu'ayb,[1543] the secretary of Sultan Abû l-Ḥasan, who was the leading philologist of his time. I recited to him the beginning of a *qaṣîdah* by Ibn an-Naḥwî,[1544] without mentioning him as the author. (The *qaṣîdah* runs:)

> I did not know when I stood near the traces of the abandoned dwelling places
> What the difference was between the new ones and those that were almost effaced.

(Ibn Shu'ayb) said to me immediately, 'That is a poem by a jurist.' I asked him how he knew that. He replied: 'Because he says: "What the difference was." That is a juridical expression and does not belong to the methods of (proper) Arab speech.' Full of admiration, I told him that it was indeed a poem by Ibn an-Naḥwî."

Secretaries and poets are not like that. They choose carefully the material they memorize. They have contact with the methods of Arab speech with regard to prose correspond-

1540 Cf. Bombaci, p. 471.

1541 'Abdallâh b. Yûsuf. Cf. *Autobiography*, pp. 22 ff., 41 ff.

1542 Cf. 1:xli, above.

1543 Aḥmad b. Shu'ayb, d. 750 [1349]. Cf. *Autobiography*, p. 48. The passage of the *Autobiography* is quoted by Aḥmad Bâbâ, *Nayl al-ibtihâj* (Cairo, 1351/1932, in the margin of Ibn Farḥûn, *Dîbâj*), p. 68.

1544 Yûsuf b. Muḥammad, 433–513 [1041/42–1119]. Cf. Ibn al-Abbâr, *Takmilat aṣ-Ṣilah*, ed. F. Codera (Bibliotheca Arabico-Hispana, No. 6) (Madrid, 1889), p. 740, No. 2098; Aḥmad Bâbâ, *Nayl al-ibtihâj*, pp. 349–51.

ence. They select the good material from (Arab) speech.

One day, I had a conversation with Abû 'Abdallâh b. al-Khaṭîb,[1545] the wazir of the rulers of Spain. He was the leading authority on poetry and secretaryship. I said to him, "I find it difficult to compose poetry when I want to, despite my understanding of (poetry) and my knowledge of the good language material in the Qur'ân, the traditions, and the various (other) branches of Arab speech, although I know
III, 349 little by heart. It may be that I am affected by my knowledge of scientific poems and the rules of (literary) composition. I have memorized the large and the small poem by ash-Shâṭibî on Qur'ân readings and Qur'ân orthography,[1546] and I know them by heart.[1547] I studied the two works of Ibn al-Ḥâjib on jurisprudence and the principles of jurisprudence,[1548] the *Jumal* on logic by al-Khûnajî,[1549] and many of the rules of scientific school instruction. That has filled my memory and harmed the habit for which I was prepared [1550] through the good material from the Qur'ân, the traditions, and (other documents of) Arab speech. It prevented my talent from developing." (Ibn al-Khaṭîb) looked at me in amazement for a while. Then he said, full of admiration: "Would anyone but you say a thing like that?"

The remarks made in this section explain another problem. They explain why both the poetry and the prose of the Muslim Arabs are on a higher level of eloquence and literary taste than those of pre-Islamic Arabs. We find that the poetry of Ḥassân b. Thâbit,[1551] 'Umar b. Abî Rabî'ah,[1552] al-

[1545] Cf. 1:xliv, above. Bulaq adds "our friend," and explains that the rulers of Spain mentioned were the Banû l-Aḥmar (the Naṣrids of Granada).

[1546] Cf. 2:441 f., above. The reference to Qur'ân orthography is added in C and D.

[1547] Bulaq omits the last statement.

[1548] Cf. 2:428 f., and pp. 19, 29 f., above.

[1549] Cf. p. 143, above. Bulaq adds: "and part of the *Kitâb at-Tashîl.*"

[1550] Ibn Khaldûn here uses the colloquial form *ista'ăddêt* (C vocalizes *ista'addaytu*), for *ista'dadtu.*

[1551] Cf. *GAL*, I, 37 f.; *Suppl.*, I, 67 f.

[1552] Cf. p. 383, above.

Ḥuṭay'ah,[1553] Jarîr,[1554] al-Farazdaq,[1555] Nuṣayb,[1556] Ghaylân Dhû r-Rummah,[1557] al-Aḥwaṣ,[1558] and Bashshâr,[1559] as well as the literary products of the ancient Arabs of the Umayyad dynasty and the early years of the 'Abbâsid dynasty, (including) their sermons, their prose correspondence, and their discussions with the rulers, are on a much higher level of eloquence than the poetry of an-Nâbighah,[1560] 'Anṭarah, Ibn Kulthûm, Zuhayr, 'Alqamah b. 'Abadah, and Ṭarafah b. al-'Abd. (They also are on a higher level) than the prose and discussions of pre-Islamic (authors). A sound taste and a healthy natural disposition[1561] will confirm the (correctness of this observation) to the intelligent critic of eloquence.

The reason for this is that (authors) who lived in Islam III, 350
learned the highest form of speech (as it is found) in the Qur'ân and in the traditions, which for human beings is inimitable. It entered into their hearts. Their souls were brought up on the (linguistic) methods (of this kind of speech). As a result, their nature was lifted, and their habits with regard to eloquence were elevated, to greater heights than had ever been reached by their pre-Islamic predecessors, who had not learned the (highest) form of speech and had not been brought up on it. Therefore, their prose and poetry were better in texture and of a purer brilliance than their (predecessors'). They were more solid in construction and more even in execution, because their (authors) had learned the high-class speech (of the Qur'ân and the traditions). When a person thinks this (explanation) over, his literary

1553 Cf. *GAL*, I, 41; *Suppl.*, I, 71.

1554 Cf. p. 383, above.

1555 Cf. *GAL*, I, 53 ff.; *Suppl.*, I, 84.

1556 Nuṣayb b. Rabâḥ. Cf. *GAL*, *Suppl.*, I, 99.

1557 Cf. p. 383, above.

1558 Cf. *GAL*, I, 48 f.; *Suppl.*, I, 80.

1559 Bashshâr b. Burd. Cf. *GAL*, I, 73 f.; *Suppl.*, I, 108 ff.

1560 For him and the other famous authors of *Mu'allaqahs* (see p. 410, below), cf. *GAL*, I, 22 ff.; *Suppl.*, I, 44 ff. For 'Amr b. Kulthûm, cf. *GAL*, *Suppl.*, I, 51 f.

1561 Cf. pp. 345 f., above.

taste will attest to its correctness, if he has taste and understands eloquence.

I once asked our *shaykh*, the sharîf Abû l-Qâsim,[1562] the (chief) judge of Granada in our day, why the Muslim Arabs were on a higher level (of eloquence) [1563] than the pre-Islamic Arabs. (Abû l-Qâsim) was the chief authority on poetry. He had studied (it) in Ceuta with certain [1564] *shaykhs* there who were pupils of ash-Shalûbîn.[1565] He had (also) made a profound study of philology and acquired a more than perfect knowledge of it. Thus, he was a man who, with his taste, could be expected not to be ignorant of (this question). He remained silent for a long while. Then he said to me, "By God, I do not know." Whereupon I said, "I shall suggest to you (an idea) concerning this problem that has come to my mind. Perhaps, it explains it." And I mentioned to him what I have noted (here). He was silent in amazement. Then, he said to me: "Doctor (*faqîh*), this is a remark that deserves to be written down in gold(en letters)." After that, he (always) treated me with deference. He listened to what I had to say
III, *351* in class and acknowledged my excellence in scholarship.

God "created man" and "taught him clarity." [1566]

[57] *An explanation of the meaning of natural and contrived speech. How contrived speech may be either good or deficient.*[1567]

It should be known that the secret and spirit of speech—that is, expression and address—lie in conveying ideas. If no

[1562] Muḥammad b. Aḥmad b. Muḥammad, as-Sabtî, 697–760 [1297–1359]. Cf. Ibn al-Khaṭîb, *al-Iḥâṭah*, II, 129–33. Other authors prefer 761 [1359/60] as the date of his death, it would seem for no good reason. Cf. Ibn al-'Imâd, *Shadharât*, VI, 192 f. Cf. also p. 408, below

[1563] Bulaq actually adds "of eloquence."

[1564] Bulaq: "a number of."

[1565] 'Umar b. Muḥammad, 562–645 [1166/67–1245]. Cf. E. Lévi-Provençal, *La Péninsule Ibérique*, p. 136; A. R. Nykl, *Hispano-Arabic Poetry* (Baltimore, 1946), pp. 324 f.

[1566] Qur'ân 55.3–4 (2–3).

[1567] This section is not found in Bulaq and A. The title reads in B: "Natural speech is more solid in construction and on a higher level of eloquence

effort is made to (convey ideas), (speech) is like "dead land" (*mawât*) [1568] which does not count.

The perfect way of conveying (ideas) is eloquence. This is shown by the literary critics' [1569] definition of eloquence. They say that (eloquence) is conformity of speech to the requirements of the situation.[1570] Knowledge of the conditions and laws governing the conformity of word combinations to the requirements of the situation is the discipline of eloquence (rhetoric). The conditions and laws were deduced from the Arabic language and have become a sort of rules. The manner in which word combinations are used indicates the relationship that exists between two interdependent (parts of an utterance). (It does so) with the help of conditions and laws constituting the main part of the rules of Arabic. The situations that apply to the word combinations —which may be earlier or later position, determination or indetermination, implicit or explicit (reference), statements used restricted or absolute, and so on—indicate the situations that envelop from outside the (existing) relationship and the persons discoursing with each other. (They do so) with the help of conditions and laws that constitute the rules of a discipline belonging to rhetoric and called the "science of idea expression" (*'ilm al-ma'ânî*). Thus, the rules of Arabic are comprised under those of the science of idea expression, because the (purpose of) indicating the (existing) relationship is part of the (purpose of) indicating the situations that envelop that relationship. Any word com- III, *352*
binations unable to indicate the requirements of a given situation because of some defect in the rules governing the vowel endings or the rules governing the ideas, are (likewise) unable to establish conformity (between themselves

than contrived speech." The text later on differs considerably in B, on the one hand, and in C and D, on the other. In this connection, one may compare the chapter on *maṭbû'* and *maṣnû'* in Ibn Rashîq, *'Umdah*, I, 108–113 (Ch. xx.)

[1568] The problem of "dead lands" has greatly occupied Muslim jurisprudence throughout its existence.

[1569] B: "philologists."

[1570] Cf. p. 333, above.

and) the requirements of the situation; they belong to the (group of things) of which no use is made, which belong in the category of "dead land."

After the requirements of a given situation have thus been indicated, there come the diverse ways in which the mind moves among the ideas with the help of different kinds of (word) meanings. In its conventional meaning, a word combination indicates one particular idea, but then the mind moves on to what might be the consequence of, or have as its consequence, that idea, or (what might) be similar to it and, thus, express (some idea) indirectly as metaphor or metonymy,[1571] as has been established in the proper places.[1572] This moving around causes pleasure to the mind, perhaps even more than (the pleasure) that results from indicating (the requirements of the situation). All these things mean attainment of a conclusion from the argument used to prove it, and attainment, as one knows, is one of the things that cause pleasure.

The different ways the (mind) moves around in this way also have (their) conditions and laws, which are like rules. They were made into a (special) craft and called "the (science of) style" (*bayân*).[1573] (This science) is sister to the science of idea expression, which indicates the requirements of a given situation. The (science of style) has reference to the ideas and meanings of the word combinations. The rules of the science of idea expression have reference to the very situations that apply to the word combinations, as far as they affect the meaning. Word and idea depend on each other and stand side by side,[1574] as one knows. Thus, the science of idea expression and the science of style are both part of rhetoric, and both (together) produce perfect indication and conformity to the requirements of the situation. Conse-

[1571] Cf. p. 335, above.

[1572] Ibn Khaldûn is not referring here to his own remarks, pp. 332 ff., above, but to works on literary criticism in general.

[1573] Cf. p. 336, above.

[1574] *Mutaḍâyifâni*, as in C and D. B has *mutaṭâbiqâni* "conform to each other."

quently, word combinations that fall short of conformity and perfect indication are inferior in eloquence. (Such word combinations) are linked by rhetoricians to the sounds dumb animals make. The preferred assumption is that they are not Arabic, because Arabic is (the kind of speech) in which III, *353* indications are in conformity with the requirements of the situation. Thus, eloquence is the basis, genius, spirit, and nature of Arabic speech.

It should further be known that in the usage of (philologists), "natural speech" means the (type of) speech that conveys the intended meaning and, thus, is perfect in its nature and genius. Just speaking is not what is meant by (natural speech) as a (kind of) expression and address; the speaker (who uses natural speech) wants to convey what is in his mind to the listeners in a complete and definite fashion.

Thus, after perfect indication (of the requirements of the situation has been achieved), the word combinations, (if expressed) according to that genius that is basic (to Arabic speech), have (their) different kinds of artistic embellishment.[1575] In a way, they give them the brilliance of correct speech. Such (kinds of artistic embellishment) include the ornamental use of rhymed prose, the use of phrases of identical structure at the end of successive cola (*muwâzanah*),[1576] allusion (*tawriyah*) to a cryptic idea by a homonym,[1577] and * antithesis, so that there will be affinity (*tajânus*) between

antithesis, and other rhetorical figures (alqâb) [1578] *invented and enumerated (by literary critics) and for which they set up con-*

[1575] Cf. p. 335, above.

[1576] Instead of *jumal . . . al-aḥkâm* (found in the margin of C and in the text of D), B simply has *al-fuṣûl*. A similar substitution, involving the same MSS, is to be found p. 408, l. 16, and p. 406, l. 20, below. Here, the literal translation is: "creating a balance between the larger portions of speech and the cola of different character into which it is divided." However, the technical meaning of *muwâzanah*, as given above, is meant. For *muwâzanah*, cf. G. E. von Grunebaum, *A Tenth-Century Document of Arabic Literary Criticism*, p. 26.

[1577] The upper text that follows is that of C and D, the lower that of B.

[1578] Cf. p. 337 (n. 1308), above.

the words and ideas (used).[1579] This gives brilliance to speech and pleasure to the ear, and sweetness and beauty, all in addition to indicating (the meaning).

This craft is found represented in the inimitable speech (of the Qur'ân) in numerous passages, as, for instance:

> By the night when it covers; and the day when it reveals itself.[1580]

Or:

> As to those who give and fear God and believe in what is most beautiful . . .[1581]

and so on, to the end of the cola division in the passage. Or:

> But as to those who deviate and prefer the life of this world . . .[1582]

and so on, to the end of the passage. Also:

> And they think that they are doing good.[1583]

There are many similar things (in the Qur'ân). (But) it

ditions and laws and which they called "the discipline of rhetorical figures" (badî').

Both the older and the more recent (literary critics), as well as those of the East and the West, have differed (with each other) in enumerating the (different) kinds and subdivisions (of the rhetorical figures), just as they have differed as to whether (the discipline of rhetorical figures) should be considered part of rhetoric or not. That (it should not) was the opinion of the Westerners. The Easterners considered it as a part of (rhetoric),

1579 *Tajânus,* as a technical term, usually refers to an etymological relationship between the expressions used. The clause introduced by "so that" seems to have been intended to apply only to "antithesis," not to all the rhetorical figures mentioned.

1580 Qur'ân 92.1–2 (1–2).

1581 Qur'ân 92.5 ff. (5 ff.).

1582 Qur'ân 79.37 ff. (37 ff.).

1583 Qur'ân 18.104 (104).

comes (only) after (the meaning) has been indicated perfectly by the word combinations (as they are) basically, before the rhetorical figures occur in them.[1584]

(Rhetorical figures) also occurred in pre-Islamic speech, but spontaneously and unintentionally. They are said to occur in the poetry of Zuhayr.[1585] III, *354*

Among the (early) Muslim (authors), they occur both spontaneously and intentionally. These (authors) did remarkable things with them. The first to have a good knowledge of the method of (rhetorical figures) were Ḥabîb b. Aws (Abû Tammâm), al-Buḥturî, and Muslim b. al-Walîd.[1586] They very eagerly set out to achieve a (contrived) technique and did remarkable things with it.

It is (also) said that the first to concern themselves with (rhetorical figures) were Bashshâr b. Burd[1587] and Ibn

---

but not as something basic to speech. They considered it as something that, after one has seen to the conformity of speech with the requirements of the situation, gives it brilliance and ornateness and provides it with sweetness and beauty. Without such conformity, a speech is not Arabic, as mentioned before, and no embellishment can dispense with it[1588] *in (speech). Moreover, (the rhetorical figures) are derived from the language of the Arabs by using it and investigating its word combinations. Partly, they are heard (used by the Arabs), and their existence is attested. Partly, they are derived and acquired.*[1589] *One knows this from the works of the authorities.*

When they speak about "contrived speech," they mean word combinations representing the different types and kinds of rhetorical figures. They also speak of natural speech in (their books) as speech possessing perfect indication. The two (things) are op-

[1584] Cf. Bombaci, p. 471.
[1585] Cf. p. 397, above.
[1586] Cf. *GAL*, I, 77; *Suppl.*, I, 118.
[1587] Cf. p. 397, above.
[1588] The suffix could refer either to "rhetorical figures" or, as indicated above, to "conformity."
[1589] *Leg. muqtabas muktasab.*

Harmah,[1590] who were the last (poets whose poems) are used as evidence for (the grammatical and lexicographical problems of) the Arabic language. They were followed by Kulthûm b. 'Amr al-'Attâbî,[1591] Manṣûr an-Numayrî,[1592] Muslim b. al-Walîd, and Abû Nuwâs. After them came Ḥabîb (Abû Tammâm) and al-Buḥturî. Then, there appeared Ibn al-Mu'tazz. He gave the whole craft of rhetorical figures its definitive form.

Let us mention examples of natural (speech) which is free from (contrived) technique, such as, for instance, the verse of Qays b. Dharîḥ:[1593]

> I go out from among the tents; perhaps, I
> Shall talk about you to my(self) in secret, being alone.

Or the verse of Kuthayyir:[1594]

> I, in my passion for 'Azzah after
> Our relationship had come to an end for me, and for her,
> Am indeed like one who hopes for shade from a cloud that, as soon as
> He settles down to his siesta, clears away.

This, indeed, is natural (poetry) that is uncontrived in its

posed to each other. This shows that the craft of (rhetorical figures) is opposed to rhetoric.

Since the craft of rhetorical figures had no (particular, defined) subject and, consequently, was not a science, the littérateurs of ancient times considered (rhetorical figures) as part of the literary disciplines and included them in literary (adab) *works.*

[1590] Cf. *GAL*, I, 84; *Suppl.*, I, 134.

[1591] Cf. p. 393, above.

[1592] I.e., Manṣûr b. Zibriqân b. Salimah (or: Salimah b. Zibriqân), an-Namarî (not an-Numayrî). Cf. *Kitâb al-Aghânî*, XII, 16–25; al-Khaṭîb al-Baghdâdî, *Ta'rîkh Baghdâd*, XIII, 65–69.

[1593] Cf. *GAL*, I, 48; *Suppl.*, I, 81.

[1594] Cf. 1:407 and p. 383, above. The verses are found in Kuthayyir's *Dîwân*, ed. H. Pérès (Algiers & Paris, 1928–30), I, 57. They are quoted, for instance, by Ibn Rashîq, *'Umdah*, II, 74; *Lisân al-'Arab*, XVI, 111.

good composition and in the solidity of its word combinations. If, later on, some (contrived) technique were added upon such a foundation, its beauty would (merely) be increased.

Contrived (speech) has been frequent since the time of Bashshâr and Ḥabîb (Abû Tammâm) and other (authors) of their class. (They were followed) by Ibn al-Mu'tazz who gave the craft of (rhetorical figures) its definitive form. (These authors) served as models to later (writers) who used the course they had prepared and wove on their loom. III, 355

People who cultivate the craft of (rhetorical figures) distinguish numerous subdivisions and use different termi-

This was done by Ibn Rashîq in the Kitâb al-'Umdah.[1595] *In it, he discussed the craft of poetry in an unprecedented manner. He showed how to produce poetry. He had this (subject) followed by a discussion of the rhetorical figures. The same was done by other, Spanish littérateurs.*

It has been said that the first to concern himself with this (contrived) technique was Abû Tammâm Ḥabîb b. Aws aṭ-Ṭâ'î. He loaded his poetry with rhetorical figures (alqâb). *The people after him followed him in this respect. Before (him), poetry had been free from (rhetorical figures). The pre-Islamic and the outstanding (early) Islamic poets had not concerned themselves with them in their poetry and had not made much use of them. They occur in their (poems), but only spontaneously as a gift of (outstanding linguistic) talent, and not as the result of constant practice and studied application. Healthy natures have a good taste for them. But (rhetorical figures) are found in (early poetry) only as the result of perfect conformity (of the words to the meaning), faithful regard for the rights of eloquence, and freedom from harmful, forced use of the rhetorical figures or from crude, studied application and constant practice (of them). Thus, innate natural disposition makes it natural that embellishment (with rhetorical figures should be found) in (that poetry).*

[1595] Cf. 2:403 and pp. 384 and 387, above, and p. 406, below.

nologies for the rhetorical figures (*alqâb*). Many of them consider them part of rhetoric, although (these figures) are not concerned with indicating (the meaning of speech), but provide embellishment and brilliance. The early representatives of the discipline of rhetorical figures considered them not to be a part of rhetoric. Therefore, they mentioned them as part of the literary disciplines (*adab*) which have no (particular, defined) subject. This was the opinion of Ibn Rashîq in his *Kitâb al-'Umdah*, and of the Spanish littérateurs. They mentioned various conditions governing the use of the (rhetorical figures). Among them, there is the condition that they should express the intended meaning in an unforced and unstudied manner.

The spontaneous occurrence of (rhetorical figures) causes no comment, because (in such cases, the rhetorical figures) are in no way forced, and the speech (in which they occur) cannot, therefore, be criticized as (linguistically) faulty. The forced and studied use of (rhetorical figures) leads to disre-

The prose of the pre-Islamic and outstanding (early) Islamic (authors), too, was a straight prose divided into cola without rhyme or meter, until the appearance of Ibrâhîm b. Hilâl aṣ-Ṣâbi',[1596] *the secretary to the Bûyids. He concerned himself with the use of rhymed prose in (his) speech and adhered to it in (his) government correspondence, in imitation of the rhyme of poetry. He was at liberty to do so, because his rulers were used to non-Arabic (speech), and he himself had the outlook of common persons, that has nothing to do with royal aspirations or with the authority of the caliphate which wants authoritative eloquence. He dealt with the lower regions of artificially adorned speech in the same way as is done in private correspondence. At the time, he was successful with it [?],*[1597] *and his fame grew. Afterwards,*

1596 Cf. p. 393, above.

1597 *Fa-shâlat yawma'idhin na'âmatuhû bi-hâ.* The phrase means "to be scattered, to blow hot and cold, to die," but I fail to see what sense any of these meanings would make in the context. It could hardly be: "He died at that time, but his fame grew." Ibn Khaldûn probably understood it in a positive sense, as indicated above.

gard of the basic word combinations of speech and thus destroys all basis for indication (of the meaning of speech). It removes outright all eloquence and leaves speech only the (rhetorical) embellishments. This (however, actually) is the situation that is preponderant among (our) contemporaries. (But) people who have taste in eloquence despise (them because of) their infatuation with the various (rhetorical figures) and consider that (propensity an indication of their) inability to do better.

(Thus,) I heard our *shaykh*, Professor Abû l-Barakât al-Ballaffîqî,[1598] who knew the language and had a natural taste for it, say: "The thing I most desire is some day to see one of III, 356
those who practice the different branches of (the craft of) rhetorical figures in poetry or prose, punished with the most severe punishment and publicly denounced, thus giving warning to his pupils not to concern themselves with this (contrived) technique. (Otherwise,) they might fall in love with it and forget all eloquence."

Another condition (governing the use of rhetorical figures) is that they be used sparingly and in no more than

the speech of later (authors) became more and more contrived. One forgot the period when straight prose was in use to express authoritative eloquence. Government correspondence came to be like private correspondence, and Arabic came to be like the common language. Good and bad became (inextricably) confused with each other, and the nature (of authors) was unable to achieve basic eloquence in speech, because little attention was paid to it. Everybody now is infatuated with the different branches and kinds of the craft of (rhetorical figures) in poetry and prose and greatly concerned with cultivating every type of it. (But) the great rhetoricians always despised it and disapproved of its cultivation at the expense of other (things).

I have seen our shaykhs *censure persons concerned with linguistic matters who occupied themselves (unduly) with (rhe-*

[1598] Cf. 1:xlii, above.

two or three verses of a poem, which suffices to adorn and give it brilliance, while the use of many (such rhetorical figures) would be a blemish. This was stated by Ibn Rashîq and others.

Our *shaykh*, the sharîf Judge Abû l-Qâsim as-Sabtî,[1599] who was the chief cultivator of the Arabic language in his time, used to say: "The different kinds of rhetorical figures may occur to a poet or a secretary, but it is ugly if he uses many of them. They belong among the things that embellish speech and constitute its beauty. They are like moles on a face. One or two make it beautiful, but many make it ugly."

Pre-Islamic and (early) Islamic prose followed the same lines as poetry. Originally, it was straight prose, considering (only) creation of a balance between the larger portions of (speech) and its word combinations, to indicate that it is balanced by means of cola into which it is divided,[1599a] without adherence to rhyme or concern for (contrived) techniques. (This was so) until the appearance of Ibrâhîm b. Hilâl aṣ-Ṣabi', the secretary to the Bûyids. He con-

torical figures). (*I noticed that*) *they had a low opinion of them.*

(*Thus,*) *I heard our* shaykh *Professor Abû l-Barakât al-Ballafîqî, who knew the language and had a natural taste for it, say: "The thing I most desire is some day to see one of those who practice the different branches of the craft of (rhetorical figures) in poetry or prose, afflicted by the most severe punishment and publicly denounced, so that his pupils will be deterred from occupying themselves with the craft of rhetorical figures." He was afraid lest eloquence suffer from it and be forgotten.*

Our shaykh, *the sharîf, Judge Abû l-Qâsim as-Sabtî, who was the chief cultivator of the Arabic language and its standard-bearer (in his time), used to say: "The different kinds of rhetorical figures may occur spontaneously to a poet or a secretary.*

1599 Cf. p. 398, above.

1599a Cf. n. 1576, above.

cerned himself with (contrived) techniques and the use of rhyme. He did marvelous things with it. (However,) people criticized him because of his propensity for (using such things) in government correspondence. He could do that only because his rulers were used to non-Arabic (speech) and had nothing to do with the authority of the caliphate which caused eloquence to flourish. Afterwards, the prose of later (authors) became more and more contrived. One forgot the III, 357
period when straight prose had been used. Government correspondence came to be like private correspondence,[1600] and Arabic came to be like the common language. Good and bad became (inextricably) confused with each other.[1601]

All these (statements) show that contrived, studied, or forced speech is inferior to natural speech, because it has little concern for what is basic to eloquence. The judge in such matters is (one's) taste.[1602]

And God created you and "taught you what you did not know." [1603] *

Still, it is ugly if he repeats them. They belong among the things that embellish speech and constitute its beauty. They are like moles on a face. One or two make it beautiful, but many make it ugly."

All the (statements) of these excellent men consider cultivation of the craft of rhetorical figures (alqâb badî'îyah) *to be (linguistically) faulty, as it might deprive speech of its high eloquence. Such statements by them show that contrived speech is inferior to natural speech. We have shown here its secret and real character. The judge in such matters is (one's) taste.*

And God knows better. He "taught you what you did not know."

[1600] Some very fine examples of such private correspondence among friends can be found in Ibn Khaldûn's *Autobiography*, pp. 103 ff.

[1601] Cf. Bombaci, p. 471. Lit., "animals guarded by a shepherd and those not guarded."

[1602] Cf. p. 386, above.

[1603] Qur'ân 2.239 (240).

[58] *People of rank are above cultivating poetry.*

It should be known that poetry was the archive of the Arabs, containing their sciences, their history, and their wisdom.[1604] Leading Arabs competed in it. They used to stop at the fair of 'Ukâẓ [1605] to recite poetry. Each would submit his product for criticism [1606] to outstanding and intelligent personalities. Eventually, (Arab poets) came to vie in having their poems hung up at the corners of the Holy Sanctuary to which they made pilgrimage, the house of their ancestor Ibrâhîm (the Ka'bah). This was done by Imru'u-l-Qays b. Ḥujr, an-Nâbighah adh-Dhubyânî, Zuhayr b. Abî Sulmâ, 'Antarah b. Shaddâd, Ṭarafah b. al-'Abd, 'Alqamah b. 'Abadah, al-A'shâ, and the other authors of the nine *Mu'allaqât*.[1607] Only a person who had enough power among his people and his group (*'aṣabîyah*) and who held the proper position among the Muḍar, was able to get so far as to have his poem hung up there. This (fact) is stated in connection with the reason why such poems were called *Mu'allaqât*.[1608]

III, *358* Then, at the beginning of Islam, the Arabs gave up the (custom). They were occupied with the affairs of Islam, with prophecy and revelation. They were awed by the (linguistic) method and form of the Qur'ân. They were (thus) silenced. For a time, they no longer discussed poetry and prose. Then, those (great happenings) continued, and right guidance came to be something familiar to the Muslims.[1609] There was no revelation (saying) that poetry was forbidden or prohibited. The Prophet listened to poetry and rewarded (the poet) for it. Under these circumstances, the Arabs returned to their old

---

1604 Cf. p. 304 (n. 1186), above.

1605 Cf. A. J. Wensinck in *EI*, *s.v.* "'Okâẓ."

1606 Lit., "to criticize its texture."

1607 The "suspended" poems, according to the traditional interpretation of the word. A recent summary of modern scholarly opinions as to its meaning may be found in *Bulletin des études arabes* (Algiers, 1946), VI, 152–58. Bulaq corrects "nine" to "seven," the number to which the *Mu'allaqât* are usually restricted. For the poets, cf. also p. 397, above.

1608 Cf. Bombaci, p. 471.

1609 For the phrase used here, cf. Qur'ân 4.6 (5).

customs with regard to poetry. 'Umar b. Abî Rabî'ah,[1610] the leading Qurashite of his time, wrote poetry of a high rank and on a high level. He often submitted his poetry to Ibn 'Abbâs,[1611] who paused to listen to it in admiration.

Then there came great royal authority and a mighty dynasty. The Arabs approached the (caliphs) with their laudatory poems, and the caliphs rewarded them most generously according to the quality of the poems and their position among their people. They were eager to have poems presented to them. From them they learned remarkable stories, history, lexicography, and noble speech. The Arabs saw to it that their children memorized the poems. This remained the situation during the days of the Umayyads and in the early days of the 'Abbâsid dynasty. One may compare the report, by the author of the '*Iqd*, about the conversation of ar-Rashîd with al-Aṣma'î, in the chapter on poetry and poets.[1612] It shows that ar-Rashîd possessed a good knowledge of the subject and was firmly grounded in it. He was concerned with the cultivation of (poetry). He was able to discern good speech from bad speech, and he possessed a wide memorized knowledge of (poetry).

Later on, people came whose language was not Arabic, III, *359*
because they had a non-Arab (background) and a deficient knowledge of the (Arabic) language, which they had learned as a craft. (Poets) did write laudatory poems for the non-Arab amirs, who did not possess the (Arabic) language, (but) they did so only in order to win their favor, and not for any other reason. This was done, for instance, by Ḥabîb (Abû Tammâm), al-Buḥturî, al-Mutanabbi', Ibn Hâni',[1613] and later (poets). Thus, the predominant purpose of producing poetry came to be mere begging and asking for favors, because the particular use that, as we have mentioned, the early (Arabs) had made of poetry no longer existed. This is

1610 Cf. p. 383, above.
1611 Cf. 1:34, above.
1612 Cf. 1:32, above.
1613 Cf. pp. 382 f. and 393, above.

why people of ambition and rank among later (Muslims) disdained poetry. The situation, thus, changed. Concern with poetry came to be (considered) a blemish or fault in leaders and people holding great positions.[1614]

God causes the change of night and day.[1615]

[59] *Contemporary Arab poetry, Bedouin and urban.*

It should be known that poetry is not restricted exclusively to the Arabic language. It exists in every language, Arabic and non-Arabic.[1616] There were poets among the Persians and among the Greeks. (The Greek poet) Homer was mentioned and praised by Aristotle in the *Logic*.[1617] The Ḥimyarites, too, had their poets in ancient times.

Later on, corruption affected the language of the Muḍar, whose forms, and whose rules governing the vowel endings, had been systematized (as the pure Arabic language). The various later dialects differed according to the (more or less close) contact with (non-Arabs) and the (larger or smaller) admixture of non-Arab (elements).[1618] As a result,
III, 360 the Bedouin Arabs themselves came to speak a language completely different from that of their Muḍar ancestors with regard to vowel endings, and different in many respects with regard to the (conventional) meanings and forms of words. Among the urban population, too, another language originated, which was different from that of the Muḍar with regard to vowel endings, as well as most meanings and grammatical inflections. It differs also from the language of

1614 R. Brunschvig, *La Berbérie orientale*, II, 404, shows that this statement is not correct. In fact, versemaking was always popular in Islam with everyone who laid claim to some degree of education.

1615 Cf. Qur'ân 24.44 (44).

1616 Cf. pp. 373 and 382, above.

1617 Ibn Khaldûn might possibly have been thinking of the perfunctory reference to Homer in the *Hermeneutics* 21*a*, or perhaps of the passages in the *Rhetoric* and the *Poetics* where Homer is mentioned. To judge from the form of Homer's name in the MSS, especially as vocalized in C and D, Ibn Khaldûn would seem to have pronounced it *Ûmatîrash*.

1618 Cf., for instance, p. 346, above.

present-day Arab Bedouins. Again, it differs within itself according to the (different) terminologies of the inhabitants of the various regions.[1619] Thus, the urban population of the East speaks a dialect different from that of the Maghribîs. And the language of the urban population in Spain differs from both of them.

Now, poetry exists by nature among the speakers of every language, since meters of a certain harmonious arrangement, with the alternation of (fixed) numbers of consonants, with and without vowels, exist in the nature of all human beings. Therefore, poetry is never abolished as the result of the disappearance of one particular language—in this case, that of the Muḍar, who, as everybody knows, were outstanding champions of poetry. In fact, every racial and dialect group among the Arab Bedouins who have undergone some non-Arab influence, or the urban population, attempts to cultivate poetry and to fit it into the pattern of their speech, as much as it suits them.

Contemporary Arab Bedouins who gave up the language of their Muḍar ancestors under non-Arab influence, produce poetry in all the meters used by their Arab ancestors. They make long poems in (those meters). (Their poems) represent all the ways and purposes of poetry,[1620] the erotic (*nasîb*), the III, *361*
laudatory, the elegiac, and the satirical (parts of the ancient *qaṣîdahs*).[1621] They switch from one subject to another in their speech (as was done in the ancient *qaṣîdahs*). They often brusquely state what they want to say at the beginning of the poem. Most of their poems begin with the name of the poet. Then, they pass on to the erotic part (*nasîb*). The Western Arabs call those poems *Aṣma'îyât*, after al-Aṣma'î,[1622] the great transmitter of Arab poetry. The Eastern Arabs call it *Baddâwî* [1623] (Bedouin) and *Ḥawrânî* and

[1619] Cf. p. 351, above.

[1620] MS. C breaks off here, though it has been continued by another hand through the first verses of the poem, p. 416, below.

[1621] Cf. p. 375, above.

[1622] Cf. p. 1:32, above.

[1623] The doubling of the *d* is indicated in B.

Qubaysî [?] [1624] poetry. In connection with it, they often use plain melodies which are not artistic musical compositions. They sing the (poems). They call such songs *Ḥawrânî* songs, after the Ḥawrân, a section of the 'Irâq and Syria where Bedouin Arabs used to live and are still living at this time.[1625]

The (Arabs) have another kind (of poetry) which is widely in use among them. It employs four lines,[1626] of which the fourth has a rhyme different from that of the first three. The fourth rhyme, then, is continued in each stanza through the whole poem, similar to the quatrains and the stanzas of five lines which were originated by recent poets of mixed Arab and non-Arab parentage (*muwallad*).[1627] These Arabs show an admirable eloquence in the use of this type of poetry. There are outstanding and less outstanding poets among them.

Most contemporary scholars, philologists in particular, disapprove of these types (of poems) when they hear them, and refuse to consider them poetry when they are
III, 362 recited. They believe that their (literary) taste recoils from them, because they are (linguistically) incorrect and lack vowel endings. This, however, is merely the result of the loss of the habit (of using vowel endings) in the dialect of the (Arabs). If these (philologists) possessed the same (speech) habit, taste and natural (feeling) would prove to them that these poems are eloquent, provided that their (own) natural dispositions and point of view were not distorted. Vowel endings have nothing to do with eloquence. Eloquence is the conformity of speech to what one wants to express and to the

---

[1624] The reference to *Ḥawrânî* and *Qubaysî* (?) is added in D. Paris reads *Qaysî*, instead of *Qubaysî*, but the latter reading should, it seems, not be changed unless there is more evidence for reading *Qaysî*.

[1625] Cf. p. 437, below.

[1626] *Ghuṣn* "branch," actually is the technical term for the first three lines of a *muwashshaḥah*, whereas the fourth is called *simṭ*. The rhyme scheme of the stanza, as a rule, is (*a-a*), *b-b-b-a*, *c-c-c-a*. On the *muwashshaḥah* see p. 440, below.

[1627] But cf. n. 1492 to this chapter, above. Cf. M. Hartmann, *Das arabische Strophengedicht* (Semitistische Studien, Ergänzungshefte zur Zeitschrift für Assyriologie, Nos. 13–14) (Weimar, 1897), p. 216.

requirements of a given situation,[1628] regardless of whether the *u*-ending indicates the subject and the *a*-ending the object, or vice versa. These things are indicated by syntactic combinations (*qarâ'in*) as used in the particular dialect used by the (Arabs).[1629] The meanings are based upon the technical conventions of people who have a particular (linguistic) habit. When the technical terminology (as it is used) in a particular (linguistic) habit is generally known, the meaning comes out correctly. And if the indicated meaning is in conformity with what one wants to express and with the requirements of the situation, we have sound eloquence.[1630] The rules of the grammarians have nothing to do with that.

The poems of (the Arabs) show all the methods and forms of (true) poetry. They lack only the vowel endings. Most words have no vowel after the last consonant, and the subject and object of verbal sentences as well as the subject and predicate of nominal sentences are distinguished from each other by syntactic means (*qarâ'in*), and not by vowel endings.

One [1631] such poem is put in the mouth of the sharîf Ibn

[1628] Cf., for instance, p. 399, above.

[1629] Cf. pp. 320 f. and 347, above. For *qarâ'in*, cf. p. 344, above.

[1630] Cf. Bombaci, pp. 471 f., who translates *dalâlah* (rendered above as "meaning"), "means of expression."

[1631] The following poems belong to the large epic cycle that became attached to the invasion of northwestern Africa by the Banû Hilâl in the eleventh century. Cf. *GAL, Suppl.*, II, 64, and *'Ibar*, VI, 18; de Slane (tr.), I, 41 f. A modern representative of the epic was published by A. Bel, "La Djazya," *Journal asiatique*, XIX 9 (1902), 289–347; XX 9 (1902), 169–236; I 10 (1903), 311–66. Cf. also G. Marçais, *Les Arabes en Berbérie du XIe au XIVe siècle* (Constantine & Paris, 1913), p. 85.

The poems are often difficult to understand. In contrast to the *muwashshaḥahs* and *zajal*s quoted below, which have often been studied by modern scholars, the epic poems have received little attention. They are a primary and invaluable source for the history of northwest African Arabic. A condition for their study—which this translator regrets not fulfilling—is an intimate knowledge of present-day northwest African dialects, such as can be acquired only through many years of daily contact with the people who speak them. Perhaps such knowledge might be less helpful than anticipated, but this can only be decided after experiment.

The printed editions are of no value so far as the text of the poems is concerned. The corrections offered by the MSS are too numerous to be listed here, and have only occasionally been noted. With the help of the

Hâshim.[1632] In it, he weeps for al-Jâziyah bint Sarḥân and mentions her departure with her people to the Maghrib. (It runs:)

Then spoke the war hero,[1633] the sharîf Ibn Hâshim, concerning
The affliction of his soul, complaining of its misfortune.
III, 363 He hastened to tell (us) how his mind has gone
After a young Bedouin who torments (his soul), already afflicted.
(He told) of how (his) spirit complains about its affliction,
(How) when the morning to say farewell had come—God may destroy him who knows about it!—
(His spirit) felt as if a man with a scalpel had sliced down through it
With a blade of pure Indian steel.
It has become a bleating (sheep) in the hand of (the man who) washes it,
Whose harshness in handling its strap is (as painful) as the thorns of an acacia.
Double (fetters) hold together its feet and its head,
And while (the washer) scrubs it, he holds it by the end of a rope [?].
My tears have begun to flow, as if
Controlled by the operator who turns the water wheels.
At the least let-up, (the tears) are made to flow all the more copiously,

correct text, as indicated in the MSS, the task of translation is not as hopeless as de Slane once thought. However, the present effort—which often follows de Slane's pioneer one—is full of uncertainties, affecting many more passages than those where question marks have been inserted.

The text of the poems ought to be published in transcription by a specialist in the field. The transcription given here in the footnotes uses the forms of classical Arabic as far as possible, and does not try to prejudice the case for correct transcription of the dialectical forms.

[1632] He reflects the historical personality of Shukr b. Hâshim, ruler of Mecca in the eleventh century. Cf. C. S. Hurgronje, *Mekka* (The Hague, 1888–89), I, 60 f.

[1633] *Abû l-hayjâ'*, as is found in the Istanbul MS. Ḥamîdîye 982, completes the opening verse, otherwise incomplete.

(Like) the rain that pours down in sheets from the rain clouds,
(That) flows from the plains at aṣ-Ṣafâ III, *364*
Heavily, blocking the lightning,[1634] it is so abundant.
This song of mine is preparation for a raid,
Which has aroused even the poor people of Baghdad.[1635]
The crier called out the departure, and people secured (their baggage),
And the money lenders of (the tribe) pressed the borrowers.
Hinder her [them?] from leaving now, O Dhiyâb b. Ghânim!
Mâḍî b. Muqarrab [1636] controls her [their?] journey.
Ḥasan [?] [1637] b. Sarḥân says to them: Go west!
Drive (before you) the herds! I am their watchman.
He urges them and drives them on, with the bleating [sheep?].

Zayyân b. ʿÂbis, the kind, left me.
He was not satisfied with the splendor and provision of (the) Ḥimyar.
He left me, who pretended to be my friend and companion, III, *365*
And I have no shield (left) to turn around.
He says to them again: The land of Ibn Hâshim
I can protect, but not if it is parched by [1638] thirst.
The entrance and territory of Baghdad are forbidden to me.

[1634] B has something like *ʿanûfạn* (D: *ʿayûfan*) *wa-taḥjâz al-barq*. The Bulaq text, which de Slane followed, is easier to translate but does not make much sense in the context.

[1635] The translation is very uncertain. The preceding line could mean: "This song of mine is like the love poetry of ʿUrwah." Baghdad is correctly equated with Mecca by de Slane.

[1636] The doubling of the *r* is indicated in A and D.

[1637] B and D vocalize Ḥasn, perhaps Ḥusn, which, however, would seem to be a female name.

[1638] Or perhaps, "causes thirst."

We cannot go in or out there, and my mount is scared
away from it.
My spirit turns away from the country of Ibn Hâshim
Because of the (parching) sun. (Otherwise), death will
come upon me in its noontime heat.
The fires of the maids continued all night to send off
sparks,
Looking for shelter [?], while they bind [1639] the captive of
their (charms) with [in?]. . . .

Another such poem is the mocking elegy in which the (Hilâl) mourned the Zanâtah amir, Abû Su'dâ al-Yafranî,[1640] their adversary in Ifrîqiyah and the land of Zâb. (It runs:)

Then spoke Su'dâ, she with the pure cheeks, while
The lament among the litter-bearing camels, kneeling
(ready to depart), renewed her grief:
III, *366* O you who ask about the grave of Khalîfah az-Zanâtî,
Take the description from me! Do not be stupid!
I see him go up the river Rân [?],[1641] above which
There is a Christian [1642] monastery [?] of a lofty construction.
I see him where the low ground turns aways from the
road up the sand hill,
The river to the east of him, and the patch of reeds indicating (where he is).
Oh, how my soul suffers because of Khalîfah az-Zanâtî,
Who was the offspring of generous ancestors.
He was killed by the fighting hero, Dhiyâb b. Ghânim,
By wounds that made (his blood) to flow (as water flows
out of) the openings of a water bag.

1639 *Yashuddû* (as indicated in B and D); *b[?]-j-r-j-'-n* (perhaps: "with prattling" = *jarjarah?*).

1640 D vocalizes Yifrinî. For the father of Su'dâ, Khalîfah az-Zanâtî, cf., for instance, G. Marçais, *Les Arabes en Berbérie du XIe au XIVe siècle*, pp. 10, 131 f., 263.

1641 De Slane: Zân?

1642 The Sufi order of the 'Îsawîyah, which de Slane had in mind in this connection, did not yet exist in Ibn Khaldûn's time. But the word "monastery" also seems uncertain. B and D have *ar-rayṭ* (?), instead of *ar-r-b-ṭ*.

O Jâziyah! [1643] Khalîfah az-Zanâtî is dead!
Do not leave, unless you want to leave!
Go, calumniator! We sent you away thirty times.
And ten and six during the day (which is) little [?].

Another such poem is put in the mouth of the sharîf Ibn Hâshim, with reference to an altercation between him and Mâḍî b. Muqarrab. (It runs:) [1644]

The excellent Mâḍî started to say:
O Shukr, we are not satisfied with you.
O Shukr, return to the Najd, and do not add any more censure!
(Only) he who cultivates his own land (really) lives.
You have kept away from us, O Shukr. You have approached others.
You have attracted (to yourself) Arabs who wear fine garments.
We have come to face what is destined for us
Just as . . .
If she-camels in the seventh month [1645] can become pregnant again in your land,
We Arabṣ here could not have more fertile ones.

Another such poem deals with the journey of (the Hilâl) to the Maghrib and how they took it away from the Zanâtah. (It runs:)

[1643] This is the reading of the MSS. De Slane corrected the text to "O my woman neighbor." In fact, since it is not clear why Jâziyah should have been addressed here by Su'dâ, the text may have originally referred to the (male rather than female) neighbor whom Su'dâ addresses. The last two lines are not clear.

[1644] This and the following poem appear in the order found in Bulaq, A, and B. D has the next poem first, but then has a long lacuna that extends to p. 426, l. 5. Bulaq has a rather different arrangement of the verses.

[1645] *Ash-shawl*, which means either "she-camels in the seventh month of their pregnancy" or "she-camels seven months after they have given birth." Such she-camels usually give very little milk. Possibly the verse should be translated: "If she-camels in the seventh month give ample milk in your land." At any rate, the meaning is: We in the East cannot compete with the fertility of the West. For *shawl*, cf. also p. 421, below.

III, 367 What a good friend have I lost in Ibn Hâshim!
(But) what men before me have lost good friends!
He and I had a proud (quarrel) between ourselves,
And he defeated me with an argument whose force did not escape me.
I remained (dumbfounded), as if (the argument) had been pure and
Strong wine, which renders powerless those who gulp it down.
Or (I could be compared) with a gray-haired woman who dies consumed by grief
In a strange country, driven out from her tribe,
Who had come upon hard times and finally was rejected
And had to live among Arabs who disregarded their guest.
Like (her), I am as the result of humiliating experience
Complaining about my soul, which has been killed by boredom.[1646]
I ordered my people to depart, and in the morning
They firmly fastened the packsaddles to the backs of their mounts.[1647]
For seven days, our tents remained folded,
And the Bedouin did not erect tent poles to set them up,[1648]
III, 368 Spending all the time upon the humps of hills parallel to each other

The following verses are from a poem of Sulṭân b. Muẓaffar b. Yaḥyâ of the Dawâwidah, a subtribe of the Riyâḥ,[1649] and one of their chieftains. He composed them when
III, 369 he was confined in al-Mahdîyah in the prison of the amir, Abû Zakarîyâ' b. Abî Ḥafṣ, the first Almohad ruler of Ifrîqiyah:

[1646] Cf. R. Dozy in *Journal asiatique*, XIV 6 (1869), 177 f.
[1647] *Sic* Dozy.
[1648] *Sic* Dozy.
[1649] D has a lacuna from here to p. 426, l. 5.

(The poet) speaks, when, with the coming of the morning, his weakness has left him:
May sleep be forbidden to the lids of my eyes!
Who will help a heart that has become the ally of pain and sorrow,
And a spirit that is tormented by love, whose illness has long been with me?
(I love) a woman from the Ḥijâz, an Arab Bedouin woman,
A young kid [?],[1650] a passionate one, who is hard to catch,
Who loves the desert and is not used to villages,
But only (to) sandy plains where the tents receive
The spring rains. There, she spends her winters,
For she is tempted by the desert and in love with it.[1651]
She spends the spring among lands green from the rain

(The lands) charm the eye, after they have received
Rain from the passing clouds.
How do (these clouds) shed tears of water, and how do III, *370*
Gushing springs with their abundance of fresh water compete with each other in murmuring? [1652]
(The lands are) a virgin bride with garment resplendent
Upon her and with a belt of camomile blossoms.
(They are) a desert, a plain, a vast expanse, a far place to travel,
A pasture where ostriches wander among animals led to pasture.
The drink of (the desert) [1653] is the pure milk of she-camels in their seventh month,[1654]

[1650] *Gh-d-'-wîyah,* if it does not refer to a proper name of a locality, ʿAḍawîyah? for instance, may be identical with *ghadawî, ghadhawî?*
[1651] Cf. R. Dozy in *Journal asiatique,* XIV6 (1869), 180.
[1652] Dozy, *loc. cit.,* suggests "crowd upon each other."
[1653] *Sic* Dozy.
[1654] Cf. n. 1645 to this chapter, above.

Which are milked in the evening.[1655] Its food is the meat of sheep [?].[1656]
It has no need of gates, nor of battles whose
Ferocity turns the hair of the young men gray.
May God water the winding valleys of al-Musayjid[1657] with rain
Continuously, so that the decayed bones there come to life again.
Their recompensation (for the happiness they brought me shall be) my love. Would that I
Could relive the days that went by in their sandy hills!
The nights when the bows of youth were in my arms,
Whose arrows never missed, when I stood up (to shoot)!
And my horse, always ready under my saddle, a mare[1658]
In the time of (my) youth in (my) prime, while my hand was holding its reins!
III, *371* And how many fleshy beauties kept me awake! I did not think
That there could be anything more splendid in the world than the rows of their teeth when they smiled.
And how many other maids with full bosoms and swaying hips,
With blackened eyelids and brilliant tattooing!
My passion for them makes (me) beat myself heavily [?]
With my hand. My heart will not forget their claims (on me)⌟[1659]
Nor the fire kindled by passion that burns in my entrails,
Burns in a flame that cannot be extinguished by the water (of my tears).
O you who gave me your promise (to set me free),[1660] until when

[1655] *ʿAtîm*, a plural or secondary form of *ʿatûm*.

[1656] *Jawâzî*, pl. of *jawzâʾ?*

[1657] *Alwâdha l-musayjid*. Whether *al-Musayjid* is a place name or means something else is not certain.

[1658] For *mushâqah*, cf. p. 435 (n. 1742), below.

[1659] A rather doubtful suggestion by Dozy, *op. cit.*, pp. 181 f.

[1660] Cf. Dozy, *op. cit.*, p. 182, who explains that the ruler who holds the poet captive is addressed.

Shall (my) life be spent in a house whose darkness makes me blind?
But I have seen the sun in eclipse for a while
And overcast, and then, the clouds (that covered it) disappeared.
Banner and flags, let them come to us and bring us luck
With the help of God! May their insignia flutter in the wind.
There come into (my) sight the warriors ready to go.
My lance on my shoulder, I march in front of them,
On the sandy plain of Ghiyâth al-Farq above Shâmis,[1661]
God's country whose hillocks I like best of all, III, *372*
To a camping place at al-Ja'farîyah, near the sands,
Staying there, as long as it pleases me.
(There) we shall meet the generous leader of Hilâl b. 'Âmir
Whose greeting will remove all my burning thirst from me.
They are proverbial (for their courage) in the West and the East.
People attacked by them are quickly routed.
Greetings to them and to everyone under their tents!
Fate may let (it) last, as long as the pigeons coo in Ghînâ!
But leave that alone! Do not be grieved by something that has gone!
In this world, nothing is permanent for anyone.

A poem by a recent (Maghribî Arab) poet is that of Khâlid b. Ḥamzah b. 'Umar, the *shaykh* of the Ku'ûb,[1662] of the Awlâd Abû l-Layl. In it, the poet censures their enemies, the Awlâd Muhalhil, and replies to verses by their poet Shibl b. Miskiyânah b. Muhalhil, in which he boasted of the superiority of his tribe to the (Ku'ûb). (It runs:)

[1661] This and the following place names cannot be verified.
[1662] Cf. R. Brunschvig, *La Berbérie orientale*, I, 171.

Thus speaks [1663]—and this is said by an unfortunate person who has smelled
III, 373 The blows of abuse of critical pundits,[1664] having had to deal with the hardest of them,
Which smell to him like the stench of drainage areas [?] [1665]
Who, however, (on his part) has selected the sweetest kinds of rhymes for recitation,
Well-embroidered,[1666] choice ones, of our own composition [?],[1667]
With which you will find me amusing myself, when my detractors are asleep.[1668]
Sieved ones (separated) from him who might criticize them [1669] as to their stanzas,
Whose ways, as well as mine, have been well established [1670] by the critical pundits.
My mentioning them (here), O noble people, serves the purpose of breaking [1671]
Blows from a young lion (Shibl), with a lamb-like answer:
O Shibl,[1672] there came to us [1673] from among nice pregnant (she-camels)
Several full-grown ones, whose possession is reassuring to those in pain,

[1663] The name of the poet should appear here somewhere, but the poem goes on, and no name is given in the introductory verses, which extend down to l. 18.

[1664] *Qîfân*, pl. of *qâ'if* "who goes after and draws conclusions from tracks and traces."

[1665] *Yarîḥu bi-hâ ja'wa* (= *jawâ?*) *al-maṣâbbi?*

[1666] *Muḥabbaratan.*

[1667] The text (*min nishâdinâ*) may not be correct.

[1668] *Tajidnî liyâ nâma l-wushâ multahân bi-hâ* (classical: *tajidunî idhâ nâma l-wushâh multahiyan bi-hâ*).

[1669] *Nâqidâ* = *nâqidihâ.*

[1670] *Muḥakkamata* = *muḥkamata.*

[1671] The MSS have *hayyaḍa*, but meter and meaning require *yuhayyiḍu.*

[1672] The translation of the remainder is mere guesswork and may be completely wrong.

[1673] B vocalizes *jatnâ*, which does not fit the meter. My translation, uncertain as it is, is based on the following reading: *a-Shiblu jâ'atnâ min ḥabâl⟨â⟩ ẓarâ'ifa—qirâḥun* . . . That is, Shibl had boasted that his tribe had robbed the Ku'ûb of some animals and, in addition, had heaped scorn upon them.

But you appropriated them and took all you could, though you were not in need.
However, you said, of the people who own them, things that make those (camels) blameworthy.
Your statement concerning the mother of . . . ,[1674] the son of Ḥamzah,
The protector of their[1675] grounds, . . . the rebuilder of their ruins, (is wrong). III, 374
Do you not know that he raised them up after he had met
The lead [?] of the Banû Yaḥyâ and . . .[1676] which he melted [?]?
A firebrand of a leader, O Shibl, a burning one.
Have you ever seen one who (dared to) approach (the fire of) Hell[1677] and warm himself at it?
(There are) Hell fires [?] which he extinguished, yet they started burning again after being extinguished,
And he extinguished them a second time, being a bold person, not fearing them.
And they started burning again after being twice extinguished. . . . [?]

As he is in demand on account of his (heroism),
Thus, the men of the Banû Ka'b, on account of whom he is feared, are to be avoided.
It has, thus, become clear to him who has sense that they stretch out to the limit
And that they belong[1678] among the greatest things he has to fear.

[1674] The word is not quite clear in the MSS. It could be something like *al-Mi'tamîn*, which does not make sense or fit the meter. Whatever it may be, the word seems to be descriptive of the poet Khâlid b. Ḥamzah, who boasts of himself and his tribe.

[1675] The suffix may refer to "mother," but apparently the whole tribe is meant.

[1676] The word *'allâq*, used here, appears to occur again below, p. 426, l. 4.

[1677] *Falaq*. Cf. *Lisân al-'Arab*, XII, 186, l. 10.

[1678] *Leg. min* instead of *'an?*

Verses on censure from the same poem:

Whenever you brag about what you possess, I possess more because [1679]
III, *375* My possession consists of the firm tie and connection of glory.
I [1680] have a dignity [?] [1681] with the help of which I can repel every group [?] [1682]
With swords from whose necks (backs) hostile people back away.
If property is the requirement for brides,
We are able to woo them with (booty gained at) the points of (our) spears.
Their dowry [1683] consists of nothing less than slender, lean,
Bluish-grey (horses), as quick in their movements as the tongues of vipers.
O my cousins, humiliation is not for young men to appreciate
(Whose very) captives ride mounted when they travel.
They know that fate will stalk them
Without doubt, since the world quickly changes.

Verses on women departing in their litters, from the same poem:

In departing women,[1684] crossing deserts, not fearing hostile people,
Cutting through tracts of land in a much feared environment,
The eye sees—tell Shibl!—(dear) acquaintances.

[1679] *Wa-lîdhâ taghânaytû 'nâ aghnâ li-annanî.*

[1680] D sets in again.

[1681] *Wanâ = anâh?*

[1682] *Mabda'*, as vocalized in the MSS, to be connected with *bid'ah?* The only mĕaning indicated in the dictionaries for *mibda'*, "knife," does not seem to fit here.

[1683] *Naqduhâ.*

[1684] *Bi-ẓa'nin* (thus vocalized in B and D), pl. of *ẓa'înah.*

Every wild cow [1685] has for friends those who are able to get her [?]! [1686] III, *376*
You see [1687] their people in the early morning [?] [1688] carry them
With every. . . .[1689]
There are some people killed every day because of them among the signs erected in the desert [?],[1690]
And the promiscuous [?] libertine has no chance to kiss them.[1691]

Here is a wise maxim from (Maghribî Arab) poetry:

It is stupid of you to seek the impossible.
It is correct to keep away from those who keep away from you.
Let people close their doors to you!
Mount the backs of (your) camels, and God will open a gate (for you).

In the following verse Shibl refers to the fact that the Ku'ûb trace their pedigree back to Tarjam:

Both the old and the young descendants of Tarjam
Make everybody complain of their violence.

The following poem is a poem by Khâlid,[1692] in which he blames his tribesmen (*ikhwân*) for allying themselves with

[1685] Used as a metaphor for beautiful women.

[1686] Possibly, *muḥtaẓîhâ*. *Ḥaẓiya*, however, is not ordinarily construed with the accusative. The MSS have *mḥtẓnh* = *muḥtaḍinhâ* "take her unto themselves (?)."

[1687] Or: "The eye sees . . ."

[1688] *Ghaṭṭâ ṣ-ṣabâḥi* = *ghadâ* . . (?)

[1689] The following words seem to refer to camels.

[1690] *Fî l-arâmâ*, probably to be connected with *'rm*, *ârâm*, but there are other possibilities (pl. of *ri'm?*), all equally dubious.

[1691] *Wa-râ l-fâjiru l-mamzûju 'annû* (= *'anhu*) *ruḍâb(a)hâ*.

[1692] The name is indicated only in D. Cf. p. 423, above. Khâlid's break with Ibn Tâfrâgîn (cf. 1:xli, above) came in A.D. 1354. Cf. R. Brunschvig, *La Berbérie orientale*, I, 175. The word *ikhwân* can hardly mean "brothers," though there were differences of opinion between Khâlid and his brothers.

the Almohad *shaykh* Abû Muḥammad b. Tâfrâgîn who had
III, 377 seized control of Tunis from his charge, the Sultan of Tunis, Abû Isḥâq, the son of Sultan Abû Yaḥyâ. This happened near our own times. (The poem runs as follows:)

Well-informed, the generous hero, Khâlid, gives a speech
Worthy of an orator. What he says is always correct,
The speech of a sage, an intelligent speech, without
Confusion. One cannot escape (the logic of) what he says.[1693]
I have conceived an intelligent idea, not for any compelling reason
And not in order to cause trouble that would result in reproaches.
I have kept (the speech) as a treasure [?].[1694] What a good thing to have it was,
A treasure of thought! Every treasure is discovered [sooner or later?].
(Now,) I openly come out with it and speak about things
Done by men related (to us) in the tribe,
The Banû Ka'b, our closest blood relatives,
Our cousins, both the old and young men.
When the country was conquered, some of (its inhabitants) were treated by us
As true friends and as hospitably received neighbors.
Others were defended by us against their adversaries.
You know that what I say is supported by the truth.[1695]
III, 378 To others we gave part of our own property
As a reward. That is written down in the official decree.[1696]
Others came to us in need. Our high-mindedness
Made us generous to them and we gave them ample (gifts).

[1693] Cf. R. Dozy in *Journal asiatique*, XIV^6 (1869), 183.

[1694] *Kanzî?* A marginal note in B, which is partly cut away in my photostat, seems to have *mustakhrij al-kanz*.

[1695] *Leg. yu'în-hu ṣawâb?*

[1696] Cf. Dozy's discussion of the verse, *op. cit.*, pp. 183 f.

Others attacked us with malice.
We reproved them,[1697] until the things with which they were concerned disappeared.

Others complained about the servants of an important person [1698]
Who closed the door to them when decisions were being made in the halls.
Against the former, we protected the latter.[1699] He required them to let them in
Against the will of the master of al-Yâlifî and Rabâb.[1700]
All the while, we sought to exalt
Them. We never let down a veil to betray (them).
We took the land of Tarshîsh (Tunis) under our protection as our possession after
We had risked (our) swift (horses) and (our own) necks for it III, *379*
. . . of possessions those which were outside
Of the control of their rulers who had . . .
With the help of the resistance of the chiefs of our tribe,
The Banû Ka'b . . .
They helped us against any hostile coalition.
They freed us from the fetters of any (unpleasant) occurrence,
Until those among them who did not have so much as a lamb came to be
Affluent and abundantly blessed with goods,
And used the captive (women) who were sold dear [1701] by the people who owned them
And dressed in different kinds of silk.
They drove (riding) animals . . .

1697 *Naqamnâhu?*

1698 That is, Ibn Tâfrâgîn.

1699 *Fa-ṣunnâhu?*

1700 As a marginal note in B explains, these men were Ibn Tâfrâgîn's officials. A reads Yâliqî, D Bâliqî.

1701 *Al-muthmanât.*

Numerous ones
They acquired large stocks of different kinds of animals,[1702]
Such as can only be met with at special times.
They came to be similar to the Barmecides of old,
III, 380 Or to the Hilâl in the time of Dhiyâb.[1703]
They came to be our shields in every important danger,
Until the enemy's fire (of war) turned into a blaze.
(Then,) they left home under the cover of darkness, but they did not fear
Blame, because the home of noble persons is never subject to censure.
They clothed the tribe in fur pelisses to cover it,
While they themselves—would that they knew it—wore mean coats.
There is also among them a spy [?] [1704] who has not got the (right) information.
My opinion about his forgetfulness [1705] is that his mind is deranged.
He holds suspicions about us that do not apply to us.
Let us wish that he may have several avenues to earn forgiveness!
He is wrong, and so are all those involved with him in his error,
As is established. Those who hold evil suspicions are blameworthy.
Oh,[1706] how to find consolation (over the death of) the hero Bû Muḥammad (b. Tâfrâgîn),
Who used to give away thousands without counting it!
(His) servants are afflicted by his (loss). They thought of

[1702] Cf. Dozy, *op. cit.*, p. 185.
[1703] Dozy, *loc. cit.*
[1704] *Jâ'isun?*
[1705] *Leg. wa-dhahlû ḥukmî lû anna* . . . (?)
[1706] The following verses assume that Ibn Tâfrâgîn is dead, and highly praise him. Thus, they must belong to some other poem, since the preceding verses, as we were told at the beginning of the quotation, are directed against him. He died in October, 1364; cf. R. Brunschvig, *La Berbérie orientale*, I, 180.

His appearance, so long as he lived, like the appearance of (rain) clouds. III, *381*
(Now, however,) they run in search of watering places under the (rain) clouds,
(But) find that all they had hoped to find is a mirage.
When he gave gifts, he knew what was appropriate.
Even when he gave little, it was right.
We have no hope ever to be consoled,
Since the arrows of death struck him down.
The broad land of Tarshîsh (Tunis) has become too strait
For him, and the setting sun is gone with the scattered clouds.
He [?] will soon depart from it

And from maids with charming eyes, slender, coquettish ones,
Who were reared behind curtains and behind veils.
He is haughty when they are, and he is gay when they are,
Under the influence of the beautiful (music of) the *qânûn* and the sound of the rebec.[1707]
They lead him astray, because he has no (longer) any certainty (of himself). And often
He talks (with them), even as though he were a young man.
He spent (happy) days with them. (His) orders were obeyed.
There was delicious food and good drinks. III, *382*
Now, past friendship no longer is available to Ibn Tâfrâgîn.
Instead of it, he received only death.
If he has outstanding intelligence, (even) a raven [?] dare enter the deep sea.
Unforeseen events require men of action,
Great ones, until the people are welded together,

[1707] Cf. 2:396, above.

And (until) the snatched lances and quivers are red (with blood),
And (until) the slave (young man) who wants to gain our royal authority comes to
Repent and does not come to be sound. . . .
O you who eat [1708] bread and like to season it,
You mixed and seasoned the good stuff with poison.[1709]

'Alî b. 'Umar b. Ibrâhîm, a contemporary chieftain of the Banû 'Âmir, one of the subtribes of the Zughbah, censures his cousins who aspire to the leadership of his clan in the following poem: [1710]

III, *383* . . . Sweet [1711] verses of poetic speech,
Well embroidered, like pearls in the hand of a craftsman
When all are in order on the silken thread (on which they are strung),
I bring them (here) [1712] to show the reasons for what happened,
While there appeared the departure [1713] of the camels with their litters, (causing) a separation [?],
That resulted in (the splitting of) the mother tribe into two tribes, and the staff
Is split—May we never meet people who would condemn (us) for it!—
But on the day, when the(ir evil) intention [1714] went away with them, my heart
Felt a sting (like) that of the thorn of the tragacanth,
Or like that of the fiery sparks the smith makes,[1715]

[1708] *Wâkilun = âkilun?*

[1709] I would not know how this verse fits the context. The only explanation that suggests itself, again, is that Ibn Khaldûn or his informant combined selections from different portions of one poem or from different poems.

[1710] B has a number of explanatory notes in the margin.

[1711] The opening half of the first verse is not given.

[1712] *Anâ jâ' bihâ minnî.*

[1713] Cf. p. 437 (n. 1758), below.

[1714] Or possibly: "their trenches (of their tents)," from the root *n'y*, or "their removal," from the same root.

[1715] *Abrâș al-bh'my*, explained in B as *sharar al-ḥaddâd.*

Kindled by them among curved tongs.
Or rather, (my) heart is in the hands of a (wood) splitter [?] [1716]
Who brought them the saw for (wood) cutting, a stupid one.[1717]
Whenever I say: Let us be spared the pain of separation, I am visited and
Encircled by someone [?] who announces the separation.
O that place, which was yesterday (still) populated
With a large tribe and group, while there were many slaves (there);
Servants who bind up (the horses) tightly for the riders [1718] in tournaments [?], III, 384
Some of whom, in the darkness of the night, are awake and (others) asleep;
And cattle whose gathering pleases those who see (the cattle),
Whenever (the cattle) appear from plain or mountain path; [1719]
And crows [1720] whose young ones frighten even (or, please only) their parents; [1721]
And herds [1722] upon herds of wild cows and ostriches.
Today, (however), there is nothing there except owls around it,[1723]
Wailing over the traces of abandoned camps there and the round hillocks.[1724]

[1716] *Leg. qâ'iḍin?* The MSS have *qâbiḍin* "the one who grasps (it)." Or *qâbiḍ* may be some unknown technical term, relative to an occupation?

[1717] *Ghushâm*, explained in B as *jâhil*.

[1718] Perhaps *li-l-khuṭṭâ*, pl. of *khâṭin*, in the sense indicated above. Or *li-l-khuṭâ* "for (causing them to go in short) steps"?

[1719] *Kuẓâm*, explained in B as *ath-thanâyâ*. Cf. also n. 1745, below.

[1720] *Ghudhf*, explained in B as *ghurâb*.

[1721] *Dayâsim-hâ yarû'û murabbîhâ*. They frighten them because they are so ugly.

[1722] *Aṭṭalâw*, or *aṭlâw*, explained in B as *jamâ'ât*.

[1723] The verse seems to be defective.

[1724] *Ḥutâm* (or rather *ḥuthâm*—cf. n. 1755, below) is explained in B as *al-kudâ al-mustadîrah*.

I stood a long time there questioning [1725] the (scene)
With a weak eye, while (my) tears flowed copiously.
All I got from it was a feeling of desolation in my heart
And sickness, for reasons that I know, and (my heart) has become deranged [?].[1726]
Now then, you should bring greetings [1727] to Manṣûr Bû 'Alî—
And after greetings, there is well-being.[1728]
Say to him: O Abû l-Wafâ',[1729] who is the evil spirit [?] of your [pl.] opinions,
You [pl.] entered dark, deep waters,
Turbulent ones, which cannot be measured with the rod. They just
III, 385 Flow over land and hills.
You were not (able to) measure off in them a measure to guide you.
Swollen waters cannot be crossed by swimmers.
There have helped—preparing for your undoing by entering them—
Certain vile men without intelligence.
O raiders,[1730] they made a mistake, and they will not
Last. There are no worlds [1731] that persist.
. . . would [1732] you could see how their opinions
Are a stopgap,[1733] and like rags [1734] that cannot be repaired,

[1725] *Nasâl-hâ* = *as'al-hâ.*

[1726] *Wa-hâma.* Or is the word the plural of *wahm* "hallucinations" or, perhaps, "nightmares"?

[1727] *Wa-min ba'di dhâ taddî* (= *tu'addî*). Both B and D have the marginal note *tḥml*, but *taddî* apparently is the necessary plural *taddîu* (modern *teddîu*). Cf. W. Marçais, *Le Dialecte arabe parlé à Tlemcen* (Paris, 1902), p. 74.

[1728] I.e., a favorable atmosphere for taking advice.

[1729] If the translation of the preceding verse is correct, he would be identical with Bû 'Alî Manṣûr.

[1730] In a note apparently referring to *yâ ghuzwatâ*, B explains the word as "O children of our father." However, the poet is said to address his cousins.

[1731] *Leg. dunân* instead of *dny'*.

[1732] The beginning of the verse is incomplete. The preserved words *a-lâ 'annâhum* make no sense to me.

[1733] It is doubtful whether *sad* (*sic* B) can be understood in this sense, as "a bad repair job."

[1734] *Rafla(h)* is explained in B as *khiraq.*

نبي ابا زيان تطلع الشتوا او تبا على تانا شر برك الطامس زمام
وكم دا تحبوا اتى ان من غشيه خليع الناس بحاج كل غشام
وارحا وتخضوا الملوك وتنعوا على الطعنه تخزى طعنه قتام
عليكم سلام الله من لسن فا تهوز ما غنت ورقا وناح حمام

ومن شعر عرب البريه بالشام ثم بنواحي حوران لامراه قتل زوجها وبعثت الى احلافه من قيس تغريهم بطلب ثاره ٥

تقول فتاة الحي ام سلامة بعين اراع الله من لا رثا لها
تبات بطول الليل ما تالف الكرى موجعه كن السفا في مجالها
على ما جرى في دارها وبالها بلحظة عين البين غير حالها
فقدنا شهاب الدين يا قيس كلكم ونمتوا عن اخذ الثار ماذا مقالها
انا قلت اذا ورد الكتاب يسرني ويبرد من نيران قلبي ذبالها
ايا حين تسريح الذوائب واللحا وبيض العذارى ما حميتوا جمالها

وامثال هذا الشعر عندهم كثير وشعرهم متداول ومن اصحابهم من يتحلاه ومنهم من يستنكفه كما قلناه في فصل الشعر مثل الكثير من ومارناه وذوقه وسلم لهذا الفن وانا الخبير ٥

الموشحات والازجال للاندلس ٥

واما اهل الاندلس فلما كثر الشعر في قطرهم وتهذبت مناحيه وفنونه وبلغ التنميق فيه الغايه استحدث المتاخرون منهم فنا منه سموه بالموشح ينظمونه اسماطا اسماطا واغصانا اغصانا يكثرون منها ومن اعاريضها المختلفه ويسمون المتعدد منها بيتا واحدا ويلتزمون عند قوافي تلك الاغصان واوزانها متتاليا فيما بعد الى اخر القطعه واكثر ما ينتهي عندهم الى سبعه ابيات ويشتمل كل بيت على اغصان عددها بحسب الاغراض والمذاهب وينسبون فيها ويمدحون كما يفعل في القصائد وتجاروا في ذلك الى الغايه واستظرفه الناس وجملة الخاصه والكافه لسهوله تناوله وقرب طريقه وكان المخترع لها بجزيرة الاندلس مقدم بن معافر القبريري من شعرا الامير عبد الله بن محمد المرواني واخذ عنه ذلك ابو عبد الله بن عبد ربه صاحب كتاب العقد ولم يظهر لهما مع المتاخرين ذكر وكسدت موشحاتهما فكان اول من برع في هذا الشان بعدهما عبادة القزاز شاعر المعتصم بن صمادح صاحب المريه وقد ذكر الاعلم البطليوسي انه سمع ابا بكر بن زهير يقول كل الوشاحين عيال على عبادة القزاز فيما اتفق له من قوله

بدر تم شمس ضحا غصن نقا مسك شم ٥

III. Poem in the vulgar language with explicatory notes From MS. B (Yeni Çami 888)

Without usefulness or desirability.[1735] At the outpost on high
There are places that are no places for them to occupy.
By the Prophet and the House and its corners that
Are visited [1736] at all times and in every year,
If life lasts in me [1737] for the . . .[1738] of the nights,
You shall taste a bitter-tasting [1739] wine.
. . .[1740] we follow [1741] the deserts perseveringly,
With every spear a narrow path, and (with every) sword, III, *386*
And (with) every horse, (quick) like the winds, that runs fast,[1742]
Worthy to carry upon itself a young man of noble birth,
And (with) every bay (steed) with short tail and mane,[1743] which gnashes its teeth,
And in harness continuously champs (the) bit.
The sterile earth will be pregnant with us for a while,
And then give birth to us [1744] from every narrow mountain path,[1745]
With heroes, and strong-bodied camels, and lances
Coming in huge numbers while the enemy assembles tumultuously.

[1735] The MSS have *khlw 'l-ghb'wbgh'*. I wonder whether this can be read *khalwu l-ghinâ wa-⟨l⟩-bughâ.*

[1736] The MSS have *alladhî—wa-mazârahâ*. This stands for classical *allatî mazârahâ*, but the dialectical form seems uncertain.

[1737] D vocalizes *biyyah = bî?*

[1738] The meaning of *budd* escapes me. It might possibly be "cutting through (the desert in) the night." The beginning of the following verse reads *w'n bdh'*, to be corrected to *wa-min buddihâ* "and as the result of cutting through (the desert in) them"?

[1739] *Khamṭ* and *ash-sh(u)kâ'* are explained in B as *al-murr* and *ash-sharâb*, respectively.

[1740] Cf. n. 1738, above.

[1741] The word is left without diacritical points in A and B. D has *ttly*, possibly *natlî* (classical *natlû*), as translated above, or *nablâ* (classical *nablû*) "we are wearing out"?

[1742] *Mushâqâ*, *shadâyâh*, and *'âbir* are explained in B as *al-faras*, *ar-riyâḥ*, and *sâbiq*, respectively. For *mushâqâ*, cf. also n. 1658 to this chapter, above.

[1743] *Muktafiḍ* (or *muktafaḍ*) has the following marginal note in B: *mukhtaram* [no diacritical points given] *shabbahahû bi-dhâlika li-qiṣar dhaylihî wa-sha'rihî.*

[1744] That is, will spew us forth.

[1745] *Kuẓâm* is explained in B as *ath-thanâyâ*. Cf. n. 1719, above.

I hold them back [?], being the commander [1746] who leads them,
With my sharp spear a sign for wars.
We [1747] shall go after your pastures like greedy falcons,[1748]
So that you will pay back the debts you owe (us, your) creditors,
When the owl of the plain, O Amir Bû ʻAlî,
Meets hungry hunters starving for meat.[1749]
III, 387 Also, Bû Ḥammû [1750] bought a stumbling race horse,
And he let precious horses in great numbers go.[1751]
He let men go whose neighbor (guest) never sees any wrong (done to him)
And who do not knuckle under, fearing [1752] the enemy, humble ones.
Why do you not set them up (help them), and they will (then be able to) follow their intended course.[1753]
They are the glory of the Zughbah, first and last.
How often has a camel-driver stirred their [1754] (women) departing in the camel litters toward the desert,
Between the level ground and the hillocks,[1755]

1746 *ʻAqîd al-qawm* is explained in B as *amîruhum.*

1747 *Wa-naḥnâ.* Cf. modern *ḥnâ.*

1748 The text reads *aḍrâsh al-buzâ,* which does not fit the meter. B explains *aḍrâsh* as *shirâr al-buzâh.* The *al-buzâ* in the verse may be an explanatory gloss that entered the text.

1749 *Qurâm* is explained in B as *shadîd ash-shahwah ilâ l-laḥm.* The meaning seems to be: When we, bloodthirsty, come to your habitat, which will be ruined by us and henceforward be inhabited only by owls.

1750 B explains: "The ruler of Tlemcen and the middle Maghrib." The ʻAbd-al-Wâdid Abû Ḥammû (see above, 1:1 f.) supported the enemies of the poet, as would appear from this passage.

1751 A and D have: *wa-khallâ l-jiyâda l-ghâliyâti kusâm.* B has: *wa-khallâ l-ghiyâda l-ghâliyâti tusâmu* "and he let the precious young (women) go and be put up for sale"?

1752 *Yarjî* = *yarjîu,* or perhaps *tarjî,* as fem. referring to the broken plural.

1753 *Wa-yaqdîu shû/awrahum. Al-qadd* and *ash-shwr* are explained in B as *al-istiqâmah* and *al-jihah al-maqṣûdah,* respectively.

1754 The MSS here have the dual, which fits the meter only with difficulty and can hardly be understood without resort to the improbable assumption that the poet is including his hostile cousins as part of his tribe.

1755 *Ḥuthâm* is explained in B as *al-kudâ,* as above, n. 1724.

After him [1756] who crosses the elevations of the desert [1757]
When the departure [?] of the camels with their litters . . .[1758]
And how much booty do they bring (back) when they follow him,
The ally of glory, the best vintage of all [?]! [1759]
And when kings come to tyrannize him and to be unfair,
He departs early in the morning, traveling [1760] while it is still dark.
Farewell [1761] to you from an eloquent (poet), who understands
The song of the dove and the wailing of the pigeon.

The following poem is a poem of the Arab Bedouins of the Syrian desert in the region of the Ḥawrân. It was (composed) by a wife whose husband had been killed and who sent to his Qaysite allies, instigating them to seek revenge for him: III, *388*

The valiant tribeswoman, Umm Salâmah, speaks
About a dear person—God frighten those who do not mourn for him!
She spends long nights unused to sleep,
Full of grief, and sorrow is wherever she turns,
Because of what happened in her house and family.
In one moment, separation (from her husband who was killed) changed her position.

[1756] As the following shows, this is the sing. *qaṭṭâ'*, and not the pl. *quṭṭâ'*.

[1757] *Aṣ-ṣuwâ* is explained in B through *jam' ṣuwah, wa-huwa al-qafr*. The *bû mayâ'il* that follows may mean "who possesses (or does) something."

[1758] *Liyâ* (= *idhâ*) *nâḍa tarku ẓ-ẓâ'inîna rumâm*. B explains *nâḍa* as *rkb li-l-ghazw*. As above, p. 432 (n. 1713), *tarku* is indicated in A and D. Could it be *barku* "kneeling camels"?

[1759] *Sajjâj* and *ghuyâm* are explained in B as *khâriq ash-sharâb* and *ash-sharâb*, respectively.

[1760] *Y-j-dh-y* is explained in B as *yasîru*.

[1761] This appears to be the last verse of the poem, but there must have been many more verses.

You have lost Shihâb-ad-dîn, all you Qays,
And you have neglected to take revenge. Is that (your) friendship for her?
I said, when they sent me a letter to cheer me
And to cool the fire burning in my heart:
"What a shame,[1762] to comb forelocks and beards,
And not to protect the beauty of white-skinned virgins!"

The following verses are by a man of the tribe of Hulubbâ,[1763] of the Judhâm Bedouins of Egypt: [1764]

Thus speaks ar-Rudaynî—ar-Rudaynî [1765] speaks the truth—
Preparing well-constructed, original verses:
O you who are coming upon a she-camel,[1766]
III, *389* A strong one, filling out the fine saddle straps,[1767]
One that (is fit to) carry a young man who does not consider sleep something to be earned without toil
By him [1768] who possesses great qualifications, is clever, and knows what is going on!
If you come from [1769] the tribe Hulubbâ, a group
Ever ready to excel in fighting when someone struts into war,[1770]

1762 *A-yâ ḥayn.*

1763 The vocalization is uncertain, but the meter seems to require a closed syllable after the *l*. The name is occasionally read Halbâ'.

1764 The following verses are found only in D. The author reproaches his tribe for not supporting him, while other tribes do.

1765 Ar-Rudaynî, apparently the poet's name, also means "spear." The meaning of the parenthesis may be something like "the sword decides."

1766 The exact meaning of the word *'ydhyh* used here escapes me.

1767 That is, a fat one. D has *mlw 'l-ls'*, which apparently is to be interpreted as *mil'i n-nisâ'*.

1768 This translation presupposes genitives depending on *maghnam*, which, however, might not be absolutely necessary, since the poem (if vocalized according to classical rules) shows also rhymes on *-fu(n)*, against the more frequent *-fi(n)*. At any rate, the endings were not, apparently, pronounced.

1769 D has the pl. *ji'tum*, while the Paris edition reads the simpler and possibly more correct sing. *ji'ta*.

1770 *Birâzîyatin in-zâfa* (in D spelled as one word) *li-l-ḥarb zâ'ifun.*

And [1771] (from) my people, the Banû Manẓûr—may I never taste the loss of them!—
A group of people representing all maṇkind, the rallying point of the weak and fearful,
I myself (personally) having all my experience from the Banû Raddâd [1772]
—May my God protect them against serious setbacks!—
(Then, let me inform you:) There has come to me, together with the caravan, confusing information
And (news of) divided intentions and contradictory opinions.
How can I (alone) stay the injustice (being done me), while you [1773] are a group,
(Riding upon and disposing over) every neighing horse with a long mane?
<I hope and pray> [1774] that you may all reach a decision,[1775]
Even if [1776] (your) property and life perish in its (execution).
I have ʿUbayd b. Mâlik (as support) among the high leaders,[1777]
In whom there is high nobility, with command over the people,
And (I have) true friends in the leaders of the Âl Muslim,
While I (suffer) from my own people many unpleasant things.[1778]

There [1779] are many such poems. They circulate among (Arab Bedouins). Some tribes cultivate them. Others, in- III, 390

[1771] The verse is not found in Paris. In D it reads:
Wa-qawmî Banî Manẓûrin lâ dhuqtu faqdahum
Lufûfi l-warâ malqâ ḍaʿîfin wa-khâʾifin.

[1772] Thus, the poet belongs to the Raddâd family, of the Manẓûr clan, of the Hulubbâ subtribe, of the Judhâm tribe.

[1773] Addressing his tribe.

[1774] The beginning of the verse is not preserved.

[1775] D: *raʾyan yalummukum.*

[1776] *Wa-law anna,* as in the Paris edition. D omits *wa-.*

[1777] D: *dhurân.*

[1778] D: *wa-ʾnâ min dhurâ qawmî kathîru l-ʿajârifi.* Paris has a different text, which may be translated "Whose amir supports all tribes."

[1779] This paragraph is not found in Bulaq.

cluding, for instance, most of the contemporary chiefs of the Riyâḥ, Zughbah, and Sulaym,[1780] and others, disdain cultivating them, as we explained in the section on poetry.[1781]

The Spanish muwashshaḥahs *and* zajals

Poetry was greatly cultivated in Spain. Its various ways and types were refined. Poems came to be most artistic. As a result, recent Spaniards created the kind of poetry called *muwashshaḥ*.[1782]

The *muwashshaḥah* consists of "branches" (*ghuṣn*) and "strings" (*simṭ*) [1783] in great number and different meters. A certain number (of "branches" and "strings") is called a single verse (stanza). There must be the same number of rhymes in the "branches" (of each stanza) and the same meter (for the "branches" of the whole poem) throughout the whole poem. The largest number of stanzas employed is seven. Each stanza contains as many "branches" as is consistent with purpose and method. Like the *qaṣîdah*, the *muwashshaḥah* is used for erotic and laudatory poetry.

(The authors of *muwashshaḥahs*) vied to the utmost with each other in this (kind of poetry). Everybody, the elite and the common people, liked and knew these poems because they were easy to grasp and understand. They were invented in Spain by Muqaddam b. Mu'âfâ al-Qabrî,[1784] a poet under the

[1780] The reference to the Zughbah and Sulaym appears only in B, not in A or D.

[1781] The reference appears to be to pp. 410 ff., above.

[1782] The following section has received much attention from modern scholars interested in Arabic lyric poetry and its relationship to the medieval poetry of Christian Europe. Two works that will be systematically referred to in the notes that follow are the pioneer study by M. Hartmann, *Das arabische Strophengedicht* (see n. 1627, above), and the recent treatment of the subject by A. R. Nykl, *Hispano-Arabic Poetry* (n. 1565, above).

[1783] Cf. p. 414, above. Hartmann, pp. 110 f., tries to give this passage too literal an interpretation.

[1784] For this rather enigmatic personality who, according to Ibn Khaldûn, must have lived *ca.* A.D. 900, cf. Hartmann, pp. 71 f.; Nykl, pp. 31, 36, 386 f.; E. Terés in *al-Andalus*, XI (1946), 156; J. Rikabi, *La Poésie profane sous les Ayyûbides* (Paris, 1949), p. 172 f.

B reads the name in a form something like Muqaddam b. Mu'âfir at-Tirmidhî. A and D have Mu'âfir al-Qabrîrî. The name of the alleged inventor of *muwashshaḥ* poetry in Spain is not altogether certain.

amir 'Abdallah b. Muḥammad al-Marwânî. Aḥmad[1785] b. 'Abdrabbih, the author of the *'Iqd*, learned this (type of poetry) from him.[1786] (Muqaddam and Ibn 'Abdrabbih) were not mentioned together with the recent (authors of *muwashshaḥahs*), and thus their *muwashshaḥahs* fell into desuetude. The first poet after them who excelled in this subject was 'Ubâdah al-Qazzâz,[1787] the poet of al-Mu'taṣim b. Ṣumâdiḥ, the lord of Almería. Al-A'lam al-Baṭalyawsî[1788] mentions that he heard Abû Bakr b. Zuhr[1789] say that all authors of *muwashshaḥahs* are indebted to the following verses which 'Ubâdah al-Qazzâz happened to make: III, *391*

Full moon—Late morning sun—Bough on a sandhill —sweet smelling musk:
How perfect—how resplendent—how exuberant—how fragrant![1790]
No doubt—he who sees her—falls in love with her—has lost out![1791]

[1785] A and D have 'Abdallâh. B has 'Abdallâh, which, however, is corrected in the margin to Aḥmad. Hartmann, p. 23, makes the very improbable suggestion that the author of the *'Iqd* and the Ibn 'Abdrabbih meant here are two different persons. Cf. also as-Suyûṭî, *Al-Wasâ'il ilâ ma'rifat al-awâ'il*, ed. R. Gosche, *Die Kitâb al-awâ'il* (Halle, 1867), pp. 18 f. As-Suyûṭî's authority is the *Mughrib* of Ibn Sa'îd. Ibn Bassâm already identified this Ibn 'Abdrabbih with the author of the *'Iqd*. Cf. his *Dhakhîrah*, I 2 (Cairo, 1361/1942), 1 f.

The particular work by Ibn Sa'îd that was Ibn Khaldûn's source for this chapter is now said to have been found, but more detailed information is not yet available. Cf. n. 1810, below.

[1786] For this passage, cf. *GAL*, *Suppl.*, I, 477.

[1787] According to S. M. Stern, "Muḥammad b. 'Ubâdah al-Qazzâz," *al-Andalus*, XV (1950), 79–109, the poet of the lines quoted would be Muḥammad b. 'Ubâdah. He lived in the eleventh century.

[1788] Abû Isḥâq Ibrâhîm b. al-Qâsim, who died in 642 or 646 [1244/45 or 1248/49]. Cf. Hartmann, p. 88 (n. 2); as-Suyûṭî, *Bughyah*, p. 185; Ḥâjjî Khalîfah, *Kashf aẓ-ẓunûn*, II, 119. His name appears as Ibrâhîm b. Muḥammad, which seems to be an error, in Ibn Farḥûn, *Dîbâj*, p. 80, in the biography of his pupil, al-Lablî, 613–691 [1216/17–1292]. Cf. *GAL*, *Suppl.*, I, 967.

[1789] Muḥammad b. 'Abd-al-Malik, who died in 595 or 596 [1199–1200]. Cf. *GAL*, I, 489; *Suppl.*, I, 893; Nykl, pp. 248 ff. His age at death is given as sixty in one source but elsewhere as close to, or over ninety. Cf. also pp. 443 ff., below. MSS. A, B, and C all have Zuhayr, instead of Zuhr.

[1790] *Leg.* with A, B, and D: *anamm.*

[1791] Nykl, p. 392, follows Hartmann, p. 89, in translating the last line (*qad ḥaram*): "falls in love—with none but her." It should be noted that B and D vocalize *ḥurim!*

It is believed that no contemporary from the time of the *reyes de taïfas* preceded ('Ubâdah) as author of *muwashshahahs.*

('Ubâdah) was followed by Ibn Arfa'-ra'sah,[1792] the poet of al-Ma'mûn b. Dhî n-Nûn, the lord of Toledo. It has been said that he did very well with the beginning of his famous *muwashshaḥah*, where he says:

> The lute sings — the most original melody. — Wild brooks running through — the lawns of gardens

and at the end, where he says:

> You are bold and do not submit — Perhaps you are al-Ma'mûn — who frightens the companies (of the enemy) — Yaḥyâ b. Dhî n-Nûn.

III, *392* There was much competition (in *muwashshaḥ* poetry) during the reign of the Veiled (Almoravid) Ṣinhâjah. Original things were produced at that time. The champions in the race were al-A'mâ at-Tuṭîlî [1793] and Yaḥyâ b. Baqî.[1794] One of the "gilded [1795] *muwashshaḥahs*" of at-Tuṭîlî is the following:

> How can I — be patient, when the way signs — (fill me with) emotion,
> And the caravan in the desert — with the chaste and tender (maids) — is gone?

A number of *shaykhs* have mentioned that Spaniards interested in (*muwashshaḥ* poetry) tell how a number of authors of *muwashshaḥahs* once gathered in Sevilla, each of them with a

[1792] Cf. Hartmann, pp. 26 f., 168; Nykl, pp. 201 f., where the name is vocalized Ibn Irfa' Ra'suh. The vocalization *ra'sah* is indicated in B and D. Poems by this author and by some of the other authors of *muwashshaḥahs* mentioned here are also found in Ibn al-Khaṭîb's *Jaysh at-tawshîḥ*. Cf. S. M. Stern, *Les Chansons mozarabes* (Palermo, 1953), pp. 51 ff.

[1793] He died in 520 [1126]. Cf. *GAL*, I, 271; *Suppl.*, I, 480; Hartmann, pp. 15 f., 160 f.; Nykl, pp. 254–58. [* *Dîwân*, ed. Beirut, 1963].

[1794] He died in 540 [1145]. Cf. Hartmann, pp. 31 ff.; Nykl, pp. 241–44; E. García Gómez in *al-Andalus*, XIX (1954), 43–52.

[1795] This is corrected in Bulaq to "refined." But "gilded" seems to be the correct reading, as a technical term for a special kind of *muwashshaḥ* poetry. Cf. Hartmann, p. 15 (n. 2).

very artistic *muwashshaḥ* poem of his own composition. Al-Aʿmâ at-Tuṭîlî stepped forward to recite his poem. He began with his famous *muwashshaḥah:*

> Laughing and revealing (teeth like) pearls — showing a face beautiful like the moon — time is too narrow to hold (the beauty of the beloved) — but my bosom incloses it.

(When the assembled poets heard that,) Ibn Baqî tore up his *muwashshaḥah*, and all the others followed suit.[1796]

Al-Aʿlam al-Baṭalyawsî mentioned that he heard Ibn Zuhr say: "The only *muwashshaḥ* poem I ever envied the poet is the following lines by Ibn Baqî:

> Look at Aḥmad — at the peak of glory — which cannot be reached (by anyone else)! — The West caused his rise — Show us someone like him — O East!" [1797]

In the time of (at-Tuṭîlî and Ibn Baqî), there lived the gifted *muwashshaḥah* poet Abû Bakr al-Abyaḍ.[1798] In their time, there also lived the philosopher Abû Bakr b. Bâjjah,[1799] the author of famous melodies. There is a famous story that relates how he attended the reception of his master Ibn Tîfalwît,[1800] the lord of Saragossa, and had one of his singing girls recite the following *muwashshaḥah* of his own composition: [1800a] III, *393*

> Let the train (of your robe) drag wherever it will — and add drunkenness (with the love of your beloved) [1800b] to drunkenness (with wine)!

1796 Cf. Nykl, p. 256. For the famous verses, cf. also Ibn Sanâ'-al-Mulk, *Dâr aṭ-ṭirâz*, ed. Rikabi (Damascus, 1949), pp. 25, 43 f.

1797 Cf. Nykl, pp. 243 f. Cf. also Ibn Saʿîd, *El Libro de las Banderas de los Campeones*, ed. and tr. E. García Gómez (Madrid, 1942), pp. 48, 193.

1798 Like most of the poets mentioned in the pages that follow, he is very little known, so far, from other sources.

1799 Cf. p. 116, above.

1800 The vocalization Tîwalfît is found in D. The recent edition of Ibn Saʿîd, *Mughrib* (Cairo, 1953), p. 61, vocalizes Tayfulwît.

1800a D adds: "beginning."

1800b A has correctly *minhu.* B, D, and Bulaq have *minka.*

This greatly moved (Ibn Tîfalwît), to whom the praise was directed. Then, (Ibn Bâjjah) finished the poem with these words:

> Let God raise the banner of victory—for the distinguished amir Abû Bakr!

When the song was over, Ibn Tîfalwît was heard to exclaim: "How moving!" He tore his garments (as a sign of joyous emotion) and said: "What a beautiful beginning and end!" And he swore the most binding oaths that Ibn Bâjjah should walk home upon gold. The philosopher was afraid that it would not end well, so he employed the ruse of putting gold in his shoes and walking home on that gold.[1801]

Abû l-Khaṭṭâb b. Zuhr [1802] mentioned that in the salon of Abû Bakr b. Zuhr, the afore-mentioned *muwashshaḥah* poet Abû Bakr al-Abyaḍ was mentioned. One of those present spoke slightingly of him, whereupon (Abû Bakr b. Zuhr) said: "How can one speak slightingly of a person who made the following poem: [1803]

> I get no pleasure out of drinking wine—on meadows of camomile flowers—unless one with slender hips—when he bends down in the morning—or in the evening
> III, *394* —says: Why does the evening drink (*shamûl*)—beat my cheek—and why does the north wind (*shamâl*) blow—so that it bends—the well-proportioned bough—that my garment covers?
>
> This is what makes hearts vanish—The way he walks throws me into confusion—O glance, sin more and more!—O red lips, and the fine teeth of his!—Cool the thirst—of a sickly lover—(who) will not give up—(his) love pact with his (beloved)—and will not cease

[1801] Cf. Hartmann, pp. 30 f., 184; Nykl, p. 253. Cf. also the version of the story given by Ibn al-Khaṭîb, *al-Iḥâṭah*, I, 244 f.

[1802] Cf. Nykl, p. 341. Hartmann, p. 7 (n. 1), suggests that Ibn Zuhr is in this case an error for Ibn Diḥyah, d. 633 [1235]. Cf. *GAL*, I, 310 ff.; *Suppl.*, I, 544 f.

[1803] Cf. Hartmann, pp. 6 ff.; Nykl, pp. 245 f., 392 f.

—in every condition—hoping to be united with him—though he is unapproachable."

Subsequently, at the beginning of the Almohad dynasty, Muḥammad b. Abî l-Faḍl b. Sharaf[1804] became famous. Alms [?][1805] b. Duwayrîdah said: "I saw Ḥâtim b. Sa'îd[1806] begin a poem thus:

A sun in conjunction with a full moon:—Wine and a boon companion.

Further, Ibn Hardûs,[1807] who made the following poem:

O night of union and happiness—by God, return!

(Further,) Ibn Mu'ahhil,[1808] who made the following poem:

A holiday is not made by a (fine) dress and scarf—and the smell of perfume—A holiday is when one meets—with the beloved."

(There was also) Abû Isḥâq ad-Duwaynî.[1809] Ibn Sa'îd[1810] said: "I heard Abû l-Ḥasan Sahl b. Mâlik say that (Abû Isḥâq) came to Ibn Zuhr when (the latter) was advanced in years. He wore rustic clothes, as he was living at Ḥiṣn Istabbah.[1811] He was not recognized. (Abû Isḥâq) sat at the very end of the room. The conversation was in progress, and he recited a *muwashshaḥah* of his own composition in which the following verses occurred: III, *395*

1804 Cf. Hartmann, p. 58. Is he identical with Abû l-Ḥasan b. al-Faḍl, quoted below, p. 448?

1805 *Sic* A and B. D has al-Ḥasan, which looks like a simplification.

1806 Cf. Hartmann, p. 21. The famous poem is quoted in full by Ibn Sanâ'-al-Mulk, *Dâr aṭ-Ṭirâz*, pp. 26, 45 f.; * as-Safadî, *Wâfî*, IV, 41 f.

1807 Cf. Hartmann, pp. 37 f.

1808 Hartmann, p. 42, and Nykl, p. 341, read Ibn Mûhal.

1809 Cf. Hartmann, p. 19.

1810 The historian, 'Alî b. Mûsâ, of the thirteenth century. Cf. *GAL*, I, 336 f.; *Suppl.*, I, 576 f. He evidently is Ibn Khaldûn's most important source for this section, as well as for certain other information. Cf. 1:22 (n. 58), 1:118 (n. 67), 1:120 (n. 80), and p. 441 (n. 1785), above.

1811 Estepa, which, however, is elsewhere spelled Iṣṭabbah. D vocalizes Astabbah.

The antimony of darkness runs—from the white eyeball of dawn—in the morn—and the wrist of the river—is clad in garments of green (plants)—from the marshes.

Ibn Zuhr stirred and asked: 'You can make such verses?' (Abû Isḥâq) replied: 'Try me.' Whereupon (Ibn Zuhr) asked who he was. He told him, and (Ibn Zuhr) said: 'Come up.[1812] Really I did not recognize you.' "

Ibn Sa'îd continued: "The champion of the whole group was Abû Bakr b. Zuhr. His *muwashshaḥahs* are known in the East and the West." He said: "I heard Abû l-Ḥasan Sahl b. Mâlik say that people asked Ibn Zuhr: 'If you were asked what is your most original *muwashshaḥah* (what would you say)?' (Ibn Zuhr) replied: 'I would say the following poem:

Why does the infatuated person—not wake up from his drunkenness?—How drunk he is—without wine! [1813] —Why is the grieved person full of longing—homesick?—Will our days along the canal—and our nights—ever return—when we enjoyed the balmy breeze—fragrant as Dârîn [1814] musk—and when we almost—received new life—from the beauty of the pleasant spot?—A river which is given shade—by splendid large trees along it—with thick green foliage—and the water runs—(carrying) on its surface and submerged under the water—fallen myrtle (leaves).' " [1815]

III, *396* Afterwards, Ibn Ḥayyûn [1816] became famous. He composed the following famous *zajal:*

[1812] That is, "take a seat of honor."

[1813] The following three cola (to "homesick") are found only in Bulaq. A, B, and D have an empty space.

[1814] "Dârîn musk" is a proverbial expression in ancient Arabic poetry. Dârîn is said to have been a seaport on the Persian Gulf to which the eastern trade brought perfumes. Cf. al-Bakrî, *Mu'jam mâ sta'jam* (Cairo, 1945–51), pp. 538 f.; Yâqût, *Mu'jam al-buldân*, II, 537; *Lisân al-'Arab*, XVII, 10.

[1815] Cf. Nykl, p. 250; J. Rikabi, *La Poésie profane sous les Ayyûbides*, p. 183. Rikabi suggests that the "canal" may be a proper name (Khalîj), and he translates *yuḥayyînâ* "were greeted" (instead of "received new life"). The first line of the poem is referred to by Ibn Sa'îd, *Mughrib*, p. 266.

[1816] Cf. Hartmann, p. 27; Nykl, pp. 342 f.

His arrow is more dangerous than death—whether shot by the hand or by the eye.[1817]

He also wrote the following couplet:

I was created beautiful and am known as a skillful archer.
Hence, I do not stop fighting for a moment.
I do, with these two eyes of mine,
What my hand does with the arrow.[1818]

Together (with Ibn Zuhr and Ibn Ḥayyûn), al-Muhr b. al-Faras became famous at that time in Granada. Ibn Sa'îd said: "When Ibn Zuhr heard his poem:

By God, what a splendid day it was—at the river of Ḥimṣ (Sevilla) on those meadows!—We then turned around to the mouth of the canal—breaking the musk seals—on (the bottles of) golden wine—while the cloak of evening was being folded up by the hand of darkness.[1819]

he said: 'We could not invent such a (beautiful comparison as that of the) cloak!' "

Muṭarrif lived in the same place as (al-Muhr). Ibn Sa'îd reported, on the authority of his father, that Muṭarrif came to Ibn al-Faras, who got up to honor him. When Muṭarrif told him not to do that, Ibn al-Faras replied: "What—not get up for the poet who made these verses:

Hearts are smitten—by well-aimed glances.
—Say, how can you remain—without emotion?" [1820] III, 397

Later, there was Ibn Ḥazmûn [1821] in Murcia. Ibn ar-Râ'is mentioned that Yaḥyâ al-Khazrajî [1822] came to his salon and

[1817] Cf. Nykl, *loc. cit.* Perhaps one might translate: "His arrow is always ready to be shot (*yufawwaq . . . ḥîn*), whether by the hand or by the eye (*'în*)." D, however, vocalizes *ḥayn* and *'ayn*.

[1818] Cf. Nykl, *loc. cit.*

[1819] Cf. Hartmann, p. 71; Nykl, p. 343.

[1820] Cf. Hartmann, pp. 72 f.; Nykl, p. 343.

[1821] Cf. Hartmann, pp. 38 ff.

[1822] Cf. Hartmann, pp. 63 f. Instead of Ibn ar-Râ'is, Bulaq reads Ibn ar-Râsîn.

recited a *muwashshaḥah* of his own composition. Ibn Ḥazmûn said to him: "A *muwashshaḥah* is not a *muwashshaḥah*, until it is entirely free from forced (artificiality)." When Yaḥyâ asked: "How, for instance?" Ibn Ḥazmûn replied: "As, for instance, the following verses of mine:

> O you who are keeping away from me — to be united with you — is there a way? Or do you think — your love can be forgotten — by the heart of the (love)sick person?" [1823]

Abû l-Ḥasan Sahl b. Mâlik in Granada.[1824] Ibn Sa'îd said: "My father used to admire his poem (which reads):

> The brook of the morning in the east — turns into a sea everywhere — and the doves cry out plaintively to each other — as if they are afraid of drowning — and they weep in the early morning among the foliage (of the trees)."

At that time, Abû l-Ḥasan b. al-Faḍl [1825] became famous in Sevilla. Ibn Sa'îd, on the authority of his father, said: "I heard Sahl b. Mâlik say to (Ibn al-Faḍl): 'O Ibn al-Faḍl, you excel (*faḍl*) among the writers of *muwashshaḥahs* with these verses of yours:

> Alas for a time that has passed — In the evening, passion is finished and gone — I am alone against my will, not willingly — I spend the night by the bright-burning fire of tamarisk coals — in my mind embracing those remnants of the abandoned camps — in my imagination kissing their traces.' "

III, 398 (Ibn Sa'îd) continued: "I heard Abû Bakr b. aṣ-Ṣâbûnî [1826] recite his *muwashshaḥahs* to Professor Abû l-Ḥasan ad-

[1823] Cf. Nykl, p. 342.

[1824] Cf. Hartmann, p. 80; Nykl, p. 350. Cf. also p. 445, above, and p. 459, below.

[1825] Cf. Hartmann, p. 35. Identical with Muḥammad b. Abî l-Faḍl, p. 445, above?

[1826] Cf. Hartmann, pp. 43 f.; Nykl, p. 247.

Dabbâj [1827] many times, but I heard (ad-Dabbâj) praise him highly only for the following verses:

> Swearing by the love of him who keeps (me) off: — The night of one consumed by longing has no dawn — The morning is frozen and does not flow [1828] — My night, I think, has no morn — Is it correct, O night, that you are eternal — Or, have the tips of the wings of the eagle [1829] been clipped — so that the stars of heaven do not run their course?"

One of the best *muwashshaḥahs* by Ibn aṣ-Ṣâbûnî runs:

> What is the matter with the person in love who pines away in grief? Woe unto him! The physician who should have cured him made him ill.
> His beloved avoids him — and then, slumber imitates the example of the beloved in this respect (and also avoids him).
> Sleep treats my eyelids cruelly, but I do not weep for it, except (that having no sleep) means loss of (seeing) the image (of the beloved in my dreams).[1830]
> The (hoped for) meeting (with the beloved) today was a disappointment for me (as it did not take place), just as he wanted it. What a sad meeting!
> But I do not blame him who keeps me off, in the form of reality or unreality.[1831]

Among the people of the (African) shore, Ibn Khalaf al-Jazâ'irî [1832] became famous. He is the author of the famous *muwashshaḥah:*

[1827] 'Alî b. Jâbir, 566–646 [1170/71–1248]. Cf. Ibn al-Abbâr, *Takmilat aṣ-Ṣilah*, p. 683, No. 1910.

[1828] *Jamada ṣ-ṣubḥu laysa yuṭṭarad*, as vocalized in D. De Slane's suggestion, "The morning is not generally praised" (because it means the end of the lovers' meeting), does not seem to fit the context here.

[1829] With reference to the constellations called *Nasr* "Eagle."

[1830] B is missing from here to p. 454, l. 17.

[1831] I.e., in reality or in dreams.

[1832] Cf. Hartmann, p. 33.

III, *399* The hand of morn has lighted—sparks of light—in the braziers of the flowers.

(Another author from northwestern Africa is) Ibn Khazar al-Bajâ'î.[1833] One of his *muwashshaḥahs* runs:

Some fortunate circumstance greeted you with a smile from the teeth of time.

A *muwashshaḥah* by a recent poet is that of Ibn Sahl,[1834] a poet first in Sevilla and later on in Ceuta. The following verses are from his poem:

Does the gazelle of al-Ḥimâ [1835] know that it inflamed (*ḥamâ*)—the heart of a lover which it has made its dwelling place?—Now, it is afire and throbbing, like a—firebrand with which the east wind plays.[1836]

Our afore-mentioned friend, the wazir Abû 'Abdallâh b. al-Khaṭîb, who was in his day the (leading) poet of Spain and the Maghrib, wove on (Ibn Sahl's) loom. He thus said: [1837]

May the abundant rain, as it pours down, benefit you,
O time of the meeting in Spain!
My meeting with you is but a dream
In (my) slumber, or a furtive moment.
Time presents such a diversity of wishes,
That proceed in a prescribed order,
One by one, or two by two,
III, *400* Like groups (of pilgrims) whom the festival calls (to Mecca).
Rain gave a generous sparkle to the meadow.
So that brilliant flowers are smiling in it.
An-Nu'mân transmits on the authority of Mâ'-as-samâ',

[1833] Cf. Hartmann, pp. 34 f. The form of this poet's name seems not quite certain. He was from Bougie.

[1834] Cf. pp. 92 and 393, above; Hartmann, pp. 71 ff.

[1835] Cf. Nykl, p. 45. Al-Ḥimâ is often used as a cover name for the place where the poet himself lives.

[1836] Cf. Nykl, pp. 344 f.

[1837] Cf. Nykl, p. 366.

Exactly as Mâlik transmits on the authority of Anas.[1838]
Beauty has clothed the (beloved) with an embroidered garment
That makes him look scornfully upon the most splendid dress,
On nights when I would have covered the secret of (my) love
With (their) darkness, had there not been the suns of gleaming white (faces).
On (such occasions), the star of the cup inclined and fell
In a straight course with happy results.
A desirable situation, with which there is nothing wrong, except
That it passed as quickly as a glance of the eye,
Just when (we) were enjoying being together,[1839] or as suddenly as
The (disappearance of the) watchful stars ushers in the morning.
Shooting stars fell upon us, or
The eyes of narcissuses affected us.
What else could a man (wish) for who has escaped (from sorrow),
So that (the beauty of) the meadow [1840] could gain a place (in him)? III, *401*
The flowers seize this opportunity
Of being safe from his trickery, and do not fear him.
Then, the water (of the brook) whispers with the pebbles.
Every lover is alone with his friend.
One beholds the rose, jealous and annoyed (because of the beauty of the beloved),
Covering itself, flushing with anger, with its (red color).
One sees the myrtle, intelligent and understanding,

[1838] I.e., an-Nu'mân b. (?) Mâ'-as-samâ', a sixth-century Lakhmid ruler of al-Ḥîrah on the Euphrates; Mâlik b. Anas, the famous jurist; *an-nu'mân* "anemone"; *mâ'-as-samâ'* "water of heaven," meaning rain. Thus, the verse means that flowers follow naturally and reliably upon rain.

[1839] Bulaq: "sleeping."

[1840] D has *ad-dahr* "fate, eternity."

Listening clandestinely with sharp ears.[1841]
Dear (fellow-)tribesmen from Wâdî al-Ghaḍâ,[1842]
In my heart there is a place where you live.
My longing for you cannot be encompassed by (even) the widest space;
I do not care to distinguish its East from its West.
Bring back the past times of intimacy,
And you will liberate (me) who cares for you from his sadness.
Fear God, and revive a passionate lover
Whose life spends itself with (each) breath.
His respect for you made his heart a prison.
Would you want that prison to be destroyed?
In my heart, one of you is near
III, *402* In wishful thought, while he is far away.
A moon whose rise in the west caused
Unhappiness (for me) who is deeply in love with him, while he himself is happy!
The virtuous and the sinners know no distinction,
When they love him, between the divine promise and the divine threat.[1843]
He charms with his eyes, with red lips sweet as honey.
He roams in the soul like (life-giving) breath.
He aimed his arrow, said: "In the name of God," [1844] and let fly.
Thus, my heart became the prey of the wild beast (of passion).
Even when he is unfair and (my) hope is disappointed,
So that the heart of the lover melts with longing,

[1841] Lit., "ears of a horse," possibly referring also to the shape of myrtle leaves?

[1842] Wâdî al-Ghaḍâ is identified by geographers with a certain place in northern Arabia called Buwayrah. Cf. al-Bakrî, *Muʿjam mâ staʿjam*, pp. 285, 999; Yâqût, *Muʿjam al-buldân*, I, 765. Here it seems to be a cover name for the river of Granada.

[1843] That is, love for him cancels the distinction between virtuous persons, to whom Paradise is promised, and sinners threatened with punishment in Hell.

[1844] Cf. R. Dozy in *Journal asiatique*, XIV ^{6} (1869), 190 f.

Still, he is the first (best) beloved of my soul.
As it is no sin to love one's beloved,
His orders are executed and obeyed
In bosoms [1845] that he has rent (with love's pain), and hearts.
(His) glance sits in judgment over them, and he has his way.
He does not heed, in connection with the poor weak souls (of his lovers),
Him who renders justice to the one who is treated unjustly, against the one who treats him unjustly,
And who rewards pious (souls) and (punishes) the evil-doer.
What is the matter with my heart? Whenever the east wind blows, III, *403*
It has a new attack of longing.
On the tablet (of destiny) was written for (my heart) [1846]
These divine words: "My punishment, indeed, will be severe." [1847]
It is worried and ill,
But, still, always very eager for torturing (emotions).
A burning (passion) is kindled in my bosom—
A fire among dry stubble.
It has left only a little of (my) lifeblood,
Just as the morn remains after the last darkness of the night.
Submit, O my soul, to the decision of destiny,
And use the time (that is left) in (thinking of) my return (to God) and repentance.
Do not think back to a time that has passed,
When (I received) alternately (from the beloved) favors long gone, and reproaches.
Address now the gracious master,

[1845] Lit., "ribs."
[1846] De Slane: "for (my beloved)." This would be correct if the verse were found before that preceding it. Was this, possibly, its original position?
[1847] Qur'ân 14.7 (7).

Who was inspired with the success (announced) in the heavenly prototype (of the Qur'ân),
Who is noble in end and origin,
The lion of the flock,[1848] the full moon of the assembly,
III, 404 Upon whom victory descends, as
The revelation descends by means of the holy spirit.[1849]

The attempts at *muwashshaḥahs* by Easterners are obviously forced. One of the best *muwashshaḥahs* they happened to produce is by Ibn Sanâ'-al-Mulk al-Miṣrî.[1850] It became famous in the East and the West. It begins:

O my beloved, lift the veil (which covers) the light—from (your) face,
So that we may behold musk (black eyebrows) on camphor (white skin)—in pomegranates (red cheeks).
Encircle, O clouds, the crowns of the hills—with ornaments,
And give them as bracelets winding brooks.

Muwashshaḥ poetry spread among the Spaniards. The great mass took to it because of its smoothness, artistic language, and the (many) internal rhymes found in it (which made them popular). As a result, the common people in the cities imitated them. They made poems of the (*muwashshaḥ*) type in their sedentary dialect, without employing vowel endings. They thus invented a new form, which they called *zajal*. They have continued to compose poems of this type down to this time. They achieved remarkable things in it. The (*zajal*) opened a wide field for eloquent (poetry) in the (Spanish-Arabic) dialect, which is influenced by non-Arab (speech habits).

[1848] That is, "a lion among sheep." However, the metaphor intended may have been "lion of the thicket," i.e., courage.

[1849] Al-Maqqarî, *Nafḥ aṭ-ṭîb* (Cairo, 1304/1886–87), IV, 199, quotes ten more verses. Cf. de Slane and Hartmann, p. 65.

[1850] Hibatallâh b. Ja'far, 545–608 [1150–1211]. Cf. *GAL*, I, 261; *Suppl.*, I, 461 f. For the following verses, cf. Hartmann, pp. 47 f., who thinks that the last two lines belong to a different poem. The verses are not found in the recent edition of Ibn Sanâ'-al-Mulk's *Dâr aṭ-ṭirâz*, cited above, n. 1796.

The first to create the *zajal* method was Abû Bakr b. Quzmân,[1851] even though *zajal* poems were composed in Spain before his time. But the beauty of the *zajal* became evident, its ideas took on their artistic shape, and its elegance became famous, only in Ibn Quzmân's time. He lived in the days of the Veiled (Ṣinhâjah Almoravids). He is (indisputably) the leading *zajal* poet.

Ibn Sa'îd said: "I saw his *zajals* recited in Baghdad more often than I had seen them recited in the cities of the West. And," continued Ibn Sa'îd, "I heard Abû l-Ḥasan b. Jaḥdar al-Ishbîlî,[1852] the leading contemporary *zajal* poet, say: 'No leading *zajal* poet has produced a *zajal* like that of Ibn Quzmân, the principal *zajal* artist, (which he made on the following occasion). He had gone to a park with some of his friends, and they were sitting in an arbor. In front of them was the marble statue of a lion. From its mouth water flowed down over blocks of stone set in steps. Whereupon Ibn Quzmân said: III, *405*

An arbor that is standing upon a platform — like a portico,
And a lion that has swallowed a snake — thick as a thigh,
And opens its mouth like a man — who loudly breathes his last,
And (the snake) goes from there on blocks of stone — making a great noise.' "

Although Ibn Quzmân had his residence in Córdoba, he often came to Sevilla and spent a good deal of time along the river there. It happened that one day a group of noted *zajal* poets came together and took a boat ride on the river for recreation. They were accompanied by a handsome lad from one of the wealthy leading families of the place. They were together in a boat fishing and made poems describing their situation. 'Îsâ al-Balîd led off with the following verses:

[1851] Muḥammad b. 'Abd-al-Malik, d. *555* [1160]. Cf. *GAL*, I, 272 f.; *Suppl.*, I, 481 f.; E. Lévi-Provençal in *Journal of the Royal Asiatic Society* (1944), pp. 105–118; Nykl, pp. 266 ff.

[1852] Cf. Nykl, p. 350, and below, p. 458.

My heart desires freedom, but cannot get it, — for love has checkmated it.

III, *406* You can see that (my heart) has become completely miserable — and is restless and also suffers greatly.

It is affected by [1853] loneliness for eyelids dark with antimony,

Those eyes are what make it miserable.[1854]

Then, Abû ʿAmr b. az-Zâhid al-Ishbîlî said:

He is caught. All those who enter the ocean of passion are caught.[1855]

You can see what causes him pain and difficulties.

He wanted to play with love.

Many people have died in that game.

Then, Abû l-Ḥasan al-Muqri' ad-Dânî said:

A nice day, everything about which pleases me: — Drinks and handsome (boys) surround me.

The finch sings in the willow tree — while a fish in the pot is my reward.[1856]

Then, Abû Bakr b. Martîn said:

You (he [?]) want(s) it to be true when you (he) say(s): "I have to go back

To the river," you (he [?]) announce(s) [?], "and recreation and fishing." [1857]

[1853] *ʿÂbû*, meaning literally, "loneliness for . . . blames it." The translation suggested by de Slane and Dozy, "It is lonely for the eyelids dark with antimony, that are absent," seems hardly possible.

[1854] Cf. R. Dozy in *Journal asiatique*, XIV 6 (1869), 194 f.

[1855] Cf. Dozy, *loc. cit.*

[1856] Cf. Dozy, pp. 196–98.

[1857] A and B read: *Al-ḥaqq trîd ḥadîth baqâ-lî ʿâd*
Fî l-wâd tajhar[?] *wa-n-nazah wa-ṣ-ṣayâd*
The word read here as *tajhar* appears in A as something like *b*[?]*-ḥ-m-y-r*. D reads the second line as follows: *Fî l-wâd an-nazîh wa-l-bûrî wa-ṣ-ṣayâd.* This does not seem possible, metrically. It means: "To the enjoyable river and the fish and fishing." However, it would seem likely that instead of *tajhar* "you announce," some adjective describing the river should be read here.

Those are not fish that he wants to hook— III, 407
The hearts of men are in his little net.

Then, Abû Bakr b. Quzmân said:

When he rolls up his sleeves to cast (his little net),
One sees the fish run in his direction.
They do not want to fall into it.
They want only to kiss his little hands.[1858]

In the eastern Spain of their time, Yakhlaf[1859] al-Aswad composed fine *zajals*, for instance:

I was caught. I was afraid to be caught:
Love has brought me into difficulties.

(Later on) in (this poem) he says:

When I look into the brilliant, resplendent face (of the beloved), its redness reaches its limit.
O student of alchemy, alchemy is in my eye.
I look with it at silver, and it turns into gold.[1860]

After these (poets) came a period in which Madghallîs[1861] was the champion. He accomplished marvelous things in *zajal* poetry. The following verses are from his famous *zajal*[1862] that goes:

[1858] Cf. Nykl, p. 313.

[1859] The first letter is indicated as *y* in A, B, and D, although Nykl, p. 351, following Bulaq, reads Mukhallaf. W. Hoenerbach and H. Ritter, "Neue Materialien zum Zacal," *Oriens*, III (1950), 275, have Yakhlaf b. Râshid, but it seems that they do not consider this man identical with the person mentioned here. Cf. also *Oriens*, III (1950), 302 (n. 1), 315.

[1860] Cf. R. Dozy in *Journal asiatique*, XIV^{6} (1869), 198 f.; Nykl, p. 351. The same idea is also expressed by other poets; cf., for instance, the verses quoted by aṣ-Ṣafadî, *al-Ghayth al-musajjam* (Cairo, 1305/1887–88), I, 12.

[1861] He lived in the second half of the twelfth century. Cf. W. Hoenerbach and H. Ritter in *Oriens*, V (1952), 269–301. The vocalization of the name is not quite certain. Hoenerbach and Ritter prefer Mudghalîs. However, a double *l* is indicated in MSS. B and D.

[1862] Cf. Nykl, p. 310; Hoenerbach and Ritter in *Oriens*, V (1952), 301. The last line is found in A and B, but not in D.

And a fine rain that falls—and beats the rays of the sun.[1863]
III, 408 The one appears silvery,[1864] and the other golden.
The plants drink and get drunk—the boughs dance and are excited.
They want to come to us—Then, they are ashamed and go back.

A fine *zajal* of his is the following: [1865]

The bright sunlight has come, and the stars are confused.[1866]—Let us get up and shake off laziness!
A little mixed [1867] wine from a bottle seems to me sweeter than honey.
O you who censure me for my behavior! May God let you behave according to your words!
You say that (wine) generates sin and that it corrupts the intellect.
Go to the Ḥijâz! It will be better for you.
What leads you into such superfluous (talk) with me?
Go you on the pilgrimage (to Mecca) and visit (Medina),
But let me be engrossed in drinking!
If one does not have the power and ability (to behave),
Intention is more effective than action.

They were succeeded in Sevilla by Ibn Jaḥdar.[1868] He
III, 409 showed himself superior to (all other) *zajal* poets on the occasion of the conquest of Majorca, when he composed the *zajal* that begins:

Those who oppose the oneness of God will be wiped out by the sword.
I have nothing to do with those who oppose the truth.[1869]

[1863] For the second colon, Nykl and also Hoenerbach and Ritter have suggested the following translation: "and the rays of the sun that beat (the air)."

[1864] Hoenerbach and Ritter read the active: "overlays with silver . . . with gold."

[1865] Cf. Nykl, p. 310; Hoenerbach and Ritter in *Oriens*, V (1952), 290 f.

[1866] Cf. p. 460, below.

[1867] *Shurayb(a)*, as vocalized in B and D; cf. also A.

[1868] Cf. p. 455, above. The event described falls in the beginning of the thirteenth century.

[1869] Cf. Nykl, p. 350.

Ibn Sa'îd said: "I met (Ibn Jaḥdar). I also met his pupil al-Ya'ya',[1870] the author of the famous *zajal* that begins:

Would that, when I see my beloved, I might tempt his ear with a little message:
Why did he adopt the neck of the little gazelle and steal the mouth of the partridge?[1871]

They were succeeded by Abû l-Ḥasan Sahl b. Mâlik,[1872] the leading littérateur. Also, (still) later, (close) to the present time, there was our friend, the wazir Abû 'Abdallâh b. al-Khaṭîb, the leading poet and a prose writer without peer in Islam. A fine poem of this type by him is the following:

Mix the goblets and fill mine, so that I may start all over again![1873]
Money was created only to be squandered.[1874]

A poem in Sufi style in the manner of the Sufi ash-Shushtarî[1875] (by Ibn al-Khaṭîb) is the following:

Between sunrise and sunset, love poems of various kinds were composed.
Gone are (the mortals) who (were created and) had not been before. There remains (God) who never ceases.[1876] III, *410*

Another fine poem in this sense by (Ibn al-Khaṭîb) is the following:

To be away from you, son—is my greatest misfortune.
When I can be near (*qurb*) you—I let my boat (*qârib*) drift.

1870 *Sic* B and D. A has no dots. Bulaq: al-Ma'ma'.
1871 Cf. Nykl, p. 350.
1872 Cf. pp. 445 and 448, above.
1873 I.e., with drinking.
1874 Cf. R. Dozy in *Journal asiatique*, XIV^{6} (1869), 202; Nykl, p. 366.
1875 'Alî b. 'Abdallâh, d. 668 [1269]. Cf. *GAL*, I, 274; *Suppl.*, I, 483 f.; Hartmann, pp. 87 f.; L. Massignon, in *Mélanges offerts à William Marçais* (Paris, 1950), pp. 251–76.
1876 Cf. Nykl, p. 364.

A contemporary of the wazir Ibn al-Khaṭîb in Spain was Muḥammad b. 'Abd-al-'Aẓîm,[1877] from Guadix. He was a leading *zajal* poet. He wrote a *zajal* in which he imitated Madghallîs' verse: "The bright sunlight has come, and the stars are confused." [1878] It runs as follows:

Dissipation is permitted, you clever fellows,
Since the sun entered into Aries.
Thus, commit a new immorality every day!
Don't let a boring period intervene between them!
Let us go after them at the Genil,[1879]
Upon the verdant meadows there!
Let Baghdad alone and do not talk about the Nile!
I like these regions here better,
A plain which is better than an expanse of forty miles.[1880]
III, *411* When the winds blow over it to and fro,
No trace of dust is found,
Not even enough to apply as antimony to the eyes.
How could it be different, since there is no pleasant spot here
Where the bees do not swarm.[1881]

At the present time, the *zajal* method is what the common people in Spain use for their poetry. They even employ all fifteen meters for poems [1882] in the vulgar dialect and call them *zajals*. For instance, we have the following verses by a Spanish poet:

A long time, years, I have loved your eyes.
But you have no pity and no softness in your heart.
You can see how my heart has become, because of you,
Like a ploughshare in the smiths' hands.

[1877] Cf. Nykl, p. 362.

[1878] Cf. p. 458, above.

[1879] The river of Granada, the Darro (Arabic: Nahr Falûm), unites at Granada with the Genil. Cf. E. Lévi-Provençal, *La Péninsule Ibérique*, p. 30.

[1880] Cf. R. Dozy, *op. cit.*, p. 202.

[1881] I.e., there are flowers everywhere. For Dozy's different suggestion, see pp. 202 f. of his article, and *Supplément aux dictionnaires arabes*, I, 549a.

[1882] Cf. p. 374, above.

Tears [1883] stream down. Fire burns.
Hammers to the right and the left.
God created the Christians to be raided,
But you raid the hearts of (your) lovers.

At the beginning of this century, an excellent representative of this method was the littérateur Abû 'Abdallâh al-Lûshî.[1884] He wrote a poem in which he praised Sultan Ibn al-Aḥmar: [1885]

Morning has come. Get up, O my boon companion, let us drink III, 412
And be gay, after we have been moved by music!
The gold ingot of dawn has rubbed (its) red color
Against the touchstone of the night. Get up and pour (the wine)!
You will find (it) to be of pure alloy, white and clean.
It is silver, but the red color of the dawn made it golden.[1886]
(Wine) is a currency that has great circulation among mankind.
The light in the eyes (of the beloved) is acquired from the light of (that currency).
This is the day, O my companion, when we can (really) live.
By God, how pleasant is a young man's life on (such a day)! [1887]
The night, too, is for kissing and embracing,

[1883] De Slane explains that the lover's tears are here compared to drops of water sprinkled on the fire in a forge, to obtain greater heat.

[1884] Muḥammad b. Muḥammad, *ca.* 678 [1279/80] to 752 [1351]. Cf. Ibn al-Khaṭîb, *al-Iḥâṭah*, II, 195–99.

[1885] Cf. Nykl, p. 343. The ruler to whom the poem is addressed is one of several Muḥammads of Granada. Cf. p. 465 (n. 1904), below. Muḥammad III reigned at the beginning of the century, from 701 to 708, but it remains uncertain whether he is meant here.

[1886] Dozy in *Journal asiatique*, XIV^6 (1869), 203–205, suggests a slightly different translation.

[1887] Cf. Bulaq. De Slane: "One has to work during the day, but rich people have it easy," makes little sense in the context.

Turning over and over on the bed of (love) union.[1888]
A good time has come now after a stingy one.
Why should it [1889] let good fortune escape its hands?
As one [1890] swallowed its bitterness in the past,
So one now drinks its delectable (wine) and eats fine food.[1890a]
The watcher asks: You littérateurs, why do we
III, *413* See you so generous [1891] with wine and love?
Those who censure me are astonished by it,
But I say: You people, why are you astonished?
Could anyone but a sensitive (poet really) love a handsome (boy),
As, by God, we find it said and stated in writing?
Beauty can be acquired only by a cultured poet
Who deflowers virginal (beauty) and does not bother with (beauty) that has belonged to others before.[1892]
The cup is forbidden, but only to those
Who do not know how to drink it.
Intelligent, delicate [?],[1893] or dissolute people
Are forgiven the sins they may commit in this respect.
There is one whose beauty captivates me, and I cannot captivate it with the choicest words.
A handsome fawn, fat enough to put out the coals (on which it is roasted),
While it sets my heart afire with (burning hot) tamarisk coal.
A (handsome) gazelle, who so moves the hearts of lions when they see it,

[1888] For this and the following verses, cf. Dozy, *op. cit.*, pp. 206 ff.

[1889] Dozy thinks that the pronoun refers to the poet, but since the poet speaks of himself in the first person, this is not probable. The reference is to "time."

[1890] The passive is indicated in B.

[1890a] To be understood figuratively: Times were bad, but now they are good.

[1891] Dozy: "produce (verses)."

[1892] Thus, a poet is entitled to love.

[1893] A, B, and D read *wa-l-khnkr*. Cf. Dozy, *Supplément aux dictionnaires arabes*, I, 410*a*.

And even when they do not see it but only imagine (they see it), they run away.
She then revives them when she smiles,
And they are gay, after having been sad.
She has a little mouth like a seal ring and a row of white teeth. III, *414*
The preacher of the people[1894] demands (in his sermon) to kiss them.
What a necklace of pearls and corals (those teeth are), O man.
Well strung and not pierced!
A darkish down on her lips,[1895] which want something.[1896]
To compare it with musk would be an insult.
Hair black as the raven's wing
Which (even) the nights when I am separated from her consider remarkable,[1897] falls down
Upon a body, milk white, whiter
Than any ever got by shepherd from his flock,
And two little breasts. I did not know before
That anything could be so firm.
Under the fat (bosom), there is a slim waist,
So slim that it could hardly be found when one looks for it.[1898]
It is slimmer than my religion, as I might say.
Come, look at your slave, my lady! I do not lie in this respect.[1898a]
What religion remains to me, and what intelligence?
You deprive those who follow you of both the one and the other.

[1894] *Khaṭîb al-ummah*, as in B and Bulaq.

[1895] De Slane translates *shârib* "eyebrow." However, even though the author clearly is speaking of a girl, he seems to use a description common in connection with handsome boys.

[1896] Namely, to be kissed.

[1897] Even in comparison with the darkness of the gloomy nights of separation, her hair must be considered remarkably dark.

[1898] Cf. Dozy, *Supplément aux dictionnaires arabes*, II, 157.

[1898a] Or rather, "Do you think that your slave is a great liar?"(?)

She has buttocks as heavy as a watcher [1899]
III, *415* When he observes and watches a lover.[1900]

The place becomes a castle when you are here,
But when you are away, it seems to me a cave.[1901]
Your good qualities are like those of the Amir,
Or like the sand, who could count it?
He is the pillar of the cities. He speaks pure Arabic.
He is outstanding in knowledge and actions.
He is an original poet, and how well he writes!
How he pierces with his lance the breasts (of the enemy)!
How he smites their necks with the sword!
Heaven envies him four of his qualities.
Who could count his (qualities), tell me, or estimate them?
The sun (envies) his light, the moon his ambition,
The rain his generosity, and the stars his position.
He rides on the steed of generosity [1902] and gives free rein
To enterprise and zeal in being (generous).
Every day, we put on the robes of honor that he gives us.
With the perfume of his high glory we consider (the day) perfumed.
His kindness is showered upon everybody who comes to him.
He lets no one who approaches him go home with empty hands.

[1899] A watcher is "heavy" in the sense of being a nuisance.

[1900] The following two verses were omitted by mistake in the Paris edition. The first, which I have not been able to translate, reads:

In lam yunaffar ghurzâ-u-yanqashiʿ
Fî ṭarf dîsâ wa-'lnby[?] *taṣlabû.*

[1901] *Qabû* = *qabw*, or perhaps = **cavo?*

For suitable meanings of *qabw*, and for its pronunciation *ɋbû* in northwestern Africa, cf., for instance, W. Marçais, *Textes arabes de Tanger* (Paris, 1911), p. 421.

[1902] The Arabic text has here an untranslatable play on words.

He brought out the truth that had been concealed. III, *416*
Falsehood can (now) no longer conceal it.
He rebuilt the crumbling pillar of piety (toward God)
Which time had ruined.
He is feared when he is met, just as one puts one's hope in him.
In spite of the kindness of his face, how forbidding he can be!
He goes to war laughing, and war is frowning.
He is superior. No one in the world is superior to him.
When he draws his sword among the engines of war,[1903]
No second stroke is needed where he strikes.
He is the namesake [1904] of the chosen (Prophet Muḥammad). God
Selected and chose him to be ruler.
One can see that he is caliph, the commander of the Muslims.
He leads his armies and is an ornament of his cavalcade.
All heads bow and obey the chief.
Indeed, they desire to kiss his hand.
His house, the Banû Naṣr, are the full moon of the time.
Their glory (steadily) rises and (never) sets.
They go far in loftiness and nobility. III, *417*
They do not go far in humbleness and shame.[1905]
Let God preserve them, as long as the firmament revolves.
And the sun rises and the stars sparkle,
And as long as this poem shall be sung to music,
O sun of the harem, that never sets.[1906]

[1903] Cf. R. Dozy in *Journal asiatique*, XIV^6 (1869), 212 f.

[1904] The poem is addressed to one of the Naṣrids of Granada, by name Muḥammad. Cf. p. 461 (n. 1885), above.

[1905] The parallelism with the preceding verses hardly permits de Slane's translation: "But they draw near (to God) through their humbleness and modesty."

[1906] Dozy, *op. cit.*, p. 213, points out that the last line occurred in an earlier poem by Ibn az-Zaqqâq, d. 528 [1134]. Cf. *GAL, Suppl.*, I, 481; Nykl, pp. 231–33. It was quoted by al-Maqqarî, *Analectes*, II, 196. Ibn az-Zaqqâq, however, probably was not the first to use it.

The urban population of the Maghrib then created a new poetical form in meters with internally rhyming couplets,[1907] similar to the *muwashshaḥah*. They wrote poetry in this form in their sedentary dialect, too. They called it "local meter." [1908] The first to create the form was a Spaniard who settled in Fez, by name Ibn 'Umayr. He wrote a fragmentary piece in the manner of the *muwashshaḥah*, in which he only rarely [1909] disregarded the rules of the vowel endings. It begins:

On the bank of the river, the plaint of a dove
Upon a bough in the garden near morn made me weep.
The palm of morning was wiping off the ink of darkness,
And the drops of dew were flowing among the teeth of the camomiles.
I had gone to the meadows early in the morning. The dew was scattered about there
Like jewels strewn over the bosoms of maidens.
The tear of the water wheels was being shed
III, *418* Like snakes wriggling around fruit.
The boughs are all twisted like an anklet around the thigh.
All of this surrounds the meadow like a bracelet.
The hands of the dew break through the folds of the calyxes,
And the winds carry a breeze from off (the flowers), which smells like musk.
The ivory of the clear sky is covered by the dark musk of the clouds.
The zephyr draws his train over (the flowers) and spreads their perfume.
I saw the dove in the foliage on a branch.
It had wetted its feathers with drops of dew.
It cooed plaintively, like a lovesick stranger.

1907 The rhyme scheme is *ab-ab-cd-cd*.
1908 Cf. 2:223, above.
1909 *Sic* D. The earlier texts have "never."

It had covered itself with its new plumage as with a cloak,
But with its beak red and its leg colored.
It had a necklace of well-arranged strings of jewels.
It was sitting between the boughs like a lovesick person,
Using one wing as a cushion, and the other to cover itself.
It had come to complain about the passion in its heart,
And, on account of it,[1910] had put its beak to its breast and cried.
I said: O dove, my eye can no longer slumber.
Please, will you not stop crying and shedding tears?
The dove replied: I cried, until my tears ran dry.[1911] III, *419*
I cry plaintively all the time, without tears,
For a young bird that flew away from me and did not return.
I have been familiar with crying and grief since the time of Noah.
This is faithfulness, I say, this is fidelity.
Look, my eyes have become (red) like sores.
But you (human beings), if one of you is afflicted, after a year,
He says: I have had enough of this weeping and mourning.
I said: O dove, if you had plunged into the ocean of misery (in which I am),
You would cry and mourn for me with tears and sighs.
And if your heart felt like mine,
The boughs upon which you are sitting would be reduced to ashes.
How many years is it today that I suffered separation (from my beloved),
So that it is altogether impossible for the eyes (of anybody) to see me? [1912]
My body is covered with thinness and disease.

[1910] *Leg. minhu?*
[1911] Cf. Dozy, *op. cit.*, p. 214.
[1912] Because I am so greatly shrunken.

My thinness conceals me from the eyes of spectators.
If death should come to me, I would die on the spot.
III, 420 Those who are dead, my friends, at last enjoy rest.
(The dove) said to me: If the rivers in the meadows[1913] were to moan
Out of the (great) fear that I harbor for (my beloved), the soul would be returned to the heart.[1914]
I am discolored by my tears. This whiteness
Will always be like a necklace around my neck to the day of the (last) convocation.
As for the tip of my beak, its story is known:
It is like a bit of flame, while (the rest of my) body is (gray as) ashes.
All[1915] kinds of doves cry and mourn for me.
He who experiences the anguish of being kept apart and separated (from his beloved) might (well) mourn.[1915a]
O joy of this world, farewell to you,
Since we find no rest or place of repose in you!

The inhabitants of Fez liked it and applied this method in their poetry. They omitted the vowel endings with which they were not familiar. This kind of poetry gained a wide diffusion among them. Many of them excelled in it. They used several forms, the *muzawwaj*, the *kâzî*, the *mal'abah*, and the *ghazal*.[1916] They differ according to the arrangement of the rhyming couplets and the contents the poets want to express in them.

A *muzawwaj* poem is that of Ibn Shujâ', an outstanding Maghribî poet, from Tâzâ:

[1913] *Al-awdâh bi-r-riyâḍ.*

[1914] The meaning of this verse seems to be that if nature were to give an audible expression of grief commensurable with the dove's feelings, it would be so tumultuous that it would wake the dead.

[1915] The remaining lines of the poem are found only in D, not in Bulaq, A, or B.

[1915a] *Nâḥ*, although D has *bâḥ*. The latter may mean, "shows (it)."

[1916] *Muzawwaj* means approximately "couplet." D reads *mamzûj*, Bulaq *muzdawij*. *Kâzî* is not known.

Mal'abah is "plaything." Cf. Greek παίγνιον. See 2:220 f., above.

Ghazal is commonly used as "love song."

Money is the ornament of the world and the strength of the soul. III, *421*
It makes faces that are not beautiful, beautiful.
Lo, anyone who has plenty of money to spend
Is made a spokesman and given a high rank.
Whoever has a great deal of money is great, even if he be small.
And the mighty man becomes small when he becomes poor.
The one thing warps my breast, and the other makes it jealous.
It would burst, if there were not the (possibility of) recourse to destiny.
A man who is great among his people may (have to) seek refuge
With a man who has no pedigree and no influence.
Such a reversal causes me sadness,
And because of it I put my garment over my head to conceal (myself) [?].
Thus, the tails have come to be in front of the heads,
And the river borrows water from the water wheel.
Did the weakness of man do that, or the corruption of time?
We do not know which we should blame more.
Someone came to be addressed [1917] as "Father of someone" III, *422*
And "please!" and how (long it took) before he replied!
We have lived, thank God, long enough to see with our own eyes
The souls of princes in the skins of dogs.
Many with very great souls may have weak (material) foundations.
They are in one place, and glory is in another.
Whereas people see them as old fools, they see themselves

[1917] In order to honor him.

As the outstanding personalities of the country and (its) solid foundation.

The (Maghribî) method is represented by the following verses from a *muzawwaj* poem by Ibn Shujâʻ:

He whose heart goes after the handsome (ones) of this day will be tired (and disappointed).
You had better leave off or beauty will use you for a plaything.
There is no handsome (beloved) [1918] among them who ever promised something and did not break his promise.
Few are those to whom you can be faithful, and who are faithful to you.
They are proud toward their lovers and refuse (them).
They deliberately set out to break people's hearts.
When they enter into a liaison, they break it up in their own good time.
When they make a promise, they break it in any case.
III, 423 There is a handsome (youth) with whom I have fallen in love. I have set my heart on him.
I have made my cheek the shoe for his foot.
I have given him a place in the center of my heart.
I said: O my heart, honor him who has taken up residence in you!
Think little of the humiliation that you suffer!
For you cannot escape being affected by the frightful power of passion.[1919]
I have given him power over me. I am satisfied to have him as my master.
If you [1920] could see my condition when I see him!

[1918] *Malîḥâ*. It is not, however, necessary to translate, with Dozy (*Journal asiatique*, XIV 6, 215): "There is none among you who ever promised something to a lover."

[1919] For this and the following verses, cf. Dozy, *loc. cit.*

[1920] I.e., the heart.

I am like a beetle upon the surface of a pond,
Which turns over in it and suffocates like a little (round fruit).[1921]
I know at once what is in his mind.[1922]
I understand what he wants before he mentions it.
I try to get (for him) what he wants, even if it be
Grape juice in spring, or early wheat in the winter.[1923]
I go to fetch it,[1924] even if it be in Iṣfahân.
Whenever he says: "I need something," I say to him: "You'll get it."

And so on.

Another (Maghribî) poet was 'Alî b. al-Mu'adhdhin of Tlemcen.

An outstanding poet in Zarhûn,[1925] in the region of Meknès, close to the present time, was a man known as al- III, 424
Kafîf (the blind one). He produced original specimens of these types of poetry. The best poem of his that sticks in my memory is a poem on the trip of Sultan Abû l-Ḥasan [1926] and the Merinids to Ifrîqiyah. In it, he describes their rout at al-Qayrawân. He consoles them about it and cheers them by describing what happened to others, but first he blames them because of their raid against Ifrîqiyah. It is a *mal'abah,* a variety of this sort of poetry. The beginning is one of the most original examples of how to indicate eloquently the purpose of a poem right at the start. This is called "excellence of beginning" (*barâ'at al-istihlâl*). His verses run:

Praised be He who holds the hearts of amirs
By their forelocks at any moment and time.
If we obey Him, He gives us much help.

[1921] *Narja' mithl dhurrûḥâ fî wajh-al-ghadîr*
Tadur bû wa-yatfaṭṭas bi-ḥâl-al-jarû.

[1922] The meter requires: <*mâ*, or *esh*> *bi-sabq-aḍ-ḍamîr.*

[1923] Cf. Dozy, *loc. cit.*, and *Supplément aux dictionnaires arabes,* II, 261*a.*

[1924] *Ñasûqû.*

[1925] Cf. G. S. Colin in *EI, s.v.* "Meknes."

[1926] The event referred to took place in 1348. Cf. 1:xxxix, above.

If we disobey Him, He punishes (us) with all kinds of
humiliation.

He goes on, until, after the transition (*takhallus̱*),[1927] he comes to inquire after the armies of the Maghrib:

Be a sheep, but do not be a shepherd!
For a shepherd is held responsible for his flock.
Start with a prayer for him who called (us)
To Islam, the gracious, exalted, perfect (Prophet),
For the right-guided caliphs, and the men of the second
generation!
Afterwards, mention whatever you like, and speak out:
III, *425* O pilgrims,[1928] cross the desert
And describe the countries with (their) inhabitants!
Where did the intention of the Sultan lead
The army of brilliant, beautiful Fez?
O pilgrims, by the Prophet whom you visited
And for whose sake you traversed the sand hills of the
desert,
I have come to ask you about the army of the West
That perished in black Ifrîqiyah,
And about the (ruler) who provided you (for your pilgrimage) by his gifts
And made the desert of the Ḥijâz a place of luxurious
living.
There[1929] has come up something like a dam facing a
slope,
And a gorge is cleft after the water of a deluge [?].[1930]
It (the army) is crushed like Sodom and trampled into the
earth [?].

[1927] *Takhallus̱* is the transition from the erotic to the laudatory part of a poem. Cf. Lane's *Arabic-English Dictionary*, p. 2786*c*, *s. rad. nsb.*

[1928] The Moroccan poet asks pilgrims returning from Mecca for information about events in a region they had to pass through. In Islam, pilgrims were always the transmitters of news and political information.

[1929] The poet now describes the obstacles that might, he imagines, prevent him from obtaining the information.

[1930] *Wa-yufyar shawṭ baʿd mâʾ ṭûfân.*

Tell me now, did Zughar [1931] become their jailer?
If the region from near Tunis
To the country of the West were an Alexandrian obstacle [1932]
Built (across the world) from the East to the West,
With one layer of iron, and a second of bronze,[1933]
Still, the birds should answer us, III, 426
Or the wind should bring us special news from them.
Vexing and bad things,
If they were recited . . .
Stones would run with blood and burst,
Hillocks [1934] would tumble and be carried away by a torrent.
Let me know with your penetrating intelligence
And think it over for me completely [?] in your heart,
If you know, whether a pigeon or messenger
From the Sultan has become known, and speak out seven times [?]
About the announcement of 'Abd-al-Muhayman al-Ghawwâṣ [?]
And (further) indications spread (from) atop the minarets.
They are indeed people, naked, unprotected,
Ignored, with no place and no power.
They do not know how to picture (their) failure,
Or how they (might have) entered the city of al-Qayrawân.
O my Lord Abû l-Ḥasan, we come to the gate (court)
On a definite matter: Let us go to Tunis!
We are enough for you, and you do not need the Jarîd and the Zâb. III, 427

1931 A daughter of Lot, after whom the Dead Sea is named *Baḥr Zughar*, here signifying the desert?

1932 Referring to the famous Dam of Gog and Magog built by Alexander. Cf. 1:162, above.

1933 Cf. 1:75 (n. 10), above.

1934 *Leg. al-qîrân.*

What do you have to do with the Arabs of dark[1935] Ifrîqiyah?
Do you not know the story of 'Umar, the son of al-Khaṭṭâb,
The Fârûq, conqueror of villages, the treacherously (assassinated caliph)?
He took possession of Syria, the Ḥijâz, and the crown[1936] of Khosraw (the 'Irâq),
And he conquered a part of the entrance to Ifrîqiyah.
He was a person of great renown [?],[1937]
And still he used to say: "In (Ifrîqiyah), our friends will be divided."[1938]
This Fârûq, the emerald of all beings,
Pronounced himself thus concerning Ifrîqiyah.
It remained quiet to the time of 'Uthmân.
Ibn az-Zubayr[1939] conquered it according to verified information.
When the spoils from it arrived at the government office,
'Uthmân died, and the atmosphere changed for us.
People were divided under three amirs.
Something (better) treated with silence came to be (considered true) faith.
If that was the situation in the days of the pious (early Muslims),
What shall we do in later times?
III, 428 The experts in *jafr*[1940] in their little booklets,
And in the history of their Mercury[1941] and Saturn,

[1935] *Ghawbas*, from the root *gh-b-s?*

[1936] The "crown of Khosraw" does not mean the Persian Empire, but "crown" *tâj* stands here for *ṭâq* "arch." The allusion is to the famous architectural monument, mentioned by Ibn Khaldûn, 1:101, 356, and 2:239, 242 f., above.

[1937] Possibly one should read:

Kân dhâ dhukrat lû kathrat dhikrâ.

[1938] Cf. 1:333, above.

[1939] According to the historians, 'Abdallâh b. az-Zubayr participated in the conquest of Ifrîqiyah and killed Gregory (Jirjîr), the Byzantine governor, in the battle of Sbeitla in 647/48. Cf. also *'Ibar*, VI, 108; de Slane (tr.), I, 209.

[1940] Cf. 2:194 and 209 ff., above.

[1941] Cf. R. Dozy, *Supplément aux dictionnaires arabes*, II, 442*b*.

Mention in their pamphlets and verses —
(Experts such as) Shiqq and Saṭîḥ [1942] and Ibn Murrânah [1943]
— That, when Merîn's creatures have to lean
On the walls of Tunis, Merîn loses its importance.
And remember what [1944] the chief minister,
The influential 'Îsâ b. al-Ḥasan, said to me.
He said to me: I ought to be the person who knows,
But when fate comes, eyes are blind.
I tell you: What brought the Merinids
From the capital of Fez to the Dabbâb Arabs?
May our lord profit from the death of Bû Yaḥyâ,
The Sultan of Tunis and master of al-'Unnâb! [1945]

Then, he began to describe the trip of the Sultan and his armies, to the end of that, and then on to the end of the whole III, 429 affair with the Arabs of Ifrîqiyah, using in his description every kind of remarkable, original (expression).

The inhabitants of Tunis also produced *mal'abahs* in their dialect. However, most of them are bad. Nothing has stuck in my memory, because they are so bad.

The common people of Baghdad also had a kind of (popular) poetry. They called these poems *al-mawâlîyâ*. (The *mawâlîyâ*) have many subdivisions. They are called *al-Ḥawfî*,[1946] *Kân-wa-kân*, and *Dûbayt*. All the different meters recognized by them are used for these poems. Most of the verses are couplets of four "branches" that rhyme with each other.

The Egyptians followed the Baghdâdîs in this respect.

1942 Cf. 1:219 and 2:202, above.

1943 Cf. 2:220, above.

1944 Or: "And we remember."

1945 "Jujube trees," referring to Bône.

1946 *Al-Ḥawfî* is known as a kind of song native to modern Tlemcen, in particular. Cf. W. Marçais, *Le Dialecte arabe parlé à Tlemcen*, pp. 205 ff. Bulaq corrects *al-Ḥawfî* to *al-Qûmâ*, and it would seem that in fact Ibn Khaldûn should not have written *al-Ḥawfî* here, but *al-Qûmâ*, as the latter is well known, like the other terms mentioned, as a kind of *mawâlîyâ*.

For the popularity of this poetry in thirteenth and fourteenth century Baghdad, cf. Ibn Kathîr, *Bidâyah*, XIII, 31; XIV, 120, 155.

They produced remarkable poems of this type. They rivaled (each other in) expressing in them all the methods of rhetorical expression as required by their dialect. They produced marvelous things.

I [1947] have seen it stated in the *Dîwân* of Ṣafî-ad-dîn al-Ḥillî that a *mawâlîyâ* has the meter *basîṭ* and consists of four rhyming "branches." It is also called *ṣawt* "tune" and *baytân* "double verse." It was invented by the people of Wâsiṭ. *Kân-wa-kân* has one rhyme (throughout) and different meters in its hemistichs. The first hemistich is longer than the second. The rhyme letter must be accompanied by one of the weak letters (*î, û, â*). It was invented by the Baghdâdîs. The following (*kân-wa-kân*) is recited:

III, 430 In the winking of the eyelids we have—a conversation that is self-explanatory.
The mother of the dumb (child) understands—the language of the dumb.[1948]

End of the quotation from Ṣafî-ad-dîn.

The most remarkable poem of the sort that has stuck in my memory is that of an (Egyptian) poet. (It runs:)

This wound is still fresh—and the blood is still flowing—and my killer,[1949] dear brother—has a good time in the

[1947] The following quotation from ʿAbd-al-ʿAzîz b. Sarâyâ al-Ḥillî, 677–749 [1278–1349]—cf. *GAL*, II, 159 f.; *Suppl.*, II, 199 f.—is not from his often-printed *Dîwân*, but from his still unpublished *ʿÂṭil al-ḥâlî*, as appears from the remarks of Hartmann, p. 218, and W. Hoenerbach and H. Ritter in *Oriens*, III (1950), 268.

[1948] B reads:

Lanâ bi-ghamz al-ḥawâjib—ḥadîth tafsîrû minnû
Wa-umm al-akhras taʿrif—bi-lughat al-khursân.

Umm al-akhras in B is a correction of *umm al-'s.* D reads *umm al-aḥdab* "mother of the hunchback," and adds a superfluous *wa-bû.* The correctness of the reading *umm al-akhras*, found also in A, and the meaning of the second verse became clear to me only after I received a copy of W. Hoenerbach's edition of al-Ḥillî's *ʿÂṭil* (Wiesbaden, 1956). Cf. there pp. 152 f.

[1949] The "killer" is the beloved, and the "wound" is caused by the pangs of love.

desert — They said: We shall avenge you — I said: This is worse — He [1950] who wounded me shall heal me — That will be better.

Another poet says:

I knocked at the door of the tent. She said: Who is knocking? — I said: One enamored, no robber or thief.
She smiled — A flash like lightning came to me from her teeth — I returned perturbed, drowned in the ocean of my tears.

Another poet says:

There was a time in our relationship when she could not guarantee me that she would not depart. And when I complained about my passion, she said: I would give (my) eye for you.
But when someone else, a handsome youth, caught her eye, I reminded her of our relationship, but she (merely) said: I am in your debt.[1951]

Another poet describes *ḥashîsh* as follows:

A choice intoxicant whose effect always lasts with me — It makes wine, wine merchant, and cupbearer superfluous. III, *431*
It is an old strumpet whose viciousness [1952] inflames me — I conceal it in my intestines, and it comes out of my eyes.

Another poet says: [1953]

You who like to be united with the children of love, *naḥ* — how much pain will separation cause to the heart, *awwah aḥ* (Oh, ouch).

[1950] The remainder of this poem is not found in Bulaq.

[1951] This refers to the eye that she promised to give him, if she were ever to be unfaithful to him. Thus, she owes him the eye, but now does not want to pay her debt.

[1952] *Leg. qubḥ-hâ?*

[1953] The following two poems are not found in D.

I deposited my heart *ḥaw-ḥaw*,[1954] and my patience is
baḥ—Everybody is *kakh* in my eye. Your person is *daḥ*.

Another poet says:

I called her, while gray hair already enveloped me: Give
me a loving kiss, O Mayyah.
She said, having burnt out the inside of my heart, I would
not think that such cotton could ever cover the mouth
of a person who is still alive.[1955]

Another poet says:

He saw me and smiled. The rain clouds of my tears
preceded the lightning (smile of his brilliant teeth)—
He withdrew the veil. The full moon seemed to rise.
III, *432* He lowered his dark hair. The heart got lost in its net—
He led us aright again with the thread of dawn coming
from where his hair was parted.

Another poet says:

O camel driver, shout at the animals—and stop at the
dwelling of my beloved ones shortly before dawn!
Call out among their tribe: Let him who wants the
(heavenly) reward—rise and pray for a deceased person who was killed by separation (from the beloved).

Another poet says: [1956]

The eye with which I was observing you, spent the night
—observing the stars, and fed on sleeplessness.
The arrows of separation hit me and did not pass me by—
My solace—Let God give you a great reward—is
dead.

[1954] *Sic* A. B has *ḥûḥû*. The sense of the meaningless words can easily be supplied by the listener or reader.

[1955] The white beard is compared to the cotton stuffed into the mouth of the corpse before burial.

[1956] In A and B the following two poems come after the *dûbayt*.

Another poet says: [1957]

In your district, O cruel pretty ones, I loved—a gazelle
that afflicts ferocious lions with pensiveness.
A bough that captivates chaste girls when it bends—and
when it lights up, the full moon cannot compare with it.

The following poem is one of the poems called *dûbayt:*

The one whom I love has sworn by the Creator—that he III, *433*
would send his apparition in the early mornings.[1958]
O fire of my desire for him, burn—all night. Perhaps he
will be guided by the fire.

It should be known that taste as to what constitutes eloquence in connection with such poetry is possessed only by those who have contact with the dialect in which (a particular poem) is composed, and who have had much practice in using it among the people who speak it. Only thus do they acquire the habit of it, as we stated with regard to the Arabic language.[1959] A Spaniard has no understanding of the eloquence of Maghribî poetry. Maghribîs have none for the eloquence of the poetry of Easterners or Spaniards, and Easterners have none for the eloquence of Spaniards and Maghribîs. All of them use different dialects and word

[1957] Instead of the next poem, D has another that runs:

The dove said to the falconer: Set me free!
*I did not harm you. So, why do you use me as bait?
You send out the falcon to wound me with its claw,
And after I have suffered all the pain, you slaughter me!

Qâl al-ḥamâm ila-l-bazdâri sarriḥnî
Mâ lî ʿalêk adhîya kam tulawwiḥnî
Wa-tursil al-bâz bi-mikhlâbû tujarriḥnî
Wa-baʿd ṣabrî ʿala-l-âlâm tudhabbiḥnî.

At the beginning of the third line, the meter requires a correction. Instead of *wa-tursil al-bâz,* one should read *wa-tursilû* (or, perhaps, *tursil al-bâz*).

[1958] The early morning slumber, when the lover dreams of his beloved, is meant here.

[1959] Cf. pp. 358 f., above.

combinations. Everybody understands eloquence in his own dialect and has a taste for the beauties of the poetry of his own people.

"In the creation of the heavens and the earth and the difference of your tongues and colors, there are, indeed, signs for those who know." [1960]

[1960] Qur'ân 30.22 (21). The quotation is omitted in D.

(CONCLUDING REMARK)

We almost strayed from our purpose. It is our intention (now) to stop with this First Book which is concerned with the nature of civilization and the accidents that go with it. We have dealt — as we think, adequately — with the problems connected with that. Perhaps some later (scholar), aided by the divine gifts of a sound mind and of solid scholarship, III, *434* will penetrate into these problems in greater detail than we did here. A person who creates a new discipline does not have the task of enumerating (all) the (individual) problems connected with it. His task is to specify the subject of the discipline and its various branches and the discussions connected with it. His successors, then, may gradually add more problems, until the (discipline) is completely (presented).

"God knows, and you do not know." [1961]

The author of the book — God forgive him! — says: I completed the composition and draft of this first part, before revision and correction,[1962] in a period of five months ending in the middle of the year 779 [November, 1377]. Thereafter, I revised and corrected the book, and I added to it the history of the (various) nations, as I mentioned and proposed to do at the beginning of the work.

Knowledge comes only from God, the strong, the wise.

1961 Qur'ân 2.216 (213), 232 (232); 3.66 (59); 24.19 (19).

1962 For this Ibn Khaldûn needed a large library, such as he did not have at his disposal at Qal'at Ibn Salâmah where the *Muqaddimah* was written. Cf. *Autobiography*, p. 230.

SELECTED BIBLIOGRAPHY

By Walter J. Fischel

'Abd al-Wahhâb, Ḥasan Ḥusnî. *Khulâṣat ta'rîkh Tûnis.* Tunis, 1953.

'Abd el-Jalîl, Jean M. *Brève Histoire de la littérature arabe.* Paris, 1947. Cf. pp. 215–16, 284–85.

Abdu-r Raḥmân, Shams al-Ulemâ', tr. *See* Allâhâbâd.

Adams, Charles Clarence. *Islam and Modernism in Egypt.* London, 1933.

Adivar, Abdülhak Adnan. "Ibn Haldûn" in *Islâm Ansiklopedisi.* Istanbul, 1943——. Cf. fasc. 47, pp. 738–43.

Aḥmad Bâbâ b. Aḥmad at-Tinbuktî. *Nayl al-ibtihâj bi-taṭrîz ad-dîbâj.* Fez, 1903. Cf. pp. 143–45.

Aḥmed Jevdet, tr. *See* Pîrî Zâdeh.

Alatas, Ḥusein. "Objectivity and the Writing of History: The Conceptions of History by Al-Ghazali, Ibn Khaldun . . . ," *The Islamic Review* (Woking), xlii (1954), no. 1. Cf. pp. 11–14.

'Alî Pâshâ Mubârak. *al-Khiṭaṭ al-jadîdah at-Tawfîqîyah.* Bulaq, 1305 [1887/88]. Cf. vol. xiv, pp. 5–6.

Allâhâbâd, Aḥmad Ḥusain, and Abdu-r Raḥmân, Shams al-Ulemâ', trs. *Ibn Khaldûn's Muqaddimah.* Lahore, 1924–1932. 3 vols. Urdu translation.

Altamira y Crevea, Rafael. "Notas sobre la doctrina histórica de Abenjaldún" in *Homenaje á D. Francisco Codera.* Saragossa, 1904, Cf. pp. 357–74.

Amari, Michele. *Bibliotheca Arabo-Sicula.* Vol. i, Lipsia [Leipzig], 1857 (Arabic texts); *Appendice* (1875); *Seconda Appendice* (1887). Cf. pp. 460–508 and Appendices.

———. Vol. ii, Turin and Rome, 1880–1881. 2 vols. in 1. Cf. pp. 163–243, 719–20.

———. "Altri frammenti arabi relativi alla Storia d'Italia," *Atti della R. Accademia dei Lincei, Classe di scienze morali, storiche e filologiche* (Rome), 4 ser., vi (1889), 5–31.

Ammar, Abbâs M. "Ibn Khaldûn's Prolegomena to History. The Views of a Muslim Thinker of the 14th Century on the Development of Human Society." Unpublished Ph. D. dissertation,

Dept. of Archaeology and Anthropology, Cambridge University, 1941.

ANAWATI, M. M. *See* GARDET (2).

ANESÎ, 'ALÎ NÛREDDÎN AL-. "Il pensiero economico di Ibn Khaldûn," *Rivista delle Colonie Italiane* (Rome), VI (1932), 112–27.

ARENDONK, CORNELIS VAN. "Ibn Khaldûn" in *Encyclopaedia of Islam* (*q.v.*). Cf. *Supplement*, p. 91.

ARNOLD, SIR THOMAS WALKER. *The Caliphate*. Oxford, 1924.

——— and GUILLAUME, ALFRED, eds. *See* GUILLAUME (3).

ARRI, G. DI ASTI. *Ebn Khaldoun da Tunisi: Storia generale degli Arabi e di alcuni celebri popoli loro contemporanei dalla loro origine fino al Kalifato di Moavia*. Paris, 1840.

ARSLÂN, SHAKÎB, EMÎR, ed. *Ta'rîkh Ibn Khaldûn al-musammâ bi-Kitâb al-'Ibar*. *See* IBN KHALDÛN (3).

ASTRE, GEORGES ALBERT. "Un Précurseur de la sociologie au XIVe siècle: Ibn Khaldoun" in *L'Islam et l'Occident*. Paris, 1947. Cf. pp. 131–50.

AWA, ADEL. *L'Esprit critique des "frères de la pureté."* Beirut, 1948.

'AYÂD, MOHAMMED KÂMIL. "Die Anfänge der muslimischen Geschichtsforschung" in *Geist und Gesellschaft: Kurt Breysig zu seinem 60. Geburtstag*. Breslau, n.d. [1928]. 3 vols. Cf. vol. III, *Vom Denken über Geschichte*, pp. 35–48.

———. *Die Geschichts- und Gesellschaftslehre Ibn Ḫaldûns*. Forschungen zur Geschichts- und Gesellschaftslehre, 2. Stuttgart and Berlin, 1930.

———. "Ibni Haldûn's Kadar Islâmda Tarih," *Iş Meçmuası* (Istanbul), 1938, no. 14, pp. 24–36, 76–79.

——— and ṢALÎBA, JAMÎL. *See* ṢALÎBA.

BABINGER, FRANZ CARL HEINRICH. *Die Geschichtsschreiber der Osmanen und ihre Werke*. Leipzig, 1927. Cf. pp. 212, 282, 369, 379.

BACHER, WILHELM. "Bibel und Biblische Geschichte in der muhammedanischen Literatur," *Jeschurun* (Bamberg), IX (1872), 18–47.

BAMMATE, HAÏDAR. *Visages de l'Islam*. Lausanne, 1946. Cf. pp. 175–79.

BARGÈS, JEAN JOSEPH LÉANDRE. "Lettre sur un ouvrage inédit attribué à l'historien arabe Ibn Khaldoun," *Journal asiatique* (Paris), 3 sér., XII (1841), 483–91.

BARNES, HARRY ELMER. "Sociology before Comte," *American Journal of Sociology* (Chicago), XXIII, no. 2 (Sept., 1917), 197–98.

———. *A History of Historical Writing*. Norman [Okla.], 1937. Cf. pp. 94–96.

——— and BECKER, HOWARD. *Social Thought from Lore to Science*. 2d ed. Washington, 1952. 2 vols. Cf. I, 266–79, 706–8.

BARTHOLD, VASILIĬ VLADIMIROVICH. *Turkestan down to the Mongol Invasion*. E. J. W. Gibb Memorial Series, N.S. V. London, 1928. Cf. pp. 3–4.

———. *Mussulman Culture*. Calcutta, 1934. Tr. Shahid Suhrawardy. Cf. pp. 66–68.

———. *La Découverte de l'Asie: histoire de l'orientalisme en Europe et en Russie*. Tr. B. Nikitine. Paris, 1947. Cf. pp. 29–31.

BAUMSTARK, ANTON. "Der Bibelkanon bei Ibn Chaldûn," *Oriens Christianus* (Rome), IV (1904), 393–98.

BECKER, CARL HEINRICH. "Ältester geschichtlicher Beleg für die afrikanische Schlafkrankheit," *Der Islam* (Strassburg), I (1910). Cf. pp. 197–98. (See also *Islamstudien* [Leipzig], II [1932], 149–50.)

BECKER, HOWARD. *See* BARNES (3).

BEL, ALFRED. "Ibn Khaldûn" in *Encyclopaedia of Islam* (*q.v.*). Cf. II, 395–96.

BELIAEV, EVGENIĬ ALEKSANDROVICH. "Istoriko-sotsiologicheskaia teoriia Ibn-Khalduna," *Istorik Marksist* (Moscow), no. 4–5 (1940), 78–84.

BEN CHENEB, MOḤAMMED. "Etude sur les personnages mentionnés dans l'Idjâza du cheikh 'Abd El Qâdir el Fâsy" in *Actes du XIVe Congrès International des Orientalistes*. Algiers, 1905; Paris, 1908. 3 pts. Cf. pt. III, sect. 335, pp. 512–15.

BERCHER, LÉON. *Initiation à la Tunisie*. Paris, 1950. Cf. pp. 191–92.

——— and SURDON, G., trs. *See* SURDON.

BERGH, SIMON VAN DEN. *Umriss der muḥammedanischen Wissenschaften nach Ibn Ḫaldûn*. Leiden, 1912.

BJÖRKMAN, WALTHER. *Beiträge zur Geschichte der Staatskanzlei im islamischen Ägypten.* Hamburg, 1928.

BOER, TJITZE J. DE. *The History of Philosophy in Islam.* London, 1903. Cf. pp. 200–208

Bolshaia Sovetskaia Entsiklopediia. Moscow, 1950——. Cf. XVII, 259, *s.v.* "Ibn Khaldûn."

BOMBACI, ALESSIO. "La dottrina storiografica di Ibn Ḫaldûn," *Annali della Scuola Normale Superiore di Pisa,* XV (1946), 159–85.

———. "Postille alla traduzione De Slane della *Muqaddimah* di Ibn Ḫaldûn," *Annali dell'Istituto Universitario Orientale di Napoli* (Naples), N.S. III (1949), 439–72.

BOSCH, KHEIRALLAH G. "Ibn Khaldun on Evolution," *The Islamic Review* (Woking), XXXVIII (1950), no. 5, p. 26.

BOUSQUET, GEORGES HENRI. *Le Droit musulman par les textes.* Algiers, 1947. Cf. pp. 93–95.

———. *L'Islam Maghrebin.* 4th ed. Algiers, 1954.

BOUTHOUL, GASTON. *Ibn-Khaldoun: sa philosophie sociale.* Paris, 1930.

———. "L'Esprit de corps selon Ibn Khaldoun," *Revue internationale de Sociologie* (Paris), XL (1932), 217–21.

———. Preface to 2d (reprint) ed. of *Les Prolégomènes d'Ibn Khaldoun. . . .* Paris, 1934–1938. Cf. I, pp. VII–XXIV. *See* SLANE (7).

———. *Traité de Sociologie: Les Guerres.* Paris, 1951. Cf pp. 388–91.

BOUVAT, LUCIEN. *L'Empire mongol.* Paris, 1927. Cf. pp. 6–7.

BROCKELMANN, CARL. *Geschichte der arabischen Litteratur.* Vol. I, Weimar, 1898; vol. II, Berlin, 1902 (in 3 pts). Cf. II, 242–45.

———. 2d ed. Vol. I, Leiden, 1943; Vol. II, 1944–1949 (6 sects. in 3 fascicules). Cf. II, 314–17.

———. *Supplementbände.* Vol. I, Leiden, 1937; vol. II, 1938; vol. III, 1942 (23 sects. in 11 fascicules). Cf. II, 342–44.

———. *History of the Islamic Peoples.* New York, 1947.

BROWNE, EDWARD GRANVILLE. *A Literary History of Persia.* London and Cambridge, 1902–1924. 4 vols. Cf. II, 86–89; III, 412; IV, passim.

BRUNSCHVIG, ROBERT. *La Berbérie orientale sous les Ḥafṣides des origines à la fin du XVe siècle.* Paris, 1940–1947. 2 vols. Cf. II, 385–94.

——— and PÉRÈS, HENRI. *See* PÉRÈS (4).

BUKHSH, SALAHUDDIN KHUDA. "Ibn Khaldûn and his History of Islamic Civilization," *Islamic Culture* (Hyderabad), I (1927), 567–607.

———, tr. *Contributions to the History of Islamic Civilization.* Calcutta, 1929–1930. 2 vols. Cf. II, 201–60; for original, *see* KREMER.

BURET, L. "Un Pédagogue arabe du XIVe siècle: Ibn Khaldûn," *Revue Tunisienne* (Tunis), V (1934), 23–32.

BUSTÂNÎ, BUṬRUS AL-. *Dâ'irat al-ma'ârif.* Beirut, 1876–1900. 11 vols. Cf. I, 460–68.

BUSTÂNÎ, FU'ÂD IFRÂM AL-. "Ibn Khaldûn: Extracts from the *Prolegomena,*" *ar-Rawâ'i* (Beirut), 1927, no. 13.

CAHEN, CLAUDE. *La Syrie du Nord.* Paris, 1940. Cf. pp. 84–85.

CAHUN, LÉON. *Introduction à l'histoire de l'Asie: Turcs et Mongols.* Paris, 1896. Cf. pp. 495–97.

CANARD, MARIUS. "Les Relations entre les Merinides et les Mamelouks au XVIe siècle," *Annales de l'Institut d'Etudes Orientales* (Algiers), V (1939–1941), 41–81.

CARO BAROJA, JULIO. "El Poder Real, según Aben Jaldûn," *Africa* (Madrid), XII (1955), no. 161, pp. 212–14.

———. "Aben Jaldûn y la ciudad musulmana," *ibid.*, XII (1955), no. 167, pp. 484–88.

CARRA DE VAUX, BERNARD, BARON. *Les Penseurs de l'Islam.* Paris, 1921–1926. 5 vols. Cf. I, 278–93.

CASANOVA, PAUL. "La Malḥamat dans l'Islam primitif," *Revue de l'Histoire des Religions* (Paris), LXI (1910), 151–61.

———. *Mohammed et la fin du monde.* Paris, 1911. Cf. pp. 45 ff.; 133 ff.

———. *See* SLANE (5).

CHAIX-RUY, JULES. "Sociología y psicología de la vida social en la Obra de Ibn Jaldun," *Revista Mexicana de Sociología* (Mexico), XXI (1954), no. 4, pp. 7–22.

COLOSIO, STEFANO. "Contribution à l'étude d'Ibn Khaldoûn," *Revue du Monde Musulman* (Paris), XXVI (1914), 318–38.

COOK, STANLEY ARTHUR. "The Semites: The Writing of History" in *The Cambridge Ancient History*. Cambridge University Press: New York, 1923–1951. 12 vols. Cf. I, 223–25.

COQUEBERT DE MONTBRET FILS, E. "Extraits des Prolégomènes historiques d'Ibn-Khaldoun," *Journal asiatique* (Paris), 1 sér., V (1824), 148–56; VI (1825), 106–13; X (1827), 3–19.

CROZAT, CHARLES. *Âmme Hukuku Dersleri*. Istanbul, 1944–1946. 2 vols.

Dâ'irat al-Ma'ârif al-Islamîyah. [Arabic translation of *Encyclopaedia of Islam*.] Cairo, 1934. Cf. vol. L, fasc. 3, pp. 152–55.

DÂGHIR, JOSEPH A. *Maṣâdir ad-dirâsah al-adabîyah*. Saïda, 1950.

DARBISHIRE, ROBERT S. "The Philosophical Rapprochement of Christendom and Islam in Accordance with Ibn Khaldûn's Scientific Criticism," *The Moslem World* (Hartford), XXX (1940), 226–35.

DELVAILLE, JULES. *Essai sur l'histoire de l'idée de progrès*. Paris, 1910. Cf. p. 115.

DERMENGHEM, EMILE. *Les Plus Beaux Textes arabes*. Paris, 1951. Cf. pp. 209–15, 225–30.

DI MATTEO, IGNAZIO. "Il 'taḥrîf' od alterazione della Bibbia secondo i musulmani," *Bessarione* (Rome), XXVI (1922). Cf. pp. 242–43.

DONALDSON, DWIGHT M. "The Shiah Doctrine of the Imamate," *The Moslem World* (Hartford), XXI (1931), 14–23.

DOUTTÉ, EDMOND. *Magie et religion dans l'Afrique du Nord*. Algiers, 1909.

DOVER, CEDRIC. "The Racial Philosophy of Ibn Khaldûn," *Phylon* (The Atlanta [Georgia] University), XIII (1952), 107–19.

DOZY, REINHART PIETER ANNE. *Historia Abbadidarum: praemissis scriptorum Arabum de ea dynastia locis nunc primum editis*. Lugduni [Leiden], 1846. Vols. II (1852) and III (1863), *Scriptorum Arabum loci de Abbadidis*. Cf. II, 206–16; III, 235–36.

———, ed. *See* MAQQARÎ (3).

———. Review of IBN KHALDÛN (4) and SLANE (6), *q.v.*, *Journal asiatique* (Paris), 6 sér., XIV (1869), 133–218.

———. *Recherches sur l'histoire et la littérature de l'Espagne pendant le Moyen Age*. 3d ed. Leiden, 1881. 2 vols. Cf. I, 89–116 and Appendices.

Dubler, César Emil. "Fuentes árabes y bizantinas en la Primera Crónica General, Intercambios cristiano-islámicos," *Vox Romanica* (Bern), xii (1951). Cf. pp. 120–22.

Enan, Muḥammad Abdullah. *Falsafat Ibn Khaldûn al-ijtimâ'îyah.* Cairo, 1925. For originals, *see* Ḥusain, Wesendonk.

———. *Ibn Khaldûn: Ḥayâtuhû wa-turâthuhu al-fikrî.* Cairo, 1933.

———. *Ibn Khaldûn.* Cairo, 1939.

———. *Ibn Khaldûn: His Life and Work.* Lahore, 1941; reprinted 1944; 2d ed., 1946.

Encyclopaedia Britannica. Chicago, London, and Toronto, 1950. 24 vols. Cf. xii, 34, *s.v.* "Ibn Khaldûn."

Encyclopaedia of Islam. Leiden and London, 1913–1934. 4 vols. *Supplement* (in 5 pts.), 1934–1938. *See* Arendonk, Bel, Gibb (3), Macdonald (4).

Encyclopedia Americana. New York and Chicago, 1951. 30 vols. Cf. xiv, 617, *s.v.* "Ibn Khaldun."

Ezzat, Abdulazîz. *Ibn-Khaldoun et sa science sociale.* Cairo, 1947.

Farrûkh, 'Umar. *Ibn Khaldûn wa-Muqaddimatuhû.* Beirut, 1943; 2d ed., 1951.

———. "Dirâsât 'an Muqaddimat Ibn Khaldûn," *Revue de l'Académie Arabe* (Damascus), xxix (1954), 67–76, 203–14.

———. *The Arab Genius in Science and Philosophy.* The American Council of Learned Societies: Near East Translation Program, Publication 10. Tr. John B. Hardie. Washington, 1954.

Ferrand, Gabriel. *Relations de voyages et textes géographiques . . . relatifs à l'Extrême-Orient du VIIIe au XVIIIe siècles.* Paris, 1913–1914. 2 vols. Cf. ii, 459–61.

Ferrero, Gugliemo. "Un sociologo arabo del secolo XIV: Ibn Kaldoun, *La Riforma sociale* (Turin), vi (1896), 221–35.

Fındıkoğlu, Ziyaeddin Fahri. "Ibn Haldun'un hayatı ve fikirleri, Ibni Haldun ve Felsefesi," *Iş Meçmuası* (Istanbul), 1939–1940 *et seq.*

———. "Les Théories de la connaissance et de l'histoire chez Ibn Ḥaldûn" in *Proceedings of the 10th International Congress of Philosophy.* Amsterdam, 1949. 2 vols. Cf. i, 274–76.

———. *La Conception de l'histoire et la théorie méthodologique chez Ibn Khaldoun.* Üçler Basımeve, Gençlik Kitabevi neşriyati. Içtimaî eserler serisi, ix. Istanbul, 1951.

FINDIKOĞLU, ZIYAEDDIN FAHRI. "Türkiyede Ibn Haldunizm" in *Fuad Köprülü Armağani.* Istanbul, 1953. Cf. pp. 153–63.

——— and ÜLKEN, HILMI ZIYA. *See* ÜLKEN (2).

FISCHEL, WALTER JOSEPH. "Ibn Khaldun and Timur" in *Actes du XXIe Congrès International des Orientalistes.* Paris, 1949. Cf. pp. 286–87.

———, *Bulletin des études arabes* (Algiers), 1950, no. 47, p. 61.

———. "Ibn Khaldûn's Activities in Mamlûk Egypt (1382–1406)" in *Semitic and Oriental Studies Presented to William Popper.* Berkeley and Los Angeles, 1951. Cf. pp. 102–24.

———. *Ibn Khaldûn and Tamerlane: Their Historic Meeting in Damascus,* A.D. *1401* (*803* A.H.). A study based on Arabic Manuscripts of Ibn Khaldûn's "Autobiography," with a translation into English, and a commentary. Berkeley and Los Angeles, 1952. For Persian translation, *see* NAFÎSÎ (2).

———. "The Biography of Ibn Khaldûn" in *Yearbook: The American Philosophical Society: 1953.* Philadelphia, 1954. Cf. pp. 240–41.

———. "Ibn Khaldûn's Use of Jewish and Christian Sources" in *Proceedings of the 23rd International Congress of Orientalists.* Cambridge, 1954. Cf. pp. 332–33.

———. "Ibn Khaldûn and Josippon" in *Homenaje a Millás-Vallicrosa.* Barcelona, 1954–1956. 2 vols. Cf. I, 587–98.

———. "Ibn Khaldûn's 'Autobiography' in the Light of External Arabic Sources" in *Studi orientalistici in onore di Giorgio Levi Della Vida.* Rome, 1956. 2 vols. Cf. I, 287–308.

———. "Ibn Khaldûn's Sources for the History of Jenghiz Khân and the Tatars," *Journal of the American Oriental Society* (Baltimore), LXXVI (1956), 91–99.

———. "Ibn Khaldûn: On the Bible, Judaism and Jews" in *Ignace Goldziher Memorial Volume.* Budapest, 1948; Jerusalem, 1956. Cf. II, 147–71.

———. "A New Latin Source on Tamerlane's Conquest of Damascus (1400/1401): B. de Mignanelli's *Vita Tamerlani* (1416), Translated into English with an Introduction and a Commentary," *Oriens* (Leiden), IX (1956), 201–232.

"Ibn Khaldûn's Contribution to Comparative Religion"

in *University of California Publications in Semitic Philology* (Berkeley and Los Angeles), in press.

FLINT, ROBERT. *History of the Philosophy of History in France, Belgium, and Switzerland.* Edinburgh, 1893. Cf. pp. 157–70.

FLÜGEL, GUSTAV LEBERECHT. "Ibn Chaldûn" in *Allgemeine Encyclopädie der Wissenschaften und Künste*, eds. Ersch and Gruber. Leipzig, 1818–1850. 3 sects. in 99, 43, and 25 pts. Cf. sect. 2, pt. 15, pp. 26–28.

FORRER, LUDWIG. *See* SPULER (2).

FRANK, HERMAN. *Beitrag zur Erkenntniss des Sufismus nach Ibn Ḫaldûn.* Inaugural-Dissertation. Leipzig, 1884.

FREYTAG, GEORG WILHELM FRIEDRICH. *Chrestomathia Arabica grammatica historica.* Bonn, 1834. Cf. pp. 150–82.

GABRIELI, FRANCESCO. "Il concetto della 'aṣabiyya nel pensiero storico di Ibn Ḫaldûn," *Atti della Reale Accademia delle Scienze di Torino* (Turin), LXV (1930), 473–512.

———. *Storia della letteratura araba.* Milan, 1951. Cf. pp. 263–65.

GABRIELI, GIUSEPPE. "Saggio di bibliografia e concordanza della storia di Ibn Ḫaldûn," *Rivista degli studi orientali* (Rome), X (1924), 169–211.

GARCIN DE TASSY, JOSEPH HÉLIODORE SAGESSE VERTU. "Supplément à la Notice de M. de Hammer, sur l'Introduction à la connaissance de l'Histoire, célèbre ouvrage arabe d'Ibn Khaledoun," *Journal asiatique* (Paris), 1 sér., IV (1824), 158–61.

GARDET, LOUIS. *La Cité musulmane: Vie sociale et politique.* Paris, 1954.

——— and ANAWATI, M. M. "La Place du Kalâm d'après Ibn Khaldûn" in *Introduction à la théologie musulmane.* Paris, 1948. Cf. pp. 121–24 and passim.

GAUDEFROY-DEMOMBYNES, MAURICE. "Ibn Khaldoun, Histoire des Benou'l-Ahmar, rois de Grenade," *Journal asiatique* (Paris), 9 sér., XII (1898), 309–40, 407–62.

GAUTIER, EMILE FÉLIX. "Un Passage d'Ibn Khaldoun et du Bayân," *Hespéris* (Paris), XLI (1924), 305–12.

———. *L'Islamisation de l'Afrique du Nord: Les siècles obscurs du Maghreb.* Paris, 1927. *See* MARÇAIS, WILLIAM.

———. *Mœurs et coutumes des Musulmans.* Paris, 1931.

GAYANGOS, PASCUAL DE, tr. *See* MAQQARÎ (2).

GIBB, HAMILTON ALEXANDER ROSSKEEN. *Arabic Literature.* Oxford, 1926. Cf. pp. 112–13.

———. "The Islamic Background of Ibn Khaldûn's Political Theory," *Bulletin of the School of Oriental Studies* (London), VII (1933–1935), 23–31.

———. "Ta'rîkh" in *Encyclopaedia of Islam* (*q.v.*). Cf. *Supplement*, pp. 233–45.

———. *Modern Trends in Islam.* Chicago, 1947.

GIESECKE, HEINZ HELMUT. *Das Werk des 'Azîz b. 'Ârdašîr Âstarâbâḏî.* Leipzig, 1940. Cf. pp. 114–15.

GOITEIN, SOLOMON DOB FRITZ. [*Extracts from Ibn Khaldûn's Muqaddima* (*On the Method of History*).] In Hebrew, with introduction, notes, and vocabulary. Jerusalem, 1943.

———. "An Arab on Arabs: Ibn Khaldûn's Views on the Arab Nation," *The New East, Quarterly of the Israel Oriental Society* (Jerusalem), I (1950), nos. 2–3, 115–21, 198–201. In Hebrew; English summary in no. 3.

GOLDZIHER, IGNAZ. "Linguistisches aus der Literatur der muhammedanischen Mystik," *Zeitschrift der Deutschen Morgenländischen Gesellschaft* (Leipzig), XXVI (1872). Cf. pp. 766–67.

———. "Über muhammedanische Polemik gegen Ahl al-Kitâb," *ibid.*, XXXII (1878). Cf. pp. 345, 361, 368.

———. "Materialien zur Kenntnis der Almohadenbewegung in Nord-Afrika," *ibid.*, XLI (1887), 30–140.

———. *Die Ẓâhiriten.* Leipzig, 1884.

———. *Muhammedanische Studien.* Halle, 1889–1890. 2 vols. in 1.

———. *A Short History of Arabic Literature.* Translated from Croatian into Hebrew by P. Shinar. Jerusalem, 1952. Cf. pp. 140–41.

GONZÁLEZ-PALENCIA, ANGEL. *Historia de la literatura Arábigo-Española.* 2nd ed. Barcelona, 1945. Cf. pp. 183–85.

GRÅBERG AF HEMSÖ, JAKOB GREFVE. *Notizia intorno alla famosa Opera istorica di Ibnu Khaldùn, filosofo affricano del secolo XIV.* Florence, 1834.

———. "An Account of the Great Historical Work of the African Philosopher Ibn Khaldun," *Transactions of the Royal Asiatic So-*

ciety of Great Britain and Ireland (London), III (1835), 387–404.

Grande Enciclopédia Portuguesa e Brasileira. Lisbon and Rio de Janeiro, 1935–1956. 33 vols. Cf. v, 488, *s.v.* "Caldune."

Grande Encyclopédie. Paris, 1886–1903. 31 vols. Cf. XX, 515–16, *s.v.* "Ibn Khaldoun."

GREEF, GUILLAUME JOSEPH DE. *Le Transformisme sociale: Essai sur le progrès et le regrès des sociétés.* Paris, 1901. Cf. pp. 115–18.

GRUNEBAUM, GUSTAVE EDMUND VON. "as-Sakkâkî: on Milieu and Thought," *Journal of the American Oriental Society* (Baltimore), LXV (1945). Cf. p. 62.

———. *Medieval Islam: A Study in Cultural Orientation.* 2d ed. Chicago, 1953.

———. "Islam: Essays in the Nature and Growth of a Cultural Tradition," *The American Anthropologist* (Chicago), LVII (1955).

———, ed. *Unity and Variety in Muslim Civilization.* Chicago, 1955.

GUERNIER, EUGÈNE LÉONARD. *La Berbérie, l'Islam et la France.* Paris, 1950. Cf. pp. 226–35, 396–402.

GUIDI, MICHELANGELO. "Ibn Khaldûn" in *Enciclopedia Italiana.* Rome and Milan, 1930–1950. 26 vols. and Appendices. Cf. XVIII, 682.

GUILLAUME, ALFRED. *The Traditions of Islam.* Oxford, 1924. Cf. pp. 89–93, 159–68.

———. "Arabian Views on Prophecy (Ibn Khaldûn)" in *Prophecy and Divination among the Hebrews and Other Semites.* The Bampton Lectures. New York, 1938. Cf. pp. 197–213.

——— and ARNOLD, SIR THOMAS WALKER, eds. *The Legacy of Islam.* Oxford, 1931.

GUMPLOWICZ, LUDWIG. "Ibn Chaldûn, ein arabischer Sociologe des 14. Jahrhunderts" in *Sociologische Essays.* Innsbruck, 1899.

———. "Un Sociologue arabe du XIVe siècle" in *Aperçus sociologiques.* Lyon and Paris, 1900. Cf. pp. 201–26.

ḤÂJJÎ KHALÎFAH, MUṢṬAFÂ B. 'ABDALLÂH. *Kashf aẓ-ẓunûn: Lexicon bibliographicum et encyclopaedicum.* Ed. G. Flügel. Leipzig and London, 1835–1858. 7 vols. Cf. II, no. 2085, p. 101 and passim.

HAMMER-PURGSTALL, JOSEPH, FREIHERR VON. *Über den Verfall des Islam nach den ersten drei Jahrhunderten der Hidschra*. Vienna, 1812.

———. "Description des nôces de Bouran" in *Fundgruben des Orients* (Vienna), v (1816). Cf. p. 389.

———. "Extraits d'Ibn Khaledoun" in *ibid.*, vi (1818), 301–7, 362–64.

———. "Notice sur l'Introduction à la connaissance de l'histoire, Célèbre Ouvrage arabe d'Ibn Khaldoun," *Journal asiatique* (Paris), 1 sér., i (1822), 267–78; iv, 158–61.

———. *Geschichte des Osmanischen Reiches*. Pest, 1827–1835. 10 vols. Cf. i, 301; iii, 489; viii, 253.

ḤAWFÎ, A. M. AL-. *Ma' Ibn Khaldûn*. Cairo, 1952.

HERBELOT DE MOLAINVILLE, BARTHÉLEMY D'. "Khaledoun" in *Bibliothèque orientale, ou Dictionaire universel. . . .* Paris, 1697. Cf. ii, 418.

HEYWORTH-DUNNE, GAMAL-EDDINE. *A Basic Bibliography on Islam*. The Muslim World Series, iv. Cairo, 1955. Cf. pp. 28-30.

ḤIMṢÎ, NA'ÎM AL-. "al-Balâgha bayn al-lafẓ wa-l-ma'nâ," *Revue de l'Académie Arabe* (Damascus), xxv (1950), 447–48.

HIRSCHBERG, H. Z. ["The Berber Heroine Known as the 'Kahena' "], *Tarbiz* (Jerusalem), xxvi (1957), 370–83. In Hebrew.

HITTI, PHILIP KHÛRI. *History of the Arabs*. London and New York, 1951.

HOOGVLIET, MARINUS. *Specimen e litteris orientalibus exhibens diversorum scriptorum locos de regia Aphtasidarum familia*. Leiden, 1839.

HORTEN, MAX. *Die Philosophie des Islam*. Munich, 1924.

HOSTELET, GEORGES. "Ibn Khaldoun, un précurseur arabe de la sociologie au XIVe siècle," *Revue de l'Institut de Sociologie* (Brussels), 1936, pp. 151–56.

HUART, CLÉMENT IMBAULT. *Littérature arabe*. Paris, 1923. Cf. pp. 345–49.

ḤUSAIN, ṬÂHÂ. *Etude analytique et critique de la philosophie sociale d'Ibn Khaldoun*. Paris, 1917. For Arabic translation, *see* ENAN (1).

ḤUṢARÎ, SÂṬÎ AL-. *Dirâsah 'an Muqaddimat Ibn Khaldûn.* Beirut, 1943–1944. 2 vols.

———. "La Sociologie d'Ibn Khaldûn" in *Actes du XVe Congrès International de Sociologie.* Istanbul, 1952.

IBN AL-FURÂT, NÂṢIR AD-DÎN MUḤAMMAD. *at-Ta'rîkh.* Beirut, 1936–1938. Cf. vol. IX.

IBN AL-'IMÂD. *Shadharât adh-dhahab fî akhbâr man dhahab.* Cairo, 1350–1351 [1931–1933]. Cf. vol. VII, pp. 76–77.

IBN AL-KHAṬÎB, LISÂN-AD-DÎN. *al-Iḥâṭah fî akhbâr Gharnâṭah.* Cairo, 1319 [1901]. 2 vols. *See* MAQQARÎ (1).

IBN 'ARABSHÂH, AḤMAD B. MUḤAMMAD. *'Ajâ'ib al-maqdûr fî akhbâr Tîmûr: Ahmedis Arabsiadae, vitae et rerum gestarum Timur, qui vulgo Tamerlanes dicitur, historia.* Ed. S. H. Manger. Leovardiae [Leeuwarden], 1767–1772. 2 vols. Cf. II, 62–70, 786–96. Other editions: Calcutta, 1841; Cairo, 1868. For English translation, *see* SANDERS.

———. *Kitâb Fâkihat al-khulafâ' wa-muâfkahât aẓ-ẓurafâ': Fructus Imperatorum.* Ed. G. Freytag. Bonn, 1832–1852. 2 pts. in 1 vol. Cf. I, 151; II, 94.

IBN FARḤÛN. *See* AḤMAD BÂBÂ.

IBN IYÂS, MUḤAMMAD B. AḤMAD. *Badâ'i' az-zuhûr fî waqa'i' ad-duhûr.* Bulaq, 1311–1312 [1893–1895]. 3 vols. Cf. vol. I.

IBN JULJUL, AL-ANDALUSÎ ABÛ DÂWÛD SULAYMAN B. ḤASSÂN. *Les Générations des médecins et des sages.* Ed. Fu'âd Sayyid. Cairo, 1955.

IBN KHALDÛN, WALÎ AD-DÎN 'ABD-AR-RAḤMÂN. [History.] *Kitâb al-'Ibar wa-dîwân al-mubtada' wa-l-khabar.* Bulaq, 1284 [1867/68]. 7 vols. For partial Turkish translation, *see* ṢUBḤÎ PÂSHÂ.

——— ———. *Histoire des Berbères et des dynasties musulmanes de l'Afrique septentrionale.* Texte arabe publ. par M. de Slane. Algiers, 1847–1851. 2 vols. Corresponds to vols. VI and VII of the preceding. For French translation, *see* SLANE (4), (5).

——— ———. *Ta'rîkh Ibn Khaldûn al-musammâ bi-Kitâb al-'Ibar.* Ed. Emîr Shakîb Arslân. Cairo, 1936. 3 vols. Corresponds to vol. II and part of vol. III of the Bulaq edition, plus a separate vol. of Appendices.

IBN KHALDÛN, WALÎ AD-DÎN 'ABD-AR-RAḤMÂN. [Muqaddimah.] *Prolégomènes d'Ebn-Khaldoun.* Texte Arabe par E. Quatremère. *Notices et Extraits des manuscrits de la Bibliothèque Impériale* (Académie des Inscriptions et Belles-Lettres), vols. XVI–XVIII. Paris, 1858. For Urdu translation, *see* ALLÂHÂBÂD. Turkish, *see* PIRI ZÂDEH. French, *see* SLANE (6), (7). English, *see* ROSENTHAL, F. (4).

———. [Autobiography.] *at-Ta'rîf bi-Ibn Khaldûn wa-riḥlathu gharban wa-sharqan.* Ed. Muḥammad b. Tâwît aṭ-Ṭanjî. Cairo, 1370 [1951]. Complete Arabic text. For French translation, *see* SLANE (1), (2). English, *see* FISCHEL (4).

——— ———. *Kitâb al-'Ibar.* Bulaq, 1860. 7 vols. Cf. VII, 379–462, for fragmentary Arabic text of the Autobiography.

——— ———. *Muqaddimah.* Cairo, 1904. Fragmentary Arabic text of the Autobiography on the margins.

———. [Treatise on Logic.] *Lubâb al-Muḥaṣṣal fî uṣûl ad-dîn* (*de Ibn Jaldûn*). Ed. and tr., Fr. Luciano Rubio. Tetuán, 1952. Arabic text only has appeared.

IBN AṢ-ṢIDDÎQ, A. *Ibrâz al-wahm al-maknûn min kalâm Ibn Khaldûn.* Damascus, 1347 [1929].

IBN TAGHRÎ BIRDÎ, ABÛ L-MAḤÂSIN YÛSUF. *an-Nujûm az-zâhirah fî mulûk Miṣr wa-l-Qâhirah.* Ed. W. Popper. University of California Publications in Semitic Philology (Berkeley), vol. VI (1915–1918). Cf. pp. 2, 122, 276.

IBRAHIM-HILMY, PRINCE. *The Literature of Egypt and the Soudan from the Earliest Times to the Year 1885.* A Bibliography. London, 1886–1887. 2 vols. Cf. I, 316–17.

IORGA, NICOLÁE. *Geschichte des Osmanischen Reiches.* Gotha, 1908–1913. 5 vols. Cf. I, 317–38.

IQBAL, SIR MOHAMMAD. *The Reconstruction of Religious Thought in Islam.* Oxford, 1934.

ISKANDARÎ, AḤMAD AL-. "Ibn Khaldûn," *Revue de l'Académie Arabe* (Damascus), IX (1929), 421–32, 461–71.

ISSAWI, CHARLES, tr. *An Arab Philosophy of History: Selections from the Prolegomena of Ibn Khaldun of Tunis (1332–1406).* The Wisdom of the East Series. London, 1950.

———. "Arab Geography and the Circumnavigation of Africa," *Osiris* (Bruges), X (1952), 117–28.

JABRÎ, SHAFÎQ. "Muṣṭalaḥât Ibn Khaldûn," *Revue de l'Académie Arabe* (Damascus), XXVI (1951), 370–76.

JOMIER, JACQUES. *Le Commentaire coranique du Manâr*. Paris, 1954.

JULIEN, CHARLES ANDRÉ. *Histoire de l'Afrique du Nord*. 2d ed. Paris, 1952. Cf. pp. 134–35.

KAY, HENRY CASSELS, ed. and tr. *Yaman: Its Early Medieval History by Najm ad-din 'Omârah al-Ḥakami, also the Abridged History of its Dynasties by Ibn Khaldûn*. . . . London, 1892. Cf. pp. 138–90.

KHADDURI, MAJID. *War and Peace in the Law of Islam*. Baltimore, 1955.

——— and LIEBESNY, HERBERT J., eds. *Law in the Middle East*. Washington, 1955. 1 vol. only has appeared: *Origin and Development of Islamic Law*. Cf. esp., ch. 10, "Judicial Organization" by E. TYAN (*q.v.*).

KHEMIRI, TAHIR. "Der 'Aṣabîja-Begriff in der Muqaddima des Ibn Ḫaldûn," *Der Islam* (Berlin), XXIII (1936), 163–88.

KHUḌR AT-TUNÎSÎ, MUḤAMMAD. *Ḥayâtu Ibn Khaldûn*. Cairo, 1925.

KHÛRI, RA'ÎF. "Ibn Khaldûn wa-Hegel," *aṭ-Ṭarîq* (Beirut), III (1944), fasc. 3, p. 5.

KÖBERT, RAIMUND. "Gedanken zum semitischen Wort- und Satzbau, No. 9: 'Ibar = I'tibâr," *Orientalia* (Rome), N.S. XV (1946), 151–54.

KRAMERS, JOHANNES HENDRIK. *Analecta orientalia: Posthumous Writings and Selected Minor Works*. Leiden, 1954–1956. 2 vols. Cf. "L'Islam et la démocratie," II, 168–83; "La Sociologie de l'Islam," II, 184–93; "L'Etat musulman," II, 194–201.

KREMER, ALFRED, FREIHERR VON. "Ibn Chaldun und seine Kulturgeschichte der islamischen Reiche," *Sitzungsberichte der Kaiserlichen Akademie der Wissenschaften, Phil.-hist. Klasse* (Vienna), XCIII (1879), 581–634. For English translation, *see* BUKHSH (2).

KURD, 'ALÎ MUḤAMMAD. "Ibn Khaldûn," *Revue de l'Académie Arabe* (Damascus), XXI–XXII (1946–1947), 396–404.

———. "Ibn Khaldûn wa-Tîmûrlank" [According to Ibn az-Zamlakânî], *ibid.*, XXIII (1948), 159.

LANCI, MICHELE ANGELO. *Dissertazione storico-critica su gli Omireni e loro forme di scrivere trovate ne' codici Vaticano. Appresso è un*

Articolo di Eben Caliduno intorno all'arabesca Paleografia. Rome, 1820.

Laoust, Henri. *Essai sur les doctrines sociales et politiques de Taḳî-d-Dîn b. Taimîya.* Cairo, 1939.

Le Bon, Gustave. *La Civilization des Arabes.* Paris, 1884.

Levi Della Vida, Giorgio. "The 'Bronze Era' in Moslem Spain," *Journal of the American Oriental Society* (Baltimore), LXIII (1943), no. 3, 183–91.

———. "La traduzione araba delle Storie di Orosio" in *Miscellanea Giovanni Galbiati.* Fontes ambrosiani, 25–27. Milan, 1951. 3 vols. Cf. III, 185–203.

———, *al-Andalus* (Madrid and Granada), XIX (1954), 257–93. Reprint of the preceding, corrected and augmented.

———. "Ibn Khaldûn" in *Collier's Encyclopedia.* New York, 1952. 20 vols. Cf. X, 326.

Lévi-Provençal, Evariste. "Note sur l'exemplaire du *Kitâb al-'Ibar* offert par Ibn Ḫaldûn à la Bibliothèque d'al-Karawîyîn à Fes," *Journal asiatique* (Paris), CCIII (1923), 161–68.

———. Communication to the Académie des Inscriptions et Belles-Lettres in *Comptes rendus: Séances de l'Année 1923.* Paris, 1923. Cf. pp. 202–3.

———. *L'Espagne musulmane au Xième siècle.* Paris, 1932.

———. *Extraits des historiens arabes du Maroc.* 3d ed. Paris, 1948.

———. *Histoire de l'Espagne musulmane.* Paris and Leiden, 1950–1953. 3 vols.

Levin, I. "Ibn-Chaldun, arabski sociolog XIV vieka," *Novyi Vostok* (Moscow), XII (1926), 241–63.

Levy, Reuben. *An Introduction to the Sociology of Islam.* London, 1931–1933. 2 vols.

———. 2d ed. *The Social Structure of Islam.* Cambridge University Press, 1957.

Lewis, Bernard. *The Arabs in History.* London, 1950.

Lichtenstädter, Ilse. "Arabic and Islamic Historiography," *The Moslem World* (Hartford), XXXV (1945), 126–32.

Liebesny, Herbert J. *See* Khadduri (2).

Luciani, J. D. "La Théorie du droit musulman (Ouçoul el-fiqh) d'après Ibn Khaldoun," *Revue africaine* (Algiers), LXIX (1928), 49–64.

MACDONALD, DUNCAN BLACK. *Ibn Khaldûn: A Selection from the Prolegomena of Ibn Khaldûn. With Notes and an English-German Glossary*. Semitic Study Series, IV. Leiden, 1905; reprinted 1948.

———. *Aspects of Islam*. New York, 1911. Cf. pp. 309–19.

———. *The Religious Attitude and Life in Islam*. 2d ed. Chicago, 1912. Cf. pp. 41–79, 95–124, 130–33, 165–74.

———. "Kalâm" and "al-Mahdî" in *Encyclopaedia of Islam* (*q.v.*). Cf. II, 673 ff.; III, 113–15.

MACHADO, JOSÉ PEDRO. "A Língua Arábica do Andaluz segundo os 'Prolegómenos' de Iben Caldune," *Boletim de Filologia* (Lisbon), VII (1944), 401–18.

MACHADO, OSVALDO A. "La historia de los Godos según Ibn Jaldûn," *Cuadernos de Historia de España* (Buenos Aires), I–II (1944), 139–53.

———. "Historia de los Arabes de España por Ibn Jaldûn," *ibid.* (1946–1948): IV, 136–47; VI, 146–53; VII, 138–45; VIII, 148–58.

MACHUEL, LOUIS. *Les Auteurs arabes*. Pages choisies des grands écrivains. Paris, 1912. Cf. pp. 342–48.

MAGALI-BOISNARD, MME. "La Vie singulière d'Ibn Khaldoun, historien des Arabes et des Berbères," *Bulletin de la Société de Géographie d'Alger et de l'Afrique du Nord* (Algiers), 1929, no. 120, pp. 497–514.

———. *Le Roman de Khaldoun*. Paris, 1930.

MAGHRIBÎ, 'ABD AL-QÂDIR AL-. "Ibn Khaldûn bi-l-madrasah al-'Âdilîyah bi-Dimashq" in *Muḥammad wa-l-Mar'ah*. Damascus, 1347 [1929]. Cf. pp. 38–82.

MAHDI, MUḤṢIN. *Ibn Khaldûn's Philosophy of History: A Study in the Philosophic Foundation of the Science of Culture*. London, 1957.

MAḤMASSÂNÎ, ṢOBḤÎ. *Les Idées économiques d'Ibn Khaldoun: Essai historique, analytique et critique*. Lyon, 1932.

MAITROT DE LA MOTTE-CAPRON, A. "Essai sur le nomadisme," *Revue internationale de Sociologie* (Paris), XLVII (1939), 321–26.

Majallat al-Ḥadîth (Aleppo), Sept., 1932. Special issue on the occasion of Ibn Khaldûn's sexcentenary.

MAQQARÎ, AḤMAD B. MUḤAMMAD AL-. *Nafḥ aṭ-ṭîb min ghuṣn al-Andalus ar-raṭîb.* Bulaq, 1279 [1862/63]. 4 vols. Cf. IV, 414–26.

———. *The History of the Mohammedan Dynasties in Spain.* Tr. Pascual de Gayangos. London, 1840–1843. 2 vols. Cf. I (Appendix B), XXVII–XLII; II (Appendix D), XLIX–LXXX.

———. *Analectes sur l'histoire et la littérature des Arabes d'Espagne.* Eds. R. Dozy *et alii.* 2 vols. Vol. I, Leiden, 1855–1860; vol. II, 1858–1861.

MAQRÎZÎ, TAQÎ AD-DÎN AḤMAD AL-. *al-Khiṭaṭ: al-Mawâ'iẓ wa-l-i'tibâr bi-dhikr al-khiṭaṭ wa-l-âthâr.* Bulaq, 1270 [1853]. 2 vols. Cf. II, 76, 190.

MARÇAIS, GEORGES. *La Guerre vue par Ibn Khaldoun.* Bulletin d'Information du Gouvernement Général de l'Algérie. Algiers, 1939. Cf. pp. 293–95.

———. *Les Idées d'Ibn Khaldoun sur l'évolution des sociétés.* Bulletin d'Information du Gouvernement Général de l'Algérie. Algiers, 1940. Cf. pp. 465–68.

———. "Les Idées d'Ibn Khaldoun sur l'histoire," *Bulletin des études arabes* (Algiers), no. 1 (1941), pp. 3–5.

———. *La Berbérie musulmane et l'Orient au Moyen Age.* Paris, 1946.

———. "Ibn Khaldoun et le livre des Prolégomènes," *Revue de la Méditerranée* (Paris and Algiers), IV (1950), no. 38, pp. 406–420; no. 39, pp. 524–34.

MARÇAIS, WILLIAM. Review of GAUTIER (2), *Revue critique d'histoire de littérature* (Paris), N.S. XCVI (1929), 255–270.

MARGOLIOUTH, DAVID SAMUEL. *Lectures on Arabic Historians.* Calcutta, 1930. Cf. pp. 156–58.

———. "Ibn Khaldûn" in *Encyclopaedia of the Social Sciences.* New York, 1942. 15 vols. Cf. VII, 564–65.

MARÍAS AGUILAR, JULIÁN. *La filosofía en los textos.* Barcelona, 1950. 2 vols. Cf. I, 450–63.

MAUNIER, RENÉ. "Les Idées économiques d'un philosophe arabe, Ibn Khaldoun," *Revue d'Histoire économique et sociale* (Paris), VI (1912), 409–19.

———. "Les Idées sociologiques d'un philosophe arabe au XIVe siècle," *Revue internationale de Sociologie* (Paris), XXIII (1915),

142–54; reprinted in *L'Egypte contemporaine* (Cairo), VIII (1917), 31–43.

MAUNIER, RENÉ. *Mélanges de sociologie nord-africaine.* Paris, 1930. Contains the two preceding titles; cf. pp. 1–35.

MENASCE, PIERRE JEAN DE. *Arabische Philosophie.* Bibliographische Einführungen in das Studium der Philosophie. Bern, 1948. Cf. p. 24.

MERAD, ALI. "L'Autobiographie d'Ibn Khaldûn," *IBLA* (Tunis), XIX (1956), 53–64.

MERCIER, ERNEST. *Histoire de l'établissement des Arabes dans l'Afrique septentrionale selon les documents fournis par les auteurs arabes et notamment par l'histoire des Berbères d'Ibn Khaldoun.* Constantine, 1875.

———. *Histoire de l'Afrique septentrionale.* Paris, 1888–1891. 3 vols.

MEYER, EDUARD. *Geschichte des Altertums.* 3d ed. Berlin and Stuttgart, 1902–1939. 5 vols. in 7. Cf. I, 83–84.

MEYERHOF, MAX. "An Early Mention of Sleeping Sickness in Arabic Chronicles," *Journal of the Egyptian Medical Association* (Cairo), XXIV (1941), 284–86.

MONTAGNE, ROBERT. *La Civilisation du désert.* Paris, 1947.

MUḤÂSIB, JAMÂL AL-. "at-Tarbiyah 'ind Ibn Khaldûn" [Ibn Khaldûn's Theory of Education], *al-Machriq* (Beirut), XLIII (1949), 365–98.

MUHTADÎ, SHUKRÎ. " 'Abd-ar-Raḥmân Ibn Khaldûn," *al-Muqtaṭaf* (Cairo), II (1927), 167–73, 270–77.

MÜLLER, AUGUST. *Der Islam im Morgen- und Abendland.* Berlin, 1885–1887. 2 vols. Cf. II, 666–70.

NAFÎSÎ, SA'ÎD. "Ibn Khaldûn" in *Farhang-nâmah-î Pârsî* [Persian Encyclopedia], ed. *idem.* Teheran, 1950. Cf. I, 528–532.

———. Persian translation of FISCHEL (4). Teheran, 1957.

NASHAAT, MOḤAMMAD 'ALÎ. "Ibn Khaldoun, Pioneer Economist," *L'Egypte contemporaine* (Cairo), XXXV (1945), no. 220, pp. 375–490.

———. *The Economic Ideas in the Prolegomena of Ibn Khaldûn.* Cairo, 1944.

NÂṢIRÎ, AḤMAD B. KHÂLID AN-. *Kitâb al-Istiqṣâ' li-akhbâr duwal al-maghrib al-aqṣâ.* Casablanca, 1954–1955. 4 vols.

NÂṢIRÎ, AḤMAD B. KHÂLID AN-. French translation of vol. IV of the preceding (*Les Mérinides*), by Ismaël Hamet, in *Archives marocaines*, XXXIII (1934). Cf. Index, p. 588, *s.v.* "Ibn Khaldoun."

NICHOLSON, REYNOLD ALLEYNE. *Translations of Eastern Poetry and Prose*. Cambridge, 1922. Cf. pp. 176–85.

———. *A Literary History of the Arabs*. London, 1923. Cf. pp. 437–40.

NOËL DES VERGERS, MARIE JOSEPH ADOLPHE, ed. and tr. *Histoire de l'Afrique sous la dynastie des Aghlabites et de la Sicile sous la domination musulmane*. Texte arabe d'Ebn Khaldoun, accompagné d'une traduction française et de notes. Paris, 1841.

NYKL, ALOIS RICHARD. *Hispano-Arabic Poetry and Its Relations with the Old Provençal Troubadours*. Baltimore, 1946.

OPPENHEIMER, FRANZ. *System der Soziologie*. Jena, 1922–1935. 4 vols. Cf. II, 173 ff.; IV, 251 ff.

ORTEGA Y GASSET, JOSÉ. "Abenjaldun nos revela el secreto. (Pensamientos sobre África Menor)" in *El Espectador*. Madrid, 1916–1934. 8 vols. Cf. VIII, 9–53.

PELLAT, CHARLES. *Langue et littérature arabes*. Paris, 1952. Cf. pp. 177–80.

PÉRÈS, HENRI. *La Poésie andalouse en Arabe classique au XIe siècle*. Paris, 1937; 2d ed., 1953.

———. *Ibn Khaldoun (1332–1406): Extraits choisis de la "Muqaddima" et du "Kitâb al-ʿIbar."* Algiers, 1947.

———. "Essai de bibliographie d'Ibn Ḫaldûn" in *Studi orientalistici in onore di Giorgio Levi Della Vida*. Rome, 1956. 2 vols. Cf. II, 304–29.

——— and BRUNSCHVIG, ROBERT. "Ibn Khaldoun: sa vie et son œuvre (Bibliographie)," *Bulletin des études arabes* (Algiers), 1943, pp. 55–60, 145–46.

PIQUET, VICTOR. *Les Civilisations de l'Afrique du Nord*. Paris, 1909.

PÎRÎ ZÂDEH, MEḤMED ṢÂḤIB, and AḤMED JEVDET. *ʿUnwân as-siyar: Tarjumen muqaddamat Ibn Khaldûni*. Constantinople, 1863. 3 vols. For original, *see* IBN KHALDÛN [Muqaddimah].

PIZZI, ITALO. *Letteratura Araba*. Milan, 1903. Cf. pp. 333–37.

PLESSNER, MARTIN. "Beiträge zur islamischen Literaturgeschichte," *Islamica* (Leipzig), IV (1931), 538–42.

PONCET, J. "L'Evolution des 'genres de vie' en Tunisie: autour d'une phrase d'Ibn Khaldoun," *Cahiers de Tunisie*, II (1954), 315–23.

PONS BOIGUES, FRANCISCO. *Ensayo bio-bibliográfico sobre los historiadores y geógrafos Arábigo-Españoles*. Madrid, 1898. Cf. pp. 350–62.

PRAKASH, BUDDHA. "Ibn Khaldûn's Philosophy of History," *Islamic Culture* (Hyderabad), XXVIII (1954), 492–508; XXIX (1955), 104–19, 184–90, 225–36.

QÂDIR, 'ABD AL-. "The Social and Political Ideas of Ibn Khaldûn," *The Indian Journal of Political Science* (Allahabad), III (1941), 117–26.

———. "The Economic Ideas of Ibn Khaldûn," *ibid.*, XXII (1942), 898–907.

QALQASHANDÎ, AḤMAD AL-. *Ṣubḥ al-A'shâ*. Cairo, 1913–1919. 14 vols. Cf. vols. IV–VII; XIII.

QAMÎR, YUḤANNÂ. *Muqaddimat Ibn Khaldûn: dirâsah, mukhtârât*. Beirut, 1947. Cf. pp. 1–47.

QUATREMÈRE, ETIENNE MARC. *See* IBN KHALDÛN [Muqaddimah].

RAPPOPORT, CHARLES. *Zur Characteristik der Methode und Hauptrichtungen der Philosophie der Geschichte*. Berner Studien zur Philosophie und ihrer Geschichte, III. Bern, 1896. Cf. pp. 75–79.

———. *La Philosophie de l'histoire comme science de l'évolution*. Paris, 1903; 2d ed., 1925. Cf. pp. 78–88.

REINAUD, JOSEPH TOUSSAINT. "Ibn-Khaldoun" in *Nouvelle Biographie Générale*, ed. Didot. Paris, 1877. 46 vols. Cf. XXV, 740–47.

RENAUD, HENRI PAUL JOSEPH. "Divination et histoire nord-africaine aux temps d'Ibn Khaldoun," *Hespéris* (Paris), XXX (1943), 213–21.

———. "Sur un passage d'Ibn Khaldoun relatif à l'histoire de Mathématique," *ibid.*, XXXI (1944), 35–47.

RIBERA Y TARRAGÓ, JULIÁN. *La ensenañza entre los Musulmanes españoles*. Saragossa, 1893.

RICHTER, GUSTAV. *Das Geschichtsbild der arabischen Historiker des Mittelalters*. Tübingen, 1933. Cf. pp. 24–25.

RITTER, HELLMUT. "Irrational Solidarity Groups: A Socio-Psychological Study in Connection with Ibn Khaldûn," *Oriens* (Leiden), I (1948), 1–44.

———. "Autographs in Turkish Libraries," *ibid.*, VI (1953), 83.

RIẒÂ, ḤAMÎD. "Ibn Khaldûn, the Philosopher of History," *Islamic Review* (Woking), XXVI (1938), 267–71.

ROSENTHAL, ERWIN ISAK JAKOB. *Ibn Khalduns Gedanken über den Staat: Ein Beitrag zur Geschichte der mittelalterlichen Staatslehre.* Munich and Berlin, 1932.

———. "Ibn Khaldûn: A North African Muslim Thinker of the 14th Century," *Bulletin of the John Rylands Library* (Manchester), XXIV (1940), 307–20.

———. "Some Aspects of Islamic Political Thought," *Islamic Culture* (Hyderabad), XXII (1948), 1–17.

———. "Ibn Jaldûn's Attitude to the Falâsifa," *al-Andalus* (Madrid and Granada), XX (1955), 75–85.

———, ed. and tr. *Averroes' Commentary on Plato's Republic.* Oriental Publications, No. 1. Cambridge, 1956.

ROSENTHAL, FRANZ. "Die arabische Autobiographie" in *Studia Arabica I.* Analecta Orientalia, 14. Rome, 1937. Cf. pp. 33 ff.

———. *The Technique and Approach of Muslim Scholarship.* Analecta Orientalia, 24. Rome, 1947.

———. *A History of Muslim Historiography.* Leiden, 1952.

———, tr. *Ibn Khaldûn: The Muqaddimah; An Introduction to History.* New York (Bollingen Series XLIII), London, 1958. 3 vols.

ROSSI, GIOVANNI BERNARDO DE. *Dizionario storico degli autori arabi.* Parma, 1807. Cf. p. 56.

RUBIO, FR. LUCIANO. "En torno à los 'Prolegomenos' de Abenjaldun: Muqaddima o Muqaddama?" *La Ciudad de Dios* (Madrid), CLXII (1950), 171–78.

———, ed. *See* IBN KHALDÛN [Treatise on Logic].

SAKHÂWÎ, MUḤAMMAD B. 'ABD AR-RAḤMÂN AS-. *al-I'lân bi-t-tawbîkh li-man dhamma ahl at-ta'rîkh.* Damascus, 1349 [1930].

———. *aḍ-Ḍau' al-lâmi' li-ahl al-qarn at-tâsi'.* Cairo, 1353–1355 [1934–1936]. 12 vols. in 6. Cf. IV, 145–49.

ṢALÎBA, JAMÎL and 'AYÂD, KÂMIL M. *Ibn Khaldoun: morceaux choisis* (*Muntakhabât*). Damascus, 1933.

SÂMÎ AL-KAYÂLÎ. "Ibn Khaldûn wa l-'Arab" in *al-Fikr al-'Arabîyah.* Cairo, 1943. Cf. pp. 13–26.

SÁNCHEZ-ALBORNOZ Y MEDUIÑA, CLAUDIO. "Ben Jaldûn ante Pedro El Cruel" in *idem* (ed.), *La España musulmana según los autores islamitas y cristianos medievales.* Buenos Aires, 1946. 2 vols. Cf. II, 422–23.

SANDERS, JOHN HERNE. *Tamerlane or Timur the Great Amir. From the Arabic Life by Ahmed Ibn Arabshah.* London, 1936. For original, *see* IBN 'ARABSHÂH (1).

SANTILLANA, DAVID. *Istituzioni di Diritto musulmano malichita, con riguardo anche al sistema sciafiita.* Rome, [1926]–1938. 2 vols.

SARKIS, JOSEPH ELIAN. *Dictionnaire encyclopédique de bibliographie arabe.* Cairo, 1928–1931. In 11 pts. Cf. cols. 95–97.

SARTON, GEORGE ALFRED LÉON. *Introduction to the History of Science.* Carnegie Institution of Washington. Baltimore, 1927–1948. 3 vols. in 5. Cf. III (pt. 2), 1767–79.

———. "Arabic Scientific Literature" in *Ignace Goldziher Memorial Volume.* Budapest, 1948; Jerusalem, 1956. 1 vol. in 2. Cf. I, 55–72.

SAUVAGET, JEAN. *Introduction à l'histoire de l'Orient musulman.* Paris, 1943. Cf. pp. 182–83.

———. *Historiens arabes: pages choisies et traduites.* Initiation à l'Islam, v. Paris, 1946. Cf. pp. 137–46.

SCHIMMEL, ANNEMARIE, tr. *Ibn Chaldun: Ausgewählte Abschnitte aus der muqaddima. Aus dem arabischen.* Tübingen, 1951.

SCHMID, JOHAN VON. "Ibn Khaldoun, philosophe et sociologue arabe (1332–1406)," *Revue de l'Institut de Sociologie* (Brussels), 1951, pp. 237–53.

SCHMIDT, NATHANIEL. "The Manuscripts of Ibn Khaldûn," *Journal of the American Oriental Society* (Baltimore), XLVI (1926), 171–76.

———. "Ibn Khaldûn" in *The New International Encyclopaedia.* 2d ed. New York, 1925. 25 vols. Cf. XI, 716–17.

———. *Ibn Khaldun: Historian, Sociologist and Philosopher.* New York, 1930.

———. "Ibn Khaldun and His Prolegomena," *The Moslem World* (Hartford), XXII (1932), 61–63.

SCHREINER, MARTIN. "Zur Geschichte der Aussprache des Hebräischen," *Zeitschrift für die Alttestamentliche Wissenschaft* (Giessen), VI (1886). Cf. pp. 251–55.

SCHULZ, F. E. "Sur le grand ouvrage historique et critique d'Ibn Khaldoun . . . ," *Journal asiatique* (Paris), 1 sér., VII (1825), 213–26, 279–300.

———. "Extrait du grand ouvrage historique d'Ibn-Khaldoun," *ibid.*, 2 sér., II (1828), 117–42.

ŞEREFEDDIN, M. "Ibni Haldun Vesilesiyle Islâm ve Türkler," *Iş Meçmuası* (Istanbul), nos. 15–16 (1938), pp. 67–71.

SHAFAQ, RÎẒA ZÂDEH. ["Ibn Khaldûn and the History of Philosophy"], *Revue de la Faculté des Lettres de Tabriz* (Tabriz), ed. Adib Ṭûṣî, III (1950), no. 7, pp. 360–69. Article in Persian.

SHERWANI, HAROON KHAN. "Political Theories of Certain Early Islamic Writers," *The Indian Journal of Political Science* (Allahabad), III (1942), 225–36.

———. *Studies in Muslim Political Thought and Administration.* Lahore, 1945. Cf. pp. 181–93.

———. "The Genesis and Progress of Muslim Socio-Political Thought," *Islamic Culture* (Hyderabad), XXVII (1953). Cf. pp. 144–48.

SILVESTRE DE SACY, ANTOINE ISAAC, BARON DE, ed. and tr. "Extraits des Prolégomènes d'Ebn-Khaldoun" in *idem, Relation de l'Egypte, par Abd-Allatif, médecin arabe de Bagdad. . . .* Paris, 1810. Cf. pp. 509–24 (translation); 558–64 (Arabic text).

———. *Chrestomathie Arabe, ou Extraits de divers écrivains Arabes.* . 2d ed. Paris, 1826–1827. 3 vols. Cf. I, 370–411; II, 168–69, 257–59, 279–336; III, 342–46.

———. *Anthologie grammaticale arabe.* Paris, 1829. Cf. pp. 167–86, 408–47, 472–76.

———. "Les Haleines de la familiarité . . . par Abd-Alrahman Djami," *Notices et Extraits des manuscrits de la Bibliothèque du Roi* (Académie des Inscriptions et Belles-Lettres), XII (1831). Cf. pp. 293–305.

———. "Ibn-Khaldoun" in *Biographie Universelle ancienne et moderne . . .* , ed. Michaud. 2d ed. Paris, 1843[–1865]. 45 vols. Cf. XX, 268–71.

SILVESTRE DE SACY, ANTOINE ISAAC, BARON DE. "Le Soufisme d'après les Prolégomènes d'Ibn Khaldoun," *Libres études* (Paris), ed: E. Bailly, 1909–1910. Cf. pp. 6–9.

SIMON, MARCEL. "Le Judaisme berbère dans l'Afrique ancienne," *Revue d'Histoire et de Philosophie religieuses* (Strasbourg), XXVI (1946), 1–31, 105–45.

SLANE, WILLIAM MACGUCKIN, BARON DE, tr. "Autobiographie d'Ibn Khaldoun," *Journal asiatique* (Paris), 4 sér., III (1844), 5–60, 187–210, 291–308, 325–53.

———, in his Introduction to *idem* (tr.), *Prolégomènes historiques d'Ibn Khaldoun, q.v.* (*infra*). Cf. XIX (1862), pp. VI–LXXXIII. Corrected version of the preceding.

———, ed. *See* IBN KHALDÛN [History].

———, tr. *Ibn Khaldoun: Histoire des Berbères et des dynasties musulmanes de l'Afrique septentrionale.* Traduite de l'Arabe. Algiers, 1852–1856. 4 vols.

———. Nouvelle édition publiée sous la direction de Paul Casanova. Paris, 1925–1934. 3 vols.

———, tr. *Prolégomènes historiques d'Ibn Khaldoun.* Traduits en Français et commentés. *Notices et extraits des manuscrits de la Bibliothèque Impériale* (Académie des Inscriptions et Belles-Lettres), vols. XIX–XXI. Paris, 1862–1868.

———. *Les Prolégomènes d'Ibn Khaldoun.* Paris, 1934–1938. 3 vols. Photomechanical reproduction of the preceding.

SOROKIN, PITIRIM ALEKSANDROVICH. *Social Philosophies of an Age of Crisis.* Boston, 1951.

———, ZIMMERMAN, CARLE C., and GALPIN, CHARLES J., eds. *A Systematic Source Book in Rural Sociology.* Minneapolis, 1930–1932. 3 vols. Cf. I, 54–68.

SPULER, BERTOLD. Review of SCHIMMEL (*q.v.*), *Vierteljahrschrift für Social- und Wirtschaftsgeschichte* (Wiesbaden), XL (1953), 63–67.

——— and FORRER, LUDWIG. *Der vordere Orient in islamischer Zeit.* Wissenschaftliche Forschungsberichte. Bern, 1954.

ṢUBḤÎ PÂSHÂ, 'ABD-AL-LAṬÎF. *Miftâḥ al-'Ibar.* Istanbul, 1276 [1859/60]. 4 vols. *See* IBN KHALDÛN [History].

SURDON, G. and BERCHER, LÉON, trs. *Recueil de textes de sociologie et de droit public musulman contenus dans les "Prolégomènes" d'Ibn Khaldoun.* Bibliothèque de l'Institut d'Etudes Supérieures d'Alger, 6. Algiers, 1951.

Suyûṭî, 'Abd ar-Raḥmân Jalâl ad-Dîn as-. *Kitâb Ḥusn al-muḥâḍarah fî akhbâr Miṣr wa-l-Qâhirah.* Cairo, 1321 [1903]. 2 vols. in 1. Cf. II, 123–24.

Syrier, Miya. "Ibn Khaldûn and Islamic Mysticism," *Islamic Culture* (Hyderabad), XXI (1947), 264–302.

Ṭanjî, Muḥammad b. Tâwît aṭ-, ed. *See* Ibn Khaldûn [Autobiography].

Terrasse, Henri. *Histoire du Maroc.* Paris, 1949–1950. 2 vols. Cf. vol. II.

Tiesenhausen, Vladimir Gustavovich, baron. "Die Geschichte der 'Oqailiden-Dynastie," *Mémoires présentés à l'Académie Impériale des Sciences de St. Petersbourg*, VIII (1859), 129–72.

———. "Recueil de matériaux relatifs à l'histoire de la Horde d'Or," *ibid.*, I (1884), 365–94. Text and translation.

Togan, Zeki Velidi. "Ibn Khaldûn et l'avenir de l'état musulman" in *Bilgi Meçmuası.* Istanbul, 1941. Cf. pp. 733–43.

———. *Tarihde Usul.* Tarih arastırmaları, 1. Istanbul, 1950. Cf. pp. 170–87.

———. "Kritische Geschichtsauffassung in der islamischen Welt des Mittelalters" in *Proceedings of the Twenty Second [International] Congress of Orientalists*, ed. *idem.* Istanbul, 1953. Only vol. I has appeared. Cf. I, 76–85.

Tornberg, Carl Johan. "Ibn Khalduni narratio de expeditionibus Francorum in terras islamismo subjectas ex codicibus Bodleianis," *Nova Acta regiae societatis scientiarum Upsaliensis* (Upsala), XII (1844), 1–154.

———. "Notitiae de populo Berberorum ex Ibn Khalduno in Primordia dominationis Murabitorum," *ibid.*, XII (1844), 315–36, 398–400.

———. "Geschichte der Franken . . ." in Reinhold Röhricht (ed.), *Quellenbeiträge zur Geschichte der Kreuzzüge.* Berlin, 1875. Cf. pp. 5–31.

Toynbee, Arnold Joseph. "The Relativity of Ibn Khaldûn's Historical Thought" in *A Study of History.* London, 1934–

1954. 10 vols. Cf. III, 321–28, 473–76. (See also x, 84–87 and Index.)

TYAN, EMILE. *Histoire de l'organisation judiciaire en pays d'Islam.* Lyon, 1938–1943. 2 vols.

———. *Institutions du droit public musulman: Le Califat.* Paris, 1954.

———. *See* KHADDURI (2).

ÜLKEN, HILMI ZIYA. *La Pensée de l'Islam.* Istanbul, 1953. Cf. pp. 557–76.

and FINDIKOĞLU, ZIYAEDDIN FAHRI. *Ibni Haldun.* Turk-Islâm Feylesofları, VI. Istanbul, 1940.

VAN DYCK, EDWARD A. *Iktifâ' al-qanû' bi-mâ huwa maṭbû'.* Cairo, 1896. Cf. pp. 76–77.

VERA, FRANCISCO. *La cultura española medieval.* Madrid, 1933–1934. 2 vols. Cf. I, 102–8.

VILLENOISY, COSSERON DE. "Un Homme d'état: historien et philosophe du XIVe siècle (Ibn Khaldoun)," *La Nouvelle Revue* (Paris), XL (1886), 545–78.

WAJDÎ, MUḤAMMAD FARÎD. "Ibn Khaldûn fî l-Mîzân," *al-Hilâl* (Cairo), XL (1932), 1234–42.

WEIL, GUSTAV. *Geschichte des Abbasidenchalifats in Egypten.* Stuttgart, 1862. 5 vols. Cf. II, 63–83, 89.

WELCH, GALBRAITH. *North African Prelude: The First 7000 Years.* New York, 1949. Cf. pp. 173–74, 390–92.

WESENDONK, OTTO GÜNTHER VON. "Ibn Chaldun, ein arabischer Kulturhistoriker des 14. Jahrhunderts," *Deutsche Rundschau* (Berlin), Jahrgang XLIX (1923), 45–53. For Arabic translation, *see* ENAN (1).

WIET, GASTON. "Les Biographies du Manhal Safi," *Mémoires présentés à l'Institut d'Egypte* (Cairo), XIX (1932). Cf. p. 199.

———. "L'Egypte Arabe de la conquête Arabe à la conquête ottomane (642–1517)" in *Histoire de la nation égyptienne,* ed. Gabriel Hanotaux. Paris, 1931–1940. 7 vols. Cf. IV, 530.

WRIGHT, WILLIAM, ed. *The Paleographical Society: Facsimiles of Manuscripts and Inscriptions.* Oriental Series. London, 1875–1883. Cf. pl. LXXXIV.

WÜSTENFELD, HEINRICH FERDINAND. "Die Geschichtschreiber

der Araber und ihre Werke," *Abhandlungen der Königlichen Gesellschaft der Wissenschaften* (Göttingen), XXIX (1882), pp. 26–31.

ZAHIDA, H. PASHA. "Ibn Khaldoun, Sociologist" in *Actes du XVe Congrès International de Sociologie*. Istanbul, 1952.

ZAYDÂN, JIRJÎ. *Ta'rîkh adab al-lughah al-'arabîyah.* Cairo, 1912–1924. 4 vols. Cf. III, 210–14.

ZMERLI, S. "La Vie et les œuvres d'Ibn Khaldoun," *Revue Tunisienne* (Tunis), XVIII (1911), 532–36.

ADDENDA (1966)

'ABBÂS, AḤMAD. "Vie et œuvre d'Ibn Ḫaldûn" in *Falâsifat al-Islâm fî-l-ġarb al-'arabî*. Association Nibrâs al-fikr. Tetuan, 1961.

ABBOTT, NABIA. *Studies in Arabic Literary Papyri. I. Historical Texts.* Oriental Institute Publications, LXXV. Chicago, 1957. Cf. pp. 5–31. ("Early Islamic Historiography.")

AFSHAR, IRAJ. See *Fehrest maqâlât-e Farsî.*

'ALÂM, MANZÛR. "Ibn Khaldûn's Concept of the Origin, Growth and Decay of Cities," *Islamic Culture* (Hyderabad), XXXIV (1960), 90–106.

A'mâl Mahrajân Ibn Khaldûn (Proceedings of the Symposium on Ibn Khaldûn, held in Cairo). Cairo, 1962.

ANAWATI, GEORGE C. "Abd el-Rahmān ibn Khaldoun, un Montesquieu arabe," *La Revue du Caire* (Cairo), XXII (1959), 175–91, 303–19.

'ÂSHÛR, MUḤAMMAD AL-FÂḌIL B. "Ibn Khaldûn," *al-Fikr* (Tunis), III (1958), no. 8, 702–7.

AYALON, DAVID. *Ibn Khaldūn's View of the Mamelukes,* in L. A. Mayer's Memorial Volume, Jerusalem, 1964. (In Hebrew.) Cf. pp. 142–44, English summary, p. 175.

———. "The System of Payment in Mamlûk Military Society," *Journal of Economic and Social History of the Orient* (Leiden), I (1957), 37–65, 257–96.

———. "Studies on the Transfer of the Abbâsid Caliphate from Baghdâd to Cairo," *Arabica* (Leiden), VII (1960), 41–59.

BADAWÎ, ʿABD AR-RAḤMÂN. *Mu'allafât Ibn Khaldûn.* Cairo, 1962.

BATSIEVA, S. M. "Sotsial' nuie osnovui istoriko-philosophskogo ucheniia Ibn Khalduna" (The social bases of Ibn Khaldûn's historical-philosophical doctrine) in *Pamiati akademika Ignatiia IUlianovich Krachkovskogo.* Leningrad, 1958. Cf. pp. 192–201.

———. "Istoriko-Philosophskoe uchenie Ibn Khaldûna" (The historical-philosophical doctrine of Ibn Khaldûn), *Akademiia nauk SSSR, Sovetskoe vostokovedenie* (Moscow), I (1958), 75–86. English summary, p. 86.

———. *Istoriko-Philosophskiy traktat Ibn Khaldûna "O prirode obchshestvennoy zhizni lyudey"* (Historical-philosophical treatise of Ibn Khaldûn on the origin of the social life of the people). (Dissertation resumé, Leningrad University.) Leningrad, 1958.

———. *Istoriko-Sotsiologicheskiy traktat Ibn Khalduna "Mukaddima."* Moscow, 1965.

BIELAWSKI, JÓSEF. "Ibn Ḫaldūn, Historyk, Filozof i Socjolog Arabski z XIV Wieku" (Ibn Khaldûn, Arab historian, philosopher and sociologist of the 14th century), *Przegląd Orientalistyczny* (Warsaw), (1957) no. 2, 127–46.

———. "Twórca socjologii w świecie Islamu . . . ," *Kultura i Społeczeństwo* (Warsaw), III (1959), no. 2, 4–34.

BOUSQUET, GEORGES-HENRI, tr. and ed. *Les Textes économiques de la Mouqaddima (1375–1379).* Paris [1961].

———. "Les Caqâliba chez Ibn Khaldûn," *Rivista degli Studi Orientali* (Rome), XL (1965), pp. 139–141.

BRUNSCHVIG, ROBERT and GRUNEBAUM, GUSTAVE EDMUND VON, eds. *Classicism et déclin culturel dans l'histoire de l'Islam.* Paris, 1957.

CAIRNS, GRACE E. *Philosophies of History:* Meeting of East and West in Cycle—Pattern Theories of History. New York, 1962. London, 1963. Cf. pp. 322–36 (New York edn.).

CARO BAROJA, JULIO. "Aben Jaldún—Antropólogo Social" in *Estudios Mogrebíes.* Instituto de Estudios Africanos. Madrid, 1957. Cf. pp. 11–58.

———. "Las Instituciones Fundamentales de los Nómadas según Aben Jaldún," *op. cit.* Cf. pp. 27–41.

CHAMBLISS, ROLIN. *Social Thought, from Hammurabi to Comte.* New York, 1954. Cf. pp. 283–312.

COHEN, GERSON D. "Ibn Khaldûn—Rediscovered Arab Philosopher," *Midstream* (New York), v (1959), 77–90.

CORCOS, DAVID. "The Jews of Morocco under the Marinides," *Jewish Quarterly Review* (Philadelphia), LIV (1964), 271–87; LV (1964), 53–81, 137–50.

DÂGHIR, YÛSUF ASʿAD. *See* IBN KHALDÛN (1).

DEMEERSEMAN, A. "Ce qu'Ibn Khaldoun pense d'al-Ghazzâlî," IBLA [Institut des belles lettres arabes] (Tunis), XXI (1958), 161–93.

EZZAT, ABDULAZÎZ. *See* ʿIZZAT, ʿABD AL-ʿAZÎZ.

FARÛKI, KEMAL A. *Islamic Jurisprudence*, Karachi, 1962.

FÂSÎ, MUḤAMMAD AL-. "Ibn Khaldûn" in *Falâsifat al-Islâm fî-l-ġarb al-ʿarabî.* Association Nibrâs al-fikr. Tetuan, 1961.

Fehrest maqâlât-e Farsî (*Index Iranicus*). Répertoire méthodique des articles persans concernant les études iranologiques, publiés dans les périodiques et publications collectives. Vol. I, 1910–1958. Ed. Iraj Afshar. Teheran, 1961.

Fikr, al-. Special Ibn Khaldûn issue on the occasion of the 555th anniversary of his death. (Tunis), VI (1961), no. 6.

FINDIKOĞLU, ZIYAEDDIN FAHRI. "L'Ecole ibn-Khaldounienne en Turquie" in *Proceedings of the Twenty-second International Congress of Orientalists, Istanbul, 1951.* Leiden, 1957. 2 vols. Cf. II, 269–73.

FISCHEL, WALTER JOSEPH. "Selected Bibliography of Ibn Khaldûn" in *Ibn Khaldûn: The Muqaddimah, an Introduction to History.* Tr. Franz Rosenthal. New York, 1958. 3 vols. Cf. III, 485–512.

———. "Ascensus Barcoch: A Latin Biography of the Mamlûk Sultan Barqûq of Egypt (d. 1399) by B. de Mignanelli in 1416," translated and annotated, *Arabica* (Leiden), VI (1959), 57–74, 152–72.

———. "Ibn Khaldûn on Pre-Islamic Iran" in *Proceedings of the 26th International Congress of Orientalists*, New Delhi (to appear in 1967).

———. "Našâṭ Ibn Khaldûn fî Miṣr al-Mamlûkîya (1382–1406)," (in Arabic) in *Dirâsât Islâmîya, Anthology of writings by Americans on Islam.* Ed. N. Ziyâda. Beirut, 1960. Cf. pp. 177–212.

———. "Ibn Khaldûn's Use of Historical Sources," *Studia Islamica* (Paris), XIV (1961), 109–119.

———. Preliminary report of the above, in *Proceedings of the Twenty-Fifth International Congress of Orientalists, Moscow, 1960.* Moscow, 1962–3. 5 vols. Cf. II, 71.

———. "Ibn Khaldûn and al-Masʿûdî," in *al-Masʿûdî Millenary Commemoration Volume.* Indian Society for the History of Science. Aligarh, 1961. Cf. pp. 51–9.

———. *Ibn Khaldûn and Tamerlane: Their Historic Meeting in Damascus,* A. D. *1401 (803 A. H.).* *See* orig. bibl. Fischel (4). For Arabic translation, *see* JAWÂD.

———. Urdu translation of the above. Sind Academy. Lahore (to appear in 1967).

———. *Ibn Khaldûn in Egypt (1382–1406). His public functions and his historical research: An essay in Islamic historiography.* Berkeley, 1967.

GIBB, HAMILTON ALEXANDER ROSSKEEN. Reprint of "The Islamic Background of Ibn Khaldûn's Political Theory" in *Studies on the Civilization of Islam.* Eds. Stanford Jay Shaw and William R. Polk. Boston, London, 1962. Cf. pp. 166–75. Cf. also orig. bibl., Gibb (2).

GONÂBÂDI, MUḤAMMAD PARVIN. *See* PARVIN-E GONÂBÂD.

GRUNEBAUM, GUSTAVE EDMUND VON. *See* BRUNSCHVIG.

GUERNIER, EUGÈNE LÉONARD. *La Berbérie, l'Islam et la France; le destin de l'Afrique du Nord.* Paris, 1950. 2 vols. Cf. I, 226–31; 396–402.

HADDAD, J. ALMANSUR. *See* KHOURY, J. and A. BIERRENBACH.

ḤARAKÂT, IBRÂHÎM. "Ibn Khaldûn's 'Kitâb al-ʿIbar' as a Historical Source," *Afâq* (Rabat), I (1963), 123–32.

HODGSON, MARSHALL G. S., ed. *See* NICHOLSON.

HOOKHAM, HILDA. *Tamburlaine the Conqueror.* London, 1962.

HOURANI, ALBERT HABIB. *Arabic Thought in the Liberal Age, 1798–1939.* New York, London, Toronto, 1962.

ḤUṢARÎ, ABÛ KHALDÛN SÂṬIʿ AL-. *Dirâsât ʿan Muqaddimat Ibn Khaldûn* [édition augmentée]. Cairo, Baghdad, 1961.

IBN KHALDÛN, WALÎ AD-DÎN ʿABD AR-RAḤMÂN. *Ta'rîkh al-ʿAllâma*

Ibn Khaldûn. Ed. Yûsuf As'ad Dâghir. Beirut, 1956–1960. 7 vols.

———. *Muqaddimat Ibn Khaldûn*. With notes and introduction by 'Alî 'Abd al-Wâḥid Wâfî. Cairo, 1957–1962. 4 vols.

———. *Muqaddimah*. For Hindi translation, *see* Rizvi. Persian, *see* PARVIN-E GONÂBÂD. Portuguese, *see* KHOURY. Turkish, *see* UGAN. For other translations, *see* orig. bibl. IBN KHALDÛN (4).

———. For French translation of the economic texts, *see* BOUSQUET.

———. *Šifâ'-us-sâ'il litahzîb-il-masâ'il.* (*Apaisement à qui cherche comment clarifier les problèmes.*) Edition, introduction et vocabulaire technique par le père Ignace Abdo Khalifé, S. J. Institut de Lettres orientales de Beyrouth, XI. Beirut, 1959.

Şifâ'u's-sâ'il litehzîbi'l-mesâ'il. Ed. Muhammed b. Tâwît aṭ-Ṭanjî. Istanbul, 1958. Ankara Üniversitesi Îlâhîyat Fakültesi Yayınları, XXII.

IBRÂSHÎ, MUḤAMMAD 'AṬÎYAH AL- and TAWÂNISÎ, ABÛ AL-FUTÛḤ MUḤAMMAD AL-. *Silsilat Tarâjim*. Cairo, 1957. Cf. II, 80–142.

Index Iranicus. See *Fehrest maqâlât-e Farsî*.

Index Islamicus, 1906–1955. A catalogue of articles on Islamic subjects in periodicals and other collective publications. Ed. J. D. Pearson, with assistance of Julia F. Ashton. Cambridge, 1958. Cf. pp. 340–1.

———. *Supplement, 1956–1960*. Ed. J. D. Pearson. Cambridge, 1962. Cf. pp. 106–7.

IRVING, T. B. "The World of Ibn Khaldûn," *The Islamic Literature* (Lahore), IX (1957), 347–51, 473–77.

———. "Peter the Cruel and Ibn Khaldûn," *op. cit.*, XI (1959), 5–17.

———. "A Fourteenth Century View of Language" in *The World of Islam*, Studies in Honour of Philip K. Hitti. Eds. J. Kritzeck and R. Bayly Winder. London, New York, 1959. Cf. pp. 185–92.

'ISSA, 'ALÎ AḤMAD. *The Arabic Society: Experimental Sociological Studies*. Cairo, 1961. Cf. pp. 179–91.

IVANOV, N. A. " 'Kitâb al-'Ibar' Ibn Khalduna kak istochnik po istorii stran Severnoy Afriki ve XIV veke" (Ibn Khaldûn's "Kitâb al-'Ibar" as a Source for the History of the North

African Lands in the 14th Century), *Arabskii Sbornik* (Moscow), XIX (1959), 3–45.

ʿIZZAT, ʿABD AL-ʿAZÎZ. *The Philosophy of History and Sociology.* Cairo, 1960. Cf. pp. 34–61.

JAFFAR, S. M. *History of History*. Peshawar City, 1961. Cf. I, 44–47.

JEAN-LÉON L'AFRICAIN. *Description de l'Afrique.* Tr. (from Italian) and ed. A. Epaulard and others. Publication de l'Institut des Hautes Études Marocaines, LXI. Paris, 1956. 2 vols.

KHALIFÉ, LE PÈRE IGNACE-ABDO, S. J. "Un nouveau traité mystique d'Ibn Ḫaldūn" in *Akten des vierundzwanzigsten internationalen Orientalisten-Kongresses, München, 1957.* Wiesbaden, 1959. Cf. pp. 330–33.

———. *See also* IBN KHALDÛN (5).

KHOURY, J. and A. BIERRENBACH, trs. *b. Haldun. Os prolegomenos ou filosofia social.* Introduction by J. Almansur Haddad. São Paulo, 1958–1960. (Portuguese translation of the *Muqaddimah.*)

KOPILEWITZ, IMMANUEL. *Aqdamot la-Historia* (Hebrew translation of the *Muqaddimah.*) Translated, with notes and introduction, Bialik Institute, Jerusalem, 1967.

KRITZECK, JAMES, ed. *Anthology of Islamic Literature, from the rise of Islam to modern times.* New York, 1964. Cf. pp. 274–84.

LACOSTE, YVES. "La grande oeuvre d'Ibn Khaldoun," *La Pensée* (Paris), LXIX (1956), 10–33.

LEVI DELLA VIDA, GIORGIO. Review of F. Rosenthal's translation of the *Muqaddimah, Oriente Moderno* (Rome), XXXVIII (1958), 1005–7.

LEWIS, BERNARD. "The Muslim Discovery of Europe," *Bulletin of the School of Oriental and African Studies* (London), XX (1957), 409–16.

———, and HOLT, P. M., eds. *Historians of the Middle East.* School of Oriental and African Studies, Historical writing on the peoples of Asia, IV. London, 1962.

LIEBLING, A. J. "The Round of History" (review article), *The New Yorker* (New York), XXXV (1959), no. 38, 213–41.

MACDONALD, J. "An Arab's Appreciation of Ibn Khaldûn and

Western Criticism of Islam," *The Islamic Literature* (Lahore), XI (1959), 187–95.

MADELUNG, WILFRED VON. "Fatimiden und Baḥrainqarmaṭen," *Der Islam* (Berlin), XXXIV (1959), 34–88.

Mahrajān Ibn Khaldūn, Casablanca, 1962. Colloque organise par la Faculté des Lettres à Rabat (Université Mohammad V).

MAHDI, MUHSIN. "Ibn Khaldûn" in *Approaches to the Oriental Classics*. Ed. William Theodore de Bary. New York, 1959. Cf. pp. 68–83.

———. *Ibn Khaldûn's Philosophy of History*. New York: Phoenix edn., 1964.

———. "Die Kritik der islamischen politischen Philosophie bei Ibn Khaldûn," in *Wissenschaftliche Politik: eine Einführung in Grundfragen ihrer Tradition und Theorie*, Freiburg im B., 1962. Cf. 117–51.

MALLÂḤ, MAḤMÛD AL-. *Daqâ'iq wa-ḥaqâ'iq fî Muqaddimat Ibn Khaldûn*. Baghdad, 1955.

———. *Naẓrah thâniyah fî Muqaddimat Ibn Khaldûn*. Baghdad, 1956.

MANZOOR, ʿALÂM. *See* ʿALÂM, MANZÛR.

MIGNANELLI, B. DE. *See* FISCHEL (2).

MULLER, HERBERT JOSEPH. *The Loom of History*. New York, 1958; London, 1960. Cf. pp. 290 ff. (New York edn.).

MÛSÂ, MUNÎR M. *General Sociology*. Damascus, 1959. Cf. vol. I, 27–36.

NADVÎ, MEVLANA MUḤAMMAD HANÎF SAHAB. *Afkâr-i Ibn Khaldûn*. Lahore, 1954. Urdu translation of the *Muqaddimah*.

NASSAR, NASSIF. "Le Maître d'Ibn Khaldūn: al-Ābilī" in *Studia Islamica*, Paris, XX (1965), 103–114.

NICHOLSON, REYNOLDS ALLEYNE. Reprint of "Ibn Khaldûn: the dynamics of history" in *Introduction to Islamic Civilization*. Course syllabus and selected reading by Marshall G. S. Hodgson. Chicago, 1958. 3 vols. Cf. II, 490–501.

NÛR, MUḤAMMAD ʿABD AL-MUNʿIM. *An Analytical Study of the Sociological Thought of Ibn Khaldûn*. Cairo, 1960.

PARVIN-E GONÂBÂD, MUḤAMMAD, tr. *Moqaddame-ye Ebn-e-Khaldûn, ta'lîf-e ʿAbdo'r-Raḥmân Ebn-e-Khaldûn*. Teheran, 1957–1959. Persian translation of the *Muqaddimah*.

PEARSON, J. D. See *Index Islamicus* and *Supplement.*

PÉRÈS, HENRI. *Le siècle d'Ibn Khaldoûn* (*VIIIe/XIVe*). (Bibliothèque de l'Institut d'études supérieures islamique d'Alger.) Algiers, 1960.

PERLMAN, MOSHE. "Ibn Khaldûn on Sufism," *Bibliotheca Orientalis* (Leiden), XVII (1960), 222–3.

PRAKASH, BUDDHA. *The Modern Approach to History.* Delhi, 1963 (University Publications).

QUIROS RODRIGUEZ, C. B. "Ibn Jaldûn, politico e historiador," *Archivos del Instituto de Estudios Africanos* (Madrid), VI (1952), no. 24, 7–9.

RALIBY, OSMAN. *On the Political and Social Ideas of Ibn Khaldūn.* Djakarta, 1962. (Indonesian texts.)

RICHTER, GUSTAV. "Medieval Arabic Historiography" (tr. and ed. M. Saber Khan), *Islamic Culture* (Hyderabad), XXXIII (1959), 148–51; XXXIV (1960), 139–151. Cf. orig. bibl., RICHTER.

RIḌWÂN, IBRÂHÎM. *Muqaddimah. Selections.* Ed. Aḥmad Zaqî. Cairo, 1960.

RIZVI, ATHAR AHBES. *Ibnî Khaladuna ka Mukadama.* Lucknow, 1961. Hindi translation of the *Muqaddimah.*

ROSENTHAL, ERWIN ISAK JAKOB. *Political Thought in Medieval Islam: an introductory outline.* Cambridge, 1962. Cf. pp. 84–109, 260–8.

ROSENTHAL, FRANZ, tr. *Ibn Khaldûn, An Introduction to History: The Muqaddimah,* ed. and abridged by N. J. Dawood. London, 1967.

SALIBI, KAMAL S. "Listes chronologiques des grands Cadis de l'Egypte sous les Mamelouks," *Revue des Etudes Islamiques* (Paris), XXV (1957), 81–125.

ṢÂLIḤ, RUSHDÎ A. *Rajul fi-l-Qâhirah* (A Man in Cairo). A fictionalized biography of Ibn Khaldûn in Cairo. Kutub li'l-Jamî'a, CXV. Cairo, 1957.

SAMÎHÎ, ʿABD AL-KARÎM. "Ibn Khaldûn and His 'Taʿrîf,' " *Revue al-Anwâr* (Tetuan), (1951), no. 26, 12–13, 19–20.

SAUNDERS, J. J. "The Problem of Islamic Decadence," *Cahiers d'Histoire mondiale* (Paris), VII (1963), 701–20.

SHARIF, M. M., ed. *A History of Muslim Philosophy, with short accounts of other disciplines and the modern Renaissance in Muslim lands.* 2 vols. Vol. I, Wiesbaden, 1963. Vol. II (in print). Cf. chs. XLVI, XLIX.

SHERWANI, HAROON KHAN. "Ibn Khaldûn—A Life Sketch," *Indian Journal of the History of Medicine* (Madras), IV (1959), 9–12.

SHIBER, SABA G. "Ibn Khaldûn—an early town planner," *Middle East Forum* (Beirut), XXX (1962), 35–39.

SIKIRIC, ŠAĆIR. "Ibn Haldûnova Prolegomena (Les 'Prolégomènes' d'Ibn Haldun)," *Prilozi za Orientalnu filologiju i istoriju Jugoslovenskih naroda pod Turskom Vladavinom* (Revue de Philologie orientale et d'Histoire des Peuples yougoslaves sous la Domination turque) (Sarajevo), V (1954–1955), 233–50. French summary, p. 250.

SIMON, HEINRICH. *Ibn Khaldûns Wissenschaft von der menschlichen Kultur.* Beiträge zur Orientalistik, II. Leipzig, 1959.

SOMOGYI, JOSEPH DE. "The Development of Arabic Historiography," *Journal of Semitic Studies* (Manchester), III (1958), 373–87.

SPULER, BERTOLD. "Ibn Khaldoun, the Historian" in *Aʿmâl Mahrajân Ibn Khaldûn.* Cairo, 1962. Cf. pp. 349–56.

SUBBA REDDY, D. V. "Sociology of Medicine in the *Muqaddimah* of Ibn Khaldûn," *Indian Journal of the History of Medicine* (Madras), IV (1959), 13–23; V (1960), 10–21.

ṬANJÎ, MUḤAMMAD IBN TÂWÎT AṬ-. "Prolégomènes d'Ibn Khaldoun" in *Proceedings of the Twenty-second International Congress of Orientalists, Istanbul, 1951.* Leiden, 1957. 2 vols. Cf. II, 262–3.

———. *See also* IBN KHALDÛN (6).

TEKINDAĞ, M. C. ŞEHABEDDIN. *Berkuk devrinde Memlûk Sultanlığı.* İstanbul Üniversitesi Ebebiyat Fakültesi Yayınlarından Mo. DCCCLXXXVII. Istanbul, 1961.

UGAN, ZAKIR KÂDIRÎ, tr. *Ibni Haldun Mukaddime.* Istanbul, 1954–1957. 3 vols. Turkish translation of the *Muqaddimah.*

ÜLKEN, HILMI ZIYA. "Ibn Khaldoun, Initiateur de la sociologie" in *Aʿmâl Mahrajân Ibn Khaldûn.* Cairo, 1962. Cf. pp. 29–40.

WÂFÎ, ʿALÎ ʿABD AL-WÂḤID. *ʿAbd ar-Raḥmân Ibn Khaldûn, ḥayâtuhu, âṯâruhu wa-maẓâhir ʿabqariyyatihi.* Cairo, 1962.

———. *See* IBN KHALDÛN (2).

WALZER, RICHARD. "Aspects of Islamic Political Thought: al-Fârâbî and Ibn Khaldûn," *Oriens* (Leiden), XVI (1963), 40–60.

WARDÎ, ʿALÎ AL-. *Manṭiq Ibn Khaldûn fî ḍaw' ḥaḍâratihi wa-šaḫṣiyyatihi; muqaddima li-dirâsât al-manṭiq al-ijtimaʿî.* Cairo, 1962.

WHITE, HAYDEN V. Review of F. Rosenthal's translation of the *Muqaddimah*, "Ibn Khaldûn in World Philosophy of History," *Comparative Studies in Society and History* (The Hague), II (1959–1960), 110–25.

WIET, GASTON. *Grandeur de l'Islam: de Mahomet à François Ier.* Paris, 1961. Cf. pp. 298–306.

———. *Cairo, City of Art and Commerce.* Tr. Seymour Feiler. The Centers of Civilization Series, XVI. Norman (Okla.), 1964.

WOLFSON, HARRY A. "Ibn Khaldûn on Attributes and Predestination," *Speculum* (Cambridge, Mass.), XXXIV (1959), 585–97.

ZIADEH, FARHAT J., tr. *The Philosophy of Jurisprudence in Islam. Comparative study of the Islamic rites and modern legal systems,* by Ṣobḥî Rajab Maḥmassânî. Leiden, 1961.

INDEXES

INDEX OF ARABIC TERMS

The entries are arranged according to the Latin alphabet. Some Persian, Turkish, Kurdish, and South Arabic words are included. For Berber words, see the General Index *s.v.* Berbers. The strange, supposedly Arabic words from poems in the Northwest African dialect are listed here in part. Homonyms, such as *maḥall*, *musnad*, etc., have not been distinguished in this index.

A

abdâl ("saints"), [2]165, 175, 187, [3]93*n*
'âbir, [3]435*n*
ablâyuh (*al-*), [1]95*n*
abrâṣ al-bh'my, [3]432*n*
abwâb al-mâl, [1]361*n*
adab, [3]404, 406
'adad, [3]124*n*
'adad ash-shakl, [3]174*n*
'adâlah, [1]38*n*, 395, 461 f., [3]25
aḍghâth al-aḥlâm, [1]211*n*
adhwâ', [1]298*n*
'âdil, [1]446, 461*n*
'adl, [3]49*n*, 61
aḍrâsh, [3]436*n*
af'âl, [3]321*n*
aḥadîyah, [3]87
'ahd, [1]410, 481*n*
ahl al-khawâṣṣ, [2]295*n*
aḥsâb, [1]188*n*
'ajam, [3]311*n*
'aks, [3]146
âl, [2]401*n*
âlah, *âlât*, [2]48, 50, 325, 364
'âlam, [3]88*n*
'alâmah, [1]xli, [2]18, 26, 62 f.
'allâq, [3]425*n*
almiland, [2]38
alqâb, [2]339*n*, [3]337*n*, 371, 401, 405 f., 409
alwâdh, [3]422*n*
'amâ'îyah (*ḥaḍrah*), [3]88, 177
'amal, *a'mâl*, [2]272*n*
'âmil, [3]322
amîr, [1]465 f., [2]11 f.
amîr al-umarâ', [2]11
'âmm(*ah*), [1]313*n*
amr, [1]lxxx & *n*
annîyah, [3]96
'aqabah ("ravine"), [3]91 f.
'aqîd al-qawm, [3]436*n*
arâmâ, [3]427*n*
'âriyah, [3]95*n*
arkân, [3]130*n*
'arrâf, [1]214, 218
'aṣabah, [1]lxxviii f.
'aṣabîyah, [1]lxi, lxxviii ff., lxxxii f., lxxxv, cx, 263*n*, [3]410
ashghâl (*ṣâḥib al-*), [1]xxxvii, [2]16, 24
'aṣr, *a'ṣâr*, see *'uṣûr*
'atîm, *'atûm*, [3]422*n*
'attâbî, [1]362*n*
aṭṭalâw, *aṭlâw*, [3]433*n*
a'wâd, [2]72*n*
'awl, [3]127*n*, 128
awliyâ', [2]146*n*
awzân, [3]188*n*
ayâmâ, [1]455*n*
'aymah, [1]181*n*
aymân al-bay'ah, [1]429
'aysh, [1]117*n*, [2]315

B

ba''âj, [3]164
badâwah, [1]lxxvii, cx
baddâwî, [3]413
badî' (*'ilm al-*), [3]336 f., 340, 402
badî'îyah (*alqâb*), [3]409
badûḥ, [3]176*n*
baghlî (*dirham*), [2]56, 58
baḥr, *buḥûr*, [3]374

bahramân (yâqût), [1]367*n*
balâghah, [2]444, 446 f., [3]335, 339, 358*n*, 370
balâṭ, [1]357*n*, [2]263
bamm, [3]184, 187
barâ'at al-istihlâl, [3]471
baradah, [2]373
barîd, [2]4*n*
barzakh, [1]199, [3]69 ff., 73, 177 f.
basṭ, [3]220*n*, 223*n*
ba'th, bu'ûth, [1]381*n*
bâṭin, [1]413
bay'ah, [1]428 f.
bayân, [2]438*n*, [3]26*n*, 117, 286, 319, 332*n*, 335 f., 358, 375, 379, 400
bayt, buyûtât, [1]273*n*
bh'my (abrâṣ al-), [3]432*n*
bisâṭ al-ḥâl, [3]344*n*
bizîdhaj, [3]135*n*
budd, [3]435*n*
bûq, [2]396
burhân, [3]140

C

châlîsh, [2]52
chatr, chitr, [2]52

D

dajl, [2]188
dalâlah, [3]415*n*
dalîl, [2]407*n*
ḍamâ'ir, [1]228*n*
dânaq, [2]56, 58, [3]180
dâr aṣ-ṣinâ'ah, [2]40*n*
ḍarar, [2]361*n*
ḍarb mufaṣṣal, [3]125*n*
ḍârib al-mandal, [2]201
dawâdâr, dawîdâr, [2]14, 28
dawlah, [1]lxxx
dawr, [3]198*n*
dêwâneh, [2]20, 407
dhawât, [3]321*n*
dhawq ("taste"), [3]79*n*, 358*n*
dhikr, [1]213, 221*n*, 222, 225, [2]422, 435*n*, [3]81 f., 181, 184, 192, 394
dhû l-wizâratayn, [2]15
dîn, [1]58*n*, [3]314
diqqah, [2]148*n*
dîwân, [2]19 ff., 64, 407, [3]324
dîwân al-jaysh, [2]9*n*
dîwân ar-rasâ'il, [2]65
du'â', [3]369
dûbayt, [3]475, 478 f.

F

falaq, [3]425*n*
fânîdh, [1]362*n*
fann, [1]cx*n*
faqîh, [2]5*n*, [3]398
farâ'iḍ, [3]22, 128
fard, [3]97*n*, 106*n*
farḍ, [3]22
farḍ al-kifâyah (al-'ayn), [1]392*n*
farq, [3]91
faṣl, [3]272*n*
faṣṣ, [3]139*n*, 254
fatq, [3]89
fatwâ, [1]452, 459 f., [2]392, 394
fawâṣil, [3]369
faylasûf, falâsifah, [3]247
fiqh, [3]3
firâsah, [1]223
fu'âd, af'idah, [2]412
furfurah, [3]244
furûḍ, [3]22 f.

G

gâmûs, [1]366*n*
ghâbir, [2]403
gharar, [1]73*n*, [2]114*n*
gharb, [2]194
gharîb, [2]450 ff.
ghawbas, [3]474*n*
ghazal, [3]468
ghazârah, [2]221*n*
ghubâr, [1]239, [3]197 f., 204 ff.
ghudhf, [3]433*n*
ghulâh, [1]406
ghushâm, [3]433*n*
ghuṣn, [3]414*n*, 440
ghuyâm, [3]437*n*

H

habâ'îyah (ḥaḍrah), [3]88
ḥaḍârah, [1]lxxx

ḥadathân, ḥidthân, [2]202
ḥadd, [2]215*n*
ḥadîth qudsî, [1]193*n*, [3]88*n*, 98*n*
ḥaḍrah, [3]88*n*
ḥâjib, [1]30, 451, [2]7, 9, 13 ff., 27, 97 f., 111*n*, 112 f.
ḥâkim, [2]18, 35
ḥâl, [3]39*n*, 344*n*
ḥalûm, [2]403*n*
ḥâlûmah, [1]212
ḥanîfîyah (*dîn al-*), [2]191
ḥaqq, [1]209
harîsah, harrâs, [2]302*n*, 348
ḥarrâr, [2]348*n*
ḥashîsh, [3]477
ḥâsib, ḥussâb, [1]241*n*, [2]201
ḥawâ'iṭ, [3]132*n*
ḥawfî, [3]475
ḥawrânî, [3]413 f.
haykal, hayâkil, [1]151*n*, 354*n*, 356 f., 359, [2]235*n*, 240, 249, 258, 260, 359, [3]132
hazaj, [2]403
ḥ-f-ẓ, [3]290*n*, 353*n*
ḥidâ', [2]348*n*
ḥidthân, ḥadathân, [2]202
ḥijâb, [2]111*n*
ḥijr, [2]249, 252, 254 f.
hilal, [2]67
ḥimyah, [2]373
ḥisâb al-jummal, [2]206
ḥisâb an-nym, [1]234 ff.
ḥisbah, [1]449, 462, [2]7
ḥiss mushtarik, [1]196*n*
ḥukmî, [3]139*n*, 227*n*
ḥurûf muqaṭṭaʿah, [2]205*n*, [3]59
ḥussâb, ḥâsib, [1]241*n*, [2]201
ḥuthâm, ḥutâm, [3]433*n*, 436*n*

ʿibârah, [3]140
ʿibiddâ, [1]276*n*
ibrâm, [1]49*n*, 379*n*
idrâk, [3]281
ʿiffah, [1]262*n*
ightirâr, [2]114*n*
iʿjâz, [1]193*n*
ijâzah, [2]449, 452
ijmâʿ, [3]23
ikhtilâṭ, [3]241*n*
ikhwân, [1]251, [3]427
iksîr, [3]228*n*
ilâhî (*ʿilm*), [3]111
ʿilhiz, [1]419
ʿillah (*naṣṣ ʿalâ l-*), [3]4, 27 f.
ʿilm al-badîʿ, [3]336 f., 340
ʿilm al-bayân, see *bayân*
ʿilm ilâhî, [3]111
ʿilm al-maʿânî, [3]399
imâm, [1]388, 464
imâmah, [1]466
imârah, [1]465, [2]316 f., 327
ʿimârah, ʿimârât, [1]lxxii*n*, 80*n*
imlâk, [1]348
inâ', [1]37*n*
inshâ', inshâ'î ("command"), [3]334
inshâ' (*ṣâḥib al-*), [2]28
iqlîm, [1]96*n*
iqtirân, iqtirânî, [3]36*n*
iʿrâb, [2]305, 444, 446*n*, 463, [3]322, 325, 334*n*, 346
irdabb, [1]365*n*, 366
ʿirfân, [3]78
ʿiṣâbah, [1]lxxviii, [2]52
ishbâʿ, [2]400*n*
ʿiṣmah, [1]185, 187, 199, 256, 403*n*, 471*n*
istibṣâr, [1]321*n*, [2]134*n*
istihlâl (*barâ'at al-*), [3]471
iṣṭilâḥ, iṣṭilâḥî, [2]384*n*
istinṭâq, [3]220 ff.
istiṣḥâb, [3]8
istiṣlâḥ, [3]24*n*
îthâr, [1]30*n*
îwân, [3]315; see also General Index *s.v.* Îwân Kisrâ
ʿiyâr, [1]464
izâr, [2]256

J

jabr, [3]124*n*
jadl, [3]141
jafr, [2]194*n*, 200, 209 f., 218 f., 225, 230, [3]474

jâh, [2]286*n*
jâ'is, [3]430*n*
jam', [3]91, 146
jarḥ (*wa-ta'dîl*), [1]72*n*
jawhar fard, [3]50 f.
jawzâ', *jawâzî*, [3]422*n*
j-dh-y, [3]437*n*
jidhm, [2]182*n*
jîl, [1]4*n*
jindâr, [2]17
jummal (*ḥisâb al-*), [2]206

K

ka'b, [3]124*n*
kâhin, [1]204
kalimah, [1]lxxx & *n*, [3]373
kalimah îmânîyah, [3]179, 182
kân-wa-kân, [3]475 f.
karâmah, [1]223, [3]179*n*
kasb, [2]340, [3]266*n*
kashf, [1]215*n*, 223, 230, [2]157, 186, 203, 210, 229, [3]81, 87
kâtib, [2]7
kâtib as-sirr, [2]14
kayfîyah, [3]354*n*
kâzî, [3]468
khabar, [1]13*n*
khabar al-wâḥid, [1]77*n*
khafârah, [1]325*n*
khafîf, [2]403
khalad, [3]64
khalîfah, [1]388, 465, 473
khamr, [3]331
khamṭ, [3]435*n*
khârijîyah, [1]279*n*
khârṣînî, [3]271
khâtam, [2]61
khâtimah, [2]61
khatm al-awliyâ', [2]189*n*
khaṭṭ ar-raml, [1]226*n*
khawâriq, [1]188*n*
khawâṣṣ (*ahl al-*), [2]295*n*
khâzindâr, [2]25
khibb, [2]306
khilṭ, [2]375
khinzîrîyah, [3]165
khirqah, [2]187, [3]93
khiṭâbah, [3]141
khitâm, [2]61
khurj, [3]306
khurq, [3]306*n*
khuṭbah, [1]3*n*
kisrawîyah, [1]417
kitâbah, [2]452
kiyân, [3]234, 238, 244
kôs, [2]52
kunbâṣ, [1]117
kundur, [2]397
kurraj, [2]404
kuẓâm, [3]433*n*, 435*n*

L

lablâyah, [1]95
lâzim, *lâzib*, [2]256
lazîq, [1]268*n*
liyâ, [3]424*n*, 437*n*

M

ma'âd, [3]45*n*
ma'ânî (*'ilm al-*), [3]399
ma'ânî (*ṣifât al-*), [3]48*n*
ma'âsh, [2]315
mabâdi', [2]402*n*
mabsûṭ, [3]122*n*
madd, [2]400*n*
madrak, [3]90*n*
maghnîsiyâ', [3]244
maghribî (*dirham*), [2]56
maḥall, [3]5*n*, 84*n*, 88*n*, 334*n*
mahd, *mahdî*, [2]185, 192
mahr, [1]349
majbûdah, [2]78
majisṭî, *mijisṭî*, [3]135
mâl, *mâl mâl*, *mâl ka'b*, [3]124*n*
mal'abah, [2]221, [3]468
malâḥim, [2]187, 200, 220
malakah, [1]lxxxiv & *n*, 383 & *n*
malakût, [1]3*n*
man', [3]146
mandal (*ḍârib al-*), [2]201
mann, [1]349, 363*n*
maq'ad, *maqâ'id*, [2]37*n*
maqâm, [3]40*n*
maqâṭi', [2]402*n*

maqṣûrah, ²69
maqṭû', ²393
maqûlât, ³140
marâkiz al-khashab, ²362n
ma'rifah, ³78, 140n
marz, ²215n
maṣâliḥ, ²447
masânîd, ²463n
mashhûd (yawm), ¹370n, 450n
maṣnû', ³399n
ma'ṣûm, see 'iṣmah
maṭâbiq, ²323n
maṭâli', ²402n
maṭbû', ³399n
mathânî, ³192, 368 f.
mathlath, ³184n, 187
mathnâ, ³184n, 187
matlûw, ¹192n, 260n, ³113, 284n
mawâhib, ³77n
mawâjid, mawâjîd, ³77n, 83n
mawâlid, ³279n
mawâlîyâ, ³475 f.
mawât, ³399
mawḍû', ¹91n
mawjûd, ³77n
mawlâ, tamwîl, ¹377, ²304
mawqûf, ²393
mayl, ³134n
mazâlim, ¹xlviii, 455n
maẓhar, maẓâhir, ³87, 88n
mazmûr, ²401n
miḍmâr, ²399 f.
miḥrâb, ²69
mîkhâl, ²239n, 363
mîl, ¹96n
minbar, ²70, 72n
miqdâr, ²305
mithâl, muthul, ³88, 90, 293
mithqâl, ¹367, ²56, 58, ³163
mi'zaf, ²396n
mîzân, ³188n
mizmâr, ²401n
mu'âhidûn, ¹481n
mu'allal, ²450
mu'allaqât, ³376n, 397n, 410
mu'arrifât, ³140n
mu'attab, ¹362n

mu'ayyan, ¹362n
mubashshirât, ¹209
mubayyiḍah, ²51
mubtada', ¹13n
mu'ḍal, ²450
mufaṣṣal, ¹202n
mufattaḥ, ²367n
muftariq, ²451 & n, 452, ³161n
muḥaddath, ¹223n
muḥâsabah, ³78
muḥawwal, ³183n
muḥdithûn, ³65n
muḥtamil, ³58n
muḥtasib, ¹41n
mujâhadah, ¹221n
mujassimah, ³68
mu'jizah, ¹188n, 193n
mujmal, ²443n
mukallaf, ¹392n
mukhallad, ³6n, 115n
mukhammasah, ³119 f.
mukhl, ²239n
mukhtalif, ²451 & n, 452
mukhtaṣar, ³32n, 143n
muktafi/aḍ, ³435n
mulk, ¹lxxx, 3n, 284
munajjim, ²201
munâsakhah, ³20
munâwalah, ²449, 452
munkar, ²450
munqaṭi', ²450
munṭaq, ³130n
muqaddamah, muqaddimah, ¹xxixn, lxviii
muqaṭṭa'ah (ḥurûf), ²205n, ³59
muqrabât, ¹19n
murabba'ah, ³119 f.
murâbiṭûn, ¹323
muraqqaq, ¹348n
murîdûn, ¹323
mursal, ²393, 450, murassal, ³368
muṣâdarah, ¹368n, ²124n
musaddasah, ³119 f.
musawwidah, ²51
mushabbihah, ³69
muṣḥaf, ²439
mushâqah, mushâqâ, ³422n, 435n

mushkil, ²451 f.
mushtarik (ḥiss), ¹196n
musnad, ²381, 393, 454n, 463n, ³282
muṭâbaqah, ¹245n
muʻtadil, ¹108n
muṭâlabah, ¹284n, ²132n
muʼtalif, ²451n, ³161n
mutamâsik, ²168
mutaṣawwifah, ³76
muthallathah, ³119 f.
muthul, see mithâl
muttafiq, ²451n
muwallad, ³314, 353, 385n, 414
muwashshaḥ, muwashshaḥah, ³414n, 440
muwâzanah, ¹204n, ³401
muzawwaj, ³468

N

nabîdh, ¹36 f., 445, ³331
nâḍa, ³437n
nafs, ³75n
naghamât, ²403n
naḥw, ³322
nâʼib, ²12, 14, 18 f.
nakaba, nakbah, ¹368n, ²124n
naqḍ, ¹49n, 379n
naqîb, nuqabâʼ, ²187, ³93n
nasab, ¹cxn
naṣb, ²403n
nashʼah, ³198n
nasîb, ³369, 388, 413
naṣṣ, nuṣûṣ, ¹405, 410, 412 f., ³4n, 24n, 27 f.
nazîʻ, ¹268n
nazîf, ¹268
nâẓir al-jaysh, ²25
nâẓir al-khâṣṣ, ²25
nîṭush (baḥr), ¹98n

Q

qâbilah, ²368
qabû, ³464n
qadar (qâla bi-l-), ³62n
qadd, ³436n
qaḍîb ("sticks," as musical instruments), ²405n
qaḍîyat al-iqtirân, ³36n
qanâh, ²362n
qânûn, ²396, ³431
qarâʼin, ³344, 415
qarn, ²192
qaṣd, ¹420n
qaṣîdah, ³373, 413, 440
qaṭʻ, ³23n
qawâṭiʻ, ³262n
qayl, ³347
qaysî, ³414n
qiblah, ²253, 258 f.
qirâʼah, ²451
qismah, ²214n
qiyâmah, qiyâmât, ³45n, 178, 180
qiyâs, ³24, 140
qiyâs iqtirânî, ³36n
qiyâs ṣûrî, ³145n
qubaysî, ³414
qubbah, ²258n
qudsî (ḥadîth), ¹193n, ³88n, 98n
qûmâ, ³475n
qummus/ṣ, qamâmis/ṣah, ²262n
qurâm, ³436n
quṭb, ²187, ³92

R

rabâb, ²396n
râbiʻ, ²213
radʻ, ¹328n
râfiḍah, ¹406
rafla(h), ³434n
raḥim (ṣilat ar-), ¹264n, ²145n
raʻîyah, raʻâyâ, ¹61n, 383, ²151
rakʻah, ¹33n
raml (khaṭṭ ar-), ¹226n
raqm, ¹364n
rasâʼil, 265, ³393
rasm, ²442
ratq, ³88
ribḥ, ²336, 340
rikâz, ²324
riṭl, ¹349, 360
rûḥ, ³75n

S

sabaj, [2]270n, 361n
ṣadr, [1]373n, [3]53n, 171n, 266n
saffâj, [2]302n
safsaṭah, [3]141
ṣaḥâḥ(an), [2]170n
ṣâḥib al-'alâmah, [1]xli, [2]18
ṣâḥib al-ashghâl, [1]xxxvii, [2]16, 24
ṣâḥib al-inshâ', [2]28
ṣâḥib al-madînah, [2]35
ṣaḥîfah, [1]117
saj', [1]204n, [3]335, 368
sajjâj, [3]437n
ṣakk, [2]4n, 392n
ṣamad, [2]55
sanjaq, [2]52
sâqah, [2]51, 68
ṣaqâlibah, [1]251n
sarayân, [3]217n
sarîr, [2]53
sawâd, [1]325n
sawâqiṭ, [3]217, 226
sayyâlah (masâ'il), [3]182n
sha'badhah, sha'wadhah, [3]159
shabah (shibh, shubah), [3]374n
shabbâbah, [2]395 f.
shadâyâh, [3]435n
shâdharwân, [2]254
shâdhdh, [2]450
shaf', shaf'îyah, [3]97n
shakl, [3]174n
shâlat na'âmatuhû, [3]406n
shârib, [3]463n
shaṭaḥât, [3]100 f.
shaṭfah, [2]52
shawâhid, [3]356n
shâwîyah, [1]251
shawl, [3]419n
shaw/ûr, [3]436n
shay', [3]124n
shî'ah, [1]402
shi'r, [3]141, 373
shiyah, shiyât, [2]73n, [3]374n
sh(u)kâ', [3]435n
shuklah, [2]221n
shûrâ, [1]430, 439
shûrmâhî, sûrmâhî, [1]364n

shurṭah, [1]457
shu'ûn, [1]221, [3]390n
ṣifât al-ma'ânî, [3]48n
ṣiḥâḥ, [2]170n
sikkah, [2]54
sîmiyâ', [3]171 f.
simṭ, [3]440
sinâd, [2]403
ṣirâṭ, [1]67, [3]349
sirr, [1]cxn
sirr (kâtib as-), [2]14
siyâsah madanîyah, [2]138
subuḥât, [3]181
ṣûfîyah, [3]76
ṣufr, [1]75n
sulṭân, [1]cxix, 469, [2]5 f., 10 f.
sûqah, [2]291n
ṣûrî, [3]145n
sûrmâhî, shûrmâhî, [1]364
ṣuwah, ṣuwâ, [3]437n

T

ta'âlîm, [3]111
ta'alluh, [1]337
ṭabarî (dirham), [2]56, 58
ta'bîr, [1]207n
ṭâbiyah, [2]360
ta'biyah, [2]76
ta'dîl, [1]72n, [3]136n
tafrîq, [3]161n
tafriqah, [3]91n
tafṣîl aḍ-ḍarb, [3]125n
taftîḥ, [2]367n
tafwîḍ (wizârat at-), [2]11n
taghbîr, [2]403
taḥaddî, [1]188 ff., 223, [3]100, 167, 170
tajallî, [3]87
tajânus, [3]401, 402n
tajnîs, [3]336
tajsîm, [3]69n, 84
takhabbaṭa, [1]218n
takhalluṣ, [3]472
takhattama, [2]61
taksîr, [3]172, 183, 225
ta'lîf, [3]161n
talkhîṣ, [3]123

tall, [1]251n
talqîn, [3]74n
tamaddun, [1]lxxv, 297
tamshiyah, [3]241n
tamwîl ("to be addressed as Sire"), [1]377, [2]304
tanfîdh, [2]19n
taqdîr, [3]22n
taqṭîr, [3]227n
taqwîm, [3]136n
ṭard, [3]146
ṭarîkh, ṭirrîkh, [1]364n
tarṣîʿ, [3]336
tarsîl, [3]340
taṣawwur, [1]198n, 203, 205, 218, [3]35, 138, 248, 273, 275 f., 281 f., 295 f., 332
taṣdîq, [1]198n, [3]138, 248
tashbîh, [3]69, 84
tashîl, [2]440n
ṭashsh, [3]82n
taṣʿîd, [3]227n
tathniyah, [3]95n
tawahhum, [3]165
tawḥîd, [3]61, 78
tawliyah, [2]5n
tawqîʿ, [2]27
tawriyah, [3]336, 340, 401
ṭawwâb, [2]360
ṭibâq, [3]336
ṭirâz, [2]65 ff.
ṭûb, [2]360n
turunj, [1]364n

U

ʿumrân, [1]lxxvi f., lxxx, cx, 3n, 253, [3]352
ʿuqûd, [1]19n
ûqyânûs, [1]96n
ʿurf, [3]24n
ʿuṣbah, [1]lxxviii, 263n
uslûb, [2]307, 402, 446n, [3]284, 303, 375
uss, [1]241n, [3]124n, 203-4n
ustâdh-ad-dâr, ustâdâr, [2]25
uṣûl, [3]130n

uṣûl al-fiqh, [3]23n
ʿuṣûr, aʿṣâr (ahl al-, aʾimmat al-), [1]14n

W

waʿd, waʿîd, [3]49n
waḥdah, [2]229n
waḥdânîyah, [3]87
wâḥid, [3]97n
wâḥidîyah, [3]87n
waḥy, [1]84n, 200
wajd, [3]77n
wajh, [3]163n
wakîl, [2]18
wâlî, [1]457, [2]36
walî, [1]455n; see also awliyâʾ
wâzîʿ, [1]lxxv & n, 328n
wazîr, [2]8
wiʿâʾ, [1]37n
wijdân, wijdânî, [1]198n, [2]48n, 340n, [3]83n, 252n, 295n
wilâyah, [2]5n, 188
wizârah, [2]6
wujûd, [1]198n

Y

yamanî (dirham), [2]56
yâqût, [1]367n
yattûʿ, [1]181n

Z

zabaj, [2]361n
ẓahr, [2]260n
zâʾirajah, [1]238-39n
zajal, [3]454
zajr, [1]217
zaman fard, [3]106n
zamm, zumûm, [1]135
ẓann (or ẓâhir), [2]140n
zarkash, [2]67
zawâqî, [2]49n
zîj, [1]239n, [3]112, 135n, 136
zimâm, [1]239, [3]188n, 190, 197n, 198, 200, 207 ff., 215n
zîr, [3]184, 187 f., 190
zulâmî, zullâmî, [2]396

GENERAL INDEX

The proper names were carefully indexed by David Horne, whose help is gratefully acknowledged, and completeness has been the aim in compiling them. The subject entries were indexed by myself, and they are highly selective. Combining in one list subject entries, names of persons mentioned in the text, authorities cited in the notes, geographical names, etc. has been my express intention. Multiple indexes are increasingly the fashion, and much can be said in their favor; however, the net result is that the user has to look in several places for what he can find at once in a large comprehensive index.

In alphabetizing, the Arabic article has been disregarded. Also, a personal name not followed immediately by an indication of the father's name is given precedence, regardless of the qualifications that may go with it, and it is followed directly by any other occurrences of the name with "b." For instance, "Muḥammad at-Taqî" precedes "Muḥammad b. ʻAbd-al-ʻAẓîm"; ʻAlî Zayn-al-ʻâbidîn b. al-Ḥusayn" (where "b." does not *immediately* follow upon ʻAlî) precedes "ʻAlî b. . . ."

The various small inconsistencies in transliteration to which I have succumbed (cf. 1:cxv), stand out starkly in the index. Another inconsistency appears here for the first time. It concerns the Arabic article in names of cities, where it was retained, and in names of countries, where it was translated. Thus we have al-Baṣrah and al-Kûfah in both the text and the index, but it is "the Ḥijâz" and "the Jarîd" in the text, with the result that these names of countries appear in the index without an article.

F. R.

A

Aaron, [1]275, 412, 474, [2]4, 259
al-Aʻazz, Abû l-Maḥâsin ʻAbd-al-Jalîl b. Muḥammad, [2]101*n*
Abaghâ b. Hûlâgû, [3]19
Abân b. Ṣâliḥ b. Abî ʻAyyâsh, [2]184 f.
ʻAbbâdân, [1]134, 146
ʻAbbâdids of Sevilla, [1]61*n*
ʻAbbâs(?), [3]186
ʻAbbâs (son of)(?), [3]195
al-ʻAbbâs (pseudo-Mahdî of the Ghumârah), [1]327, [2]197
(al-)ʻAbbâs b. ʻAbd-al-Muṭṭalib, [1]29, 186, 271, 352, 410, 436, [2]183 f.
al-ʻAbbâs b. ʻAṭîyah (of the Tûjîn), [1]271
al-ʻAbbâsah (sister of ar-Rashîd), [1]28 ff., 269*n*
al-ʻAbbâsî (author of *Âthâr al-uwal fi tartîb ad-duwal*), [2]74*n*
ʻAbbâsid(s): origins, [2]132; and Hâshimîyah Shîʻah, [1]409 f.; moral qualities, [1]29 f., 35 f., 423 f.; splendor and power of their golden age, [1]348 f., 352, 369 ff., [2]236, 384, 404; literary ambitions, [3]341, 411; flourishing of literature under them, [3]386 f., 397; promoted Greek science,

[3]115 f., 130, 134, 147, 250; education of their princes, [3]306 f.; originally used title "imam," [1]409, 467; led prayer in person, [1]451, [2]71; employed doorkeepers, [2]112 f.; used the Prophet's cloak and stick, [2]65, *ṭirâz*, [2]65, black flags, [2]50 f., 173 f., 180, and green flags, [2]51; created office of police, [2]36; honorific surnames of, [1]467; reliance on non-Arabs, [1]373 f., [3]314; gave titles to non-Arab rulers, [1]469, [2]11; never entered Maghrib in person, [1]271; relations with Idrîsids, [1]48 ff., [2]115, 127, with Fâṭimids, [1]42, 45 f., 319, [2]115, 128, [3]11, with Almoravids, [1]470 f.; decay of their power, [1]285 f., 314 f., 468, [2]10 f., 92, 114 f., 121, 127 ff., 386, [3]19; caliphate in Egypt, [1]334; "'Abbâsid" sermon, [2]72

Abbott, N., [2]392*n*

'Abd b. Ḥumayd, [2]455

'Abd-al-'Azîz (Merinid ruler), [1]li f.

'Abd-al-'Azîz b. 'Abd-as-Salâm, 'Izz-ad-dîn, *see* Ibn 'Abd-as-Salâm, 'Izz-ad-dîn

'Abd-al-'Azîz b. Mûsâ b. Nuṣayr, [2]121

'Abd-al-Ghanî an-Nâbulusî, [3]108*n*, 109*n*

'Abd-al-Ḥakam b. 'Abdallâh b. 'Abd-al-Ḥakam, [3]10*n*

'Abd-al-Ḥamîd, S. Z., [2]44*n*

'Abd-al-Ḥamîd b. Yaḥyâ, [2]23, 29

'Abd-al-Ḥaqq (b. 'Abd-ar-Raḥmân al-Ishbîlî), [2]60

'Abd-al-Ḥaqq b. Sab'în, *see* Ibn Sab'în

'Abd-al-Jabbâr b. Aḥmad al-Asadâbâdî, [3]29

'Abd-al-Karîm b. Munqidh, [2]44

'Abd-al-Malik b. Abjar, [2]373*n*

'Abd-al-Malik b. Ḥabîb, [3]14, 16

'Abd-al-Malik b. al-Manṣûr b. Abî 'Âmir, al-Muẓaffar, [1]380*n*

'Abd-al-Malik b. Marwân, [1]304, 423 f., 427, 432, 433*n*, 438, 447, 451, [2]9, 22, 40, 55 ff., 59, 68, 76, 112, 253 f., 301, [3]61

'Abd-Manâf, Banû, [1]318, 444, [2]114, 121

'Abd-al-Masîḥ (of the Saṭîḥ legend), [1]219, [2]202

'Abd-al-Muhayman al-Ghawwâṣ(?), [3]473

'Abd-al-Muhayman b. Muḥammad al-Ḥaḍramî, [1]xl

'Abd-al-Mu'min (Almohad ruler), [1]472, [2]43, 305

'Abd-al-Muṭṭalib, [1]360, [2]178, 189, 251, 257

'Abd-al-Qâdir al-Qurashî, [3]33*n*

'Abd-al-Qâhir al-Baghdâdî, [1]407*n*, [3]69*n*

'Abd-al-Qâhir al-Jurjânî, [3]286, 334*n*

'Abd-al-Qawî b. al-'Abbâs, Banû, [1]271

'Abd-al-Qays b. Rabî'ah, Banû, [1]441

'Abd-ar-Raḥîm b. 'Umar al-Mawṣilî, Jamâl-ad-dîn, [2]230

'Abd-ar-Raḥmân I ad-Dâkhil, [2]115

'Abd-ar-Raḥmân II b. al-Ḥakam, [2]405*n*

'Abd-ar-Raḥmân III an-Nâṣir, [1]365, 393, 456, 468, [2]40

'Abd-ar-Raḥmân b. 'Abdallâh b. 'Abd-al-Ḥakam, [2]71*n*, [3]10*n*

'Abd-ar-Raḥmân b. Abî Ḥâtim, ar-Râzî, *see* Ibn Abî Ḥâtim

'Abd-ar-Raḥmân b. al-Ash'ath, [2]22

'Abd-ar-Raḥmân b. 'Awf, [1]59*n*, 420, 430–31

'Abd-ar-Raḥmân b. al-Manṣûr b. Abî 'Âmir, an-Nâṣir, [1]380

'Abd-ar-Raḥmân b. Muḥammad b. Munqidh, Abû l-Ḥârith, [2]44*n*

'Abd-ar-Raḥmân b. Rabî'ah, [1]290

'Abd-ar-Raḥmân b. Ziyâd b. An'um, [2]380
'Abd-ar-Razzâq, Ḥâjj, [1]xcvii
'Abd-ar-Razzâq b. Hammâm, [2]180
'Abd-as-Salâm al-Kûmî (Almohad Wazir), [2]15
'Abd-al-Wâdids, *see* Zayyânids
'Abd-al-Wahhâb (Mâlikite judge), [2]265, [3]11, 14, 17
'Abdallâh al-Baghdâdî (author of *Kitâb al-Kuttâb*), [1]lxxvi*n*, [2]20*n*
'Abdallâh b. (al-)'Abbâs, [1]29, 34, 444, 447, [2]71, 158, 179, 204, 253, 380, 402*n*, 444*n*, [3]56 & *n*, 411
'Abdallâh b. 'Abd-al-'Azîz b. 'Abdallâh b. 'Abdallâh b. 'Umar b. al-Khaṭṭâb. [1]33*n*
'Abdallâh b. 'Abd-al-Ḥakam, [3]10*n*, 14
'Abdallâh b. 'Adî, *see* Ibn 'Adî
'Abdallâh b. Aḥmad b. Ḥanbal, [2]181, 456
'Abdallâh b. Farrûkh, *see* Ibn Farrûkh al-Qayrawânî
'Abdallâh b. al-Ḥârith, [2]166
'Abdallâh b. al-Ḥârith b. Jaz', [2]158, 180
'Abdallâh b. al-Ḥasan Walad al-Fakhûrî, *see* Ibn al-Fakhkhâr, 'Abdallâh b. Ḥasan
'Abdallâh b. Ḥasan b. al-Ḥasan b. 'Alî b. Abî Ṭâlib, [1]119
'Abdallâh b. Ḥasan b. Shihâb, [1]xci
'Abdallâh b. Ja'far b. Abî Ṭâlib, [2]404
'Abdallâh b. Jaḥsh, [1]466
'Abdallâh b. Jud'ân, [2]380
'Abdallâh b. Khâlid, [2]256*n*
'Abdallâh b. Lahî'ah, [2]175 f., 180 f., 184
'Abdallâh b. Marwân, [1]424
'Abdallâh b. Mas'ûd, *see* Ibn Mas'ûd
'Abdallâh b. Muḥammad al-Marwânî, [3]441
'Abdallâh b. Muḥammad b. al-'Arabî, [1]470
'Abdallâh b. Qilâbah, *see* Ibn Qilâbah
'Abdallâh b. Saba', [1]407*n*
'Abdallâh b. Sa'îd b. Kullâb, [3]63
'Abdallâh b. Salâm, [1]439, [2]445
'Abdallâh b. Ṭâhir, [1]80*n*, [2]139, Pl. VII
'Abdallâh b. 'Umar, [1]34, 426, 432, 439, 442, 444, 447, [2]158, 183, [3]61
'Abdallâh b. 'Umar al-'Umarî, [2]184
'Abdallâh b. Wahb, *see* Ibn Wahb, 'Abdallâh
'Abdallâh b. Ziyâd, [2]177*n*, 178
'Abdallâh b. az-Zubayr, *see* Ibn az-Zubayr
'Abdî, 'Abdallâh al-Bosnawî, [1]323*n*
al-Abharî, Abû Bakr, [3]13–14
al-Âbilî, Muḥammad b. Ibrâhîm, [1]xl, xlv, [2]197, 339
al-Abîwardî, [1]46
al-Ablaq al-Asadî, [1]220
Abraham, [1]20, 43, 133, 275, 281, [2]250, 253 f., 258*n*, 263 f., [3]410
al-Abraq, [3]377
Abû l-'Abbâs (Ḥafṣid ruler), [1]l, lvi ff., lxii, cv, [2]17, 93*n*, 117*n*, 246*n*, 304*n*
Abû l-'Abbâs ash-Shî'î, [1]41*n*
Abû 'Abd-al-Ilâh, *see* Muḥammad, Abû 'Abdallâh (al-Waththâb)
Abû 'Abdah, Banû, [2]99
Abû 'Abdallâh (Ḥafṣid of Bougie), [1]xlvii, l f.
Abû 'Abdallâh ash-Shî'î, [1]41, 413, [2]133, 210 f.
Abû l-'Alâ' al-Ma'arrî, *see* al-Ma'arrî, Abû l-'Alâ'
Abû 'Amr b. az-Zâhid al-Ishbîlî, *see* Ibn az-Zâhid al-Ishbîlî
Abû l-Aswad ad-Du'alî, *see* ad-Du'alî, Abû l-Aswad
Abû l-'Atâhiyah, [1]427*n*
Abû Bakr, [1]187, 223 f., 272, 389, 396*n*, 404 ff., 418, 422*n*, 430 f., 433, 435 f., 450, 465 f., [2]7 f., 61,

186, 194, 255, 257, 264, [3]39*n*, 82, 93, 103
Abû Bakr, Abû Yaḥyâ (Ḥafṣid ruler), [1]lxxxvi*n*, 368, [2]17*n*, 93*n*, 101*n*, 222, [3]428, 475
Abû Bakr, Judge, *see* al-Bâqillânî
Abû Bakr al-Iskâf, [2]159
Abû Bakr b. Abî Khaythamah, *see* Ibn Abî Khaythamah
Abû Bakr b. 'Ayyâsh, [2]163
Abû Bakr b. aṣ-Ṣâ'igh, *see* Ibn Bâjjah
Abû l-Baqâ' Khâlid, [2]222*n*
Abû l-Barakât Hibatallâh al-Baghdâdî, [1]91*n*
Abû Budayl, [2]219
Abû Burdah (Hâni' b. Niyâr), [1]256 f.
Abû d-Dalfâ', *see* Shaybân b. 'Abd-al-'Azîz al-Yashkurî
Abû d-Dardâ', [1]453
Abû Dâwûd (author of the *Sunan*), [2]59*n*, 157, 159 & *n*, 160, 162 f., 164 & *n*, 165 ff., 171, 173, 181 f., 207 ff., 257, [3]104*n*, 169*n*
Abû Dâwûd, *see* Sulaymân b. Najâḥ, Abû Dâwûd
Abû Dhu'ayb, [2]102*n*
Abû l-Faḍl (b. Khaldûn), [1]xxxii*n*
Abû l-Faraj al-Iṣfahânî, [1]lxxvi*n*, 48*n*, 220*n*, 282*n*, 338*n*, 407*n*, 411*n*, [2]167*n*, 225*n*, [3]341, 366–67, 377*n*, 378*n*, 383, 404*n*
Abû l-Fatḥ al-Bustî, [1]297*n*
Abû Firâs, [3]383
Abû Ḥammû (Zayyânid ruler), [1]l ff., 424*n*, [3]436
Abû Ḥanîfah, [2]265, 460 f., [3]4, 6, 8 f., 14, 31
Abû Hârûn al-'Abdî, [2]170 f.
Abû l-Ḥasan (Merinid ruler), [1]xxxix f., xli, 182, 367, [2]45 & *n*, 51, 52*n*, 164, 240, [3]264, 395, 471, 473
Abû l-Ḥasan b. al-Faḍl, [3]445*n*, 448
Abû Hâshim b. Muḥammad b. al-Ḥanafîyah, [1]409
Abû Ḥâtim ar-Râzî, Muḥammad b. Idrîs, [2]161, 168, 173, 177 f., 182, 209
Abû Ḥayyân, *see* Ibn Ḥayyân, Ḥayyân b. Khalaf
Abû Ḥayyân at-Tawḥîdî, *see* at-Tawḥîdî, Abû Ḥayyân
Abû Ḥâzim, [1]47*n*
Abû Ḥudhayfah, [1]397
Abû l-Hudhayl al-'Allâf, [3]62
Abû Hurayrah, [2]21 & *n*, 158, 160, 181 f., [3]22
Abû l-Ḥusayn, Banû (Banû Sa'îd), [2]24
Abû l-Ḥusayn, Banû (Kalbite governors of Sicily), [2]42
Abû l-Ḥusayn al-Baṣrî, *see* al-Baṣrî, Abû l-Ḥusayn Muḥammad b. 'Alî
Abû l-Ḥusayn an-Nûrî, [3]179*n*
Abû Idrîs al-Khawlânî, [1]456
Abû 'Inân (Merinid ruler), [1]xl ff., xlvii f., liii, 182*n*, 369 f., [2]52*n*
Abû Isḥâq, *see* al-Isfarâyinî, Abû Isḥâq
Abû Isḥâq ad-Duwaynî, *see* ad-Duwaynî, Abû Isḥâq
Abû Isḥâq Ibrâhîm I (Ḥafṣid ruler), [2]72*n*, 116
Abû Isḥâq Ibrâhîm II (Ḥafṣid ruler), [3]428
Abû Isḥâq as-Sabî'î, *see* as-Sabî'î, Abû Isḥâq
Abû Kâmil Shujâ' b. Aslam, *see* Shujâ' b. Aslam, Abû Kâmil
Abû Karib, *see* As'ad Abû Karib, Tibân
Abû l-Khalîl, Ṣâliḥ, [2]165 f.
Abû l-Khaṭṭâb b. Zuhr, [3]444
Abû l-Khayr Aḥmad, [1]xcviii
Abû l-Layl, Awlâd, [3]423
Abû Madyan, [1]lii, [2]198 & *n*
Abû Mahdî 'Îsâ b. az-Zayyât, *see* Ibn az-Zayyât, Abû Mahdî 'Îsâ
Abû Ma'shar, [2]214, 218, 368*n*
Abû Mûsâ al-Ash'arî, [1]419, 453, [2]401*n*

Abû Muslim, [1]410, [2]47, 215
Abû Muslim ('Amr ['Umar?] b. Aḥmad, b. Khaldûn,) [1]xxxiv, [3]126–27
Abû Naḍrah, [2]166
Abû Nu'aym al-Iṣfahânî, [3]22
Abû Nuwâs, [1]36, 45*n*, 349, [3]383, 404
Abû l-Qâsim Muḥammad b. Aḥmad as-Sabtî, *see* as-Sabtî, Muḥammad b. Aḥmad
Abû l-Qâsim ash-Shî'î, *see* al-Qâ'im, Abû l-Qâsim (Fâṭimid ruler)
Abû l-Qâsim b. Abî Bakr b. Zaytûn, [2]427–28
Abû l-Qâsim b. Dâwûd as-Salawî, [1]240*n*
Abû Qilâbah al-Jarmî, [2]180
Abû Qudâmah, 'Ubaydallâh b. Sa'îd, [2]174
Abû Rîdah, M. 'A., [1]lxxii*n*, 44*n*, 176*n*
Abû Sa'îd (Merinid ruler), [1]367, [2]240*n*, 339
Abû Sa'îd al-Kharrâz, [3]96
Abû Sa'îd al-Khudrî, [1]439, 445, [2]158, 166 ff., 208
Abû Ṣakhr al-Hudhalî, 'Abdallâh b. Salm, [1]338*n*
Abû ṣ-Ṣalâḥ Muḥammad al-Ḥanafî al-Qaṭarî, *see* al-Qaṭarî, Abû ṣ-Ṣalâḥ Muḥammad al-Ḥanafî
Abû Sâlim (Merinid ruler), [1]xlviii f., lii f.
Abû Salimah al-Khallâl, [1]410
Abû ṣ-Ṣiddîq an-Nâjî, [2]167, 169 ff.
Abû Su'dâ al-Yafranî, *see* Khalîfah az-Zanâtî, Abû Su'dâ al-Yafranî
Abû Sufyân b. Ḥarb, [1]187, [3]42
Abû Ṭâlib b. 'Abd-al-Muṭṭalib, [1]318, [2]51, 121
Abû Tammâm, [3]377*n*, 383, 393, 403 ff., 411
Abû Tâshfîn ('Abd-al-Wâdid ruler), [1]368
Abû ṭ-Ṭufayl, [2]162, 176
Abû 'Ubayd al-Âjurrî, [2]167
Abû 'Ubayd ath-Thaqafî, [2]85
Abû 'Ubaydah b. al-Jarrâḥ, [1]59*n*
Abû Usâmah, Ḥammâd b. Usâmah, [2]174
Abû Wâ'il, [2]161, 257
Abû l-Wâṣil, 'Abd-al-Ḥamîd b. Wâṣil, [2]171 f.
Abû Wâṣil at-Tamîmî, [2]171*n*
Abû Yaḥyâ, *see* Abû Bakr, Abû Yaḥyâ (Ḥafṣid ruler)
Abû Yaḥyâ Zakarîyâ' b. Aḥmad (b.) al-Liḥyânî (Ḥafṣid ruler), [2]101 f., 222
Abû Ya'lâ al-Mawṣilî, [2]157, 182, 455
Abû Ya'qûb al-Bâdisî, [2]195
Abû Ya'qûb Yûsuf (Almohad ruler), [2]43, Pl. I
Abû Ya'qûb Yûsuf (Merinid ruler), [2]197 f., 240*n*
Abû Yâsir b. Akhṭab, [2]206 f.
Abû Yazîd (the Man of the Donkey), [2]211
Abû Yazîd al-Bisṭâmî, [3]102, 179, 191*n*, 194
Abû Yûsuf Ya'qûb (Merinid ruler), [2]72 f., 427*n*
Abû z-Zinâd, [2]55
Abû Zakarîyâ' Yaḥyâ I (Ḥafṣid ruler), [1]xxxv, xxxvii, [2]72, [3]420
Abû Zakarîyâ' Yaḥyâ II (Ḥafṣid ruler), [2]116
Abû Zayd ad-Dabûsî, [3]28, 30, 32
Abû Zur'ah ad-Dimashqî, [2]173*n*, 181 f.(?)
Abû Zur'ah ar-Râzî, [2]161, 168, 173*n*, 181 f.
al-Abyaḍ, Abû Bakr, [3]443 f.
Abyssinia, Abyssinian(s), [1]99, *following* 110, 121 f., 169, 171, 173, 219, 329, 397, 481, [2]8, 202, 457, [3]186, 343, 346*n*
Abyssinian Sea (= Indian Ocean), [1]99
Acco, [1]133, [2]42
accounting, *see* bookkeeping

Achaemenids, *see* Kayyanids
acrobatics, [2]348 f., [3]166*n*
'Âd, [1]26 ff., 298, 308, 343, 356 f., 359, [2]239 f., 268, 354
Adam, [1]279, 389, 415, [2]250, 266, 316
Aden, [1]26 f., 124
Adhanah, [1]143
Adhkish, [1]*following* 110, 157
Adhri'ât, [1]133 & *n*
Adhwâ', [1]298, [2]354; *see also* Tubba's of the Yemen
Adıvar, A. Adnan, [1]lxvii*n*, [3]273*n*
Adriatic Sea (Gulf of Venice, Straits of the Venetians), [1]99, 139, 151 f.
adultery, fornication, [1]28 ff., 47 ff., 79, [2]107, 185*n*, 295 f., [3]42
Aegean islands, [2]42
al-Afḍal b. Badr al-Jamâlî, [1]365*n*, 366 & *n*
Affifi, A. E., [3]88*n*
'Afîf-ad-dîn Sulaymân b. 'Alî at-Tilimsânî, [3]92*n*
Africa, Northwestern, *see* Ifrîqiyah; Maghrib; Morocco
Africa, Roman province of, *see* Ifrîqiyah
Afrîqus b. Qays b. Ṣayfî, [1]21 f.
al-Afṭas, *see* al-Ḥusayn b. al-Ḥasan b. 'Alî b. 'Alî Zayn-al-'âbidîn
Aga-Oglu, M., [1]75*n*
Aghânî (*Kitâb al-*), *see* Abû l-Faraj al-Iṣfahânî
Aghlabids, [1]42, 46, 48 ff., 351, 382, [2]40, 70, 121, 128, 133, 240, 289 f.
Aghmât, [1]129
agriculture, [1]lxxvii, 183, 249, 251, 289 f., 308 f., [2]90, 93 ff., 102, 105, 136, 247, 269, 271, 278 f., 314 ff., 320, 330, 335 f., 341, 355 ff., [3]151 f., 280; *see also* *Nabataean Agriculture*
al-Aḥdab (mathematician), [3]123
Ahlwardt, W., [3]95*n*, 110*n*
Aḥmad Bâbâ, [1]xxx*n*, xliv*n*, 128*n*, [3]20*n*, 129*n*, 395*n*
Aḥmad aṣ-Ṣiqillî, [2]43
Aḥmad b. 'Abd-as-Salâm, [3]264
Aḥmad b. 'Abdallâh b. Yûnus, [2]163
Aḥmad b. Ḥanbal, [1]38, 384*n*, [2]160, 163, 167 f., 173 ff., 177 f., 181*n*, 185*n*, 192*n*, 209, 265*n*, 453, 455 f., 460–61, [3]8 f., 41*n*, 64
Aḥmad b. al-Ḥârith b. Miskîn, [3]11*n*
Aḥmad b. Muḥammad b. 'Abd-al-Ḥamîd, [1]361
Aḥmad b. Muḥammad b. Ḥanbal, *see* Aḥmad b. Ḥanbal
Aḥmad b. 'Umar b. Surayj, [3]332*n*
Aḥmad b. Yûsuf b. al-Kammâd, [3]136*n*
al-Aḥmar, Banû, *see* Naṣrids (of Granada)
al-Aḥqâf, [1]99 f., 124, 169
Ahrens, W., [3]163*n*, 168*n*
al-Aḥsâ', [1]134
al-Ahwânî, A. F., [1]lxxiv*n*, [3]139*n*, 142*n*
al-Aḥwaṣ, [3]397
al-Ahwâz, [1]135, 362, [2]21*n*
Aila (Aylah), [1]100, 132 f., [2]250
'Â'ishah, [1]17, 185, 201, 223 f., 438, 440, 442 f., [2]253 f., [3]58, 160, 168
al-'Ajamî, Muḥammad b. Aḥmad, [1]lxvii
Ajdâbiyah, [1]131
al-Âjurrî, *see* Abû 'Ubayd al-Âjurrî
'Akkâ, *see* Acco
Akmal-ad-dîn, Muḥammad b. Maḥmûd, [2]229
'Alâ'-ad-dawlah (Kâkôyid of Iṣfahân), [3]250*n*
al-A'lam al-Baṭalyawsî, [3]441, 443
Alamanni, [1]152, 159; Alamâniyah, [1]*following* 110
Alans, [1]101, *following* 110, 160, 172
al-'Alâyâ, [1]144
Alcalá, [2]24
Alcántara, [1]141

Alcazarquivir, [1]129*n*
alchemy, [1]lxxiii, [2]295*n*, [3]157, 172 ff., 180, 188, 215, 218, 220, 223 ff., 227 ff., 267 ff., 457
Aleppo, [1]143
Alexander, [1]73, 162 f., 382, 475, [3]113, 114*n*, 115, 249, 473
Alexander of Aphrodisias, [3]115
Alexandretta, [1]143
Alexandria, [1]lviii, lxii, 41 f., 48, 73, 98, 102, 121, 132, 420, 479 f., [2]38, 44, 101, 133, 248 f., [3]17 f., 114*n*
Alfonso, [3]185
Alfraganus, *see* Ibn al-Farghânî
Algeciras, [1]139 f., 182
Algeria, [2]115
Algiers, [1]129, [2]273 f.
'Alî, I., [1]81*n*
'Alî al-Hâdî, [1]414
'Alî al-Hilâlî, [2]158
'Alî Pasha Damad, [1]xcvii
'Alî ar-Riḍâ, *see* ar-Riḍâ, 'Alî
'Alî Zayn-al-'âbidîn b. al-Ḥusayn b. 'Alî b. Abî Ṭâlib, [1]405, 410, 412
'Alî b. 'Abd-ar-Raḥmân (b. Khaldûn) (son of Ibn Khaldûn), [1]xlvi
'Alî b. 'Abdallâh b. (al-)'Abbâs, [1]29
'Alî b. Abî Ṭâlib, [1]80*n*, 402, 403 & *n*, 404 ff., 410, 412, 418, 421, 426, 430*n*, 431, 433, 435 f., 438 ff., 441 ff., 447, 456, 466, [2]8 f., 21*n*, 70*n*, 71, 82, 158, 162 ff., 174 ff., 178, 181, 183 f., 186 f., 192, 213, 225, 257, 351, [3]39*n*, 82, 93, 322
'Alî b. Isḥâq, Abû l-'Abbâs, *see* Ibn Isḥâq, Abû l-'Abbâs 'Alî
'Alî b. al-Madînî, *see* Ibn al-Madînî
'Alî b. al-Mu'adhdhin, *see* Ibn al-Mu'adhdhin, 'Alî, of Tlemcen
'Alî b. Muḥammad b. al-Ḥanafîyah, [1]409
'Alî b. Mujâhid (ruler of Denia and the Baleares), [3]329, *cf. also* [2]442
'Alî b. Mûsâ b. Ja'far aṣ-Ṣâdiq, *see* ar-Riḍâ, 'Alî
'Alî b. Nufayl, [2]165
'Alî b. Rabban aṭ-Ṭabarî, *see* aṭ-Ṭabarî, 'Alî b. Rabban
'Alî b. 'Umar b. Ibrâhîm (chieftain of the Banû 'Âmir-Zughbah), [3]432
'Alî b. Zengi, *see* al-Walî al-'Ajamî, 'Alî
'Alî b. Ziyâd al-Yamâmî, [2]177 f.
Alicante, [1]141
'Alids, *see* Shî'ah
al-'Allâf, *see* Abû l-Hudhayl al-'Allâf
al-'Allâqî, [1]122
Allouche, I. S., [1]129*n*
al-'Almawî, [3]284*n*
Almería, [1]140 f., [2]40, [3]441
Almohads, [1]xxxv, 53 & *n*, 273, 315, 321 ff., 330 ff., 335, 342, 351, 368, 393, 471, [2]13, 15 f., 23 f., 37, 43 ff., 51, 57, 66, 69 f., 116, 130, 134, 219 ff., 240, 283, 290, 305, 350, 387, 427 & *n*, Pl. I, [3]185, 420, 428, 445
Almoravids, [1]53, 240, 316, 321, 323, 470 ff., [2]43, 82, 83*n*, 93, 134, 386, [3]442, 455; *see also* Lamtûnah
Alms(?) b. Duwayrîdah, [3]445
Almuñécar, [1]140
alphabet, *see* writing
Alps, [1]151
'Alqamah b. 'Abadah, [3]397, 410
'Alqamah b. Qays, [2]172, 174
Alṭunbughâ al-Jûbânî, [1]lix
'Alwah, [1]121
al-'Alwî, Muḥammad b. Aḥmad, [1]xlii
al-A'mâ at-Tuṭîlî, [3]442 f.
Amalekites, [1]23, 288, 298, 308, 334, 357 f., [2]240, 251, 264, 268, 288, 354
Amanus, [1]133 f., 142 ff., 155
Amari, M., [1]94*n*, [2]40*n*, 42*n*, 43*n*
al-A'mash, [2]161
Âmid, [1]144, 155

al-Âmidî ('Alî b. Abî 'Alî), Sayf-ad-dîn, [1]79n, [3]29, 148
al-Âmidî (al-Ḥasan b. Bishr), [1]45n
al-'Amîdî (Muḥammad b. Muḥammad) [3]33
al-'Âmilî, [1]356n
al-Amîn ('Abbâsid caliph), [1]324, [3]306–7
Amîn, A., [2]372n
'Âmir, Banû (Zughbah subtribe), [1]270 f., [3]432
'Âmir b. Ṣa'ṣa'ah, Banû, [1]283, [3]348
al-'Âmirî, Abû l-Ḥasan (Muḥammad b. Yusûf), [1]lxxvin, [2]74n, 244n
'Âmirids, *see* Ibn Abî 'Âmir, al-Manṣûr
'Ammâr ad-Duhnî, [2]177
Amminadab, [1]18
Ammonites, [1]474
Amorium, [1]153 f., 352
'Amr b. Abî Qays, [2]163 f.
'Amr b. al-'Âṣ, [1]384, 404, 440, 466, [2]9, 39, 53, 70n, 71
'Amr b. Jâbir al-Ḥaḍramî, Abû Zur'ah, [2]175, 180 f.
'Amr b. Kulthûm, [3]397
'Amr b. Muḥammad al-'Anqazî, *see* al-'Anqazî
'Amr b. Sa'd b. Abî Waqqâṣ, [1]373
'Amr b. az-Zubayr, [2]64
Amram, [1]18
Amu Darya, [1]136n
Âmul, [1]137, 148
Anak, [1]357 f., [2]240
Ananias (Patriarch of Alexandria), [1]479
Anas b. Mâlik, [1]445, [2]158, 172, 177 f., 184–85
Anatolia, [1]lxv, 102, 144, 153 f., [2]307
Anawati, M.-M., [3]142n
al-Anbâr, [1]145, [2]380
al-Anbârî, *see* Ibn al-Anbârî
'Anbasah (a copyist at the time of the caliph al-Mahdî), [2]219
Andrae, T., [1]4n, 186n
angels, [1]29, 43, 186, 191, 195 ff., 205, 208, 211 f., 216, 230 f., 437, 444, [2]194, 255, 419 ff., 423, [3]43, 55, 59, 69 f., 72, 74, 81, 87, 99, 108, 157, 159
animals: a subject of the science of physics, [3]111, 147; affected by generation and decay, [1]278; minerals, plants, and, [2]414, [3]238 f.; higher and lower, [1]195, [2]423; compared to man, [1]84, 90 ff., 168 f., 252, 291, 295, 301, [2]276 f., 377, 411, 412n, 416 ff., 424, [3]77 f., 90, 138; subjected to man, [2]311, 416; hunting and fishing, [2]315, 367, 377, [3]436, 456 f., 479n; products of, used for barter by Bedouins, [1]309; skins used as clothing and currency, [1]168, as writing material, [2]392; used for military purposes, [1]24, [2]77; depicted on non-Arab coins, [2]55; used as sacrifices, [1]256, [2]274; protected in the sacred territory, [2]256; trained for entertainment, [2]348, 432; of the temperate zones, [1]167; contrasts between wild and domestic, [1]178 f., 282 f.; beasts of prey do not cohabit in captivity, [1]301; if not milked, udders dry up, [2]314, [3]387
spontaneous generation, [3]245, 273, 277; used in soothsaying, [1]203, 214, 216 f., 231, 234; waste matter used in alchemy, [3]227, 235, 237 ff., 268; dream interpretation, [3]107 ff.; on talismans, [2]224n, [3]163; easily affected by magic, [3]161, 164 f.; sea monsters, [1]73
ants, [2]275; bees, *see main entry;* beetles, [1]418, [3]471; birds, [1]203, 214, 217, [2]220, 275, 323, 348, 391, 432, [3]279, 473; calves, [3]273; camels, [1]19n, 26 f., 83n, 138, 178, 182 f., 251 f., 265, 350,

366n, 419 f., [2]49, 68, 78 f., 210, 222, 247, 269, 348, 353, 364, 402, [3]373, 377, 418 f., 421, 424 ff., 432, 435 ff., 478; cats, [1]316, 470, [2]275; chickens, [1]183, 244, 419, [3]242; cows (oxen, buffaloes, cattle), [1]90, 178, 249, 251 f., 366n, 408, [2]170, 247, 271, 282, [3]433, wild cows, [1]178, 282, [3]427, 433, *see also below*, *gâmûs* cows; crows, [3]433; dogs, [2]163, [3]364, 469; donkeys, [1]90, 178, 282, [2]68, 211, 348, 432; doves (pigeons), [1]4, [3]423, 437, 466 ff., 473, 479n; eagles, [3]449; elephants, [1]90, 370n, [2]77 f.; falcons, [1]364, [3]436, 479n; fawns, [3]462; finches, [3]456; fish, [1]35 f., 74, 357, 364, [2]240, 365, [3]456 f.; foxes, [2]175; *gâmûs* cows, [1]366n; gazelles, [1]178, 282, [3]450, 459, 462, 479; giraffes, [1]178; goats, [1]117, 178, 182, 249, [2]247, 250, [3]164; horses, [1]19, 90, 350, 360, 366n, 419 f., [2]32 f., 49, 68, 81, 84, 121n, 126, 131, 316, 358, 377, 404, [3]72, 222 f., 374, 422, 426, 429, 433, 435 f., 439, 464; lambs, [1]256, [2]210, [3]424; lions, [1]90, 316, 470, [2]42, 83, 171, 224n, 322, [3]163, 335, 424, 454 f., 462, 479; locusts, [1]84, 92; monkeys, [1]195, [2]423; moths, [1]327; mules, [1]349, 364, 366n; nightingales, [3]194; onagers, [1]178; ostriches, [1]178, [3]421, 433; owls, [2]104 f., [3]436; parrots, [1]49; partridges, [3]459; pigeons, *see above*, doves; rats, [1]371, [2]275; ravens, [3]463; scorpions, [1]31, 418, [3]163, 273, 277; sheep, [1]138, 249, 251 f., 256, 290, 371, 420, [2]210, 247, 250, [3]164, 416 f., 422, 424, 454n, 463, 472; shellfish, [1]195, [2]423; silkworms, [1]249, 297, [2]315; snails, [1]195, [2]423; snakes, [1]138, [2]224n, [3]107 ff., 163, 273, 277, 426, 455, 466; spiders, [1]4; starlings, [1]74; wolves, [1]197; worms and insects, [2]275, 320

Ankara, [1]144 & *n*

Anmâr b. Nizâr (tribe), [1]219

Anôsharwân, *see* Khosraw I Anôsharwân

al-ʿAnqazî, ʿAmr b. Muḥammad, [2]177

Antalya, [1]144

ʿAnṭarah b. Shaddâd, [3]397, 410

Anṭarsûs (Anṭarṭûs, Antaradus), [1]143

Antichrist, [2]156, 159, 188, 190, 192, [3]69

Antioch, [1]143

Antuña, M. M., [1]xlii*n*

Apollonius, [2]365

Apulia, [1]152*n*

Aq-Qoyunlu, [1]235*n*

al-ʿAqabah (near Mecca), [1]429

al-ʿAqabah (seaport), [1]133

ʿAqîl b. Abî Ṭâlib, [2]21

al-ʿAqîq, [1]420

aqueducts, *see* water

Aquileia, [1]99, 152, 159

Arabian Nights, [1]75*n*, [2]244*n*

Arabian Peninsula, [1]lxxvii, 21, 23, 100 f., 122, 169, [2]264, [3]18*n*

Arab(s): identical with nomads and peasants, [1]250; camel nomads, [1]251 f.; unwilling to subordinate themselves, [1]304 ff.; unfamiliar with crafts and sciences, [2]353 f., 377, 381, 445, [3]230, 311 ff.; unskilled in navigation, [2]39; unable to select proper site for cities, [2]247 f., 269 f.; use of tents, [2]67 f.; technique of warfare, [2]74; form of writing, [2]381 f.; use of poetry, [2]401 f.; purity of lineage, [1]260; differences in hardiness among tribes, [1]282 f.; becoming civilized, [1]347 f.; their character influenced by religion, [1]305 ff.; gain world domination, [1]299,

330, 400; overpower Berbers in the Maghrib, ¹64, ²266, 289, with ruinous consequences, ¹305; religious reformers among Maghribî A., ²199 f.; A. battle music in the Maghrib, ²49; Arabic language, *see* language, linguistics; *see also* Bedouins

Arabs, non-: mainly peasants, ¹251; drawn to urban life, ²267 ff.; cultivate the crafts, ²353 f., music, ²401, principles of jurisprudence, ³30, theology, ³53; coinage, ²55; use of the *ṭirâz*, ²66; military music, ²49; technique of warfare, ²74, 78; employed by early Muslims as bookkeepers, ²8, as sailors, ²39; affect the purity of Arab pedigrees, ¹266 f.; the sounds of their speech, ¹66; cause of corruption of the Arabic language, ³321 f., 325, 343, 346, 352 f., 363, 366, 412; constitute the majority of scholars in Islam, ³311 ff., 319

Arabs, pre-Islamic: uncivilized, ¹441; their buildings and civilization, ¹26, ²268 f., 354, 378 ff.; avoid wine and viniculture, ¹35; soothsayers, ¹218 f., ²202; poetry, ³376, 403 ff.; Jews and Christians among, ¹66n, ²203, 206 f., 445

al-'Arâ'ish, *see* Larache

Aral, Lake, ¹103, 136, 157

Aramaic language, ¹200n, 212n, 213n

Arberry, A. J., ¹xciii, ³80n, 96n

architecture, ¹168, 249 f., 354, 356 ff., 420, ²69 ff., 75, 82, 238 ff., 247, 252 ff., 260 f., 268, 270 f., 300, 355, 357 ff., 414 f., 435, ³132, 379 f.; *see also* monuments

Arcila, ¹129

Arcos (de la Frontera), ¹323

Ardabîl, ¹155

Ardashîr, ²215

van Arendonk, C., ¹406n

'Arfajah b. Harthamah al-Azdî, ¹55, 268, ²39

Arguin, ¹118n

'Arîf, Awlâd, ¹liii

Arîs, well of, ²61

al-'Arîsh, ¹100, 132

Aristotle, Pseudo-Aristotle, ¹78, 81 f., 91n, 120n, 235 f., 238, 275n, ²frontispiece, 35n, 48, 415n, ³85, 115 f., 131n, 139, 140n, 147, 153, 248 ff., 254 f., 272n, 284n, 287, 412

arithmetic, algebra, ¹xliv, 19n, 91n, 237 f., 241n, 244, ²407, 426, ³20 ff., 112, 118 ff., 136, 162, 187 f., 198 ff., 215, 221 ff., 299, 304, 326 f.

Arius, ¹479

al-'Arj, ¹134

Armant, ¹125

Armenia, Armenian(s), ¹102, *following* 110, 143 f., 146, 154 f., 334, 364, 474

Arnold, T. W., ¹391n

'Arqah, ¹133 & n, 143

Arrajân, ¹135

Arran, ¹155

Artaxerxes, *see* Bahman (Artaxerxes)

Artemidorus, ³103n, 105n, 108n

Arzan, ¹154

'aṣabîyah, *see* group feeling

Asad, Banû, ¹266, 446, ³343

As'ad Abû Karib, Tibân, ¹22, 25, ²251

Asad b. al-Furât, ²40, ³14 f.

Asad b. Mûsâ, ²170 f.

al-Aṣamm, ¹391

Aṣbagh b. al-Faraj, ³16

Ascalon, ¹132 f., ²42

Asclepius, ³109n

Asfî, Ribâṭ, ¹129

al-A'shâ, ²252, ³410

al-'Asharah al-mubashsharah, ¹59n

al-Ash'arî, ¹314n, ³49 ff., 63, 144, 266 f.
Ash'arite(s): replaced Mu'tazilah, ³63; views on primevalness of the Qur'ân, ³63 f., on fraudulent miracles, ¹190, on the divine attributes and the articles of faith, ³49 f., 63, 67, 69, 145, on importance of premises and arguments, ³51 f., 145, on atoms and accidents, ³50 f., 144, 146; their doctrines opposed, ³266 f.; their doctrines followed by the Mahdî of the Almohads, ¹471; A. doctrine and Abû Isḥâq al-Isfarâ'inî, ³100, 144 f., al-Bâqillânî, ³50 f., 144 f., Ibn Mujâhid, ³50 f., the Imâm al-Ḥaramayn, ³28 f., 50 f., al-Ghazzâlî, ³28 f.
al-Ash'ath b. Qays, ¹282
Ashhab b. 'Abd-al-'Azîz, ³11, 14
Ashîr, ¹129, ²116
al-'Ashsh, Yûsuf, ¹75n
al-Ashtar, ²82
'Âṣim (b. Abî n-Najûd), ²159 ff.
Asín Palacios, M., ¹322n, ²138n, ³88n, 114n
al-'Askarî, Abû Hilâl, ¹451n, 466n, ²53n
Aslam b. Sidrah, ²379
Asmâ' bint Abî Bakr, ¹224
al-Aṣma'î, ¹32, ²256, ³411, 413
Assassins (Neo-Ismâ'îlîyah), ¹143, 413, ³92
Assuan, ¹121
Assyut, ¹125
Astarâbâdh, ¹136, 147 f.
astrolabes, ³134
astrology, ¹lxxii f., 206, 226 ff., 234 f., 241, 343, ²193 ff., 201, 203, 211 ff., 221, 224, 282, 323, 371, ³112 f., 116, 137, 151, 156, 162, 166 f., 169, 172 f., 176 ff., 186 f., 189, 193, 196 ff., 220 ff., 246, 258 ff., 274n, 474

astronomy, ¹96 f., 104 f., 113 ff., 357, ²240 f., ³112, 131, 133 ff., 196, 274n
Ateş, Ahmed, ¹xcvii, ³273n
Atlantic Ocean, ¹95n
Atlas Mountain (Daran), ¹128 ff.
'Attâb b. Bashîr, ²172
al-'Attâbî, Kulthûm b. 'Amr, ³393, 404
Audisio, G., ¹33n
Augustus (Roman Emperor), ¹476
Aumer, J., ¹ci
L'Aurès, see Awrâs, Mount
Avars, see Sarîr
Avempace, see Ibn Bâjjah
Avenzoar, see Ibn Zuhr
Averroes (Ibn Rushd), ¹xliv, 108 f., 275 f., ²415n, ³16n, 51n, 67n, 116, 135, 139n, 142, 147, 153, 166n, 254
Avicenna (Ibn Sînâ), ¹lxxiv, 91n, 171, ²224, 371 f., ³36n, 73, 116, 121, 130, 135, 142, 147 ff., 153, 157n, 166n, 217n, 250, 254, 256, 272 ff., 277, 280
Ávila, ¹xln, 150
'Awâṣim, ¹266, 364n
'Awf al-A'râbî, ²169
Awlîl, ¹118
Awrabah (Berber tribe), ¹318, ²115
Awrâs, Mount, ¹129 f., ²116
Aws, Banû, ¹25, ²264
Awthân, Cape, ¹131
'Awwâd, J.(K.), ¹348n, ²189n
al-Awzâ'î, ³46n
'Aydhâb, ¹100, 126
Aylah, see Aila
'Aylân, ³348n
'Ayn Zarbah, ¹143 f.
Ayyûbids, ²435n, ³12; see also Ṣalâḥ-ad-dîn, Yûsuf b. Ayyûb
Azd, Banû, ¹55, 268, 441, ²82
al-Azdî, 'Alî b. Ẓâfir, ¹366n
Azerbaijan, ¹23, 101 f., *following* 110, 146, 155, 364, ²226
Azgâr (Berber tribe), ¹125

al-Azhar University, [1]lx
Azîlâ, *see* Arcila
al-ʿAzîz, Nizâr (Fâṭimid ruler), [2]51
al-ʿAzl, [3]377
Azov, Sea of, [1]164*n*
al-Azraqî, [2]257

B

Bâb al-Mandeb, [1]99 f., 122 f.
Babel, [3]113*n*, 156, 159 f.
Babinger, F., [1]lxvii*n*, xciv*n*, cvii*n*, cviii*n*
Babylon, [1]475
Babylonia, Babylonian(s), [1]78, [3]156
Bacon, Roger, [1]81*n*, 235*n*, [2]48*n*, [3]249*n*
Badajoz, [1]140
Badawî, ʿA., [1]80*n*, 81*n*, 91*n*, 235*n*, [2]48*n*, 415*n*, [3]139*n*, 142*n*, 274*n*
Badakhshân, [1]136
al-Badîʿ al-Hamadhânî, [3]393
Bâdis, [1]129, 140, 327, [2]197
Bâdîs, Banû, *see* Zîrids
Bâdîs b. al-Manṣûr (Zîrid ruler), [2]116
al-Bâdisî, *see* Abû Yaʿqûb al-Bâdisî
Badr, [2]176, [3]74
Badr al-Jamâlî, [1]366*n*
Bagharghar, *see* Tughuzghuz
Baghdad, [1]33*n*, 39, 42, 45 f., 50, 101 f., 145 f., 154, 315, 324 f., 334, 349, 361, 412, 434, 470*n*, 471*n*, [2]115, 133 f., 178, 194*n*, 218 f., 227, 236, 299, 384 ff., 404 f., 431, 434, 460, [3]9, 11, 17, 19, 114*n*, 289, 324, 417 & *n*, 455, 460, 475 f.
al-Baghdâdî, *see* ʿAbd-al-Qâhir al-Baghdâdî
al-Baghdâdî, *see* ʿAbdallâh al-Baghdâdî
Bahdalah, Banû, [2]171
al-Bahlawîyîn, *see* al-Bahlûs
Bahlûl, *see* Buhlûl
al-Bahlûs, [1]*following* 110, 146 f.
Bahman (Artaxerxes), [2]260
al-Baḥr al-Muḥîṭ, *see* Surrounding Sea
Bahrâm (Mars), [3]189
Bahrâm b. Bahrâm, [1]80, [2]104
al-Baḥrayn, [1]24, 25*n*, 100 f., 126, 134, [2]21, 128, 354
al-Bajâʾî, Ibn Khazar, *see* Ibn Khazar al-Bajâʾî
al-Bâjarbaqî, [2]225, 229 f.
Bajâyah (Bijâyah), *see* Bougie
al-Bâjî, Abû l-Walîd, [3]10
Bajîlah, Banû, [1]55, 268, [2]39
Bâkhamrâ, [1]411*n*
Bâkiyâk, *see* Bâyakbâk
Bakkah, *see* Mecca
Bakr b. Wâʾil, Banû, [1]441
al-Bakrî, [1]16*n*, 64, 74, 75*n*, [2]244 f., [3]446*n*, 452*n*
al-Balâdhurî, [1]21*n*, 333*n*, 417*n*
Balanjar, [1]161
Baʿlbakk, [1]134
Baleares, [2]441; *see also* Ibiza; Majorca; Minorca
Balkh, [1]101 f., 136 f.
Balkhâ River, [1]137
al-Ballafîqî, Abû l-Barakât Muḥammad b. Muḥammad, [1]xlii, [2]459, [3]269, 407 f.
Ballahrâ, [1]127
Balwâṭ, *see* Carpathian Mountains
al-Bâmiyân, [1]137
banners, *see* flags
al-Bâqillânî, [1]43, 44*n*, 189*n*, 397*n*, 398, [3]50 & *n*, 51 f., 56, 59*n*, 144 f., 332
al-Barâdhiʿî, Abû Saʿîd, [3]15, 286
Barca (Barqah), [1]98, 131, 365, [2]248, 282 f.
Barcelona, [1]142, 150, [3]185
Bardhaʿah, [1]154
Bârimmâ, Mountain of, [1]146, 154
al-Barjî, Muḥammad b. Yaḥyâ, [1]xlii
Barkiyâruq b. Malikshâh, [2]101
Barmecides, [1]28 ff., 30 ff., 63, 272, 277 f., 360, 373, [2]23, 63, 99, 242, 392*n*, [3]430

Barqah, *see* Barca
Barqûq, al-Malik aẓ-Ẓâhir, [1]lix ff., lxiv, xci, xcvi, 368, [2]227, Pl. I, [3]18
Barthold, W., [1]17*n*, 124*n*, 155*n*
al-Basâsîrî, [1]42
Bashîr b. Nahîk, [2]182
Bashqirs, [1]*following* 110, 161, 165
Bashshâr b. Burd, [2]275*n*, [3]397, 403, 405
al-Baṣrah, [1]23, 41*n*, 100 f., *following* 110, 134, 363, 384*n*, 410, 420, 441, 443, 453, [2]71, 247, 269, 299, 384, 431, 434, 452, [3]289, 323 f.
al-Baṣrî, Abû l-Ḥusayn Muḥammad b. ʻAlî, [3]29
al-Baṣrî, al-Ḥasan, *see* al-Ḥasan (b. Abî l-Ḥasan) al-Baṣrî
al-Baṭḥâ', [1]102
baths, [1]174, [2]236, 302, 348, [3]384
Baṭn Namirah, [2]256
al-Battânî, [3]136
battle-day literature, [3]339 ff., 367
Bâṭûs, land of, *see* Anatolia
Baumgartner, W., [2]260*n*
Bâyakbâk, [1]374
Bayʻat ar-riḍwân, [1]429*n*
Bâyazîd Yıldırım, [1]lxv
Baybars, [1]366, [2]225*n*, 226, 230
Baybars Institute, [1]lxii
al-Bayḍâwî, [1]4*n*, 173*n*, [3]29, 53
al-Bayhaqî (Aḥmad b. al-Ḥusayn), [2]185
al-Bayhaqî (ʻAlî b. Zayd), [1]22*n*
al-Bayhaqî (author of the *Kitâb al-Kamâ'im*), [1]22
al-Bayhaqî (Ibrâhîm b. Muḥammad), [1]427*n*, [3]307*n*
al-Baylaqân, [1]*following* 110, 146, 154, 160
Bayonne, [1]150
al-Baysânî, *see* al-Qâḍî al-Fâḍil al-Baysânî
Baza, [1]140 f.
al-Bazdawî, Sayf-al-Islâm (Fakhr-al-Islâm), [3]30, 33
al-Bazzâr, [2]157, 181 f., 455
de Beaurecueil, S. de Laugier, [3]95*n*
beauty, [1]39, [2]398 f., [3]194, 384, 388, 404 f., 408 f., 438, 443, 446, 451, 454, 462, 470
Bedouins: defined, [1]lxxvii, 250 ff.; strength and vitality, [1]295 f., [2]297, 376 f.; modesty, [2]89 f., 111, 122, 293; mostly illiterate, [2]8, 22, 378, 382 f., 444 f.; always prepared for self-defense, [1]257 f.; care little for the crafts, [3]32; agriculture their main craft, [2]357; little food, [1]177; no ready cash, [1]309; healthier than sedentary people, [1]178 f., 282 f., and basically as intelligent, [2]433; able to gain control only over easily accessible territory, [1]302; their way of life destructive to civilization, [1]302 ff., but not considered blameworthy by the Prophet, [1]255 ff.
urban life: disliked, [2]267; dominated by, [1]308 f.; attracted to, [1]252 f., [2]236, 291; difficulties of entering into, [2]279 f.; changes under the influence of urbanization, [2]68, 79, 236
bees: spontaneous generation, [3]273, 277; remarkable instincts and social organization, [1]84, 92, [2]371; indicate the presence of flowers, [3]460; honey, [1]363 f., 408, [2]94, 315, 341, [3]151, 273, 452, 458
Beeston, A. F. L., [1]95*n*
Behemoth, [1]4
Beirut, [1]134
Beja, [1]99 f., *following* 110, 122 f.
Bel, A., [1]xcii, 272*n*, [2]57*n*, [3]415*n*
Belacazar, [1]140*n*
Bell, R., [3]97*n*
Belqâ', [1]409*n*
Ben Cheneb, M., [1]239*n*
Beni Saf, [1]lii
Benjamin, [1]475, [2]259

Berbera, ¹99, 123
Berber(s): alleged origin of the name, ¹21 f.; alleged Ḥimyarite connections, ¹22; pre-Islamic, ¹382, ²289; East African "Berbers," ¹99; tribes, ¹125, 128 f.; mainly peasants or nomads, ¹251 f., ²266; unfamiliar with the crafts, ²353; built few cities, ²266 f., 353; food cheap in B. countries, ²279; rebelliousness, ¹333, ²289; soothsayers, ²202; technique of warfare, ²74, use of music in battle, ²49; "students" as treasure hunters and alchemists, ²320 f., ³270; Qur'ân teachers, ³301; poor copyists of books, ²394

successive rule of different B. tribes, ¹298, 315, 318 f., 331; B. tribes claiming noble Arab descent, ¹270 f.; overpowered by the Arabs, ¹64, ²266, 289, *cf.* also ³415 ff.; support of Idrîsids, ¹47 f., ²115, 121, of Fâṭimids, ¹41, 45, 382; rule in Spain, ¹316, 335, ²386, group feeling there, ¹61

sounds of the language, ¹cxv, 66 ff., 128n, 129n, ³129n; words: *adrar, idraren*, ¹128n, *afrâg*, ²68, *agrur*, ¹119n, *ameswar*, ²17n, *ait*, pl. of *u*, ¹271n, *Buluggîn*, ¹67, 68n, *Daran, Dren*, ¹128n, *mizwâr*, ²17 f., *tazouggit*, ²49n, *tâzûgâit*, ²49; a statement translated, ¹272; poems, ²202; influence of the language upon Arabic, ³252, 386; B. rarely master Arabic, ³372

Bercher, L., ¹lxxiin, cix, 247n, 264n, 272n, 322n, 372n, 385n, 414n, 428n, 448n, 454n, ²3n, 5n, 75n, 108n, 399n, ³48n

Berenice, desert of, ¹*following* 110, 131

Bergh, S. van den, *see* van den Bergh

Bergin, T. G., ¹lxxxin, cxivn
Bergsträsser, G., ¹67n, ²443n, ³59n, 168n
Berthelot, M., ³242n
Berthels, E., ³95n
Bethlehem, ¹lxiii, ²262
Biârma, ¹165n
Bible: the Torah, ¹4, 18, 20, 170, 192, 475 ff., ²258, 260, 438, 445 f., ³284; the Psalms, ²401n; the Gospel, ¹4, 192, 476 ff.; Books of the Old Testament, ¹477 f., the New Testament, ¹478; its study forbidden to Muslims, ²438 f.

passages mentioned: Gen. *9:25*, ¹170n; Exod. *6:16* ff., ¹18n; Exod. *20:5*, ¹281; Num. *1:46*, ¹16n; Judg. *7:6*, ²176n; I Kings *10:26*, ¹19n; Job *40:15*, ¹4n; Matt. *6:21*, ³339n

Israelite stories, ¹19, 230; Noah, the first carpenter, ²365 f., his long life, ¹343; Negroes, descendants of Ham, ¹169 ff.; the story of Og, ¹357 f., ²240; *see also* Israelites; Jews

Bilâl b. Abî Burdah b. Abî Mûsâ al-Ashʿarî, ¹373
Bilâq, ¹121n
Birge, J. K., ¹xxiii
Birjîs (Jupiter), ³189, 193
al-Bîrûnî, ¹108n, 112n, 124n, 367n, ²270n, ³119n, 121n, 134n
al-Birzâlî, ¹366n, 367n
al-Bisâṭî, Shams-ad-dîn, ²398n
Bîshâpûr, ²Pl. I
Bishr b. Marwân, ²177
Bishtâsp, *see* Yastâsb
Biskra, ¹xliii, 1 ff., lviii, 130, 238n, ²274, 304, ³196n
Bisṭâm, ¹147, ³191, 194
Bisṭâm b. Qays, ¹282
al-Bisṭâmî, *see* Abû Yazîd al-Bisṭâmî
Bithynia, ¹98
Blachère, R., ¹81n, ²214n, 365n, 368n, ³126n, 247n

Black Death, [1]xxxviii, xl, 64
Black Sea [1]98, 140, 146, 153 ff., 159 f., 162, 164
Black Sea (= Surrounding Sea), [1]96
Black Volta, [1]118n
Blochet, E., [1]cin
Boaz, [1]18
Bodin, J., [1]lxvii
Bohemia, [1]*following* 110, 159
Boll, F., [1]112n
Bombaci, A., [1]xxv, cviii, 6n, 9n, 19n, 25n, 52n, 54n, 62n, 181n, 198n, 206n, 234n, 264n, 392n, 397n, 421n, [2]131n, 237n, 286n, 300n, 318n, 345n, 349n, 350n, 358n, 393n, 437n, [3]5n, 9n, 26n, 32n, 36n, 66n, 68n, 79n, 82n, 102n, 103n, 108n, 115n, 117n, 134n, 138n, 146n, 154n, 162n, 164n, 165n, 169n, 171n, 176n, 178n, 228n, 251n, 253n, 254n, 259n, 260n, 261n, 264n, 270n, 271n, 280n, 288n, 297n, 298n, 315n, 337n, 340n, 341n, 349n, 356n, 358n, 368n, 373n, 374n, 375n, 379n, 382n, 384n, 386n, 393n, 395n, 403n, 409n, 410n, 415n
Bône, [1]xxxvii, lviii, 130, [2]248, [3]475
bookkeeping, accounting, [1]354, [2]8, 10, 15 f., 18 f., 22, 24 f., 31, 407n; business arithmetic, [3]112, 122, 126 f.
books: production, [2]347 f., 355 f., 385 f., 391 ff.; copying, [2]119, 227 f., 347n, 348, 352, 385, 387; binding, [2]347n, 348; textual accuracy, [2]348, 387, 392 ff., 457; last forever, [3]6, 115; valuable possessions, [2]101; suppressed by censorship, [3]6; destroyed by Muslims during the Conquest, [3]114, by Mongols, [2]219, [3]114n; the Torah burned by Nebuchadnezzar, [2]260
    purposes of scientific, [3]284 ff.; their overwhelmingly large number, [3]288 ff.; abridgments, [3]287; uselessness of short handbooks, [1]xlv, 10, [3]290 f.; Muslim scientific books written in languages other than Arabic, [2]307
Bornu, [1]*following* 110, 125n
Bouché-Leclerq, A., [3]163n
Bougie, [1]xli, xlviii, l ff., lviii, 129, 315, 332, [2]57, 116, 236, 248, 273, 429, [3]19, 126n, 185, 450n
Bourges, [1]151
Bouthoul, G., [1]xcii f., cviii
Bräunlich, E., [3]327n
brass, *see* metals
Breysig, K., [1]lxviin
bridges, [1]357, Pl. IIIa, [2]244n
Brittany, [1]*following* 110, 158
Brockelmann, C., [1]xxv, cxiv, 35n, [2]22n, [3]96n, and *passim* as the author of *GAL*
bronze, *see* metals
Bronze City, *see* Copper City
Browne, E. G., [2]104n, [3]391n
Brünnow, R., [1]338n
Brunschvig, R., [1]xxxii, xxxvin, xxxviin, xlin, xlvn, lvin, lviin, [2]16n, 17n, 38n, 72n, 77n, 101n, 198n, 200n, 246n, 248n, 361n, 428n, 429n, [3]136n, 264n, 412n, 423n, 427n, 430n
Brussa, *see* Bursa
Büchner, V. F., [1]93n
Bughâ, [1]49, 374
Buhl, F., [1]207n
Buhlûl (al-Majnûn, an early Sufi), [3]194
Buhlûl b. 'Ubaydah at-Tujîbî, [2]381
al-Buḥturî, [3]383, 403 f., 411
building, *see* architecture
Bukhârâ, [1]103, 148 f., [3]68
al-Bukhârî, [1]21, 38 & n, 56, 185n, 186n, 187n, 188n, 192n, 205n, 208n, 209n, 211n, 254n, 255 & n, 256n, 276n, 281n, 289n, 290n, 359n, 397n, 398n, 415n, 435n, 447n, [2]61 & n, 157n, 158, 159n,

162, 163*n*, 164*n*, 167 & *n*, 169 & *n*, 170 & *n*, 171, 173*n*, 174, 176 f., 179, 182, 183*n*, 189, 204*n*, 208 & *n*, 209, 240, 249*n*, 253*n*, 257, 324*n*, 336, 380*n*, 401*n*, 444*n*, 453*n*, 454, 457 ff., 462, [3]42 & *n*, 43*n*, 56*n*, 58*n*, 61*n*, 68, 73*n*, 74*n*, 96*n*, 98*n*, 151*n*, 229*n*, 262*n*
Bulgaria, [1]159*n*
Bulgars (Bulghâr, Burjân), [1]98, *following* 110, 160 ff., 165
al-Bulqînî, Sirâj-ad-dîn, [3]12
Buluggîn b. Zîrî, [1]332, [2]42
Bûnah, *see* Bône
al-Bûnî, [3]168*n*, 172, 174, 177*n*, 178, 181, 226
Bûrân (wife of al-Ma'mûn), [1]39, 348 f., 359
al-Burâq (Muḥammad's horse), [3]72
Burayd, [1]466*n*
Burd, Banû, [2]99
Buret, L., [3]292*n*
Burgos, [1]150, 151*n*
Burgundy, [1]151, 159
Burjân, *see* Bulgars
Bursa (Brussa), [1]xc, xcvii, 153
Burṭâs, [1]161
Bûshanj, [1]136
al-Bûṣîrî, [1]xliv*n*
Bust, [1]135
al-Bustî, *see* Abû l-Fatḥ al-Bustî
Buttam Mountains, [1]136 ff., 148
Buwayrah, [3]452*n*
al-Buwayṭî, [3]10
Bûyids, [1]269*n*, 373, 378, [2]128, [3]250, 406, 408
Buzurjmihr, [1]83, [2]216
Byzantine Sea (= Mediterranean), [2]38
Byzantines (ar-Rûm), [1]12, 23 f., 57, 98 f., 102, 143, 153, 172, 329 f., 333, 347, 419, 441, 456, 474, [2]7, 38 f., 41, 50, 61, 76, 78, 134, 193, 263, 268, 288, 301, 307, 319, 362 f., 404, [3]115 f., 186, 249, 283 f., 343, 346*n*, 361, 372, 474*n*

C

Cacella, [3]364*n*
Cadiz, [1]140, [2]43
Caesarea, [1]133
Cahen, C., [1]lxxxix*n*
Cairo, [1]lviii, lx, lxii, lxv, xciv, xcvi*n*, 41, 100*n*, 123, 131 f., 180, 468, [2]133, 137, 224, 236 f., 263, 274 f., 321, 349, 378, 386, 431, 435, 436*n*, Pl. I, [3]19, 315
Calabria, [1]*following* 110, 142, 151 f.
Calatayud, [1]141
Calatrava, [1]141
Caleb, [1]275
caliphate, [1]lxxx, 314, 385 ff.; derivation of term, [1]388 f.; title "Commander of the Faithful," [1]465 ff., [2]45 & *n*; only kind of just government, [2]285; its necessary character, [1]389 f.; conditions governing choice of caliph, [1]394 ff., [2]189; one of articles of faith, [3]50; possibility of more than one caliph at same time, [1]392 ff.; oath of allegiance, [1]428 ff.; succession, [1]430 ff.; institutions connected with, [1]448 ff., [2]4; first four caliphs, [1]39, 59*n*, 404 ff., 418, 430 f., 433, 435 f., 465, [2]8, 186, [3]82, 93; Shî'ah doctrine, [1]402 ff., 435 f., 466 f., 471, [2]186, [3]5, 50, 93 f.
calligraphy, *see* writing
Callisthenes (Pseudo-), [1]73*n*
Camel, Battle of the, [1]440
camels, *see* animals
Canaan, Canaanites, [1]21, 23, 333, 357 f., 474, [2]240
Canaan, T., [3]162*n*, 176*n*
Canard, M., [1]142*n*, 153*n*, [2]44*n*, 193*n*
Canaries (islands), [1]116 ff., 125
cannibalism, [1]119, 168

Canton, [1]124, 127*n*
Cape Blanco, [1]118*n*
Carcassonne, [1]142, 150
Carmody, F. J., [2]214*n*
Carmona, [1]xxxiii, lviii
Carpathian Mountains, [1]159
carpentry, [1]89, 309, [2]271, 313, 316, 347*n*, 348, 354 f., 363 ff., [3]132, 355, 433
Carra de Vaux, B., [1]226*n*, [3]72*n*, 156*n*
Cartagena, [1]141
Carthage, [1]357, Pl. IIIb, [2]38, 239 ff., 243
Casanova, P., [1]ciii*n*
Casiri, M., [1]xxx*n*, [3]365*n*
Caspian Sea, [1]17, 101, 146 f., 155 f., 161 f.
Castilla, [1]il, 150
Cataracts, Mountain of the, [1]121
causality, [1]194, [2]414 ff., [3]34 ff., 260 f.
Ceuta, [1]xxxvi, il, lviii, 129, 139 f., [2]38, 220, 248, 273, 305, [3]365, 398, 450
Ceylon, [1]123, [2]266
Chain Mountain (Taurus), [1]142 ff., 155
Chaldaeans, [1]78, [2]288, [3]113, 156, 160, 283
Cherchel, [1]357, [2]38, 239
chess, [2]217, 416
children: newborn, [2]356, [3]68 ff.; "belong to the bed," [1]50; greatly desired, [1]54; born in natural state, follow parents' religion, [1]254, 306; speaking in cradle, [2]185 f., 192, 370; enjoyment of sense perceptions, [3]253, 256; defective perception, [1]215; linguistic habit yet unformed, [3]318, 321, 342 f., 360 ff., 391; weak and dependent, [1]257, 345, [2]69, 79; fond of fortune tellers, [2]201; the "folly of youth," [3]304 f.; imitate fathers, [1]62, 299 f.; responsibility toward one's, [2]296; provided for by acquisition of real estate, [2]284 f., and establishment of *waqf* foundations, [2]436*n*; as rulers, [1]43, 50, 377 f., [2]113; *see also* education; orphans
  in letter magic, [3]190; "young ones" as alchemical cover name, [3]239
China, Chinese, [1]23, 99, *following* 110, 122 f., 127, 138, 168, 172, [2]121, 281, 325, 353, [3]9, 271*n*
Chinchilla, [1]141
Chinese Sea (= Indian Ocean), [1]99
Christensen, A., [3]168*n*
Christian(s), [1]254, [2]445, [3]284, 418(?), 461; survey of early C. history, [1]476 ff.; the Pope, [1]151, 480 f.; the Patriarch and other religious ranks, [1]478 ff.; C. church in Jerusalem, [1]42, [2]262 f.; divisions of Christianity, [1]480 f.; C. Abyssinians, Slavs, and Turks, [1]169; humiliated by God, [2]150*n*; ascetics, [3]82; Nicene Creed, [1]479; doctrine of incarnation, [1]406, [3]86; religion transmitted from parents to children, [1]254; Christianity averse to science, [3]115, but C. clergymen transmitted Greek scientific heritage to Muslims, [3]115; philosophy cultivated in contemporary C. countries, [3]117 f.
  polemics with Muslims, [1]4*n*; fighting against Muslims, [1]19, for Muslims in the contemporary Maghrib, [2]80; employed by early Muslims as bookkeepers, [2]8 f.; Muslim struggle against them in Spain, [1]335, [2]290, 386; economic and cultural consequences for Muslims of their reconquest of Spain, [2]278 f., [3]302, 364 f.; the Crusaders, [2]42 ff., 100, 263; wealth of contempo-

rary C. merchants, [2]281; Ibn Khaldûn's attitude toward, [1]il
see also European Christians; Jesus
cities, *see* urban life
civilization, [1]lxxvi f., 8*n*, 84 f., [3]111; defined, [1]89; exists in varying degrees, [1]369; most strongly represented in temperate zones, [1]104, [2]357, least developed in southern half of the earth, [1]107 f., 119, [2]367; requires co-operation, [2]301; depends on size of population, [2]236 f., 270 f., 272 ff., 351, 434 f., [3]117, 149; nomadic anarchy its antithesis, [1]303 f., 306 f.; development from primitive to highest state, [1]249 f., 347; sedentary culture, [2]286 ff., 349 ff., 427, 432 f., [3]115, 315, is civilization's final goal, [1]lxxx f., [2]291 ff., 347; requiring leisure, [3]364
development influenced by taxation, [2]89 ff.; flourishes under a benevolent government, [2]135, 146; ruined by government interference with business, [2]95, by government injustice, [2]103 ff.; affected by epidemics, [1]64, [2]136 f.; harmed by astrology, [3]362 f.
measure of historical truth, [1]8, 72 f., 76 f., 368 ff.
see also population; urban life
Clement of Alexandria, [3]252*n*
Clement of Rome, [1]477
climate, [1]104 ff., 169 ff., 174 f., 226, [2]136 f., 235, 244 ff., 269, 357 f., 367, 376, [3]259 f.
cloths (clothes), [1]34, 36, 167 f., 186, 249 f., 299 f., 338 f., 347 f., 350, 360, 362 ff., 366 ff., 425, 471, [2]16, 33, 65, 117 f., 126, 168, 194, 251 f., 255 f., 272, 274, 276, 302, 312, 323, 336, 340 f., 354, 366 f., [3]77, 161, 163 f., 194, 238, 429 f., 445, 447, 451, 469
Codera, F., [2]380*n*, 381*n*, [3]395*n*
Cohen, B., [1]4*n*
Coimbra, [1]141
coins, coinage: office of the mint, [1]464, [2]3, 7, 54 ff., Pl. I; currency manipulations in political warfare, [1]50; protection of currency the task of the government, [1]464, [2]3, [3]270; the various metals used as media of exchange, [1]168; Bedouins have no ready cash, [1]309; coins forged by alchemists, [3]269 ff.
Colin, G. S., [1]42*n*, 96*n*, 128*n*, [3]197*n*, 471*n*
Collo, [2]248
colocynths, [1]183
color: depends on light, [3]90; distinguishing quality of metals, [3]272, 461; fast colors of garments, [2]350 f.; color distinctions in Arabic, [3]330; ethical meaning of different colors, [1]186; dynastic colors, [2]50 f.; color and race, [1]170 ff.; of Saturn, [2]221; in magic, [2]323, [3]163 f.; as an alchemical term, [3]236, 238, 242; dyeing with saffron, [2]238
Comans, [1]160, 164 f.
commerce: defined, [2]316 f., 336 f., 340, [3]280; corrupt business practices, [2]293; legality of cunning, [2]110, 317, 343 f.; by sea, [2]38; with remote countries, [1]118, [2]338; to be encouraged by the ruler, [1]294; flourishes with the help of government spending, [2]103, 291; ruined through price fixing, [2]110; adversely affected by prolonged prevalence of unfair prices, [2]340 ff.; advantage of trading in medium-quality and much needed goods, [2]337; gold and silver its standard of value, [3]277; customs duties, [2]19, 90,

92 f., 123, 136, 278 ff., 292 f., 340; positions of power advantageous for merchants, [2]327, 330; wealth of non-Muslim merchants, [2]281 f.; engaged in by the ruler, [2]93 ff.; a livelihood for government officials, [2]102; business arithmetic, [3]112, 122, 126 f.; *see also* prices
Comte, A., [1]lxvii*n*
Condorcet, M. J. A. N. C. de, [1]lxvii*n*
consensus (general), [1]389 ff., 396, 431, 438, 447, [2]59 f., 449, [3]7, 23 ff.
Constantine (Northwest African city), [1]xli, xlv–vi, xlviii, il, l, lviii, 129, [2]116, 221, 248*n*, 274
Constantine (Roman emperor), [1]478 f., 261
Constantinople (Istanbul), [1]lxvii*n*, xc, xcv, 23, 98, 153, 159, 329, [2]191, 193, 362
Constantinople, Straits of, [1]139, 153 ff., 160
copper, *see* metals
Copper City, [1]74*n*, 75
Copts, [1]12, 18, 23, 57, 78, 288, [2]19, 53*n*, 268, 288, 319, 325 f., 354, [3]113, 156, 186, 197*n*
Corbin, H., [2]372*n*
Córdoba, [1]xxxiii, xxxv, lviii, 140, 357, Pl. IIIa, [2]121, 236, 427, 429, 434, [3]16, 288–89, 455
Coria, [1]141
Cossyra, [2]40*n*
Creswell, K. A. C., [1]xx
Crete, [1]98, 139, 142, [2]41 f.
Crusaders, *see* Christians
Ctesiphon (al-Madâ'in), [1]101, 301, 329, [2]78, 299
culture, *see* civilization
Cureton, W., [1]403*n*, [3]69*n*
custom, habit, [1]lxxxiv; determines character, [1]254, 283; man "a child of custom," [1]258, [2]318; a second nature, [2]117; difficult to replace or uproot, [2]349, 354 f., [3]294 f., 304, 318, 363, 371 f.; determines human tolerance for foodstuffs, [1]181; changed gradually through political conditions, [1]58; disregarded or broken through by prophets, [1]437, 444, [2]118, through miracles, [1]21; luxury customs, *see* luxury
habits as qualities and colors of soul, [2]344, 354 f.; good habits the key to success, [3]218; the habit of faith, [3]40 ff.; crafts as habits, [2]346, 354 f., [3]318; definition of scientific habit, [2]426, [3]394, its acquisition, [3]294
Cyprus, [1]98, 132, 139, [2]41
Cyrillus (of Alexandria), [3]253*n*
Cyrus, *see* al-Muqawqis

D

Dabbâb, Banû, [3]475
ad-Dabbâj, Abû l-Ḥasan, [3]448–49
Dabîl (Dwîn), [1]154
ad-Dabûsî, *see* Abû Zayd ad-Dabûsî
Dageou, [1]120*n*
Dahâgh, [3]168*n*
aḍ-Ḍaḥḥâk b. Qays, [2]79
Dahlak, [1]123
Dalâṣ, [1]126, 131
Damascus, [1]lxii f., 27, 134 & *n*, 266, 357, 365, [2]101, 121, 194, 229 ff., 262 f., 299, 362, Pl. I
Damietta, [1]121, 132
ad-Damîrî, [3]103*n*
Dammar (Mount Demmer), [1]130
Danby, H., [2]261*n*
ad-Dânî, Abû 'Amr, [2]441 ff.
ad-Dânî, Abû l-Ḥasan al-Muqri', [3]456
Daniel, [1]83, 229, [2]228
ad-Dâniyâlî, [2]227 f.
Darâbjird, [1]135
Dar'ah, [1]*following* 110, 128
Daran, *see* Atlas Mountain
ad-Dâraquṭnî, [2]162 f., 168
ad-Dârimî, [2]455

Dârîn, [3]446
Darius, [3]113
Darro, [3]460n
Darwinism, [1]195, [2]423
ad-Daryûsh, Khâlid, [1]324 f.
dates: palms, [1]180; doom palms, [2]250; fecundation, [3]150; liquor (*nabîdh*), *see* wine drinking; as revenue, [1]362; given by Abû Bakr to 'Â'ishah, [1]223 f.; pits used in soothsaying, [1]214, 216
David, [1]18, 391, 422, 474, [2]53, 249, 259 f., 401, [3]114n
Dawâwidah (subtribe of the Riyâḥ), [1]1, 272, [3]420
Dâwûd al-Jawâribî, [3]69n
Dâwûd b. 'Alî (aẓ-Ẓâhirî), [3]5 f.
Dâwûd b. 'Alî b. 'Abdallâh b. (al-)'Abbâs, [1]32 & n
Dâwûd b. al-Muḥabbar b. Qaḥdham, [2]183
Daylam, [1]31, 42, 101, 156, 315, 351, 412, [2]115, 128, 133, 217, 306, [3]367
ad-Dayyân, Banû, [1]282
Dead Sea, [3]473n
Deccan, [1]127n
Dedering, S., [1]240n, [2]230n, [3]13n
Defrémery, C., [1]369n
Delafosse, M., [1]118n
Delhi, [1]370
Demmer, Mount, *see* Dammar
Denia, [1]98n, 141, [2]41, 441, [3]329
Deny, M. J., [1]74n
Derbend ("Gates"), [1]17, 155, 161, 290
Derenbourg, H., [3]376n
devils, satans, [1]186, 205 f., 211 f., 218, 222, 292, 385, 415, [2]20, 143, 326, 407, [3]72, 108, 158 f., 167
adh-Dhahabî, [2]40n, 68n, 162, 164, 172, 174, 178, 180 & n, 230n, 401n
Dharwân, well of, [3]160
Dhât al-abwâb, [1]75n
Dhât as-salâsil, [1]404n

Dhiyâb b. Ghânim, [3]417 f., 430
Dhû l-Adh'âr, [1]22, 25
Dhû l-Jaddayn, [1]281
Dhû n-Nûn al-Miṣrî, [3]191
Dhû r-Rummah, [3]383, 397
Dhûbân, [2]217
dialectics: legal, [3]31 ff., 304; philosophical, [3]141, 357
Dieterici, F., [2]138n, 415n, 423n, [3]131n
Dietrich, A., [1]361n
aḍ-Ḍimâr, [1]134n
ad-Dîmashqî, Ja'far (author of *al-Ishârah ilâ maḥâsin at-tijârah*), [2]93n, 336n, [3]378n
(ad-)Dînawar, [1]146, 263n
Diogenes, [3]115n
Djérid, *see* Jarîd
Dongola, [1]121
D'Ooge, M. L., [3]120n
doorkeeper (*ḥâjib*), [1]451, [2]7 ff., 13 ff., 24, 27, 37, 97 f., 112 f.
Doutté, E., [2]226n, [3]160n, 170n, 171n, 183n
Dozy, R., [1]xxxivn, lxvin, cii, cviii, 46n, 94n, 174n, 263n, 268n, 282n, 342n, 362n, 381n, 408n, [2]14n, 16n, 37n, 50n, 157n, 170n, 221n, 302n, 359n, 362n, 403n, 432n, [3]11n, 77n, 163n, 258n, 263n, 265n, 304n, 314n, 341n, 366n, 386n, 390n, 420n, 421n, 422n, 428n, 430n, 452n, 456n, 457n, 459n, 460n, 461n, 462n, 463n, 465n, 467n, 470n, 471n, 474n
dreams, dream interpretation, [1]163, 207 ff., 219, [2]200 f., 420, [3]70 ff., 91, 103 ff., 252, 374, 449 f., 479n
ad-Du'alî, Abû l-Aswad, [3]322 f.
Dûmat al-Jandal, [1]133
Dunlop, D. M., [1]94n, 240n, 290n, [2]138n
ad-Durûb, [1]142n, 143 f.
Dusares, [1]133n
Dussaud, R., [1]143n
ad-Duwaynî, Abû Isḥâq, [3]445 f.

dynasties, *see* government, leadership; group feeling; political science

E

Eber, [3]283
Ecija, [1]140
economics, *see* coins, coinage; commerce; labor; poverty; prices; profit; taxation; wealth
Edessa, [1]144
Edomites, [1]334, 474
education: various local methods of elementary, [3]300 f.; faulty teaching methods, [3]293 f., 300; limitation of corporal punishment, [1]261, 463, [3]306; harmful severity, [3]305 ff.; memorizing, [2]307, 430, [3]339, 353, 362, 364, 383, 392 ff.; practice in discussion, [2]429 f.; higher, scientific, [2]426 ff., [3]288 f., 292 ff., 307 f.; length of college attendance, [2]430; traveling for educational purposes, [2]434, [3]8, 12, 14, 17 f., 307 f.; endowments for higher, [2]435, 439; "he who is not educated by his parents will be educated by time," [2]419; harmful to courage and self-reliance, [1]259 f., [2]296 f.
changing prestige of teachers, [1]58 f.; teachers as a rule not wealthy, [2]334; supervision of teachers, [1]452, 463; teaching of classical Arabic, [3]353 f., 363, 365, the philological sciences, [3]301, 303 f., calligraphy, [2]378, 385 f., [3]301 f., 328, poetry, [3]301, 303 f., 307, history, [3]307, 411, music, [2]348, arithmetic, [3]122, 304; Greek education, [3]303*n*
egg: earth compared to, [1]95*n*; treating eggs to produce large chickens, [1]183; as an alchemical term, [3]242 f.
Egypt, Egyptian(s), [1]xxx f., xlvi, lviii ff., lxxxviii, xcvi, cv, 16, 18, 23 f., 41 f., 45, 48*n*, 67*n*, 100, 102, *following* 110, 121 ff., 125 f., 131 ff., 175, 180, 288, 318 f., 329, 331, 334, 344, 351, 357, 359 f., 365 f., 368, 378*n*, 413, 420, 441, 443, 456, 463, 467, 479 ff., [2]12, 14 f., 18 f., 36, 39, 42 f., 45, 53, 66 f., 71, 101, 115, 128 f., 133, 139, 224, 226 f., 229 ff., 236, 239, 243, 258, 263, 267, 274 f., 281, 283, 288, 290, 307, 321 f., 325 f., 348 ff., 378, 382, 385 f., 395, 428, 432, 435, 447*n*, 452, [3]6*n*, 10 ff., 17 ff., 113, 117, 156, 160, 289, 315, 324, 346, 438, 475 f.
Ehrenkreutz, A. S., [2]44*n*
Eilers, W., [3]135*n*
El Eubbad, *see* al-'Ubbâd (El Eubbad)
Elder, E. E., [2]312*n*
Elgood, C., [3]150*n*
Eli, [2]259
Elias, *see* Ulyûs
Elias (commentator on Aristotle), [3]131*n*
Emesa, [1]134, 143, 364*n*
Emesa (= Sevilla), [3]447
Empedocles, [3]114*n*
Enan, M. A., [1]xxxi
engineering, *see* mechanics
England, [1]68*n*, 159, 163
Enoch, [1]229*n*, [3]213*n*
Ephraim, [2]259
epistemology, *see* philosophy
Erzerum, *see* Arzan
Esau, [1]333
Escott, E. B., [3]162*n*
Esna, [1]125
Estella, [1]150
Estepa, [3]445
Estonia, [1]164
Eternal Islands, *see* Canaries

ethics, ¹78, 253 f., 261 f., 291, 385, 391, ²139, 141 ff., 192, 343 f., ³39 f., 249, 256
Ettinghausen, E. S., ¹xix
Ettinghausen, R., ¹xxiv
Euclid, ²365, ³116, 130
euphorbia, ¹181n, 183
Euphrates, ¹25n, 101 f., 134, 144 ff., 153 f., 364, ²78, 217, ³451n
European Christians, ¹57, 66, 117, 150 f., 159, 168 f., 172, 302, 330, 333, 382, 481, ²38 f., 41 f., 46, 52, 80, 101, 263, 266, 288–89, 319, 325, ³118, 283, 319, 352, 372; *see also* Christian(s)
evil eye, ³170 f.
Évora, ¹140
existence: four levels, ³69 ff., 172; order of the *existentia*, ¹lxxiv, 194 ff., ²356, 413 f., 422 f., ³81, 83, 99, 138; common to all *existentia*, ²398; subject to generation and decay, ¹278; has no reality but is created by human perception, ³86, 90 f.; not entirely encompassed by intellect, ³35 ff., 246 ff.; believed by Sufis encompassed by their mystical perception, ²82; and the religious law, ¹402; and magic, ³217 f., 226
Ezra, ²260

F

Faḍl, Âl, ¹269n, 272n
(al-)Faḍl b. ʿÎsâ, ²168
al-Faḍl b. Yaḥyâ b. Khâlid al-Barmakî, ¹31 f., 137, ²63, 392
al-Fahraj, ¹135
Fakhkh, ¹48
Fakhr-ad-dîn ar-Râzî (Ibn al-Khaṭîb), ¹xliv & n, 213n, 402, ²428, ³26n, 29, 52, 54, 143, 146, 148, 153, 164, 315
fame, ¹339, 354, ²288 f.
Fârâb, ¹149

al-Fârâbî, ²138n, 371 f., ³116, 131n, 142, 250, 254, 272, 274n, 277n, 280
Faraj (son of Barqûq), al-Malik an-Nâṣir, ¹lxii f., ²229
al-Faramâ, ¹132
Fârân (Paran), ¹100, 132, ²250
al-Farazdaq, ³397
Farghânah, ¹103, 138, 148 f.
al-Farghânî (Alfraganus), *see* Ibn al-Farghânî
al-Farghânî, Saʿîd-ad-dîn Muḥammad b. Aḥmad, ³87 & n, 88n
al-Fâriʿah bint Ṭarîf, ³378n
Fâris b. Wadrâr (Merinid wazir), ¹370 f.
al-Fârisî, Abû ʿAlî, ³313, 323, 361
Farmer, H. G., ²395n, 396n, 399n, 401n, 403n, 404n, 405n, ³184n
Fârs, ¹17, 23, 100, *following* 110, 134 f., 147, 350, 362, ²85, 115, 128, 133, 307
Fasâ, ¹135
al-Fâsî, Taqî-ad-dîn, ¹lxvin
Fâṭimah, ¹44, 405, 407n, ²165, 195
Fâṭimid (Expected), *see* Mahdî, Mahdism
Fâṭimids: origins, ¹41 ff., 413; ²210 f.; how they came into power, ²133; wealth and splendor, ¹350, 360 f., 365 f., ²51, 53; buildings, ²239; heretical beliefs, ¹44; legal system, ³11, 17 f.; able to predict the future, ²210 f.; originally used title "imam," ¹467; led prayer in person, ¹451; attitude toward the wazirate, ²13; used title "*ḥâjib*," ²15; police, ¹456; *ḥisbah*, ¹463; used the *maqṣûrah*, ²70, *ṭirâz*, ²66, umbrella, ²65; honorific surnames of, ¹467, of their amirs, ¹469 f.; Berber supporters, ¹318 f., 331, 382, 428, ²115; relations with ʿAbbâsids, ¹42, 45 f., 319, ²115, 128, ³11, with Spanish Umayyads, ¹42, 240, with Ḥamdânids, ¹286,

with Sicily, ²42; decay, ²42, 92, 263; duration of rule, ¹332
Fayyûm, ¹131, ²133
Ferguson, J., ¹lxviin
Ferrand, G., ¹22n, 75n, 118n, 120n, ³185n
Fez, ¹xxxix, xli ff., xlv, xlvii ff., li ff., lviii, lxiv, lxxxix, xci ff., xcv, cii f., 47n, 51 f., 129, 175, 180, 182n, 367n, 411, ²52n, 134, 137, 221, 236 f., 246, 273 f., 299, 339, 387, 429, ³129, 466, 468, 472, 475
Fezzan, ¹*following* 110, 125
finance, *see* coins, coinage
Fındıkoğlu, Z. F., ¹lxviin
Finland, Finns, ¹161n, 164
al-Firkâwî, Maḥmûd, ³95n
Fîrûz Shâh (of Delhi), ¹370n
Fîrûzâbâd, ¹370n
Fîrûzgûh, ¹370n
Fisch, M. H., ¹lxxxin, cxivn
Fischel, W. J., ¹xxiii, xxxi, xliin, xlivn, xlvin, xlviin, lxivn, lxxn, xcv, c, 13n, 368n, 388n, 475n, 477n, ²195n; *see also* ³484 ff.: Selected Bibliography of Ibn Khaldûn
Fischer, Frank V., ²337n
Fiṭr b. Khalîfah, ²162 f.
flags (banners), ¹471, ²48 ff., 77 f., 82, 176, 304, ³423, 444; the Darafsh-i-Kâviyân, ³168; the "tradition of the flags," ²173 f., 180
Flanders, ¹159
fleets, *see* navigation, navy
Fleischer, H. L., ¹135n
flowers, ¹37, ²295, 397, ³460n; house decoration compared to flower beds, ²361; as code writing, ²391; in poetry, ³421, 444, 446, 450 f., 466; stimulate poets, ³384; *see also* oleander; orange trees

Flügel, G., ¹10n, 27n, ²365n, 379n, ³63n, 110n, 129n, 272n, 322n, 336n
food: production requires co-operation, ¹89 f., ²271 f.; scarcity and abundance, ¹177 ff.; sources to be located near cities, ²247, 269; trading in grain, ²336, 340 f., in sugar and honey, ²341; hoarding of, ¹175, ²278, 339 f.; supervision of foodstuffs, ¹463, ²3, 7; will be plentiful in the days of the Mahdî, ²168, 170, 181 ff.
 man's taste for, ²397, ³361; only essential for his existence, ²357; necessary, ²276, 347; luxury, ¹249, 338, ²33, 274, 295, 376, ³431, 462; source of illness, ¹35 f., 180 f., ²373 ff.; fasting, ²422; absorbed by animals and plants, ³238
Forget, J., ³73n, 93n
fornication, *see* adultery, fornication
de Foucauld, C., ²49n
Fraga, ¹141
France, ¹98, *following* 110, 159
Francis, ³185
Frank, H., ¹cxiiin, ³76n
Franks, *see* European Christians
Frisia, ¹159
Frye, R. N., ¹116n
Fuḍâlah b. 'Ubayd, ¹439
al-Fuḍayl b. 'Iyâḍ, ¹33
Fück, J., ³62n
Fulton, A. S., ¹81n
Fumm aṣ-ṣilḥ, ¹348
Fusṭâṭ, ¹100, ²236n

G

Gabès, ²42, 244 ff., 304
Gabriel (archangel), ¹202, 261n, ³191
Gabrieli, F., ¹lxxviiin, ³141n
Gabrieli, G., ¹lxxxixn, c, ciiin, civn
Gafsa (Qafṣah), ¹130, ²304

Galen, ¹74n, 90, 175, 210, ³149
Galicia, Galicians, ¹150, 168, 300, 302, ²45, 52, ³352
Gandhâra, ¹127
Gandz, S., ³162n, 197n
García Gómez, E., ¹316n, ³442n, 443n
Gascogne, ¹*following* 110, 142, 150 f.
Gate City, ¹74, 75n
"Gates," *see* Derbend
Gates, Mountains of the, ¹161
Gaudefroy-Demombynes, M., ²44n, 45n, 402n, 405n
Gauthier, L., ¹108n, ³67n
Gawgaw, ¹67n, *following* 110, 118n, 119, 169
Gaza, ¹lxv
generatio aequivoca, ³245, 273, 277
Genil, ³460
Genoa, ¹151, ²41 & n
geography: shape of earth, ¹94 f., 110; distribution of land and water, ¹95 f., 108, 110; cultivated part of the earth, ¹96 f., 103 ff.; equator, ¹96 f., 108 f., 110; seven zones, ¹cvi, 96 f., 110 ff., 116, ²357, 367, 430; temperate and intemperate zones, ¹167 ff.; length of degree, ¹96 & n, 113; oceans, ¹97 ff.; main rivers, ¹101 ff.; its role in planning of cities, ²235; influence of Greek geography, ¹lxxi f.; Ibn Khaldûn's Description of the Maghrib, ¹xliii, lxiv
geomancy, ¹226 ff., ²201
geometry, ¹91n, ²363, 365, ³111 f., 116, 128 ff., 243 f.
Germany, Germans, ¹*following* 110, 152, 159 & n
Gerona, ¹142, 150
Geyer, R., ²252n
al-Ghaḍâ, Wâdî, *see* Wâdî al-Ghaḍâ
Ghadâmes, ¹130
Ghadîr Khumm, ¹403n
Ghâfiq, ¹140
Ghalwah, *see* ʿAlwah

Ghamrasen, ¹272n
Ghânah, ¹*following* 110, 118 f., 125, ³185n
Ghassân, Ghassânids, ¹266, ²264, ³343
Ghassâsah, ¹129
Ghaṭafân, Banû, ³343
al-Ghawr, *see* Ghôr
Ghâyat al-ḥakîm, *see* al-Majrîṭî, Maslamah b. Aḥmad
Ghaznah, ¹136, ²217
Ghaznawids, ²130, 133–34
al-Ghazzâlî, ¹lxxvin, 44n, 223n, 297n, 419n, 427n, ²373n, ³29, 32, 39n, 52, 54, 75, 80, 82, 92n, 143, 146, 149n, 153, 229
al-Ghazzâlî, Aḥmad, ³97n
Ghînâ, ³423
Ghiyâth al-Farq, ³423
Gh-n-w-n, Lake, ¹165
Ghôr, ¹133
Ghumârah (Berber tribe), ¹179, 327, ²197
Ghumart (Berber tribe), ²202
al-Ghûr, ¹136 f.
Ghurghûn, Lake and Mountain of, ¹157
al-Ghuzûlî, ¹xxxn, ³99n
Ghuzz, ¹*following* 110, 156 f.
Gibb, H. A. R., ¹lxxivn, ²44n
Gibbon, E., ¹lxvii
Gibeon, ²259
Gibraltar, Straits of, ¹98, 129, 140
Gideon, ²176n
Gidmîwah (Berber tribe), ¹128
Gildemeister, J., ¹94n
Gilgal, ²259
Girgashites, ¹334
Gnâwah, ³185n
de Gobineau, J. A., ¹lxviin
God, ¹lxxii f., 3 f., 261, 292 f., 299, ²32, ³252 f.; oneness, ¹53, 471, ³34 ff., 144; attributes, ³44 ff., 55, 60 ff.; beautiful names, ³176, 191, 194; divinity of Shîʿah imams, ¹406, ²186; *see also* theology

de Goeje, M. J., [1]lxxviii*n*, 21*n*, 74*n*, 94*n*, 135*n*, 220*n*, 364*n*, [2]39*n*, 380*n*
Gog and Magog, [1]96, *following* 110, 137, 149, 157 f., 161 ff., 166, 172, [3]473*n*
Goguyer, A., [1]349*n*
Goichon, A.-M., [1]91*n*, 196*n*, 197*n*, 198*n*, [3]36*n*, 73*n*, 93*n*, 217*n*
Goitein, S. D., [2]6*n*
Goldziher, I., [1]44*n*, 186*n*, 403*n*, 407*n*, [2]21*n*, 224*n*, [3]5*n*, 6*n*, 8*n*, 13*n*, 24*n*, 27*n*, 30*n*, 150*n*, 303*n*
Goliath, [1]474
Gosche, R., [3]441*n*
Gospel, *see* Bible
Goths, [1]330, [2]38, 78, 288 f., 350
Gottheil, R. J. H., [1]453*n*
Gottwaldt, I. (J.) M. E., [1]22*n*, [2]214*n*
government, leadership: the "restraining influence," [1]lxxv, 79, 84, 91 f., 260 f., 284, 305, 381, 390, 426 f., 433, [2]3, 137, 300, 343; origin of new dynasties, [2]128 ff., 298, causes of their decay and disappearance, [1]lxxx ff., 285, 296 f., 317, 328 f., 342, 346, 352, 355, 373, 376, [2]92, 95, 98, 104, 110, 113 ff., 297 ff.; harmed by astrology, [3]262 f.; the government "the world's market place," [1]46 f., [2]102 f., 287, 352; "the common people follow the religion of the ruler," [1]58, 300, [2]123, 306; mainly based on the army, [1]80, 82; oppressive rule breeds apathy, [1]258 f., [2]103 f., [3]305 f.; construction of cities, [2]235 ff.; independent city governments, [2]302 ff.; emblems, prerogatives of the ruler, [1]379, [2]48 ff., 304; duties and functions of, [2]3 ff.; protection of the currency, [1]464, [2]3, [3]270; proper style of government correspondence, [3]369 ff.; officials unable to escape from serving a decaying dynasty, [2]99 ff.
only one leader possible, [1]337, 392 ff., 421; good and bad qualities of leaders, [1]280, 291 ff., 306, 337, 353 ff., 378, 382 ff., 395 f., [2]89 f., 95, 111 f., 122, 140 ff., 297, [3]464 f.; leaders must not take unnecessary risks, [1]73; leaders favor the crafts, [2]352, 356, respect scholars and pious men, [1]292 ff., 459, [2]142, 155, disdain to be scholars themselves, [1]60, [3]314; leadership is goal of group feeling, [1]284 ff., [2]118, is vested only in members of one family, [1]54, 268 f., or in fully accepted members of tribe, [1]55; rulers dominated by others, [1]377 ff., [2]10, 113, rule with the help of clients, [1]372 ff.; law of generations for ascendancy and decay, [1]lxxxii, 278 ff., 343 ff.; financial position of ruler, [2]97 f.; advantage of obsequiousness toward leaders, [2]331 ff.; ruler pictured as an ocean in dreams, [3]107 ff.; predictions concerning the future of dynasties and rulers, [2]200 ff.
see also group feeling; political science; taxation
Gozzo, [1]142
Gråberg af Hemsö, J., [1]xcii
Graefe, M., [2]243*n*
Graf, G., [1]480*n*
grammar, [2]428, [3]187, 286, 299, 319 ff., 329, 333 f., 339, 379 f., 405; defined, [3]322, 346 f.; works on, [2]444, [3]289 ff., 313, 323 f., 356; the three vowels, [1]7; its significance for the interpretation of the Qur'ân, [1]27 f., [3]57, 323, of the *ḥadîth*, [1]200 f., 204 f., [2]463, for jurisprudence, [3]26 f.; grammatical knowledge insufficient for teaching the idiomatic

use of a language, [3]354 ff., 360, 363; grammatical terms in the title of Ibn Khaldûn's work, [1]13n
grammarians: do not recognize linguistic change, [3]345, 351, 357, 414 f.; write inferior poetry, [3]395
see also language, linguistics
Granada, [1]xxx, xxxiii, xxxv, xliii, xlivn; il, l, liii, lviii, 140, 334 f., [2]24, 447n, 458, Pl. IIb, [3]185n, 365, 396n, 398, 447 f., 452n, 460n, 461n, 465n
Greece, Greek(s), [1]lxxi, 12, 78, 136n, 153, 168n, 172, 298, 334, 382, 475, [2]203, 261, 266, 288, 326, 354, 365, [3]113 ff., 133 ff., 139, 142, 151, 197n, 319, 412; Greek language, translations from it, [1]lxxv, lxxxiv, 89, [2]22, 239n, 417, [3]115 f., 130 f., 142n, 147, 149, 151, 171n, 228n, 229n, 237n, 250; education, [3]303n; *see also* Byzantines
Green Gulf (= Persian Gulf), [1]100
Green Sea (= Surrounding Sea), [1]96
Gregory (Jirjîr), [3]474n
Griffini, E., [3]230n
Grohmann, A., [2]53n, 65n, 241n
group feeling, [1]lxi, lxxviii ff., lxxxii f., lxxxv, cx; based on blood or close client relationship, [1]264 f., 374, [2]120, 267, 302 f.; exists in different degrees of strength, [1]269n, 284 f., 328, 332 ff., 336 f., 381 f., [2]87, 119; provides protection and defense, [1]263, 313, 374, 381, [2]238; relation to nobility, [1]273 f.; not affected by a long-forgotten foreign origin, [1]55; of clients, [1]276 ff.; favors desert life, [2]267; urban, [2]303; leads to royal authority, [1]284 ff., 336, 414, sustains it, [2]97, 119, 195, but a dynasty may outlast its own, [1]314 f., 318, 372 f., [2]122; decay, [1]236 ff., 317, 344 f., [2]47, 118 f., 301
necessary for successful religious propaganda, [1]55 f., 263, 322 ff., [2]195 f., 198; strengthened by religion, [1]319 ff.; enjoyed by prophets, [1]188; of pre-Islamic poets, [3]410; undesirable, of pre-Islamic times, [1]lxxviii f., 416, 441; importance overshadowed by beginnings of Islam, [1]436 f., 444; relation to the caliphate, [1]397 ff.
see also government, leadership
Grünert, M., [2]415n
von Grunebaum, G. E., [1]44n, 249n, 417n, [3]336n, 338n, 401n
Guadalajara, [1]141
Guadix, [1]140, [3]460
Gudâlah (Berber tribe), [1]125, [2]197
Guijo, [1]140n
Guillaume, A., [3]64n
Gurganj, [1]103, 148
Guzûlah (Berber tribe), [1]125n, [2]197

H

Haarbrücker, T., [1]403n, 407n, [3]62n, 63n, 69n
Ḥabîb b. Aws, *see* Abû Tammâm
habit, *see* custom, habit
al-Hâdî ('Abbâsid caliph), [1]48 & n, 467
ḥadîth: science of, defined, [2]437, explained, [2]447 ff., systematized, [3]80; collections of, [2]393, 453 ff., [3]312; criticism, [2]158 ff., 393, 448 ff., 460, of transmitters ("personality criticism"), [1]38 f., 72, 76 f., 461n, [2]158 ff., 208 f., 449 f., [3]25, 312; abrogation, [2]447 f., 455 f., [3]25; "ambiguous," [3]46n, 101; divine (*ḥadîth qudsî*), [1]193n, [3]87 f., 98; inimitable linguistic form of, [3]397; teaching, [3]301 f., 304, 307; Ibn Khaldûn as a teacher of, [1]lxii, cv; as a

source of law, ¹60, 231 f., 454,
²459 f., ³3 ff., 23 ff., 150 f., 285,
309, 311 f., 316, 319, for the articles of faith, ³44, 301; used in
magic, ³181; important for littérateurs, ³340, 353; traditions
quoted, ¹21 & n, 44, 50, 184 ff.,
192, 200 ff., 204 f., 209, 211, 223,
227n, 228n, 229, 231 f., 254 ff.,
261, 264 f., 273, 276, 281, 289 f.,
322, 324, 343, 359, 384, 387,
392, 396 f., 403 f., 408, 414 f.,
435, 447, 459 f., ²75, 86, 131,
156 ff., 185 f., 191 ff., 203 ff.,
207 f., 249, 257, 263, 265, 285,
312, 324, 332, 335 f., 373, 375,
401, 421n, 438 f., 444n, 457 f.,
³22, 36, 41 ff., 58, 60 f., 67, 74,
78, 88n, 96n, 103 f., 107 f., 109,
128, 150 f., 160, 168 f., 262, 300,
312 f., 321, 345
al-Ḥadîthah, ¹145
Ḥaḍramawt, ¹xxxviii, 124, 169
Ḥafṣids, ¹xxxv, xxxvii, xxxix ff.,
xlv, xlvii f., l, lvi, lxxxvin, ciii,
cv, 332, 335, 342, 368, 472,
²16 ff., 24, 27, 72 f., 93n, 101 &
n, 116, 117n, 221 f., 304, ³329
Hagar, ²249 ff.
Hajar, ¹126, 134
Ḥājib b. Zurârah, ¹281 f.
al-Ḥājirî, M. Ṭ., ²3n
al-Ḥajjâj b. Yûsuf, ¹58 & n, 60,
63, 255 ff., 304, 350, 359, 373,
²22 f., 55 f., 68, 77, 253 ff., Pl. I
al-Ḥajjâj b. Yûsuf b. Maṭar, ³130n
Ḥājjî Khalîfah, ¹lxvii, 10n, 323n,
³21n, 129n, 136n, 172n, 230n,
272n, 441n
al-Ḥakam b. Hishâm b. 'Abd-ar-
Raḥmân I, ²405
al-Ḥâkim an-Nîsâbûrî, ¹187, 374n,
²71n, 157, 160, 165 ff., 176 f.,
179, 185, 451, 456
Halbâ (Arab tribe in Egypt), ³438
Halkin, A. S., ¹4n, ³69n
al-Ḥallâj, ³102, 192, 278

Ḥaly b. Ya'qûb, ¹123
Ham, ¹169 ff.
Hamadhân, ¹146, 363
Ḥamdân the Qarmaṭian, ¹42n
al-Hamdânî, ²380n
Ḥamdânids, ¹286, ²115, 129
Ḥammâd (founder of Ḥammâdid
dynasty), ²116
Ḥammâd b. Isḥâq al-Mawṣilî, ²404
Ḥammâd b. Salamah, ²170 f.
Ḥammâdids, ¹315n, ²70
Hammer-Purgstall, J., ¹c
Ḥammûdids, ¹116, ²220
Ḥamzah al-Iṣfahânî, ¹22n, ²214n,
³327n
Ḥamzah b. 'Abd-al-Muṭṭalib, ²178
Ḥanafites, ¹36n, 445, ²229, 462,
³10, 21, 28, 30, 32, 67 f., 129,
284; see also Abû Ḥanîfah
Ḥanbalites, ¹38n, ²230, ³9, 21,
65 f., 129; see also Aḥmad b.
Ḥanbal
al-Harawî, 'Abdallâh b. Muḥammad
al-Anṣârî, ³92, 95
Ḥarb b. Umayyah, ²379 f.
Harghah (Berber tribe), ¹55, 273
al-Ḥarîrî, ¹349n, ²316
al-Ḥârith b. Ḥarrâth, ²164
al-Ḥârith b. Hishâm, ¹200
al-Ḥârith b. Ka'b, Banû, ¹282
al-Ḥârith b. Kaladah, ²373n, ³150
al-Ḥârith b. Miskîn, ³11, 14, 17
Ḥarrân, ¹144, 221n
al-Ḥarrânî (alchemist), ³237
Hartmann, M., ³414n, 440n, 441n,
442n, 444n, 445n, 446n, 447n,
448n, 449n, 450n, 454n, 459n,
476n
Hartner, W., ¹4n
Hârûn ar-Rashîd, see ar-Rashîd
Hârûn b. al-Mughîrah, ²163 f.
Hârûn b. Sa'îd (Sa'd) al-'Ijlî,
²209 f.
al-Ḥaṣâ'irî, Muḥammad b. al-
'Arabî, ¹xxxviii
al-Ḥasan (doorkeeper of the caliph
al-Mahdî), ²219

al-Ḥasan al-ʿAskarī, ¹414
al-Ḥasan (b. Abī l-Ḥasan) al-Baṣrī, ¹lxxv, lxxvi*n*, ²184 f., 187, ³61, 194
al-Ḥasan b. ʿAlī b. Abī Ṭālib, ¹52, 406, 407*n*, 410, 412, 426, ²63, 163, 178, 192, 225
al-Ḥasan b. ʿAlī b. al-Ḥasan b. ʿAlī b. ʿUmar, *see* al-Uṭrūsh, an-Nâṣir
al-Ḥasan b. ʿAlī b. Muḥammad b. al-Ḥanafīyah, ¹409
al-Ḥasan b. Muḥammad (b. Khaldūn), ¹xxxvi f.
al-Ḥasan b. Muḥammad aṣ-Ṣabbâḥ, ¹413
al-Ḥasan b. Sahl, ¹39 f., 348, 349 & *n*
Ḥasan(?) b. Sarḥân, ³417
al-Ḥasan b. Yazīd as-Saʿdī, ²171 f.
al-Ḥasan b. Zayd b. Muḥammad b. Ismāʿīl b. al-Ḥasan b. Zayd b. al-Ḥasan b. ʿAlī b. Abī Ṭālib, ¹411
Hâshimite(s), ¹282, 318 f., 325, ²51, 121, 172, 176, ³307
Hâshimīyah, *see* Shīʿah
Haskūrah (Berber tribe), ¹128
Hasmoneans, ¹475 f., ²261
Ḥassān b. an-Nuʿmân, ²40
Ḥassān b. Thâbit, ¹439, ³396
al-Ḥaṣṣâr (Muḥammad b. ʿAbdallâh b. ʿAyyâsh), ³123
Ḥassūn b. al-Bawwâq (Merinid minister of finance), ¹367
Ḥâtim b. Saʿīd, ³445
Hauber, A., ³156*n*
Hausherr, J., ¹43*n*
al-Ḥawfī, Abū l-Qâsim, ³21, 128 f.
al-Ḥawqalī, *see* Ibn Ḥawqal
al-Ḥawrâʾ, ¹132
Ḥawrân, ¹133, ³414, 437
al-Hawshinī (author of a "play-poem"), ²223
Hawwârah (Berber tribe), ¹130, 318
Hay, D., ¹211*n*

Hayduck, M., ²415*n*
Hayyib (tribe), ¹131
al-Ḥazlajīyah, *see* Kharlukh
Hebrew(s), *see* Jews
Hebron, ¹lxiii
Hegel, G. W. F., ¹lxvii*n*
Helena (mother of Emperor Constantine), ²261 f.
Hell, J., ²102*n*
Heller, B., ¹357*n*, ³114*n*
Hennig, R., ¹117*n*, 118*n*
Heracleia, ¹98, 160
Heraclius (Byzantine emperor), ¹187 f., 321, ²301, ³42
Heraclius (Patriarch of Alexandria), ¹480
Herât, ¹136, 148, ³117
Herder, J. G., ¹lxvii*n*
Hermes, ¹83, 229*n*, ²246*n*, 368
Herod, ¹476, ²261
Herzfeld, E., ¹xix
Hesronita, Ioannes, ¹94*n*
Hezron, ¹18
highway robbery, ²108; safety of roads, ²3, 140, 149, 199
Ḥijâz, Ḥijâzī(s), ¹18, 42, 45, 100 f., 106, *following* 110, 122, 126, 132 f., 169, 177, 295, 319, 330 f., 365, 407, 410, 418, 441, 444, 447, 465, 467 f., 474, ²56, 115, 196, 207, 240, 247, 264, 266, 379, 404, 452 ff., 457, 461, ³4, 6, 8, 12 f., 321, 341, 421, 458, 472, 474
al-Ḥijâzī (chief of the Banū ʿÂmir), ¹271
al-Ḥijr, ¹133
Hilâl, Banū, ¹305, ²289, ³415*n*, 418 f., 430
Hilâl b. ʿÂmir, ³423
Hilâl b. ʿAmr, ²164
al-Ḥillah, *see* al-Jâmiʿayn
al-Ḥillī, Ṣafī-ad-dīn, ³476
Ḥimṣ, *see* Emesa
Ḥimyar, Ḥimyarite(s), ¹22 f., 266, 283, 296, 298, 308, ²241, 354,

379 ff., 445, ³282 f., 347, 412, 417
Hind, ¹32
Hind (daughter of an-Nuʿmân of al-Ḥîrah), ²252n
al-Hind, see India
Hintâtah (Berber tribe), ¹128
al-Ḥîrah, ¹24, 25n, 101, 134, 145, ²252n, 379, ³451n
Hishâm (b. ʿUrwah), ²166
Hishâm al-Muʾayyad, b. al-Ḥakam, ¹61, 380, ³328
Hishâm b. ʿAbd-al-Malik, ¹424,

history, historians: defined, ¹6, 71; authoritative histories, ¹7 f., 63 f.; uselessness of short historical handbooks, ¹10; highly regarded in early Islamic times, ¹56; historical knowledge needed by secretaries, ²31; studied by littérateurs and poets, ³340 f., 367, 410 f.; teaching of history, ³307; Ibn Khaldûn as teacher of, ¹lx f., cv
  historical truth, ¹7, 71 ff., 75 f., 358 f., 371; errors with figures, ¹16 ff., 321, 330, 352, 371; fondness for slandering historical personalities, ¹28 ff., 40; fame depends on historians, ²88 f.; historians tradition-bound, ¹9 f., 62 f.; knowledge and insight required of historians, ¹55 f.; their need for careful observation of changes in conditions, ¹56 ff., 368 ff.; history and philosophy, ¹12, 16; need for a new approach to writing history, ¹65
Ḥiṣn al-Khawâbî, see Maṣyât
Hît, ¹145
Hitti, P. K., ¹lxvin, 407n
Hoenerbach, W., ¹94n, 130n, 131n, 151n, 152n, 159n, ²244n, ³457n, 458n, 476n
Holmyard, E. J., ³272n

Holy Land, ²259; an alchemical cover name, ³244
Holy War, see military science, warfare
Homer, ³412
homosexuality, ¹38 f., ²295 f.; in poetry, ³444, 449, 451 ff., 461 f., 470 f., 478
Honigmann, E., ¹97n, 112n, 154n
Horovitz, J., ¹4n, 21n, 26n, 356n, ²61n, 84n, 185n, 203n, 438n, 445n, ³369n
Horovitz, S., ³62n
horses, see animals
Horten, M., ¹lxxivn
Hourani, G. F., ²39n
Houtsma, M. T., ¹403n
Hrbek, J., ¹161n
Hubert, A., ³96n
Hûd, ²380
Ḥudayr, Banû, ²99
Ḥudhayfah b. Badr al-Fazârî, ¹281 f.
Ḥudhayfah b. al-Yamân, ²207 f.
Hudhayl, Banû, ¹266, 441, ³343
Hûdites of Saragossa, ¹317, 335, ³185n
Huesca, ¹150
Huete, ¹141
Hujwîrî, ³39n, 76n, 91n
Hûlâgû b. Ṭûlî b. Dûshî Khân, ²128, 219, ³19
Hulubbâ (Arab tribe in Egypt), ³438
Ḥulwân, ¹146, 362
humor, ¹27 f., 33 f., 326, 361n, ³266n, 370
Hunayn, ¹lii f., lviii, 129
Ḥunayn, ¹419
Ḥunayn b. Isḥâq, ³130, 303n
Hungary, ¹159
Hurgronje, C. S., ³416
al-Ḥûrînî, Naṣr, ¹xxv, xcii, cii f., 237n
Hurmus (= the following?), ³186
Hurmuz, ¹135
al-Hurmuzân, ²21 & n
Hurmuzdâfrîd, ²215

al-Ḥusayn b. ʻAlî b. Abî Ṭâlib, [1]325, 406, 407*n*, 410, 412, 426, 435, 438, 443 ff., [2]178
al-Ḥusayn b. al-Ḥasan b. ʻAlî b. ʻAlî Zayn-al-ʻâbidîn al-Afṭas, [2]257–58
al-Ḥuṣayn b. Numayr as-Sakûnî, [2]252
al-Ḥusayn b. al-Qâsim b. Wahb, *see* Ibn Wahb, al-Ḥusayn b. al-Qâsim
al-Ḥuṣrî, [3]389*n*, 390*n*, 391*n*
al-Ḥuṭay'ah, [3]396–97
Ḥuyayy b. Akhṭab, [2]206 f.
Hyacinth (Ruby) Island, [1]138

Ibañez, E., [2]17*n*, 68*n*
Ibiza, [1]139, [2]41
Ibn ʻAbbâd, *see* ʻAbbâdids of Sevilla
Ibn al-Abbâr (author of a prediction poem), [2]221 f.
Ibn al-Abbâr (historian), [2]222*n*, 380 f., [3]395*n*, 449*n*
Ibn (al-)ʻAbbâs, *see* ʻAbdallâh b. (al-)ʻAbbâs
Ibn ʻAbd-al-Barr, [1]266*n*, [2]463, [3]48
Ibn ʻAbd-al-Ḥakam, [3]10 f., 14; *see also* ʻAbd-ar-Raḥmân b. ʻAbdallâh b. ʻAbd-al-Ḥakam
Ibn ʻAbd-al-Munʻim, *see* Ibn Munʻim
Ibn ʻAbd-al-Muʻṭî az-Zawâwî, *see* Ibn Muʻṭî
Ibn ʻAbd-as-Salâm, 'Izz-ad-dîn, [3]12
Ibn ʻAbd-as-Salâm, Muḥammad al-Hawwârî, [1]xxxix, xlii, lxxii*n*, [2]428, [3]19–20
Ibn ʻAbdrabbih, [1]32, 37*n*, 39, 266*n*, 304*n*, 407*n*, 417*n*, 424*n*, 427*n*, [2]102*n*, 403*n*, 419*n*, [3]364, 378*n*, 411, 441 & *n*
Ibn ʻAbdûn (author on *ḥisbah* in Sevilla), [1]261*n*
Ibn Abî ʻÂmir, al-Manṣûr, [1]61, 63, 316, 378, 380, [2]14, 441
Ibn Abî l-ʻAqb, [2]224 f.
Ibn Abî Du'âd, [1]456
Ibn Abî l-Faḍl, *see* Muḥammad b. Abî l-Faḍl b. Sharaf
Ibn Abî Ḥafṣ, *see* Ḥafṣids
Ibn Abî Ḥajalah at-Tilimsânî, [1]80*n*, 356*n*, [3]99*n*
Ibn Abî Ḥâtim, [2]161, 169*n*, 172, 178*n*, [3]56*n*
Ibn Abî Jamrah, Abû Bakr, [2]381
Ibn Abî Khaythamah, [2]158–59
Ibn Abî Khinzîr, [3]165*n*
Ibn Abî Maryam (court jester of ar-Rashîd), [1]28*n*, 33 f.
Ibn Abî Maryam, Saʻîd (*ḥadîth* transmitter), [2]207, 209
Ibn Abî Rabîʻah, *see* ʻUmar b. Abî Rabîʻah
Ibn Abî Sarḥ, [1]333
Ibn Abî Ṭâhir Ṭayfûr, [2]139*n*
Ibn Abî Ṭâlib al-Qayrawânî (author on dream interpretation), [3]110
Ibn Abî ʻUmârah, [1]xxxvii
Ibn Abî Uṣaybiʻah, [1]35*n*, 81*n*, 240*n*, 361*n*, [2]214*n*, 373*n*, [3]130*n*, 150*n*
Ibn Abî Wâṭîl, [2]188, 190 ff.
Ibn Abî Zayd, Abû Muḥammad al-Mâlikî al-Qayrawânî, [1]lxxii, 208*n*, 223, 261, 264*n*, 333, [2]75*n*, 108*n*, 399*n*, [3]15 f., 48, 286, 306
Ibn Adham, *see* Ibrâhîm b. Adham
Ibn ʻAdî, [2]169, 173 f., 180, 209
Ibn al-ʻAfîf (Muḥammad b. ʻAfîf-ad-dîn at-Tilimsânî), [3]92
Ibn al-Aḥmar, *see* Naṣrids (of Granada)
Ibn al-Aḥmar, Ismâʻîl b. Yûsuf, [1]xxx
Ibn al-Aḥmar, Muḥammad b. Yûsuf, *see* Muḥammad I (of Granada)
Ibn al-Akfânî (tenth-century Baghdâdî jurist), [1]46

Ibn Aktham, *see* Yaḥyâ b. Aktham
Ibn al-'Amîd, *see* al-Makîn
Ibn 'Ammâr (of Tripoli), [2]101
Ibn al-Anbârî, [3]329
Ibn 'Aqb, *see* Ibn Abî l-'Aqb
Ibn (al-)'Arabî, [1]lxxi, 240*n*, 322*n*, 323*n*, [2]187, 189 f., 224, 398*n*, [3]39*n*, 88*n*, 92, 95*n*, 97*n*, 98*n*, 172, 214*n*
Ibn al-'Arabî, *see* 'Abdallâh b. Muḥammad b. al-'Arabî
Ibn al-'Arabî, Abû Bakr Muḥammad b. 'Abdallâh al-Mâlikî al-Ishbîlî, [1]423*n*, 446, 470, [3]10, 32, 284*n*, 303 f.
Ibn 'Arafah al-Warghamî, [1]lvi f.
Ibn Arfa'-ra'sah, [3]442
Ibn al-'Arîf, [1]322*n*
Ibn 'Asâkir, [1]26*n*
Ibn al-'Âṣî, Abû Bakr, [2]381
Ibn 'Aṭâ'llâh (Mâlikite jurist), [3]18
Ibn 'Aṭîyah (Almohad wazir), [2]15
Ibn 'Aṭîyah, Abû Muḥammad ('Abd-al-Ḥaqq b. Ghâlib), [2]446
Ibn al-Athîr, [1]lxx f., lxxix, cvi, 22*n*, 23*n*, 32*n*, 33*n*, 45*n*, 46*n*, 48*n*, 409*n*, [2]52*n*, 82*n*, 101*n*, 121*n*, 139*n*, 140*n*, 143*n*, 144*n*, 145*n*, 147*n*, 148*n*, 149*n*, 227*n*, 228*n*
Ibn al-Athîr, Majd-ad-dîn, [1]lxxv*n*, 204*n*, 229*n*, [2]194*n*, 336*n*, [3]22*n*, 346*n*
Ibn al-'Aṭṭâr, [2]463
Ibn 'Awf (Ismâ'îl b. Makkî), [3]18
Ibn al-'Awwâm, [3]152
Ibn al-Azraq, Muḥammad b. 'Alî b. Muḥammad, [1]lxvi*n*
Ibn Bâdîs, Abû 'Alî (judge of Constantine), [2]221
Ibn Bâjjah (Avempace), [1]240*n*, [2]138*n*, [3]116, 272*n*, 443 f.
Ibn Bakkâr (Bakr) (Muḥammad b. Yaḥyâ, judge of Granada), [2]458 & *n*, 459
Ibn al-Bannâ', Abû l-'Abbâs al-Marrâkushî, [1]235*n*, 238, [2]383*n*, [3]121, 123, 126*n*, 137
Ibn Baqî, Yaḥyâ, [3]442 f.
Ibn Bashîr (Mâlikite jurist), [3]15, 16*n*, 288
Ibn Bashkuwâl, [2]381*n*
Ibn Bashrûn, 'Uthmân b. 'Abd-ar-Raḥîm, [3]230*n*
Ibn Bassâm, [1]lxxvi*n*, 316*n*, 350, [2]351*n*, [3]11*n*, 364*n*, 441*n*
Ibn al-Baṭḥâwî ('Alid jurist), [1]46
Ibn Baṭṭâl ('Alî b. Khalaf), [2]459
Ibn Baṭṭûṭah, [1]369 f.
Ibn al-Bawwâb, [2]385, 388
Ibn Bishrûn, Abû Bakr, [3]230, 245
Ibn Bukayr, [2]453
Ibn Bukhtîshû', *see* Jibrîl b. Bukhtîshû'
Ibn Burrâl, Muḥammad b. Sa'd, [1]xxxviii
Ibn Buṭlân, [1]45*n*
Ibn Daqîq-al-'îd, Taqî-ad-dîn, [3]12
Ibn Darrâj al-Qasṭallî, [3]364
Ibn Dhî n-Nûn, *see* al-Ma'mûn b. Dhî n-Nûn
Ibn Dhî Yazan, [1]360
Ibn Dihâq (Dahhâq), Ibrâhîm b. Yûsuf, [3]90 f.
Ibn Diḥyah, [1]8*n*, [3]444*n*
Ibn Durayd, [2]336*n*, [3]329
Ibn Duwayrîdah, *see* Alms(?) b. Duwayrîdah
Ibn al-Faḍl, *see* Abû l-Ḥasan b. al-Faḍl
Ibn Faḍlallâh al-'Umarî, [3]127*n*
Ibn al-Fakhkhâr, 'Abdallâh b. Ḥasan, [1]xcii f., ic
Ibn al-Faqîh, [1]75*n*
Ibn al-Faraḍî, [1]456*n*
Ibn al-Farghânî (Alfraganus), [3]135
Ibn Farḥûn, [1]xli*n*, 34*n*, 471*n*, [2]265*n*, 428*n*, [3]11*n*, 13*n*, 14*n*, 15*n*, 16*n*, 18*n*, 441*n*
Ibn al-Fâriḍ, [3]87, 92
Ibn Farrûkh al-Qayrawânî, 'Abdallâh, [2]207, 209, 380 f.
Ibn Fûrak, [3]46*n*
Ibn Gorion, [1]477

Ibn Ḥabîb, *see* ʻAbd-al-Malik b. Ḥabîb
Ibn Ḥajar, ^{1}xlii & *n*, liv, lxvi & *n*, xcv, xcvi*n*, 8*n*, 26*n*, 27–28*n*, 33*n*, 38*n*, 39*n*, 200*n*, 207*n*, 255*n*, 256*n*, 398*n*, 439*n*, 456*n*, ^{2}21*n*, 40*n*, 55*n*, 158*n*, 159*n*, 160*n*, 161*n*, 162*n*, 163*n*, 164*n*, 165*n*, 166*n*, 167*n*, 168*n*, 169*n*, 170*n*, 171*n*, 172*n*, 173*n*, 174*n*, 175*n*, 177*n*, 178*n*, 179*n*, 180*n*, 181*n*, 183*n*, 184*n*, 198*n*, 207*n*, 209*n*, 229*n*, 230*n*, 246*n*, 257*n*, 265*n*, 380*n*, 401*n*, 453*n*, 458*n*, ^{3}13*n*, 14*n*, 16*n*, 29*n*, 61*n*, 117*n*, 229*n*, 324*n*, 365*n*, 366*n*
Ibn al-Ḥâjib, Abû ʻAmr, ^{1}198*n*, ^{2}428 f., ^{3}16, 18 f., 29 f., 288 ff., 324
Ibn al-Ḥakîm, Muḥammad, ^{1}xlv f., 368
Ibn Ḥamdûn (author of the *Tadhkirah*), ^{1}361*n*, 419*n*, 453*n*, ^{2}29*n*, 31*n*, 33*n*
Ibn al-Ḥammâd (astronomer), ^{3}136*n*
Ibn Ḥammâd (historian), ^{2}57, 210*n*, 211*n*
Ibn al-Ḥanafîyah, ^{1}406, 407 & *n*, 409, 444, ^{2}174, 176 f.
Ibn Ḥanbal, *see* Aḥmad b. Ḥanbal
Ibn Hâni', ^{1}45*n*(?), ^{3}393, 411
Ibn Hardûs, ^{3}445
Ibn Harmah, ^{3}403–4
Ibn Hârûn (ʻAbdallâh b. Muḥammad), ^{3}20
Ibn Hâshim, *see* Shukr b. Hâshim
Ibn Ḥawqal, ^{1}116, 131*n*, ^{2}367*n*
Ibn Ḥawshab, ^{2}211
Ibn al-Haytham, ^{3}133
Ibn Ḥayyân, Ḥayyân b. Khalaf, ^{1}xxxiii, xxxiv*n*, 8, 9*n*, 350, ^{3}364, 446 f.
Ibn Ḥázm, Abû Muḥammad, ^{1}xxxiii, 21*n*, 52*n*, 189*n*, 208*n*, 219*n*, 282*n*, 322*n*, 414, ^{2}60, 171(?), 463, ^{3}6, 26*n*, 348*n*
Ibn Ḥazmûn, ^{3}447 f.
Ibn Ḥibbân, ^{1}39 & *n*, ^{2}170, 171*n*, 172, 178, 181
Ibn Ḥijjî, Yaḥyâ, ^{1}xcviii
Ibn Hishâm, ^{1}21*n*, 22*n*, 23*n*, 25*n*, 219*n*, 360*n*, 396*n*, 404*n*, 429*n*, 436*n*, ^{2}158*n*, 206*n*, 251*n*, ^{3}74*n*
Ibn Hishâm, Jamâl-ad-dîn, ^{1}349*n*, ^{3}289 f., 324
Ibn Hubayrah, ^{1}373, ^{2}55
Ibn Hûd, *see* Hûdites of Saragossa
Ibn Ḥudayr (*ḥâjib* of Spanish Umayyads), ^{2}14 & *n*
Ibn Hudhayl al-Andalusî, ^{1}19*n*, 183*n*
Ibn ʻIdhârî al-Marrâkushî, ^{1}42*n*, 95*n*
Ibn al-ʻImâd, ^{2}164*n*, 230*n*, 442*n*, 458*n*, ^{3}11*n*, 18*n*, 29*n*, 50*n*, 398*n*
Ibn al-Imâm, Abû l-Faḍl, ^{1}240*n*
Ibn al-Imâm, Abû Mûsâ ʻÎsâ, ^{2}428
Ibn al-Imâm, Abû Zayd ʻAbd-ar-Raḥmân, ^{2}428
Ibn Isḥâq, ^{1}7, 25, 56, 401, ^{2}183, 206
Ibn Isḥâq, Abû l-ʻAbbâs ʻAlî (astronomer), ^{3}136 & *n*, 137
Ibn Jâbir (Spanish littérateur), ^{3}365
Ibn Jaʻd aṣ-Ṣiqillî, ^{3}21*n*
Ibn Jaʻfar (Muḥammad b. Jaʻfar b. Abî Ṭâlib?), ^{1}426
Ibn Jaḥdar al-Ishbîlî, Abû l-Ḥasan, ^{3}455, 458 f.
Ibn Jaḥsh, *see* ʻAbdallâh b. Jaḥsh
Ibn Jâmiʻ (Almohad wazir), ^{2}15
Ibn al-Jawzî, ^{1}27*n*, 45*n*, 46*n*, 370*n*, ^{2}456, ^{3}14*n*, 29*n*, 64*n*, 179*n*
Ibn al-Jayyâb, ^{3}365
Ibn Jinnî, ^{3}289, 325
Ibn Juljul, ^{1}81*n*, 82*n*
Ibn Jurhum, Ma/uḍâḍ, ^{2}252
Ibn al-Kalbî, ^{1}7, 22
Ibn al-Kammâd, ^{3}136
Ibn Kathîr, ^{1}4*n*, 16*n*, 44*n*, 186*n*, 229*n*, 419*n*, 426*n*, 466*n*, ^{2}86*n*, 176*n*, 185*n*, 229 f., 241*n*, 259*n*, 379*n*, 381*n*, ^{3}18*n*, 88*n*, 92*n*, 475*n*

Ibn Khafâjah, [3]386

Ibn Khalaf al-Jazâ'irî, [3]449

Ibn Khaldûn (*see also* Abû l-Faḍl, b. Khaldûn; Abû Muslim 'Amr ['Umar?] b. Aḥmad, b. Khaldûn; 'Alî b. 'Abd-ar-Raḥmân, b. Khaldûn; al-Ḥasan b. Muḥammad, b. Khaldûn; Kurayb, b. Khaldûn; Muḥammad, brother of Kurayb b. Khaldûn; Muḥammad b. 'Abd-ar-Raḥmân, b. Khaldûn; Muḥammad b. al-Ḥasan b. Muḥammad, b. Khaldûn; Muḥammad b. Muḥammad, b. Khaldûn; Muḥammad b. Muḥammad b. al-Ḥasan, b. Khaldûn; Muḥammad b. Muḥammad b. Muḥammad, b. Khaldûn; Yaḥyâ b. Muḥammad, b. Khaldûn): birth, [1]xxxviii; racial background, [1]xxxiv; ancestors, [1]xxxiii ff., xxxviii; father, [1]xxxviii, xl, [2]222; mother, [1]xl; brothers, [1]xxxviii, xl f., l; family, [1]xlv ff., il, liii, lviii, lxi f., lxiv*n*, 368*n*

first position, as *ṣâḥib al-'alâmah*, [1]xli; relations with the Merinids, [1]xl ff., xlvii ff.; secretary to Abû 'Inân, [1]xlvii; imprisoned in Fez, [1]xlvii; secretary of state of Abû Sâlim, [1]xlviii; in charge of the *maẓâlim* in Fez, [1]xlviii; in Granada, December 1362 to February 1365, [1]il f.; visit to Sevilla in 1364, [1]il; in Ḥafṣid service, March 1365, [1]l; relations with Abû Ḥammû of Tlemcen, [1]li f.; in charge of tribal affairs for the Merinid 'Abd-al-'Azîz, [1]lii; second stay in Fez, autumn of 1372 to autumn of 1374, [1]lii; in Qal'at Ibn Salâmah, 1375–78, [1]liii, lv f.; in Tunis at the court of Abû l-'Abbâs, November/December 1378 to October 1382, [1]lvi ff.; in Egypt December 8, 1382, [1]lviii; relations with Barqûq, [1]lix, lxii; judgeships, [1]lxi ff., lxv; pilgrimage to Mecca, [1]lviii, lxii, to the holy places in Palestine, [1]lxii f.; visits to Damascus, [1]lxii f., [2]229 f.; contact with Timur, [1]xliii, xliv*n*, lxiii ff.; encounter with the Ottoman ambassador, [1]lxv; death, [1]lxv

personality and character, [1]xlvi, xlviii, li, lix, lxi, lxiii, lxv; attachment to Spain, [1]xxxvi ff., lxxxvi; teachers, [1]xxxviii ff., xliii f., lxxii*n*; personal contacts with scholars, [1]238 & *n*, 369*n*, [2]195, 197, 220, 221*n*, 229, 334, 339, 458 f., [3]94, 99, 196*n*, 269, 340, 395 f., 398, 407 f.; the *Muqaddimah*, [1]liii ff., lx f., lxviii ff., 77, 83, [2]124; the *'Ibar*, [1]liv f., ciii, 10 ff., 65, 269*n*, and *passim*; the *Autobiography*, [1]xxix, xliii, lxviii, cxv, and *passim*; the *Lubâb al-Muḥaṣṣal*, [1]xxix*n*, xlv, xcv f.; his work on Sufism, [1]xlv*n*; works not yet recovered, [1]xxx*n*, xliii ff.; handwriting, [1]xcii ff., Pl. I; style, [1]lxviii f., cviii, cxi f.; interest in poetry, [1]xxxix, xlii, xlv, lxiv, xcii, xcvi, cv, cvii; personal observations of the wealth of officials, [1]368, of a person fasting for forty days, [1]182, of magic, [1]213, 238*n*, 243, [3]160 ff., 164 f., 218*n*; scholarship, [1]xliii, lxx f., lxxxvi, cv ff., cxii f., cxiv*n*; principal sources, [1]lxxxiv ff.; originality, [1]xliii, lxxxvi; influence of his work, [1]lxv ff., xc; teaching positions in Tunis, [1]lvi, at al-Azhar, [1]lx, at Qamḥîyah College, [1]lx f., at Ẓâhirîyah College, [1]lx, lxii, at Ṣurghatmishîyah College, [1]lx, lxii, 34*n*; President of Baybars Institute, [1]lxii

Ibn Khallikân, [1]365, 366*n*, [2]225, 379*n*, [3]33*n*

Ibn al-Khaṭîb, *see* Fakhr-ad-dîn ar-Râzî

Ibn al-Khaṭîb, Lisân-ad-dîn, Abû ʻAbdallâh, [1]xxix f., xlii & n, xliv f., il f., liii, lxxix, xcii, [2]54n, 320n, 429n, 458n, [3]98–99, 143n, 365n, 366, 396, 398n, 442n, 444n, 450, 459 f., 461n

Ibn Khazar al-Bajâ'î, [3]450

Ibn Khirâsh, [2]162

Ibn Khurradâdhbih, [1]74n, 95n, 116, 127n, 135n, 137n, 145n, 146n, 153n, 163, 363n, 364n

Ibn Khuwâzmandâd (Khuwayrmandâd), [3]13 & n

Ibn Kisrâ al-Mâlaqî, [1]xxxivn

Ibn Kulthûm, *see* ʻAmr b. Kulthûm

Ibn Lahîʻah, *see* ʻAbdallâh b. Lahîʻah

Ibn al-Lahîb, [3]17 & n

Ibn al-Liḥyânî, *see* Abû Yaḥyâ Zakarîyâ' b. Aḥmad (b.) al-Liḥyânî

Ibn al-Madînî, [2]177

Ibn Maʻîn, [2]163, 167 f., 173 f., 177 f., 181 f., 185, 209

Ibn Mâjah, [2]157, 165, 167 f., 172, 174, 177, 180, 257, [3]42n

Ibn al-Mâjishûn, [3]16

Ibn Mâlik, [3]289, 291, 323 f., 337

Ibn Manẓûr, *see Lisân al-ʻArab*

Ibn Mardanîsh, [1]335

Ibn Martîn, Abû Bakr, [3]456

Ibn Marzûq, Muḥammad b. Aḥmad, [1]xl

Ibn Masʻûd, [1]lxxivn, [2]158 f., 172, 174

Ibn al-Mawwâz, [3]11

Ibn al-Mu'adhdhin, ʻAlî (poet from Tlemcen), [3]471

Ibn Mu'ahhil (Mûhal), [3]445

Ibn Mufarrij, Abû ʻAbdallâh, [2]381

Ibn al-Mughayribî, [3]229, 269n

Ibn al-Muhallab (commentator on al-Bukhârî), [2]459

Ibn Muḥriz (Mâlikite jurist), Abû l-Qâsim, [3]15

Ibn al-Muḥtasib (ancestor of Ibn Khaldûn), [1]xxxv, xxxvii

Ibn Mujâhid, *see* ʻAlî b. Mujâhid (ruler of Denia and the Baleares)

Ibn Mujâhid, Muḥammad b. Aḥmad aṭ-Ṭâ'î, [3]50

Ibn al-Munammar aṭ-Ṭarâbulusî (Mâlikite jurist), [3]21, 129

Ibn Munʻim (Muḥammad b. ʻÎsâ b. ʻAbd-al-Munʻim), [3]123

Ibn al-Muntâb, [3]13

Ibn al-Muqaffaʻ, [1]82, 357n, [3]393

Ibn Muqlah, [2]385

Ibn al-Muraḥḥal, *see* Mâlik b. al-Muraḥḥal

Ibn Murrânah, [2]220, [3]475

Ibn al-Muʻtazz, [3]393, 404 f.

Ibn Muʻṭî (Yaḥyâ b. ʻAbd-al-Muʻṭî az-Zawâwî), [3]324

Ibn Muyassar, [3]17

Ibn an-Nabîh, [3]393

Ibn an-Nadîm, [1]27n, 221n, 235n, 361n, [2]365n, 379n, [3]63n, 110n, 139n, 229n, 282n, 322n, 336n

Ibn an-Naḥwî, [3]395

Ibn an-Nuʻmân (Shîʻah jurist), [1]46

Ibn Qâḍî Shuhbah, [1]xlvin

Ibn Qasî, [1]322, 323 & n, [2]187

Ibn al-Qâsim (Mâlikite jurist), [3]11, 14 ff., 286

Ibn al-Qaṣṣâr, Abû l-Ḥasan (Mâlikite jurist), [3]14, 32

Ibn al-Qaṣṣâr, Aḥmad (teacher of Ibn Khaldûn), [1]xxxix

Ibn Qayyim al-Jawzîyah, [3]95n

Ibn Qilâbah, [1]26 f.

Ibn al-Qirrîyah, [2]225

Ibn Qutaybah, [1]47n, 58n, 80n, 220n, 427n, 433n, [2]102n, 246n, 275n, 351n, 402n, 415n, [3]340

Ibn Quzmân, [3]455, 457

Ibn ar-Rafʻah, [3]12

Ibn ar-Râ'is, [3]447

Ibn ar-Râmî, [2]361n

Ibn ar-Raqîq, [1]9, 360, [2]210, [3]363

Ibn ar-Raqqâm (Muḥammad b. Ibrâhîm?), [3]224

Ibn Râshid (Muḥammad b. 'Abdallâh al-Qafṣî), [3]20, 110
Ibn Rashîq, [1]10, 316n, [2]402n, 403, [3]321n, 336n, 338, 364, 381n, 384 & n, 385n, 387, 388n, 389n, 390n, 391n, 399n, 404n, 405 f., 408
Ibn Rashîq, al-Ḥasan b. 'Atîq (Mâlikite jurist), [3]17 f.
Ibn ar-Râsîn, [3]447n
Ibn Riḍwân al-Mâlaqî, Abû l-Qâsim 'Abdallâh b. Yûsuf, [1]xl, [3]395
Ibn Rumâḥis, [2]40
Ibn Rushd, *see* Averroes
Ibn Rushd, Muḥammad b. Aḥmad (grandfather of Averroes), [3]16, 288
Ibn as-Sâ'âtî, [3]30, 32
Ibn aṣ-Ṣabbâgh, Muḥammad b. Muḥammad, [1]xl
Ibn Sab'în, [2]187–88, [3]92, 172n
Ibn aṣ-Ṣâbûnî, Abû Bakr, [3]448 f.
Ibn Sa'd, [1]256n, 398n, 422n, 466n, [2]161
Ibn aṣ-Ṣaffâr, Muḥammad, [1]xlii
Ibn Sahl al-Isrâ'îlî, *see* al-Isrâ'îlî, Ibrâhîm b. Sahl
Ibn Sa'îd, [1]xcvin, 22n, 101n, 118n, 120, 316n, [2]24n, [3]441n, 443n, 445 f., 446n, 447 f., 455, 459
Ibn aṣ-Ṣalâḥ, Abû 'Amr, [2]168n, 448n, 451 & n, 454n, 455 f., 459
Ibn aṣ-Ṣalt (mathematician), [3]130, 135
Ibn as-Samḥ (Aṣbagh b. Muḥammad), [3]126, 135, 230
Ibn as-Sammâk, [1]33
Ibn Sanâ'-al-Mulk, [3]443n, 445n, 454
Ibn Ṣayyâd, [1]205, 207
Ibn Sayyid-an-nâs, [1]xcvin, 186n, 330n, 404n
Ibn Sebuktigîn, *see* Ghaznawids
Ibn Sha'bân, Abû Isḥâq, [3]11
Ibn Shâhîn (author on dream interpretation), [3]108n, 109n
Ibn Sharaf, [1]316, 470, [3]364
Ibn Shâs, [3]18
Ibn Shibrîn, [3]365
Ibn Shu'ayb, Abû l-'Abbâs, [3]395
Ibn Shu'ayb ad-Dukkâlî (al-Haskûrî?), Abû 'Abdallâh, [2]428
Ibn Shujâ' (poet from Tâzâ), [3]468, 470
Ibn Sîdah, [3]329
Ibn as-Sikkît, [3]331
Ibn Sînâ, *see* Avicenna
Ibn Sîrîn, [3]108n, 109n, 110
Ibn Ṣulayḥah (judge of Jabalah), *see* 'Ubaydallâh b. Manṣûr, Ibn Ṣulayḥah (judge of Jabalah)
Ibn Surayj (jurist), [3]332
Ibn Surayj (singer), [2]404
Ibn Tâfrâgîn, [1]xli, [3]427n, 428, 429n, 430 f.
Ibn Taghrîbirdî, [1]366n, 368n
Ibn Ṭarîf, al-Walîd, [3]378
Ibn Tâshfîn, *see* Yûsuf b. Tâshfîn
Ibn Taymîyah, [1]lxxivn
Ibn Thâbit (Mâlikite jurist), [3]21, 128
Ibn Tîfalwît, [3]443 f.
Ibn at-Tilimsânî, [3]84
Ibn at-Tîn (commentator on al-Bukhârî), [2]459
Ibn aṭ-Ṭiqṭaqâ, [1]348n
Ibn Ṭufayl, [1]108n, [2]372n
Ibn Ṭûlûn, Aḥmad, [1]374
Ibn Tûmart (Mahdî of the Almohads), [1]53 ff., 273, 322 f., 471 f., [2]57, 66, [3]185(?)
Ibn al-Ukhûwah (Ukhuwwa), [1]324n, 328n, 362n, 453n
Ibn 'Ulayyah, [2]161
Ibn 'Umar, *see* 'Abdallâh b. 'Umar
Ibn 'Umayr (Fâsî poet from Spain), [3]466
Ibn 'Uthmân, *see* Ottomans
Ibn Wahb, 'Abdallâh, [2]453 & n
Ibn Wahb, al-Ḥusayn b. al-Qâsim ('Abbâsid wazir), [2]228
Ibn Waḥshîyah, [3]151n, 156n, 226; *see also Nabataean Agriculture*

Ibn Yûnus (Mâlikite jurist), ³15 f., 288
Ibn Yûnus, Abû Sa'îd (historian), ²381 & n
Ibn Zabâlah, ²453n
Ibn az-Zâhid al-Ishbîlî, Abû 'Amr, ³456
Ibn az-Zamlakânî (Zamalkânî), Muḥammad b. Aḥmad b. Muḥammad, ¹lxvin
Ibn Zamrak, ¹liii, ²447n
Ibn az-Zaqqâq, ³465n
Ibn Zarzar, Ibrâhîm, ¹xlii
Ibn Zaytûn, see Abû l-Qâsim b. Abî Bakr b. Zaytûn
Ibn az-Zayyât ('Abbâsid wazir), ³393
Ibn az-Zayyât, Abû Mahdî 'Îsâ, ³94 f., 98 f.
Ibn Zîrî, see Buluggîn b. Zîrî
Ibn az-Zubayr, 'Abdallâh, ¹27 f., 426n, 432, 435, 438, 440, 444, 446 f., ²56, 64, 252 ff., ³474
Ibn Zuhr (Avenzoar), ³149
Ibn Zuhr, Abû Bakr, ³441, 443 ff.
Ibn Zuhr, see Abû l-Khaṭṭâb b. Zuhr
Ibn Zûlâq, ¹28n
Ibrâhîm, see Abraham
Ibrâhîm (b. Suwayd), ²172, 174
Ibrâhîm al-Mawṣilî, ²404, 405n
Ibrâhîm b. 'Abd-aṣ-Ṣamad (Ibn Bashîr), ³15, 16n, 288
Ibrâhîm b. 'Abdallâh b. Ḥasan b. al-Ḥasan b. 'Alî b. Abî Ṭâlib, ¹410 f., ²167, 209n
Ibrâhîm b. Adham, ¹427n, ³98n
Ibrâhîm b. Khalîl as-Sa'dî ash-Shâfi'î al-Miṣrî, ¹xcviii
Ibrâhîm b. al-Mahdî, ¹40, 324n, 325 f., 433, ²404, 419n
Ibrâhîm b. Muhâjir, ²179
Ibrâhîm b. Muḥammad b. al-Ḥanafîyah, ²174
Ibrâhîm b. Muḥammad b. 'Alî b. 'Abdallâh b. (al-)'Abbâs, ¹409, 467

Ibrâhîm b. Sahl al-Isrâ'îlî, see al-Isrâ'îlî, Ibrâhîm b. Sahl
Ibrâhîm b. aṣ-Ṣalt, ³130n
Ibrâhîm b. Yazîd an-Nakha'î, ²172n, 174, 256
Ibrâhîm b. Zarzar, see Ibn Zarzar, Ibrâhîm
Iceland, ¹163n
Idlelten, see Yadlaltin (Idlelten), Banû
Idrîs, ¹229, 240n, ²317, 367 f., ³213n
Idrîs b. 'Abdallâh b. Ḥasan b. al-Ḥasan b. 'Alî b. Abî Ṭâlib, ¹47 ff., 411, 467, ²115, 289
Idrîs b. Idrîs (son of the preceding), ¹47 ff., 411, 467, ²115, 289
al-Idrîsî, ¹94n, 95n, 97 & n, 103, 109, 116 f., 119, 120n, 121n, 124n, 133n, 134n, 135n, 137n, 144n, 149n, 152n, 154n, 156n, 163n, 164n, 166n
Idrîsids, ¹47 ff., 271 f., 318 f., 411, 467, ²115, 127, 289
Ifren, see Yafran (Ifren), Banû
Ifrîqiyah, Ifrîqî, ¹9, 21, 42, 48 f., 98, *following* 110, 130, 142, 180, 305, 315, 318 f., 329, 331 ff., 335, 343, 351, 360, 365, 368, 467 ff., 472, ²13, 15 f., 24, 35, 37 f., 40, 43, 93, 101, 115 ff., 121, 128, 133, 196, 200, 211, 239, 244 f., 247 f., 266 f., 282 f., 288 ff., 304, 319, 325, 384, 386 f., 405, 428, ³14 f., 302 f., 338, 352, 357, 363 ff., 418, 420, 471 f., 474
al-Îjî, ¹198n
al-'Ijlî (Aḥmad b. 'Abdallâh b. Ṣâliḥ, or 'Abdallâh b. Ṣâliḥ), ²161, 163, 173
al-'Ijlî, see Muḥammad b. Marwân al-'Ijlî
Ikhshîdids, ¹351, 378n, ²115, 133
Ikhwân aṣ-ṣafâ', ¹95n, 172n, 188n, 220n, ²214n, 423n, ³214n
'Ikrimah, ³56
'Ikrimah b. 'Ammâr, ²178

Îlâq, [1]148
Îlâwush (Helios, Sun), [3]189
illiteracy: Bedouins mostly illiterate, [2]378; of Muḥammad, [2]383 f.; of the early Muslims, [2]8, 22, 382 f., 445, [3]4, 311, 317
Ilyâs, Banû, [1]28
Ilyasaʿ (Midrârid of Sijilmâsah), [1]42
al-ʿImâd al-Iṣfahânî, [2]44*n*, 45 & *n*, [3]393
Imâm al-Ḥaramayn, [1]189*n*, 393 & *n*, [3]21, 28, 51, 56, 85, 129
Imâmîyah (Twelver Shîʿah), *see* Shîʿah
ʿImrân, Banû (of Fez), [1]52
ʿImrân al-Qaṭṭân, [2]166, 167 & *n*
ʿImrân b. Muḥammad b. al-Ḥasan b. Yaḥyâ b. ʿAbdallâh b. Muḥammad b. ʿAlî b. Muḥammad b. Yaḥyâ b. Ibrâhîm b. Yaḥyâ al-Jûṭî, [1]52–53
Imru'u-l-Qays, [1]99, [3]376*n*, 377*n*, 410
India, Indian(s) (al-Hind, as-Sind), [1]83, 99 f., *following* 110, 120, 126 f., 136, 138 f., 168, 172, 222, 296, 329, 360, 362, 370, [2]121, 128, 217, 281, 307, 325, 353, [3]9, 156, 161, 186, 191, 193, 245, 283
Indian Ocean, [1]23, 99 ff., 104, 122 & *n*, 123 f., 126 f., 132
Indus, [1]127
injustice, *see* justice, injustice
insanity: administration of the property of the insane, [1]455; supernatural perceptions, [1]214, 218, 224 f.
intellect: thinking and action, [2]413 ff., [3]35, 275, 295; its limitations, [3]38, 246 ff., 276 f.; unable to encompass God and the world, [3]35 ff., 252 f.; the discerning, [2]413; the experimental, [2]413, 417 ff., 424; experience giving intelligence, [2]406, a shortcut to knowledge, [2]418 f.; the speculative, [2]413, 425; acquired through the study of geometry, [3]130 f.; strengthened through practice of the crafts, [2]406 f., 432; the intellectual sciences, [3]111 ff., 314; spiritual essences called "intellects," [2]420; *see also* reasoning
intelligence service, *see* postal service
Ioannes Philoponus, [2]415*n*
ʿ*Iqd*, *see* Ibn ʿAbdrabbih
Iram, [1]26 f.
ʿIrâq, ʿIrâqî(s), [1]12*n*, 24 f., 42, 58*n*, 100 f., *following* 110, 139, 144 ff., 168, 223, 266, 283, 295 f., 304, 324, 329, 333, 370, 384, 413, 420, 441, 444, 451*n*, 467, 475, [2]21*n*, 22, 26, 55 f., 65*n*, 85, 128, 165, 226, 231, 247, 256, 288, 307, 350, 379, 382, 385, 391, 405, 435, 446 f., 454, 457, 461, [3]4, 6, 8 ff., 17 f., 94, 148, 313, 315, 346 & *n*, 414, 474; the two ʿIrâqs, [1]17 & *n*, 351, 360, [2]115, 133; non-ʿArab ʿIrâq, [2]236, 267, 281, 431, 446*n*, 447, [3]117, 148*n*
al-ʿIrâq, Mountain of, [1]145 ff.
Ireland, [1]163*n*
iron, *see* metals
ʿIrqah, *see* ʿArqah
ʿÎsâ, *see* Jesus
ʿÎsâ al-Balîd, [3]455
ʿÎsâ b. al-Ḥasan, [3]475
ʿÎsâ b. ʿUmar ath-Thaqafî, [3]334*n*, 345
ʿÎsâ b. Zayd b. ʿAlî Zayn-al-ʿâbidîn, [1]410–11
ʿÎsâ b. az-Zayyât, Abû Mahdî, *see* Ibn az-Zayyât, Abû Mahdî ʿÎsâ
Isaac, [1]20, 281, [2]249, 258
ʿÎsawîyah (Sufi Order), [3]418*n*
Isbîjâb, [1]149
Iṣfahân, [1]135, 146 f., 475, [2]128, 133, 299, [3]250, 471

Iṣfahân, Mountain of, [1]145
al-Iṣfahânî, Abû l-Faraj, *see* Abû l-Faraj al-Iṣfahânî
Isfarâyin, [1]136
al-Isfarâyinî, Abû Ḥâmid, [1]46
al-Isfarâyinî, Abû Isḥâq, [1]189 f., 223, 393, [3]100, 145
al-Isfarâyinî, Abû l-Muẓaffar, [1]189n, 190n, [3]43n, 69n
al-Isfîjâbî, Muḥammad b. Yûsuf b. Muḥammad, [1]xciv, xcvii
Isḥâq b. ʿAbdallâh (eighth-century *ḥadîth* transmitter), [2]178
Isḥâq b. al-Ḥasan al-Khâzinî, *see* al-Khâzinî
Isḥâq b. Ibrâhîm al-Mawṣilî, [2]404, 405n
Isḥâq b. Qabîṣah b. Dhu'ayb, [2]207n
Ishmael, [2]249 ff.
al-Iskâf, *see* Abû Bakr al-Iskâf
al-Iskâfî, Abû Bakr Muḥammad b. Muḥammad b. Mâlik, [2]159n
Islam, early Muslims: extraordinary situation created by the coming of, [1]436 f.; military success explained, [2]86, 134 f.; strength and courage of early M., [1]260, 320 f., 329 f.; simplicity and austerity, [2]50, 53, 403 f., [3]93, 311; wealth, [1]419 f.; illiteracy, [2]8, 22, 382 f., 445, [3]4, 311, 317; knowledge of Arabic, [3]338; model character, [1]441, 445, 448, 460, [2]141, 382, [3]93, 266; quarrels, [1]434 ff.
spread of early Islam by teaching, [1]59 f.; promoted Arabic language, [2]305 f., [3]317 f.; political norms, [2]139; just rule, [1]301, 391, 426; favors education, [3]300; attitude toward building activity, [2]267 ff., 362 f., toward science, [3]116 f.; its duration, [2]204 ff., 213 ff.; in Negro Africa, [1]169
Ismâʿîl, Judge, [1]38, 39n, [3]13 & n, 17
Ismâʿîl b. Ibrâhîm b. Muhâjir, [2]179
Ismâʿîl b. Jaʿfar aṣ-Ṣâdiq, [1]41, 43, 45, 412 f., 467
Ismâʿîl b. Makkî b. ʿAwf, [3]18n
Ismâʿîl b. Yûsuf b. al-Aḥmar, *see* Ibn al-Aḥmar, Ismâʿîl b. Yûsuf
Ismâʿîlîyah, *see* Shîʿah
Israel, Israel-Allâh (Jacob), [1]18
Israelites, [1]12, 16 ff., 20 f., 24, 57, 132, 172 f., 275, 287 f., 333 f., 344, 357 f., 408, 422, 473 f., [2]191, 202, 258 ff., 264, 354, [3]283 f.; *see also* Bible; Jews
al-Isrâʾîlî, Ibrâhîm b. Sahl, [3]92n, 393 & n, 450
al-Isrâʾîlî, Najm-ad-dîn, [3]92
Issawi, C., [1]xxvi, cix, 19n, 56n, 66n, 71n, 76n, 77n, 85n, 89n, 91n, 95n, 107n, 108n, 167n, 172n, 174n, 177n, 194n, 195n, 249n, 252n, 253n, 257n, 262n, 264n, 265n, 266n, 284n, 287n, 299n, 300n, 302n, 305n, 306n, 308n, 313n, 314n, 319n, 320n, 322n, 327n, 328n, 332n, 336n, 338n, 339n, 343n, 347n, 348n, 351n, 368n, 372n, 374n, 380n, 382n, 385n, 414n, 427n, 472n, [2]3n, 46n, 89n, 102n, 103n, 126n, 135n, 146n, 271n, 277n, 281n, 283n, 287n, 293n, 300n, 302n, 311n, 313n, 314n, 315n, 325n, 326n, 340n, 342n, 343n, 346n, 351n, 353n, 354n, 355n, 378n, 406n, 411n, 412n, 416n, 427n, 431n, 434n, [3]34n, 37n, 81n, 82n, 137n, 253n, 290n, 292n, 296n, 298n, 305n, 306n, 307n, 308n, 311n, 342n, 346n, 353n, 354n, 359n, 379n
Istabbah (Ḥiṣn), [3]445
Iṣṭakhr, [1]135
Istanbul, *see* Constantinople
al-Itlîdî, [1]37n
Ivanow, W., [1]41n, 405n, [2]157n
Îwân Kisrâ, [1]101, 356, Pls. IIa-b, [2]239, 242 f., [3]474
Iyâd, Banû, [1]266, [2]379, [3]343

'Iyâḍ, Judge, ²459, 463, ³50n
Izhar, ¹18n
'Izz-ad-dîn b. 'Abd-as-Salâm, *see* Ibn 'Abd-as-Salâm, 'Izz-ad-dîn

J

Jabalah, ¹143, ²101
Jâbir b. 'Abdallâh, ¹445, ²159, 169, 175
Jâbir b. Ḥayyân, ³116, 157, 180, 188, 228, 246, 269, 278 f.
Jâbir b. Samurah, ²159n
Jabrâghûn, Mount, ¹148
Jacob, ¹18 ff., 281, ²258
Jacobites, ¹480 f.
Jacoby, F., ³253n
al-Ja'dî, ³21, 129
Jaén, ¹140
Ja'far al-Muṣaddiq, ¹413
Ja'far aṣ-Ṣâdiq, ¹41, 43, 406, 411 ff., ²203, 209 f., 218, ³109n
Ja'far b. Abî Ṭâlib, ¹426n, ²178, 196n
Ja'far b. Qudâmah, ³336n
Ja'far b. Yaḥyâ (= the following?), ³336
Ja'far b. Yaḥyâ b. Khâlid al-Barmakî, ¹28 f., 31, 277, 349n, ²10, 27, 63, ³336
al-Ja'farîyah, ³423
Jahier, H., ¹171n
al-Jâḥiẓ, ¹lxxiin, lxxvin, cxi, 451n, ²3n, 35n, ³62, 287, 336, 340
al-Jahshiyârî, ¹361n, 362n, 363n, 364n, 365n, ²29n, 31n, 33n, 35n
Jakoubovsky, A., ¹147n
al-Jâlinûs, ¹259
Jalûlâ', ¹146
Jalûlâ (in Northwestern Africa), ²38
James, W., ¹lxviin
al-Jâmi'ayn, ¹145, 408
al-Jammâ'îlî, ²161n
Janad, ¹126
Janâwah, ³185n
Japan, ¹99n
Japheth, ¹172

Jarîd, ¹*following* 110, 130, 175, ²93, 117, 244, 304 f., 386, ³473
Jarîr, ¹55, 268, ³383, 397
Jarjarâyâ, ¹145
Jarmânîyah, ¹*following* 110, 159
Jarwâsiyâ, ¹152
Jathûliyah, ¹*following* 110, 159
Játiva, ¹141, ²441
Jaubert, P. A., ¹94n
Java, ¹101n, 123
al-Jawâlîqî, ²244n
al-Jawâribî, *see* Dâwûd al-Jawâribî
Jawhar al-Kâtib, ¹360, ²133, 283
al-Jawharî (author of the *Ṣiḥâḥ*), ³328
Jaxartes, *see* Syr Darya
Jayḥân, ¹144, 154
Jayḥûn, *see* Oxus
Jayruft, *see* Jîruft
al-Jayyânî, Muḥammad b. 'Abdallâh, ¹xxxix
al-Jazâ'irî, *see* Ibn Khalaf al-Jazâ'irî
Jazîrah, ¹102, 142, 144 ff., 334, 364, 475n, ²115, 354
Jazîrat Ibn 'Umar, ¹145
al-Jâziyah bint Sarḥân, ³416, 419
Jeffery, A., ¹27n, ²158n
Jerba, ²43
Jerez (de la Frontera), ¹140
Jericho, ¹288
Jerusalem, ¹lxiii, 17, 133, 358, 474 f., ²42, 44, 171, 249, 258 f., 262 ff., 362
Jesse, ¹18
Jesus, ¹406, 476, ²156, 185 f., 192, 194 f., 261 f., 370, ³86, 149
Jevdet Effendi (Pasha), Ahmet, ¹cviii
jewelry, *see* pearls; stones (precious)
Jews: survey of Jewish history to Roman times, ¹473 ff.; the Kohen, ¹473 f.; history of the Tabernacle and the Temple in Jerusalem, ²249, 257 ff., the *dᵉbîr*, ²260n; nobility of the Patriarchs, ¹281, of David and Solomon, ¹391 f., 417, 422; numbers during

the Exodus, [1]16 ff.; sojourn in the desert, [1]133, 288, 344; Solomon's army, [1]19; Hebrew language, [1]66, 212*n*, 476; Hebrew script, [3]283 f.

highly developed culture, [2]287 f., 354; pride in ancestors, [1]275; rebellious spirit of the ancient Jews, [1]334; meekness they acquired in Egypt, [1]287 ff., 344; humiliated by God, [1]275, [2]150*n;* deceitful character, [3]306; laws of cleanliness (*Mishnâh Pârâh*, iii, 6), [2]260 f.; Sambation legend, [1]22; religion transmitted from parents to children, [1]254

polemics with Muslims, [1]4*n;* alleged alteration of the Torah, [1]20; founding of the Ka'bah, [2]249 ff.; brief control over Medina, [2]264; in pre-Islamic Arabia, [1]66*n*, [2]203, 206 f.; as informants for early Muslims, [2]445, employed by them as bookkeepers, [2]8 f.; legend of Jurayj, [2]185, 192; an astronomical work by a Sicilian Jew, [3]137; a prediction poem ascribed to a Jew of Fez, [2]221

see also Bible; Israelites

Jibrîl b. Bukhtîshû', [1]35 f.

Jidda(h), [1]ic, 100, 126, [2]252, 256

Jîlân, [1]364

jinn, [1]73, 185, [3]59, 69, 161, 165

Jirâb ad-dawlah, [1]361

al-Ji'rânah, [2]256

Jirâsh b. Aḥmad al-Ḥâsib, [2]213 ff.

Jirjîr, [3]474*n*

Jirjis b. al-'Amîd, *see* al-Makîn

Jîruft, [1]135

John, son of Zebedee, [1]476 f.

Jordan, [1]133

Jordan Depression, *see* Ghôr

Jordan Province, [1]18, 365, [2]22

Joseph, [1]18, 281, [3]103, 194

Joshua, [1]275, 473, [2]259

Josippon (Pseudo-), [1]477*n*

al-Jûbânî, Alṭunbughâ, *see* Alṭunbughâ al-Jûbânî

Jubayr b. Muṭ'im, [2]21

al-Jubbâ'î, Abû Hâshim 'Abd-as-Salâm, [3]62

al-Jubbâ'î, Muḥammad b. 'Abd-al-Wahhâb, [3]62

Jucar, [1]141

Judah, [1]19, 275, 475

Judhâm, Banû, [1]266, [3]343, 438

Juhaynah, [1]83*n*

al-Junayd, [2]187, [3]54, 191, 194

Jundîshâbûr, [1]135

Jung, C. G., [1]221*n*

Jupiter (planet), [2]211, 215 f., [3]189*n*, 193*n*

Jurash, [1]126

Jurayj, [2]185, 192

Jurhum, Banû, [2]249, 251, 380

jurisprudence, jurists, judiciary, [1]452 ff., [3]3 ff., 80, 286, 288 ff., 299, 301, 304, 309, 313, 396; defined, [2]438, [3]3, 13, 26; science of the principles of jurisprudence defined, [2]437, [3]23 f., 27 f.; hard to master, [3]263; the juridical habit, [3]394; the law to preserve society, [1]79 f.; differences of the legal schools, [1]445, [2]296, 399 f., [3]3 ff., 30 ff.; Mâlikism the best school, [2]296, 400; and language, [1]78, [3]25 ff., 56, 282*n*, 316, 319 f., 331 f., 350, science of *ḥadîth*, [2]452, 454, 459 ff., [3]150 f., 285, Qur'ân recitation, [2]359 ff., Sufism, [3]79 f., 83, 99, magic and sorcery, [3]159, 169 ff., 178 ff., 246, poetry, [3]395; legal maxims, [1]232, 432, 438, [2]400, [3]26 f.; legal disputations, [3]31 ff.; legal monetary standard, [2]58 ff.; Ibn Khaldûn's work on jurisprudence, [1]xliv; influence of jurisprudence upon his thinking, [1]lxxix, lxxxii f., lxxxv, cix

'Umar's Instructions to the Judge, [1]453 f.; the office of

judge, ¹449, 452 ff., ²149 f., 246n, 272 f., mufti, ¹449, 451 f., ²334, 392, 394, official witness, ¹461 f., market supervisor (ḥisbah), ¹449, 462; inheritance laws, ³20 ff., 112, 127 ff.; building laws, ¹455, 463, ²361 f.; business litigation, ²343; crime investigation, execution of punishments are tasks of police, ²36; jurists concerned with political theory, ²5 f., 23, with political reforms, ¹323, not permitted to take an effective part in government policy, ¹459 ff., ³308 ff.; influential under the Almoravids, ¹53, opposed by the Mahdî of the Almohads, ¹53 f.; changing prestige of judges, ¹60 f., 452, 454 ff.; jurists to be respected by rulers, ²142, 147; salaries of judges, ²273 f., 334, 339 f.; their use of seals, ²63; jurisprudence no longer cultivated in Spain, ²430
Jurjân, ¹101, 147 f., 363
al-Jurjânî, see ʿAbd-al-Qâhir al-Jurjânî
al-Jurjânî (ʿAlî b. ʿAbd-al-ʿAzîz), ¹22
justice, injustice ¹lxxv, 79 ff., 262, 304, 320n, 391, 408, 424, 453 f., ²74, 95 f., 103 ff., 140, 142, 145, 149, 151, 163 ff., 284, 330, ³305
Justinard, L., ¹128n
al-Jûzjân, ¹136 f., 148, 410, ²210
al-Jûzjânî (Ibrâhîm b. Yaʿqûb), ²163, 168, 173

K

Kaʿb, Banû (subtribe of the Sulaym), ²200, ³423, 425, 427 ff.
Kaʿb al-aḥbâr, ¹26, ²203, 205, 445
Kaʿb b. Mâlik, ¹439
Kaʿb b. ʿUjrah, ¹439
Kaʿbah, ¹12, 33, 186, ²165, 249 ff., 258, 264, 458n, ³410, 435
al-Kaʿbî, ʿAbdallâh b. Aḥmad, al-Balkhî, ³62
Kâbul, ¹127, 136
al-Kafîf (Moroccan poet), ³471
Kâfûr al-Ikhshîdî, ¹63, 378
Kahlân, Banû, ¹266, 283, ³349
Kairouan, see al-Qayrawân
kalâm, mutakallimûn, see theology
Kalb, Banû, ²165, 226
Kalbfleisch, K., ²415n
Kamil, M., ¹477n
Kanauj, ¹127
Kânim, Kanem, ¹following 110, 119 f.
Kanûri, ¹125n
Karaj, ¹364
al-Karkh, ¹364n
Karpinski, L. C., ³125n, 284n
Kashmir, ¹127
Kaskar, ¹362, 363n
Kâvagh, ³168n
Kawâr, ¹following 110, 125
Kay, H. C., ¹123n
al-Kaylânî, I., ¹403n
Kayqâwûs, ¹25
Kaysân, ¹406; Kaysânîyah, see Shîʿah
Kayyanids (Achaemenids), ¹22, 23n, 25, 298, 475, ²288, ³114
Keller, H., ²139n
Kennedy, E. S., ³135n
Kerbelâʾ, ¹407, 445, ²198
Khâbûr, ¹145, ³378
Khadîjah, ¹186 f.
Khalaf (b. Hishâm), ¹67
Khalaf b. Aḥmar, ³306 f.
Khalaj, ¹136, 149n
Khaldûn (ancestor of Ibn Khaldûn), ¹xxxiii
Khâlid, see ad-Daryûsh, Khâlid
Khâlid b. ʿAbdallâh al-Qasrî, ¹373, ²55
Khâlid b. Barmak, ¹356n
Khâlid b. Ḥamzah b. ʿUmar (chieftain of the Kuʿûb), ³423, 425, 427 f.
Khâlid b. al-Walîd, ²21 & n.

Khâlid b. Yazîd b. Mu'âwiyah, [3]229 f.
Khalîfah az-Zanâtî, Abû Su'dâ al-Yafranî, [3]418 f.
al-Khalîl b. Aḥmad al-Farâhîdî, [3]323, 325 ff., 334*n*
Khallukh, *see* Kharlukh
al-Khalwatî, [3]168*n*
Khânkû (Khânqû, Khânjû, Khânfû), [1]124*n*, 127*n*
Khârijites, [1]333, 391, 397*n*, 398, [2]69, 79, 114, 167, [3]5, 378
Kharkhîr, *see* Kirghiz
Kharlukh, [1]103, *following* 110, 136*n*, 138, 149
Kharnâb River, [1]136
al-Kharrâz, *see* Abû Sa'îd al-Kharrâz
al-Kharrâz, Muḥammad b. Muḥammad, [2]443
Kharshanah, [1]154
Khartum, [1]121*n*
al-Khaṭîb al-Baghdâdî, [1]8*n*, 33*n*, 37*n*, 38*n*, 75*n*, 349*n*, [2]159*n*, 160*n*, 161*n*, 162*n*, 174*n*, 177*n*, 178*n*, 183*n*, 207*n*, 236, 460*n*, [3]10*n*, 14*n*, 29*n*, 50*n*, 56*n*, 62*n*, 68*n*, 169*n*, 192*n*, 332*n*, 404*n*
al-Khaṭṭ, [1]134
al-Khaṭṭâbî, [2]59
Khaybar, [1]18, 133
al-Khaybarî, [2]79
Khayghûn, [1]127
Khazars, [1]98, 101, 155 f., 161 f., 172
Khâzarûn, [1]148
al-Khâzin, Abû Ja'far, [1]110*n*, 115
al-Khâzinî, Abû Ja'far, *see* al-Khâzin, Abû Ja'far
al-Khâzinî, Isḥâq b. al-Ḥasan, [1]110 f., 114 f. (= al-Munajjim?)
al-Khazlajîyah, *see* Kharlukh
Khazraj, Banû, [1]25, [2]264
al-Khazrajî, *see* Yaḥyâ al-Khazrajî
Khazrûn, Banû (rulers of Tripolitania), [2]42
al-Khiḍr, [1]407
Khifshâkh, *see* Qipchaqs
Khilâṭ, [1]102, 154
Khirkhîr, *see* Kirghiz
Khosraw (I or II, or Persian Emperor), [2]20, 257, 407
Khosraw (Reception Hall of), *see* Îwân Kisrâ
Khosraw I Anôsharwân, [1]80 f., 83*n*, [2]216, 301
Khosraw II Aparwêz, [1]219, 281 f., [2]202, 214, 216
al-Khuḍayrî, M. M., [1]44*n*, [3]142*n*
Khujandah, [1]148 f.
al-Khulkh, *see* Khaḷaj
al-Khullajân b. al-Qâsim, [2]380
Khûlukh Turks, [1]136*n*, 161
Khûnajân, [1]146
al-Khûnajî, [3]143, 291, 396
Khurâsân, [1]17, 102 f., *following* 110, 135 ff., 147 & *n*, 148, 324, 325*n*, 362, 410, 434, [2]115, 128, 132, 134, 307, 431, [3]10, 18, 117, 315
Khuttal, [1]136 ff.
Khuwârizm, [1]101 ff., *following* 110, 148 f., [2]446
al-Khuwârizmî (author of *Mafâtîḥ al-'ulûm*), [2]215*n*, [3]119*n*, 134*n*, 227*n*
al-Khuwârizmî (mathematician), [3]125 & *n*, 284
Khûz, *see* Ghuzz
Khuzâ'ah, Banû, [1]266, [2]251, [3]343
Khuzaymah (b. Thâbit), [1]256 f.
Khûzistân, [1]135
Kimäk, [1]*following* 110, 138, 149, 157
Kimble, G. H. T., [1]109*n*
Kinânah, Banû, [1]28, 266, 441, [2]251, [3]322, 343
Kinâwah, [3]185
Kindah, Banû, [1]282, 441
al-Kindî, Abû 'Umar, [1]453*n*
al-Kindî, 'Alâ'-ad-dîn, [2]246*n*
al-Kindî, Ya'qûb b. Isḥâq, [1]lxxii*n*, 175, 176*n*, [2]191, 194, 212*n*, 215, 218 f., [3]334*n*
Kirghiz, [1]138

Kirmân, [1]100, *following* 110, 135, 362
al-Kirmânî (Abû Isḥâq Ibrâhîm, author on dream interpretation), [3]108n, 110 & n
al-Kisrawîyah, *see* Sassanians
Kister, M. J., [1]37n
Knust, H., [1]lxxxiin, 80n, 320n, [2]3n, 246n
Köbert, R., [1]13n, [3]46n
Koehler, L., [2]260n
Kohath, [1]18
Korea (as-Sîlâ), [1]124
Kraemer, J., [3]325n
Kramers, J. H., [1]102n, 116n, 131n, [2]367n
Kraus, P., [1]67n, 82n, 103n, [2]3n, 38n, 157n, 173n, 188n, 228n, 233n, 242n, 271n, 273n
Krehl, L., [1]185n, [2]61n, 458n, [3]43n
von Kremer, A., [1]lxxiin, 361n, 362n, 363n
Krenkow, F., [2]385n
Kroll, W., [1]73n
Kühn, C. G., [1]90n
al-Kûfah, [1]101 f., 145, 261n, 363, 410, 420, 441 ff., 453, [2]64, 173, 236, 247, 268 f., 299, 384, 431, 434, 452, [3]289, 323 f.
Kûfich, *see* al-Qufṣ
Kûhistân, [1]135
Kulthûm b. ʿAmr al-ʿAttâbî, *see* al-ʿAttâbî, Kulthûm b. ʿAmr
al-Kunâsah, [1]410
Kunjdih, [1]149n
Kurâʿ, ʿAlî b. al-Ḥusayn, [3]329
Kurayb (b. Khaldûn), [1]xxxii, xxxiv
Kurd ʿAlî, M., [2]29n
Kurds, [1]135, 146, 252, 295, [2]37, 74
Kurds, Mountain of the, [1]135, 146, 154
Kutâmah (Berber tribe), [1]22, 41, 45, 129, 286, 298, 318, 331, 350, 413, [2]43n, 115, 133, 289
Kutâmah, Mountain of the, [2]116
Kuthayyir, [1]407, [3]383, 404

al-Kutubî, [1]xxxivn, 220n, 366n, [2]230n
Kuʿûb, *see* Kaʿb, Banû

L

Labîd b. Rabîʿah, [1]466n, [3]96
al-Lablî, [3]441n
labor, [1]lxxxi; source of all profit, [1]109, 303, [2]272, 280, 282, 313 f., 315 f., 328, 334, 351 f.; its availability the basis of prosperity and civilization, [2]272 ff., 281, 314, 347, 355, 378, 434; officials, scholars, pious men profit from free use of labor of others, [2]327 f.; collaboration greatly increases production, [2]271 f., 281; needs for the construction of large monuments, [1]357, [2]238, 241; little available in decaying governments, [2]81; expensive in large cities, [2]277, 279; costs increase food prices, [2]278 f., 314; concealed costs, [2]313 f.; forced, [1]303, [2]107 ff., 329
Labouret, H., [1]118n
al-Lâhûn, [1]126, 131
Lakhm, Banû, [1]266, [3]343; Lakhmids, [1]25n, 268n, [2]379n, [3]451n
al-Lakhmî (Mâlikite jurist), [3]15, 288
Lamlam, [1]*following* 110, 118
Lammens, H., [1]49n, 58n, [2]258n
Lamṭah (Berber tribe), [1]*following* 110, 125
Lamtûnah (Berber tribe), [1]53, 118, 125, 240, 316, 321, 323, 335, 351, 470, 472, [2]43, 82, 134, 220, 386; *see also* Almoravids
land ownership: as an investment, [2]283 ff.; surveying, [3]132
de Landberg, C., [2]45n
Lane, E. W., [2]121n, [3]335n, 387n, 472n

language, linguistics: language defined as a habit of the tongue, [3]318, 320 f., 342, 371 f., 391; articulation of sounds, [1]66, [3]327 f., 348 ff.; confusion of sound and letter, [1]65 f.; conventional character of the meanings of words, [1]172; language a social necessity, [1]79; communication of information through speech, [2]390, [3]281, 296 f., 316, 398 ff.; the right of language to change, [3]345 ff.; linguistic "taste," [3]338, 345, 354, 358 ff., 386, 397 f., 405, 409, 414, 480; memorizing as a means to acquire mastery of a language, [3]339, 353, 362, 364, 383, 392 ff.; nations of the past had own languages and terminologies, [1]57, [3]321; language and jurisprudence, [1]78, [3]25 ff., 56, 282*n*, 316, 319 f., 331 f., 350, theology, [3]64 ff., 83 ff., Sufism, [3]79, 97, 101 f., magic, [3]172, 175 f.; cover names of alchemists, [3]228 f., 239 ff.; the philological sciences, [2]437 f., 444, 446, 463, [3]289 ff., 299, 301, 303 f., 319 ff., 354 ff., 365

good Arabic: not natural but acquired by training, [3]283, 342 f., 353 f., 359; cannot be acquired by studying the Qur'ân [3]303, *but cf.* [3]338, 340, 397; does not result from grammatical knowledge alone, [3]354 ff.

Arabic: requires scientific treatment, [2]444; promoted by Islam, [2]305 f., [3]317 f.; pronunciation of the Qur'ân, [1]67, [2]400, 449; adoption of, as government language, [2]22 f.; corruption of, [2]9 ff., 26, 305 ff., 444, [3]26, 304, 312, 321 f., 325, 343, 345 f., 352 f., 363 ff., 412; dialects, [1]68*n*, [2]221, 223, 305, [3]343, 351 f., 396*n*, 412 ff., 454 ff., 479, Pl. III; urban and rural usages of, [2]306 f., [3]348 ff., 360 f., 363 ff., 412 ff.; etymologies, [1]21 f., 200, 388 f., 402, 428 f., 465, [2]20, 210, 256 f., 315, 368, 373, 403, 407, [3]22 f., 50, 63, 76 f., 152 f., 247, 329; transliteration of non-Arabic sounds, [1]65 ff., 128*n*, 129*n*, 481*n*; compared to other languages, [3]321, 344, 401; rarely mastered by non-Arabs, [3]318 f., 361 f., 372; replaced by other languages, [2]307, [3]367; translation of Greek works into, [3]115 f., 130 f., 135, 140 f., 147, 149, 151, 317

see also grammar; literature, literary criticism

Laoust, E., [1]119*n*, 125*n*, [2]68*n*, 360*n*

Laoust, H., [3]64*n*

Larache, [1]129

Laribus, [1]130

Latin language, [1]476 f., [3]185, 284; script, [3]283

Lattakiyah, [1]143, [2]101*n*

Le Strange, G., [1]349*n*

lead, *see* metals

leadership, *see* government, leadership

leather work, [2]348, 353

Lérida, [1]141

León, [1]150

Leon, H. M., [2]225*n*

Leon, *see* Ulyûs

Levi, [1]18

Levi Della Vida, G., [1]lvn, 75*n*, 151*n*, 205*n*, 219*n*, 417*n*, [3]149*n*, 197*n*

Lévi-Provençal, E., [1]xxxiii*n*, xxxvii, xli*n*, xcii f., 42*n*, 61*n*, 75*n*, 95*n*, 116*n*, 128*n*, 140*n*, 141*n*, 261*n*, [2]41*n*, 201*n*, 302*n*, 381*n*, 441*n*, 458*n*, [3]364*n*, 398*n*, 455*n*, 460*n*

Leviathan, [1]4*n*

Levy, R., [1]324*n*, 361*n*

Lewicki, T., [1]94*n*, 159*n*
Lewis, B., [1]45*n*
lexicography, [2]463, [3]63, 319 f., 325 ff., 339, 405, 411
Lichtenstädter, I., [1]xxiv, [3]369*n*
Lieberman, S., [2]261*n*
Lippert, J., [2]214*n*, 365*n*, [3]115*n*
von Lippmann, E. O., [3]244*n*, 269*n*, 273*n*
Lisân al-'Arab, [1]lxxv*n*, lxxviii*n*, 19*n*, 74*n*, 205*n*, 220*n*, [2]84*n*, 121*n*, 256*n*, 401*n*, 403*n*, [3]23*n*, 61*n*, 348*n*, 404*n*, 425*n*, 446*n*
Lisbon, [1]141
literature, literary criticism, [1]204, [2]438, [3]319, 332 ff., 339 ff., 358; literature defined, [3]340; literary criticism defined, [3]336 f.; works on literary criticism, [3]286 f., 336 f.; poetry, [3]375 ff., and prose, [3]368 ff.; rhymed prose, [1]203 ff., [3]335, 339, 368 ff., 380, 406 ff.; Arabic literary and speech methods (*uslûb*), [2]307, 443 f., 446, [3]358 ff.; clarity of expression, [2]390, 429; harmony of speech, [2]402; natural and contrived speech, [3]398 ff.; figures of speech, [3]65, 329, 335 ff., 340, 370 f., 400 ff.; knowledge of literary criticism needed by Qur'ân commentators, [3]338 f.; still cultivated in Spain, [2]430, [3]303, 357, 365 f.
locusts, social organization of, [1]84, 92
Löfgren, O., [2]380*n*
logic, [1]91, 203, [3]28, 33, 36*n*, 51, 56, 71, 89, 137 ff., 249 ff., 291, 295 ff., 299, 310, 357, 396; defined, [3]111 f., 137, 247, 295 f.; the Aristotelian Organon, [1]78, 275*n*, [3]139 ff., 254, 412; logical terminology, [1]9, 77, 371, [2]431, [3]90, 272, 274; theologians' attitude toward, [3]51, 143 ff.; Ibn Khaldûn's work on, [1]xliv
Lombardy, Lombards, [1]142, 151 f.
Lorca, [1]141
Lorraine, [1]159
Lot, [1]334, [3]473*n*
Loth, O., [2]191*n*, 212*n*, 215*n*
love, [2]398, [3]98 f., 194, 384; love poetry, [3]369, 373 f., 376 f., 390 f., 404, 413, 417*n*, 421, 441 ff.; love magic, [3]162, 193
Luciani, J.-D., [1]cxiii*n*, [3]23*n*, 24*n*, 27*n*
Luckey, P., [3]124*n*
al-Lujj, [2]252
Luke, St., [1]476
al-Lukkâm, *see* Amanus
Luqmân, [2]3*n*, [3]114
al-Lûshî, Abû 'Abdallâh, [3]461
luxury, and customs of, [1]lxxx f., 29, 36, 60, 85, 180, 249 f., 252 ff., 257, 282 f., 286 f., 296 ff., 309, 317, 320, 336, 338 ff., 344 f., 347 f., 351 f., 378, 397, 418, 424, 458, [2]34, 50, 69 f., 79, 90 ff., 98, 111, 114, 117, 119 ff., 123, 125, 127, 131, 235, 237, 243, 267 f., 272 ff., 276, 279 ff., 284 f., 287, 289, 292 ff., 298, 302, 317, 321, 335, 346 ff., 352, 354, 364, 367, 376, 378, 387, 401, 404 f., 434, 439, [3]150, 337

M

al-Madâ'inî, [2]55
Madghallîs, [3]457, 460
Madhḥij, Banû, [1]282*n*
Mâḍî b. Muqarrab, [3]417, 419
Madkûr, I., [3]142*n*
Madyan, *see* Midyan, Midyanites
Maggara, *see* Maqqarah
Maghîlah (Berber tribe), [1]318, [2]115
Maghrâwah (Berber tribe), [1]298, 428, 470, [2]134; *see also* Maghzâwah
Maghrib, [1]lviii, xcv, xcvi*n*, cv, cxv, 11 f., 21 ff., 42, 47 ff., 61, 64 f., 75, 98 f., 103, 118 f., 125, 168 f., 175, 177, 179 f., 239, 271, 290, 296, 298, 305, 308, 315, 319, 321, 323, 329 ff., 335, 351, 357, 360, 369 f., 382, 393, 411, 413, 428, 456, 463, 467, 469 ff., 479, [2]15, 17, 26, 37 f., 40, 43 ff., 49, 51, 58, 64 ff., 68, 70, 74, 80 f., 115 f., 121, 127 f., 130, 133 f., 137, 190, 195 f., 198 f., 202, 211, 219 ff., 239, 244, 266 f., 273 f., 281 ff., 288 ff., 299, 305, 307, 320 ff., 325, 339, 349, 353, 378, 386 f., 394 f., 405, 427 ff., 432 f., 435, 439, 441, 443, 446, 459, [3]10, 12 f., 16 f., 19, 32, 110, 117, 122, 136 f., 164, 218, 270, 289, 301 ff., 324, 337, 346, 352, 357, 363, 413, 416, 419, 423, 427, 436*n*, 450, 466, 468, 470 ff., 479
Maghzâwah (*or* Maghrâwah?), [1]*following* 110
Magians, Majûs, [1]93, 124, 139, 254, 390; *see also* Zoroastrianism
magic, sorcery, [1]lxxii f., 27, 189, 202 ff., [2]57, 200 ff., 244 f., 319 ff., [3]82, 113, 116, 151 f., 156 ff., 278, 474; defined, [3]156; various types enumerated, [1]214, 216, 231, 234; talismans, [2]224*n*, 319 f., 322 ff., [3]113, 116, 158, 162 ff., 171, 174 ff.; magic squares, [2]224, [3]163 f., 168 f., 174, 176 f., 185, 188, 193; letter magic, [3]171 ff., 245; *Za'irajah*, [1]238 ff., [3]182 ff., 224, 227; evil eye, [3]170 f.; reality of magic and sorcery, [3]159 ff., 178 f.; degrees of magical ability, [3]158 f.; magic and astrology, [3]156, 158 f., 162 ff., 176 ff., 186 f., 189, 193, 196 ff., 220 ff.; and alchemy, [3]157, 172 ff., 180, 188, 228 f., 245 f., 280; relationship to miracles, [3]167 ff., 278; distinction between sorcery and talismans, [3]165 ff.; magic in Egypt, [2]321 f., [3]156, 160, 168, 245; magic observed or experienced by Ibn Khaldûn, [1]213, 238*n*, 243, [3]160 ff., 164 f., 218*n*
magnesia, an alchemical substance, [3]244
Magog, *see* Gog and Magog
Maguzawa Country, [1]*following* 110
Mâh-al-Baṣrah, [1]363*n*
Mâh-al-Kûfah, [1]363*n*
Mahdî, Mahdism, [1]lxxx, 408, [2]156 ff., 220; expected appearance in the Maghrib, [2]190, 196 f.; will require group feeling to be successful, [2]195 f., 198; descent in Damascus, [2]194; will destroy Constantinople, [2]193; discussed by Sufis, [2]157, 186 ff., 197, [3]94; pseudo-Mahdîs in Northwestern Africa, [1]326 f., [2]197
al-Mahdî: of the Almohads, *see* Ibn Tûmart; Fâṭimid ruler, *see* 'Ubaydallâh al-Mahdî; *see also* Muḥammad b. 'Abdallâh b. Ḥasan b. al-Ḥasan b. 'Alî b. Abî Ṭâlib, an-Nafs az-Zakîyah; *and* Muḥammad b. al-Ḥasan al-'Askarî
al-Mahdî ('Abbâsid caliph), [1]29, 34, 40*n*, 432, 467, [2]216*n*, 219, 255
Mahdi, M., [1]xliv*n*, xlv*n*

al-Mahdîyah, [1]130, 315, [2]41 f., 77*n*, 211, 236 f., 289, 386, [3]420
Maḥmûd (Mameluke amîr), [1]368
Maḥmûd (of Ghaznah), [2]134*n*
al-Maḥramî, 'Alî b. Yaḥyâ, [2]86*n*
Maimonides, [1]4*n*, [2]261*n*
Majnûn Laylâ, [2]225
Majorca, [1]98 & *n*, 139, [2]41, [3]458
al-Majrîṭî, Maslamah b. Aḥmad, [1]xxxiv, 204*n*, 212, 221, [2]191*n*, 415*n*, [3]116, 127, 152, 156*n*, 157, 162, 163*n*, 164, 175, 178, 180, 182*n*, 228 ff., 242 f., 245 f., 268*n*, 269, 278
al-Majûsî, 'Alî b. al-'Abbâs, [3]149
Makhramah b. Nawfal, [2]21
al-Makîn, [1]480
Malabar, [1]127
Málaga, [1]116, 140
Malatya, [1]102, 144
Malay Archipelago, [1]101*n*, 123
Malga, [2]239, 243
Mâlî, [1]118 f., 169
al-Malik an-Nâṣir, Faraj, *see* Faraj (son of Barqûq)
al-Malik an-Nâṣir, Muḥammad b. Qalâ'ûn, [1]366, [2]101 f.
al-Malik aẓ-Ẓâhir Barqûq, *see* Barqûq, al-Malik aẓ-Ẓâhir
Mâlik b. Anas, [1]xlii, lx, ic, 34, 224*n*, 423, 429, 447, [2]159, 178, 265, 296, 380, 399 f., 453, 460, [3]4, 6 ff., 12 ff., 16 f., 31, 66, 128, 286, 312*n*, 451
Mâlik b. al-Muraḥḥal, [3]365
Mâlik b. Wuhayb, [1]240 ff., [3]200*n*, 214, 224
Mâlikites, [1]lxi f., 3*n*, 370, 445, [2]230, 265*n*, 296, 380, 459, [3]10 ff., 21, 32, 128 f., 286, 288 f.
al-Malîlî, Abû l-Ḥasan (judge of Fez), [2]339
Malinke, *see* Mandingo
Mallorca, *see* Majorca
Malta, [1]142, [2]41 f.
Malwîyah River, *see* Moulouya River
Mamelukes, [1]xxx, lviii, 342; *see also* Turks
al-Ma'mûn ('Abbâsid caliph), [1]37 & *n*, 39, 49, 78 & *n*, 324 f., 348 f., 352, 356*n*, 361, 413, 433 f., 456, [2]51, 139, 156, 217 f., 236, 243, 335, [3]116, 134, 147
al-Ma'mûn b. Dhî n-Nûn, [1]350, 359, [3]442
man, [1]lxxi ff.; subject of the science of physics, [2]356, [3]147; has retained same size throughout ages, [1]357 ff., [2]239 ff., 363; beauty of the human form, [1]167, 178, [2]398, [3]444, *see also* women; sustenance, [2]311; years of growth and decay, [2]291 f.; senility, [2]117, 296; artificial creation of man, [3]276; *see also* medicine
preservation of the human species divinely ordained, [1]79, 91, 381, 390, 448, [2]107, 295 f., 329, 371 f.; human qualities, [1]385, 415 f., [2]122, 293 f., 344, [3]157, 305 f.; basically evil, [1]lxxiv, 262, but inclined toward goodness, [1]291; "a child of custom," [1]258, [2]318; obsequious to tradition, [2]298; never satisfied, [2]153; made apathetic by loss of independence, [1]300 f., 339, [3]305; weaker than many animals, [1]90; aggressiveness and animal nature, [1]lxxiv, 91 f., 380 f., 385; God's representative on earth, [1]91, 95, 292, 301, 389, [2]311, 416
in need of co-operation and social organization, [1]lxxiv f., 89 f., [2]137, 235, 271, 300, 329, 411*n*, 417; social stratification, [2]29, 328 ff.; character of servants, [2]317 ff.; occupies stage immediately above monkeys, [1]195, [2]423; distinguished from animals by ability to perceive, [3]77 f.; essentially ignorant, [2]424 ff.; ability to think, [1]lxxvi, 84, [2]357,

411 ff., 436, ³78, 111, 138 f., 247, 281, 295 ff., exists in different degrees, ²357, 416, 431 ff., limits, ³35 ff., 276 f.; requires studying and teachers for all his knowledge and qualities, ³307

four levels of human existence, ³69 ff.; nature encompassed by human soul, ³175; exchange of humanity for angelicality, ¹195 f., 199, 208, ²423, ³75, 81, 157 f.; fulfillment of human reality lies in man becoming pure intellect, ²413

Manbij, ¹102, 143
Mandeville, D. C., ³272n
Mandingo, ¹118n
Manṣûr (in traditions concerning the Mahdî), ²164
al-Manṣûr ('Abbâsid caliph), ¹29, 31, 34, 410 f., 424–25, 432, 467, ²47, 179, 255, ³115, 130, 312n
al-Manṣûr (Fâṭimid ruler), ²211
al-Manṣûr (Ḥammâdid ruler), ²57
Manṣûr, Bû 'Alî, ³434, 436
al-Manṣûr, Ya'qûb (Almohad ruler), ¹239, ²44, 45 & n, 70, ³185n
al-Manṣûr b. Abî 'Âmir, see Ibn Abî 'Âmir, al-Manṣûr
Manṣûr b. 'Ikrimah b. Khaṣafah b. Qays b. 'Aylân, ³348
Manṣûr b. Zibriqân an-Namarî, ³404
al-Manṣûrah, ²240
Manẓûr, Banû, ³439
maps: ¹frontispiece, 23, 96n, 102n, 103, 109, 116n, 133n, 134n, 137n; sea charts, ¹117; southern orientation of Arabic maps, ¹120n
Maqqarah, ¹130
al-Maqqarî, ¹xxxn, xlivn, lxvi & n, xcii & n, 316n, ³366n, 454n, 465n
al-Maqqarî, Muḥammad b. Muḥammad, ¹xlii
al-Maqrîzî, ¹lxvi

al-Marâghah, ¹143, 146, 154
Mar'ash, ¹144
Marbella, ¹140
Marçais, G., ¹xln, lin, ²240n, ³415n, 418n
Marçais, W., ³434n, 464n, 475n
Margoliouth, D. S., ¹lxxixn, 297n, 453n, ²275n
Ma'rib, ¹126, ²241
Marj Râhiṭ, ²79n
al-Marjânî, Jamâl-ad-dîn 'Abd-al-Malik b. 'Abdallâh, ¹239n, ³196n
Mark, St., ¹477, 479
Markwart (Marquart), J., ¹74n, 136n
Marrakech, ¹129, 239, 335, ²43, 134, 299, 351, 427
Mars (planet), ²213, 217, ³173, 189n
Ma'rûf al-Karkhî, ³192
Marw-ar-rûdh, ¹136
Marw ash-Shâhijân, ¹147
Marwân I b. al-Ḥakam, ¹423, 427, 443, 447, ²70, 79, 177n, ³229n, 230
Marwân II, ²79n, 213
Mary (Maryam), mother of Jesus, ²185, ³194
Mâsabadhân, ¹363, 364n
al-Mashaddâlî, 'Imrân b. Mûsâ, ²429
al-Mashaddâlî, Nâṣir-ad-dîn, Abû 'Alî, ²428–29, ³19
al-Masîlah, see Msila
Maskawayh, ¹xcivn, ²86n, 217n
Maslamah al-Majrîṭî, see al-Majrîṭî, Maslamah b. Aḥmad
Maslamah b. Makhlad, ¹439
Maṣmûdah (Berber tribe), ¹54 f., 128, 179, 273, 298, 315, 322, 327, 331, ²197
Mâssah, Monastery of, ¹128, 326, ²196 f.
Massé, H., ²332n
Massignon, L., ¹4n, 42n, 193n, 322n, ²193n, ³77n, 93n, 97n, 98n, 100n, 102n, 459n

al-Maṣṣîṣah, [1]143 f.
Massûfah (Berber tribe), [1]125
Mas'ûd I of Ghaznah, [2]134*n*
Mas'ûd b. Mawdûd b. Zengi, [1]xciv*n*
al-Mas'ûdî, [1]7 f., 16, 17*n*, 18, 22 & *n*, 28*n*, 35 f., 49*n*, 63 ff., 73 & *n*, 74 & *n*, 75 & *n*, 80 & *n*, 97*n*, 116, 175, 176*n*, 219 & *n*, 220*n*, 295*n*, 321*n*, 348, 352 & *n*, 356*n*, 358 & *n*, 359*n*, 407*n*, 419 & *n*, 420, 424, 425*n*, 426*n*, [2]104, 243*n*, 251*n*, 266, 336*n*, 368*n*, 380*n*, [3]88*n*, 307*n*, 321*n*
Maṣyât (Maṣyâd, Maṣyâf, Maṣyâb), [1]143 & *n*
Maṭar al-Warrâq, [2]170 f.
mathematical sciences, [3]111, 115 f., 121, 123, 130, 135, 157, 257; *see also* arithmetic, algebra; astrology; astronomy; geometry; optics
matter and form, [1]214, [2]104, 291, 300 f., 305, 421, [3]266, 274
Matthew, St., [1]476
al-Mâwardî, [1]lxxvi*n*, lxxxv, 391*n*, 450, 452*n*, [2]5*n*, 6, 11*n*, 20*n*, 21*n*, 22*n*, 54*n*, 59, 252*n*, 254*n*, 256*n*
Maymûn, Banû (of Cadiz), [2]43
Maysarah al-Maṭgharî, [2]289
Mayyâfâriqîn, [1]154 f.
al-Mazammah, [2]197
al-Mâzarî (Muḥammad b. 'Alî, Mâlikite jurist), [1]393, 394*n*, [2]459
Mâzin b. Ghassân (tribe), [1]219
Mazzara, [1]142
McCarthy, R. J., [1]314*n*
Mecca, [1]xxxvi f., lviii, lxii, lxvi*n*, xcv, 4*n*, 33, 43*n*, 48*n*, 126, 133, 171, 202, 209, 255 f., 404, 465, [2]133, 165, 177 & *n*, 196, 198, 249 f., 252 f., 256 ff., 262 ff., [3]416*n*, 417*n*, 450, 458, 472*n*; *see also* Ka'bah
mechanics, engineering, [1]39, 357 f., [2]238 f., 241, 363, 365, [3]132
medicine: defined, [3]148; a craft, [2]355 f., 373 ff., [3]148, a science, [3]148 ff., a subdivision of physics, [3]112; specialization (ophthalmology), [3]149; midwifery, [2]355 f., 368 ff.; hospitals, [2]153; epidemics, [2]136 f., [2]244 ff., 269, 376; physicians found in cities, [2]246*n*, 377, [3]149 f.; Avicenna's poem on, [1]171
man's embryonic stages, [2]368, 425, [3]275; human brain, [1]197, 210, [2]412, [3]105, 254, 295; heart, [1]210, 329, [3]104; vital spirit, [1]74, 174, 210 f., 329, [2]136, 374, 397, [3]104; digestive process, [2]122, 373 ff., [3]268, 278; preserving fish for human consumption, [1]35 f.; bad physical and mental effects of food, [1]178 ff., [2]373 ff.; effects of wine, [1]174, of *ḥashîsh*, [3]477; fevers, [2]374 f.; life determined by temper, [1]331, 358 f., its length, [1]343, [3]232; death from suffocation, [1]74, from starvation, [1]181 f., [2]136; artificial creation of man, [3]276
the Prophet's medical knowledge, [2]373, [3]150 f.; epidemics predicted by astrology, [2]213; talismans against bladder stones, [3]163*n*; letter magic and medicine, [3]173 f., 188 f., 222 f.; pulse an alchemical term, [3]233; medicine in love poetry, [1]220, [3]449, 476 f.
see also Galen
Medina (Yathrib), [1]4*n*, 12, 18, 25, 126, 202, 209, 223 f., 255 ff., 290, 295, 398*n*, 420, 439 ff., 453, 466, [2]70*n*, 133, 165, 194, 196, 249, 256, 262, 264 f., 362, 404, 453, 461, [3]6 ff., 12, 160*n*, 341, 458
Medinaceli, [1]141
Mediterranean, [1]23, 97 ff., 102, 117, 120 f., 129 ff., 139 ff., 150 ff., 159, 305, 326, [2]38 ff., 281, 283, 350, 353

Mehmet Muezzinzade, [1]xcvii
Mehren, A. F., [2]372*n*, [3]273*n*, 336*n*
Meknès, [1]129, [3]471
Melchites, [1]480 f.
Menelaus, [2]365, [3]131
Mensing, J. P., [1]xxv, and *passim* as the author of *Concordance*
Mercier, G., [1]128*n*, [2]17*n*
Mercier, L., [1]19*n*, 183*n*
Mercury (planet), [2]323, [3]474
Mérida, [1]140
Merinids, [1]xxxix ff., xlv, xlvii f., li ff., lxiv, 331, 335, 367, 369, [2]17, 24, 37, 45, 51, 66, 72 f., 130, 134, 198, 240*n*, 299, 387, 427*n*, [3]395, 471, 475
Mesemvria, [1]160*n*
Mesopotamia, *see* ʿIrâq
Messiah, *see* Jesus; Mahdî, Mahdism
Messina, [1]142
metals: nature of, [3]272 f.; origin of gold, [3]274 f.; do not exist in large quantities, [1]76; found in temperate zones, [1]168; their existence the result of civilization, [2]325; the seven malleable, [3]271; as media of exchange, [1]168; gold and silver as standard of value, [2]313, [3]277; gold mines, [1]124, [2]282; gold firmly embedded in its ore, [2]175; gold and silver, the treasures of the earth, [2]179, decay like other metals, [2]325; gold listed in inventory, [1]367 f., 420, [2]257; silver ingots as revenue, [1]362 f.; objects, ornaments, gifts of silver or gold, [1]26, 36, 47, 350, 360, 366*n*, 425, [2]53, 65, 116 f., 251, 253, 257, 259 f., 326, [3]392, 444; the Prophet's silver seal ring, [2]61; gold embroidered flags, [2]51 f., [3]168, cloth, [2]65, 67, carpets, [1]349; metal vessels, [2]349; iron stamps for coinage, [1]464, [2]54, 56; iron unknown in the Canaries, [1]117; bronze, brass, [1]75*n*, [2]259, [3]473; blacksmiths, [1]89, 309, [2]271, 302, 347*n*, 348, [3]432 f., 460 f.; goldsmiths, coppersmiths, [2]302, 348, 352
  bed of the Tiber paved with copper, [1]151; "Copper City," [1]75; magical copper vessels sealed with lead, [2]244 f.; use of metals in magic, [3]163, 168, 193, in alchemy, [3]175, 227 f., 234, 242*n*, 245, 267 ff., 457; "copper," "lead" as alchemical cover names, [3]244; "gold brick," "silver brick" to denote prophets and saints, [2]189 f.
metaphysics, *see* philosophy
Meyerhof, M., [1]118*n*, [3]114*n*
Mez, A., [1]174*n*, 221*n*, 352*n*, 364*n*, [2]27*n*, 65*n*, 392*n*, [3]102*n*
Midrârids, [1]42, 46
midwifery, [2]355 f., 368 ff.
Midyan, Midyanites, [1]100, 132, 334
Mihrajân, [1]48
Miknâsah, *see* Meknès
Miles, G. C., [1]xxiv
military science, warfare: a political craft, [2]347*n*; knowledge of, required of the caliph, [1]395; military administration in the government, [2]4, 6, 9 f., 17, 19 ff., 391; relative importance of military and civilian administration, [2]46 f.; judges participating in army campaigns, [1]61; position of soldiers in the state, [1]316 f., 340 ff., 354 f., [2]81, 92, 119 f., 123, 126, 299 f., 341; size of army contributes to extent of the realm, [1]17 f., 328, [2]124 f.; army main support of government, [1]80, 82, [2]23, used against Bedouins, [1]251 f., for the protection of the sedentary population, [1]256, [2]237 f.; cities constructed for defense purposes, [1]249, [2]237 f., 244, 248, 358; naval warfare, [2]38 ff., 248 f.; causes of war, [1]313, 381, [2]73 f.,

417; Holy War, ¹54, 449, 454, 456, 465, 473, ²40, 43, 45, 74, 79 f., 134, 263
    limitations to size of army, ¹16 f.; logistics, ¹23 ff.; weapons, ²84, of Bedouins, ²364, a human substitute for natural equipment of animals, ¹90; naphtha, mangonels, ¹370, ²253; matching military equipment of enemy, ¹417, ²87; warfare requires money, ¹340; battle order, ²76, of Mamelukes, ²81; fighting technique of attack and withdrawal, ²75, 77, 79 f., 404 f.; fighting in closed formation, ²74 f., 77, 79 f.; use of tents, ²67 f., military music, ²48 ff., trenches, ²81, 84, elephants, ²77 f., "thrones" for commanders, ²78; surprise attacks at night, ¹262, ²358; fleeing in battle and desertion, ¹263, 383, ²21, 75 & n, 81, 85, 87; concern for soldiers' morale, ¹259, ²149, 151; advice to fighters, ²82, 84 f.; Bedouins incapable of sustained fighting, ¹302, but Bedouin life produces better soldiers, ²297; foreign mercenaries, ¹343; use of trickery, ²85 f., 131; decisive character of non-material factors, ²85 ff., 130 f.; elegies for warriors, ³378; poetic descriptions of raids and battles, ³416 ff.; predictions of military happenings by means of magic, ¹236, astrology, ²213; warfare referred to in letter magic, ³173, in the *Zâ'irajah*, ¹240n

Miller, K., ¹109n, 116n
Minorca, ¹139, 241
Minorsky, V., ¹98n, 99n, 101n, 103n, 124n, 127n, 135n, 136n, 137n, 138n, 146n, 148n, 149n, 154n, 155n, 157n, 160n, 161n, 162n, 165n, 363n
mint, *see* coins, coinage

(al-)Miqdâd, ¹420
miracle(s): "miracles" and "wonders" defined, ¹188 f.; "miracles" and "acts of divine grace," ¹223, ³100 f.; prophetical, ¹184, ²365, ³160, 279; not required as proofs of the prophetical mission, ¹187; the Qur'ân Muḥammad's greatest, ¹192 f.; increase in number of Israelites, ¹20 f.; miraculous births, ²370; cannot serve as analogy for ordinary affairs, ²135; and sorcery, ³167 ff., 179 f., alchemy, ³245, 278 ff.; *see also* prophecy; saints
mirrors, ³82 f., 96; used by soothsayers, ¹214, 216 f., 231, 234
Miskawayh, *see* Maskawayh
Misrâtah, ¹125n
al-Mizzî, ¹38, ²161n
Moabites, ¹474
Môbedhân, ¹80 ff., 219, ²104 f., 202
Mogadishu, ¹99, 122n, 123
Moksha-Mordva, ¹161n
Mongol language, ¹lxiv
Mongol(s), ²128, 194n, 307; *see also* Tatar(s)
monkeys, ¹195, ²423
Mont Jûn (Mons Jovis, Montjoux), ¹151n
Montemayor, ¹150
Montemor-o-velho, ¹150n
de Montesquieu, C. L., ¹lxvii
Montillo, ¹140n
monuments: attest to civilization of past nations, ¹57, 369, ²239 ff., 268 f., 363; great monuments of the world, ¹356 ff., ²238 ff., of Rome, ¹151, of Constantinople, ¹153, of Northwestern Africa, ¹305, 357, ²239; pyramids, ¹356n, 357, ²239, 243; temples of Upper Egypt, ³160
Moon, Mountain of the, ¹101n, 120, 122
Morgenstern, J., ²258n

Morocco, [1]xlii*n*, xlvii & *n*, xlviii, 47, 49, *following* 110, 117 f., 129, 318, 367, [2]115, 223, 283, 289, 387, 430
Moses, [1]16, 18, 21, 275, 287 f., 322*n*, 357*n*, 412, 473 f., [2]258 ff., 439, [3]156, 160, 168
mosques, [1]51, 326 f., 357, 450, 452, [2]69 ff., 194, 231, 239 f., 249 ff., 362 f., Pls. III–VI
Mosul, [1]xciv*n*, 23, 102, 145, 334, 364, 375*n*, [2]52*n*, 115, 129, [3]325
mother: "Mother of the Book," [3]57; an alchemical cover name, [3]239
motion: of the spheres, [1]104, 194 f., [3]111 f., 131, 133 f., 136, 147, 248
Moulouya River, [1]128, [2]116
Msila (al-Masîlah), [1]129, 315*n*, [2]116
Mu'ammar as-Sullamî, [3]62
Mu'âwiyah b. Abî Sufyân, [1]26, 384*n*, 417, 421 ff., 426 f., 431 ff., 438 ff., 446 f., 451*n*, [2]9, 39 f., 53, 63 f., 69, 70*n*, 112, 192, [3]150*n*
Mu'âwiyah b. Ḥudayj, [1]440, [2]40
al-Mu'ayyad, *see* Hishâm al-Mu'ayyad, b. al-Ḥakam
Mu'ayyadîyah Library, [1]lxvi*n*
al-Mubarrad, [3]340
al-Mubashshir b. Fâtik, [1]lxxix*n*, lxxxi*n*, lxxxii*n*, 80*n*, 81*n*, 320*n*, 328*n*, [2]3*n*, 35*n*, 246*n*, 368*n*, [3]115*n*
Muḍar (tribe), [1]28, 57, 219, 266, 283, 298 f., 308, 319, 330, 352, 400, 418, 435, 442, 444, [2]114, 288, 305, 381 f., [3]282 f., 343 f., 346 f., 349, 351 ff., 363 f., 391, 410, 412 f.
Mudghalîs, *see* Madghallîs
Müller, A., [1]35*n*, 81*n*, [2]214*n*, 365*n*, [3]115*n*, 130*n*, 378*n*
al-Mufaḍḍal b. Salamah, [2]403*n*
Mufliḥ (official of al-Muqtadir), [2]228
al-Mughayribî, [3]229*n*, 269
al-Mughîrah b. Shu'bah, [1]426, 439, 466
Mugojar Mountains, [1]157*n*
al-Muḥabbar b. Qaḥdham, [2]183
Muhalhil, Awlâd, [3]423
al-Muhallab b. Abî Ṣufrah, [1]373; Muhallabites, [1]63
Muḥammad, [1]4 f., 43 f., 59, 76, 173*n*, 184 ff., 187 & *n*, 188, 192 ff., 200 ff., 204 f., 208 f., 211, 219, 223, 229, 254 ff., 260, 261*n*, 264, 273, 276, 279, 281, 289, 324, 330, 352, 359, 384 & *n*, 387 f., 396 f., 399 ff., 402*n*, 403 f., 410, 414 ff., 428, 429*n*, 432, 435 ff., 443, 448, 450, 458 ff., 466*n*, [2]7 f., 61, 65, 75, 86, 107, 134 f., 141 f., 159, 162 ff., 168 ff., 178 ff., 184 ff., 188 ff., 203 ff., 208, 210, 213 f., 249, 253, 255, 257, 263 ff., 306, 312, 326, 336, 339, 370, 373, 380, 383 f., 401, 425, 437 f., 440, 443 f., 450, 452, 461, [3]3 f., 7 f., 23 ff., 35 ff., 41 ff., 46, 55, 59 f., 67 f., 74, 78, 88*n*, 96, 103 f., 107, 150, 151*n*, 154, 160, 161*n*, 168 f., 182 f., 191, 196, 256, [3]262, 311 f., 321, 338, 345, 350, 367, 410, 435, 465, 472
Muḥammad (brother of Kurayb b. Khaldûn), [1]xxxv
Muḥammad, Abû 'Abdallâh (al-Waththâb) (brother of the Ḥafṣid Abû Yaḥyâ Abû Bakr), [2]223
Muḥammad I (of Granada), [1]xxxv
Muḥammad III (of Granada), [3]461*n*
Muḥammad V (of Granada), [1]xliv*n*, il
Muḥammad 'Alî (of Egypt), [1]cvii*n*
Muḥammad al-Bâqir, [1]405, 412

Muhammad al-Ḥabîb (father of 'Ubaydallâh al-Mahdî), [1]413, [2]211
Muhammad al-Mahdî, *see* Muhammad b. 'Abdallâh b. Ḥasan, an-Nafs az-Zakîyah
Muhammad Pasha, [1]183*n*
Muhammad al-Qaṣîr (teacher of Ibn Khaldûn), [1]xxxix
Muhammad as-Sajjâd, *see* Muhammad b. 'Alî b. 'Abdallâh b. (al-)'Abbâs
Muhammad Shâh (of Delhi), [1]370
Muhammad at-Taqî, [1]413
Muhammad b. 'Abd-al-'Aẓîm (poet from Guadix), [3]460
Muhammad b. 'Abd-ar-Raḥmân (b. Khaldûn) (son of Ibn Khaldûn), [1]xlvi
Muhammad b. 'Abd-ar-Raḥmân aḍ-Ḍârib, [1]ic
Muhammad b. 'Abd-ar-Razzâq (Moroccan jurist), [1]xlii
Muhammad b. 'Abd-as-Salâm, *see* Ibn 'Abd-as-Salâm, Muhammad al-Hawwârî
Muhammad b. 'Abdallâh b. 'Abd-al-Ḥakam, [3]10*n*
Muhammad b. 'Abdallâh b. Ḥasan b. al-Ḥasan b. 'Alî b. Abî Ṭâlib, an-Nafs az-Zakîyah, [1]31, 410 f.
Muhammad b. Abî l-Faḍl b. Sharaf, [3]445, 448*n*
Muhammad b. Abî l-Ḥusayn (Northwest African philologist), [3]329
Muhammad b. 'Alî b. 'Abdallâh b. (al-)'Abbâs, [1]29, 409
Muhammad b. Baḥr (teacher of Ibn Khaldûn), [1]xxxix
Muhammad b. Dâwûd (aẓ-Ẓâhirî), [3]5*n*
Muhammad b. Fuḍayl, [2]173
Muhammad b. al-Ḥanafîyah, *see* Ibn al-Ḥanafîyah
Muhammad b. al-Ḥasan (al-Wâsiṭî al-Muzanî?), [2]453
Muhammad b. al-Ḥasan al-'Askarî, [1]408, 414
Muhammad b. al-Ḥasan b. Muhammad (b. Khaldûn), Abû Bakr, [1]xxxvii
Muhammad b. Hishâm b. 'Abd-al-Jabbâr b. 'Abd-ar-Raḥmân an-Nâṣir, [1]380
Muhammad b. Isḥâq, *see* Ibn Isḥâq
Muhammad b. Ismâ'îl b. Ja'far aṣ-Ṣâdiq, [1]45, 412 f.
Muhammad b. Ja'far b. Abî Ṭâlib, [1]426*n*
Muhammad b. Khâlid al-Janadî, [2]184 f.
Muhammad b. Marwân al-'Ijlî (al-'Uqaylî), [2]181
Muhammad b. Maslamah, [1]442
Muhammad b. Muhammad (b. Khaldûn) (brother of Ibn Khaldûn), [1]xxxviii, xli
Muhammad b. Muhammad b. al-Ḥasan (b. Khaldûn), [1]xxxvii
Muhammad b. Muhammad b. Muhammad (b. Khaldûn), [1]xxxviii
Muhammad b. Muhammad b. Muhammad b. 'Imrân (chief of the Banû 'Imrân in Fez), [1]53
Muhammad b. Muhammad b. al-Qûṣawî, [1]ic
Muhammad b. al-Munkadir, [2]159
Muhammad b. Mûsâ b. an-Nu'mân, [2]381
Muhammad b. Qalâ'ûn, *see* al-Malik an-Nâṣir, Muhammad b. Qalâ'ûn
Muhammad b. al-Qâsim b. 'Alî b. 'Umar b. 'Alî Zayn-al-'âbidîn, [1]411
Muhammad b. Sa'd, *see* Ibn Sa'd
Muhammad b. Shu'ayb, *see* Ibn Shu'ayb aḍ-Dukkâlî (al-Haskûrî?), Abû 'Abdallâh
Muhammad b. Sîrîn, *see* Ibn Sîrîn
Muhammad b. Ṭalḥah, [1]440
Muhammad b. Tûmart, *see* Ibn Tûmart

Muḥammad b. ʽUbâdah al-Qazzâz, [3]441*n*
Muḥammad b. Yaḥyâ adh-Dhuhlî, [2]207
Muḥammad b. Zayd b. Muḥammad b. Ismâʽîl b. al-Ḥasan b. Zayd b. al-Ḥasan b. ʽAlî b. Abî Ṭâlib, [1]411
Muḥammad b. al-Ḥakîm, *see* Ibn al-Ḥakîm, Muḥammad
Muhanna' (chief of Âl Faḍl), [1]269*n*, 272
al-Muḥâsib, Jamâl, [3]292*n*
al-Muḥâsibî, [3]63, 80
al-Muhjam, [1]124
al-Muhr b. al-Faras, [3]447
al-Muḥsin (alleged son of ʽAlî and Fâṭimah), [1]407*n*
al-Muhtadî (ʽAbbâsid caliph), [1]456
al-Muʽizz (Fâṭimid ruler), [1]332, [2]133
al-Muʽizz (Zîrid), [3]15*n*
Mujâhid (ruler of Denia and the Baleares), [2]41, 440–41, 442
Mujâhid (b. Jabr), [2]179, 256, [3]56
Mukhallaf al-Aswad, *see* Yakhlaf al-Aswad
al-Mukhtâr b. Abî ʽUbayd, [1]406
Mukrân, [1]100, *following* 110, 126, 135, 362
al-Muktafî (ʽAbbâsid caliph), [1]42*n*
Multân, [1]127
al-Munajjim, Isḥâq, [1]116
al-Mundhir (ʽAbbâsid in Mahdî traditions), [2]179
al-Mundhir (Lakhmid ruler), [1]268, [2]379; *cf. also* an-Nuʽmân b. Mâ'-as-samâ'
Mundhir b. Saʽîd, [1]456
Munk, S., [1]lxxxiv*n*, [3]144*n*
al-Munqaṭaʽ, [2]256
Munqaṭaʽ al-ʽashâ'ir, [2]256
Munqidh, Banû, [2]44
Muqaddam b. Muʽâfâ al-Qabrî, [3]440 f.
Mûqân, [1]364*n*
al-Muqaṭṭam, Mountain, [1]125 f.
al-Muqawqis, [2]53 & *n*
al-Muqtadir (ʽAbbâsid caliph), [2]227 f.
al-Murâbiṭûn (followers of Ibn Qasî), [1]323
Murâd I b. Orkhan, [1]144*n*
Murajjâ b. Rajâ' al-Yashkurî, [2]182
Murcia, [1]141, 335, [3]447
Murghâr, Mount, [1]157
al-Murîdûn (followers of Ibn Qasî), [1]323*n*
Murnâq, [2]38
al-Murtaḍâ, *see* ash-Sharîf al-Murtaḍâ
al-Murtaḍâ az-Zabîdî, [2]385*n*, [3]32*n*
Mûsâ al-Kâẓim, [1]412 f.
Mûsâ b. Nuṣayr, [1]75; 333, 373
Mûsâ b. Ṣâliḥ (Berber soothsayer), [2]202
Muṣʽab b. az-Zubayr, [2]55
Musannâh, [1]160
al-Musayjid, [3]422
Musaylimah, [1]207
music, [1]348, [2]347*n*, 355 f., 395 ff.; defined, [2]395, [3]112; musical instruments, [2]48 f., 51 f., 348 f., 395 ff., 403 f., [3]194, 431, 442; teaching of, [2]348; effects of harmony, [2]49, 356, 395 ff.; animals influenced by, [2]49; effects of military, [2]48 f.; conducive to Sufi experiences, [1]230; practice of, unsuitable for princes, [1]40, 434; Negroes fond of dancing and, [1]174; singing in the bath, [1]174
origin of Arabic, [2]402 ff.; introduction of, into Spain, [2]405, still practiced there, [2]349; and Qur'ân recitation, [2]141, 399 ff., poetry, [3]341, 384, 442 f., 465, magic, [3]184 ff., 190, 194, 215, 225
Muslim (subtribe of the Riyâḥ), [2]200
Muslim, Âl (Egyptian Bedouins?), [3]439

Muslim b. al-Ḥajjâj, [1]187n, 324n, 392n, 394, [2]157n, 158, 159n, 162, 167, 169 f., 173, 176 ff., 182, 192n, 208n, 209, 249, 454, 458n, 459, 462, [3]43n, 61n
Muslim b. al-Walîd, [3]403 f.
al-Musta'în ('Abbâsid caliph), [1]49n
al-Musta'în (Hûdite of Saragossa), [1]317
al-Mustanṣir ('Abbâsid caliph), [3]18 f.
al-Mustanṣir (Ḥafṣid ruler), [2]72, 222, [3]329
Mustanṣirîyah College, [3]19n
al-Musta'ṣim ('Abbâsid caliph), [2]219, [3]18
al-Mustaẓhir ('Abbâsid caliph), [1]470 f.
al-Mu'taḍid ('Abbâsid caliph), [1]42, 46, [2]127; in Spain, [1]316, 470
al-Mutanabbi', [1]262n, [3]382, 386, 411
Muṭarrif (poet from Granada), [3]447
Muṭarrif b. 'Alî (Mâlikite jurist), [3]16
Muṭarrif b. Ṭarîf, [2]164
al-Mu'taṣim ('Abbâsid caliph), [1]314, 352, 411, 427, 456, [2]217; in Spain, [1]316, 470
al-Mu'taṣim (b. Ṣumâdiḥ, of Almería), [3]441
al-Mutawakkil ('Abbâsid caliph), [1]427, [2]127, 213
Mu'tazilah: history of, [3]61 f.; interpretation of the Qur'ân, [2]446 f., [3]339; views on the Qur'ân, [3]49, on acts of divine grace and fraudulent miracles, [1]190, on the divine attributes, [3]48 f., 61 ff., 68, on "sustenance," [2]312, on human actions, [1]188, on predestination, [3]48, 61 f., on the caliphate, [1]390 f., on the opponents of 'Alî, [1]441; knowledge of philosophy, [3]62; authors on the principles of jurisprudence, [3]29; Zayd b. 'Alî Zayn-al-'âbidîn suspected of M. leanings, [1]406
al-Mu'tazz ('Abbâsid caliph), [1]36
al-Muthannâ b. aṣ-Ṣabbâḥ, [2]184
al-Muttaqî al-Hindî, [1]397n
al-Muẓaffar, *see* 'Abd-al-Malik b. al-Manṣûr b. Abî 'Âmir
al-Muẓaffar (b. al-Musta'în, Hûdite of Saragossa), [1]317
al-Muzanî, [3]10
mysticism, *see* Sufism
von Mžik, H., [1]361n, [2]29n, 177n

N

Nallino, C. A., ¹96n, 97n, ²40n, 42n, 43n, 212n, 214n, ³62n, 135n, 221n, 262n
Naples, ¹151
Narbonne, ¹142, 150
Nasâ, ¹148
an-Nasafî ('Umar b. Muḥammad), ³34
an-Nasâ'î, ²162 f., 167 f., 171, 175, 177, 455
an-Nâshî, ³387n, 389
Nâshir, *see* Yâsir
Nashîṭ al-Fârisî, ²404
an-Nâṣir ('Abbâsid caliph), ²128
an-Nâṣir, *see* 'Abd-ar-Raḥmân b. al-Manṣûr b. Abî 'Âmir
an-Nâṣir, *see* al-Malik an-Nâṣir, Muḥammad b. Qalâ'ûn
an-Nâṣir, al-Uṭrûsh, *see* al-Uṭrûsh, an-Nâṣir
Naṣîr-ad-dîn aṭ-Ṭûsî, *see* aṭ-Ṭûsî, Naṣîr-ad-dîn
Naṣr, Banû (= Naṣrids?), ³185
Naṣr b. Sayyâr, ¹373
Naṣrids (of Granada), ¹xxxv, 334 f., ²51, 66, ³185n, 365, 396n, 461, 465
an-Nâṭulus, *see* Anatolia
navigation, navy, ¹117 f., ²37 ff., 365
an-Nawawî, ¹393, 394n, ²21n, 451, 456, 459, 463, ³12, 18
Nawbakht, Banû, ¹63, 277, 373, ²23, 99
Nawfîl, *see* Theophilus
an-Nawsharî, 'Îsâ, ¹41
Nawwâr (family of), ²226
an-Naẓẓâm, Ibrâhîm, ³62
Nebuchadnezzar, ¹17, 475, ²260
Nefzoua, ¹130
Negroes, ¹99, 102, 118 f., 121, 123, 125, 168 ff., 301, 397, 411, 424 f., ²367, ³185n, 245; *see also* Sudan
Nemours, ¹lii
Neo-Ismâ'îlîyah, *see* Assassins; Shî'ah

Neo-Platonism, *see* Plato
Nero, ¹479
Nestorians, ¹480
Nicea, ¹479
Nicholson, R. A., ¹cix, 15n, 77n, 84n, 262n, 305n, 343n, ³39n, 76n, 88n, 102n, 179n
Nicomachus of Gerasa, ³120n
Niebla, ¹140
Niger, ¹102n
Nihâwand, ¹363 & n
Nile, ¹lviii, 101, 102 & n, 118 ff., 125 f., 131, ²321, ³460
Nîsâbûr, ¹147, ³68n
Nîsar, desert of, ¹125, 128
Nisibis, ¹144
Niẓâm-al-Mulk, ²213
Niẓâm-al-Mulk (Bûyid?), ³250n
Niẓâmî, ²104n
Nizâr, Banû, ¹28
Noah, ¹44, 169 f., 343, ²365 f., ³467
Nob, ²259
Nöldeke, T., ¹67n, 220n, ²443n, ³59n, 378n
nomads, *see* Arab(s); Bedouins
Normandy, ¹159
Norway, ¹164
Noun, ¹128
Noureddine, A., ¹171n
Nûbah, *see* Nubia, Nubian(s)
an-Nubâhî, ¹140n, ²458n, ³365n
Nubia, Nubian(s), ¹102, *following* 110, 120 ff., 424 f.
Nûl, *see* Noun
an-Nu'mân (Lakhmid ruler), ¹281 f., ²252n
an-Nu'mân (*leg.* al-Murdhir?) b. Mâ'-as-samâ', ³450, 451n
an-Nu'mân b. Bashîr, ¹439 f.
an-Numayrî, *see* Manṣûr b. Zibriqân an-Namarî
numbers, numerals: *ghubâr* (dust) numerals, ¹10, 239, ³197 f., 204 ff.; *zimâm* numerals, ¹239, ³188n, 190, 197n, 198, 200, 207 ff., 214n; numerical value of

the letters of the alphabet, [1]236n, [2]190 ff., 194, 205 f., 225, 230, [3]173 f., 221 ff., predictions from this value, [1]236 ff., 241, [2]205 f., 215; magical properties of, [3]158, 162, 166, 173 f.; loving numbers, [3]162; the elemental ogdoad, [3]220; the ten spheres of the world, [3]249; the lucky number seven, [2]51; *see also* arithmetic, algebra; history, historians
an-Nûrî, *see* Abû l-Ḥusayn an-Nûrî
Nuṣayb b. Rabâḥ, [3]397
Nyberg, H. S., [1]441*n*, [2]423*n*, [3]39*n*, 62*n*, 88*n*, 96*n*
Nykl, A. R., [3]398*n*, 440*n*, 442*n*, 443*n*, 444*n*, 445*n*, 446*n*, 447*n*, 448*n*, 450*n*, 455*n*, 457*n*, 458*n*, 459*n*, 460*n*, 461*n*, 465*n*

O

Oases (Inner), *see* Siwa; *cf. also* [1]102, 121
Oases, Mountain of the, [1]125
Obed, [1]18
Og, [1]357 f., [2]240
oleander, [2]295
Oman, [1]100 f., *following* 110, 126, [2]39, 354
ophthalmology, [3]149
Opitz, K., [1]171*n*
von Oppenheim, M., [1]272*n*
optics, [3]132 f.
Oran, [1]liii, lviii, 129, [2]273 f.
orange trees, [1]364*n*, [2]295
Orosius, [1]95*n*
orphans, [1]455, [3]39 f.
Ottomans, [1]lxv, lxvii, xc, 144, 153
Ouargla, [1]119
Ousselat, Mount, [1]130
Oxus, [1]101 ff., 136 & *n*, 137, 139, 148, 157

P

paganism, [1]93, 117 f., 127, [2]258, 264, 266; *see also* Magians, Majûs
painters, painting, pictures, [1]300, [2]55 ff., 66, 224, 322, 352, [3]163
Palermo, [1]142
Palestine, [1]lxii, 18, 333, 357*n*, 365
Palmyra, [1]134
Palmyrenian language, [1]200*n*
Pamplona, [1]150
Pantelleria, [2]40 f.
paper manufacture, [2]392
Paran, *see* Fârân
Pareja Casañas, F. M., [2]217*n*
Parthia, [1]146*n*
Paul, St., [1]151
Pauly-Wissowa, *Real-Encyclopädie*, [1]128*n*
pearls, [1]349, 365*n*, 366 ff., [2]194, 325, [3]432, 443, 463; mother-of-pearl, [2]361, [3]392
Pechenegs, [1]*following* 110, 161, 165
Pechina, [2]40
Pedersen, J., [2]70*n*, 71*n*
Pedro the Cruel, [1]xlii, il
Pedroche, [1]140*n*
Pellat, C., [1]lxxvi*n*, 316*n*, 453*n*
Peloponnesos, [1]139, 142
Peñuela, J. M., [3]390*n*
perception: sense, [1]196 ff., 210 f., [2]346, 406, 412 f., 419 ff., [3]71, 137; intellectual, [2]413, 419 ff., [3]35; range of human, [3]77 f., 247 ff.; reality created by human, [3]86, 90 f.; defective sense, [3]37, 154; of animals, [2]416, 421; sense, of the dead, [3]74; supernatural, [1]184 ff., [2]420 ff., [3]72 f., 81 f., 103 ff., 252; "the inability to perceive is perception," [3]39; *see also* sense perception
Pérès, H., [1]c, 407*n*, [2]15*n*, 89*n*, 315*n*, 335*n*, 356*n*, [3]151*n*, 404*n*
Perez, [1]19
perfume: produced on the islands of the Indian Ocean, [1]124; not used during the pilgrimage, [2]367; perfumers, [2]302, 348; names of perfumes used in code

writing, [2]391; used in magic, [2]323, [3]164; in poetry, [3]441, 445, 464; musk, [2]61 f., [3]441, 446 f., 454, 463, 466

Périgueux, [1]151*n*

Peripatetics, [3]114

Perlmann, M., [1]26*n*

Persia, Persian(s), [1]12, 17, 24 f., 57, 78, 83, 172 f., 219, 267, 273*n*, 278, 298, 301, 304, 315, 321, 329 f., 333 f., 347 f., 350 f., 356, 360, 382, 386, 417, 419, 429, 441, 475, [2]7, 20, 22, 48, 50, 52*n*, 53, 55 f., 67, 76 ff., 84, 95, 104 f., 134, 138, 193, 202, 215*n*, 216, 251, 257, 260 f., 266, 268, 288, 301, 307, 319, 354, 404, [3]9, 113 ff., 135*n*, 168 f., 186, 313 ff., 319, 337, 343, 346*n*, 352, 361, 412

Persian Gulf, [1]23, 25*n*, 100, 102, 122, 124, 126, 134 f., 146, [3]446

Peter, St., [1]151, 476 f., 479 f.

Petra, [2]240

Philae, [1]121*n*

Philistines, [1]474, [2]259

philology, *see* grammar; language, linguistics; lexicography; literature, literary criticism

philosophy, [3]111 ff., 246 ff., 299; defined, [3]246 f.; the philosophical sciences defined, [2]436; etymology of "philosopher," [3]247; history of, [3]114 ff., 139 ff., 248 f.; epistemology, [1]198*n*, [2]411 ff., [3]77 f., 86, 91, 137 ff.; all human knowledge acquired, [2]424 ff.; metaphysics, [2]420, [3]34 ff., 53, 83, 85, 111 f., 152 ff., 167, 250, 252, 257, 299

philosophical views on existence, [2]398, on the permanence of the species, [2]371 f., on politics, [2]138, on prophecy, [1]lxxiv f., 79, 92 f., 190 f., 390, [2]417, [3]73, on the Resurrection, [3]256 f.; and theology, [3]51 ff., 143 ff., 153 ff., 246 ff., the Mu'tazilah, [3]62, Sufism, [3]155, history, [1]12, 16, dream visions, [3]72 f., magic, [3]158 f., 165 ff., 170, 218, 229, alchemy, [3]218, 229 f., 232 f., 236 f., 242, 271 ff., 280; inferior poetry of philosophers, [3]395; translation of Greek philosophical works, [2]203, [3]140 ff., 152; Ibn Khaldûn's works on, [1]xliv

see also ethics; logic; matter and form; physics

physics, [1]lxxvii f., 91*n*, 104, 107 f., 336*n*, [2]356, [3]52, 89 f., 116, 147 f., 151, 155, 250 f., 257, 275, 278, 299; defined, [3]111 f., 147, 152 f.

pilgrimage, [1]xxxvi f., lviii, lxii, lxiv; legal problems concerning circumambulation of the Ka'bah, [2]254 f.; reason for restrictions to be observed during the, [2]367; pilgrims transmitters of news, [3]472, taxed, [2]92; instituted by Abraham, [2]250; performed by Tubba's, [2]251, by Persians, [2]251, 257; prohibited by Spanish Umayyads, [2]100

Pinto, O., [1]417*n*

Pirizade Effendi, [1]cvii

Pisa, [1]151

Plato, [1]xxiv, lxxxi*n*, lxxxii*n*, 320*n*, 381*n*, [3]85, 115, 131, 249, 252; Neo-Platonism, [1]4*n*

Plessner, M., [1]lxxxix*n*, 81*n*, 212*n*

Pliny, [1]128*n*

Plooij, E. B., [3]130*n*

Plutarch (Pseudo-), [3]274*n*

poetry: defined, [3]381 f.; Arabic, defined, [2]402; various types of, [3]368, 373, 388 ff., 413; relationship of, and prose, [3]368 ff.; poetical method (*uslûb*), [2]307, [3]341, 369, 375 ff.; prosody, [2]223, [3]187, 386, 374 f., 381, 413 f., 440, 460, 466, 475 f.

easy to memorize, [2]441, 443;

importance of memorizing good, [3]362, 383, 392 ff.; ideal conditions for composing, [3]383 ff.; poems set to music, [2]403 f., [3]341; poets are proud and haughty, [2]331, sensitive to beauty, [3]384, 462; natural aptitude for, [2]399, [3]375, 387, 413; changing social position of poets, [3]410 ff., 440; use of poetic license, [3]385, of clichés, [3]386; teaching of, [3]301, 303 f., 307; linguistic skill of poets, [3]330; must be known by secretaries, [2]30, [3]341; used to encourage fighters, [2]49; inferior, of scholars and scientists, [3]394 ff.; Ibn Khaldûn's interest in, [1]xxxix, xlii, xlv, lxiv, xcii, xcvi, cv, cvii

Aristotelian Poetics, [3]141 f., 412*n;* believed by some people to exist only in Arabic, [3]373*n*, 382, 412; originally the only Arab art, [2]401 f.; "archive of the Arabs," [2]402, [3]304, 374, 410; Muḥammad's attitude toward, [3]410; 'Abbâsid and Umayyad, at times superior to pre-Islamic, [3]367, 396 ff.; influence of Arabic, upon the poetry of Christian Europe, [3]440*n*

the *Mu'allaqât*, [3]377*n*, 397*n*, 410; evidential verses, [3]356 f., 404; poems on: Qur'ân reading, [2]441, Qur'ân orthography, [2]442 f., Sufism, [3]87, 92, 95, 386, calligraphy, [2]388 f., poetry, [3]387 ff., grammar, [3]324, alchemy, [3]229, 269, the *Zâ'irajah*, [3]183 ff., how to make water disappear in the ground, [2]322 f., astrology and theology, [3]264 ff.

prediction poems, [2]219 ff., in the Berber language, [2]202; *rajaz* poems, [1]117, [2]219, 443; in Northwestern Africa, [3]364, in Spain, [3]364 ff.; popular, from Northwestern Africa, [3]415 ff., from Egypt, [3]438 f., 454, 475 f., from Syria, [3]437 f., from the 'Irâq, [3]455, 475 f.; *zajals*, [2]221, [3]415*n*, 440, 446 f., 454 ff.; *muwashshaḥ* poetry, [3]414*n*, 415*n*, 440 ff.; "gilded" *muwashshaḥahs*, [3]442; "play poems" (*mal'abah*), [2]221, 223, [3]468, 471 ff.; *muzawwaj* poetry in the Maghrib, [3]468 ff.; popular *ghazal* poetry in the Maghrib, [3]468; *kâzî*, [3]468; *mawâlîyâ*, [3]475 f.; *ḥawfî*, [3]475 & *n; qûmâ*, [3]475*n; kân-wa-kân*, [3]475 f.; *dûbayt*, [3]475, 478 f.; *Aṣma'îyât*, [3]413; *baddâwî*, [3]413; *Ḥawrânî*, [3]413 f.; *Qubaysî* (*Qaysî?*), [3]414

verses quoted: [1]xxxiv*n*, cxi, 32, 37, 43, 45, 220, 236, 240, 262, 297, 316, 338, 349, 407 ff., 427, 470, [2]83 f., 102, 252, 275, 322 f., 379 f., 388 f., [3]95 f., 183 ff., 211, 213 f., 224, 264 ff., 310, 376 ff., 387 ff., 404, 416 ff., 441 ff.

Poitou, [1]151, 158

Poland, [1]159, 164

police, [1]456 ff., [2]4, 35 ff., 97; private citizens taking over police duties, [1]325

political science, [1]lxxvi*n*, 56, 78, 80 ff., 89, 235, 337, 386 f., [2]5 f., 105, 138 ff., 347*n*, 417, [3]309

pomegranates: seeds removed by magic, [3]161; cheeks compared to them, [3]454; pomegranate marmalade as revenue, [1]363

Poole, S. Lane, [2]55*n*

Pope, *see* Christian(s)

Popper, W., [1]368*n*

population, [1]lxxvi f.; its size depends on business, [2]104, determines wealth and prosperity, [2]272 ff., 280 ff., 290 f., 299, 314, influences prices, [2]276 ff.; growth in successive generations, [1]18 f.;

replenished in cities from the countryside, ²236, 270; transfer at change of dynasties, ²299 f.; denseness causes epidemics, ²136, 376, produces a healthy climate, ²245 f.; *see also* civilization; urban life

Porphyry, ³139n, 142n, 252n, 253n

postal service, ¹451, ²4, 9, 14

poverty, ²153, 274 f., 282, 293, 330 ff., ³39 f., 280

prayer, ¹449 ff.; important religious activity, ¹418, 436, 449 f., 466, ²141, ³41 f.; teaches discipline, ¹307, ²74; the Friday prayer, ¹42, 450, ²70 ff.; enclosure (*maqṣûrah*), ²69 f., Pls. IV–V; pulpit (*minbar*), ²70 f., Pls. IV–V; calculation of time, ¹105, 112; the rows formed for, ²74, ³76n; for rain, ¹450, ³377; ar-Rashîd's fondness for, ¹33; salaries of prayer leaders and muezzins, ²334 f.; means to supernatural perception, ²422; used in magic, ³165, 178, 180 f., 187, 193

preachers, preaching, ¹33, ²71, 208, 334, 463, ³368 f.

predestination, ¹4, 292 f., ³43, 45, 48, 61 f., 260, 265 ff., 475

prediction of the future, ¹207, 219, 221, 240, 411, ²46, 187, 190 ff., 200 ff., ³258 f., 474 f.; *see also* astrology; magic, sorcery

Pretzl, O., ¹67n, ²443n, ³59n

prices: fixed by the government, ²94 ff., 109 f.; urban price structure, ²276 ff., 292; of grain, ²136, 339 ff., real estate, ²284; determined by customs duties and all other costs, ²293; cost of food pushed up by labor costs, ²278 f., 314; raised by scarcity of goods, ²338; prolonged prevalence of unfair, ²340 ff.

principles of jurisprudence, *see* jurisprudence, jurists, judiciary

prisons, ¹31, 36, 74, 221, 371, 396, 411, ²17, 194, 299, ³420, 452

profit: defined, ²312, 336; various ways of earning a living, ²315 f.; obtained through labor, ¹303, ²272, 280, 282, 313 f., commerce, ²336 ff., no human effort, ²311; augmented through prestige or power, ²326 ff.; measured in silver and gold, ³277

prophecy: its mechanics and psychology, ¹184 ff., ²422 ff., ³70, 72 f., 75, 157 f., 179; essential for human society, ¹lxxiv f., 79, 390, ²417, not essential, ¹92 f.; does not exist in extreme north and south, ¹167n, 169; suspends the ordinary course of affairs, ¹437, 444, ²134 f.; prophets may disregard custom, ²118, enjoy social prestige, ¹188, 322, 414

must be true, ¹205; infallibility (*'iṣmah*) of prophets, ¹185 f., 403, ³42; the light of prophecy, ¹4n, 206; prophets possess perfect perception, ³38, 72 f., 87, 154; Muḥammad's perfection, ²383 f.; prophetical miracles, ¹188 ff., 223, ²134 f., 185 f., 192, 365 f., 370, ³100, 167, 279; distinction between prophecy and sainthood, ²189; and Sufism, ¹224, dream visions, ¹208 f., ³72 f., 107, 110, magic, soothsaying, ¹206, ³167, 179, geomancy, ¹227n, 229 ff., astrology, ³258 f., 262

see also religion; science and scholarship

psychology, *see* soul

Ptolemais, *see* Ṭulaymithah

Ptolemy, ¹lxxiin, 96n, 97 & n, 101n, 103, 110 ff., 116, 122,

149*n*, 164*n*, 226 ff., 235 & *n*, [3]135, 259 ff.
pulleys, [1]39, [2]238, 363, [3]132
pyramids, *see* monuments
Pyrenees, [1]141, 150
Pythagoras, [1]235*n*

Q

Qâbis, *see* Gabès
Qabîṣah b. Dhu'ayb, [2]207, 209
al-Qâbisî, [1]lxxiv*n*
al-Qabrî, *see* Muqaddam b. Mu'âfâ al-Qabrî
al-Qâbûn, [2]230
al-Qâḍî al-Fâḍil al-Baysânî, [2]44, 45*n*, [3]393
Qâḍîkhân, [2]244*n*
al-Qâdir ('Abbâsid caliph), [1]46
al-Qâdisîyah, [1]17, 101, 134, 145, 259, 321, 466, [2]77 f., [3]168
Qafṣah, *see* Gafsa
Qaḥṭabah, Banû, [1]31, [2]99
Qaḥṭân (tribe), [1]330, 352
al-Qâ'im, Abû l-Qâsim (Fâṭimid ruler), [1]41, 467, [2]41
al-Qal'ah, *see* Qal'at Ibn (Banî) Ḥammâd
al-Qalandarîyah, [2]229
al-Qalânisî, Abû l-'Abbâs (Mu'tazilite), [3]63
Qal'at Ibn (Banî) Ḥammâd, [1]315, 332, [2]70, 116, 237, 239, 289, 351
Qal'ât Ibn Salâmah, [1]liii, lv f., lviii, lxxi, [3]481*n*
Qalâ'ûn (descendants of), [1]368
Qalhât, [1]126
al-Qâlî, Abû 'Alî, [3]341
al-Qalqashandî, [1]lxvi, [2]29*n*, 31*n*, 35*n*, 45*n*, 48*n*, 52*n*, [3]334*n*
Qamḥîyah College, [1]lx f.
Qamnûriyah, [1]125
al-Qa'nabî, [2]453
Qanâwah, [3]185
al-Qandahâr, *see* Gandhâra
Qara-Qoyunlu, [1]235*n*
al-Qarâfî, Shihâb-ad-dîn, [2]429, [3]18, 29
Qaraqum, Lake of, [1]157*n*
Qârib b. al-Aswad, [1]207
Qarmaṭians, [1]42, [2]51
Qâshân, [1]136, 147
al-Qâsim, Banû (Ait), *see* Zayyânids
al-Qâsim b. Abî Bazzah, [2]162
Qâsim b. Marâ b. Aḥmad (of the Banû Ka'b), [2]200
al-Qâsim b. Muḥammad b. Abî Bakr, [1]422
al-Qâsim (b. Muḥammad) b. Idrîs (alleged ancestor of the Zayyânids), [1]271
Qaṣr Ibn Hubayrah, [1]145
Qaṣr Kutâmah, [1]129
Qaṣr al-Majâz, [1]139
al-Qaṣr aṣ-ṣaghîr, [1]129, 139*n*
Qastâllah, *see* Estella
Qasṭallat Darrâj, [3]364*n*
al-Qasṭallî, *see* Ibn Darrâj al-Qasṭallî
Qatâdah b. Di'âmah, [2]166
al-Qaṭarî, Abû ṣ-Ṣalâḥ Muḥammad al-Ḥanafî, [1]ic, 192*n*, 230*n*
Qaylah, [2]264 f.
al-Qayrawân (Kairouan), [1]xxxix, lviii, 9, 41 f., 46, 130, 360, 382, 413, 428, [2]13, 38*n*, 70, 116, 236 f., 240, 247, 269, 283, 289, 351, 386, 427, 429, 434, Pls. IV–VI, [3]14, 15 & *n*, 16 f., 110, 264, 288, 363, 471, 473
al-Qayrawânî, *see* Ibn Abî Ṭâlib al-Qayrawânî
Qays ([b.] 'Aylân), Banû, [1]281, 441, [3]348*n*, 437 f.
Qays b. 'Âṣim (al-Minqarî), [1]282
Qays b. Dharîḥ, [3]404
Qazwîn, [1]146 f., 156
al-Qazwînî, Jalâl-ad-dîn, [3]337
al-Qifṭî, [2]214*n*, 216*n*, 365*n*, 368*n*, [3]115*n*, 136*n*
Qinnasrîn, [1]143, 266, 364 & *n*
Qipchaqs, [1]162, 166

Qirqîsiyâ', [1]145
al-Qônawî, Ṣadr-ad-dîn, [2]189*n*, [3]88*n*
Quatremère, E. M., [1]xxvi, xci, xcvii, c ff., cviii, 132*n*
Qubâqib, [1]153 f.
Qubâqib, Mount, [1]154
al-Qubbashî, Abû Bakr b. Mufarrij (Mufarraj), [2]381*n*
Quḍâ'ah, Banû, [1]266, [3]343
Qudâmah b. Ja'far, [3]336
Qudâmah b. Maẓ'ûn, [1]439
al-Qudûrî, [1]46
Qûfâyâ Mountains, [1]149, 157 f., 162 ff.
al-Qufṣ, [1]135
Qûhistân, *see* Kûhistân
al-Qull, *see* Collo
al-Qulzum, [1]100, 132
al-Qulzum, Sea of, *see* Red Sea
Qûmis, [1]363
Qumm, [1]147
Qumr, Mountain of the, [1]101, 118, 120, 122
Qur'ân, [2]439 ff.; the Qur'ânic sciences defined, [2]437; Qur'ân interpretation, [1]25 ff., [2]443 ff., 458, [3]23, 56 ff., 65, 80, 257, 299, 312 f., 337 ff., 369; the seven readings, [1]67, [2]440 f.; its orthography, [2]382 f., 442 f., [3]301, 396; use of *saj'*, [1]204*n*, [3]368 f.; proper recitation, [2]141, 399 ff., 403; distinction between Meccan and Medinese *sûrahs*, [1]202; the letters at the beginning of certain *sûrahs*, [2]191 f., 205 ff., 215, [3]55, 57, 59; teaching of the Qur'ân, [3]300 ff., 307; Qur'ân "readers," [2]31, 440 f., [3]3 f., 311
its inimitability, [1]193, [3]303, 338 f., 397, 402; Muḥammad's greatest miracle, [1]192 f.; believed created by the Mu'tazilah, [3]49; primeval but its recital created, [3]64 f.; "ambiguous" verses, [3]45 f., 55 ff., 101; as a source of law, [1]60, 454, [3]3 f., 23 ff., 309, 311 f., 316, 319, for the articles of faith, [3]45 ff.; used in magic, [3]177 f., 181, 194, 217, 226; significance for Arabic littérateurs, [3]303, 338, 340, 353, 402, 410
passages quoted (the numbering of verses here is that of the Egyptian edition only): **1**, [3]192, 217*n*; *1.6*, [1]67*n*, [3]349; *1.6–8*, [3]41; **2**.*1*, [3]59*n*; *2.20*, [2]243; *2.29*, [1]276, [2]81; *2.30*, [1]91*n*, 95*n*, 389, [2]416; *2.32*, [2]349; *2.37*, [3]176*n*; *2.67 ff.*, [1]408*n*; *2.102*, [1]40, [3]113, 159 f.; *2.103*, [1]40; *2.106*, [2]448; *2.125*, [2]458; *2.125 ff.*, [2]249*n*; *2.127*, [2]250; *2.142*, [1]176, 234, [2]266, 345, [3]20, 75, 129, 170, 290, 294, 308, 354, 362; *2.151*, [3]392; *2.163*, [3]315; *2.164*, [1]166; *2.212*, [2]109, 326, 328; *2.213*, [1]176, 234, [2]266, 345, [3]20, 75, 129, 170, 290, 294; *2.216*, [1]245, [2]199, [3]481; *2.231*, [2]81; *2.232*, [1]245, [2]199, [3]481; *2.233*, [3]294, 297, 409; *2.245*, [2]302; *2.247*, [1]287, 317, 378; *2.249*, [2]176*n*; *2.251*, [1]285, [2]343; *2.253*, [1]230; *2.259*, [1]408*n*; *2.275*, [1]218*n*; **3**.*6*, [3]56 f., 66; *3.7*, [2]206; *3.13*, [3]117; *3.26*, [2]145*n*; *3.37*, [2]109, 326, 328; *3.47*, [1]258, 385, [2]241, 363, 436, [3]315, 353; *3.49*, [1]476*n*, [3]279; *3.66*, [1]245, [2]199, [3]481; *3.68*, [1]377, [2]46, [3]35; *3.76*, [1]255; *3.96*, [2]256*n*; *3.97*, [1]336, [2]276; *3.109*, [3]67*n*; *3.110*, [1]40, 167*n*; *3.173*, [1]14; *3.182*, [2]108; *3.190*, [1]166, [2]52; **4**.*6*, [3]410*n*; *4.11 f.*, [3]127*n*; *4.17*, [2]426; *4.40*, [1]424; *4.46*, [1]40; *4.59*, [1]392, 403; *4.66*, [1]40; *4.92*, [2]426; *4.104*, [2]426; *4.111*, [2]426; *4.157*, [1]476*n*; *4.170*, [2]426; **5**.*3*, [1]202*n*; *5.17*, [1]258, [3]353; *5.22–24*, [1]288; *5.26*, [1]288*n*; *5.29*, [1]327, [2]442; *5.54*, [1]224 f., [3]290; *5.60*, [3]339;

5.77, ³339; *5.109*, ³110; *5.110*, ¹476*n*, ³279; *5.116*, ³110; **6.3**, ³67; *6.11*, ¹295; *6.18*, ¹213, 261, 310, 382; *6.61*, ¹310, 382; *6.73*, ¹213, 261; *6.91*, ³35; *6.92*, ²256; *6.96*, ²58; *6.97*, ³368; *6.98*, ³368; *6.112*, ³117; *6.126*, ³368; *6.137*, ³117; *6.165*, ¹389, ²329*n*; **7.**10, ²407, 419; *7.43*, ³69, 258; *7.54*, ³47, 65; *7.110 ff.*, ²322*n*; *7.117*, ³168; *7.118*, ³169; *7.185*, ³291; *7.187*, ³59; **8.**7, ²60; *8.51*, ²108; *8.63*, ¹193, 319; **9.**4, ¹255; *9.7*, ¹255; *9.33*, ¹295; *9.40*, ¹4*n*; *9.47*, ²442; *9.78*, ³110; **10.**35, ³94; *10.82*, ²60; **11.**46, ¹44; *11.66*, ¹430, ²69; *11.92*, ³280; **12**, ³103; *12.14*, ¹263; *12.21*, ¹322, 334, 472, ²113, 130, 238, 285, 305, 394, 430, ³34; *12.39*, ²297; *12.44*, ¹211, ²420, ³105 ff.; *12.76*, ¹65, ²48, 447, ³148, 310; **13.**2, ²311*n*; *13.11*, ¹295; *13.16*, ²297*n*; *13.31*, ¹300; *13.33*, ¹185; *13.38*, ²122; *13.41*, ¹319, ²270, 286, 291, 387, ³305; *14.*7, ³453; *14.19 f.*, ¹280, ²301; *14.32 f.*, ²311; **15.**9, ¹193; *15.17 ff.*, ¹205*n*; *15.75*, ³319; *15.86*, ¹175, 252, 353, ²50, 351 f., 356 f., 366, 368, 372, 405, ³331; *15.87*, ³192, 369; **16.**8, ¹169, ³250; *16.12*, ²311*n*; *16.41*, ¹40; *16.44*, ²443; *16.68*, ¹84*n*; *16.78*, ²407, 412, 419, 425, ³71; *16.93*, ¹414, 481; **17.**1, ²258, 262*n*; *17.9*, ³288; *17.16*, ¹293, ²294; *17.70*, ²417; *17.85*, ¹79, ³36, 178; **18**, ¹408*n*; *18.77*, ³65; *18.104*, ³402; **19**, ³194; **20.**1, ³59*n*; *20.28-32*, ²4; *20.50*, ¹84, 92; *20.114*, ¹372; **21.**5, ¹211, ²420, ³105 ff.; *21.22*, ¹337, 394; *21.89*, ¹305, 308, 355, ²67; **22.**5, ²425, ³275; *22.10*, ²108; *22.47*, ²204; *22.56*, ¹434; *22.65*, ²311*n*; *23.14*, ³275;

23.15, ¹386; *23.36*, ³256; *23.78*, ²407, 419; *23.91*, ³66; *23.115*, ¹293*n*; **24.**19, ¹245, ²199, ³481; *24.35*, ¹83, ³124; *24.38*, ²109, 326, 328; *24.40*, ¹387; *24.44*, ²97, 53, ³412; *24.45*, ¹258, ³353; **25.**2, ¹115, ²60; *25.20*, ²329*n*; *25.23*, ³317*n*; **26.**45, ³168; **27.**21, ²383, 442; *27.44*, ²259*n*; *27.69*, ¹295; **28.**68, ¹258, 293, ³118, 353, 367; *28.88*, ²128; **29.**6, ²276*n*; *29.17*, ²311, 313; *29.20*, ¹295; *29.41*, ¹40; *29.45*, ²141; *29.46*, ²438; *29.61*, ²311*n*; *29.64*, ¹40; **30.**4, ¹300; *30.7*, ¹387; *30.22*, ²52, ³480; *30.42*, ¹295; *30.54*, ¹258, ³353; **31.**6, ¹20; *31.20*, ²311*n*; *31.22*, ¹56; *31.29*, ²311*n*; **32.**9, ²407, 419; **33.**4, ¹44; *33.33*, ¹50*n*; *33.40*, ²61; *33.52*, ²73; *33.62*, ¹173, ²99, 134, 377; *33.63*, ³59; **34.**1, ¹213, 261; *34.48*, ³110; **35.**1, ²433, ³126, 325; *35.8*, ¹414, 481; *35.13*, ²311*n*; *35.16 f.*, ¹280, ²301; *35.39*, ¹389; *35.43*, ¹173, ²99, 134, 377; **36.**22, ¹33; *36.38*, ²58; *36.81*, ¹175, 252, 353, ²50, 351 f., 356 f., 366, 368, 372, 405, ³331; **37.**7 *ff.*, ¹205*n*; *37.96*, ²345, 372; *37.159*, ³66; *37.164*, ¹230; **38.**24, ¹461; *38.35*, ¹417; *38.38*, ¹386; *38.65*, ²297; **39.**4, ¹258, ²297; *39.5*, ²311*n*; *39.23*, ¹185, ³368; *39.36*, ¹185; **40.**33, ¹185; *40.85*, ¹54, 57, 332; **41.**6, ²424; *41.12*, ²58; *41.46*, ²108; *41.54*, ²280; **42.**7, ²256; *42.11*, ³66 f.; *42.19*, ¹430, ²69, 93; *42.24*, ²60; *42.49*, ¹258, ³353; *42.53*, ¹386; **43.**32, ²329; *43.35*, ¹297; **45.**3-5, ¹166; *45.12*, ²311*n*; **46.**15, ¹344; *46.30*, ³94; **47.**21, ¹40; *47.38*, ²311; **48.**23, ¹173, ²99, 134, 377; **49.**5, ¹40; *49.13*, ¹278, 415; **50.**29, ²108; **51**, ¹202; *51.47*, ²383, 442; *51.58*, ²102, 337 f., 342, ³280; **52.**4,

²250; 55, ¹202; 55.3 f., ²390, ³398; 57.21, ¹224 f., ³290; 59.9, ²148; 59.17, ¹327, ²442; 60.3, ¹416; 61.4, ²75, 82n; 61.9, ¹295; 62.4, ¹224 f., ³290; 64.16, ²148; 66.3, ³246; 67.23, ²407, 419; 68.1, ¹4n; 68.33, ¹40; 68.42, ³60; 72.26, ³264; 73.5, ¹185, 201; 73.20, ¹296, 346, 428, ²67, 88, 122, 279, 300, 307, 315, 439; 74, ¹202; 74.31, ¹414, 481; 75.16 f., ¹193; 75.16–19, ³107; 79.37 ff., ³402; 81.15, ³265; 82.19, ¹300; 83.26, ²61; 85.20, ³38; 89.3, ³97n; 89.6 f., ¹26; 90.10, ¹261 f.; 91.8, ¹262; 92.1 f., ³402; 92.5 ff., ³402; 93, ¹202; 93.11, ²35n; 95.5, ³305; 96, ¹202; 96.1–5, ²425; 96.5, ²422, ³135; 96.18, ³58; 99.1, ¹318; 107.4 f., ³41; 110.1, ²444; 112, ³36; 112.1 f., ²55; 112.3, ³66; 113.4, ³160, 168
al-Qurashî, Abû l-Qâsim of Bougie (mathematician), ³126
Quraysh, Qurashite(s), ¹28, 60, 187 f., 219, 266, 319, 360, 380, 395 ff., 407, 419, 432, 435, 441 f., 444, 472, ²21, 164 f., 188 f., 192, 196, 198, 251 ff., 379 f., ³74, 343 f., 411
Qurrah b. Iyâs, ²158, 182
al-Qurṭubî, Muḥammad b. Aḥmad b. Farḥ, ²446
Qûṣ, ¹126
Quṣayy b. Kilâb, ²252
al-Qushayrî, ¹460, ²185n, ³76, 77n, 80, 82, 85, 92n, 102, 179n

R

Rabâb (an official of Ibn Tâfrâgîn), ³429
Rabâb, Awlâd, ¹270
Rabat (Ribâṭ al-Fatḥ), ²240
ar-Rabb(?), ¹145n
ar-Rabîʿ (b. Yûnus), ²219
Rabîʿah b. Naṣr (Yemenite ruler), ¹219, ²202

Rabîʿah b. Nizâr, Banû, ¹28, 283, 418, ³343, 378
race, ¹3 & n; origin of racial distinctions, ¹170 ff.; Berbers and Arabs, the two races of the Maghrib, ¹11
Raddâd, Banû, ³439
ar-Radhdh, ¹364n
ar-Raḍî, see ash-Sharîf ar-Raḍî
Raḍwâ, Mountain of, ¹133, 407 f.
Râfiʿ b. Khudayj, ²265
ar-Râfiʿî, ³12, 18
ar-Râfiqah, ¹144
ar-Râghib al-Iṣfahânî, ¹45n, 262n, 427n, 451n, 452n, ²35n, 86n, 246n, ³165n
ar-Rahawî, Abû l-Qâsim (Tunisian poet), ³264
ar-Raḥbah, ¹145
Rahman, F., ¹197n
rain: rainfall of varying intensity, ²136; falling raindrops seem to form a straight line, ³133; in poetry, ²223, ³377, 417, 421, 430, 450, 458, 464, 478; through prayer, ³377; through magic, ³162, 245; will be plentiful in the days of the Mahdî, ²170 f., 181 f., 194; "from the divine throne to light rain," ³82; see also water
Ram, ¹18
Râmhurmuz, ¹135
ar-Rân, see Arran
ar-Raqqah, ¹102, 144, ²139
Râshid (client of the Idrîsids), ¹47 f.
ar-Rashîd (ʿAbbâsid caliph), ¹28 ff., 48 & n, 49, 269n, 277, 356, 361n, 365, 424, 427, 432–33, 467, ²10, 27, 63, 127, 218 f., 242 f., 301, ³306 f., 312, 323, 341, 378n, 411
Rashîd-ad-dîn, Faḍlallâh, ¹lxxii
Raslândah, ¹163, 164n
Rawḥ b. Zinbâʿ, ²68
ar-Rayy, ¹147, 363

ar-Rayyân, ³363
ar-Râzî, *see* Abû Ḥâtim ar-Râzî, Muḥammad b. Idrîs
ar-Râzî, *see* Fakhr-ad-dîn ar-Râzî
ar-Râzî, *see* Ibn Abî Ḥâtim
ar-Râzî, Abû Bakr Muḥammad b. Zakarîyâ', ³149, 237n
reasoning: its limits, ³352 f.; not safe from error, ¹58, ³309 f.; logical, ³137 ff.; as a source of law, ¹454, ³4, 24, 27 f., 285; and tradition, ³8 f., 13; and theology, ³154; *see also* intellect
Red Sea, ¹23, 100, 122, 124, 126, 132 f.
Reinaud, M., ¹120n
religion, ¹lxxiii; the "form" of political existence, ²305; role in politics, ¹80, 386 f., 448, ²105, 137 ff.; depends on group feeling for its success, ¹55 f., 263, 322 ff., ²195 f., 198; makes possible the foundation of powerful realms, ¹319 ff.; fulfillment of religious duties incumbent upon leaders, ¹292; makes Bedouins social beings, ¹305 ff.; basic Arab (Bedouin) indifference to, ²199 f.
   degrees of faith, ³41 ff., 55, 59 f.; stimulated by hunger, ¹179 f.; undermined by customs of luxury, ²292, 297; averse to science, ³115 ff.; unessential for the cultivation of the sciences, ³111; opposes magic and sorcery, ³113, 156, 159, 169 f., 178 ff., 246, 262 f., counteracting, ³168 f.; religious poetry, ³386, 395
   see also God; prophecy; theology
Renaud, H. P. J., ¹xln, xliin, xciin, cxiiin, 238n, 239n, ³21n, 123n, 126n, 136n
Rescher, O., ¹226n

reyes de taïfas, ¹315 ff., 351, 469 f., ²13, 15, 23, 41, 66 f., 70, 92, 99 f., 116, 129, 350, 405, ³364, 442
Rhazes, *see* ar-Râzî, Abû Bakr Muḥammad b. Zakarîyâ'
rhetoric, ¹78, 83, 275 f., ³141 f., 307, 335, 339, 368n, 370, 399, 401 ff., 412n
Ribâṭ Mâssah, *see* Mâssah, Monastery of
Richter, G., ²139n
ar-Riḍâ, 'Alî, ¹325, 413, 433
Rikabi, J., ³440n, 443n, 446n
Ripaia, ¹149n
Ritter, H., ¹lxxviiin, xcv f., 204n, 212n, 213n, ²93n, 191n, 336n, 415n, ³156n, 164n, 378n, 457n, 458n, 476n
Riyâḥ, Banû, ¹1, 272, ²200, ³420, 440
Riyâḥ b. 'Ijlah, ¹220
Robbins, F. E., ¹lxxiin
Robson, J., ²395n, 399n, 403n
Roger II, ¹94n, 116, ²43, ³123n
Roman Sea (= Mediterranean), ¹98
Romania (Rumania), ¹159n, ²42n
Rome, Roman(s), ¹lxvi, 74, 98, 151, 168n, 334, 474, 476 f., 479 ff., Pls. IIIa-b, ²38, 53, 191, 261, 268, 288, 298, 319, 354, ³115, 117, 283 f.
Ronda, ¹182
Rosen, F., ³284n
Rosenthal, E. I. J., ¹cix, ²138n, 413n, ³139n, 256n
Rosenthal, F., ¹livn, lxixn, lxxixn, cvn, cxin, 19n, 28n, 41n, 78n, 116n, 163n, 174n, 250n, 264n, 265n, 385n, 446n, 447n, ²21n, 22n, 55n, 74n, 161n, 163n, 191n, 228n, 263n, 365n, 439n, ³62n, 109n, 115n, 135n, 284n, 289n, 304n, 312n, 322n, 334n
Rosetta, ¹121, 132

royal authority, *see* government, leadership
Rubio, L., [1]xxix*n*, xlv
ar-Rudaynî, [3]438
ar-Rûdhân, [1]135
Ruelle, C. E., [3]242*n*
ar-Rûm, *see* Byzantines; Greece, Greek(s); Rome, Roman(s)
ar-Rûmâniyah, islands of, [1]159*n*, [2]42*n*
Rûmî, Jalâl-ad-dîn, [3]39*n*, 88*n*
Ruska, J., [1]19*n*, [3]121*n*, 237*n*
Russia, Russian(s), [1]98, 159 f., 164 f.
Rustum, [1]17, 307, 348*n*, [2]78, [3]168
Ruwâḥah (tribe), [1]131
ar-Rûyân, [1]363

S

Sa'âdah (of the Muslim-Riyâḥ), [2]200
Saba', [1]126
Saba' b. Yashjub, [2]241
as-Saba'îyah, *see* Shî'ah
Sabasṭiyah, *see* Samaria
aṣ-Ṣabbâḥ, *see* al-Ḥasan b. Muḥammad aṣ-Ṣabbâḥ
Sabbath River, [1]22*n*
aṣ-Ṣâbi', Ibrâhîm b. Hilâl, [3]393, 406, 408
Ṣâbians, [1]221*n*, [2]258, 264; *see also* al-Ḥarrânî (alchemist)
as-Sabî'î, Abû Isḥâq, [2]163 f.
as-Sabtî, Abû l-'Abbâs (alleged author of the *Zâ'irajah*), [1]239, 240*n*, 243, [3]182*n*, 183, 185*n*
as-Sabtî, Muḥammad b. Aḥmad, Abû l-Qâsim, [1]xlii, [3]398, 408
as-Sabtî, Sîdî Aḥmad, [1]239*n*
Sâbûr, [1]135
Sachau, (C.) E., [1]108*n*, 256*n*, [2]161*n*
Sa'd, Banû (chieftains of the Banû Yazîd-Zughbah), [1]272
Sa'd b. 'Abd-al-Ḥamîd b. Ja'far, [2]177 f.
Sa'd b. Abî Waqqâṣ, [1]17, 59*n*, 255, 259, 301, 420, 430*n*, 439 f., 465, [3]114
Sa'd b. 'Ubâdah, [1]396 f.
Ṣa'dah, [1]124, [2]51
Ṣadghiyân (Berber tribe), [2]43
Sadwîkish (Berber tribe), [2]43
aṣ-Ṣafâ, [3]417
Ṣafad, [1]lxv
aṣ-Ṣafadî, [1]240*n*, [2]230*n*, [3]13*n*, 457*n*
safety of roads, *see* highway robbery
as-Saffaḥ ('Abbâsid caliph), [1]282*n*, 410, 432, 467, [2]179
Ṣaffârids, [2]128
Ṣafî-ad-dîn al-Ḥillî, *see* al-Ḥillî, Ṣafî-ad-dîn
Sahl b. 'Abdallâh, *see* at-Tustarî, Sahl b. 'Abdallâh
Sahl b. Hârûn, [3]393
Sahl b. Mâlik, Abû l-Ḥasan, [3]445 f., 448, 459
Sahl b. Nawbakht, Banû, *see* Nawbakht, Banû
Sahl b. Sa'd, [1]445
Sahl b. Salâmah al-Anṣârî, Abû Ḥâtim, [1]325 f.
as-Sahmî, [2]169*n*
Saḥnûn, [3]14 ff., 286
Sâ'ib Khâthir, [2]404
Sa'îd, Banû (Banû Abî l-Ḥusayn, of Alcalà), [2]24
Ṣâ'id al-Andalusî, [1]81*n*, [2]214*n*, 365*n*, 368*n*, [3]126*n*, 127*n*, 247*n*
Sa'îd b. Abî Maryam, *see* Ibn Abî Maryam, Sa'îd
Sa'îd b. al-'Âṣ, [1]442
Sa'îd b. al-Musayyab, [2]22, 55, 165
Sa'îd b. Zayd, [1]59*n*, 430*n*, 439 f.
Sâ'idah, Banû, [1]396*n*
Saint Bernard, [1]151*n*
saints, [1]305, [2]165, 175, 188 ff., 382, [3]93 f.; their perceptions, [1]198, [2]201, 203, [3]87; acts of divine grace (*karâmât*), [1]189 ff., 411, [3]99 f., 167, 179 f., 182, 279; sainthood of fools, [1]224 f.

as-Sakhâwî, [1]xxxn, xlvin, lviin, lxin, lxvi, lxxiin, xcvn, xcviiin, cvn, [2]429n, [3]229n
as-Sakkâkî, [1]249n, [3]286, 336 f.
Saksîwah (Berber tribe), [1]128
as-Saksîwî, ʿUmar, [1]327, [2]197
Ṣalâḥ-ad-dîn (Saladin), Yûsuf b. Ayyûb, [2]43 ff., 92, 263, 435, [3]11
Salâm (Sallâm) (the dragoman), [1]163
Salâmah, Banû (chieftains of the Banû Yadlaltin-Tûjîn), [1]272; *see also* Qalʿat Ibn Salâmah
Salamah b. al-Abrash, [2]183
Salamah b. al-Akwaʿ, [1]255 ff.
Salamanca, [1]150
Salamîyah, [1]143
Salé (Salâ), [1]129, [2]248
Ṣâliḥ, Banû (of Ghânah), [1]119
Ṣâliḥ b. ʿAbd-ar-Raḥmân (secretary of al-Ḥajjâj), [2]22 f.
Ṣâliḥ b. ʿAbdallâh b. Ḥasan b. al-Ḥasan b. ʿAlî b. Abî Ṭâlib, [1]119
Ṣâliḥ b. Abî Maryam, Abû l-Khalîl, *see* Abû l-Khalîl, Ṣâliḥ
Ṣâliḥ b. Sharîf (Spanish littérateur), [3]365
Sâlim (client of Abû Ḥudhayfah), [1]397 f.
Sâlim al-Ḥarrânî, [3]237n
as-Sâlimî (Muḥammad b. Aḥmad b. ʿUmar, author on dream interpretation), [3]110
Salîṭ (b. Qays), [2]85
Saljûqs, [1]42n, 315, 351, [2]115, 128, 130, 133 f., 217, 299, 306, [3]367
Sallâr (Mameluke amîr), [1]366
Salmon, [1]18
as-Samʿânî, [2]159n, 164n, 177n, [3]69n
Sâmânids, [2]115, 128 f., 133
Samaria, [1]474 f.
Samarkand, [1]23, 103, 148
as-Samaw'al al-Maghribî, [2]415n
Sambation legend, [1]22n
aṣ-Ṣammân, [1]134
Samosata, [1]144
Samuel, [1]474
Ṣanʿâ', [1]23, 124, [2]253
Sanad (b. ʿInân, Mâlikite jurist), [3]18
Sánchez Pérez, J. A., [3]197n
Sand River, [1]22, 24
sand writing, *see* geomancy
as-Sandûbî, Ḥ., [1]451n
Sanguinetti, B. R., [1]369n, [3]150n
Santamaria, [1]140
Sant'Angelo (de' Lombardi), [1]99
Santarem, [1]141
Santarîyah, *see* Siwa
Santiago, [1]150
Santillana, D., [1]lxxivn, lxxixn, 50n, 284n, 453n, [3]8n, 15n, 20n, 22n, 84n
Saragossa, [1]141, 317, 335, [3]185n, 443
Sarah, [2]250
as-Sarâh, Mount, [1]133n
Sarakhs, [1]135
as-Sarakhsî, Aḥmad b. aṭ-Ṭayyib, [1]67n
Sarandîb, *see* Ceylon
Sardinia, [1]98, 139, 142, [2]41
Sarḥûn (Sarjûn, secretary of ʿAbd-al-Malik), [2]22
as-Sarî as-Saqaṭî, [3]192
Sarîr, [1]155 f.
Sâriyah b. Zunaym, [1]223
Sarjûn (Sergios), *see* Sarḥûn
as-Sarrâj (author of *al-Lumaʿ fî t-taṣawwuf*), [3]179n
as-Sarrâj (author of *Maṣâriʿ al-ʿushshâq*), [1]220n
Sarûj, [1]144
Ṣaṣṣah b. Dâhir, [2]217
Sassanians, [1]25, 80n, 269n, 298, [2]55n, 215, 288, [3]168n
satan, *see* devils, satans
Saṭîḥ, [1]219, [2]202, [3]475
as-Saṭṭî, Abû ʿAbdallâh Muḥammad (b. ʿAlî) b. Sulaymân, [1]xl, [3]129
Saturn (planet), [1]4, [2]211, 213, 221, [3]474

Saul, ¹474, ²176, 177n, 259
Sauvaget, J., ¹71n, 302n, 306n, ²52n
Sawâd, ¹325n, 361
Ṣawl, ¹126
Saxony, ¹159
Sayf-ad-dawlah (Ḥamdânid ruler), ³250
Sayf-ad-dîn Ghâzî I (of Mosul), ²52n
Sayf b. 'Umar al-Asadî, ¹7, 17
Sayfawayh, ¹27, 28n
Sayḥân, ¹144, 154
Sayılı, A. (M.), ²429n, ³272n
Ṣaymarah, ¹146
aṣ-Ṣaymarî (al-Ḥusayn b. 'Alî), 146
Sayqawayh, Sîqawayh, see Sayfawayh
aṣ-Ṣayrafî, Abû Bakr, ²82, 83n, 85
Sayram, see Isbîjâb
Sayyid, F., ¹82n
as-Sayyid al-Ḥimyarî, ¹409
Sbath, P., ¹81n
Sbeïtla, ¹130, ²38, ³474n
Schacht, J., ¹261n, 423n, 429n, 438n, ³24n
Schiaparelli, C., ¹94n
Schimmel, A., ¹lxviin, cix, 178n, 328n, ²98n
Schmidt, N., ¹lxxxixn
Schoonover, K., ³80n
Schreck, M., ¹199n
Schrieke, B., ³72n
Schwally, F., ¹67n, 427n, ²443n, ³59n, 307n
Schwarz, P., ¹32n, 362n
science and scholarship: scientific habit, ²426, ³394; mastery of more than one craft or science, ²355, ³294 f., 318, 363, 371 f.; natural to human civilization, ²411n; accessible to all human beings regardless of their religion, ³111; sciences in the temperate zones, ¹167, 172; intellectual processes in the acquisition of scientific knowledge, ³281, 291 ff., 295 ff.; progress in scholarship, ³289n; purposes of scholarly authorship, ¹34, ³284 ff., 481; overwhelming amount of scholarly literature, ³288 ff.; division of the sciences, ²436 ff., ³11 ff., 298 f.; historical survey of intellectual sciences, ³113 ff., 314; translation of Greek scientific works, ³115 f., 130 f., 135, 140 f., 147, 149, 151, 229n, 250; sciences of pre-Islamic nations largely lost, ¹78, ³103, 114

scholars: have little voice in, or aptitude for, politics, ¹458 ff., ³309 f., 314; their pride and haughtiness, ²331; compared to prophets, ²191; "the heirs of the prophets," ¹459 f.; as a rule not wealthy, ²332, 334 f.; their handwriting imitated, ²382; non-Arab origin of most Muslim scholars, ³311 ff., 319; "the farâ'iḍ one-third of scholarship," ³22 f., 128

see also education
Scotland, ¹163n
Sea of the Khazars, see Caspian Sea
seal, ¹62 f., ²60 ff., 304, ³247; sealing clay, ¹362, ²26, 64 f.; "seal of the prophets," ²61, 189 f., ³183, of the saints, ²189 f.; magical, ³192, "lion seal," ³163
Sebuktigîn, see Ghaznawids
secretaries (kâtib), ²6 f., 8 f., 22 f., 26 ff., 97 f., 155, 390 f., 407, ³341, 369 ff., 394 ff., 408 f.
sedentary culture, see civilization; urban life
Sées, ¹158
Segovia, ¹150
Segura, ¹141
Seldon, E. S., ¹xxiv
Selefke, ¹143 f.

Senegal, [1]102*n*
sense perception: agreeable sensations, [2]397 f.; "common sense," [1]196 f., 211, [3]72 f.; *see also* perception
Serbia, [1]159*n*
Serjeant, R. B., [2]65*n*, 354*n*
servants, [1]62, 277, [2]317 ff., [3]108*n*, 305, 352
Seth, [1]80*n*
Seven Sleepers, [1]408
Sevilla, [1]xxxiii ff., xxxvii, xlii, il, lviii, 61, 140, 261*n*, 470, [2]405, [3]365, 442, 447 f., 450, 455, 458
sex: sexual relations forbidden during the pilgrimage, [2]367; beasts of prey do not cohabit in captivity, [1]301; *see also* adultery, fornication; homosexuality; love; women
Sfax, [2]42
ash-Sha'bî, [3]56
ash-Shâbushtî, [1]348*n*
Shaddâd (of the Iram legend), [1]26
Shâdhân al-Balkhî (b. Baḥr, Abû Sa'îd), [2]214
Shadîd (of the Iram legend), [1]26
ash-Shâfi'î, [1]8*n*, [2]185, 265, 399, 448, 453, [3]4, 6, 8, 10 & *n*, 11, 28, 31, 63, 129, 285
Shâfi'ites, [1]445, [2]230, [3]10, 12, 18 f., 21, 32; *see also* ash-Shâfi'î
ash-Shâhijân, [1]135
ash-Shahrastânî, [1]403*n*, 407*n*, 413 f., [3]62*n*, 63*n*, 64*n*, 69*n*
Shahrazûr, [1]146, 364; Mountain of, [1]146
ash-Shahrazûrî, [1]lxxiv f.
Shahrbarâz, [1]290
Shâkir, Banû, [3]132
ash-Shalûbîn, [3]398
Shâmis, [3]423
ash-Shammâkh, [1]48
ash-Sharâh, [1]409, 420; Mount, [1]133
ash-Sharîd (subtribe of the Banû Sulaym), [1]271
ash-Sharîf al-Murtaḍâ, [1]46
ash-Sharîf ar-Raḍî, [1]45, [3]378*n*, 383, 393
ash-Shârimsâḥî, [3]18 f.
ash-Sharîshî, [1]lxxvi*n*, [3]307*n*
ash-Shâsh, *see* Tashkent
ash-Shâṭibî, Abû l-Qâsim b. Fîrruh, [2]441 ff., [3]396
Shaṭṭanawf, [1]131
Shaybah b. 'Uthmân, [2]257
Shaybân, Banû, [1]282
Shaybân b. 'Abd-al-'Azîz al-Yashkurî, Abû d-Dalfâ', [2]79
Shayzar, [2]44
Sheba, Queen of, [2]259*n*
Shelah, [3]283
Shem, [1]173
Shî'ah: derivation of term, [1]402; doctrine of prophecy, [1]4*n*, the caliphate, [1]402 ff., 435 f., 466 f., 471, [2]186, [3]5, 50, 93 f.; the Hidden (Concealed) Imam, [1]45, 408, 412, [2]186; views on the Mahdî, [2]194 f., pro-Shî'ah bias of transmitters of Mahdî tradition, [2]163 f., 173, 177, 180; Shî'ah law, [3]5, 11, 17, 19, 350; and Mu'tazilah, [1]406; influence on Sufism, [2]186 f., [3]86, 92 ff.
sects, [1]404 ff.: Extremists, [1]406, 408, [2]186, [3]92 ff.; Hâshimîyah, [1]409; Imâmîyah (Twelver Shî'ah), [1]404 ff., 408, 412 ff., 436, [2]186, [3]50, 86 Ismâ'îlîyah, [1]143, 412 f., [2]186, [3]92 ff.; Kaysânîyah, [1]406, 409; Saba'îyah, [1]407*n*, [2]175; Wâqifîyah, [1]406 ff. Zaydîyah, [1]124, 405, 410 ff., [2]51, 115, 133, 209
death of al-Ḥusayn, [1]443 ff.; favored by the Barmecides, [1]31; caused difficulties for the 'Abbâsids, [2]127; against Ḥanbalites in the 'Irâq, [3]9; used

white flags, ²51; 'Alids have foreknowledge of the future, ¹411, ²203, 209 ff., 218, 225; Fāṭimid descent of the Mahdî of the Almohads, ¹54 f.; 'Alid dynasty of Ghânah, ¹119; surviving Ṭâlibid group feeling, ²196 *see also* Fâṭimids; Idrîsids

ash-Shi'b, ²256

Shibl b. Miskiyânah b. Muhalhil (poet of the Awlâd Muhalhil), ³423 ff.

ash-Shiblî, Abû Bakr, ³192

ash-Shiḥr, ¹100, *following* 110, 122, 124, 126

ash-Shî'î, *see* Abû l-'Abbâs ash-Shî'î; Abû 'Abdallâh ash-Shî'î

Shiloh, ²259

ships, *see* military science, warfare; navigation, navy

Shiqq, ¹219, ²202, ³475

ash-Shîrajân, ¹135

Shîrâz, ¹135

Shirmasâḥ, ³18n

Shiyâh, Mount, ¹156 f., 161 f.

Shu'ayb b. Khâlid, ²163

Shu'bah (b. al-Ḥajjâj), ²160 ff., 168 f., 172 f.

Shuhayd, Banû, ²99

Shujâ' b. Aslam, Abû Kâmil, ³125

Shukr b. Hâshim, ³415–16, 417 ff.

Shurayḥ, Judge, ¹261, 453

ash-Shushtarî, ³459

Sîbawayh, ³186, 289, 313, 323, 356, 361

Sîbawayh al-Miṣrî, ¹28n

Sibṭ Ibn al-Jawzî, ³149n

Sicily, ¹98, 116, 139, 142, ²40 ff., ³123n, 137, 149, 165n

Siddiqi, M. Z., ²246n, 415n

Sîdî Aḥmad, *see* as-Sabtî, Sîdî Aḥmad

Sidon, ¹133 f.

Sierra (de Guadarrama), ¹141

Ṣiffîn, ¹102, 145; battle of, ¹440, ²82

Siggel, A., ³244n, 271n

Sijilmâsah, ¹42, 46, 75, 128, 413, ²248

Sijistân, ¹127, 135 f., 362

Sila, ¹118

as-Sîlâ, *see* Korea

as-Silafî, ¹481n

Sili, ¹118n

silver, *see* metals

Silves, ¹140

Silvestre de Sacy, A. I., ¹c, 13n, ²325n, ³77n, 334n, 356n

Simplicius, ²415n

Sinai, Mount, ¹132

as-Sind, *see* India

Ṣinhâjah (Berber tribe), ¹22, *following* 110, 118, 125, 128, 177 f., 285, 295 f., 298, 315, 318, 330 ff., 360, 382, 428, 468 ff., ²51, 57, 70, 83, 115 f., 197 & n, 239, 283, 289 f., 305, 350, ³442, 455

Sinope, ¹160

Sionita, Gabriel, ¹94n

Sîrâf, ¹135, ²65

Sirte, ¹131

Siwa, ¹*following* 110, 125

Siyâh Kûh, *see* Shîyah, Mount

de Slane, W. M., ¹xxvi, xxxi, xxxvii, xxxviiin, xln, xlin, xciii, c, cin, cii, ciiin, cviin, cviii, cx, cxiii f., 4n, 22n, 53n, 66n, 75n, 91n, 95n, 99n, 118n, 119n, 128n, 131n, 134n, 140n, 150n, 152n, 189n, 232n, 235n, 240n, 281n, 322n, 327n, 328n, 333n, 362n, 364n, 366n, 471n, ²15n, 24n, 44n, 49n, 72n, 83n, 87n, 93n, 102n, 116n, 117n, 163n, 177n, 202n, 198n, 200n, 211n, 214n, 220n, 222n, 225n, 240n, 244n, 246n, 260n, 272n, 289n, 316n, 323n, 325n, 379n, 451n, ³5n, 20n, 21n, 33n, 44n, 59n, 68n, 77n, 98n, 133n, 150n, 267n, 324n, 329n, 374n, 377n, 415n, 416n, 417n, 418n, 419n,

449*n*, 453*n*, 454*n*, 456*n*, 461*n*, 463*n*, 465*n*, 474*n*
slaves, slavery: Ham's descendants, [1]170; slavery accepted in the hope of gain, [1]301 f.; trade, [1]117 ff., 139, [2]336; part of tax revenues, [1]363 f.; part of an inventory, [1]366*n*, 367; unreliable advisers, [2]95; develop bad qualities if harshly treated, [3]305; easily affected by magic, [3]165; eligible for the caliphate, [1]397
Slavs, [1]169, 171 ff., 251, [2]38, 42, 325
sleep, *see* dreams, dream interpretation
Smith, M., [3]80*n*
"Snow Mountain," *see* Murghâr, Mount
sociology, *see* civilization; man; urban life
Socrates, [1]328*n*, [3]85, 115
Sodom, [3]472
Soghd, Soghdians, [1]23, *following* 110, 137, 148
Solomon, [1]18 f., 22, 391, 417, 422, 474, [2]53, 249, 259 ff., 263 f.
de Somogyi, J., [3]103*n*
sophistry, [3]33, 141
sorcery, *see* magic, sorcery
soul, psychology, [1]195 f., 201 ff., 207, 209, 214 ff., 254, 381*n*, [2]3, 50, 77, 81, 86, 102, 130, 292 f., 339 f., 344, 397 f., 406, 413, 421, 432, [3]35, 39, 75, 81 f., 105 f., 111, 147, 157 f., 165 f., 170, 175 f., 217, 219, 226, 232 f., 240, 244 f., 248, 252, 255, 260, 280, 295
Sourdel, D., [1]lxxvi*n*, [2]20*n*
Sousse, [1]130
South Arabia, *see* Yemen
Spain, [1]xxxiii ff., xxxviii, xl*n*, xlv f., il, lii, lviii, lxxxi*n*, lxxxv f., cxv, 42, 54*n*, 61, 95*n*, 98, 140 f., 149 f., 168, 179 f., 267, 296, 300, 302, 313, 315 f., 323, 329 f., 332, 334 ff., 351, 365, 378, 393, 428, 463, 468 ff., [2]12, 14, 18, 23 f., 35 f., 38, 40, 45 f., 66, 70, 78, 82, 92, 99 f., 115 f., 121, 127, 129, 191, 220, 267, 278 f., 288, 290, 307, 349 f., 371, 378, 384 ff., 391, 393 f., 405, 427, 430, 440 f., 446, [3]12 ff., 21, 94, 116 f., 126, 135, 142, 149, 153, 157, 185, 301 ff., 324, 328 f., 338, 351 f., 357, 364 ff., 386, 396, 406, 413, 440, 450, 454 f., 457, 460, 479
Spitaler, A., [1]218*n*
Spuler, B., [1]361*n*
Stählin, O., [3]252*n*
Starling, Statue of the, [1]74
Steele, R., [1]81*n*, 235*n*, [2]48*n*
Steinschneider, M., [1]81*n*, [2]214*n*, 415*n*, [3]103*n*, 162*n*
Stern, S. M., [2]83*n*, [3]441*n*, 442*n*
Stevenson, W. B., [1]94*n*, 163*n*
Stinking Land, [1]*following* 110, 161 f., 165
Stoics, [3]114
stones (precious): origin, [3]230; diamonds, [1]367; emeralds, [1]26, 367, [2]65, [3]474; emerald mines, [1]124; hyacinths (rubies), [1]26, 349, 367, [2]65; the Hyacinth (Ruby) Island, [1]138; turquoise, [2]65; ring-stones, [1]365*n*, 366 ff.; jet, [2]270, 361
Storey, C. A., [3]117*n*
Strabo, [1]128*n*
Streck, M., [1]363*n*
Suakin, [1]100, 123
Subayṭilah, *see* Sbeïtla
Ṣubḥî Pasha, 'Abd-al-Laṭîf, [1]cviii*n*
as-Subkî, Taqî-ad-dîn, [3]12
Sudan, Sudanese, [1]118*n*, 121, 125, 171, 173, 296, 305, [2]282 f., 338, 367*n*, [3]161, 185*n*
Suez, [1]23 f., 100, 123, 132; Canal, unsuccessful attempts to build, [1]100; Sea of, *see* Red Sea
Sufâlah, [1]99, 123

Sufism, [1]4*n*, 191, 198, 221*n*, 323, 327*n*, [2]229, 434*n*, 435*n*, [3]39 f., 76 ff., 459; defined, [3]76, 80; derivation of term, [3]76 f.; the mystical "habit," [3]394; states and stations, [3]39 f., 43, 78 f., 91, 99; "taste" (mystical experience), [3]79; ecstatic experiences, [3]77 f., 100 ff., 155; *dhikr* exercises, [1]213, 422, [3]81 f., 181, 184, 192; abstinence from food, [1]182, [3]82; supernatural perceptions, [1]213, 216, 222 ff., 230, [3]81, 100 ff., 254 acceptance of Shî'ah ideas, [2]186 f., [3]86, 92 ff.; opinions on the Mahdî, [2]157, 186 ff., 197, [3]94; monism, [2]229*n*, 398*n*, [3]83, 85 ff., 95 ff.; S. attitude toward metaphysics and theology, [3]54, 155; S. and magic, [1]243, [3]167, 171 f., 179 f., 191 ff., 278; the cloak, [2]187, [3]93; training of novices, [3]78 f.; al-Bâjarbaqîyah, [2]230; al-'Îsawîyah, [3]418*n*; al-Qalandarîyah, [2]229; attitude of jurists toward, [3]83, 99; Ibn Khaldûn's work on, [1]xlv*n*

Sufyân ath-Thawrî, [1]33*n*, [2]160, 178, [3]56

Sufyân b. Umayyah, [2]379

Sufyân b. 'Uyaynah, [1]33, [2]177

as-Suhaylî, [2]158 f., 204 ff., 215

Suḥnûn, *see* Saḥnûn

as-Suhrawardî ('Umar b. Muḥammad), [3]77*n*, 80

Ṣûl, [1]156

as-Sulamî (author on Sufism), [1]37*n*

Sulaym (b. Manṣûr), Banû, [1]270 ff., 283, 305, [2]200, [3]348, 440

Sulaymân, *see* Solomon

Sulaymân b. 'Abd-al-Malik, [1]47*n*, 424, 432, [2]121

Sulaymân b. 'Abîd ('Ubayd?), [2]170

Sulaymân b. 'Alî at-Tilimsânî, *see* 'Afîf-ad-dîn Sulaymân b. 'Alî

Sulaymân b. Kathîr, [1]410

Sulaymân b. Najâḥ, Abû Dâwûd, [2]442 f.

Sulaymân b. Sa'd, [2]22

as-Sulaymânî, Aḥmad b. 'Alî b. 'Amr, [2]164

aṣ-Ṣûlî, [2]379*n*

sultan: defined, [2]5, 11; usage of the term, [1]cxi*n*, 469, [2]10

Sulṭân b. Muẓaffar b. Yaḥyâ (chieftain-poet of the Dawâwidah), [3]420

aṣ-Ṣumân(?), [1]134*n*

Sumatra, [1]99*n*

Sunken Land, [1]165

Surdon, G., [1]cix, 247*n*, 272*n*, 322*n*, 372*n*, 385*n*, 414*n*, 428*n*, 448*n*, 454*n*, [2]3*n*, 5*n*

Ṣurghatmishîyah College, [1]lx, lxii, 34*n*

Surrounding Sea, [1]95, 98 f., 102, 110 f., 116 ff., 121, 123, 124–25, 157 & *n*, 128 f., 138 ff., 149 f., 152, 157 ff., 162 ff., 166

Surt, *see* Sirte

as-Sûs (al-aqṣâ), [1]*following* 110, 128, 179, 326, 330, [2]196 f., 283

Susa (as-Sûs), [1]135

Sûsah, *see* Sousse

sustenance, [1]3 f., [2]311 ff.

Suter, H., [3]136*n*

Suwayd, Banû (subtribe of the Zughbah), [1]liii

Suwayqat Ibn Mathkûd, [1]130

as-Suyûṭî, [1]lxvi*n*, 37*n*, 202*n*, [2]246*n*, 383*n*, 398*n*, 400*n*, 440*n*, 443*n*, [3]3*n*, 10*n*, 11*n*, 17*n*, 18*n*, 46*n*, 56*n*, 57*n*, 58*n*, 59*n*, 327*n*, 366*n*, 441*n*

Syr Darya, [1]103*n*, 148

Syracuse, [1]142

Syria, Syrian(s), [1]liv, lxiii, 12, 16, 18, 23 f., 42, 45, 57, 78, 98, 100 ff., *following* 110, 129, 132 f., 142 ff., 155, 168, 266, 269*n*, 288, 305, 319, 321*n*, 329, 331, 333 f., 357 ff., 404*n*, 409, 413, 417, 441,

444, 467, 475n, ²21 f., 26, 38, 40, 42 ff., 51, 67, 115, 128 f., 133, 165, 175, 217, 226 f., 230 f., 250, 259, 263, 267, 281, 287 f., 307, 325, 350, 382, 435n, 452, 454, 457, ³6n, 9, 12, 18, 113, 115, 156, 160, 283, 346, 414, 437, 474

Syrian Sea (= Mediterranean), ¹98, 139, ²38

T

Tabâlah, ¹126

aṭ-Ṭâbarân, see aṭ-Ṭawbarân

aṭ-Ṭabarânî, ²157, 158n, 171, 175, 181 ff.

aṭ-Ṭabarî, ¹lxx, lxxviiin, cvi, 7, 17n, 22 & n, 26, 31, 33, 34n, 35 f., 56, 223n, 259n, 268n, 290n, 295n, 307n, 321n, 324n, 325n, 348, 397n, 404n, 419n, 426n, 436n, 440, 445n, 456n, ²39n, 48n, 61n, 63 f., 79, 82n, 85n, 139, 140n, 142n, 143n, 144n, 145n, 147n, 148n, 149n, 151n, 152n, 176n, 204 & n, 205 & n, 219, 258n, 259n, 380n, 444

aṭ-Ṭabarî, 'Alî b. Rabban, ¹37n, ²246n, 415n

Ṭabaristân, ¹101, following 110, 147, 156, 363, 411 f., ²51, 115, 133; Sea of, see Caspian Sea

Ṭab'î Bey, ¹lxvii

Tabrîz, ¹146, ²447

Tabûk, ¹133, 202, 330

Tâdlâ, ¹129

at-Taftazânî, Sa'd-ad-dîn, ³117, 315

aṭ-Ṭagharghar, see Tughuzghuz

at-Tahânawî, ³8n, 146n, 220n

aṭ-Ṭaḥâwî, Aḥmad b. Muḥammad, ²462

al-Tahir, Ali Nasuh, ³59n

Ṭâhir b. al-Ḥusayn, ¹lxx f., cvi, 324 f., ²139, 156, 217, Pl. VII

Ṭâhirids, ¹373n, ²99, 128

aṭ-Ṭâhirîyah, ¹148

aṭ-Ṭâ'if, ²256, 379

tailoring, ¹34, 309, ²222, 302, 316, 348, 354 f., 366 ff., ³354 f.

Tâj-al-mulk (Tâj-ad-dawlah, Bûyid), ³250n

Tâjirah, ¹120

Tajo, ¹141

at-Tâjuwîn, ¹following 110, 125

Takrît, ¹145

Takrûr, ¹118, 169

aṭ-Ṭalamankî, Abû 'Umar, ²381

Talas, see Ṭarâz

Talavera, ¹141

Ṭalḥah (b. 'Ubaydallâh), ¹59n, 420, 426, 430n, 438, 440, 442 f., ²158, 184

aṭ-Ṭâliqân, ¹136, 411

talismans, see magic, sorcery

Tallgren, A. M., ¹94n

Tallgren (Tuulio), O. J., ¹94n, 149n, 164n, 165n

Tamerlane, see Timur (Tamerlane)

Tamîm, Banû, ¹281, 282n, 441, ²184, ³343

Tangier, ¹98, following 110, 129, 139 f., 369, ²38; Straits of, see Gibraltar, Straits of

at-Tan'îm, ²256

aṭ-Ṭanjî, M. T., ¹xxv, xxixn, xln, lxxxix, xcv, icn, civ

Tannery, P., ¹226n, 227n, 229n, 233n, 235n, ³156n

aṭ-Ṭantadâ'î, Aḥmad b. Ḥasan, ¹xcv; Badr-ad-dîn Ḥasan, ¹xcv; Bahâ'-ad-dîn Muḥammad b. Ḥasan, ¹xcv; Yaḥyâ b. Ḥasan, ¹xcv

aṭ-Ṭâq, ¹135

Ṭarafah b. al-'Abd, ³397, 410

Taranto, Gulf of, ¹152n

Ṭarâz, ¹149

Tarde, G., ¹lxviin

Tarifa, ¹98, 139 f., ²458

Tarjam (ancestor of the Ku'ûb), ³427

Tarnût, ¹132

Tarragona, ¹141

Tarshîsh (= Tunis), ³429, 431

Tarsûs, ¹143 f.
Tâshfîn b. ʿAlî b. Yûsuf (Almoravid ruler), ²82 f.
Tashkent, ¹103, *following* 110, 148 f.
Ṭâshköprüzâdeh, ¹lxvii, ³162n
Tatar(s), ¹lxiii f., 68n, 315, 351, 413, ²128, 134, 219, 307, ³9, 114n, 186
Taurus, *see* Chain Mountain
Tavast, ¹164
Tawât, *see* Touat
aṭ-Ṭawbarân (aṭ-Ṭâbarân), ¹126–27
at-Tawḥîdî, Abû Ḥayyân, ¹403n, ²185n, ³304n
taxation, ¹49 f., 80, 286, 289 f., 304, 307, 328, 340 f., 353, 361 ff., 381, 465, ²4 f., 7 f., 16, 19 ff., 89 ff., 102 f., 105 f., 111, 118, 122 f., 126, 131, 136 f., 146, 150 f., 281, 283, 287, 291, 297, 304, 315 f., 324n, 336, 339 f., 390, ³126, 132; customs duties, *see* commerce
aṭ-Ṭayâlisî, ²455
Taymâʾ, *see* Tema
Ṭayy, Banû, ¹266, 272, 283
Tâzâ, ¹129, ³468
teachers, teaching, *see* education
Tebessa, ¹130
Tema, ¹133
tents, ¹28, 250, 303, ²67 ff., 78 ff., 258n, 259, 267, 364, ³187, 404, 420, 423, 477
Terés, E., ³440n
Terrasse, H., ²198n, 246n, 289n
Tetuan (Tîṭṭâwîn), ¹140
ath-Thaʿâlibî, ¹327n, ²83n, 351n, ³330
ath-Thaʿâlibî (= ath-Thaʿlabî), ¹26, ²444
Thâbit b. Qurrah, ³130
Thaʿlab, ³331
ath-Thaʿlabî (ath-Thaʿâlibî), ¹26, 357n, ²176n, 259n, 365n, 380n, 444

Thamûd, ¹133, 298, 308, 343, 356 & n, 357, 359, ²240, 268, 354
Thapsia garganica, ¹183
Thaqîf, Banû, ¹60, 266, 441, ³343
Thawbân (b. Bujdud), ²158, 179 f.
ath-Thawrî, *see* Sufyân ath-Thawrî
Themistius, ³115
Theodosius, ³131
theology (*kalâm*), ³34 ff., 299; defined, ²438, ³34, 53; origin, ³45; explanation of its name, ³50, 62 f.; created by the Muʿtazilah, ³62 f.; the articles of faith, ³43 ff., 55, 59 f., 145 f., 152 f.; concept of God, ³83 ff., 144, 261 f.; doctrine of the "voluntary agent," ¹188 f., ²372; the divine attributes, ³44 ff., 55, 60 ff., 144; essential speech, ¹199, 201, ³39, 49 f., 62 ff.; degrees of faith, ³41 ff., 55, 59 f.; the theory of "states," ³144 f.; on the Resurrection, ³45, 50, 55, 60, 69, 73 f., 256 ff.

theological theory of human perception, ³75, of dream visions, ³72, of the distinction between miracles and sorcery, ³167 ff.; its relation to Sufism, ³155, to the principles of jurisprudence, ³28 ff., to philosophy, ³51 ff., 143 ff., 153 ff., 246 ff., 266 f.; no longer a necessary subject, ³54; cultivated by non-Arabs, ³313; poem against, ³265 ff.; in love poetry, ³452 f., 459; the inferior poetry of theologians, ³395
Theophilus (Nawfîl), ²216 & n
Thorbecke, H., ¹349n
Thorndike, L., ²214n
Thouvenot, R., ¹128n
thrones, ¹155n, 296, ²253, 78, 304, ³184; divine throne, ³82 f., 88, 99, 266
Tibân Asʿad Abû Karib, *see* Asʿad Abû Karib, Tibân
Tiberias, ¹133

Tibet, [1]23, 25, 136 ff., 148
aṭ-Ṭîbî, Sharaf-ad-dîn, [2]447
Tiflis, [1]154
Tigris, [1]101 f., 134, 144 ff., 154, 349, 362, [2]219, [3]114n, 179
Tîgûrârîn, [1]119
at-Tîh, [1]132
Tihâmah, [1]123 f., 126n
Tilimsân, *see* Tlemcen
Timur (Tamerlane), [1]xliii, xlivn, xlvi, lxiii ff., 388n
Tînmallal (Berber tribe), [1]128
(at-)Tirmidh, [1]103, 136 f.
at-Tirmidhî, [1]38, 408, [2]157, 159 f., 167 ff., 208, 455
Tîṭṭerî, Mount, [1]129, [2]116
Titus (Roman Emperor), [2]261
Tlemcen, [1]xxxix, xlviii, l ff., lviii, 129, 271, 272n, 367 f., [2]72, 116, 198, 240, 273 f., 428 f., [3]436n, 471
Togan, A. Zaki (Zeki) Validi (Velidi), [1]lxviin, 161n, 251n
Tokhma Su, *see* Qubâqib
Toledo, [1]141, 350, [3]442
Torah, *see* Bible
Torki, M., [2]385n
Torrey, C. C., [2]71n
Tortosa, [1]141 & n
Touat, [1]119
Toulouse, [1]150
Toynbee, A. J., [1]cxvn
Tozeur (Tûzar), [1]130, [2]197, 304
traditions, *see* *ḥadîth*
Transoxania, [1]17, 23, [2]115, 128 f., 133, 164, 307, 431, [3]9 f., 117, 315
Trapani, [1]142
treasure hunting, [2]243, 319 ff.
Trebizond, [1]155
Trimingham, J. S., [1]121n, 122n
Tripoli (Syria-Lebanon), [1]133, 143, [2]42, 101
Tripoli, Tripolitania, [1]130, 333n, [2]42, 248 f., 304
Ṭ-r-m-y, Lake of, [1]164
Trujillo, [1]140
Trummeter, F., [1]xcvin, 22n
Tubba'îyah (poem), [2]220
Tubba's of the Yemen, [1]21 ff., 57, 296, 298, 308, 360, [2]84, 251 268, 288, 354, 379
Tudela, [1]150
Türgish, [1]*following* 110, 162
aṭ-Ṭughrâ'î, [3]228, 269, 273 f., 277
Tughrilbek, [1]42n
Ṭughsh, Banû, *see* Ikhshîdids
Tughuzghuz, [1]*following* 110, 138, 172
Tûjîn (Berber tribe), [1]271 f.
Tukulor, [1]118n
Ṭulayḥah al-Asadî, [1]207
Ṭulaymithah, [1]131
Ṭûlûnids, [1]374, [2]115, 128 f.
Ṭumṭum the Indian, [3]156
Tunis, [1]xxxvii ff., xlv ff., l, liii, lvi ff., lx, lxii, cii f., cv, 130, [2]38n, 40, 43, 72, 101, 116, 221 ff., 243, 290, 350 f., 386 f., 428, 430, Pl. III, [3]20, 110, 136n, 185, 264, 302, 329, 428 f., 431, 473, 475
at-Tûnisî (Abû Isḥâq Ibrâhîm b. Ḥasan), [3]15
aṭ-Ṭûr, *see* Sinai, Mount
Turkomans, [1]144, 153, 155, 251 f., 295, [2]74
Turks, [1]lx, lxvii, lxxxviii, xc, cvii f., 12, 23 ff., 57, 66, 98, 101, 103, 136 ff., 149, 156 f., 161 f., 164 f., 169, 172, 251 f., 277, 285, 286n, 302, 315, 330, 334, 342, 351, 366, 373, 378, 413, 458, [2]12 ff., 18 f., 25 f., 28, 35, 37, 52, 67, 74, 81, 128, 133, 217, 225, 227, 353, 435, 436n, [3]9, 162, 186, 245, 283, 319, 352, 361
aṭ-Ṭurṭûshî, [1]lxxxv, 83, 316 f., [2]87, [3]17
Ṭûs, [1]148
aṭ-Ṭûsî, Naṣîr-ad-dîn, [1]xlv, [3]148, 315
Tustar, [1]135
at-Tustarî, Sahl b. 'Abdallâh, [1]243

Tuwât, *see* Touat
aṭ-Ṭuwayjin, Ibrâhîm as-Sâḥilî, [3]366
Ṭuways, [2]404
at-Tuwayzirî (pseudo-Mahdî at Ribâṭ Mâssah), [1]326, [2]197
Tûzar, *see* Tozeur
Tyan, E., [1]xlviii*n*, 453*n*
Tyrambe, [1]164*n*
Tyre, [1]133, [2]42

U

'Ubâdah al-Qazzâz, [3]441 f.
'Ubayd b. Mâlik, [3]439
'Ubaydallâh al-Mahdî (Fâṭimid ruler), [1]41, 45 f., 413, 467, [2]210 f.
'Ubaydallâh b. Manṣûr, Ibn Ṣulayḥah (judge of Jabalah), [2]101
'Ubaydallâh b. 'Umar (al-'Umarî), [1]33*n*
'Ubaydallâh b. Ziyâd b. Abî Sufyân (Abîhi), [1]373
'Ubaydids, *see* Fâṭimids
al-'Ubbâd (El Eubbad), [1]lii f., [2]198 & *n*
Úbeda, [1]140
al-Ubullah, [1]100, 134
al-'Udhrî (geographer), [1]116
Ülken, H. Z., [1]lxvii*n*
Uḥud, [1]466*n*
'Ukâẓ, [1]126, [3]410
Ulyûs, [2]216 & *n*
'Umar al-Khayyâm, [3]126*n*
'Umar as-Saksîwî, *see* as-Saksîwî, 'Umar
'Umar b. 'Abd-al-'Azîz, [1]422 ff., [2]192, [3]312*n*
'Umar b. Abî Rabî'ah, [1]32*n*, [3]383, 396, 411
'Umar b. al-Fâriḍ, *see* Ibn al-Fâriḍ
'Umar b. al-Khaṭṭâb, [1]55, 78, 223, 259 f., 261*n*, 264*n*, 266, 268, 295, 307, 333, 384, 397 f., 403 ff., 417, 419, 430 f., 433, 435, 437, 453 f., 456*n*, 465 f., 481*n*, [2]8 f., 21, 39, 56, 61, 71, 85, 186, 193 f., 257, 262, 268, 306, 438, [3]74, 82, 93, 114, 306, 474
al-'Umarî, [1]33
al-'Umarî, *see* 'Abdallâh b. 'Umar al-'Umarî
Umayyad(s): original power, [2]121; moral qualities, [1]421 ff., 434 f.; frugality and simplicity, [1]36, 350, 468; reliance upon Arabs, [1]373; group feeling, [1]432 f., 435, 444; science in their time, [3]229 f.; flourishing literature, [3]386 f., 397; led prayer in person, [1]451; originated the office of doorkeeper, [2]9, 112; did not use honorific surnames, [1]468; coinage, [2]Pl. I; decay of power, [1]424, [2]133
Umayyad(s), Spanish, [1]380, [2]288; origin of rule, [2]115, 127; wealth, [1]365; supported by Arab group feeling, [1]61, 315, 334 f.; relations with Berbers, [1]382, 428; use of the position of wazir, [2]12 f., of doorkeeper, [2]14 f.; police, [2]36 f.; market supervision (*ḥisbah*), [1]463; used *ṭirâz*, [2]66; battle technique, [2]77; aided development of a special Spanish Arabic script, [2]385; honorific surnames, [1]468; prohibited the pilgrimage, [2]100; relations with the Fâṭimids, [1]42, [2]40; decay of power, [1]332, [2]42, 70, 127, 129
Umayyah b. Abî ṣ-Ṣalt (early poet), [1]207
Umayyah b. Abî ṣ-Ṣalt, Abû ṣ-Ṣalt (scientist), [3]130*n*; *see also* Ibn aṣ-Ṣalt
Umm Ḥabîbah, [2]158, 183
Umm Salimah, [2]158, 165 f.
Underwood, P. A., [1]xix ff., xxiii
al-'Unnâb, *see* Bône
'Uqayl, Banû (of Mosul), [2]115

al-ʿUqaylî, Abû Jaʿfar, ²162, 165, 174

urban life, ¹lxxv ff., lxxx f.; planning of towns, ¹76, 249, ²235, 243 ff., 268 f., 358, *see also* jurisprudence: building laws; growth and decay of cities, ²270 f., 292 ff.; cities built only by compulsion, ²235 ff.; capital cities most prosperous, ²287; change of capitals, ²298 ff.; ideal cities, ²138; independent city governments, ²302 ff.

different standards of living, ²273 f.; urban price structure, ²276 ff., 292; no true nobility to be found in cities, ¹274 ff.; weakens the resistance to hunger and certain types of food, ¹183, ²376 f.; has an effeminating influence, ¹257, 342, 345, 458, ²125, 248, 266, 296 f., 376; not conducive to religious feeling, ¹180; moral decay of population, ²293 f., 296; crafts not equally represented in all cities, ²301 ff., 347; crafts and sciences, depending on demand, disappear from decaying cities, ²351 f., 362, 378, 387, 391, 394, 405, 426, 434 f., ³34, 113, 117, 149, 315, 324, 365

see also Bedouins; civilization; population

al-Urbus, *see* Laribus
al-Urmawî, Sirâj-ad-dîn, ³29
al-Urmawî, Tâj-ad-dîn, ³29
ʿUrwah b. Ḥizâm al-ʿUdhrî, ¹220n, ³417n(?)
Usâmah b. Munqidh, ²102n
Usâmah b. Zayd, ¹404, 439, 442
Usâmah b. Zayd al-Laythî, ²207, 209
Usrûshanah, ¹137, 148
Utâmish, ¹374
al-ʿUtbî, ³14, 286

ʿUthmân b. ʿAffân, ¹lxxvin, 333n, 418 f., 426, 430n, 431, 439 ff., ²8, 61, 255, ³82n, 474
ʿUthmân b. Ayyûb al-Maʿâfirî at-Tûnisî, ²381
ʿUthmân b. Khâlid aṭ-Ṭawîl (Muʿtazilite), ³62
al-Uṭrûsh, an-Nâṣir, ¹412
ʿUwayf al-Qawâfî, ¹281

V

Vacca, V., ¹207n
Vajda, G., ¹115n, 235n, ³149n
Valencia, ¹141, 335
Validi, A. Zaki (Zeki), *see* Togan, A. Zaki (Zeki) Validi (Velidi)
van den Bergh, S., ¹cxiiin, 196n, ²409n, ³51n, 166n, 252n, 258n
Venetians, Straits of the, *see* Adriatic Sea
Venice, ¹98 f., *following* 110, 142, 152; Gulf of, *see* Adriatic Sea
Venus (planet), ¹234, ²214 ff., ³162; temple of, ²258, 264
Vettius Valens, ³135n
Vico, G. B., ¹lxviin, lxxxin, cxivn
Virgil, Polydore, ¹211n
Vishtâspa, *see* Yastâsb
Vitelli, G., ²415n
Volga, ¹156, 161 f., 165
Vonderheyden, M., ²210n

W

Waddân, ¹125, 130 f.
Wâdî al-Ghaḍâ, ³452
Wâdî l-Qurâ, ¹419
Wâdî as-Sabt, ¹22n
Wâḍiḥ (governor of Alexandria), ¹48
al-Wâdiyâshî, Shams-ad-dîn Muḥammad b. Jâbir b. Sulṭân, ¹xxxix, lxxiin
Wahb b. Munabbih, ²203, 205, 445
Wakhân, ¹136
Wakhsh, ¹136 f.
Wakhshâb, ¹136 f.
Wakîʿ b. al-Jarrâḥ, ²174

al-Walî al-ʿAjamî, ʿAlî, ²385
al-Walîd b. ʿAbd-al-Malik, ¹357, ²40n, 255, 262 f., 362
al-Walîd b. Ṭarîf, see Ibn Ṭarîf, al-Walîd
al-Walîd b. ʿUqbah, ¹442
Walker, J., ²55n
Walzer, R., ¹82n, 176n, ³139n, 149n
Wangârah, ¹67n, 119 f.
waqf foundations, ¹455, ²435, 436n, 438
al-Wâqidî, Pseudo-Wâqidî, ¹7 f., 321 & n, ²444
Wâqifîyah, see Shîʿah
al-Waqqashî, Abû l-Walîd, ²381
al-Wâqwâq, ¹99, 123
warfare, see military science, warfare
Wargalân, see Ouargla
Waṣîf, ¹49, 374
Wâṣil b. ʿAṭâʾ, ¹406, ³61 f.
Wâsiṭ, ¹102, ³476
Waslât, Mount, see Ousselat, Mount
Waste Country, ¹*following* 110, 166
water: source of fertility, ²287; irrigation, ²295, ³151; wheels, ³416, 466, 469; importance for town planning, ²246, 269; springs, wells, ponds, ²250, 314 f., 322, 361, ³389, 421, 455, 471; aqueducts, ¹357, Pl. IIIb, ²239 ff., 243; running, in houses, ¹250, 339, 361, 363; bags, ³418; use of the water of the Thamûd forbidden by the Prophet, ¹359; stimulates poets, ³384; swimming, ³310, 434

distribution of land and, ¹95 f., 108, 110; formation of circles when water is struck, ¹328; and oil, ²235, 242; elemental functions, ¹194, ³172 f., 220, 223 f., 234 f., 238, 240, 242 f., 265; influenced by moon, ³259; use in magic, ¹214, 216 f., 231; walking upon, ³279; rose water, ¹362, ³173

see also rain

al-Wâthiq (ʿAbbâsid caliph), ¹163, 314
al-Waththâb see Muḥammad, Abû ʿAbdallâh (al-Waththâb)
Watrîgah (Berber tribe), ¹125
Watt, W. M., ¹4n, ³63n
wazirate: defined, ²5; derivation of term, ²6; used in the Qurʾân, ²4; usage of term, ²8; history of office, ²9 ff.; duties defined, ²6 f.; wazirs trying to take over control, ¹377 f., ²27; historically important wazirs, ¹63, 373 f., ²99; among the Mamelukes, ²25; contemporary wazirate in Northwestern Africa and Spain, ¹61, ²12 f.
wealth: poem in praise of personal, ³469; acquired through power or prestige, ²326 ff.; synonymous with power, ¹187n; depends upon political protection, ²285 f.; of early Muslims, ¹419 f., officials, ¹368, ²98 ff., 123 ff., 155; should not be hoarded, ²146, ³459; influences attitude toward alchemy, ³280; see also commerce
weaving, ²313, 316, 347n, 348, 353, 355, 366 ff., ³379; silk, ²348; brocade, ²302; *ṭirâz*, ²65 f., Pls. IIa-b; "wove on the loom," ¹9n, 62n, ³375n
Wellhausen, J., ¹477n
Wensinck, A. J., ¹xxv f., 26n, 36n, 59n, 407n, ²254n, 317n, 361n, 74n, 88n, 410n, and *passim* as the author of *Concordance*
Weysi (Wissi) Effendi, ¹lxvii, xciv f.
Whitting, C. E. J., ¹348n
Wiedemann, E. ³168n, 272n
Wieschhoff, H. A., ¹120n
Wiet, G., ¹133n
wine drinking, ¹28 f., 33 ff., 39, 349, 425, 442, ²61 f., 107, ³304n, 331, 420, 435, 443 ff., 451, 456, 458 f., 461 f., 477; reason for its

effect, [1]174; stimulates poets, [3]384; effect of music compared to intoxication, [2]48 f.; customs duties on wine, [2]340; *nabîdh*, [1]36 f., 445, [3]331
Woepcke, F., [3]126*n*
Wolfson, H. A., [3]253*n*
women: status according to religious law, [1]402; female beauty described, [3]422, 463 f.; weak and dependent, [1]257, 345, 402, [2]69, 79, 140; fond of fortune tellers, [2]201; marriage arrangements, [1]349, 455; childbirth, [2]368 ff.; pictured in dreams as vessels, [3]108 f.; the Prophet fond of, [3]41*n*
woodwork, [2]364
Wright, R. R., [1]112*n*, [3]119*n*
Wright, W., [1]xcvi*n*
writing, [2]316, 331, 352, 355 f., 377 ff.; defined, [2]377; an urban craft, [2]378; communication of information through, [2]390, 406 f., [3]281 f., 296, 316 f.; useful for acquisition of intelligence, [2]406 f.; all scripts not natural but conventional, [3]283; teaching of calligraphy, [2]378, 385 f., [3]301 f., 328; its technical aspects, [2]388 f.; learned by word method, [2]378
history of Arabic, [2]378 ff.; the various Arabic scripts, [2]384 ff.; non-Arabic scripts, [3]283 f., 319; transliteration of non-Arabic sounds, [1]65 ff., 128*n*, 129*n*, [3]129*n*; code, [2]390 f.; letters used for cryptic references, [2]226 ff., 322, 441, [3]184 ff., 189, 192 f., 229; numerical value of letters of Arabic alphabet, [1]236 ff., [2]190 ff., 194, 205 f., [3]173 f., 221 ff.; elemental interpretation of letters, [3]172 f., 220, 223 ff.; letter magic, [3]171 ff.; sand writing, *see* geomancy; *al-qâfîṭûs* "alphabetos," [3]219
Wüstenfeld, F., [1]22*n*, 75*n*, 120*n*, [2]21*n*, 206*n*, 225*n*, 257*n*, [3]18*n*, 74*n*

Y

Yadlaltin (Idlelten), Banû (Berber tribe), [1]272
Yafran (Ifren), Banû (Berber tribe), [1]428, [2]202
Yaghamrâsin b. Zayyân (Zayyânid ruler), [1]272, [2]72
Yaḥyâ (Ḥammâdid ruler), [2]57*n*
Yaḥyâ, Abû Zakarîyâ', *see* Abû Zakarîyâ' Yaḥyâ I and II (Ḥafṣid rulers)
Yaḥyâ al-Jûṭî b. Muḥammad b. Yaḥyâ al-'Addâm b. al-Qâsim b. Idrîs b. Idrîs, [1]52
Yaḥyâ al-Khazrajî (poet from Murcia), [3]447 f.
Yaḥyâ al-Qaṭṭân (b. al-Qaṭṭân), [2]162 f., 167, 209
Yaḥyâ b. 'Abdallâh (grandson of Abû Ya'qûb al-Bâdisî), [2]195
Yaḥyâ b. 'Abdallâh b. Ḥasan b. al-Ḥasan b. 'Alî b. Abî Ṭâlib, [1]31 f.
Yaḥyâ b. Aktham, [1]37 & *n*, 38, 456
Yaḥyâ b. Baqî, *see* Ibn Baqî, Yaḥyâ
Yaḥyâ b. al-Biṭrîq, [1]81*n*
Yaḥyâ b. Khâlid al-Barmakî, [1]30, 356, [2]63, 242
Yaḥyâ b. Ma'în, *see* Ibn Ma'în
Yaḥyâ b. Muḥammad (b. Khaldûn) (brother of Ibn Khaldûn), [1]xxxviii, l f., 272*n*
Yaḥyâ b. Muḥammad b. Khushaysh, [2]381
Yaḥyâ b. Sa'îd, *see* Yaḥyâ al-Qaṭṭân
Yaḥyâ b. Yaḥyâ al-Laythî, [3]14
Yaḥyâ b. Zayd b. 'Alî Zayn-al-'âbidîn b. al-Ḥusayn b. 'Alî b. Abî Ṭâlib, [1]410 f., [2]210
Yakhlaf al-Aswad, [3]457
Ya'lâ b. Munyah, [1]420
Yalamlam, Mountain of, [1]126
al-Yâlifî (an official of Ibn Tâfrâgîn), [3]429
Yamâmah, [1]100 f., *following* 110, 122, 126, 134, 169, 220

al-Yanbu', [2]196
Ya'qûb, Abû Yûsuf, *see* Abû Yûsuf Ya'qûb (Merinid ruler)
Ya'qûb al-Manşûr, *see* al-Manşûr, Ya'qûb (Almohad ruler)
Ya'qûb b. 'Abd-al-Ḥaqq, *see* Abû Yûsuf Ya'qûb (Merinid ruler)
Ya'qûb b. Shaybah, [2]178
Ya'qûb b. Sufyân, [2]161
al-Ya'qûbî, [1]403*n*
Yâqût, [1]lxxix*n*, 75*n*, 120 & *n*, 123*n*, 124*n*, 131*n*, 134*n*, 297*n*, 316*n*, 364*n*, [2]225*n*, 275*n*, [3]18*n*, 185*n*, 446*n*, 452*n*
Yâqût al-Musta'şimî, [2]385
Yarmûk, [1]321
Yâsîn al-'Ijlî, [2]174
Yâsir (Tubba' of the Yemen), [1]22
Yastâsb, [1]23, 25
Yathrib, *see* Medina
Yathrib b. Mahlâ'îl (Mahalalel), [2]264
al-Ya'ya', [3]459
Yazdjard, [1]329, [3]186; era of, [2]217, 218*n*
Yazdshîr, [1]135
Yazîd, Banû (subtribe of the Zughbah), [1]272
Yazîd ar-Raqâshî, [2]168
Yazîd b. 'Abd-al-Malik, [2]55
Yazîd b. Abî Ziyâd, [2]172 ff.
Yazîd b. Mazyad, [3]378*n*
Yazîd b. Mu'âwiyah, [1]422 f., 431 f., 434 f., 438, 443 ff., [2]252 f., [3]229*n*
Yazîd b. Zuray', [2]167
yeast, [3]268, 276, 278
Yemen, [1]xxxiii, xxxviii, 21, 23 f., 27, 42, 99 ff., *following* 110, 122 ff., 126*n*, 169, 171, 177, 219, 282 f., 296, 304, 330, 360, 365, 370, 418, 441, 474, [2]51, 65*n*, 202, 211, 226, 288, 354, 380, 382, [3]5, 282, 343
yogis, [1]222
Yulâq, [1]121
Yûnus b. Abî Isḥâq, [2]177
Yûsuf (father of al-Ḥajjâj), [1]60
Yûsuf, Abû Ya'qûb, *see* Abû Ya'qûb Yûsuf
Yûsuf al-'Ashrî b. 'Abd-al-Mu'min, *see* Abû Ya'qûb Yûsuf (Almohad ruler)
Yûsuf b. Ayyûb, *see* Şalâḥ-ad-dîn (Saladin), Yûsuf b. Ayyûb
Yûsuf b. al-Ḥajjâj, [3]130
Yûsuf b. Qorqmâs Amîr al-ḥâjj al-Ḥalabî, [1]235*n*
Yûsuf b. Tâshfîn (Almoravid ruler), [1]470 f., [2]93
Yûsuf b. 'Umar (governor of the 'Irâq), [2]55
Yûsuf b. Ya'qûb, *see* Abû Ya'qûb Yûsuf (Merinid ruler)
Yver, G., [1]118*n*, 119*n*

Z

Zâb (Northwestern Africa), [1]130, [2]117, 196, 211, 304, [3]418, 473
Zâb, Greater, [1]145 f.
Zâb, Lesser, [1]145 f.
az-Zâb (or ar-Rabb?), [1]145
Zabîd, [1]99, 124
Zâbulistân, [2]217
Zâdânfarrûkh (secretary to al-Ḥajjâj), [2]22
Ẓafâr, [1]124
Zaftah, *see* Zifta
Zaghâwah, *see* Zaghây
Zaghây, [1]*following* 110, 120, 125
aẓ-Ẓâhir, *see* Barqûq, al-Malik aẓ-Ẓâhir
Ẓâhirites, [3]4 ff.
Ẓâhirîyah College, [1]lx, lxii, [2]332*n*
az-Zahrâwî ('Alî b. Sulaymân), [3]126
Zâ'idah b. Qudâmah, [2]159, 160 & *n*
Zâ'irajah, [1]238 ff., [3]182 ff., 224, 227, Pls. I, II
az-Zajjâj, Abû Isḥâq, [2]403, [3]313
az-Zajjâjî, Abû l-Qâsim, [3]323
Zakarîyâ', Abû Yaḥyâ, *see* Abû Yaḥyâ Zakarîyâ' b. Aḥmad (b.) al-Liḥyânî

az-Zamakhsharî, [1]26, [2]446 f., [3]59, 258*n*, 324, 329, 337 ff., 361
de Zambaur, E., [1]368*n*
Zamm, [1]148
Zamora, [1]150
Zamzam, well of, [2]250 f., 257
Ẓanâgah, *see* Ṣinhâjah
Zanâtah (Berber tribe), [1]12, 125*n*, 128*n*, 252, 270 ff., 286, 290, 295, 298, 318, 322, 331, 335, 343, 351, 360, 382, 428, 469, 472, [2]17, 45, 49, 51, 69, 115, 134, 202, 306, [3]185, 418 f.
az-Zanâtî, Abû 'Abdallâh, [1]229
Zanj, [1]99, 123, 171, 173, 411
Zarhûn, [3]471
az-Zarzâlî, Muḥammad b. ash-Shawwâsh, [1]xxxviii
Zawâwah, [2]429
az-Zawâwî (Aḥmad b. Muḥammad, teacher of Ibn Khaldûn), [2]401*n*
az-Zawâwî, Abû 'Alî Nâṣir-ad-dîn, *see* al-Mashaddâlî, Nâṣir-ad-dîn, Abû 'Alî
aẓ-Ẓawdî, 'Abdallâh b. Abî Bakr b. Yaḥyâ, [3]129
Zawîlat Ibn Khaṭṭâb, [1]131
Zayd al-'Ammî, [2]167 f., 169*n*
Zayd b. 'Alî Zayn-al-'âbidîn b. al-Ḥusayn b. 'Alî b. Abî Ṭâlib, [1]405 f., 410 ff., [2]210
Zayd b. Arqam, [1]445
Zayd b. Thâbit, [1]420
Zaydîyah, *see* Shî'ah
Zayla' (Zâla'), [1]100, 122 f.
Zayn-al-'âbidîn, *see* 'Alî Zayn-al-'âbidîn b. al-Ḥusayn b. 'Alî b. Abî Ṭâlib
Zayyân b. 'Âbis, [3]417
Zayyânids, [1]xxxix f., xlviii, 271 f., [2]18, 72
Zetterstéen, K. V., [1]34*n*, 396*n*, [2]21*n*
Ziada, M. Mostafa, [1]cvii*n*
Zibaṭrah, [1]144*n*
Zifta, [1]131
zîj, [3]112, 135 ff.
Zion, [2]260
Zîrids, [1]332, 360, [2]42, 70, 116, 283, 350
Zirr b. Ḥubaysh, [2]159 ff.
Ziryâb, [2]405
Ziyâd b. Abî Sufyân (Abîhi), [1]384, 451*n*, [2]64
Ziyâdat-Allâh I b. Ibrâhîm b. al-Aghlab, [2]40
zodiacal signs, [1]104 ff., 113, 227, 239, 241, [2]194, 211 ff., 323, [3]156, 163, 180, 198 ff., 206, 210 f., 221, 259, 460
zones, *see* geography
Zoroastrianism, [1]80*n*, 93*n*, 278, [2]55*n*, 104 f., 202, 266; *see also* Magians, Majûs
az-Zubaydî, Abû Bakr, [3]327*n*, 328
az-Zubayr, [1]59*n*, 420, 426, 430*n*, 438, 440, 442 f.
Zughar, [3]473
Zughbah, Banû, [1]liii, 270, 272, [3]432, 436, 440
Zuḥal, *see* Saturn (planet)
Zuhayr b. Abî Sulmâ, [1]43*n*, [3]397, 403, 410
Zuhrah b. Ḥawîyah, [1]259
az-Zuhrî, [1]17, [2]22, 257, 448
az-Zurqânî, [1]ic
Zwemer, S. M., [1]193*n*

Translation

of the *Zâ'irajah* (obverse)

(see plate I, following 3:204)

In this translated schema of the *Zâ'irajah*, the direction of letters and numerals has in general been left unchanged, i.e., it is the same as in the Arabic original. It has seemed advisable, however, to change it in the circle in the lower left-hand corner; there, numerals and letters appear in the direction required by the Latin alphabet.

Since some of the signs are rather similar to each other, the transliteration is not always absolutely certain. *Zimâm* numerals are transcribed by italics, in order to distinguish them from *ghubâr* numerals. In both systems, 5 has the same form, and 7 nearly identical forms.

NOTES

§ The Arabic words seem meaningless.

§§ This reading is indicated in the table included in the edition of the Turkish translation of the *Muqaddimah*.

* The following Arabic words are found in the table of the Turkish translation:

mazîd *jayb*
mazîd al-janûb ajma' 5 70 5 mazîd jayb
kullî
mazîd *jayb* *tamâm*

** It is not quite clear whether the signs visible to the right of *f* belong to the table here.

*** The table of the Turkish translation has the letters *t th kh* in the circle and a full complement of letters on the chord.

The reverse side of the chart (see Plate II, following 3:204) is not translated as it can be deciphered easily with the help of note 882 to Chapter VI (3:197). The squares show letters of the Arabic alphabet as well as *ghubâr* and *zimâm* numerals.

DIAGRAM BY LIAM DUNNE

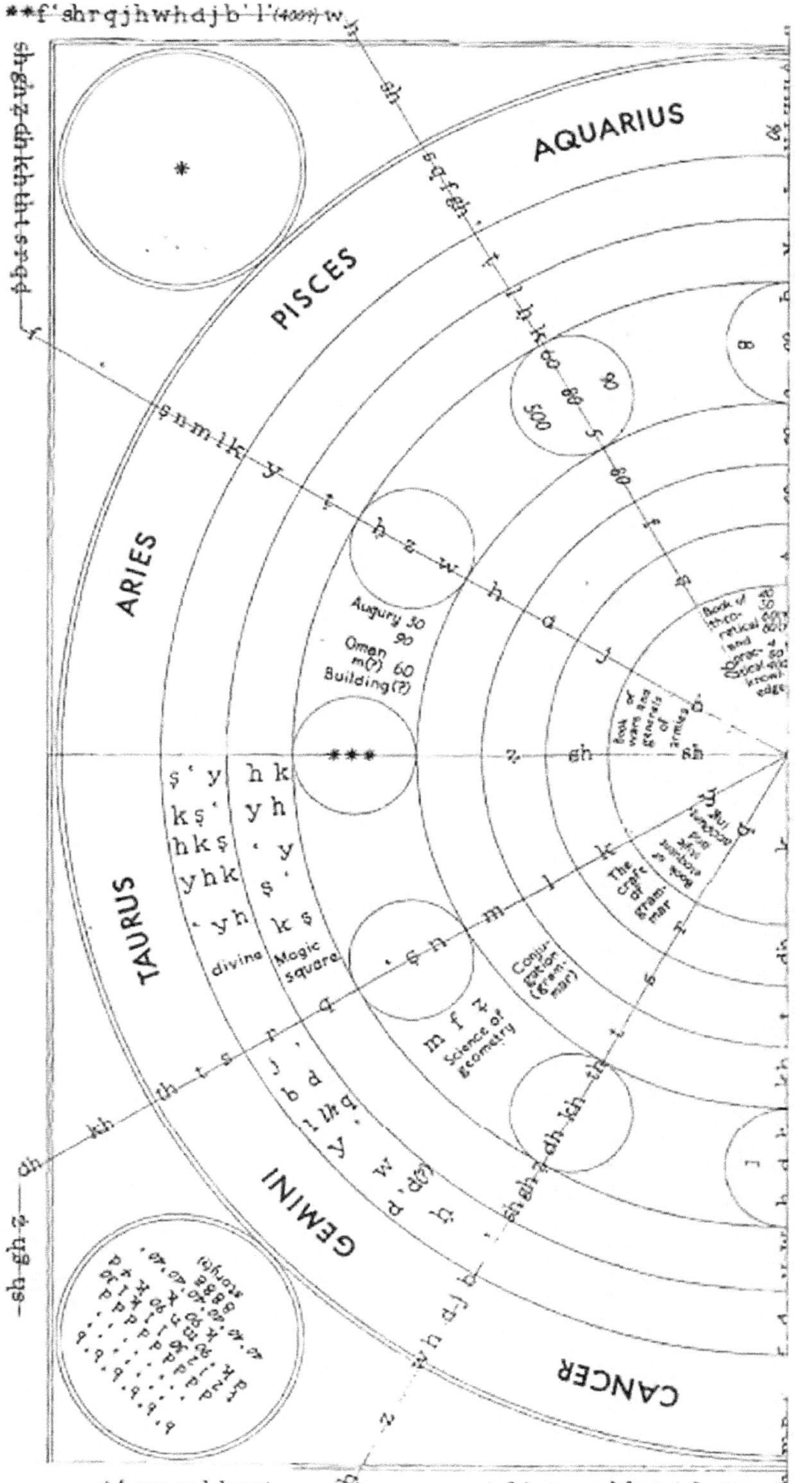

**f'shrqjhwhdjb'l'(400?) w
AQUARIUS
PISCES
ARIES
TAURUS
GEMINI
CANCER
Augury 30
90
Omen
m(?) 60
Building(?)
Book of wars and generals of armies
divine
Magic square
Science of Geometry
Conjugation (grammar)
The craft of grammar
d f ' ṣ z m l k y ṭ ḥ z w

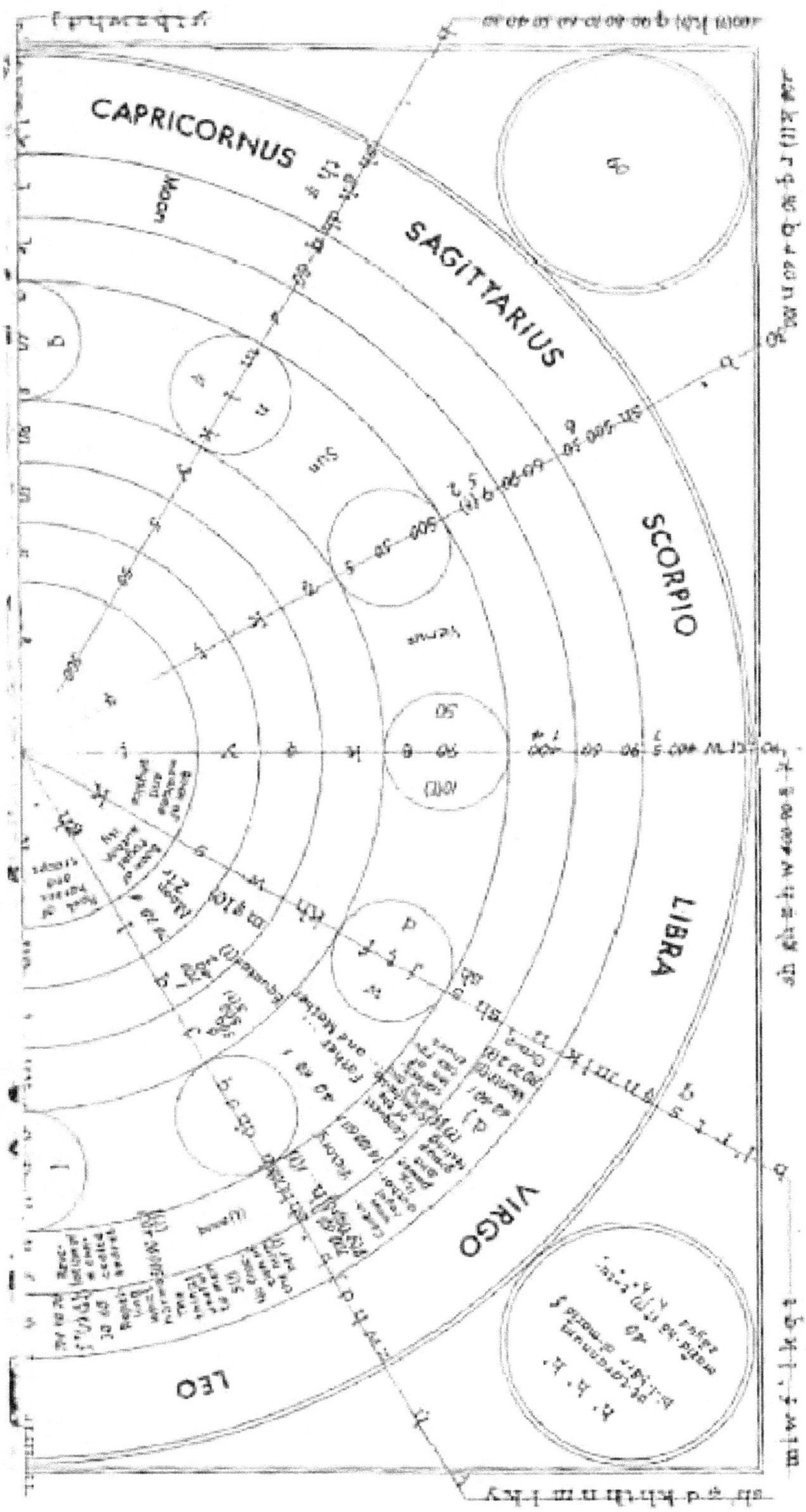

CAPRICORNUS
SAGITTARIUS
SCORPIO
LIBRA
VIRGO
LEO
Moon
Sun
Venus

www.ingramcontent.com/pod-product-compliance
Lightning Source LLC
Chambersburg PA
CBHW080846090526
44397CB00064B/1102
9789390804764